Psychology Applied to Modern Life
ADJUSTMENT IN THE 80s 2ND EDITION

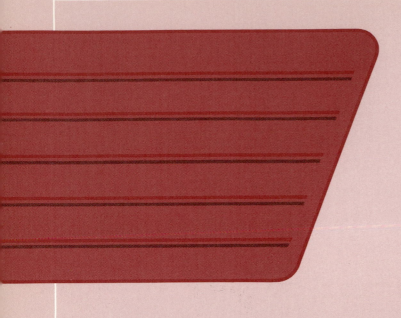

Psychology
Applied to Modern Life
ADJUSTMENT IN THE 80s 2ND EDITION

Wayne Weiten

COLLEGE OF DUPAGE
ILLINOIS SCHOOL OF PROFESSIONAL PSYCHOLOGY

Brooks/Cole Publishing Company
Monterey, California

*We need to see
that the very complexity of life
is a source of its beauty,
rather than a source of anxiety.*

MICHAEL SCOTT CAIN

Psychology
Applied to Modern Life
ADJUSTMENT IN THE 80s 2ND EDITION

Consulting Editor: Lawrence S. Wrightsman, University of Kansas

Brooks/Cole Publishing Company
A Division of Wadsworth, Inc.

Printed in the United States of America

10 9 8 7 6 5 4 3 2 1

Library of Congress Cataloging in Publication Data

Weiten, Wayne, [date]
Psychology applied to modern life.

Bibliography: p.
Includes index.
1. Adjustment (Psychology) 2. Interpersonal
relations. 3. Adulthood—Psychological aspects.
4. Self-help techniques. I. Title.
BF335.W42   1985   158   85-11645

ISBN 0-534-05412-9

Sponsoring Editor: *Claire Verduin*
Editorial Assistants: *Pat Carnahan and Linda Wright*
Production Coordinator: *Fiorella Ljunggren*
Manuscript Editor: *Rephah Berg*
Permissions Editor: *Carline Haga*
Interior and Cover Design: *Vernon T. Boes*
Cover Photo: *Alfred Gescheidt, Image Bank West*
Art Coordinator: *Judith Macdonald*
Interior Illustration: *Brenda Booth and Maggie Stevens*
Photo Editor: *Judy K. Blamer*
Photo Researcher: *Judy Mason*
Typesetting: *Allservice Phototypesetting Company, Phoenix, Arizona*
Cover Printing: *Phoenix Color Corporation, Long Island City, New York*
Printing and Binding: *R. R. Donnelley & Sons Company, Willard, Ohio*

(Credits continue on p. 565)

To two pillars of stability in this era of turmoil — my parents

PREFACE

TO THE INSTRUCTOR

Many students enter adjustment courses with great expectations. They've ambled through their local bookstores, and in the "Psychology" section they've seen innumerable self-help books that offer highly touted recipes for achieving happiness for a mere $3.95. After paying (usually) far more money to enroll in a bona fide collegiate course that deals with many of the same issues as the self-help books, many students expect a revelatory experience. However, the majority of us with professional training in psychology or counseling take a rather dim view of these self-help books and the pop psychology that they represent. We tend to view this literature as grossly oversimplified, intellectually dishonest, and opportunistic. Often we summarily dismiss the pop psychology that so many of our students have embraced. We then try to supplant it with our more sophisticated academic psychology, which is inevitably much more complex and much less accessible. Far too often, students spurn the academic psychology that we love and respect in favor of the glitter of pop psychology.

In this textbook, I have tried to come to grips with this problem of differing expectations between student and teacher. My goal has been to produce a comprehensive, research-oriented, academically rigorous treatment of the topic of adjustment that nonetheless acknowledges the existence, relevance, and potential contribution of so-called pop psychology. This integration involves the following:

- In Chapter 1 I confront the phenomenon of popular self-help books. I try to take the student beneath the seductive surface of such books and analyze some of their typical flaws. My goal is to make the student a more critical consumer of this kind of literature without writing it off as worthless.
- I try to provide the student with a better appreciation of the merit of the empirical approach. This effort to clarify the role of research, which is rare for an adjustment text, also appears in the very first chapter, where the value of scientific data is illustrated by reviewing Freedman's research on happiness and contrasting his findings with commonsense notions about the ingredients of happiness.
- While encouraging a more critical attitude toward self-help books, I do *not* suggest that they should all be dismissed. Instead, I argue that some of them offer authentic insights. With this in mind, I highlight some of the better books in

Recommended Reading boxes sprinkled throughout the text. These recommended readings tie in with the adjacent topical coverage and show the student the interface between academic and popular psychology.
- Recognizing that adjustment students want to leave the course with concrete, personally useful information, I have ended each chapter with a section called "Applying Psychology to Your Life." These application sections are "how to" discussions that address everyday problems. They focus on issues that tie in with the content of the particular chapter, and they contain more explicit advice than the text proper.

In summary, I have tried to make this book both rigorous and applied. It is hoped that the strategies outlined above will help the student to bridge the gap between popular and academic psychology.

PHILOSOPHY

A certain philosophy is inherent in any systematic treatment of adjustment as a topic. My philosophy can be summarized as follows:

- *I believe in theoretical eclecticism.* This book will not indoctrinate your students along the lines of any single theoretical orientation. The psychoanalytic, behavioristic, and humanistic schools of thought are all treated with respect.
- *I believe that an adjustment text should be a resource book for students.* I have tried to design this book so that it encourages and facilitates the pursuit of additional information on adjustment-related topics. It should serve as a point of departure for more learning.
- *I believe that effective adjustment requires "taking charge" of one's own life.* Throughout the book I try to promote the notion that active coping efforts are generally superior to passivity and complacency.

CONTENT

Although I have tried to integrate pop psychology into the text, let me emphasize that this is a rigorous and research-oriented treatment of the topic of adjustment. Illustrative of this reality is the fact that this book has substantially more references than any other adjustment text currently available! Now, we all know that a great number of references does not necessarily yield a high-quality textbook—the number of references simply offers some concrete evidence that this book is comprehensive in coverage and thoroughly grounded in research. I also think you will find it very up to date. However, I have tried to avoid the tendency, common in textbooks, to ignore older research simply because it is older. I believe that an obsession with currency derogates our heritage and gives students an impression of instability in the field. With these thoughts in mind, let me outline some of the specifics of content coverage and highlight some of the changes from the first edition.

THE TEXT PROPER

- Chapter 2 provides a succinct review of the psychoanalytic, behavioristic, and humanistic approaches to personality. If you enroll students who have not had an introductory psychology course, this chapter should quickly put them on more even ground with those students who have had such a course (throughout the book I assume that this may be the student's first course in psychology). A unique feature of this coverage is my analysis of the contributions and shortcomings of each of the three schools of thought.
- There has recently been an explosion of research on stress. Reflecting that reality, an entire chapter (Chapter 3) is devoted to the nature of stress and our reactions to it.
- Theories of psychological health tend to be ignored in research-oriented adjustment texts. I have chosen, however, to provide extensive coverage of many such theories (more than just Maslow's).
- An entire chapter is devoted to communication. It focuses on both verbal and nonverbal communication and delves into the important issue of self-disclosure.
- There is very heavy coverage of interpersonal behavior, with an emphasis on intimate relationships.
- Consistent with the great increase in academic interest in sexuality, a full chapter (Chapter 12) is devoted to sexual behavior.
- The chapter on psychopathology uses up-to-date DSM-III terminology and emphasizes etiology in order to relate the topic clearly to the adjustment process.
- Many students are very curious about esoteric topics such as hypnosis, meditation, and yoga. These and other topics are examined respectfully but critically in Chapter 15.

APPLICATION SECTIONS

The sections titled "Applying Psychology to Your Life" should be of special interest to most students. They are tied to chapter content in a way that should show students how practical applications emerge out of theory and research. Although some of the material covered in these sections shows up frequently in adjustment texts, much of it is unique. The unusual application sections include:

- Being intelligent about drugs
- Building self-esteem
- Dealing constructively with interpersonal conflict
- Understanding the games couples play
- Improving sexual functioning
- Coping with shyness
- Understanding and preventing suicide

CHANGES AND NEW MATERIAL IN THE SECOND EDITION

To me, one of the exciting things about psychology is that it is not a stagnant discipline. It continues to progress at what seems a faster and faster pace. A good textbook must reflect this metamorphosis and evolve with the discipline. Although the professors and students who used the first edition of this book did not clamor for change, I have made some significant alterations in the contents of the second edition—adding new topics that reflect recent trends in the field, condensing and reorganizing other material to make room for the additions. The major alterations from the first edition include the following.

- There is an entirely new chapter (Chapter 4) devoted to health psychology. Interest and research in this area have blossomed in recent years, and if one subscribes to a holistic view of human functioning, this research is very relevant to the adjustment process. Although this coverage is unprecedented in adjustment/applied psychology texts, I suspect that it will become a standard topic in the future. My decision to add this chapter blending psychology and medicine was greatly facilitated by the fact that I was able to coax a collaboration out of my wife, a physician in family practice.
- Interest in adult development has grown gradually over the last decade. About three-quarters of Chapter 10 is new material on this topic. The recent theoretical contributions of Levinson and Gould are discussed in some detail.
- This increased emphasis on adult development also led me to alter the perspective from which I cover several other topics. Material from the first edition on vocational, marital, and sexual adjustment has been restructured somewhat to reflect a developmental perspective. These topics are pulled together in a new section focusing on adult development. I believe that this consistent thematic treatment integrates these topics into a more coherent whole.
- Research on stress has continued to proliferate at a dizzying pace. For this reason, you will find the chapter on stress (Chapter 3) revised substan-

tially, as I have tried to incorporate a great deal of new research.

- The growing interest in stress has led to an accompanying expansion in research on coping. This is decidedly fortunate for those of us interested in adjustment, because coping lies at the very core of the adjustment process. Although only about half of the material is new, coping processes now require an entire chapter (Chapter 5) for adequate coverage.

- To facilitate some of the changes outlined above, material from the first edition on academic adjustment, the healthy personality, and self-modification has been compressed and moved. The more applied elements of the discussion of academic adjustment have been converted into the application section appended to Chapter 1 so that your students can benefit from this advice earlier in the course. The discussion of the healthy personality has been incorporated into the description of the three major models of personality in Chapter 2. The explanation of self-modification has been shortened a bit and converted into the application section for Chapter 5.

WRITING STYLE

I have tried to integrate the technical jargon of our discipline into a relatively informal and down-to-earth writing style. The book has been written with the student reader in mind. The chapters were pretested with my own students, who were urged to slash away at any pompous verbiage. Concrete examples are used extensively to clarify complex concepts, as well as to help maintain student interest.

FEATURES

In addition to the application sections, this text contains a number of other features intended to stimulate student interest.

RECOMMENDED READING BOXES

As I mentioned earlier, students tend to be very interested in self-help books. I have sifted through hundreds of them to identify some that may be especially useful. These are highlighted in boxes that briefly review the book and include a provocative excerpt or two. These Recommended Reading boxes are placed in the text so as to be germane to the material being covered at that point. A few of these boxes examine books that aren't self-help books as such but are relevant to adjustment issues. Some of the recommended books are very well known, while others are obscure. I think they all have something worthwhile to offer, although I certainly don't intend to endorse every idea in every book. This feature replaces the conventional suggested readings list that usually appears at the ends of chapters, where it is almost universally ignored by students. Parenthetically, let me add that I consider these boxes to be an important element of this book and I invite your participation in suggesting self-help books to recommend in the next edition. If you have a self-help book or two that you and/or your students find exceptionally useful, please write to me about it (in care of Brooks/Cole Publishing Company, Monterey, Calif. 93940). Many suggestions from users of the first edition turned out to be helpful and were incorporated into this revision.

SIDELIGHT BOXES

The remaining boxes are used to present a wide variety of supplementary materials. They include human-interest news items, questionnaires, discussions of controversies, and so forth. These boxes contain interesting sidelights and generally are not used to present crucial concepts.

ILLUSTRATIONS

Photographs and figures are used extensively. Although these are intended to make the book attractive and help maintain student interest, they are not merely decorative. They have been carefully selected so as to support and enhance the educational goals of the text.

CARTOONS

Because a little comic relief usually helps keep a student interested, numerous cartoons are sprinkled throughout the book. Like the figures, most of these have been chosen to reinforce ideas in the text. Some of them do exceptional jobs of driving points home.

LEARNING AIDS

Because this book is rigorous, substantive, and sizable, quite a number of instructional aids have been incorporated into the text to help your students digest the wealth of material.

- The *outline* at the beginning of each chapter provides the student with a preview and overview of what will be covered.
- *Subtitles* are employed *very* frequently in order to keep material well organized for the student.
- *Vocabulary* items are identified with boldface type to alert the student that these are key terms to learn.
- A *running glossary* in the page margins provides on-the-spot definitions of vocabulary items as they appear in the text for the first time (and occasionally the second time if a term comes many chapters later and is critical at that point). The index at the back of the book is set up to allow students to quickly relocate these glossary entries when necessary. All the terms for which

there are running glossary entries appear in boldface in the index.

- *Italics* are used liberally throughout the book to emphasize important points.
- *Chapter summaries* are provided to give the student a quick review of the chapter's major points.

A new feature in this edition is the inclusion of review materials at the end of each chapter: a list of detailed learning objectives for the chapter, a list of vocabulary terms that students should know, and a list of important theorists and researchers whose contributions students should be familiar with. As you may know, these structured guidelines for review appeared in the Study Guide in the first edition. Because students reported that they were very helpful, I decided to make them available to all students, rather than just those who buy the workbook. New review exercises have been incorporated into the workbook for students who need additional help.

SUPPLEMENTARY MATERIALS

INSTRUCTOR'S MANUAL

An instructor's manual is available as a convenient aid for your educational endeavors. It provides a brief overview of each chapter along with a list of relevant films. It also includes questions for class discussion and/or essay exams. Most important, it contains an extensive collection of multiple-choice questions for objective tests. I feel very strongly about the quality of test-item pools. I believe that it is critical that students be tested fairly with sensible, unambiguous questions. I am confident that you will find this to be a dependable and usable test bank. With the assistance of William Gnagey of Illinois State University, it has been expanded to about twice its size in the first edition.

STUDY GUIDE AND PERSONAL EXPLORATIONS WORKBOOK

A combination study guide and workbook is also available for your students. The study guide portion of the book is designed to help students master the information contained in the text. It has been revised by William Gnagey and contains a programmed review, as well as several other kinds of review exercises and a self-quiz. The personal explorations portion contains some exercises designed to aid your students in achieving personal insights. There are also some psychological tests or scales that your students can administer and score for themselves. Most students find these interesting and exciting. The personal explorations portion also contains probing questions intended to help students think about themselves relative to the issues raised in the text. The pages in the study guide/workbook are perforated so that you can assign particular exploration exercises, which the students can then submit to you. I think the personal explorations part of this book has exciting possibilities, and I strongly urge you to take a good look at it.

ACKNOWLEDGMENTS

This book has been an enormous undertaking, and I want to express my gratitude to the innumerable people who have influenced it both directly and indirectly. To begin with, I must cite the contribution of the hundreds of students who have taken the Adjustment course with me over the last ten years. It is trite to say that they have been a continuing inspiration—but they have. Moreover, many of them have taken the time to read and critique individual chapters; their collective contribution to the book's readability has been substantial. I am also very deeply indebted to Pat Polonus, who typed every word of the original manuscript. She has been a great friend and buoyant morale booster. Let me also commend the staff at the College of DuPage Library; they have been helpful and patient as I have plundered their facility of hundreds upon hundreds of books. I am also indebted to colleagues—especially Ray Olson, Sally Hadley, and Barb Lemme—who have allowed me to borrow extensively from their personal libraries, and to Jeff Sculley, who prepared the indexes for the book.

Although their contributions are less direct, I want to thank the various psychologists who have influenced my career development, including Claire Etaugh, Rick Stalling, Don Gottschalk, Harry Upshaw, and Shari Diamond. I am also grateful to a variety of friends for their support, but especially Jerry Mueller, Craig Himmelman, and John Weiss, who have provided encouragement when my energies have flagged. My greatest debt is to my wife, Beth Traylor, who has been a steady source of emotional support and a wonderful companion while enduring the grueling rigors of her medical career.

The quality of a textbook depends greatly on the quality of the prepublication reviews by psychology professors around the country. The following persons have greatly influenced the development of this book by providing exacting and constructive reviews of various portions of the manuscript: John R. Blakemore of Monterey Peninsula College, Dennis Coon of Santa Barbara City College, Richard Fuhrer of the University of Wisconsin at Eau Claire, Michael Hirt of Kent State University, Fred J. Hitti of Monroe Community College, William T. McReynolds of the University of Tampa, James Prochaska of the University of Rhode Island, Joan Royce of Riverside City College, Thomas K. Saville of Metropolitan State College at Denver, Norman R. Schultz of Clemson University, Kenneth L. Thompson of Central Missouri State University, David L. Watson of the University of Hawaii, Raymond Wolfe of the State University of New York at Geneseo, and Norbert Yager of Henry Ford Community College. For their helpful reviews of the present edition I thank the following people: M. K. Clampit of Bentley College, Robert Higgins of Central Missouri State University, Joseph Horvat of Weber State College, Walter Jones of the College of DuPage, Wayne Joose of Calvin College, Susan Kupisch of Austin Peay State University, Barbara Hansen Lemme of the College of DuPage, Harold List of Massachusetts Bay Community College, Frederick Meeker of California State Polytechnic University, Pomona, John Moritsugu of Pacific Lutheran University, Gary Oliver of the College of DuPage, Joseph Philbrick of California State Polytechnic University, Pomona, Dale Simmons of Oregon State University, Deborah Weber of the University of Akron, and Raymond Wolf of Moraine Park Technical Institute.

Insightful professional review has also been provided by Larry Wrightsman, the consulting editor on this project. With his vast experience in textbook writing and his encyclopedic store of information on psychology, he has contributed an abundance of perceptive suggestions for improvement.

Superlatives are also in order for the people at Brooks/Cole. I am very pleased that Kevin Howat, Ray Kingman, and Claire Verduin talked me into writing this book for Brooks/Cole. Claire, who has served as supervising editor on the project, has been a great source of encouragement and has provided innumerable insights about publishing as she has fielded my endless questions. She has also become a treasured friend. Senior production coordinator Fiorella Ljunggren has handled the production of the book with great dexterity, efficiency, and enthusiasm. Manuscript editor Rephah Berg has added new meaning to the word *meticulous;* her eye for detail has never ceased to amaze me. Carline Haga (permissions editor), Judy Blamer (photo editor), and Judy Macdonald (art coordinator) have also made significant contributions to the book. Finally, Vernon Boes deserves great credit for rising to the challenge of creating an attractive, new design for the book.

Wayne Weiten

A NOTE TO THE STUDENT

In most college courses students spend more time with their textbook than with their professor. Given this reality, it helps if students *like* their textbook. Making textbooks likable, however, is a tricky proposition. By its very nature, a textbook must introduce students to a great many new concepts, ideas, and theories. If it doesn't, it isn't much of a textbook, and instructors won't choose to use it, and so you'll never see it anyway. In any case, what I want you to realize is that I have tried to make the book as likable as possible without compromising the academic content that your instructor demands. Thus, I have tried to make the book lively, informal, engaging, well organized, easy to read, concrete, practical, and occasionally humorous. Before you plunge into Chapter 1, let me explain some of the key features of the book.

ORGANIZATION

The book is divided into four major parts. In the first section, entitled "The Dynamics of Adjustment," you will be introduced to key concepts, methods of investigation, theories of personality, the dynamics of stress, the interface between behavior and physical health, and the nature of coping. In the second section, "The Interpersonal Realm," you will learn about the complexities of social relationships. Topics such as how we see others, communication, sex roles, friendship, and love will be explored. In the third section, "Transitions and Challenges in Adult Life," we will look at patterns of development in adulthood. A broad overview of adult development will be followed by more specific information on vocational development, transitions in intimate relationships, and the expression of one's sexuality. Finally, in the fourth section, "Crisis and Growth," we will consider the nature of psychological disorders and discuss psychotherapy and other approaches to personal growth.

LEARNING AIDS

This text contains a great deal of information to be digested. To facilitate this learning process, a number of instructional aids are incorporated into the book to facilitate your learning and enhance the effectiveness of the teaching process.

1. *Outlines* at the beginning of each chapter will provide you with both a preview and an overview of the chapter.
2. *Italics* are used liberally throughout the text to emphasize crucial points more clearly.
3. *Vocabulary* items are identified with **boldface** type to alert you that these are key psychological terms that you should know.
4. A *running glossary* in the margin provides on-the-spot definitions of vocabulary items as they are introduced in the text. It is often difficult for students to adapt to the jargon used by scientific disciplines. However, learning this terminology is an essential element in the educational endeavor. The running glossary is meant to make this learning process less painful. If you subsequently need to return to a running glossary entry, just look the term up in the index. All the glossary items are printed in boldface along with the page number identifying the location of the definition.
5. *Chapter summaries* are included to give you a brief review of the chapter's key points.
6. *Review materials* can be found at the end of each chapter. You should use these to help you master the material in the chapter. The *learning objectives* are particularly important, as they represent precise statements of what you should know after reading the chapter. You will also find a list of terms that you should know, as well as a list of theorists or researchers who are important. It would be wise for you to go over these lists to make sure you have effectively digested the information in the chapter.

RECOMMENDED READING BOXES

This text should function as a resource book. To facilitate this goal, potentially useful or particularly interesting books are highlighted in boxes within the chapters. Each box provides a brief description of the book and a provocative excerpt. Of course, I do not agree with or approve of everything in these recommended books. They are merely offered to you as potentially useful or intriguing. Although these recommended books will not be limited to self-help books, the main purpose of this feature is to introduce you to the better self-help books available.

ENTERTAINMENT FEATURES

Most textbooks tend to be dismayingly effective sedatives. To counteract this tendency to put you to sleep, boxes containing interesting (I hope) sidelights will be interspersed throughout the book. These boxes are intended to give you a break from the principal reading task. Additionally, because I believe that the ability to laugh at ourselves is a sign of psychological health, numerous cartoons are spread throughout the text to help illustrate certain points and to provide another type of break.

WORKBOOK

A *Study Guide and Personal Explorations Workbook* is available to accompany this text. The workbook has two general purposes. First, it is designed to assist you in mastering the information contained in the text. To accomplish that goal, it includes additional review exercises to help you organize information and a self-quiz to permit you to assess your mastery. Second, it includes various activities, projects, and self-tests to aid you in achieving some personal insight. The exercises in the workbook are closely tied to the content of the text. The workbook itself contains a much more detailed description of its features.

I sincerely hope that you find the book enjoyable. If you have any comments or advice that might help me improve the next edition, please write to me in care of the publisher (Brooks/Cole Publishing Company, Monterey, California 93940). Finally, let me wish you good luck—I hope you enjoy your course and learn a great deal.

Wayne Weiten

ABOUT THE AUTHOR

Wayne Weiten is a graduate of Bradley University and received his Ph.D. in psychology from the University of Illinois at Chicago in 1981. He has conducted research on the functional specialization of the cerebral hemispheres, jury behavior, attribution theory, and educational measurement issues and is currently interested in pressure as a form of stress and the measurement of stress. At present, he teaches at the College of DuPage and is an adjunct faculty member at the Illinois School of Professional Psychology.

BRIEF CONTENTS

CONTENTS

2 *THEORIES OF PERSONALITY AND BEHAVIOR*   *36*

3 STRESS AND ITS EFFECTS 76

BEHAVIORAL FACTORS
4 AND PHYSICAL HEALTH
(with Beth A. Traylor, M.D.)

114

5 CONFRONTING STRESS: COPING PROCESSES

158

6 PERSON PERCEPTION: HOW WE SEE OURSELVES AND OTHERS

208

7 INTERPERSONAL COMMUNICATION 236

8 WOMEN AND MEN RELATING TO EACH OTHER: SEX DIFFERENCES AND SEX ROLES 264

9 INTERPERSONAL ATTRACTION: FRIENDSHIP AND LOVE

294

OVERVIEW OF
10 ADULT DEVELOPMENT   **328**
AND VOCATIONAL ADJUSTMENT

11 TRANSITIONS IN MARITAL AND INTIMATE RELATIONSHIPS 370

12 THE DEVELOPMENT AND EXPRESSION OF SEXUALITY

406

13 PSYCHOLOGICAL DISORDERS

442

14 PSYCHOTHERAPY   **478**

15 ESOTERIC APPROACHES TO PERSONAL GROWTH

508

Box 15.1 *RECOMMENDED READING: Inside Groups,* by T. R. Verny   512

Box 15.2 *RECOMMENDED READING: New Mind, New Body,* by B. Brown   516

Box 15.3 *RECOMMENDED READING: The Nature of Human Consciousness,* edited by R. Ornstein   525

Box 15.4 *RECOMMENDED READING: Integral Yoga—Hatha,* by Y. S. S. Satchidananda   525

Psychology
Applied to Modern Life
ADJUSTMENT IN THE 80s 2ND EDITION

The Dynamics of Adjustment

1

INTRODUCTION

A book no more contains reality than a clock contains time. A book may measure so-called reality as a clock measures so-called time; a book may create an illusion of reality as a clock creates an illusion of time; a book may be real, just as a clock is real (both more real, perhaps, than those ideas to which they allude); but let's not kid ourselves — all a clock contains is wheels and springs and all a book contains is sentences.

TOM ROBBINS

The Paradox of Progress

The immense, glistening Boeing 747 lumbers into position to accept its human cargo. The eager passengers-to-be scurry on board. In a tower a few hundred yards away, air traffic controllers diligently monitor radar screens, radio transmissions, and digital readouts of weather information. In the airport terminal, escalators silently convey pedestrians to the main concourse. At the reservation desks, congenial clerks punch up the appropriate ticket information on their computer terminals and quickly process the steady stream of passengers. Mounted on the wall behind the desks are television screens displaying up-to-the-minute information on flight arrivals, departures, and delays. Around the corner, travelers and friends cautiously edge their way through metal detectors under the watchful eyes of the security staff. Back in the cockpit of the plane, the flight crew calmly scans the complex array of dials, meters, and lights to assess the aircraft's readiness for flight. In a moment, this gravity-defying projectile will slice into the cloudy, snow-laden skies above Chicago. In a mere three hours it will transport its passengers from the piercing cold of a Chicago winter to the balmy beaches of the Bahamas. Another everyday triumph for technology will have taken place.

We are the children of technology. We completely take for granted an impressive feat such as transporting 300 people over 1500 miles in a matter of hours. After all, we live in the Space Age—a time of unparalleled progress. Our society has taken extraordinary strides in transportation, energy, agriculture, and medicine. However, this enormous progress is often accompanied by equally enormous difficulties. Our progress sometimes seems ironic in view of the innumerable social problems that continue to plague us.

Let us return to the airport scenario, which seemed harmless enough, to consider some of the personal adjustment problems that might trouble the actors in our scenario.

In the past only flying was sometimes stressful. Today the stress begins long before the plane takes off.

Peter L. is an air traffic controller. He is well paid and has a lovely family waiting for him at home. Unfortunately, he does not get to see much of his family. He constantly has to work overtime because there are not enough trained air traffic controllers available. He used to like his job, but the longer hours and heavier air traffic are taking their toll. His stomach feels tied in knots all day. He is sure he will have an ulcer before the year is over.

Melanie R. is a passenger on the flight to the Bahamas. She is going to attend a business meeting in Nassau, where she will be wined and dined by people trying to solicit business from her company. She should be in a good mood, but actually she is miserable. Melanie is terrified of flying. As she clenches her fourth glass of bourbon, she is literally dizzy with fear. This is the second time this month that her job has required an agonizing flight. She desperately wants to quit her job but cannot afford to do so.

Harold M. is also a passenger on the flight to Nassau. Unlike Melanie, he is in a giddy, expectant mood. He is going to a well-known resort spa that promises an abundance of sunshine, sand, and casual sex. His buoyant optimism temporarily dulls the feelings of despair that have devoured him for the last two months. He has been extremely depressed about the demise of a love affair for which he had high hopes. He has been "burned" in relationships three times in the last two years and is beginning to wonder whether he will ever find a satisfactory love. Although he is enthusiastic about the trip at the moment, in the deeper reaches of his consciousness he is aware that the excursion will probably be a disappointment.

Linda T. is a security guard at the airport. She watches people parade through the metal detectors all day. She finds her job extremely boring. Especially frustrating is the fact that she is qualified for much more interesting work. She has a bachelor's degree in business, and until recently she worked for a fabric company. However, she quit the job in disgust three weeks ago because of the company's sexist promotion policies. Although her work at the fabric company was evaluated very favorably, the promotions consistently went to less experienced males. She daydreams of a career in management but has no idea how she is going to convert her dreams into reality.

Neil C. spends his time hanging around the main concourse in the airport terminal. He sells literature and solicits contributions for the Hare Krishna. His task is a frustrating one, since few people are receptive to his overtures. Neil joined the Krishna group about a year ago. At that time he was lonely and depressed, and he found the gentle, friendly demeanor of the Krishnas very appealing. For the first nine months he floated along happily, buoyed by the camaraderie among the members. However, in the last few months he has begun to have doubts. He cannot imagine what his life will be like ten years from now. He is a very, very confused young man.

The people described above are imaginary, but their problems are all too common. In spite of our great progress, personal adjustment problems seem more prevalent and more prominent than ever before. For example, a startling indication of the collective difficulty we experience in adjusting to the challenging world around us is our enormous reliance on drugs. For instance, in 1983 more than 69 million prescriptions were filled for tranquilizers (IMS, 1983), which are usually prescribed to alleviate feelings of anxiety. Small wonder then, that some pundits have christened our era the "age of anxiety." Also illustrative of this point is the fact that the three leading brand-name prescription drugs (in terms of sales dollars) in the United States, Tagamet, Inderal, and Valium (Baum et al., 1985), are used primarily to treat three problems (ulcers, high blood pressure, and anxiety, respectively) for which *personal stress* is often a major contributing factor. These drugs were just part of the estimated 87 *billion* prescribed pills (about 375 per person) doled out in 1983 (Glaser, 1984). Thus, it is clear that we are depending more and more on pills to solve our problems, and the number of pills consumed suggests that we are experiencing an overdose of problems.

There are many symptoms of our collective distress that I could talk about. Pressure to succeed in climbing the corporate or academic ladder continues to intensify. However, the availability of good jobs and places in graduate school cannot keep pace with the growing demand. Moreover, many of those fortunate enough to snare "good" jobs (those requiring a college degree) report surprisingly high levels of dissatisfaction (Campbell, 1981), and "job burnout" is becoming a major concern in the 1980s (Maslach & Jackson, 1981). Similarly, it appears that marital satisfaction is on the decline. The divorce rate in the United States doubled between 1963 and 1975 (Bell, 1979). Furthermore, it is estimated that as many as half of the married couples in the country may be struggling with sexual difficulties (McCary & McCary, 1982). Finally, studies of mental health in the United States suggest that as many as one in five Americans suffer from full-fledged psychological disorders (Altrocchi, 1980). Thus, it is clear that the tremendous progress of the 20th century has not led to the disappearance of personal problems. Why not? There are probably many reasons. Let us turn now to the analyses of Fromm and Toffler, who put our era into historical perspective.

FROMM'S HISTORICAL PERSPECTIVE

ERICH FROMM

It seems trite and somewhat self-centered to carry on about how we live in "troubled times." Certainly, our ancestors had their share of problems, and I do not mean to idealize the "good old days." In some respects, the problems of the past seem to have been more threatening than our own, in that they often centered on survival. Coping with famine, plague, war, and economic depression was obviously a formidable challenge.

In *Escape from Freedom*, Erich Fromm (1941) has described how the character of personal problems has changed as we have evolved from a static, agricultural society into a modern industrial world marked by instability. Taking a long-range, historical point of view, Fromm points out that, until a couple of centuries ago, people's lives tended to be clearly laid out for them. For instance, a peasant in a feudal society knew that he was going to practice the same religion his father practiced, pledge allegiance to the same feudal lord who ruled his father, and plow the same field that his father plowed. *According to Fromm's analysis, people had relatively little personal freedom in a static society.* Our prototype peasant probably even had his marriage arranged for him! In regard to his lifestyle, he had few major decisions to make and virtually no alternative pathways to ponder.

With the advent of the Renaissance, the Industrial Revolution, and the Reformation, the static quality of society began to erode. The yoke of economic, political, and religious bondage was thrown off, and gradually, across generations, people acquired more and more personal freedom. According to Fromm, this trend toward greater individual freedom has continued unabated, peaking in our present society. Today we must face a vast array of decisions about how to lead our lives. We have *economic freedom* and must choose a career that we hope to find rewarding. We have *geographic freedom* and must decide where to live, whether to stay near our parents or move on to pastures that promise to be greener. We have *political freedom* and must decide whether to be apathetic or concerned, liberal or conservative, Democrat, Republican, or independent. We have freedom in regard to *religion* and *values*. We must decide how we feel about changing sex roles, the new morality, and abortion. The list could go on and on. Every time we walk into a grocery store, we must choose from six brands of tuna fish, 20 brands of soda, and 40 brands of cereal. Thus, Fromm argues, we have more personal freedom than ever before.

Unfortunately, Fromm suggests, *while our personal freedom has been growing, our old sources of emotional sustenance and security have diminished in effectiveness.* Fromm notes that the church, the village, and the family used to provide us with a more solid security base. In a static society there usually was only one church. People tended to have a resolute faith in this single church, which told them exactly how to behave in order to gain eternal salvation. Today, in our era of religious pluralism, the church provides a clear value system for far fewer people. Fromm further points out that the residential stability of the old villages permitted solid friendship networks to develop over generations. Today, our tendency to pick up and move over and over leads us to live in ever-shifting communities where we may barely know our next-door neighbor. Fromm also cites the family as a declining source of security. The closely knit extended family, encompassing aunts, uncles, grandparents, and cousins, has become a relic of the past. Today, with our penchant for divorce and mobility, even the nuclear family is a less dependable reservoir of emotional support.

The analysis just outlined leads Fromm to a rather startling conclusion. He argues that the diminution of our old sources of security has made it rather difficult for us to cope with our new-found freedom. He suggests that, *rather than embracing our increased freedom, many of us find it scary, threatening, and therefore aversive.* In fact, he asserts that many of us find our freedom so aversive that we try to escape from it. This escape often takes the form of submitting passively to some authority figure, such as a political or religious leader. Writing in the 1940s, Fromm cited Germany's ready submission to Hitler as a prime example of this tendency to abandon freedom. At the time of Hitler's ascendance to power, Germany was in a state of chaos and confusion. According to Fromm, it was this confusion and uncertainty that made the German populace surprisingly willing to give up its freedom to a dictator who offered simple solutions.

Fromm's thesis, that many of us wish to give up our personal freedom, is controversial and is certainly open to question. What I wish to stress is Fromm's insightful analysis of historical trends and their effect on our collective psyche. Fromm's analysis suggests that the progress we value so much has undermined our sense of security, scrambled our value systems, and confronted us with difficult new adjustment problems. It should be stressed that Fromm does *not* believe that progress is inherently bad or undesirable. He simply feels that it is important to understand the nature of the challenge we face in our modern era.

TOFFLER'S FUTURE SHOCK

FUTURE SHOCK.
Psychological disorientation and distress attributable to rapid evolution into the future and extensive cultural change.

Alvin Toffler (1970) has provided another analysis of contemporary society that merits some attention. Toffler coined the term **future shock** to describe the disorientation experienced by people who are overwhelmed by rapid and excessive social change. Citing our remarkable residential mobility, our affection for plastic, throwaway goods, and our ever-mounting stacks of scientific literature, Toffler provides an alarming description of the runaway train we call progress. According to Toffler, we live in a confusing, turbulent era of impermanence. Sophisticated job training today is obsolete tomorrow. Dramatic disparities in values exist in our society. Behavior that is considered immoral by some is considered healthy by others. Technological advances such as "test-tube babies" frighten and disturb many of us.

Toffler further describes the inability of many people to cope with this avalanche of change. He argues that many of our social problems can be attributed to the whirlpool of change that engulfs us.

> Despite its extraordinary achievement in art, science, intellectual, moral and political life, the United States is a nation in which tens of thousands of young people flee reality by opting for drug-induced lassitude; a nation in which millions of their parents retreat into video-induced stupor or alcoholic haze; a nation in which legions of elderly folk vegetate and die in loneliness; in which the flight from family and occupational responsibility has become an exodus, in which masses tame their raging anxieties with Miltown, or Librium, or Equanil, or a score of other tranquilizers and psychic pacifiers. Such a nation, whether it knows it or not, is suffering from future shock [1970, p. 366].

The Search for Direction

We live in a time of unparalleled social mutation. According to social critics such as Fromm and Toffler, the kaleidoscope of change that we see around us creates feelings of restlessness, anxiety, and uncertainty. *Hence, the basic challenge of life becomes the search for a sense of direction.* This search involves struggling with such problems as developing a solid sense of identity, a coherent philosophy of life, and a clear vision of a future that realistically promises fulfillment. Centuries ago, problems of this kind were probably much simpler. Today, however, many of us are floundering in a sea of confusion.

The manifestations of this search are many. I shall briefly examine just three of its more striking expressions: the recent popularity of "unorthodox" religious groups, the spectacular success of best-selling "self-help" books, and the expanding popularity of "self-realization" programs.

UNORTHODOX RELIGIOUS GROUPS

Since the mid-1960s, a host of unconventional religious groups have attracted the allegiance of numerous young Americans. These groups are commonly called "cults." However, that term is so hopelessly vague, and its connotation so thoroughly negative, that I prefer not to use it. Many of these so-called cults are spinoffs from centuries-old religious traditions (for example, Hare Krishna, Zen Buddhism) that are highly respected in many regions of the world. It seems unfairly derogatory to label all these groups "cults."

It is very difficult to estimate just how many people have turned to these new religions. Many of the groups remain quite obscure. For instance, the People's Temple, founded by Jim Jones, made little impact on the public consciousness until the unimaginable sequence of events ending in the staggering, dreadful carnage at Jonestown, Guyana. Cox (1977) has estimated that as many as several million Americans may have had some serious encounter with an unconventional religious organization.

The popularity of religious groups such as Reverend Moon's Unification Church, Guru Mahara Ji's Divine Light Mission, Jim Jones's People's Temple, and the Hare Krishna is perplexing and disconcerting for many people. It is this confusion, as well as the utter disbelief that one's child or friend could voluntarily join such a group, that leads to the allegations about "brainwashing." Although some of these groups occasionally use ethically questionable techniques to solicit members, brainwashing is definitely not the key to their success. Virtually all the members appear to join voluntarily. (Their continued allegiance later is more often of an involuntary nature.) I shall try to shed some light on this riddle by addressing two questions: (1) What exactly are the converts to these groups searching for? and (2) Will they find it?

WHAT ARE MEMBERS SEARCHING FOR?

Cox (1977) has extensively investigated the recent American interest in "Eastern" religions with roots in Oriental cultures. He reports that most of the devotees, when asked to explain their conversion, cite *personal* reasons that usually have little to do with the official dogma of the religion. Cox notes four themes that emerged in his discussions with members of neo-Oriental movements.

- Many are simply looking for *friendship,* warmth, and intimacy that they apparently are not finding at home, at school, or elsewhere.
- Many are attracted by the *immediacy* of the techniques, such as meditation or chanting, in contrast to the abstract sterility of conventional Western religious instruction.
- Many are looking for an *authority* figure with a doctrine that they can embrace to dispel their feelings of uncertainty and confusion.
- Many see the Eastern spirituality as more *natural* than the technology-bred Western traditions, which they regard as artificial.

Some of these themes can be seen in the stories of former converts to unconventional religious groups described in Box 1.1. Cox's findings, especially the first and third points listed above, make sense in view of the social critiques by Fromm (1941) and Toffler (1970). Both these theorists stress the transient and unsatisfactory quality of modern friendship networks and the common desire for an authority figure to help us cope with our overabundance of freedom and decisions.

It thus appears that the increasing popularity of unconventional religions is an outgrowth of social undercurrents that affect many of us. Consistent with this belief is Cox's (1977) conclusion that the people turning to unconventional religions are not all that different from most of us. "They are looking for what many other people in America are looking for today. They have merely chosen a more visible and dramatic way of looking. The real question, of course, is will they find it?" (p. 40).

WILL THEY FIND IT?

Are these new religious movements a worthwhile solution for the feelings of loneliness and confusion that plague so many people? There is no simple answer to this question. *Some* people *may* fruitfully end their search for a sense of direction by joining these groups. Certainly, some of these religious movements, such as Zen Buddhism or Sufism, have some worthwhile insights to offer to their new Western adherents. For most people, however, conversion to an unorthodox religion will turn out to be a short-lived pseudo solution. Three major problems are apparent.

1. For many people, joining a tightly knit religious group is an escape from various adjustment problems encountered at home, at work, or at school. Rather than meeting their problems head on, these people are engaging in avoidance behavior. Basically, they are trying to run away and hide from the problems of conventional life. Escape is generally an unhealthy response and rarely solves one's problems.

2. While many Americans are turning to Eastern religions, Cox (1977) notes that many Asians are turning to Western technologies and lifestyles. Many of these newly popular religious movements are ancient versions of religions that are no longer practiced widely in their Eastern homelands. Thus, in some respects, the new converts are not *turning East* so much as *turning back,* probably in a response to future shock. However, the clock cannot be turned back. Trying to turn back time is an ineffectual response to the admittedly difficult challenge of living in modern society.

3. Many con artists and **charlatans** are capitalizing on young Americans' fumbling search for a sense of direction. Many unorthodox religious groups are

CHARLATANISM. *The act of claiming knowledge, skill, or abilities that one does not have.*

led by charismatic and compelling figures who are more interested in exploiting their followers than in providing religious enlightenment. Many groups really provide nothing more than the opportunity to be manipulated, used, and then discarded.

SELF-HELP BOOKS

As a second example of our search for a sense of direction, I will discuss the current proliferation of self-help books. A glance at the best-seller lists of recent years reveals that our nation has displayed a voracious appetite for "self-help" books such as *I'm OK—You're OK* (Harris, 1967), *Your Erroneous Zones*

1.1 CONVERTS TO RELIGIOUS "CULTS"

The young people who are drawn into unconventional religious groups generally do not appear to be substantially different from most of us. They merely seem to be searching for a little friendship, some security, and a clearly defined sense of direction. Many are lured into these groups during a period in their lives when they are experiencing an emotional low. The following three descriptions of conversions are excerpted from a book on "cults," *All Gods Children* (1977), by journalists Carroll Stoner and JoAnne Parke.

Peter Boyle was a lonely young man when he first met the Krishnas on the Boston Common. They tried to sell him a magazine, but he didn't have any money. They gently, and promptly, invited Peter to come to their commune to share a "free feast."

Peter Boyle's mother was near death in a Boston hospital. He had no friends in that city and was lonely. Peter had been unhappy with his job as a merchant seaman and had not been able to find more satisfying work.

"I went to their dinner and brought some of their literature back with me to the YMCA where I was living," Peter recalls. "A week later I saw them in the park and again they invited me to dinner.

"They were very nice and paid a lot of attention to me. I began to increase my visits to twice a week and ultimately one guy told me they wanted me to stay." Peter told them he couldn't stay because of his mother's illness and his financial obligations to her. "They told me, and they believed it, that Krishna would take care of everything. I guess I believed it too."

Charlie tells the story of his recruitment. It is similar to those told by many others. "I met a girl in front of a bank in the town where I was going to school. She asked me, 'What are the three most important subjects in your life?'

"I answered, 'Health, environment and philosophy.'

"She said, 'You should buy the book, *Dianetics,* and read it if you really mean that.'

"She was pretty and I like pretty girls. I enjoyed talking with her so I bought the book from her for two dollars and I gave her my phone number.

"That was a mistake because she and her Scientology friends began calling me twice a week. I always avoided talking with them when they called. But one day I was in my room, feeling sick with a cold and all my friends were in classes when she called. I was very down so when she called I talked to her. She invited me to come to the church to see a film.

"My roommate said that I was crazy to go, but I went anyway. The film turned out to be an old BBC interview with Ron Hubbard. After the film they had a discussion of the riddle of why people have problems with mental or physical health when it is the soul that is really in trouble.

"They told me how pleased they were to have someone of 'my caliber' in Scientology and took me to see some of the organization's higher-ups when they were in town. I was flattered," Charlie says.

"I took their first course in communication techniques. Then I really jumped in and tried to spend all my spare time in Scientology. My grades began to suffer. Eventually, I left school and went home to live so I could continue working with the group. The only important thing in my life was getting 'clear' which I figured would take a few years. My relationship with my family deteriorated and I stopped seeing all my old friends."

Sylvia can now sit back and quietly reflect on the sequence of events that led up to her emotional low that month before she became a Moonie. After college Sylvia had worked as a substitute teacher, "It was very depressing seeing kids in algebra classes who couldn't add. They meandered through the halls of the schools smoking cigarettes and grass." She became further depressed by a job with an employment agency that not only deceived job seekers, but "ripped me off financially." She had broken up with her boyfriend. "It wasn't a really serious relationship, but I had been honest with him and he had lied to me. After we broke up he immediately started dating the girl I thought was my best friend. I really hadn't had any close emotional ties since college."

Sylvia was open for the Moon experience when she answered a blind-ad in a Denver newspaper for a "Creative, conscientious individual to work for the betterment of mankind." When Sylvia responded to the ad, she thought she was applying for a job, not a lifetime religious commitment.

© 1983 United Feature Syndicate, Inc. 2-3

© 1983 UNITED FEATURE SYNDICATE, INC.

(Dyer, 1976), *How to Be Awake and Alive* (Newman & Berkowitz, 1976), *Winning through Intimidation* (Ringer, 1978), *How to Get Whatever You Want out of Life* (Brothers, 1978), *Living, Loving & Learning* (Buscaglia, 1982), *Sexual Chemistry* (Fast & Bernstein, 1983), and *The Art of Self-Fulfillment* (Litwack & Resnick, 1984). These books, with their simple recipes for achieving happiness, have generally not been timid about promising to change the quality of the reader's life. Consider the following excerpt from the back cover of a recently popular self-help book entitled *Self Creation* (Weinberg, 1979).

> More than any book ever written, SELF CREATION shows you who you are and reveals the secret to controlling your own life. It contains an action blueprint built around a clear-cut principle as basic and revolutionary as the law of gravity. With it you will discover how to conquer bad habits, solve sexual problems, overcome depression and shyness, deal with infuriating people, be decisive, enhance your career, increase creativity. And it will show you how to love and be loved. You created you. Now you can start to reap the boundless benefits of self-confidence, self-reliance, self-determination with SELF CREATION.

If only it were that easy! If only someone could hand you a book that would solve all your problems! Unfortunately, it is not that simple. The mere act of reading a book is not likely to turn your life around. If the consumption of these literary narcotics were even remotely as helpful as their publishers claim, we would be a nation full of serene, happy, well-adjusted people. Realistically, however, it is clear that serenity is not the dominant national mood. Quite the contrary, our modern era has been labeled the "age of anxiety." The vast array of self-help books that crowd bookstore shelves represents just one more symptom of our collective distress and our groping search for a sense of direction.

VALUE OF SELF-HELP BOOKS

It is somewhat unfair to lump all self-help books together for a critique, because they vary tremendously in quality. There are some excellent books that offer authentic insights and sound advice. Your author does not share the view of the many psychologists who dismiss *all* these books as shallow drivel. In fact, I shall highlight some of the better self-help books in the Recommended Reading boxes that will appear throughout the text. Unfortunately, however, the few gems are dwarfed by the mountains of rubbish.

The bulk of self-help books offer relatively little of real value to the reader. Generally, they tend to have four fundamental shortcomings.

First, *they are dominated by "psychobabble."* The term *psychobabble,* coined by Rosen (1977), seems appropriate to describe the "hip" but hopelessly vague language used in many of these books. Statements such as "It's beautiful if you're unhappy," "You've got to get in touch with yourself," "You have to be up front," "You gotta be you 'cause you're you," "You need a real high-energy experience," and "Let it all hang out, baby" are typical examples of this new language. The problem is that the terminology is ill defined at best and totally meaningless at worst. Consider the following example, taken from a question/answer booklet promoting Werner Erhard's *est* training.

> The EST training doesn't change the content of anyone's life, nor does it change what anyone knows. It deals with the context or the way we hold the content. . . . Transformation occurs as a recontextualization. . . .
>
> "Getting it" means being able to discover when you have been maintaining (or are stuck with) a position which costs you more in aliveness than it is worth, realizing that you are the source of that position, and being able to choose to give up that position or hold it in a way that expands the quality of your life.

What exactly did those two paragraphs say? Who knows? The statements are so ambiguous and enigmatic that you can read virtually any meaning into them. Therein lies the problem with psychobabble: it is often so obscure that it is unintelligible. Clarity is sacrificed in favor of a hip jargon that prevents, rather than enhances, effective communication.

A second problem is that *self-help books tend to place more emphasis on salability than on scientific soundness.* The advice offered in these books is far too rarely based on solid, scientific research. Instead, the ideas are frequently based on the author's intuitive analyses, which may be highly speculative. Moreover, even when responsible authors provide scientifically valid advice and are careful not to mislead their readers, sales-hungry publishers often slap outrageous, irresponsible promises on the books' covers (much to the dismay of some authors).

The third shortcoming is that *self-help books rarely provide explicit directions about how to change your behavior.* These books tend to be smoothly written and "touchingly human" in tone. They often strike respondent chords in the reader by aptly describing some common problem that many of us experience. The reader says "Yes, that's me!" Unfortunately, when the book focuses on how to deal with the problem, it usually provides only a vague

---

1.2   WHY DO SELF-HELP BOOKS SELL?

The following was excerpted from an article by Daniel Henninger that appeared in the *Wall Street Journal* of October 11, 1977.

In 1901 Charles Wagner wrote a book called "The Simple Life." One million people bought it. It is not known how many of that million successfully used Mr. Wagner's prescriptions to uncomplicate their lives. It seems, however, that improving oneself through books is a little like maintaining a car, an enterprise that requires periodic tune-ups and eventually, an overhaul. When that day arrives, one wants a reliable mechanic to rebuild the clunkered you. Fear not. The self-help industry is ever writing, improving the old models.

In fact, contemporary man and woman seem to be about as durable as a Tinker-Toy truck, since a new, thunderously successful self-help book has appeared almost annually the past 10 years. They are so successful that a best-selling author of self-helpdom now weighs in quickly with a sequel, and it sells, no matter that the sequel is Hamburger Self-Helper, fancying up the author's leftover nostrums.

A reading expedition through a thicket of self-help's most successful books suggests . . . that many Americans, for no immediately apparent reason, are continuously disenchanted with who they are. It isn't so much a sense of personal failure (although the implicit premise of every self-help book is: you schlemiel). It is a restlessness, as if America was, for many of us, an oddly shaped living room—familiar, yes, but one never seems able to arrange the furniture properly.

It is a phenomenon that appears to be peculiarly American. When Harper and Row, for instance, published "I'm OK—You're OK" in Great Britain under another title, it flopped. Americans, it seems, go weak in the knees for anyone who can Explain Everything, or at least something having to do with some aspect of their immediate lives—their minds, their souls, bodies, flab, food, pets.

And we would prefer that the man or woman with the answer (Robert Ringer likes to call himself "the expert from afar") not be too concise or straightforward. The systems and philosophies in self-help books hold out the promise of a simple, shared view of experience. They explain life the way Cliff Notes explain Tolstoy.

distillation of simple common sense, which often could be covered in two rather than two hundred pages. These books often fall back on inspirational cheerleading in the absence of sound, explicit advice.

Finally, *these books often encourage a selfish **narcissistic** approach to life.* Although there are numerous exceptions, the basic message of many of these books is "Do whatever you feel like doing, and don't worry about the consequences for other people." This "me first" philosophy emphasizes **hedonism** and self-determined ethics. Although neither of these is altogether without merit, many of these books seem to endorse a regrettably self-centered and even exploitative approach to interpersonal relations.

WHAT TO LOOK FOR IN SELF-HELP BOOKS

In view of the great variability in quality among self-help books, it seems a good idea to provide you with some guidelines about what to look for in seeking genuinely helpful books. The following thoughts give you some criteria for judging books of this type.

1. Clarity in communication is absolutely essential. Advice won't do you much good if you can't understand it. Try to avoid drowning in the murky depths of psychobabble.

NARCISSISM. *A term originated by Freud, used today to describe a condition involving excessive self-love, which leads to immature and self-centered interactions with others.*

HEDONISM. *Devotion to the pursuit of pleasure.*

1.3 RECOMMENDED READING
Psychobabble
by R. D. Rosen (Atheneum, 1977)

This book is a scathing indictment of the popular psychological jargon that permeates many of the best-selling self-help books. Rosen, a journalist, christens this hip, new terminology "psychobabble" and argues that it has muddled our thinking about ourselves and devitalized our communication. The book also contains penetrating (though one-sided) criticism of a number of "schools" of therapy.

Psychobabble, as a style of speech (as opposed to the jargon of certain specific therapies . . .), is more than anything else a feature of contemporary decorum, a form of politesse, a signal to others that one is ready to talk turkey, to engage in real dialogue. Unfortunately, in the rush for revelation, real dialogue often turns out to be real monologue. When I asked a man to whom I had just been introduced at a party recently, "How are you?" (no doubt an early, but harmless, form of psychobabble!), he responded by describing, with an utter disrespect for brevity, his relationship with his wife. Confession, alas, is the new handshake [p. 12].

2. This may sound backward, but look for books that do *not* promise too much in the way of immediate change. The truly useful books tend to be appropriately cautious in their promises and realistic about the challenge of altering one's behavior.

3. Try to select books that mention, at least briefly, the theoretical or research basis for the program they advocate. It is understandable that you may not be interested in a detailed summary of research that supports a particular piece of advice. However, you *should* be interested in whether the advice is based on published research, widely accepted theory, or pure speculation by the author.

4. Intellectually honest authors not only talk about what we know—they also discuss what we do *not* know. There is much to be said for books that are candid about the limits of what the so-called experts really know.

5. Look for books that provide detailed, explicit directions about how to alter your behavior. Generally, these directions represent the crucial core of the book. If they are inadequate in detail, you have been shortchanged.

6. More often than not, books that have a relatively narrow focus on a particular kind of problem tend to deliver more than those that promise to cure all of life's problems with a few simple ideas. Books that cover "everything" are usually superficial and disappointing. Books that devote a great deal of thought to a particular topic tend to be written by authors with genuine expertise on that topic. Such books are more likely to pay off for you.

SELF-REALIZATION PROGRAMS

As a third example of our pervasive search for a sense of direction, I will examine the growing popularity of what I will label "self-realization" programs. These are various kinds of training programs that are supposed to provide profound enlightenment and turn one's life around, usually in a very brief period. They vary greatly in orientation, format, and themes, but they share a propensity to promise participants spectacular benefits. Some of these training regimens have enjoyed enormous success, earning glowing testimonials from thousands of converts. I will describe three programs (*est,* Scientology, Silva Mind Control) that have attained a fair amount of popularity and will evaluate their worth.

EST

Est stands for Erhard Seminars Training (in January 1985 the name was changed to The Forum), a growth method put together by a fellow who goes by the name Werner Erhard. The training consists of intensive 16-hour-a-day seminars, usually conducted on two successive weekends, with about 250 people present. The goal of *est* is "getting it." The "it" is rather mysterious, and most *est* graduates have difficulty describing or explaining it. "It" allegedly involves some devastating insight that revolutionizes the graduate's life.

The seminars are led by an *est* trainer who is usually impressively articulate, with a commanding presence. The trainer lectures and leads discussion. The basic strategy is to break down the trainees' self-esteem and then gradually rebuild it. The trainees are told that they are clods, bunglers, and idiots. They are intimidated, confused, and made to feel foolish. After they have their self-esteem lowered, they are offered a variety of insights borrowed primarily from mainstream psychology. For example, much is made of Fritz Perls's (1969) cardinal idea that one should take responsibility for one's own life. *Est* emphasizes that it is useless to blame your problems on others; you can solve problems only if you accept responsibility for them.

Although many *est* graduates complain afterward that they don't feel any different, many others rave about the experience. Many prominent professionals claim that their lives have been changed in significant ways by the training.

The changes most commonly reported include improvements in self-image, accompanied by reductions in anxiety and feelings of dependency.

SCIENTOLOGY

Scientology is a quasi-religious organization founded in the early 1950s by Ron Hubbard. The goal in Scientology is to become "clear." Getting "clear" involves reaching a point where you are free of all programming in your mind that is not under your control. What exactly does that mean? Well, according to Hubbard, people acquire automatic behavior patterns, called engrams, which can be problematic. These engrams often involve nonadaptive emotional responses to situations. Hubbard asserts that you can rid yourself of a troublesome engram by consciously and completely reliving the original experience that created it, under the guidance of an "auditor." An auditor will help you identify crucial engrams by monitoring your emotional responding during a session with a **GSR device,** similar to a lie detector.

GSR DEVICE. A physiological recording device that monitors a person's galvanic skin response. This is an index of how easily electricity will travel across the surface of the skin. It is often used as an indicator of emotional arousal.

Like *est,* Scientology borrows liberally from the mainstream of psychological theory. An engram is very similar to the conditioned response described by Pavlov some 80 years ago. The notion that you can relive emotional experiences and thereby discharge the emotion is rooted in Freud's concept of catharsis, which is at least 90 years old.

Getting *clear* through Scientology requires a greater investment of both time and money than getting *it* through *est. Est* takes only two weeks and costs around $300. Scientology training may take a couple of years and can cost several thousand dollars.

SILVA MIND CONTROL

Silva Mind Control courses have been available to the public since the mid-1960s. Developed by José Silva, the courses allegedly train participants to gain great control over their brain activity. Silva maintains that it is optimal to operate at the lower rather than the higher brain-wave frequencies. Trainees are taught to use relaxation exercises and visual imagery in order to win conscious control over brain activity.

Once this mind control is acquired, behavioral self-control is supposed to follow. Silva graduates allegedly can use their power of visualization to achieve great self-control. Supposedly, they can eat less, sleep less, work harder, or do whatever is necessary to achieve their goals in life. The mind-control training is also supposed to provide graduates with at least some extrasensory perception (ESP) capabilities.

The Silva Mind Control courses resemble *est* in cost and time commitment. The sequence of four courses costs about $200 and requires about a week's time. Generally, the courses are conducted in small groups.

CRITIQUE

Although their teachings are very different, *est,* Scientology, and Silva Mind Control have much in common. First, they are, above all else, money-making propositions for their developers. None of them offers self-realization free; it costs, and the fees aren't cheap. All three organizations seem to be more interested in making money than in spreading enlightenment. Second, the inventors of all three systems have little or no formal training in the behavioral sciences. In itself, that is not reason for condemnation. One does not have to have academic credentials in order to arrive at worthwhile insights. And, in their own fashion, these persons are undeniably bright, or they wouldn't have so many followers. What *is* disturbing, however, is the realization that these gentlemen appear to have emerged from the ranks of hucksterism rather than science. Werner Erhard, for instance, was previously a door-to-door salesman whose real name was Jack Rosenberg. He has had a long history of involvement with sales schemes that have been characterized as questionable (Brewer, 1975). Third, all three systems are ultimately intellectual mush. They all offer a few worthwhile insights, but these either are borrowed from mainstream psychology or are simple common sense. Most of the material, however, is meaningless psychobabble or intellectual rubbish that is easily refuted by available scientific data. Fourth, in light of their very questionable utility and validity, the popularity of these programs demonstrates the widespread need in our modern culture to search for that elusive secret that will ensure happiness and success. The fact that a great many people will expend considerable amounts of money and effort on such dubious intellectual mush provides another illustration of the lengths to which people will go in seeking a sense of direction.

While *est,* Scientology, and Silva Mind Control share the rather uncomplimentary features described above, they also have one other perplexing thing in common. All three have many disciples who claim that their training revolutionized their lives. If the systems appear to have little real merit, how do we account for this puzzling reality? In all probability, it is primarily a matter of *expectancy effects.* Numerous studies show that if people believe an intervention or program will affect them in certain ways, then they are prone to see the expected effects. For instance, many a patient has been "cured" of some physical illness by the administration of mere sugar pills. Such expectancy effects may occur even when people are disposed to observe themselves very objectively. This objectivity generally is *not* present when people are seeking self-realization. People who take *est,* Scientology, or Silva training are clearly searching for something. They want, sometimes desperately, to see improvement in themselves. After investing considerable time, money, and hope in some pathway to growth, they want very badly to believe that it has paid off. Thus, they are exceedingly biased observers who are predisposed to see the effects that they have been led to expect. With this strong bias, it is not surprising that many participants offer glowing endorsements of *est,* Scientology, and Silva Mind Control. Unfortunately, many of their gains turn out to be illusory and short-lived.

The Approach of This Textbook

As you can see from the previous section, in spite of our impressive technological progress, we are a people beset by a great variety of personal problems. Clearly, living in our complex, modern society is a continuous and formidable challenge. This book is all about that challenge. It is about you. It is about life. It is about psychology. Specifically, it will summarize for you the scientific research on human behavior that appears relevant to the challenge of living effectively in the 1980s. It will draw primarily, but not exclusively, from the science we call psychology.

It will deal with the same kinds of problems addressed by self-help books and self-realization programs: anxiety, frustration, loneliness, depression, self-control, and so forth. However, it makes no boldly seductive promises about solving your personal problems, turning your life around, or helping you achieve inner tranquility. Such promises are pretentious and unrealistic. Psychologists have long recognized that changing one's behavior is an arduous task, fraught with frustration and failure. Psychologists sometimes do intensive therapy with a person for years without solving that person's problem.

However, let us not be too pessimistic about your potential for personal growth. You most certainly *can* change your behavior. Moreover, you can often change it on your own without consulting a professional psychologist. I would not be writing this text if I did not believe that *some* of the readers *might* experience some personal benefit from this literary encounter. But it is important that you have realistic expectations. Reading this book will not be a revelatory experience. There are no mysterious secrets about to be unveiled before you. All this book can do is give you some potentially useful information and point you in some potentially beneficial directions. The rest is up to you.

In view of my rather negative discussion of unorthodox religious groups, self-help books, and self-realization programs, it seems essential that I lay out explicitly the philosophy that underlies the writing of this text. The following five statements summarize the assumptions and goals of this book.

1. *It is based on the premise that accurate knowledge about the principles of psychology may be of some value to you in everyday life.* It has been said that knowledge is power. It seems reasonable that greater awareness of why people behave as they do should help you in interacting with others as well as in trying to understand yourself.

2. First and foremost, *it is a course textbook.* The main purpose of this book is to instruct you about the theory and research of psychology relevant to adjustment. Just as if you were reading a physics textbook, you will be asked to learn many new concepts, some of which are quite complex. Reading this book will require some effort.

3. *It is committed to eclecticism.* Eclecticism involves choosing what appears to be the best from a diversity of sources. Although this is primarily a psychology textbook, the topic transcends disciplinary lines. Information from other disciplines, such as sociology, anthropology, and biology, will be included. Additionally, this book will not be dominated by any particular theoretical orientation. The psychoanalytic, behavioristic, and humanistic schools of thought within psychology will be treated with equal respect.

4. *It should open doors.* The coverage of this book is very broad; we will tackle many topics. Therefore, there may be places where it lacks the depth or detail that you would like. However, you should think of it as a resource book that can introduce you to other books or techniques or therapies, which you can then pursue on your own.

5. *It assumes that the key to effective adjustment is to "take charge" of your own life.* If you are dissatisfied with some aspect of your life, it does no good to sit around and mope about it. You have to take an active role in attempting to improve the quality of your life. This may involve learning a new skill or pursuing a particular kind of help. In any case, it is generally best to meet problems head on rather than trying to avoid them.

An Introduction to Key Concepts

Now that I have spelled out my approach in writing this text, it is time to turn to the task of introducing you to some basic concepts. In this section, I will discuss the nature of psychology and explain the advantages of the scientific approach to understanding behavior. I will also introduce you to the controversial concept of adjustment and will direct attention to the role of personality as it relates to the process of adjustment.

WHAT IS PSYCHOLOGY?

PSYCHOLOGY. *The scientific study of behavior and the physiological and cognitive processes that underlie it.*

Psychology is usually defined as the scientific study of behavior and the physiological and cognitive processes that underlie it. Thus, it is a discipline of study, just like history or chemistry. Unlike history, it embraces the scientific method. Science involves a particular approach to investigating the world around us that depends on objective observation. The key features and advantages of the scientific method will be discussed momentarily. At this point, it is sufficient to note that psychology is an area of scientific study, much like biology or physics. Whereas biology focuses on life processes, and physics on matter and energy, the focus of psychology is on *behavior.*

WHAT IS BEHAVIOR?

BEHAVIOR. *The activities and responses of an organism.*

Behavior is typically defined as any response or activity by an organism. This definition is very broad in scope; practically speaking, it means that psychologists study a vast array of phenomena. Psychologists are interested in maze running in rats, salivation in dogs, and brain functioning in cats, as well as visual perception in humans, play in children, and social interaction in adults. Psychology does not confine itself to the study of *human* behavior. Many psychologists believe that the principles of behavior are much the same for animals and humans. These psychologists often prefer to study animals because they can exert more control over the factors influencing the animals' behavior.

If you have taken an introductory psychology course, you are well aware of the great diversity encompassed by the term *behavior.* You probably studied the nervous system, visual and auditory perception, the physiology of motivation, simple and complex learning, thinking processes, personality, and abnormal behavior. Occasionally, students report that they are disappointed with the content of their introductory psychology course. The reason is usually that they mistakenly thought that psychology dealt only with personality and social interaction, and they were unpleasantly surprised by all the seemingly irrelevant material on animals and physiology. Those students were probably interested in that portion of psychology that is the subject matter of this book. The behavior on which the psychology of adjustment focuses is the *human* effort to deal with the demands of *everyday* life.

WHAT IS ADJUSTMENT?

The term *adjustment* has been used extensively thus far without clarifying its exact meaning. Actually, the term has a couple of meanings in psychology, and I shall discuss both of these.

ADJUSTMENT AS AN ACHIEVEMENT

ADJUSTMENT. *May refer to a person's psychological health or to the psychological process by means of which a person copes with demands and pressures.*

When we talk about someone's being well adjusted or maladjusted, we are viewing **adjustment** as an achievement. Most of us have probably used the term *adjustment* in this manner, which represents a practical rather than a theoretical perspective. Statements about the quality of someone's adjustment are essentially assertions about that person's psychological or mental health.

This use of the term *adjustment* has generated much controversy over the years. There has been much debate among psychologists and other interested parties regarding the criteria of psychological health and psychological disorders (see Chapters 2 and 14). Various critics (for example, Szasz, 1960) have stressed that looking at adjustment as an achievement necessarily involves value judgments. Some psychologists, to disassociate themselves from such value judgments, have suggested that the concept of adjustment should be discarded. For example, O'Connell and O'Connell (1974) summarize these feelings as follows.

> Small wonder, then, that psychologists have become increasingly embarrassed by the word *adjustment,* especially when some are saying that it is our society which is sick and needs to be treated as the patient. They argue, moreover, that such terms as *adjustment, mental health, mental illness,* etc. are not only meaningless, arbitrary, and mythical, but downright dangerous [p. 11].

Those critics who argue that evaluations of adjustment or psychological health implicitly involve value judgments are clearly correct. They quite accurately pinpoint as a misconception the commonly held notion that the criteria of good psychological health are as clear as the criteria of good physical health. However, repudiating terms such as *adjustment* or *mental health* hardly seems an authentic solution to this problem. The people who advocate purging *adjustment* from our vocabulary often turn around and use equally value-laden terms, such as *the integrated personality, the wholesome individual,* or *personal growth.* It seems inevitable that people are going to make judgments about adjustment as an achievement, and it appears equally inevitable that these assessments will be influenced by their values. While we can encourage people to be less judgmental, it seems more important to emphasize the debatable and fallible nature of the criteria of good adjustment and to make explicit the values that underlie these criteria. I shall make efforts along these lines in Chapters 2 and 14, which deal with psychological health and psychopathology.

ADJUSTMENT AS A PROCESS

The concept of adjustment was originally borrowed from biology. It was modeled after the biological term *adaptation,* which refers to efforts by a species to adjust to changes in its environment. Just as a field mouse has to adapt to an unusually brutal winter, a person has to adjust to changes in circumstances such as a new job or a financial setback. Accordingly, Lazarus (1969) has defined *adjustment* as the psychological processes by means of which the individual manages or copes with various demands or pressures.

From this viewpoint, adjustment is seen as an *ongoing process.* This perspective is more theoretical than practical. The emphasis is on understanding the dynamics of adjustment rather than on evaluating the quality of adjustment. Generally speaking, when the term *adjustment* is used in this text, it will refer to the *process* of coping with the demands of modern life.

WHAT IS PERSONALITY?

PERSONALITY. *A person's characteristic or consistent patterns of behavior.*

What does it mean when you say that a friend has an "outgoing" personality? Such a statement usually implies that your friend has a fairly consistent tendency to behave in a friendly, extroverted, and gregarious manner in a variety of situations. The quality of *cross-situational consistency* is probably most crucial to the concept of **personality.** The numerous definitions of personality that have enjoyed some acceptance generally share two features: (1) that personality involves characteristics that lie "within" the person and (2) that the stability of these characteristics predisposes the person to certain consistent behavioral tendencies.

Imagine that you are hurtling upward in an elevator with three other persons when suddenly there is a power blackout and the elevator grinds to a halt 45 stories above the ground. Your three companions might react quite differently. One might display considerable fear and start making ominous predictions about your impending demise. Another might take it rather casually and crack a joke to release tension. The third might systematically start reviewing the possible courses of action for getting all of you safely out of the elevator. This little scenario illustrates how personality and adjustment are interrelated. These three persons are reacting very differently to the *same* stressful situation. Such differential reactions to the same situation are usually attributed to personality differences. A person's patterns of adjustment are influenced greatly by his or her personality. Conversely, an integral part of one's personality consists of one's typical patterns of adjustment. Thus, personality and adjustment are intimately related concepts. Because of this intimate relationship, I will give considerable attention to the topic of personality. In fact, all of Chapter 2 will be devoted to theoretical models of personality.

WHAT IS THE NATURE OF SCIENCE?

We all expend a great deal of mental effort in trying to understand our own behavior as well as the behavior of others. We ask ourselves such questions as: Why am I so anxious when I interact with new people? Why am I depressed so often? Why is Sam always trying to be the center of attention at the office? Why does Joanna cheat on her wonderful husband?

Given that psychologists' principal endeavor is to understand behavior, how are their efforts different from everyone else's? The key difference lies in the psychologist's commitment to the scientific method. The investigations into behavior conducted by psychologists and other social scientists are formal, systematic, and objective, whereas the speculation of the layperson is informal, unsystematic, and usually very subjective or biased. To introduce you to the nature of the scientific endeavor, I will briefly describe the assumptions, goals, and procedures of scientific research.

ASSUMPTIONS

A number of crucial assumptions lie at the heart of the scientific approach to the understanding of behavior. Among these, the most important are the assumptions of **determinism** and **empiricism.**

DETERMINISM. *The premise or philosophical stance that events (including behavior) are governed by some lawful order.*

EMPIRICISM. *The premise that knowledge should be acquired through actual observation or experience.*

Determinism.   The psychologist assumes that your behavior is determined in some lawful manner by the events and circumstances that you are exposed to, just as the movement of matter is governed by the law of gravity. Although the behavior of people may not *seem* as consistent or lawful as the behavior of planets or molecules, the psychologist assumes that there are some laws of behavior and that they can be uncovered by systematic investigation. It should be noted that most of the "laws" derived in the social sciences are *probabilistic.* That is, they involve a statement about a behavioral *tendency* (for example, "Men *tend* to be more aggressive than women") rather than a statement that is *universally* true (for example, "Dissolving a solid in liquid will raise the boiling point of the liquid").

Empiricism.   The scientific endeavor is predicated on the belief that empiricism is the best, or at least the most dependable, route to knowledge. When we say that science is empirical, we mean that it is based on *observation.* Instead of just speculating about a relationship such as that between certain child-rearing techniques and adolescent personality, the psychologist goes out and collects information, or data, on the question. This observation is as *systematic* and *objective* as possible.

GOALS

Scientific investigation is aimed at achieving three sets of goals. These goals are described below as they relate to psychology.

Measurement and description.   One cannot investigate a question about behavior, such as whether men are more or less aggressive than women, without developing some means of measuring aggressiveness. Hence, the first goal of psychology is to develop measurement techniques that permit a clear description of behavior.

Understanding and prediction.   A higher-level goal involves the desire to understand or explain behavior. We understand behavior when we can identify the reasons for its occurrence. We usually test our tentative understanding by making a prediction, such as "If I manipulate variable A, then it will have a certain effect on variable B." If our prediction is verified, this increases our confidence in our explanation; however, it does not guarantee that we truly understand the behavior. In any case, the second goal of psychology is to achieve an understanding of why we behave as we do.

Application.   Ultimately, most psychologists hope that the information they gather will be of some practical use in helping to solve everyday problems. They would like to contribute to the efforts to reduce crime or poverty or alienation in our society, and they would like to help people become brighter, healthier, and happier. Thus, the final goal of scientific psychology is to apply the findings, or newly acquired knowledge, to practical problems.

STEPS IN A SCIENTIFIC INVESTIGATION

Your best friend has been raving for weeks about a meditation group that he has joined. He says it has turned his life around! He claims to be happier, more energetic, less anxious, and in better control of his life. You are skeptical. The only clear behavioral change you can see is that meditation is all he ever talks about. You are doubtful about the wonderful effects he ascribes to meditation. At the same time, you are genuinely curious, and you wonder whether meditation might indeed be beneficial. This is the point of departure for any research endeavor. It begins with a question or a problem. The question stimulates the scientist to seek information that may provide at least a partial answer. Social scientists use a variety of procedures to answer questions about behavior. Although it is beyond the scope of this text to go into the details of these techniques, it is important that you understand the two key steps that take place in any scientific investigation.

HYPOTHESIS. *A tentative explanation of the relationship between two or more variables. Usually stated in an if-then format, which makes a prediction that if variable* X *is manipulated in a certain way, variable* Y *will be affected in a certain way.*

1. *Formulate a testable hypothesis.* In order to use the scientific method, one must have a testable **hypothesis,** which is submitted to a critical evaluation. The hypotheses of the layperson are often vaguely stated and rarely subjected to any kind of empirical test. In contrast, scientific hypotheses must be precisely stated to facilitate testability. For example, in an investigation of meditation, you might hypothesize that people who meditate at least four hours a week should score lower on the Taylor Manifest Anxiety Scale than comparable people who do not meditate.

SUBJECTS. *The persons or animals studied in empirical research. Members of the sample.*

2. *Gather the appropriate data.* After you have clearly stated your hypothesis, the second step in a scientific investigation is to put it to a test. This involves procuring a sample of **subjects** and doing some kind of systematic observation that will allow you to support or disprove your hypothesis. It is this systematic data collection that ultimately differentiates the scientific endeavor from other approaches to understanding behavior. To test the hypothesis about meditation formulated above, you would assemble a group of meditators and a similar group of nonmeditators. You would then administer your measure of anxiety to see whether there was a substantial difference between the two groups, as predicted in your hypothesis.

WHAT ARE THE ADVANTAGES OF THE SCIENTIFIC APPROACH?

Science is not the only means we can use to draw conclusions about behavior. We all use logic, good old-fashioned common sense, and casual observation to arrive at beliefs about behavior. Since the scientific method often requires a great deal of effort in data collection, it seems reasonable to ask what the advantages of the scientific approach are.

Basically, the scientific approach has two major advantages. The first is its clarity and precision. Common-sense notions about behavior tend to be very vague or ambiguous. Consider the old truism "Spare the rod and spoil the child." What exactly constitutes sparing the rod? How do you assess whether a child qualifies as spoiled? This statement about rod sparing and child spoiling means different things to different people. When two persons disagree about this assertion, it may be because they are talking about altogether different things. In contrast, the scientific approach requires that we develop precise **operational definitions** of all relevant variables. We must specify *exactly* what we are talking about when we formulate scientific hypotheses. This greater clarity enhances communication about ideas.

OPERATIONAL DEFINITION. *A very specific definition of a concept or variable, usually stated in terms of the operations used to measure it.*

The second advantage offered by the scientific approach is its intolerance of error. Scientists are trained to be skeptical. They not only subject their ideas to empirical test; they also scrutinize one another's findings with a hypercritical eye. There is a place in science for speculation, which often yields intriguing hypotheses, but the scientist ultimately demands objective data and documentation. When the findings of two studies conflict, the scientist tries to ascertain which is correct. In contrast, common-sense analyses often tolerate contradic-

1.4 SCIENTIFIC DESCRIPTION: CORRELATION

Scientists often use various kinds of statistics to summarize the results of their empirical observations. One of the most commonly used statistics is the correlation coefficient. You will see it mentioned frequently throughout this book. The correlation coefficient provides a convenient means for indicating what kind of relationship exists between two variables and how strong that relationship is. Correlation coefficients are usually represented by the letter *r* (for example, *r* = .68).

There are two *kinds* of relationships that can be described by a correlation. A *positive* correlation means there is a *direct* relationship between the two variables—say, X and Y. This means that people who score high on variable X tend to score high on variable Y, while people who score low on variable X tend also to score low on variable Y. For example, there is a positive correlation between high school grade-point average (GPA) and subsequent college GPA (Scannell, 1960). People who do well in high school tend to do well in college, and those who perform poorly in high school tend to perform poorly in college. A *negative* correlation means there is an *inverse* relationship between the two variables. This means that the people who score high or low on variable X tend to score the opposite on variable Y. For example, there is a negative correlation between subjects' test anxiety and test performance (Sarason, 1960). Higher anxiety scores are associated with lower test scores, and vice versa.

While the positive or negative sign indicates what *kind* of relationship exists (direct or inverse), the ac-

tual coefficient indicates the *strength of the tendency* for the two variables to be associated. This coefficient can vary between 0 and ±1.00. A coefficient of zero tells us that there is no relationship between the variables, and a coefficient of 1.00 tells us that there is a *perfect,* one-to-one correspondence. In most cases, the coefficient will be somewhere in between these two extremes. The closer the coefficient is to either +1.00 or −1.00, the stronger the relationship. Thus, a correlation of .90 represents a stronger tendency for variables to be associated than does a correlation of .40. It should be noted that these figures are not percentages, and it is inappropriate to interpret a coefficient of .80 as being twice as strong as a coefficient of .40. It is also important to remember that a high correlation between two variables does not necessarily indicate that there is a causal link between the variables. Correlations often tempt people to draw inferences about causality. For instance, the previously mentioned negative correlation between test anxiety and test performance often leads people to conclude that anxiety causes one to perform poorly on exams. That conclusion may or may not be accurate. One might argue that the causation is in the opposite direction. It may be that people who perform poorly on exams are painfully aware of that fact, and their anticipation of poor performance causes them to be anxious. Whatever the case, the crucial point is that a correlation, in and of itself, does not provide a sound basis for conclusions about causation. Examples of various correlation coefficients yielded by research can be seen below.

Variables yielding correlations of different magnitudes

First variable (X)	Correlation coefficient	Second variable (Y)
Form "L" of 1937 Stanford-Binet Intelligence Scale correlates	.92	with Form "M" of 1937 Stanford-Binet
Artists' Vocational Interest Scale correlates	.85	with Architects' Vocational Interest Scale
Height of fathers correlates	.56	with height of sons
Otis Self-Administering Intelligence Test correlates	.56	with productivity of bookkeepers
Empathy Test scores correlate	.44	with sales records of automobile salesmen
Number of children in family correlates	−.18	with intelligence
Permissiveness of mothers correlates	−.25	with anti-Semitism in their daughters
Test anxiety in male students correlates	−.34	with final grade in introductory psychology course
Peer ratings of likability correlates	−.41	with peer ratings of depression among sixth-grade boys
Masculinity on Strong Vocational Interest Blank correlates	−.49	with ratings of creativity
Wholesale price of cotton correlates	−.70	with number of lynchings in the South, 1882–1930

tory generalizations (for example, "He who hesitates is lost" and "Look before you leap") and involve little effort to verify ideas or detect errors. What all this adds up to is that the scientific approach tends to yield more accurate information than common-sense analyses. This is not to say that science has a copyright on truth. However, the scientific approach does tend to produce information that is well grounded in reality.

It should be emphasized that science is not the only route through which one can acquire knowledge about behavior. Novelists, poets, playwrights, and philosophers often offer penetrating insights about the nature of human behavior. However, the scientist is the only one of these who is required to empirically verify his or her hypotheses and theories. This means that science is less speculative than other approaches to understanding behavior. Thus, a knowledge of scientific data can provide a useful benchmark against which to judge other kinds of analyses.

A Scientific Analysis of Happiness

To illustrate the utility of the scientific approach to understanding behavior, I will discuss some recent research on the determinants of happiness. Obviously, virtually all of us want to achieve happiness. But what exactly makes a person happy? This question has been the subject of much speculation. Common-sense hypotheses about the roots of happiness abound. For example, we have all heard that money cannot buy happiness. But do you believe it? A television commercial tells us "If you've got your health, you've got just about every-

---

1.5 COMMON SENSE VERSUS SCIENCE

People often say that psychology involves nothing more than common sense. This assertion reflects the undeniable fact that scientifically derived generalizations about behavior often coincide with simple common-sense statements about behavior. It is true that some psychological studies are elaborate and elegant empirical verifications of the obvious. For example, research showing that a person's level of physical attractiveness influences heterosexual attraction (see Chapter 9) admittedly does not represent a dazzling new insight into social behavior.

However, this correspondence between common sense and scientific psychology has generally been overestimated and misinterpreted. The fact that there is some correspondence does not mean that scientific research is a waste of time and effort. This correspondence simply indicates that, at least some of the time, common-sense generalizations about behavior turn out to be accurate. It is difficult to estimate just how often common-sense formulations are accurate, because they are so vague. Nonetheless, it is quite clear that common-sense notions about behavior are often wrong or at least in conflict with scientific data. For example, Vaughan's (1977) study of misconceptions about behavior indicates that the following statements, which are *not* supported by research, are commonly believed by many students in introductory psychology courses.

- To change people's behavior toward members of ethnic minority groups, we must first change their attitudes.
- The basis of the baby's love for his mother is the fact that his mother fills his physiological needs for food and other necessities.
- The more highly motivated you are, the better you will do at solving a complex problem.
- A schizophrenic is someone with a split personality.
- Fortunately for babies, human beings have a strong maternal instinct.
- Children memorize much more easily than adults.
- Boys and girls exhibit no behavioral differences until environmental influences begin to produce such differences.
- Genius is closely akin to insanity.

In Vaughan's study, each of the above statements was endorsed by at least half the students. Thus, it is clear that there is often a gap between common sense and scientific psychology.

When there *is* such a gap between common sense and scientific data, the latter seems more likely to be correct. Common-sense notions about behavior tend to be based on mere speculation and are rarely subjected to any kind of test of accuracy. In contrast, scientifically derived generalizations are based on systematic observation, which usually includes some test of accuracy.

thing." Is health indeed the key? What if you're healthy but poor, unemployed, and lonely? We often hear about the joys of parenthood, the joys of youth, and the joys of the simple, rural life. Are these the factors that promote happiness?

In recent years, social scientists have begun putting these and other hypotheses to empirical test. A number of large-scale studies have been conducted to ascertain the determinants of happiness. In these studies people are asked to evaluate their overall happiness, as well as their satisfaction with many specific aspects of their lives. The researchers then look for correlations (see Box 1.4) between subjects' general happiness and their feelings about specific areas of their lives. Although this research is still in its infancy, with much more work to be done, the preliminary returns are fascinating. The empirical data, summarized concisely by social psychologist Jonathan Freedman (1978), shed considerable light on what is and what is not important in the pursuit of happiness. I review this research for two reasons. First, it nicely illustrates the value of collecting scientific data and putting ideas to an empirical test. As you will see momentarily, many common-sense notions about happiness appear to be inaccurate. Second, evidence on what makes people happy is of direct relevance to adjustment issues. Insofar as this text is concerned with learning to live life more fully and effectively, it certainly would be worthwhile to find out whether there is any simple recipe for achieving happiness.

WHAT ISN'T VERY IMPORTANT?

Let us begin by discussing those things that turned out to be less important than one might have expected. The list is rather lengthy. Many factors that were commonly believed to be crucial to one's sense of well-being appear to bear only a slight relationship to general happiness.

Money. Money is important only when you don't have any. People at the very bottom of the economic ladder *are* relatively unhappy. However, once you ascend above the poverty level, there is little relation between income and happiness. In this modern era of voracious consumption, most of us find a way to spend all our money and come out short, no matter how much money we make. Wealthy people generally are no happier than the middle classes.

Health. The situation is essentially the same in regard to physical health. Very poor health does make it difficult (although not impossible) to be happy, but good health does not, by itself, produce happiness. It appears that people take their good health for granted.

Age. It has been suggested that adolescence is both a great time for fun and a period of turmoil, self-doubt, and misery. Neither of these assertions was confirmed. Generally, age and happiness were found to be unrelated. The only exception involved old age, and here the findings were mixed. After age 65 the number of people who report themselves as unhappy increases. Surprisingly, however, so does the number of people who say they are very happy.

Parenthood. Although children can be a tremendous source of joy and fulfillment, they can also be a tremendous source of headaches and hassles. Apparently, the good and bad aspects of parenthood cancel each other out, because the evidence indicates that having children does not appreciably influence the happiness of most people.

Community. When asked where they would most like to live, people showed a clear preference for the stereotype of the tranquil, pastoral life believed to exist in rural areas. However, when actual reported happiness was related to community type, it was found that people living in urban, suburban, and rural areas were equally happy.

Religion. Although members of the clergy reported themselves as exceptionally happy, religious convictions were not a major determinant of happiness for most people. Atheists were as happy as conventional religious believers. Moreover, even the belief in an afterlife did not enhance people's happiness.

Sex. Generally, sex is like money: it has a significant effect on your happiness only if you don't have any. Frequency of sexual encounters and number of sexual partners were unrelated to level of happiness, with the exception that people who have *no* sex life at all were extremely unhappy. The data suggest that the quality of one's sex life is more important than quantity, at least for women. Among females, the report of specific sexual problems (mostly inability to achieve orgasm) was related to being less happy. However, males' reports of specific sexual problems were not related to lower levels of happiness. Homosexuals were found to be just as happy as heterosexuals.

WHAT IS IMPORTANT?

The list of factors that turned out to be very important is surprisingly short. Freedman uncovered only a handful of items that were consistently related to overall happiness.

Love. While sex may not be all that important, love certainly is. Everyone—whether male or female, young or old, heterosexual or homosexual—indicated that love was a very important determinant of his or her happiness. Among people who were very happily in love, over 90% were very happy in general, and a mere 1% were very unhappy. More than any other single thing, the unhappy people mentioned love as the one element of life that could make them happy.

What makes a person happy? It is an elusive research question, but love certainly seems to be an important factor.

Marriage.   Surprisingly, in this era of widespread divorce, the evidence indicates that marriage is a significant determinant of happiness. Among both men and women, married people are happier than people who are single. The reason appears quite simple: single people are much more prone to feelings of loneliness. However, Freedman points out that it would be premature at this point to conclude that marriage itself *causes* this greater happiness. It may be that people who are already happy tend to get married, while people who are already unhappy tend to remain single. Thus, although it is difficult to tease out the causal relationships here, the data suggests that marriage provides an important foundation for happiness.

Work.   Job satisfaction turned out to be highly related to general happiness. One study found that, among people who were happy with their jobs, 70% were happy with life as a whole, while only 14% were unhappy with life in general. Work is important for both sexes; however, it is somewhat less important for married people than for singles. Interestingly, among married women, those who work are happier than those who do not. As one might expect, there is a relationship between job status and happiness; people who have higher-status jobs (professions, services) report greater happiness than people who have lower-status jobs (clerical and blue-collar occupations). However, there were a couple of startling exceptions to this generalization. Lawyers and physicians, who have *very* high-status jobs, indicated that they were relatively unhappy! Freedman speculates that these professions might demand such a high level of involvement that the lawyers and doctors have no time left over to enjoy themselves. He also points out that these results should be viewed with caution because a relatively small number of attorneys and physicians were involved in the research on happiness.

CONCLUSIONS

In putting the research on happiness into an overall perspective, Freedman draws several interesting conclusions. First, he stresses what you have probably already begun to realize: *there is no simple recipe for achieving happiness*. Says Freedman:

> Alas, the one overwhelming finding of all the research is that there is no easy solution for finding it. I can suggest no religious beliefs, mystical practices (I suppose it helps to have a guardian angel or spirit, but I don't know how to find one), meditative exercises (the TM publicity to the contrary), strange diets, biofeedback procedures, or system of philosophy that will produce happiness. Nor can I propose that the power of positive thinking, looking out for number one, deciding that you and I are OK, becoming your own best friend, or anything of that sort will guarantee happiness. There is no evidence that any of these ideas (many of which have been pushed by popular books) has any substantial effect on happiness for most people [1978, p. 9].

Second, Freedman points out that in many respects *happiness appears to be relative*. In other words, you evaluate what you have relative to what the people around you have and relative to what you expected to have. In comparing ourselves with others, we use as our **reference group** people who are similar to us. Thus, people who are wealthy assess what they have by comparing their possessions with those of their wealthy friends and acquaintances. This is probably one reason that it is quite possible to be wealthy and dissatisfied. You might have a lovely home, but if it sits next door to someone else's palatial mansion, it might be a source of more dissatisfaction than happiness. Consistent with this analysis, Freedman points out that, among high school and college graduates who earn about the same income, the college graduates are less happy than the high school graduates, presumably because the latter have a

REFERENCE GROUP.
According to social comparison theory, the particular group of people against whom you compare yourself in order to better understand your attitudes, values, beliefs, and behavior.

lower standard of comparison. In addition to comparing ourselves with other people, we compare what we have with what our expectations were. When we exceed our expectations, we tend to be happy. Thus, the people living in the lovely home next door to the much lovelier mansion could still be quite happy—if they never expected to live in anywhere near such an affluent neighborhood. Thus, it seems that, to a large degree, happiness is measured on a relative, rather than an absolute, scale.

The third point of Freedman's worth noting is an encouraging one. He concludes that the quest for happiness is never hopeless. There is nothing, short of terminal illness—no setback, shortcoming, difficulty, or inadequacy—that makes happiness impossible. The evidence indicates that some people find happiness in spite of seemingly insurmountable problems. Unhappy children often become happy adults. Although Freedman was unable to discover any simple shortcuts to happiness, he did find that this important goal is not beyond the grasp of any of us. No matter how unhappy you might be presently, you can still realistically nurture the hope that someday your pursuit of happiness will bring fulfillment.

Summary

In spite of great progress in our modern era, personal problems have not been eliminated. In fact, theorists such as Fromm and Toffler suggest that our progress brings new, and possibly more difficult, adjustment problems. The popularity of unorthodox religious groups, self-help books, and self-realization programs represents three of the more interesting manifestations of our struggle to find a sense of direction in our confusing world. Although this text deals with many of the same issues as the self-help books, its philosophy and approach are quite different.

Psychology is the scientific study of behavior. Adjustment is a broad area of study in psychology that focuses on how people adapt effectively or ineffectively to the demands and pressures around them. These adaptation, or adjustment, efforts are greatly affected by one's personality.

The scientific approach to understanding behavior is predicated on the assumptions of determinism and empiricism and strives to achieve an accurate description and explanation of behavior. Most psychologists hope that better understanding of behavior will have some applicability to practical problems. Scientific research involves formulating a testable hypothesis and gathering appropriate data to assess its validity. The scientific approach is advantageous in that it puts a premium on clarity and has little tolerance for error.

A scientific analysis of happiness reveals that many common-sense notions about happiness appear to be incorrect. The only life factors that are clearly and strongly related to happiness for most people are love, marriage, and work. Happiness appears to be a relative concept, and there are no approaches to life that can guarantee happiness.

Improving Academic Performance

Indicate whether the following statements about study techniques are true or false.

_____ 1. If you have a professor who delivers chaotic, hard-to-follow lectures, there is little point in attending class.

_____ 2. In taking lecture notes you should try to be a human tape recorder (that is, take down everything exactly as said by your professor).

_____ 3. Once you have memorized information perfectly, there is no point in continuing to practice it.

_____ 4. Outlining reading assignments tends to be a waste of time.

_____ 5. "Cramming" the night before an exam is an efficient way to maximize one's mastery of material.

All the above statements are false. If you answered them all correctly, you may already be fairly knowledgeable about good study habits. If so, however, you are probably in a small minority. Today an amazing number of students enter college with very poor study skills and habits. Actually, that is not so surprising when you consider that our educational system generally does *not* provide much in the way of formal instruction on study techniques. For some inexplicable reason this seemingly fundamental topic tends to "slip between the cracks" and gets very little attention. In this first application section, I will try to remedy that situation a little bit by sharing with you some insights that psychology can provide on how to improve your academic performance. I'll discuss how to study effectively, how to get more out of your reading and lectures, and how to improve your memory. For those who have trouble taking exams, I also make a recommendation for additional reading (see Box 1.7) that can help you to improve your **testwiseness.** Studies (for example, Rowley, 1974; Weiten, Clery, & Bowbin, 1980) indicate that differences among students in testwiseness *can* influence performance on classroom exams.

TESTWISENESS. *The ability to take exams skillfully, so as to maximize one's score, given a certain amount of content knowledge.*

DEVELOPING SOUND STUDY HABITS

Effective study is crucial to success in college. You may occasionally run into a few classmates who brag about how well they do without studying. However, you can dismiss their boasting as a lot of hot air. If they perform well on exams, they study. Outside of cheating (which, in addition to being immoral, is often more work than studying), there are no shortcuts. Those who claim that they do well without studying simply want to be seen as brilliant, rather than hard-working and diligent. That's their prerogative, but don't let them mislead you into thinking that you can learn without studying.

More often than not, studying is an unpleasant task. The first step toward effective study is to face up to this ugly reality. Let's not kid ourselves about the joys of learning. Although learning can be immensely gratifying, it's generally hard work. For example, your author loves to play tennis. In spite of my affection for the sport, I find the task of learning to make certain shots more effectively through repetitive practice very boring and aversive. If an enjoyable activity such as tennis can become aversive, it is easy to understand how studying for some dull, required course can become unbearable torture. Hence, there is no reason to feel guilty if you don't look forward to studying. People rarely do. Once you recognize this reality, it should be apparent that you have to set up a program to force yourself into adequate study. Such a program should involve the following steps.

1. *Set up a schedule for studying.* It is important that you allocate certain times to studying. If you wait until the urge hits you, you'll still be waiting when the exam rolls around. Instead, you should review your various time obligations and figure out in advance when you can study. In allotting certain times to study, keep in mind that you need to be wide awake and alert. You should not plan on studying at times when you're likely to be very tired (for example, just after getting off work), and you should be realistic about how long you can study at any one time. Your schedule should be written down. This serves as a reminder and increases your commitment to the schedule. Since time management is so crucial to good study habits, you might want to consider reading *How to Get Control of Your Time and Your Life* (Lakein, 1973), highlighted in Box 5.4.

2. *Find a place to study where you can concentrate.* Where you study is crucial to your success. The key is to find a place where distractions are likely to be minimal. Most people cannot study effectively while watching TV, listening to the stereo, or overhearing conversations. Do not depend on willpower to carry you through such distractions. It is much easier to plan ahead and avoid the distractions altogether. Libraries tend to be conducive to study, but they too can become social centers. Accordingly, it is generally a good idea to conceal yourself in a study carrel away from the flow of human traffic.

Whether you should study alone or in a group depends on the task at hand. If the task simply involves digesting and storing information, you're often in better shape if you study alone. The problem is that many study groups tend to degenerate into "bull sessions." However, working in a group may be valuable for certain problem-solving tasks on which brainstorming might help, such as working calculus problems.

There is evidence (Beneke & Harris, 1972) that it helps to set up one or two specific places for study *that are used for nothing else.* Those places tend to become strongly associated with studying, so that they serve as cues to evoke good study behavior.

3. *Reward your studying.* One of the reasons it is so difficult to study is that the payoff, or reward, is too distant. The ultimate reward, a degree, is often years away. Even more short-term rewards, such as an A in the course, may be weeks or months away. To combat this problem, you should plan short-term rewards for your studying. It is easier to motivate yourself to study if there is some immediate tangible reward, such as a snack, TV show, or phone call, waiting when you finish. Thus, you should set realistic study goals for yourself and then reward yourself when you meet them. The behavior modification techniques introduced in Chapter 5 can be extremely valuable in increasing study behavior.

For this young man, a tree provides the ideal place to study—quiet and certainly away from the flow of human traffic.

IMPROVING YOUR READING

Much of your study time is spent reading and absorbing information. *These efforts must be active.* If you engage in passive reading, the information will pass right through you. Many students delude themselves into thinking that they are studying when they are really using their textbooks as coloring books. They take a pastel felt-tip pen and run it through a few sentences here and there, often with no selectivity, and pretend that that constitutes studying. Underlining in your text can be very useful, but it must be done in a discriminating manner.

There are a number of ways of actively attacking your reading assignments. One of the more worthwhile of these techniques is Robinson's (1970) SQ3R method. This is a five-step procedure to promote effective reading and studying. Its name is an abbreviation of the five steps in the procedure.

Step 1: Survey. Before you plunge into the actual reading, glance over the topic headings in the chapter and try to get a general overview of the material. Try to understand how the various chapter segments are related. If there is an outline or summary, consult it to get a general feel for the chapter. You need to know where the chapter is going in order to appreciate and organize the information you are about to read.

Step 2: Question. Now that you have an overview, you're going to tackle the chapter one section at a time. Take a look at the heading of the first section and convert it into a question. This is usually quite simple. If the heading is "Sources of Stress," your question should be "What are the sources of stress?" If the heading is "Stereotyping," your question should be "What is stereotyping?" Asking these questions gets you actively involved in the reading you are about to do.

Step 3: Read. Only now, in the third step, are you ready to read. Read only the material under the first section heading. You should read it with an eye toward answering the question that you just formulated. Read it and reread it if necessary until you can answer that question.

Step 4: Recite. Now that you can answer the question, recite the answer out loud to yourself in your own words. It is important to use your own words because that requires understanding rather than simple memorization of the text. Don't go on to the next section until you thoroughly understand the main idea(s) of the present section. You may want to write down these ideas for subsequent review. When you have digested the main ideas of the first section, then you may go on to the next section. Repeat steps 2, 3, and 4 with the next section. Once you have mastered the crucial points there, you may go on again. Keep repeating steps 2 through 4, section by section, until you have read the entire chapter.

Step 5: Review. When you have read the chapter, test and refresh your memory by going back over the key points. Repeat your questions and try to answer them without consulting your book or notes. This review should fortify your memory of the main ideas and should help you see their overall relations to one another.

The SQ3R technique need not be applied rigidly. For example, it is often wise to break your reading assignment down into smaller segments than those separated by topic headings. In fact, SQ3R should probably be applied paragraph by paragraph for many textbooks. Obviously, this will require you to formulate questions without the benefit of topic headings. These headings are not necessary to use the technique. In these situations you can simply reverse the order of steps 2 and 3. Read the paragraph and then formulate a question that addresses the basic idea of the paragraph. Then work at answering your question in your own words.

It is a bit easier to use the SQ3R technique when a text has plenty of topic headings. This brings up another worthwhile point about improving your reading. You should take advantage of the various organizational aids incorporated into many modern textbooks. If a book offers you an outline at the beginning of a chapter, don't ignore it. It is important to have an overview of where the chapter is going and how the parts are interrelated. If your book furnishes learning objectives, use them. These should tell you with some specificity what you are expected to get out of your reading assignment. Good learning objectives practically formulate the question in the SQ3R process for you. Finally, if your book provides a chapter summary, don't skip it. It provides a very convenient means for reviewing the main ideas of a chapter, and it allows you to check whether you missed any key ideas that the author considered important. In summary, a lot of work usually goes into these organizational aids. They are not superfluous decoration. It is foolish not to take advantage of them when they are available.

The SQ3R technique is intended to get you actively involved in your reading. It is not the only way to accomplish this, but it does have a proven track record. What makes it successful is that it breaks a reading assignment down into manageable segments and requires understanding before you move on. Any procedure that accomplishes these goals will enhance the effectiveness of your reading.

GETTING MORE OUT OF LECTURES

Although lectures are sometimes boring and tedious, it is a simple fact that poor class attendance is associated with poor academic performance (Lindgren, 1969). Even when you have an instructor who delivers chaotic, hard-to-follow lectures from which you derive little information, it is still important to go to class. If nothing else, it helps you to get a feel for how the instructor thinks. This can help you anticipate the content of exams and can help you respond on exams in the manner expected by your professor.

Books on study skills (Pauk, 1962; Pivar, 1978) offer a number of good suggestions on how to get more out of lectures. Some of these are summarized below.

- Extracting information from lectures requires *active listening procedures,* which are described in some detail in Chapter 7. You should attend physically and mentally to the speaker. Try to anticipate what's coming and to search for "deeper" meanings. Also pay attention to nonverbal signals.
- When the course material is complex and difficult, *it is often a good idea to prepare for the lecture by reading ahead in your books*. Then you have less information to digest that is brand new.
- Whenever practical and acceptable to the instructor, *you should ask questions*. This can keep you actively involved in the lecture and help you

---

1.6

RECOMMENDED READING

The Whole Earth Textbook: A Survival Manual for Students
by William H. Pivar (W. B. Saunders, 1978)

This is an excellent book on how to surmount the trials and tribulations of college life. It proceeds in an exceptionally logical fashion, covering topics such as curriculum planning, study techniques, how to take exams, how to write papers, and how to finance your education. It is easy to read and includes a variety of useful self-analysis exercises. It also includes an impressive bibliography that lists other rel-

evant books that tackle specific topics in greater detail. Its only major flaw is a hopelessly superficial appendix on drug use.

You may not be another Ben Franklin, but if you set daily goals and follow them, you will find you are able to get a great deal more accomplished in one day than you felt possible. By setting daily goals you will reach your intermediate goals, and if your inter-

mediate goals are relevant to your career goal, then that too is within your reach. The Chinese have a proverb: "A journey of a thousand miles starts with the first step." Accomplishing your career goal should start now.

Goals may be redefined, and routes to reach them may change, but without goals, you will drift aimlessly. Don't leave to chance that which is within your grasp [pp. 23–24].

avoid daydreaming. It can also help you clarify points that you may have misunderstood. The vast majority of professors welcome these questions, and generally you need not be bashful about this.

- You are not supposed to be a human tape recorder. Insofar as possible, *try to write down thoughts in your own words.* Your crucial task is to organize the material in a manner that makes sense to you.
- *Pay attention to clues about what is important.* Many instructors give both subtle and not-so-subtle clues about what information is most crucial. These clues may range from simply repeating things to saying "You'll run into this again." Try to take note of these clues.
- It's easy to miss points in a lecture. Therefore, *it's a good idea to review your notes sometime soon after the lecture.* If something appears to be missing, consult some of your classmates.

APPLYING THE PRINCIPLES OF MEMORY

RETENTION. *A measure of memory referring to the amount or proportion of material remembered.*

Scientific investigation of memory processes dates back to at least the latter part of the 19th century, when Hermann Ebbinghaus (1885/1913) published a series of insightful studies. Thus, memory has been an important topic in psychology for about a century. This work has led to the derivation of numerous principles that are relevant to the question of how to study effectively. This section will review some of the major factors that affect **retention** and will relate them to academic endeavors.

REPETITION

There is an old saying that "practice makes perfect." Well, the evidence indicates that practice may not guarantee perfection, but it sure improves performance. Assuming that the quality of the practice is reasonably stable, *retention of verbal material improves with repetition* (Deese & Hulse, 1967). Moreover, there is evidence that continued practice after you have reached apparent mastery of the material leads to further enhancement of retention.

OVERLEARNING. *Continuing to practice something after one first appears to master it.*

This additional repetition that occurs after mastery has apparently been achieved is called **overlearning.** In a classic study of overlearning, Krueger (1929) required subjects to memorize a list of nouns. Some of the subjects quit practicing as soon as they got through the list once without error (apparent mastery, no overlearning); others continued practicing for half again as many trials as it took to achieve that criterion of mastery (50% overlearning); a third group continued working until it doubled the number of trials to mastery (100% overlearning). Measuring retention at intervals up to 28 days, Krueger found that *greater overlearning led to better recall of the material.* The practical significance of this finding should be obvious: you should not quit working on memorizing material as soon as you appear to have achieved mastery. Additional repetition will pay off in better retention.

1.7
RECOMMENDED READING
How to Take Tests
by Jason Millman and Walter Pauk (McGraw-Hill, 1969)

This is far and away the best book available on how to improve your test-taking skills. The first author has done extensive research on testwiseness, and the second has expertise in reading and study skills. Together, they have written a very thorough analysis of how to maximize performance on exams. If you're one of those people who have a hard time showing how much you know on exams, this is very worthwhile reading.

Students tend to place too little emphasis on the necessity for carefully reading directions and questions. A perfectly "correct" and well-written answer to a question not asked will receive no credit. Frequently, understanding what is wanted—understanding the question—may be more difficult than the idea or concept being tested for. Surely it makes good sense to look at the question before you leap into an answer [p. 23].

DISTRIBUTION OF PRACTICE

Assuming that you are going to study a certain number of hours for an exam, let us say eight, is it better to "cram" all the study into one eight-hour period (massed practice) or distribute it among, say, four two-hour periods (distributed practice)? The scientific evidence suggests that the age-old tradition of cramming, or massed practice, is less than optimal. Although there are some qualifications, *it appears that distributed practice promotes better retention than massed practice* (Greeno, 1964; Underwood, 1961). This does *not* mean that you shouldn't conduct a very thorough review the night before an exam. At that point, however, you should be consolidating your information, not learning it for the first time.

ORGANIZATION

Material that is organized in some way tends to be remembered better than material that is not put into some kind of organizational framework (Bower et al., 1969). This is one of the major reasons that the SQ3R technique makes study more effective. The survey step and the question/answer framework in SQ3R serve to organize the material. One of the most potent weapons in your arsenal of study techniques is to *outline* reading assignments. This is probably too time-consuming to do for every class; however, it is worth the effort in particularly important or particularly difficult classes. Outlining forces you to organize material in a way that makes sense to you. This will generally lead to improved retention.

MEANINGFULNESS

The effect of meaningfulness on memory is substantial. Let's look at a couple of simple illustrations of meaningfulness. It should be apparent that English words are more meaningful than random strings of letters. Similarly, words that form a sentence are more meaningful than a scrambled, nonsensical list of words. An enormous volume of evidence (McGeoch, 1930; Miller & Selfridge, 1950) indicates that *as material becomes more meaningful, our retention improves.*

The practical significance of this finding is simple. The more personally meaningful you can make the material, the more likely you are to remember it. When you read your textbooks, try to relate the information to your own life and experience. For example, when you read about a particular personality dimension, let us say submissiveness, you should try to think of someone you know who is very submissive. There is ample evidence that efforts to make material more meaningful lead to sizable gains in retention (Raugh & Atkinson, 1975).

MNEMONIC DEVICES

MNEMONIC DEVICE. *A technique used to help one remember something by relating the new material to familiar material.*

Making material more meaningful is sometimes easier said than done. For example, it is much more difficult to make chemistry personally meaningful than psychology. In dealing with abstract material, it is often wise to use **mnemonic devices.** These are clever little memory tricks that can help you impose meaning and organization on abstract material. You probably are already familiar with some of the simpler mnemonic devices. I will illustrate a few of these. To learn more tricks, you may want to consult *The Memory Book* by Lorayne and Lucas (1974).

ACROSTIC. *A mnemonic device involving a meaningful and easy-to-remember phrase, sentence, or poem wherein the first letter of each word or line (in a poem) serves as a reminder of something specific.*

1. *Rhymes.* An old trick that you have surely employed is the use of rhymes. Your author has probably repeated "*I* before *E* except after *C*" a hundred thousand times. Another old standby is "Thirty days hath September . . ."
2. *Acrostics.* These are sentences or phrases wherein the first letter of each word functions as a cue to help you recall specific material. "Every good boy does fine" is a classic that helps people remember the order of musical notes.
3. *Narrative methods.* Acrostics give you only the first letter of each word in

a list to be memorized. If you want the words themselves in a more meaningful arrangement, invent an entire story that includes the words in order. Simple examples of this technique in action can be seen in Table 1.1. Bower and Clark (1969) found that this procedure tremendously enhanced subjects' retention of 12 lists of ten unrelated words.

TABLE 1.1 Word lists to be memorized and stories constructed from them

Word lists	Stories
Bird Costume Mailbox Head River Nurse Theater Wax Eyelid Furnace	A man dressed in a *Bird Costume* and wearing a *Mailbox* on his *Head* was seen leaping into the *River.* A *Nurse* ran out of a nearby *Theater* and applied *Wax* to his *Eyelids,* but her efforts were in vain. He died and was tossed into the *Furnace.*
Rustler Penthouse Mountain Sloth Tavern Fuzz Gland Antler Pencil Vitamin	A *Rustler* lived in a *Penthouse* on top of a *Mountain.* His specialty was the three-toed *Sloth.* He would take his captive animals to a *Tavern* where he would remove *Fuzz* from their *Glands.* Unfortunately, all this exposure to sloth fuzz caused him to grow *Antlers.* So he gave up his profession and went to work in a *Pencil* factory. As a precaution he also took a lot of *Vitamin* E.

4. *Using visual imagery.* There are a number of ways to use visual imagery to enhance retention. One way is to simply imagine an unusual scene that includes the various elements that you need to remember. For example, let's say that you're going to stop at the drugstore on the way home to pick up a newsmagazine, shaving cream, film, and pens. To remember these few items, you might visualize a photographer taking a picture of some public figure who will be in the newsmagazine (for example, the president) shaving with a pen. The utility of such imagery has been demonstrated in research (Lesgold & Goldman, 1973), and it appears that the more bizarre you make the image, the more helpful it will be.

LOCI SYSTEM. *A mnemonic device developed in ancient Greece. It involves taking an imaginary walk along a familiar path where certain images have been associated with certain locations.*

A more elaborate technique involving visual imagery is the **loci system.** In this procedure, you imagine yourself walking along some familiar path—say, in your home. You visualize a number of specific locations in your home; these will serve as your loci. You then put each thing on your list into one of these locations, forming a vivid image of the item sitting in that location. When you need to remember the items, you simply initiate a mental walk through your home, which should stimulate recall of the images you formed. Like the narrative method, this procedure allows you to memorize things in a particular order. Studies (Bower, 1973; Groninger, 1971) show that this is a powerful procedure for augmenting memory capacity.

CHAPTER 1 REVIEW

IDEAS: REVIEW OF LEARNING OBJECTIVES

When you have mastered the material in this chapter, you should be able to do the following.

1. Summarize the theme of Fromm's book *Escape from Freedom*.
2. Summarize the theme of Toffler's book *Future Shock*.
3. List four factors that appear to draw people to unorthodox religious groups (based on research by Cox).
4. Discuss some of the reasons that unorthodox religious groups generally do not provide satisfactory solutions to the search for direction.
5. List four problems that are common in popular "self-help" books.
6. Summarize advice about what to look for in quality "self-help" books.
7. Describe *est*.
8. Describe Scientology.
9. Describe Silva Mind Control.
10. Summarize the text's critique of *est*, Scientology, and Silva Mind Control.
11. List the assumptions on which the scientific endeavor is based.
12. List the three sets of goals for the science of psychology.
13. Describe two major steps in a scientific investigation.
14. Describe two advantages of the scientific approach to understanding behavior.
15. List seven factors that do not appear to be crucial determinants of happiness.
16. Discuss the relationship between love and happiness.
17. Discuss the relationship between marriage and happiness.
18. Discuss the relationship between work and happiness.
19. Summarize Freedman's conclusions about the determinants of happiness.
20. List three steps for developing sound study habits.
21. Describe the SQ3R method of reading.
22. Briefly list six tips for getting more out of lectures.
23. Specify how retention of verbal material is influenced by repetition, distributed practice, organization, and meaningfulness.
24. Describe several mnemonic devices.

TERMS: REVIEW OF NEW VOCABULARY

When you have mastered the material in this chapter, you should be able to define the following terms.

Acrostic	Future shock	Mnemonic device	Psychology
Adjustment	GSR device	Narcissism	Reference group
Behavior	Hedonism	Operational definition	Retention
Charlatanism	Hypothesis	Overlearning	Subjects
Determinism	Loci system	Personality	Testwiseness
Empiricism			

PEOPLE: REVIEW OF MAJOR THEORISTS AND RESEARCHERS

When you have mastered the material in this chapter, you should be able to summarize the principal contributions and/or ideas of the following people.

Hermann Ebbinghaus	Erich Fromm	F. P. Robinson	Alvin Toffler
Jonathan Freedman			

2 THEORIES OF PERSONALITY AND BEHAVIOR

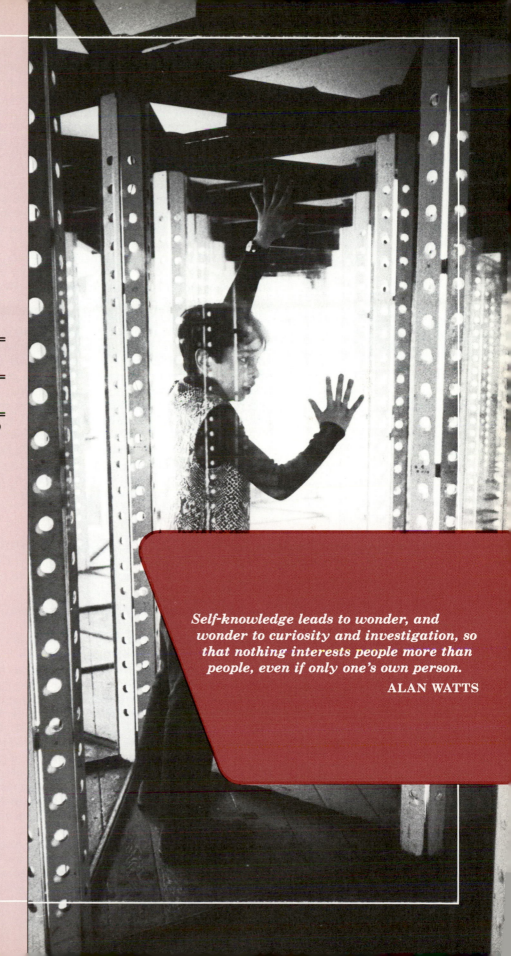

Epilogue

Summary

Applying Psychology to Your Life: Learning about Yourself through Psychological Testing

Self-knowledge leads to wonder, and wonder to curiosity and investigation, so that nothing interests people more than people, even if only one's own person.

ALAN WATTS

In class, I am often asked such questions as "What do psychologists say about letting children watch violent TV shows?" or "What do psychologists say about spanking children?" Questions such as these seem to be based on the inaccurate assumption that psychologists stand united with a single answer for each controversial question. Nothing could be further from the truth. On the contrary, psychologists are very diversified in their opinions about various issues. To a large degree, the answer to a particular question depends on which psychologist you ask!

A variety of schools of thought, or theoretical orientations, exist in psychology. A psychologist's theoretical orientation tends to markedly influence his or her analysis of most questions. In this chapter I will use a review of personality theory to acquaint you with the three major schools of thought in psychology: the psychoanalytic, the behavioristic, and the humanistic theoretical orientations. These theoretical approaches represent conceptual models that help us explain behavior. You need some familiarity with them in order to fully understand many of the explanations that you will encounter in this book, as well as other books about psychology.

I should probably warn you that this is a lengthy chapter that is packed with relatively abstract information. It is necessitated by the fact that the courses for which this text is used are remarkably diversified. For many readers, this is your very first psychology text, while many others will have had one or more previous classes in psychology. Thus, the goal of the chapter is to make sure that you have a reasonable familiarity with certain major theories, concepts, and principles that you will need in order to understand the material in the following chapters. To fulfill that goal, I have had to cram a great deal of information into the chapter, and I introduce an exceptionally great number of technical terms in psychology. If you have had other psychology courses, you may find this to be largely a review, and if you are new to the field, you may feel overwhelmed. If you should happen to fall in the latter category, let me assure you now that the remaining chapters are less technical, theoretical, and abstract.

Introduction to Personality Theory
THE NATURE OF THEORY

THEORY. *A set of interrelated hypotheses that state the relations believed to exist among certain variables so as to explain certain phenomena.*

CONSTRUCT. *A theoretical concept used for explanatory purposes. It should be defined in terms of observable behavior, although the construct itself is not observable.*

To discuss theories of personality intelligently, I must digress momentarily to consider the nature of theories. Recall from Chapter 1 that psychology attempts to discover general laws of behavior. **Theories** attempt to unify and integrate these "laws," or principles, into a coherent whole. In other words, theories try to sort out the interrelations between separate empirical facts and then bring them together into a sensible overall picture.

Consider an example drawn from Sigmund Freud's (1920/1924) early efforts to theorize about personality. Freud made several observations that he put together to arrive at the theoretical **construct** of the unconscious. He noted that commonplace slips of the tongue (such as "I decided to take a summer school curse") often appeared to expose a person's true underlying feelings rather than being meaningless mistakes. He also noticed that people's dreams sometimes expressed feelings that they appeared to be keeping bottled up and that people troubled by psychological disturbances rarely recognized the underlying causes of their disturbed behavior. Seemingly unrelated observations such as these led Freud to develop the theory that behavior is influenced by unconscious wishes and desires, which may surface in slips of the tongue or dreams. Although most people today take the idea of the unconscious for granted, this was a revolutionary, new theoretical concept in Freud's era.

Theories serve three functions, all of which are illustrated in the present example. First, as stressed above, they unify and integrate apparently unrelated principles or facts. Second, by organizing separate facts into a coherent picture, theories enable us to make the leap from the first goal of psychology, the *description* of behavior, to the second goal, the *understanding* of behavior. You can see how Freud's concept of the unconscious not only united several observations about behavior; it also made those observations more understandable by suggesting a reason for their occurrence. Third, theories serve to guide future research. Freud's construct of the unconscious influenced the direction of his further investigations and inspired an enormous amount of research by other social scientists.

DEFINITION OF PERSONALITY

A great variety of definitions have been proposed for the concept of personality. This variety suggests that there is great disagreement among psychologists regarding this concept. In reality, however, much of this diversity involves relatively superficial differences in terminology or emphasis, and there actually is a reasonable consensus about the construct of personality. When these definitions are reduced to their basics, the core of the concept is really quite simple: *personality* is a hypothetical construct used to both describe and explain one's consistent behavioral tendencies.

Now that we have seen the concept's essential simplicity, let us turn to some of its complexities.

INFERENTIAL NATURE OF THE CONCEPT

The first chapter pointed out that "the stability of these [personality] characteristics predisposes the person to certain consistent behavioral tendencies." It is important to understand that these personality characteristics that are assumed to govern behavior are hypothetical *constructs*, which cannot be observed directly. Rather, they are *inferred* from *behavior*—which, of course, *is* observable. For example, you might choose to describe a friend as "insecure." This assertion about your friend's personality might be based on your observation of his tendency to make negative remarks about himself, his inability to ask out dates because of his often-voiced fear of rejection, and his constant solicitation of reassurance from you that you really like him. Note that his insecurity is not a tangible personal feature like his hair color; it is a personal feature that you *infer* from a certain pattern of behavior. Thus, personality can be known only indirectly, from behavior. Therein lies the title of this chapter, "Theories of Personality *and Behavior*." Any theory of personality is necessarily a theory about behavior.

THE ISSUE OF CONSISTENCY

I have emphasized that behavioral consistency is crucial to the concept of personality. In recent years, however, some psychologists have argued that people exhibit far less consistency in behavior than is commonly assumed. To some extent, these assertions call into question the usefulness of the concept of personality.

For instance, Walter Mischel (1969, 1973) argues that years of research on personality have failed to uncover substantial cross-situational consistency in behavior. For example, studies show that a person who is honest in one situation may be dishonest in another. Someone who wouldn't dream of cheating in school might engage in wholesale cheating when filling out her tax return. Similarly, some people are quite shy in some situations and quite outgoing in others (Zimbardo, 1977). In one rather old study of "punctuality" (Dudycha, 1936) as a personality trait, students' time of arrival for various college functions correlated only .19 (on the average) across different situations.

In contrast, Epstein (1979) has argued that certain methodological considerations in this kind of research have led to an underestimation of the extent of cross-situational consistency in behavior. In any case, a viable concept of personality does not require that people display anything approaching *complete* consistency in behavior. Indeed, theorists such as Mischel generally have not contended that we should discard the construct of personality. Rather, they have advocated that we pay more attention to the situational determinants of behavior. Their point has considerable merit. Thus, you should be aware that most people are far from entirely consistent in their behavior and that situational factors can be very influential in moderating behavior.

GENERAL LAWS APPLIED TO PARTICULAR PEOPLE

Theories of personality necessarily deal with "people in general." For instance, if a Freudian theorist states that a child who is subjected to severely punitive toilet training is relatively likely to have sex-related anxiety later in life, this assertion refers to a *tendency* among people *in general*. Freudian theory does *not* suggest that this causal sequence is inevitable for all people under all conditions.

Theories of personality attempt to identify general uniformities in how personality is shaped and how it then shapes behavior. It should be obvious that *the general laws of personality will not always apply accurately to particular individuals*. It is important that you understand this limitation. Personality theories, by themselves, permit little in the way of predictions about the behavior of particular individuals.

OVERVIEW AND HISTORICAL BACKGROUND

Before embarking on a review of the major theoretical orientations used by psychologists to explain personality and behavior, it is necessary to provide you with an overview and historical perspective.

There are many theories of personality. A comprehensive review of all the influential theories is far beyond the scope of the present book, as it usually requires an entire course by itself. However, most of the theories can be fit into one of three categories reflecting the three major schools of thought in psychology. The theories within each category are similar enough to be described collectively. Therefore, in succession I will outline the principal facets of psychoanalytic, behavioristic, and humanistic theories of personality. For each theoretical orientation, I will discuss its views on (1) the structure of personality, (2) the development of personality, (3) the crucial motivational forces that govern behavior, and (4) the nature of the healthy personality. The description of each school of thought will be followed by an analysis of that school's significant contributions to psychology and a critique of its flaws or shortcomings.

Historically, the psychoanalytic and behavioristic models became prominent long before the humanistic movement. The *psychoanalytic* model was pioneered by Sigmund Freud during the latter part of the 19th century and early part of the 20th. Although Freud's ideas failed to gain immediate acceptance, psychoanalytic theories gradually became quite influential. Prominent theorists who followed in the psychoanalytic tradition include Carl Jung, Alfred Adler, Erich Fromm, and Erik Erikson.

The *behavioristic* model grew out of the functionalist school of thought, emerging in its own right in the 1920s. Early contributors of significance included Ivan Pavlov, E. L. Thorndike, and John B. Watson. Subsequent efforts at refinement of behavioristic theories were spearheaded by Clark Hull, B. F. Skinner, and Albert Bandura. In the 1950s, dissatisfaction with the psychoanalytic and behavioristic models surfaced, and a third theoretical force emerged in the form of *humanism*. While rooted in earlier work by Kurt Lewin and

Gordon Allport, the humanistic perspective developed by Abraham Maslow and Carl Rogers represented a significant departure from the psychoanalytic and behavioristic traditions.

The Psychoanalytic Model

PSYCHOANALYTIC MODEL. *A major theoretical orientation in psychology, developed by Sigmund Freud, which emphasizes unconscious determinants of behavior.*

PSYCHOANALYSIS. *The psychoanalytic, or Freudian, approach to therapy, which emphasizes the recovery of unconscious conflicts through techniques such as free association and transference.*

The **psychoanalytic model** was shaped by the genius of Sigmund Freud (1901/1960, 1920/1924, 1959), a physician practicing in Vienna around the turn of the century. Freud was trained in neurology, but when, in collaboration with Josef Breuer, he stumbled onto a successful treatment for a mental disorder known as hysteria, his interest turned to psychiatry. The new treatment procedure went through much revision and eventually was called **psychoanalysis.** Freud's decades of intimate experience with his patients in psychoanalysis provided the basis for his theory of personality.

Freud's theories attracted little attention at first, and when he published his classic *The Interpretation of Dreams* (1900/1953) at age 44, it sold fewer than a thousand copies—a humble beginning for a theorist who would greatly influence modern intellectual thought! Gradually his great insight was recognized by other scholars, and his theories began to gain prominence. However, this success was not without its costs. The fact that his theory centered on sexuality was repugnant to many people, and Freud had to endure a great deal of condemnation, ridicule, and hatred before he earned the praise and respect that his work deserved.

STRUCTURE OF PERSONALITY

COMPONENTS OF PERSONALITY

Freud divided personality into three structural components: the id, the ego, and the superego. These elements were viewed as separate but interacting systems within the individual personality. A person's behavior was seen as the outcome of the interaction among these three components.

ID. *In psychoanalytic theory, the primitive, instinctive portion of the personality, which operates according to the pleasure principle.*

PLEASURE PRINCIPLE. *In psychoanalytic theory, the principle by which the id operates, emphasizing immediate and complete gratification of its desires.*

Id. Freud referred to the **id** as the reservoir of psychic energy. By this he meant that the id housed the raw biological urges (to eat, sleep, defecate, copulate, and so on) that energize, or motivate, our behavior. These primitive drives were considered instinctual; and two in particular, the sexual and aggressive impulses, were thought to be of greatest importance. According to Freudian theory, the id exists at an unconscious level, its desires reaching our awareness indirectly through the ego. Finally, the id operates according to the **pleasure principle,** which means that it desires *immediate* gratification of its urges.

EGO. *In psychoanalytic theory, the part of the personality that deals with the external world, operating according to the reality principle.*

REALITY PRINCIPLE. *In psychoanalytic theory, the principle by which the ego operates. It takes into consideration social realities that may require the delay of gratification.*

Ego. The **ego** has been characterized as the "executive" of the personality. This description emphasizes the involvement of the ego in making decisions as it mediates between the id, with its forceful desires for immediate satisfaction, and the external social world, with its regulations and expectations regarding acceptable behavior. Operating at a conscious as well as an unconscious level of awareness, the ego learns about society's values, norms, and etiquette and the rules and restrictions that they involve. The ego takes these social norms into consideration and, operating according to the **reality principle,** tries to get the id to *delay* gratification of its passionate urges until an appropriate or socially acceptable time. In so doing, the ego strives (1) to avoid negative consequences, such as punishment, from society and its representatives (parents, teachers, and employers, among others) and (2) to achieve long-range goals, which often require temporary delays of gratification. In the long run, the ego, like the id, wants to maximize gratification. However, unlike the id, the ego recognizes the necessity of suppressing certain desires in certain situations.

Superego. The **superego** is the "moral arm" of personality. Throughout our lives, but particularly during childhood, we are trained about what represents appropriate behavior in our culture. Many of these societal norms are eventually *internalized*. This means that we embrace them as suitable guidelines for the governance of our behavior without external coercion from society. In other words, we truly *accept* certain rules, and then *we* put pressure on *ourselves* to adhere to these regulations or expectations. Thus, the superego consists of the values and ideals about right and wrong that are implanted in us by our society, primarily through its very influential representatives, our parents.

According to Freudian theory, behavior is governed by the interaction of the three structural components described above. The following scenario provides a concrete illustration of how this interaction might take place.

> Imagine your alarm clock ringing obnoxiously as you lurch across the bed to shut it off. It's 5:45 A.M. and time to get up for work. However, your id (operating according to the pleasure principle) urges you to return to the immediate gratification of additional sleep. Your ego (operating according to the reality principle) points out that you really *must* go to work. It tries to sway you by asserting that you'll never get the promotion that you want if you start missing work. Your id (in its typical unrealistic fashion) smugly assures you that you *will* get the promotion eventually and suggests lying back to dream about how nice things will be when you get the promotion. Your ego panics and shrilly points out that you cannot simply fail to show up for work. It suggests that you at least have to go to the trouble of calling in sick. The id eagerly accepts this compromise strategy. However, the superego now jumps into the fray, refusing to be a party to any immoral untruthfulness about being sick.

LEVELS OF AWARENESS

In addition to the three interacting components described above, *Freud theorized that personality structure is characterized by three levels of awareness: the conscious, the preconscious, and the unconscious.* The **conscious** includes whatever you are aware of at a particular point in time. For example, at this moment your conscious may include the present train of thought in this text and a dim awareness in the back of your mind that your eyes are getting tired and you are beginning to get hungry. The **preconscious** houses material bubbling just beneath the surface of awareness. You are not currently aware of it, but it can be readily retrieved into conscious awareness. Examples might include your middle name, what you had for supper last night, and the fight you had with your boyfriend yesterday.

According to psychoanalytic theory, the **unconscious** contains material which is well below the surface of conscious awareness but which nonetheless influences our behavior. The unconscious is thought to dwarf the conscious and preconscious in size (see Figure 2.1), and material stored there is often quite difficult to retrieve. For example, stored in your unconscious might be a vivid (but presently repressed) memory of some traumatic childhood event that, according to Freud, probably still influences your behavior many years later.

MOTIVATION

INSTINCTUAL AND SOCIAL NEEDS

Freud divided motivational forces into two categories: instinctual and social. He proposed that we are born with a relatively small number of *instinctually based needs* to eat, to sleep, to defecate, to aggress, to copulate, and so forth. He further proposed that as we progress toward adulthood, we acquire a larger variety of *socially based needs,* such as those for power, status, achievement, approval, independence, and order.

Although Freud devoted considerable attention to the acquisition of socially based needs, he believed that the two most important motivational forces were part of the original complement of instinctual needs. *He thought that the sexual and aggressive impulses were particularly influential for two reasons.* First, he thought that they appeared to be subject to more pervasive, more complex, and more ambiguous societal controls than other basic motivational forces. Thus, Freud believed that these two drives were especially significant because they tended to be associated with a great deal of confusion. Second, Freud noted that the sex and aggression drives are *thwarted* more regularly than other basic urges. Think about it. Although a department store clerk may annoy you immensely, you are not likely to lunge across the counter and slug the clerk, because this is socially unacceptable behavior. Likewise, when you see an attractive person who inspires lustful urges, you do not walk up and suggest a tryst in a nearby broom closet. When basic needs such as hunger or thirst are activated, you can head for a drinking fountain or a nearby vending machine—but there is nothing comparable to a vending machine for the satisfaction of sexual and aggressive urges. Thus, Freud ascribed great importance to these needs because social norms dictate that they are routinely frustrated in spite of their very basic nature.

THE CONFLICT MODEL

Freud's theory is essentially a tension-reduction, conflict model. Behavior is seen as the outcome of an ongoing series of conflicts. According to the model, when a drive is activated, this produces an unpleasant tension in the personality system. The person then acts to satisfy the drive in some way so as to release the tension.

With considerable regularity, the activation of drives produces a *conflict* between internal urges and societal expectations. For example, you might feel an urge to clobber a coworker who constantly irritates you; however, because society generally does not approve of such actions, you would experience conflict. You might be experiencing conflict at this very moment! Your id may be

SIGMUND FREUD

FIGURE 2.1 Conscious and unconscious processes. This rather odd-looking diagram illustrates Freud's belief that most of the important personality processes occur below the level of conscious awareness. In examining people's conscious thoughts and their behaviors, we can see some reflections of the ego and the superego. But whereas the ego and superego are partly conscious and partly unconscious, the primitive id is the unconscious, totally submerged part of the "iceberg."

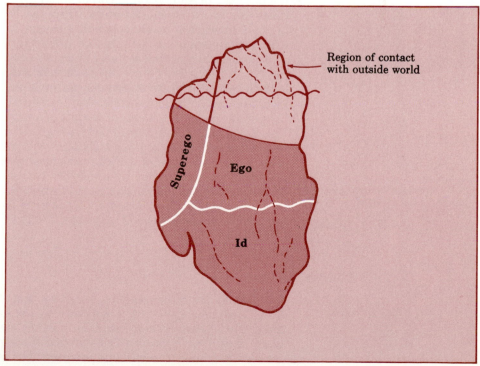

Region of contact with outside world

Superego

Ego

Id

secretly urging you to abandon reading this chapter in favor of a more immediately gratifying activity, such as watching television. Your ego may presently be weighing this appealing possibility against your society-induced need to excel in school.

As you can see, *these conflicts involve the interaction of the three structural components of personality*. To better understand how Freud's conflict model supposedly works, consider another imaginary scenario:

> Imagine that you've been dating someone for several months. You enjoy the person as a companion, and you have developed a very satisfactory sexual liaison. However, this person has limited appeal to you, and there is no way that the relationship will ever progress beyond its current level of commitment. This dating partner clearly does not meet your ideals for a potential spouse. You are experiencing conflict about whether to terminate the relationship now or let it run its course indefinitely. Your id is campaigning for a continuation of the relationship because it does not want to give up the readily available sexual outlet. Your superego argues that you should end the relationship because you are being unfair to the other person, who harbors hopes that the relationship will become permanent. Your superego accuses you of "using" the other person. The ego is caught between the id and the superego and has concerns of its own. The ego points out that as long as you maintain the present relationship you will not be actively pursuing a new and possibly more meaningful one. In the long run, the ego sees this consequence as counterproductive. However, the ego is worried about the potential embarrassment if you end the relationship and then can't find anyone to go out with. There is a certain social status associated with always having a companion for parties and such events. The ego values this status highly. What should you do? The id and the superego are sure they know, but the ego is hopelessly confused, and so goes the conflict.

DEFENSE MECHANISMS

According to the psychoanalytic model, then, your behavior is believed to be the outcome of an ongoing series of conflicts, sometimes significant and sometimes trivial. On some occasions when the conflict *is* significant, it may be difficult to reach a resolution, and a savage battle may be waged among the various components of personality. Although this battle may be entirely unconscious, *anxiety* often surfaces at a conscious level. The anxiety may involve the fear that the id will get out of control and do something terrible that will lead to severe negative consequences, or it may involve fear of the guilt that violating one's own moral code would produce.

DEFENSE MECHANISM. *A largely cognitive procedure used to defend against unpleasant emotions through self-deception and the distortion of reality.*

In either case, the arousal of anxiety is a very crucial event in Freud's model. The experience of anxiety is distressing, and people try to rid themselves of this unwelcome emotion through whatever means they can use. This effort often involves the use of **defense mechanisms**—a variety of largely unconscious mental procedures by which the person reduces or gets rid of anxiety. Unfortunately, defense mechanisms often involve self-deception, and they may be counterproductive. Because the defense mechanisms have become such important and widely used concepts, I will discuss them in detail later (see Chapter 5).

DEVELOPMENT OF PERSONALITY

Freud made the rather startling assertion that the basic foundation of an individual's personality is firmly laid down by the tender age of 5! To shed light on these crucial early years, Freud formulated a **stage** theory of development. Years later, Erik Erikson (1963) proposed a sweeping revision of Freud's developmental model, and this revision has attained considerable promi-

STAGE. *A period in human development during which (1) certain critical experiences must be dealt with, (2) certain characteristic patterns of behavior are exhibited, and (3) certain capacities become established or consolidated.*

FIXATION. *In psychoanalytic theory, the failure to move forward from one developmental stage to another. Thought to be due to either excessive satisfaction or deprivation of important needs at that stage. Believed to lead to overemphasis on those needs later in life.*

OEDIPAL COMPLEX. *In psychoanalytic theory, a child's erotic desire for the opposite-sex parent, accompanied by hostility toward the same-sex parent. Originally, Freud used the term* Oedipal complex *to denote this syndrome in boys only, calling the comparable syndrome in girls the Electra complex. Use of a separate term for the female form of this syndrome has diminished over the years.*

IDENTIFICATION. *The perception of oneself as essentially similar to another person; also, a defense mechanism wherein feelings of self-esteem are enhanced by forming a real or imaginary alliance with an admired person or group. In either case, it tends to lead to some imitation of the target of identification.*

nence. Unlike Freud, Erikson believed that significant development continued throughout the entire life span. He also shifted emphasis from sexual to social determinants of development. I will summarize Freud's developmental theory in the present section and examine Erikson's revision in Chapter 10, on adult development.

Freud outlined a series of five "psychosexual" stages. During each of these stages the child's sexual energy is directed to a particular erogenous zone of the body, and this focus of erotic energy provides the name (oral, anal, and so on) for the stage.

According to Freud, the way certain events are dealt with during the first five years shapes one's subsequent adult personality. The notion of **fixation** plays a particularly important role in this process. Fixation involves an overinvestment of instinctual energy in a particular erogenous zone. This is usually the result of parents' overindulgence of a child's needs at a particular stage, or it may be due to excessive frustration experienced by the child at that stage. In either case, fixations left over from childhood are thought to have a tremendous impact on one's psychological functioning as an adult.

The oral stage. This stage typically encompasses the first year of life, during which the main source of erotic stimulation is the mouth (in sucking, biting, chewing, and so on). The way the child's feeding experiences are handled is thought to be very influential in molding the foundation for adult personality.

The anal stage. Around age 2, children supposedly get their erotic pleasure from their bowel movements, through either the expulsion or the retention of feces. The crucial event at this time involves toilet training, which represents society's first systematic effort to regulate the child's instinctual impulses. Severely punitive toilet training is thought to have a variety of potential outcomes. For example, excessive punishment might produce a latent feeling of hostility toward the "trainer," who is usually the mother, and this hostility might generalize to women as a class. Another possibility is that excessive reliance on punitive measures might lead to the pairing of the aroused anxiety with genital concerns. This genital anxiety derived from toilet training might be manifested as sexual anxiety later in life.

The phallic stage. From age 3 through age 5, the genitals become the focus of erotic experience, largely through experimentation with masturbation. During this *very* crucial phase, the **Oedipal complex** emerges. The child develops erotically tinged desires for the opposite-sex parent, accompanied by feelings of hostility toward the same-sex parent. How the child copes with these sexual and aggressive conflicts is of paramount importance in Freud's theory. It is imperative that the child "resolve" the Oedipal dilemma by purging the sexual longings for the opposite-sex parent and by crushing the hostility felt toward the same-sex parent. This resolution of the Oedipal complex was believed to be a precondition for appropriate **identification** with the same-sex parent. Without such identification, Freudian theory predicts, the child's superego development and sex-role development are not likely to progress as they should. Thus, the Oedipal conflict is a pivotal event, since healthy psychosexual development hinges on its resolution.

The latency and genital stages. From age 5 to 6 to about 11 or 12, the child's sexuality is largely repressed—it becomes "latent." Important events during this period center on expanding social contacts beyond the immediate family. With the advent of puberty, the child evolves into the genital stage, wherein erotic impulses focus on the genitals once again. However, at this point the sexual energy is channeled toward members of the other sex, rather than toward oneself as in the phallic stage.

NEO-FREUDIAN REVISIONS OF PSYCHOANALYTIC THEORY

Freud eventually gained a legion of followers, many of them brilliant scholars in their own right, who proposed numerous revisions of his original theory. Given that Freud was exploring new and uncharted frontiers in psychodynamics, it is not surprising that many of his followers would feel the need to make certain revisions and refinements in the theory. Freud himself modified his formulations in many ways during his 50 years of theory building. Nonetheless, Freud expressed great displeasure when some of his disciples proposed their own revisions while he was still alive. Considerable bitterness surfaced when Freud's former students, such as Carl Jung and Alfred Adler, developed dissenting views about personality.

Over the years, many scholars such as Erik Erikson have proposed influential theories of their own, which, though fitting in the general psychoanalytic tradition, have often involved substantial departures from the original Freudian model. Many of these theorists, such as Alfred Adler (1927), Carl Jung (1916/1960), Karen Horney (1937), Harry Stack Sullivan (1953), Erich Fromm (1947), Erik Erikson (1963), Robert White (1959), and David Rapaport (1967), have acquired sizable followings of their own. Thus, psychoanalytic theory has become somewhat fragmented. There are actually quite a number of psychoanalytic theories of personality. These revised versions are usually called **neo-Freudian** theories of personality. The number and complexity of these neo-Freudian theories are great, and even a semicomprehensive review of them is beyond the scope and mission of this text. However, some of the major trends that have appeared with some consistency in these neo-Freudian theories are worth noting.

NEO-FREUDIAN. *Used to describe theories of personality that are essentially psychoanalytic but diverge to varying degrees from Freud's original formulations.*

1. Emphasis on coping with one's sexuality as a determinant of personality has lessened. Jung and Adler were the first to break with Freud on this point, and this deemphasis of sexuality is probably the most consistent theme in revised versions of psychoanalytic theory.

2. The preeminent importance of childhood experience in shaping adult personality has also been deemphasized. This trend is exemplified by Erikson's expanded model of development, which proposes that significant evolution in personality continues throughout adulthood.

3. Much more attention has been devoted to the influence of social factors on personality. Adler advocated this revision as early as 1911. Many prominent theorists, including Horney, Sullivan, Fromm, and Erikson, have cast their lot with Adler on this issue. Sullivan, in particular, stressed that personality cannot be isolated from interpersonal relations. He pointed out that most personality traits principally describe a person's *characteristic modes of social interaction* (for example, warm, shy, extroverted, suspicious, assertive).

4. The role of the ego and its *conscious* thought processes has been enlarged at the expense of the id and its unconscious motivational forces. Again, it was Adler who first diverted thought along these lines.

5. Whereas Freud affirmed the importance of the instinct-based sexual and aggressive impulses, subsequent theorists have stressed the prominence of other motivational forces. Adler argued for the preeminence of the drive toward superiority and power (mastery over one's world). Similarly, White saw the drive toward competence as the most fundamental motivational force governing personality.

THE HEALTHY PERSONALITY

Psychoanalytic theorists have been criticized for paying too little attention to the question of psychological health. Actually, this charge seems a little unfair when applied to the psychoanalytic school of thought. Although the Freudian theorists have never confronted this issue with the same enthusiasm shown by the humanists, it is nonetheless true that various psychoanalytic theorists commented about the nature of psychological health decades before it became fashionable to do so.

FREUD

It is true that Freud (1959) was much more interested in psychological disorders than in psychological health. However, it is inaccurate to say that Freud saw psychological health simply as the absence of any pathology. When asked about the capacities associated with psychosexual maturity, Freud replied that the mature person should be able "to love and to work." In addition to these two explicit guidelines, it is implicit throughout Freud's theory that the key to psychological health is ego strength. Specifically, then, Freud thought that the healthy personality was characterized by the following traits.

1. *Ego strength.* The ego must be strong enough to handle the dangerous impulses of the id as well as the sometimes excessive demands of the superego. Socially unacceptable impulses from the id must be suppressed or rechanneled. Extravagant demands for perfection from the superego must be assessed realistically. Conflicts should be confronted consciously.

2. *Ability to work productively.* Freud used the term *work* in a general way, to refer to more than one's job. He thought it was important to rechannel instinctual energy (through a process called **sublimation**) into socially valuable activities. Such activities might include anything from effective parenting to one's occupational endeavors. These efforts were thought to give meaning to one's life.

3. *Ability to love.* According to Freud, the ability to love depends on progressing through the early stages of psychosexual development to reach the genital stage. Although Freud stressed the importance of developing a satisfactory sexual relationship in the context of marriage, his concept of the ability to love involved more than sexual adequacy. He also emphasized the altruistic quality of this ability to love. He thus believed that psychological health entailed being able to give of oneself to people generously and unselfishly.

SUBLIMATION. *In psychoanalytic theory, the process of redirecting instinctual energy into socially acceptable or valuable activities.*

JUNG

Carl Jung (1916/1960, 1964) believed that the key to psychological health was continued personal growth, as opposed to stagnation. In therapy, Jung treated many middle-aged people whose lives had gone stale; they lacked a sense of direction and were experiencing doubts about the meaning of their lives. Jung's remedy was to encourage these people to explore their psychic interior (through such techniques as dream analysis) to get more in touch with their "true" selves. He stressed the importance of pursuing new interests and activities as they were suggested by this process of self-exploration. As you will see later, Jung's emphasis on self-discovery and growth anticipated two of the more popular themes in subsequent humanistic models of the healthy personality.

Jung was also one of the first theorists to acclaim the importance of "balance" in the healthy personality. He thought that psychological health required balancing our introverted and extroverted tendencies. He further believed that it was necessary to evenly integrate what he called the four basic ways of experiencing the world (sensing, intuiting, feeling, and thinking). This theme of balance also turned up in many later theories of psychological health.

ADLER AND FROMM

Though years apart, *Alfred Adler and Erich Fromm both focused on the social dimension in formulating their theories of psychological health.*

Adler (1939) believed that human nature is basically selfish. However, through their upbringing, some people develop a strong "social interest." This entails seeing other people as worthy, being responsive to their needs, and controlling the basic urge to compete irrationally against others for power.

Fromm (1955) called his version of psychological health the "productive orientation" toward life. This orientation included a number of features, many of which involved interpersonal sensitivity. Thus, Fromm proposed that the healthy personality is receptive to others, open, tolerant, trusting, and nonmanipulative. In particular, he stressed the significance of being able to express love for others without worrying about what we will get in return.

SIGNIFICANT CONTRIBUTIONS

Without a doubt, psychoanalytic theory has had an extraordinary impact not just on psychology but on the entire spectrum of modern intellectual thought, including artistic as well as scientific endeavors. The *ground-breaking* nature of Freud's theory was its greatest accomplishment. In this section I will enumerate some of its innovative contributions.

Behavioral determinism.   Today most people take for granted the premise of determinism, that present behavior is determined by past events. However, during Freud's era this doctrine was not commonly accepted. Freud's demonstration of the link between childhood events and adult behavior contributed tremendously to making the notion of determinism commonplace.

The unconscious.   Although the unconscious determinants of behavior remain extremely difficult to investigate, Freud's assertion that we are not aware of all the forces governing our behavior has largely been confirmed. Once again, it is hard to convey to students in the 1980s, for whom this is no grand insight, that people just did not think this way before Freud.

Conflict-induced pathology.   Freud was the first to recognize the role of conflict in generating psychological distress and disorders. Today we no longer focus exclusively on sexual and aggressive conflicts, and we use different conceptual models to analyze the role of conflict (see Chapter 3); nonetheless, we continue to view conflict as a chief contributor to psychopathology.

Influence on psychology as a discipline.   Although Freud was not a psychologist, and his theories were not eagerly accepted by most psychologists of his era, he indirectly affected the course of development of the discipline. Around the turn of the century, psychology was primarily interested in the topics of physiology, sensation, perception, and learning. If psychology had continued to focus only on these subjects, the science of psychology would have virtually nothing to say about the question of adjustment, which concerns us. Although there were many forces within psychology propelling it toward the much broader science it is today, Freud certainly contributed to this movement. His controversial theories created a certain tension within psychology that provoked psychologists to examine new areas and aspects of behavior.

CRITIQUE

Innumerable critical attacks have been launched on psychoanalytic theory (Hall & Lindzey, 1978). Freudian theory is antagonistic to the values of many people and hence has inspired brutal and sometimes malicious opposition. A great number of people were disconcerted by Freud's emphasis on sexuality and his belief that human behavior was dominated by instincts in a manner that made us little better than animals. Moreover, he pulled the rug out from under us when he exposed our unconscious and irrational nature. Irrespective of these emotional issues, psychoanalytic theory does have its shortcomings. The principal flaws are outlined below.

Lack of testability. In the first chapter, I stressed that scientific investigation requires *testable* hypotheses. Many psychoanalytic concepts are so hazy and imprecise that they defy empirical investigation. Constructs such as instinctual energy are impossible to measure. Moreover, Freud was lax about clarifying the proposed interrelations among traumatic childhood experiences, guilt feelings, Oedipal complexes, and so forth. On many issues, psychoanalytic theory is too vague to generate clear predictions about behavior.

Inadequate evidence. Freudian theory is *not* based on an impressive empirical base of scientific data. Most of the data come from clinical case studies, which are a poor to mediocre source of information in that they rely on (1) patients' verbal reports, which are of dubious accuracy, (2) relatively subjective clinical observation, wherein it is very easy to see what you expect to see on the basis of your theory, and (3) a sample of subjects who are not particularly representative. In spite of these problems, the evidentiary situation may not be as grim as some critics suggest. Some portions of psychoanalytic theory *are* testable and often *are* supported. In a review of theory-testing empirical research, Kline (1972) concluded that a reasonable proportion of the central psychoanalytic hypotheses had been supported.

Overemphasis on sexual and aggressive drives. Freud has come under heavy fire for assigning too much significance to the sexual and aggressive drives. Although these drives are clearly important, they do not have the overpowering and far-reaching influence originally suggested. This charge has been partly defused by the neo-Freudian revisions of psychoanalytic theory, which have deemphasized these two instinctual drives.

Negative view of human nature. The psychoanalytic model has been criticized for taking an excessively negative and pessimistic view of human nature. The Freudian view, which sees the human as driven by a crude, instinctual eagerness to maximize physical pleasure, is not very complimentary. The theory has also been attacked for being overly deterministic. In particular, humanistic theorists have argued that the psychoanalytic model is unduly pessimistic about our irrationality and does not give us credit for having some control over our lives.

The Behavioristic Model

BEHAVIORISM. *A major theoretical orientation in psychology that argues that only observable behavior can be studied scientifically.*

Behaviorism has been a major school of thought in psychology since the 1920s. John B. Watson was an early and vocal champion of the behaviorist position. His contribution consisted in formalizing the behaviorist philosophy and campaigning very forcefully for it. *Watson (1913) argued that scientific psychology should study only observable behavior* (hence the name *behaviorism*). He contended that consciousness or mental processes could not be studied in an objective, scientific manner because they are private events that are not accessible to public observation. In completely rejecting conscious experience as suitable subject matter for scientific investigation, Watson took a "radical" position that is no longer dominant among modern behaviorists. Nonetheless, the emphasis on studying observable behavior rather than conscious experience remains a basic premise of modern behaviorism.

Research in the behavioristic tradition has focused primarily on the subject of learning, and behaviorists have devoted relatively little attention to turning their ideas into formal theories of personality. The most influential efforts at translating the principles of behaviorism into a systematic theory of personality have been those of John Dollard and Neal Miller (1950), Albert Bandura (1977; Bandura & Walters, 1963), and Walter Mischel (1973). There is no single, unified behaviorist theory of personality. As in all three major schools of thought, there are a *number* of viewpoints that share certain central themes while disagreeing on a variety of peripheral issues. In spite of this fragmentation, however, we can sketch a general overview of the behavioristic approach to personality.

STRUCTURE OF PERSONALITY

Unlike both the psychoanalytic and humanistic theorists, *the behaviorists have generally shown a distaste for, and lack of interest in, structural aspects of personality.* Behaviorists shun structural concepts because such concepts tend to focus on unobservable mental events, which they are reluctant to consider.

How, then, do behaviorists conceptualize the stable and durable characteristics of the person? Many see personality as a collection of stimulus-response bonds. These are response tendencies that exist for various stimulus situations. Often a stimulus situation is associated with several habitual responses, which may vary in strength. In this case, the stimulus situation is said to be associated with a **habit hierarchy** (see Figure 2.2), which lists the various potential responses in order of probability. As an example, consider a rather general stimulus situation, such as a large party where you know relatively few people. Your habit hierarchy in this situation might consist of the following responses, in descending order of likelihood: (1) circulate, asking people questions about themselves to display your interest in them, (2) stick close to the few people present whom you already know, making no effort to meet anyone new, and (3) politely withdraw by focusing your attention on your host's book or record collection (or whatever else is available). According to the behaviorists, habit hierarchies such as these are acquired through learning, are based on past experience, and are subject to change in the future, as a result of new experience.

In recent years, some behaviorists (Bandura, 1977; Mischel, 1973; Rotter, 1972) have added a **cognitive** element to the behavioristic picture of personality structure. Although they acknowledge that personality is largely shaped by experience, they argue that humans do not passively absorb their environmental conditioning. Instead, they assert that humans actively seek out and process information about how to maximize their outcomes. In focusing on information-processing strategies, these behaviorists have returned to the point of view that unobservable mental events have significance. Advocates of

HABIT HIERARCHY. *A collection of response tendencies that exist for a particular stimulus situation. The hierarchy orders the potential responses according to their relative strength.*

COGNITIVE. *Pertaining to thought or mental processes.*

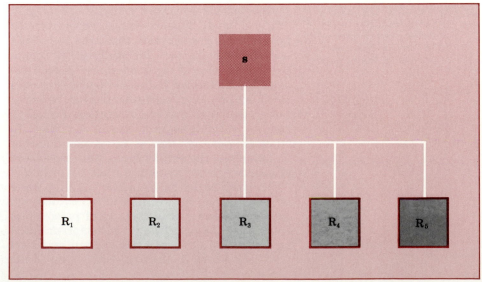

FIGURE 2.2 A hierarchy of responses to the same stimulus. The responses are ranked according to their tendency to be evoked by the stimulus (S). R_1 has a greater probability of being evoked than R_2, which, in turn, has a greater probability of being evoked than R_3, and so on.

this position call their approach "cognitive social-learning theory." Essentially, they still view personality as a collection of response tendencies. However, they would point out that your hierarchy of responses for a particular situation would depend on your *personal beliefs* about what kinds of outcomes various responses are likely to produce. Thus, they focus on *subjective expectancies* rather than habits, which are assumed to be automatic or reflexive.

DEVELOPMENT OF PERSONALITY

Although behaviorists have shown relatively little interest in personality structure, they have focused extensively on personality *development*. They have erected an elaborate network of principles to explain how our response tendencies and habit hierarchies are acquired through learning. Some behaviorists (for example, Dollard & Miller, 1950) concur with Freud on the tremendous importance of early childhood experiences, but most see personality development as a lifelong journey. They stress that personality is shaped through a continual, evolutionary process, and they see little value in proposing developmental stages.

The behaviorists explain this ongoing acquisition of characteristic modes of responding through the principles of learning. For the most part, they study learning at its most fundamental and molecular level by examining a process called conditioning. **Conditioning** deals with the formation, strengthening, and weakening of response tendencies. There are two types of conditioning, *respondent conditioning* and *operant conditioning*, both of which will be described in this section. In addition to these, we will examine the notion of vicarious conditioning, or *observational learning*, which proposes that either respondent or operant conditioning can take place *indirectly* through the observation of another's conditioning experience.

CONDITIONING. *A learning process involving the formation, strengthening, and weakening of response tendencies.*

RESPONDENT CONDITIONING

Pavlov's demonstration.   Ivan Pavlov was a prominent Russian physiologist who did Nobel Prize–winning research on digestion. While studying digestive processes in dogs, he stumbled onto the fact that the dogs could be trained to salivate in response to the sound of a bell. This may not sound like a particularly brilliant discovery, but in fact Pavlov's (1906) humble little demonstration of **respondent conditioning** is considered a major turning point in the history of psychology.

What was so significant about a dog's salivating when a bell was rung? Well, the key was that the bell started out as a *neutral* stimulus. In other words, initially it had no association with, or impact on, the response of salivation. However, Pavlov changed that by pairing the ringing of the bell with another stimulus (meat powder), which *was* associated with the salivation response. After the bell and meat were presented together a number of times, Pavlov presented *only* the bell, and he found that it had acquired the capacity to trigger the salivation response by itself. What Pavlov demonstrated was the formation of a new **stimulus-response bond** where none had existed previously!

RESPONDENT CONDITIONING. *A type of conditioning that describes how involuntary responses come to be evoked by certain stimuli. Also called classical conditioning.*

Terminology.   There is a unique vocabulary associated with the respondent conditioning model (see Figure 2.3) that often looks intimidating but is really not very mysterious. The association between the meat powder and salivation is a "natural" one that does not have to be conditioned. It is therefore called an *unconditioned* association. In natural, unconditioned bonds such as this one, the stimulus (meat powder in this case) is labeled the **unconditioned stimulus** (abbreviated UCS), and the response (salivation) is called the **unconditioned response** (UCR). In contrast, the link between the bell and salivation was established through conditioning and is therefore called a

STIMULUS-RESPONSE BOND. *An association, or link, between an external event (the stimulus) and an organism's reaction to the event (the response).*

UNCONDITIONED STIMULUS (UCS). *In respondent conditioning, a stimulus that evokes a particular response without previous training or conditioning.*

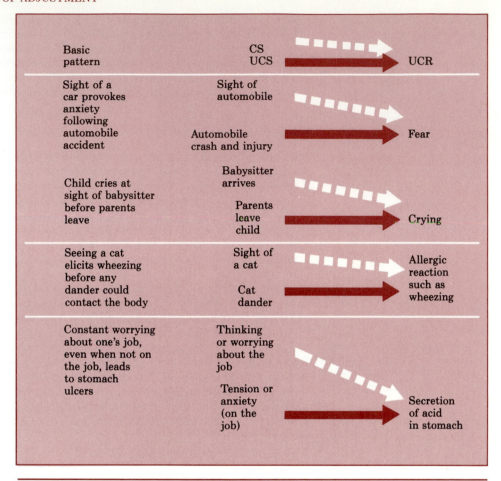

FIGURE 2.3 Diagrams of classical conditioning.

conditioned association. In acquired, or conditioned, bonds, such as this one, the stimulus (bell) is called the **conditioned stimulus** (CS), and the response (salivation) is now labeled the **conditioned response** (CR).

There are a handful of additional vocabulary items that you will encounter in discussions of classical conditioning.

1. Responses are said to be **elicited** in respondent conditioning. This word is intended to convey that the response is triggered automatically or reflexively.

2. During the **acquisition** phase, the CS and UCS are paired so as to strengthen the connection between the CS and the CR. There is great variability in how quickly a response may be acquired. In some cases, especially when an aversive UCS is involved, a single pairing may be sufficient to produce a new stimulus-response bond.

3. These conditioned associations are not necessarily permanent. After conditioning, repeated presentations of the CS alone tend to weaken the bond between the CS and CR. This weakening process is called **extinction.**

4. After conditioning has taken place, there is often a tendency to respond not only to the exact CS used but also to other, similar stimuli. This tendency to respond to similar stimuli is called **generalization.** The more similar the new stimuli are to the original CS, the greater the likelihood of generalization. For example, many people who have been ticketed for speeding violations while driving have acquired the following response. At the sight of a police car,

ACQUISITION. *The first phase of the conditioning process. In respondent conditioning, a new bond between a stimulus and response is formed and strengthened. In operant conditioning, the tendency to emit a response is strengthened through reinforcement.*

EXTINCTION. *In both respondent and operant conditioning, the weakening of a tendency to make a response. In operant conditioning, also used to denote the procedure wherein reinforcement for a response is terminated (thus weakening the response tendency).*

GENERALIZATION. *In both respondent and operant conditioning, the tendency to respond to different (although usually somewhat similar) stimuli with the same response.*

DISCRIMINATION. *In conditioning, the tendency to respond differentially to similar though not identical stimuli.*

IVAN PAVLOV

their heart "skips a beat," and their foot reflexively leaps off the accelerator (even if they are within the speed limit). Many of these people respond this way when they catch a momentary glimpse of a tow truck, which has lights on top that are similar to those on most police vehicles. This response to the similar stimulus of the tow truck is an example of generalization.

5. The generalization response in the above example will typically leave the driver feeling rather foolish. This motivates some drivers to become more skillful at distinguishing between tow trucks and police cars. Those who learn to respond *only* to police cars have developed a discrimination. **Discrimination** involves responding *differentially* to similar stimuli. Establishing a discrimination may be quite difficult if the stimuli are substantially similar.

Respondent conditioning in everyday life. What is the role of respondent conditioning in shaping personality in everyday life? It appears that *respondent conditioning is involved primarily in the acquisition of emotional responses.* This may represent a relatively small class of responses; however, it is a particularly important class in that maladaptive emotional reactions underlie many common adjustment problems.

For example, the author once had a student whose lifestyle was cramped greatly by her fear of bridges. Her fear was so excessive that she was incapable of driving on interstate highways because of all the viaducts that had to be crossed. This fear was acquired through respondent conditioning early in her childhood. Years before, when her family would drive to visit her grandmother, they had to cross a rickety, old, dilapidated bridge. Her father, in a misguided attempt to be amusing, made a major production out of these crossings. He would stop short of the bridge and carry on about the enormous danger of the imminent crossing. Obviously, the bridge was reasonably safe, or it would have been closed down. However, the naive young girl was terrified by her father's scare tactics, and the bridge became a conditioned stimulus eliciting great fear. Moreover, she generalized from this single bridge to *all* bridges, and 40 years later she was still carrying the burden of a troublesome fear of bridges. As you may already know, unrealistic fears are called phobias. What you may *not* know is that many psychologists believe that respondent conditioning leads to the formation of most phobias.

In addition to phobic fears, respondent conditioning also appears to account for more realistic anxiety of more moderate intensity. For example, imagine a news reporter in a high-pressure job where he consistently gets negative feedback about his performance from his superiors. The negative comments from supervisors function as a UCS eliciting anxiety. These reprimands are paired with the auditory and visual stimulus of the newsroom, so that the newsroom becomes a CS eliciting anxiety, even when the supervisors are not present. Our poor reporter might even reach a point at which the *thought* of the newsroom triggers anxiety, even when he is at home. Depending on his physiological makeup, this constant anxiety might very well lead to a physical symptom, such as ulcers.

OPERANT CONDITIONING

OPERANT CONDITIONING. *A type of conditioning that describes how voluntary responses are controlled by their consequences. Also known as instrumental conditioning.*

EMIT. *In operant conditioning, to express a response that is controlled by its consequences.*

The second variety of conditioning is called **operant conditioning,** a term proposed by B. F. Skinner (1938, 1971). This type of conditioning process largely governs *voluntary* responses, which are therefore said to be **emitted** rather than elicited. The fundamental principle of operant conditioning is uncommonly simple: we tend to repeat behaviors that lead to positive consequences, and we tend not to repeat behaviors that lead to neutral or negative consequences. Operant responses, rather than being triggered automatically by a stimulus, are emitted voluntarily with an eye toward gaining a favorable outcome of some kind. This type of behavior is therefore said to be controlled by its consequences.

Because operant conditioning deals mostly with voluntary responses, it appears to govern a greater share of human behavior than respondent conditioning does. Of course, some behavior may be simultaneously regulated by both. In any case, the distinguishing feature of operant behavior is that it is controlled primarily by its consequences. I will turn now to a discussion of what those consequences may be and how they regulate our behavior.

POSITIVE REINFORCEMENT. *In operant conditioning, the strengthening of a response tendency by virtue of the fact that the response leads to the delivery of a pleasant or desired stimulus.*

Positive reinforcement. A **positive reinforcer** is defined as any event that serves to increase the strength (the tendency to repeat) of a response by virtue of its presentation after the response. It is roughly synonymous with the concept of reward. Notice that reinforcement is defined *after the fact,* in terms of its effect on behavior. This is because reinforcement is subjective; an event may be reinforcing for one person and not for another. For example, approval from one's peers is a potent reinforcer for some people, while others (a minority) are relatively indifferent to such approval.

The principle of positive reinforcement seems to influence personality development in a very straightforward way. Those responses that produce positive reinforcement are strengthened and tend to become habitual patterns of behavior. For example, a youngster might "clown around" in class and gain appreciative comments and smiles from his schoolmates. This social approval will probably reinforce "clowning-around behavior," which may gradually become an integral element of the youth's personality. Similarly, whether or not a youngster becomes independent or assertive or hard-working depends on whether the child is reinforced for such behaviors by parents and other influential persons. Of course, a response tendency shaped by positive reinforcement may be situationally specific. For instance, a young girl's reinforcement history might lead her to be very assertive in school but very nonassertive at home.

NEGATIVE REINFORCEMENT. *In operant conditioning, the strengthening of a response tendency by virtue of the fact that the response leads to the removal of an unpleasant or undesired stimulus.*

Negative Reinforcement. When a response is strengthened by virtue of the fact that it leads to the removal of something unpleasant, it is said to be **negatively reinforced.** Do not let the word *negative* here confuse you. Negative reinforcement *is* reinforcement; it does strengthen a response. Consider, for example, a parent who gives in to a child's whining and begging. The parent's response of surrender is negatively reinforced (and therefore strengthened) by virtue of the fact that it leads to termination of the unpleasant whining.

Negative reinforcement appears to play a major role in the development of avoidance tendencies. Many people have a fondness for avoiding facing up to their problems. This unfortunate habit is usually acquired because avoidance behavior gets rid of anxiety and is therefore negatively reinforced. Recall our friend the newspaper reporter, whose work environment elicits anxiety (through respondent conditioning). This reporter might have a mild headache one morning and call in sick. His spontaneous decision to skip work that day might be negatively reinforced when he finds that his anxiety immediately evaporates. Thus, the response of "calling in sick" might be strengthened so that he starts using it whenever he has even the most feeble excuse. If this avoidance response continues to be negatively reinforced by successful removal of anxiety, it might become very frequent, and the avoidance pattern might carry over to other areas of behavior.

Extinction. As was the case in respondent conditioning, *extinction* refers to the weakening of a learned response. In the operant conditioning model, extinction consists in termination of reinforcement. If a previously reinforced response stops producing positive consequences, it tends to gradually wear out and become infrequent. Thus, the reinforced response tendencies making up one's personality are not necessarily permanent. For example, the youngster who found that his classmates reinforced "clowning around" in grade school might find that his attempts at comedy earn nothing but indifferent stares in high school. This termination of reinforcement would probably lead to the gradual extinction of the "clowning around" behavior. How quickly a response extinguishes depends on many factors in the person's earlier reinforcement history.

B. F. SKINNER

PUNISHMENT. *In operant conditioning, the presentation of an unpleasant, or noxious, stimulus. Responses that are followed by punishment tend to be weakened.*

Punishment.   When a reponse leads to negative consequences, it is said to be punished. The concept of **punishment** in the operant conditioning paradigm confuses many students on two counts. First, it is often mixed up with negative reinforcement. Please note that they are altogether different events with opposite outcomes! In negative reinforcement, a response leads to the *removal* of something aversive, and this response is *strengthened*. In punishment, a response leads to the *arrival* of something aversive, and this response tends to be *weakened*.

The second source of confusion involves viewing punishment as *only* a disciplinary procedure used by parents and teachers. In the operant paradigm, the term *punishment* is applicable any time a response leads to negative consequences. For example, imagine a young girl who gets ridiculed by her peers every time she tries her hand at sports. In the operant model of conditioning, it would be appropriate to say that this girl's athletic efforts led to punishment.

The impact of punishment on personality development is complex. Generally speaking, those patterns of behavior that lead to punishing (that is, negative) consequences tend to be weakened. However, some theorists believe that the habit-weakening effects of punishment are relatively temporary. This issue has been a subject of heated debate among psychologists. Additionally, punishment may (through respondent conditioning) produce emotional side effects, such as anxiety. This anxiety may then set the stage for the negative reinforcement of avoidance behavior, as previously discussed. Thus, you can see how respondent and operant conditioning govern behavior in a complex, interactive fashion.

DISCRIMINATIVE STIMULI. *Stimuli whose presence influences behavior by indicating the probable consequences (reinforcement or nonreinforcement) of a particular response.*

Stimulus control of operant behavior.   Although operant behavior is ultimately controlled by its consequences, stimuli play an important role in this process. *Environmental stimuli often serve as signals or cues indicating to a person whether reinforcement for a response is likely or unlikely.* Complex social behavior involves extensive use of these cues, which are called **discriminative stimuli.** Imagine yourself at a party where you are conversing with someone you have just met. In this situation you will probably tune in to various subtle social signals to see whether the other person is enjoying the conversation, is indifferent, or wishes you would go away. Prolonged eye contact is usually a good signal, indicating a high probability that you will be reinforced (by polite attention, complimentary remarks, and so on) for your conversational responding. However, if your new acquaintance continually glances around the room and doesn't face you squarely, he or she is signaling that your social overture is not likely to gain much reinforcement.

Discriminative stimuli allow us to *anticipate* the consequences of our actions. In this way, discriminative stimuli extend the control of consequences over our behavior. A discriminative stimulus that signals that reinforcement is likely for a particular response influences behavior by increasing the probability of that response. Consider the behavior of asking someone out for a date. Many people emit this behavior only very cautiously, after receiving many signals (eye contact, smiles, encouraging conversational exchanges) that reinforcement (an affirmative answer) is fairly likely. Learning to read subtle discriminative stimuli in social interaction is a significant part of developing adequate social skills. Personality traits such as shyness or introversion may be due in part to personal feelings of inadequacy in this area.

OBSERVATIONAL LEARNING

OBSERVATIONAL LEARNING. *The process of being conditioned through the observation of another, usually called the model. Also known as the modeling process or vicarious conditioning.*

Both respondent and operant conditioning can occur through a process called **observational learning,** which has been described by Albert Bandura (1977). Essentially, this involves being conditioned indirectly by virtue of observing someone else's conditioning. For example, your tendency to deal assertively with salespeople might be strengthened by observing a friend being reinforced for such behavior by getting an exceptionally good buy on an automobile. Although your friend and not you receives the reinforcement, you may also have this response tendency strengthened vicariously.

MODEL. *In observational learning, the person whose conditioning is observed and whose behavior may be imitated.*

Observational learning produces what are sometimes called *modeling effects*. In essence, people imitate the behavior of a **model** whom they have observed. Current evidence suggests that such modeling effects are quite common. Observational learning can lead to acquisition or extinction of virtually any kind of response. For instance, studies have shown that modeling can lead to an *increase* in aggressive behavior (Bandura, Ross, & Ross, 1963) or to a *decrease* in it (Chittenden, 1973).

Of course, our modeling or imitative tendencies are not automatic. We tend to model ourselves after people whom we respect and consider competent and people whom we see as similar to ourselves. It also appears that those of us who are relatively low in self-esteem are more prone to imitate others. These tendencies clearly show that cognitive factors are intimately involved in modeling processes.

MOTIVATION

DRIVE. *An internal state that serves to activate and direct one's behavior toward the pursuit of certain goal objects.*

Behaviorist theories generally use a rather simple model of motivation. Behavior is thought to be activated by a **drive** that creates a certain tension in the personality system. This tension can be reduced by securing some reinforcer that satisfies the activated drive. This tension-reduction model is somewhat similar to that used by psychoanalytic theory. However, Freud focused primarily on internal conflict as the source of tension, whereas the behaviorists see our hedonistic pursuit of reinforcement as the major source of tension.

PRIMARY DRIVES. *Unlearned, usually physiological needs that activate and direct behavior.*

SECONDARY DRIVES. *Learned needs acquired through conditioning that activate and direct behavior.*

A person's drives are usually divided into two classes: primary drives and secondary drives. **Primary drives** are unlearned and tend to be tied closely to physiological systems (hunger, thirst, sex, possibly curiosity, and so on). **Secondary drives** are acquired through learning and tend to be independent of physiology (for example, achievement, approval, power).

THE HEALTHY PERSONALITY

Generally, the behaviorists have been rather evasive about confronting the question of what constitutes the healthy personality. They tend to see it as a messy, value-laden issue that is not amenable to scientific analysis. *Thus, they believe that the question lies beyond the scope of their mission,* which is simply to discover and elucidate the basic laws governing behavior.

Insofar as behaviorists have addressed this issue of psychological health, two common themes have emerged. First, noting that views of psychological health vary from one culture to another, they argue that health involves the ability to adapt effectively to the requirements of one's society. Second, they regard as healthy those persons who can learn to exert some control over their environment and thereby gain control over their own behavior. In other words, they maintain that psychological health consists in the ability to engage in competent self-management. The means through which they believe that this admirable goal can be achieved will be discussed in detail in the application section of Chapter 5, which deals with behavior modification.

SIGNIFICANT CONTRIBUTIONS

The role of experience.   It is impossible to deny that one's personality is shaped to a large degree by one's experience. A sound theory of personality must account for the way personality is transformed by experience, and the behavioristic model probably does a better job of this than any other theoretical orientation. The concepts associated with respondent and operant conditioning and with observational learning permit a detailed analysis of how personality develops and changes. For the most part, the behaviorists' account of the learning process is characterized by attractive simplicity, great explanatory power, and solid scientific documentation.

Situational determinants of behavior.   The behaviorists have also provided the most thorough account of how situational factors govern behavior. It has always been clear, even to casual observers, that people are not altogether consistent in their behavior. The other models of personality either ignore this troublesome inconsistency or offer rather vague explanations for it. In contrast, behaviorists have eagerly confronted the challenge of explaining this inconsistency with their doctrine of situational specificity.

Behavior modification.   The last two decades have witnessed a revolution in psychotherapy, brought on by the behaviorists' innovative approaches to the treatment of psychological disorders. Even therapists of the psychoanalytic and humanistic persuasions have borrowed specific behavior modification techniques. Moreover, many of these techniques are so simple that they can often be used profitably by the layperson without costly professional help. Later in this text, I will devote much attention to the application of behavior modification principles to one's own problems.

ALBERT BANDURA

Influence on psychology as a discipline.   The behaviorists have had an enormous impact on psychology, transforming the discipline from the study of *consciousness* to the study of *behavior.* Admittedly, Skinner's radical behavioristic position, which completely ignores conscious experience, has been the target of much scathing criticism. Nonetheless, this evolution from the study of consciousness to the study of behavior has enhanced the scientific and empirical quality of the discipline while broadening its scope of interest. Thus, like Freud, the behaviorists altered the direction of psychology's growth in ways that many people consider beneficial.

CRITIQUE

Although behaviorism has had a profound and pervasive impact on psychology and related disciplines, it has not done so without being subjected to a great deal of vigorous criticism. Many of the objections raised have been justified, although you should keep in mind that much of this criticism has been aimed at the *radical* behavioristic philosophies propounded by Watson and Skinner, which no longer represent the dominant point of view among behaviorists. The principal shortcomings of the behaviorist model are enumerated below.

Neglect of cognitive processes.   While there is something to be said for focusing mainly on observable behavior, it is obvious that humans are conscious, feeling, thinking beings. Radical behaviorists, such as Skinner, are not so foolish as to deny the existence of conscious experience; rather, it is the *value* of speculating about inaccessible conscious experience that they repudiate. However, critics have argued, rightfully, that in neglecting cognitive processes the traditional behaviorists have chosen to ignore the most distinctive and important feature of human behavior. Over the last several decades, ample evidence has accumulated that clearly shows the significant role that cognitive processes play in governing behavior. In deference to this evidence, most behaviorists have gradually followed the lead of theorists such as Rotter, Bandura, and Mischel and have returned to considering mental events in their analyses.

Failure to view personality as a whole.   The behaviorist model takes a very analytical approach to personality, seeking to break it down into a collection of stimulus-response bonds. Critics have argued that, in carving up personality in this way, the behaviorists are guilty of a form of mutilation. The person, as a whole, becomes unrecognizable. The resulting mosaic of interrelationships between fragments of behavior is said to be artificial and confusing. This piecemeal analysis of behavior does have its shortcomings. Unfortunately, the behaviorists have not dealt adequately with the *integration* of the stimulus-response associations said to make up one's personality.

Overdependence on animal research.   Many people are bothered that so much of the behaviorists' research has involved the study of animal behavior in very artificial situations. Actually, the problem is not just the decision to study animal behavior so much as the tendency to make unwarranted extrapolations from this animal research to issues concerning human behavior. If it can be shown that a principle of behavior derived through the study of animals also applies to humans, it hardly seems worthwhile to complain about how the principle was originally discovered. However, some behaviorists have been a bit too eager to generalize from animal behavior to human behavior without verifying the applicability of the principle to humans. These unwarranted extrapolations *do* represent a problem.

Negative view of human nature.   Like Freud, the behaviorists paint a rather uncomplimentary picture of human nature. The greatest source of irritation to most people is the behaviorists' assertion that free will is nothing more than an illusion. The issue of free will is a metaphysical question that may keep philosophers arguing for centuries to come. However, whether it is an illusion or reality, people believe that they are free and behave accordingly. The author fails to see any payoff in trying to undermine or destroy this belief in personal freedom. Instead, the behaviorists' premise creates a depressing picture of human "robots" or "puppets" who are not responsible for their own behavior. It seems likely that it would be more productive to take an optimistic view of human nature and encourage people to take more responsibility for their behavior.

The Humanistic Model

HUMANISM. *A major theoretical orientation in psychology that emphasizes the unique qualities of humans, especially their freedom and their potential for personal growth.*

During the first half of the 20th century, psychology was dominated by the psychoanalytic and behavioristic perspectives. However, many psychologists found these theoretical orientations unsatisfactory. The principal charge hurled at these two models was that they were "dehumanizing." Psychoanalytic theory was chided for its belief that behavior is dominated by instinctual and animalistic drives, while behaviorism was maligned for its preoccupation with the study of animal behavior. *The overriding concern for most critics was their belief that both schools of thought failed to recognize the unique qualities of human behavior.* More specifically, critics expressed disenchantment with the mechanistic quality of these models and their extremely pessimistic views of human nature. During the 1950s this diverse opposition blended into a loose alliance that was christened the "third force" in psychology. This third force came to be known as **humanism** because of its exclusive interest in the unique dynamics of human behavior.

The humanistic school of thought is probably characterized by even more diversity and fragmentation than the psychoanalytic and behavioristic coalitions. The common bond of discontent with psychoanalytic and behavioristic theories brought together a rather heterogeneous collection of theorists under the banner of humanism. The theorists most clearly associated with the humanistic movement are Carl Rogers (1951, 1961) and Abraham Maslow (1962, 1970). Other prominent theorists who are considered to share a kindred spirit with Rogers and Maslow include Eric Berne (1964) and Thomas Harris (1967), who pioneered transactional analysis; Albert Ellis (1973), who developed the rational-emotive approach to therapy; Fritz Perls (1969), who was associated with a point of view called Gestalt therapy; and existential psychologists such as Viktor Frankl (1962) and Rollo May (1969). Although each of these theorists tends to focus on different facets of the human experience and has his own unique emphasis and terminology, there is considerable agreement among them on many fundamental issues. In this segment of Chapter 2 I will describe the theories of Rogers and Maslow in order to introduce you to the humanistic orientation. The thoughts of the other humanistic theorists mentioned above will surface in subsequent chapters where their ideas are particularly relevant.

THE HUMANISTIC PHILOSOPHY

The various humanistic theories of personality are united by a common philosophy about the human condition and the appropriate ways to study it. The development of this philosophy has been described in detail by Buhler and Allen (1972), who suggest that the recent emergence of humanism is a response to the confusing turmoil in our modern society and the resulting search for a sense of direction. Some of the major principles of this humanistic philosophy are outlined below.

1. Humanistic psychologists are interested *only* in the human being and only in issues that are important to human existence (such as love, creativity, loneliness, and death). They are not interested in animal behavior.

2. The humanists take an *optimistic* view of human nature, emphasizing that we can rise above our biological or animal heritage and that we have the freedom to chart our own courses of action. In particular, the existentialists, such as Viktor Frankl, stress that we *choose* our personality and that we should accept responsibility for that choice. The humanists believe that we all are worthwhile persons with the capacity for self-direction.

PHENOMENOLOGICAL APPROACH. *An approach to understanding behavior that emphasizes the significance of an individual's personal, subjective view of events, as opposed to objective reality.*

3. The humanists believe in the **phenomenological approach,** which assumes that an individual's personal, subjective view of the world is more important than objective reality. For instance, if you erroneously believe that certain people do not like you, you are likely to behave as if these people *really* disliked you. Thus, the humanists argue that we must attempt to understand a person's subjective point of view in order to truly understand his or her behavior.

4. Humanistic psychology assumes that we are largely *conscious* and *rational* beings and that we usually have access to our feelings, intentions, and states of mind. Rather than ignoring conscious experience and cognitive processes, the humanists enthusiastically focus on internal, mental affairs.

5. The humanists believe in a holistic, rather than analytic, approach to the understanding of personality. They are interested in getting an overview of the person as a whole, as opposed to breaking the personality into component parts, which they believe are meaningless when standing alone.

STRUCTURE OF PERSONALITY

The humanists have shown a moderate fondness for structural constructs. The most fully elaborated model of personality structure in the humanistic camp is that put together by Carl Rogers (1951, 1959). Most humanistic theories either explicitly or implicitly use a construct similar to Rogers's "self" to account for personality structure.

SELF-CONCEPT. *A collection of beliefs and judgments about one's own nature, typical behavior, strengths, and weaknesses.*

Rogers believes that our behavior is influenced greatly by our sense of *self,* or **self-concept.** The self-concept is your own mental picture of yourself. It consists of a collection of beliefs about your unique characteristics and typical behavior. For example, a self-concept might include beliefs such as "I am a nice person" or "I am smart" or "I am pretty" or "I am shy" or "I am boring." According to Rogers, the self-concept is available to awareness (that is, it is *not* buried in the unconscious); however, we tend to take it for granted as it floats innocuously in the background of our consciousness. In other words, we do not think about thinking about our self-concept very often, but we *can* do so. Although the self-concept tends to be reasonably stable, it does have a fluid quality and is subject to change.

INCONGRUENCE. *In Rogers's theory of personality, any disparity between one's self-concept and actual experience.*

Rogers stresses that *the self-concept involves a subjective picture of oneself.* Therefore, it may not be altogether consistent with people's actual experience of themselves. To put it more bluntly, *your self-concept may be inaccurate.* Most people are prone to distort their experiences so as to promote a relatively favorable self-concept. For example, you may believe that you are exceptionally bright, but your grade transcript might suggest otherwise. This inconsistency between the self-concept and the actual experience of the person is called **incongruence.** The amount of incongruence between one's self-concept and reality plays a vital motivational role in Rogers's theory.

DEVELOPMENT OF PERSONALITY

CARL ROGERS

Humanistic theories have not focused on personality development as extensively as the psychoanalytic and behavioristic models. Rogers has some worthwhile insights about developmental trends, but he does not provide a particularly thorough or systematic overview of development.

Rogers is concerned mainly with how childhood experiences promote incongruence between the self-concept and actual experience. According to Rogers, early in infancy we develop a fundamental need for positive regard (approval) from others. Early in life this positive regard is provided largely by parents, and the child quickly learns which behaviors lead to parental approval and which to parental disapproval. Thus, certain actions come to be seen as "worthy" by the child, while others are viewed as "unworthy." Because children want to believe that they merit positive regard from their parents and others, they tend to *block out* of their self-concept experiences that they view as unworthy. For example, a young girl might be scolded occasionally for teasing the family dog. Since she wants to protect her belief that she is a nice little girl, she might deny to herself that the teasing is really teasing. She might convince herself, in spite of strong evidence to the contrary, that the dog enjoys these encounters.

Rogers theorizes that as we grow up, we distort more and more of our experiences in order to feel worthy of positive regard from a wider and wider array of significant others. Thus, the gap between our self-concept and reality gradually expands as a reaction to the judgmental behavior of people around us. Rogers maintains that when parents make their affection very *conditional* (contingent on the child's conforming exactly to their expectations), the likelihood of reality distortion and incongruence increases. In contrast, when children are accustomed to relatively *unconditional* positive regard, the admission of unworthy experiences into their self-concept is less threatening, because they are less worried about rejection from significant others. Therefore, Rogers maintains, *unconditional positive regard reduces the tendency toward distortion of reality and thereby fosters a more accurate and congruent self-concept.*

MOTIVATION

The humanistic model of motivation differs markedly from those seen in psychoanalytic and behavioristic theory. Rogers and Abraham Maslow have both developed innovative approaches to motivation whose central notion is that humans are propelled by a basic force toward personal growth or self-actualization. In this section, I will finish my description of Rogers's theory and then turn to Maslow's provocative analysis of motivation.

ROGERS

SELF-ACTUALIZING TENDENCY. *In Rogers's theory of personality, the tendency to behave consistently with one's self-concept.*

According to Rogers, the key motivational force that governs our behavior is the **self-actualizing tendency.** In Rogers's system this consists in self-imposed pressure to behave consistently with one's self-concept. Rogers believes that people do not feel comfortable when they "act out of character." For example, let us say that you see yourself as a reserved, sober person, but one night you happen to get carried away, and you start getting "rowdy." Rogers's theory suggests that this rowdy behavior would make you feel uneasy.

According to Rogers, this need to be true to one's self-concept often gets misdirected by society, leading to self-defeating behavior. As you may recall from his views on personality development, Rogers believes that the conditional quality of much affection in our society leads many of us to construct an overly favorable self-concept in order to continue to feel worthy of others' positive regard. Unfortunately, our self-actualizing tendency instills in us a great loyalty to our self-concept, whether it is accurate or not! Thus, we feel threatened by informational input that is inconsistent with our sense of self. *The greater the incongruence between our self-concept and reality, the more often we are likely to feel threatened.*

This perception of threat leads us to experience anxiety. *To combat this anxiety, we behave defensively and try to reinterpret our experience so that it appears consistent with our self-concept.* Thus, we ignore, deny, and twist reality to suit our purposes. Consider a young lady who, like most of us, considers herself a "nice person." Let us suppose that in reality she is rather conceited and selfish, and she gets negative feedback from both boyfriends and girlfriends that she is a "snotty little bitch." How might she react in order to protect her self-concept? She might ignore or block out those occasions when she behaves selfishly, deny the allegations by her friends that she is self-centered, attribute the girlfriends' comments to their envy of her good looks and the boyfriends' comments to their disappointment because she stopped dating them, and start doing volunteer work with handicapped children to show everyone (including herself) that she is really a wonderful person.

As you can see, we often go to great lengths to defend our self-concept. However, this reality distortion tends to be counterproductive in the long run because it only maintains or increases the incongruence between the self-concept and real experience. As this incongruence grows, so does the need to protect the progressively less accurate self-concept. Thus, defensive behavior breeds more defensive behavior in a cyclical fashion.

MASLOW

ABRAHAM MASLOW

Hierarchy of needs. Maslow (1962, 1970) proposed that human needs were organized into a hierarchy according to priority. Figure 2.4 shows this hierarchical arrangement. According to Maslow, the needs at the bottom of the pyramid are the most basic, and we must satisfy these fairly well before we become concerned about higher needs. When we manage to satisfy a level of needs reasonably well (complete satisfaction is not necessary), the next level of needs is activated. Thus, Maslow proposes that physiological needs must be taken care of before safety/security needs become relevant. Similarly, *both* physiological and safety/security needs must be gratified before the love/belongingness needs become salient. The following example clarifies how the hierarchy works. Suppose that you have a factory job that carries relatively little prestige, and you complain to your spouse that your self-esteem needs are not being met. A month later there are massive layoffs in your industry, and you begin to fear that you may soon be unemployed. The satisfaction of your physiological and security needs is now threatened, and you will probably stop worrying about your less basic esteem needs.

Ordering of needs. Maslow theorized that all the levels of needs, and their ordering, were biologically built into human nature. However, he recognized that some people might get their hierarchy scrambled owing to unusual circumstances. For instance, he noted that the most common reversal of levels was seen in people who gave higher priority to their esteem needs than to their love needs, which are ordinarily more basic. Such people tend to show more concern about their career advancement than about their marriage or family. Thus, the ordering of needs tends to be similar to that in Figure 2.4 for *most* people; but some people have their own unique ordering, which is a function of their unique experience and history.

Metaneeds
Need for self-actualization
Ability to direct one's own life,
a sense of meaning to one's life,
fulfillment

Esteem needs
Self-esteem, esteem of others, achievement,
recognition, dignity

Belongingness and love needs
Love, affection, belongingness; need for
family and friends

Safety needs
Security, stability, freedom from
anxiety and chaos; need for structure, order,
and so on

Physiological needs
Homeostasis; specific hungers; food, water, air,
shelter, and general survival

FIGURE 2.4   Maslow's hierarchy of needs.

SELF-ACTUALIZATION. *The highest need in Maslow's hierarchy, the need to fulfill one's potential. Also used by Maslow to refer to the entire group of higher growth needs (see Metaneeds).*

Self-actualization needs. Maslow summarized his concept of the need for **self-actualization** with a very simple statement: "What a man *can* be, he *must* be" (1954, p. 46). Thus, in Maslow's theory, self-actualization concerns the inherent need of humans to evolve forward in an effort to reach their fullest potentials. According to Maslow, a person must do whatever he or she, *individually*, is fitted for. Obviously, this varies from one person to another and encompasses virtually the entire range of human experience. Whether one is married or single, plumber or physician, secretary or theologian, one may come close to using one's maximum capabilities. The crucial issue is whether you are doing what you were "cut out for," as shaped by both heredity and experience. If you have musical talent but must work as an accountant, or if you have great intellectual ability but must work as a sales clerk, your need for self-actualization is being thwarted.

In addition to this need for self-actualization, Maslow proposed that we have other **metaneeds**—that is, higher, growth needs. Among these, Maslow attributed considerable importance to *cognitive* needs for *knowledge and understanding*. He believed that some people develop an urgent need to systematize the world around them, to probe intriguing questions, to experiment, to satisfy

METANEEDS. *The higher, growth needs in Maslow's hierarchy of needs. Also called the self-actualization needs.*

their curiosity. Although such people would tend to follow academic pursuits, one does not have to be highly educated to manifest this need. I once taught a fiftyish central Illinois coal miner who had little education and was quite happy to remain a coal miner but who was driven by a profound urge to understand his world. This charming gentleman read frequently, took collegiate courses for sheer enjoyment, and devoted considerable thought to abstract, philosophical questions. In addition, Maslow proposed that some of us develop *esthetic needs* for beauty and symmetry. These needs often lead people into artistic endeavors.

Maslow believed that the metaneeds, though not essential to survival, were very important. He asserted that satisfaction of these metaneeds brought more profound happiness and serenity than did satisfaction of the lower needs. He further maintained that gratification of these higher needs was the key to psychological health and that it promoted strong individuality. He also claimed that people's pursuit of metaneeds often produced, as a side effect, positive consequences for society as a whole. Specifically, he thought that such pursuits would make people better parents, teachers, leaders, and so forth.

THE HEALTHY PERSONALITY

Because of their keen interest in the question of psychological health, humanistic theorists have generated a great number of very detailed models of the healthy personality. Their optimistic view of human nature has led them to paint very appealing pictures of the heights to which we can soar.

ROGERS'S "FULLY FUNCTIONING PERSONALITY"

Rogers (1961) did not see psychological health as an end state but as a continuous, never-ending *process*. Thus, psychological health was thought to involve movement or *growth* in a particular direction. Rogers outlined a number of personal qualities that tend to be associated with growth in a healthy direction. I will describe three of these qualities that are central to Rogers's picture of the "fully functioning person."

First and foremost, Rogers believed that *the fully functioning person is characterized by a sense of freedom.* Such poeple feel that they have the power to control their own destiny. They approach life creatively, without worrying particularly about how others will react to them. They have emancipated themselves from the usual addictive dependence on others for approval, affection, and positive regard.

Second, Rogers believed that *the fully functioning person is open to experience.* This is simply the opposite of being defensive. Instead of blocking out and distorting certain experiences, the healthy personality is open to *all* experience, even that which may sometimes be threatening. This openness produces a flexible, rather than rigid, approach to life. Ultimately, this openness leads one to approach each experience as fresh, new, and exciting.

Third, *the fully functioning person is one who can trust his or her intuitive feelings.* Rogers pointed out that the objective, rational approach to decisions is fallible and that sometimes it should be subjugated to less rational intuitive feelings. He noted that occasionally we have a gut-level feeling that we should do this or that, without being able to put our finger on any rational basis for that feeling. According to Rogers, the psychologically healthy person does not simply dismiss these mysterious feelings. Instead, the healthy personality knows when to go with such intuitive, irrational feelings.

MASLOW'S "SELF-ACTUALIZING PERSONALITY"

The most elaborate work on the healthy personality has been done by Maslow (1970). *He is one of the few theorists to actually study healthy people!* Most

By satisfying the need to grow, anyone can achieve some form of self-actualization.

of the other theorists have derived their ideas about psychological health from their therapeutic work with people who generally manifest less than optimal adjustment.

In a number of studies, some rather casual and others more formal, Maslow tried to identify unusually healthy people so that he could investigate their characteristics. In one case, he used psychological tests and interviews to sort out the healthiest 1% of a sizable population of college students. In other cases, he focused on historical figures or secretly studied personal acquaintances who he thought were exceptionally healthy. Over a period of years, he formed loose, global impressions about the characteristics of psychologically healthy people.

Maslow saw his research as a preliminary probe into this difficult question, and he regarded his conclusions as tentative. He was the first to admit that his casual data-collection procedures were not marked by great scientific rigor, noting that "the following report is presented with due apologies to those who insist on conventional reliability, validity, sampling, etc." (1970, p. 149). In spite of this humility, Maslow's investigation was probably more systematic than most on this issue, and he deserves credit for studying people who appeared to be healthy.

Maslow called his healthy subjects "self-actualizing people." *On the basis of his theory of motivation, he attributed their health to their ability to satisfy both their basic needs and their higher metaneeds.* Maslow believed that gratification of one's basic physiological, security, love, and esteem needs was essential to foster personal growth. However, he thought that it was the satisfaction of one's metaneeds for knowledge, order, beauty, and meaningfulness that produced exceptionally healthy people. Ultimately, of course, he felt that psychological health depended on the satisfaction of one's need for self-actualization. Fulfilling one's potential was assumed to be a crucial feature of the healthy personality.

Like Rogers, Maslow saw psychological well-being as a *process* rather than a static state. Even self-actualizing people are still growing. In his efforts to describe self-actualizing people, Maslow published several slightly different lists of their characteristics. The following list is adapted from two of Maslow's books (1962, 1970) and is modified slightly to reduce overlap among the items.

1. *Efficient perception of reality.* Self-actualizers tune in to reality well. They are not particularly prone to distortion or seeing what they want to see. They can be detached and objective even when their own interests or needs are at stake. They are particularly penetrating observers of other people and can quickly see through a facade and detect dishonesty in others.

2. *Self-acceptance.* Self-actualizing people have an accepting attitude toward themselves. They recognize both their strengths and their flaws, without becoming too self-congratulatory about the former or too depressed about the latter. This does not mean that they are complacent about their flaws. If something can be done, they will work to improve on their shortcomings. But they are not crippled by guilt or shame over their weaknesses. They accept all of their personal nature, even the more animalistic aspects. According to Maslow (1954), healthy personalities "tend to be good animals" (p. 156). By this he meant that they heartily enjoy their food, their sleep, their sex, and so forth, without developing neurotic aversions to biological functions.

3. *Spontaneity.* These healthy people are not afraid to express their emotions openly. They are not guarded in their interactions, carefully playing certain roles. Instead, they avoid pretense and artificiality in favor of natural, creative expression.

4. *Problem-centered.* Maslow described self-actualizers as problem-centered, as opposed to ego-centered. This was intended to convey that they do not focus most of their attention and energy on themselves. Rather, the bulk of their energies are focused on their *work* (whether it is housework or

artistic work). They adopt a mission in life and work intensely to further it. They enjoy their work because if fulfills their metaneeds, not because it leads to prestige or financial reward.

5. *Autonomy and a lack of dependency on others.* Like Rogers, Maslow believed that healthy people are not particularly dependent on others for their satisfaction. They do not need other people around to provide them with approval and guidance. Instead, they enjoy solitude and seek privacy. A closely related characteristic is self-actualizers' ability to function autonomously. They believe in self-determination, make their own decisions, and take responsibility for them. They are not very pliable or susceptible to social influence. They do not have a strong need to conform, although they are not rebellious merely for the sake of being rebellious.

6. *Continued freshness of appreciation.* Self-actualizers have an unusual capacity to maintain a fresh appreciation of the world around them. They can listen to a symphony or gaze across a lake for the hundredth time and still authentically appreciate the beauty. They manage to remain childlike (in a positive sense) and naive, instead of becoming jaded and cynical.

7. *Peak experiences.* More often than most people, self-actualizers experience profound, intense feelings of awe, wonder, and ecstasy. These peak experiences may ascend to such dizzying heights that they have a mystical or religious quality—but Maslow also included milder peak experiences, such as getting genuinely excited about an especially beautiful sunset. In either case, these peak experiences are more frequent in psychologically healthy people.

8. *Strong social interest and social relationships.* Like Adler and Fromm, Maslow argued that the healthy personality is characterized by a strong feeling of kinship with humanity. Self-actualizers are accepting toward others, sympathetic to their plight, and sensitive to their needs. At the same time, they tend to have fewer, but deeper and more intimate, friendships than most people. They are capable of great love, and they give their love unselfishly without much worry about reciprocity.

9. *Unhostile sense of humor.* These healthy individuals have a somewhat unusual sense of humor. They are not particularly amused by jokes made at someone's expense (for example, one-upmanship, ethnic jokes) or the typical "dirty" jokes that play on our sexual anxieties. They prefer more thoughtful, dry, and subtle humor. They don't take themselves too seriously, and they are capable of laughing at themselves.

10. *Balance between polarities.* Like Jung, Maslow believed that one achieves a healthy personality by striking a balance between many basic polarities evident in the human condition. According to Maslow, self-actualizers are able to resolve fundamental dichotomies such as that between reason and intuition or between mysticism and realism. Thus, he suggests that self-actualizing people are able to be both selfish and unselfish, hard-working and playful, childlike and mature, conforming and rebellious, objective and subjective, serious and humorous, conventional and unconventional, rational and irrational. In summary, self-actualizers are able to integrate antagonistic tendencies within themselves to achieve a balanced personality.

INTIMIDATING NATURE OF THE MODELS

I should probably express a word of caution about the rather intimidating nature of these humanistic theories regarding the healthy personality. For many people, Rogers's and Maslow's descriptions of psychological health are awesome and intimidating, in that they seem to describe *perfect* people. They conjure up pictures of flawless, efficient, completely happy people who never fail in any endeavor. Such images may make some people feel inferior and may make the pursuit of psychological health seem a hopeless mission. You should not be put off by these models of perfection. Bear in mind that most of the theorists were describing hypothetical, rather than real, people. When Maslow tried to identify real people of exceptional health, the results were so disappointing that he turned to the study of historical figures. Thus, if you thought these models of psychological health were a bit unrealistic, you were quite correct. Nonetheless, they can provide worthwhile goals for people to pursue.

SIGNIFICANT CONTRIBUTIONS

Importance of subjective views. The humanists' argument that a person's subjective views may be more significant than objective reality seems undeniable. Even though it may be quite difficult to achieve an understanding of another's internal frame of reference, it seems clear that we have to take into consideration more than objective reality if we expect to truly understand much behavior. The phenomenological approach is fraught with interpretive problems, but to ignore subjective experience is to omit a crucial variable from the behavioral equation.

Value-laden nature of psychological diagnosis. Chapter 1 mentioned that classifying behavior as abnormal or pathological constitutes a value judgment. The campaign to make clear the value-laden nature of psychodiagnosis has been spearheaded by the humanists. There is no simple solution to this problem, as you will see when I discuss it in detail later. However, the humanists' compelling arguments about the arbitrary nature of diagnostic labels, such as "neurotic" and "psychotic," have made us more sensitive to this very real and very serious problem.

INSIGHT THERAPY. *Any therapy involving a verbal relationship with a mental-health professional that has as its primary goal improved self-understanding.*

Innovations in psychotherapy. During the first half of this century, **insight therapy,** wherein a client and a therapist sit down and talk things over, was dominated by psychoanalytic dogma. Although Freud had some brilliant ideas, psychoanalysis clearly had its limitations and certainly was not the right treatment for all people or all problems. While psychoanalytic thought has grown stale, the humanistic movement has provided a fertile breeding ground for creative, new approaches to insight therapy. In the last three decades, most of the successful new insight therapies have emerged from the humanistic camp.

Influence on psychology as a discipline. The humanistic movement has influenced the growth of psychology, first, by helping to focus more attention on the uniquely human problem of living in our crazy, mixed-up modern world. Second, it has diverted serious attention to the study of psychological health as well as pathology. And, with its positive view of human nature, it has provided a refreshing counterpoint to the pessimistic views propagated by the behavioristic and psychoanalytic models.

CRITIQUE

Lack of testability. Humanistic theory has generated many intriguing hypotheses that are extremely difficult to put to a sound, scientific test. Like the psychoanalytic model, the humanistic model is troubled by its focus on private, inner experience, which is not easily susceptible to investigation. For example, the very existence of the pivotal self-actualization tendency is difficult to verify.

Inadequate evidence. Similarly, like Freudian theory, humanistic theorizing does not rest on a solid foundation of empirical research. The inspiration for much of humanistic theory has come from careful, discerning, but *uncontrolled* observation in clinical settings. Although case studies may be invaluable in generating hypotheses, they are ill suited for building an empirical data base. Compounding this problem is the fact that many humanists are rather nonchalant about, and even scornful of, the need to verify their ideas, principles, and hypotheses through research.

Unrealistic view of human nature. After criticizing the behavioristic and psychoanalytic models for their pessimistic view of human nature, it may seem somewhat inconsistent to object to the optimistic view taken by the humanists. Unfortunately, however, it seems that all three schools of thought take overly extreme positions in describing the essence of human nature. Some aspects of the humanists' view of human nature seem overstated or unrealistically optimistic. For instance, while the psychoanalytic and behavioristic models probably *underestimate* how free and rational we are, the humanistic model probably *overestimates* our freedom and rationality.

Encouragement of narcissism. The term *narcissism*, which was coined by Freudian theorists, refers to excessive self-love, typically accompanied by a lack of concern for others' welfare. As discussed in Chapter 1, many of the recently popular self-help books have endorsed and promoted self-centered, narcissistic attitudes. This deplorable trend has its roots in the humanistic movement. Specifically, it is based on analyses such as that by Rogers, who suggested that it is unfortunate that, in order to gain others' positive regard, we often develop into what *others* want us to be, rather than what *we* truly want to be. Although there is much to be said for becoming less dependent on others' approval, some self-styled "humanists" seem to have misread Rogers and Maslow, and they have become carried away advocating casual disregard for the welfare of others. In reality, this narcissism is quite inconsistent with the philosophy of humanism, as outlined by theorists such as Rogers and Maslow.

Epilogue

You have now been introduced to the three major models of personality and behavior in psychology. At this point you may be staggering under the burden of trying to keep the theories straight and relate them to one another. Furthermore, you may be wondering why we have three conflicting models of behavior. Well, actually we have *more* than just three! I have reviewed only the three most influential theoretical orientations. There are still other theories of personality, which did not emerge out of these three major theoretical traditions. For example, there are *constitutional,* or biological, theories of personality (Eysenck, 1967; Sheldon, 1942), *trait* theories of personality (Allport, 1937; Cattell, 1965), and *cognitive* theories of personality (Kelly, 1955), which cannot be readily fit into any of the three principal theoretical groupings that this chapter covered.

Thus, a multiplicity of theoretical models coexist. Why? Because no single model can adequately explain everything that we know about behavior, and because each model appears to have some validity and usefulness. There is more than one way to look at something. Is the glass half full or half empty? Obviously, it is both. There is no single answer.

It is an oversimplification to expect one theory to be right and the others wrong. It would be nice if life were that simple, but it is not. In view of the immense range of phenomena studied by psychology, it is not surprising that many theories exist. Actually, this is true in most, if not all, sciences.

Thus, it is not unreasonable or unusual to find several explanations for one phenomenon, all of which might be partly correct. *It is probably best to think of the various theoretical orientations as different viewpoints or perspectives on behavior. Each probably has some validity.* The three major models described in this chapter would not have endured for decades unless they had some explanatory utility. I have tried to emphasize that all three schools of thought have made significant contributions to our understanding of behavior *and* that all three models have their shortcomings. Moreover, all three are currently popular frameworks for the explanation of behavior. You cannot expect to understand these explanations without having some familiarity with the conceptual models they employ.

Summary

Personality theories provide explanatory models that help us in our effort to understand behavior. Most personality theories can be categorized under one of three very broad theoretical orientations: the psychoanalytic, behavioristic, and humanistic models of behavior.

The psychoanalytic model, developed by Sigmund Freud, analyzes personality into three interacting components—the id, ego, and superego—which operate at three different levels of awareness. Freud believed that the sexual and aggressive drives were the most important, and he proposed a conflict model to account for our behavior. His stage theory of development outlined how our early years shape our adult personality. Later Erikson expanded and modified Freud's developmental model. Various other neo-Freudians have revised psychoanalytic theory, shifting emphasis from sexual to social determinants of behavior. Psychoanalytic theorists offer rather diversified views on the nature of the healthy personality.

Behavioristic theory focuses on observable behavior and puts little emphasis on structural constructs. Instead, attention is devoted to how our personality is shaped by conditioning. Respondent conditioning is thought to govern our emotions and operant conditioning to govern most other aspects of behavior. Either type of conditioning may occur vicariously through observational learning. According to Skinner, our main motivation is to pursue reinforcement. Behavioral theorists tend to shy away from the concept of the healthy personality, although they do seem to admire adaptability and self-management skills.

Humanistic theory assumes that humans are free, conscious, and rational beings and therefore approaches behavior from a holistic, phenomenological viewpoint. Our self-concept is thought to be of prime importance in influencing our behavior. Rogers describes why we often tend to develop an inaccurate self-concept and how this may lead to defensive behavior. Maslow and Rogers both assume that we have a built-in tendency toward personal growth, and Maslow integrates this into his hierarchal model of motivation. Both theorists, like most other humanists, have very elaborate theories about the nature of the healthy personality.

The upcoming application section discusses how you can use psychological testing to learn more about your personality and abilities. It describes the logic, the limitations, and the fundamentals of psychological tests.

Learning about Yourself through Psychological Testing

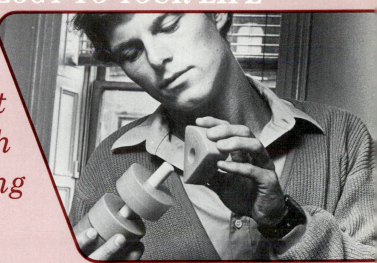

True or false? Choose one.

_____ 1. Psychological tests may be culturally and/or sexually biased.
_____ 2. Psychological-test scores are often misinterpreted.
_____ 3. Psychological testing is sometimes an invasion of privacy.
_____ 4. Psychological tests sometimes seem dehumanizing.
_____ 5. Psychological tests may be quite useful in helping people to learn more about themselves.

If you answered "true" to all five questions, you earned a perfect score. Yes, psychological tests may be biased, open to misinterpretation, dehumanizing, and an invasion of your privacy. Nonetheless, the use of psychological tests continues to grow, because psychological tests can be very useful in spite of these shortcomings. Psychological tests are an invaluable diagnostic tool for clinicians, and *you* may be able to use them to learn more about yourself.

Let us not underestimate the gravity of the problems mentioned above. Bias in testing can lead to unfair hiring practices in industry or unfair admissions decisions in education. These are indeed very serious social problems. However, it should be pointed out that these and most other problems related to psychological testing emerge when *institutions* use the tests to make decisions affecting our lives. In many instances, it has been the *misuse* of a test, rather than the test itself, that has come under fire. In any case, it has been institutional use of tests that has unleashed the current torrent of controversy.

Although bureaucratic abuse of testing is a very real danger, psychological tests can nonetheless be quite valuable in helping people to know themselves better, as long as they understand the logic and limitations of the tests.

Insofar as psychological tests can help you to form a realistic picture of your capabilities and personal qualities, they should facilitate personal growth. Consistent with this philosophy, a variety of psychological tests and scales have been included in your workbook. It is hoped that you may gain some personal insight by responding to these scales. To facilitate your use of these and other tests, this section discusses some of the basic facets of psychological testing and provides you with the opportunity to take one such test.

TYPES OF PSYCHOLOGICAL TESTS

At various points in your life, you may choose or be required to take a diverse array of psychological tests. Generally these tests fall into one of two broad categories: they measure either some cognitive ability or some aspect of personality.

TESTS OF COGNITIVE ABILITIES

This category comprises tests designed to measure some intellectual capacity. They include IQ tests, which measure general intellectual ability; achievement tests, which measure a person's mastery of various school subjects; and aptitude tests, which assess a person's potential talent for specific types of tasks. As you have progressed through school, you have probably taken many such tests.

These tests are important because they often serve as gateways to further schooling, training programs, and new jobs. Learning how to perform effectively on such cognitive tests is of critical significance if you want to avoid having the gates slammed in your face. Unfortunately, many people are unable to display their true talents on such tests. Typically, they are thwarted by one of two problems. For some people, the problem is that their intellectual functioning is disrupted by excessive test anxiety (Gaudry & Spielberger, 1971). For others, the problem is that they have failed to acquire sound test-taking skill, sometimes called "testwiseness" (Sarnacki, 1979).

PERSONALITY SCALES

If you had to describe yourself in a few words, what words would you use? Are you conscientious? Sincere? Introverted? Shrewd? Anxious? Practical? Frivolous? Hard-working? Domineering? Dependable? You would probably find yourself using words such as these, which refer to what psychologists call personality **traits.** They represent the dimensions along which we measure personality. They are used to describe, and in some cases explain, the consistency in our behavior.

TRAIT. A distinguishing quality of an individual; a personality characteristic.

Psychologists use personality scales to systematically measure these personality traits. Of course, psychologists are not the only people interested in assessing personality. In shaping and modifying our self-concepts, we all engage in a much less systematic sort of personality assessment. We also size up *other* people and make descriptive statements about their personalities. Thus, personality assessment is an inevitable activity in our lives. In your workbook you will find some of the formal tests used by psychologists to measure personality. These are intended to give you an opportunity to compare your casual observations about yourself with the results of more systematic measurement. As noted earlier in the chapter, Rogers (1959) believes that we have a fundamental tendency to make distorted observations about ourselves. Insofar as this is true, these comparisons may give you some interesting insights and food for thought.

Most personality scales are self-report inventories. These tests use the rather direct strategy of simply asking subjects to answer questions about themselves. Some of these tests measure only one dimension of personality; others measure many dimensions simultaneously (see Figure 2.5). The unidimensional tests are used more in research, the multidimensional tests more in clinical work. For the most part, the tests in your workbook are research instruments that measure a single, specific dimension of personality.

Self-report inventories have some weaknesses that merit mention. Although these tests can assess personality more precisely and systematically than our casual observations, they are only as accurate as the information we give them. Most of these inventories require subjects to review a series of statements and check those that apply to themselves. In responding to such tests, some subjects consciously answer inaccurately to create a certain impression; others are

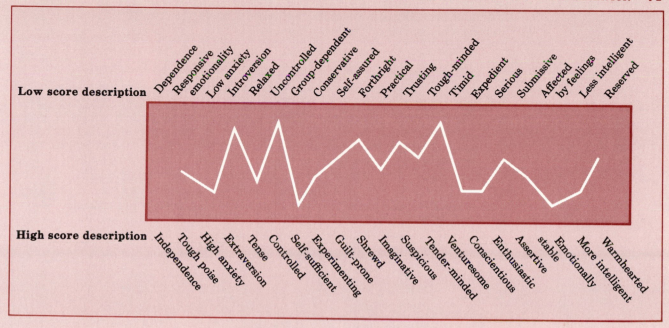

FIGURE 2.5 Sample profile from the 16 Personality Factor Questionnaire (PFQ), a personality test that measures 16 "personality factors," or traits. (© 1975, 1979, 1982, *Institute for Personality and Ability Testing, Inc., P. O. Box 188, Champaign, Illinois, USA. All rights reserved. Reprinted by permission.*)

unconsciously influenced by the social desirability or acceptability of the statements. If you really want to learn something about yourself, it is essential that you respond to the test items with serious thought and with as much candor as possible. Finally, it should be stressed that you should not regard these test results as the final word about your personality. Since the tests are susceptible to unconscious distortion on your part, the results should be regarded as suggestive rather than definitive.

KEY CONCEPTS IN PSYCHOLOGICAL TESTING

You should be familiar with a number of concepts in order to better understand both the tests in your workbook and those that you will encounter throughout life. Therefore, I will briefly review some of the fundamentals of psychological testing.

A psychological test consists of a standardized measure of a sample of a person's behavior. Testing is somewhat analogous to taking a blood sample, but the psychologist wants a *behavior* sample. This sampling interpretation of testing should alert you to one of the major limitations of psychological tests: it is always possible that the sample is not representative of your behavior as a whole. We all have our "bad days." A stomachache, a fight with your boyfriend, a shift in mood—all might affect your responses to a test on a particular occasion. Because of this "sampling" problem, test results must always be interpreted cautiously.

STANDARDIZATION

STANDARDIZATION. *The uniformities in administration and scoring of a psychological test.*

Psychological tests are **standardized.** This means that uniform procedures are used in the administration and scoring of the test. Different subjects get the same instructions, the same questions, the same time limits, and so forth. This standardization is essential because psychological tests are *relative* measures. There are no "absolute" scales along which we can measure personal qualities. Traits such as extroversion, anxiety, or creativity cannot be measured in inches or decibels or quarts.

NORMS

NORMS. *Information indicating what represents a high or low score on a psychological test; usually based on data collected from a large standardization group.*

Although it often is not made explicit, psychological tests tell you how you score *relative to other people*. They tell you that you are average or slightly above average or extremely below average in some trait or ability. The test **norms** are the framework in which your scores are interpreted. A raw score, by itself, is largely meaningless. The norms provide information about what represents a high or low score on the test. Typically, they convert your raw score into a percentile. The percentile figure tells you how many people out of 100 score *below* you on the particular trait in question. For example, if you scored at the 64th percentile on a test of assertiveness, that would indicate that you were more assertive than 64% of the sample of people that provided the basis for the norms. Obviously, then, it is important to know what kind of sample was used to arrive at the norms.

RELIABILITY

RELIABILITY. *The consistency of measurement that a test provides. A reliable test is one that obtains similar results upon repetition.*

Reliability is *the consistency of a test's measurement*. If your butcher were to slap a steak on his scale three times instead of the usual once, he would probably get three slightly different weights. This is because even expensive scales are not perfectly reliable. There is some measurement error. Butchers' scales are supposed to have minimal measurement error and therefore could be described as having relatively high reliability. A reliable measure is one that yields fairly consistent results. It is important that any measurement instrument be as reliable as possible because reliability is essential for accuracy.

Reliability can be measured in several ways, all of which involve correlation. One can correlate subjects' scores on two administrations of the test, two parts of the test, or two forms of the test, in order to estimate how consistent the test is. There are no clearly established guidelines about acceptable levels of reliability, since what is acceptable depends on the nature and purpose of the test. In any case, you should be aware that tests vary in measurement error, and you should be particularly cautious in interpreting the results of tests that have relatively low reliability.

VALIDITY

VALIDITY. *The ability of a test to measure what it was designed to measure.*

Validity is *the degree to which a test measures what it claims to measure*. The validity of a test is very difficult to estimate because psychological tests generally purport to measure very abstract qualities (for example, submissiveness, dependency, spatial aptitude), which are not readily observable. Validity is usually estimated by correlating test scores with some independent criterion measure of the trait or ability that the test is supposed to assess. For instance, if you developed a test to measure aptitude for becoming an airplane pilot, you could assess its validity by correlating subjects' scores on the test with subsequent ratings of their performance in the pilot training program. If the test is a valid measure of pilot aptitude, you should find a fairly high positive **correlation** between the test scores and the ratings. There are many other more complex procedures for validating a test, which are beyond the scope of our discussion. The crucial point is that tests vary in regard to how well validated they are. The validity of many tests is thoroughly documented. Others are used even though there is only very tenuous evidence about their validity. This happens not because psychologists are lazy or unconcerned but because some tests measure extremely abstract dimensions that defy validation. In any case, you should inquire about the validity of a test before you attribute too much significance to your scores.

CORRELATION COEFFICIENT. *A number, usually symbolized by the letter r, that is an index of the kind and degree of relationship between two variables (see Box 1.4).*

AN EXAMPLE OF A PSYCHOLOGICAL TEST: THE SAD SCALE

Now that I have introduced you to some basic concepts in psychological testing, you are ready to see psychological testing in action. In Box 2.1 you will find the SAD Scale, complete with instructions for administration and scoring. If you want to, follow the instructions in Box 2.1 and figure your score on the SAD Scale. You should respond to the scale first and then return to this section to learn more about the scale.

What the scale measures.   *SAD* stands for *social avoidance and distress.* As its name implies, this scale measures avoidance and distress in social interactions. David Watson and Ronald Friend (1969) developed the scale to assess the extent to which individuals experience discomfort, fear, and anxiety in social situations and the extent to which they therefore try to evade many kinds of social encounters. Essentially, the scale measures a couple of aspects of excessive caution in interpersonal relations—a condition discussed in Chapter 9, under shyness.

2.1   THE SAD SCALE

Instructions
The statements below inquire about your personal reactions to a variety of situations. Consider each statement carefully. Then indicate whether the statement is true or false in regard to your typical behavior. Record your responses (true or false) in the spaces provided on the left.

The Scale

_____ 1. I feel relaxed even in unfamiliar social situations.

_____ 2. I try to avoid situations which force me to be very sociable.

_____ 3. It is easy for me to relax when I am with strangers.

_____ 4. I have no particular desire to avoid people.

_____ 5. I often find social occasions upsetting.

_____ 6. I usually feel calm and comfortable at social occasions.

_____ 7. I am usually at ease when talking to someone of the opposite sex.

_____ 8. I try to avoid talking to people unless I know them well.

_____ 9. If the chance comes to meet new people, I often take it.

_____ 10. I often feel nervous or tense in casual get-togethers in which both sexes are present.

_____ 11. I am usually nervous with people unless I know them well.

_____ 12. I usually feel relaxed when I am with a group of people.

_____ 13. I often want to get away from people.

_____ 14. I usually feel uncomfortable when I am in a group of people I don't know.

_____ 15. I usually feel relaxed when I meet someone for the first time.

_____ 16. Being introduced to people makes me tense and nervous.

_____ 17. Even though a room is full of strangers, I may enter it anyway.

_____ 18. I would avoid walking up and joining a large group of people.

_____ 19. When my superiors want to talk with me, I talk willingly.

_____ 20. I often feel on edge when I am with a group of people.

_____ 21. I tend to withdraw from people.

_____ 22. I don't mind talking to people at parties or social gatherings.

_____ 23. I am seldom at ease in a large group of people.

_____ 24. I often think up excuses in order to avoid social engagements.

_____ 25. I sometimes take the responsibility for introducing people to each other.

_____ 26. I try to avoid formal social occasions.

_____ 27. I usually go to whatever social engagements I have.

_____ 28. I find it easy to relax with other people.

Scoring the Scale
The scoring key is reproduced below. You should circle your true or false response each time it corresponds to the keyed response below. Add up the number of responses you circle, and this total is your score on the SAD Scale. Record your score below.

1. False	8. True	15. False	22. False
2. True	9. False	16. True	23. True
3. False	10. True	17. False	24. True
4. False	11. True	18. True	25. False
5. True	12. False	19. False	26. True
6. False	13. True	20. True	27. False
7. False	14. True	21. True	28. False

MY SCORE _____

Research on the scale.   Watson and Friend (1969) report very satisfactory estimates of internal reliability and review convincing evidence that the scale is not unduly contaminated by social desirability bias. To check the validity of the scale, they used it to predict subjects' social behavior in experimentally contrived situations. As projected, they found that people who scored high on the SAD Scale were less willing than low scorers to participate in a group discussion. The high scorers also reported anticipating more anxiety about their participation in the discussion than the low scorers. Additionally, Watson and Friend found a strong negative correlation ($-.76$) between the SAD and a measure of affiliation drive (the need to seek the company of others).

Interpreting your score.   Our norms are based on data collected by Watson and Friend (1969) on over 200 university students. The preponderance of people score relatively low on the scale, as you can see from the norms in Table 2.1.

TABLE 2.1   **Norms for the SAD Scale**

High score	16–28	(more than 0.75 standard deviations above the mean)
Intermediate score	6–15	(from 0.50 standard deviations below the mean up to 0.75 standard deviations above the mean)
Low score	0–5	(more than 0.50 standard deviations below the mean)

High scorers: A high score on the SAD Scale means that you report considerable distress about a variety of social situations and probably go out of your way to avoid many of these situations. To put it more bluntly, you are probably above average in shyness. A high score suggests that you may be timid, reticent, and very self-conscious in dealing with people other than those you know very well.

Intermediate scorers: A score in this range indicates that you have a moderate amount of social anxiety. As will be discussed in Chapter 9, research indicates that shyness is situational for most people. Thus, your score probably means that you are socially anxious in some situations but not others.

Low scorers: A low score means that you generally do not experience tension and anxiety in social interactions. Watson and Friend emphasize that this does *not* mean that you are necessarily extroverted, outgoing, and socially aggressive. It means only that you do not feel threatened when socializing with new people. Instead, you tend to feel calm, relaxed, and comfortable when dealing with others.

CHAPTER 2 REVIEW

IDEAS: REVIEW OF LEARNING OBJECTIVES

When you have mastered the material in this chapter, you should be able to do the following.

1. Explain the three functions of a theory.
2. List the three major theoretical orientations in psychology.
3. Discuss certain limitations inherent in the concept of personality (its inferential, general nature and the issue of consistency).
4. Describe the three structural components of personality proposed by Freud.
5. Describe Freud's three levels of awareness.
6. Identify the drives that Freud thought were most significant in governing behavior and explain why he thought they were so important.
7. Explain the operation of Freud's conflict model of personality.
8. List and describe the first three stages of psychosexual development proposed by Freud.
9. List the major trends in neo-Freudian theories of personality.
10. List and describe three characteristics of psychological health as theorized by Freud.
11. Describe Jung's point of view on psychological health.
12. Describe the similar views of Adler and Fromm on psychological health.
13. List four significant contributions of psychoanalytic theory.
14. List four shortcomings of psychoanalytic theory.
15. Summarize behaviorists' view on structural constructs in personality theory.
16. List three types of conditioning.
17. Explain how responses are acquired through respondent conditioning.
18. Describe the kinds of responses that tend to be governed by respondent conditioning in everyday life.
19. Explain how responses are acquired through operant conditioning.
20. Summarize how discriminative stimuli influence operant behavior.
21. Describe observational learning.
22. Describe the behaviorist model of motivation.
23. Describe the view on psychological health taken by the behaviorists.
24. List four significant contributions of behavioristic theory.
25. List four shortcomings of behavioristic theory.
26. List the major principles of humanistic philosophy.
27. Describe Rogers's construct of the self-concept.
28. Summarize Rogers's views on why people develop incongruence between their self-concept and reality.
29. Describe the operation of Rogers's self-actualizing tendency.
30. Describe Maslow's hierarchy of needs and how it works.
31. List several metaneeds proposed by Maslow.
32. Describe three characteristics of Rogers's fully functioning person.
33. Discuss Maslow's research on psychological health.
34. List ten characteristics of Maslow's self-actualizing person.
35. List four significant contributions of humanistic theory.
36. List four shortcomings of humanistic theory.
37. List the two general categories into which psychological tests fall.
38. Summarize the problems associated with personality self-report inventories.
39. Explain why psychological tests should be reliable and valid.

TERMS: REVIEW OF NEW VOCABULARY

When you have mastered the material in this chapter, you should be able to define the following terms.

Acquisition	Emit	Observational learning	Self-actualization
Behaviorism	Extinction	Oedipal complex	Self-actualizing tendency
Cognitive	Fixation	Operant conditioning	Self-concept
Conditioned response	Generalization	Phenomenological	Stage
Conditioned stimulus	Habit hierarchy	Pleasure principle	Standardization
Conditioning	Humanism	Positive reinforcement	Stimulus-response bond
Conscious	Id	Preconscious	Sublimation
Construct	Identification	Primary drives	Superego
Correlation coefficient	Incongruence	Psychoanalysis	Trait
Defense mechanism	Insight therapy	Psychoanalytic model	Theory
Discrimination	Model	Punishment	Unconditioned response
Discriminative stimuli	Metaneeds	Reality principle	Unconditioned stimulus
Drive	Negative reinforcement	Reliability	Unconscious
Ego	Neo-Freudian	Respondent conditioning	Validity
Elicit	Norms	Secondary drives	

PEOPLE: REVIEW OF MAJOR THEORISTS AND RESEARCHERS

When you have mastered the material in this chapter, you should be able to summarize the principal contributions and/or ideas of the following people.

Alfred Adler	Sigmund Freud	Ivan Pavlov	B. F. Skinner
Albert Bandura	Carl Jung	Carl Rogers	John B. Watson
Erik Erikson	Abraham Maslow		

3

STRESS AND ITS EFFECTS

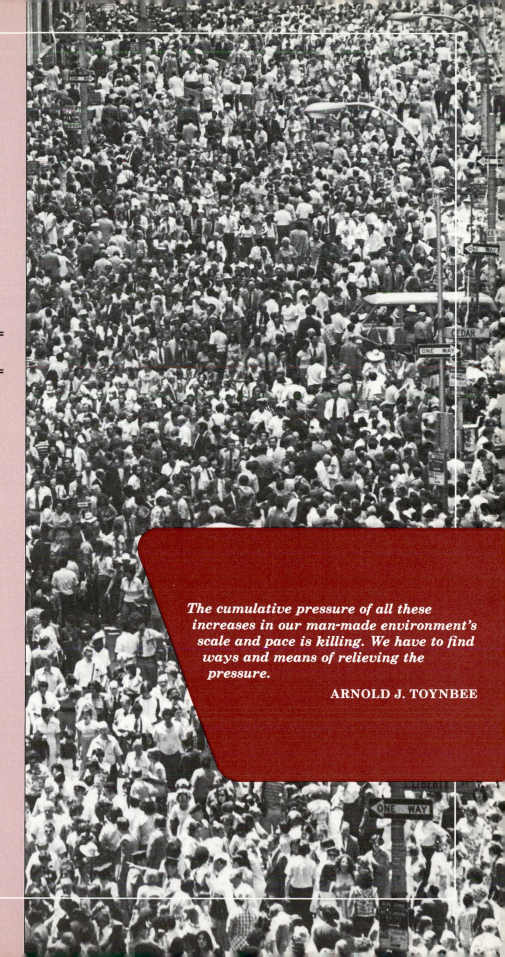

Summary

Applying Psychology to Your Life: Monitoring the Stress in Your Life

PROBLEMS WITH THE SOCIAL READJUSTMENT RATING SCALE

THE LIFE EXPERIENCES SURVEY

QUALIFICATIONS

The cumulative pressure of all these increases in our man-made environment's scale and pace is killing. We have to find ways and means of relieving the pressure.

ARNOLD J. TOYNBEE

"I had a wonderful relationship with a married man for three months. One day when we planned to spend the entire day together, he called and said he wouldn't be meeting me. Someone mentioned me to his wife, and he said that to keep his marriage together, he would have to stop seeing me. I cried all morning and then went shopping to get him off my mind. The grief was like losing someone through death. I still hurt and wonder if I'll ever get over him."

"My little brother died of leukemia recently. I had a *very* hard time accepting it when it happened, and I feel that I still have not completely accepted it. The most stressful aspect of his illness was seeing how unhappy he was having to be in the hospital *constantly,* when he didn't fully understand the seriousness of his illness, or that it would result in his death. He was only 12 years old."

"I had a boyfriend over at my apartment who thought he was the one and only. Then another boyfriend, who also thought that *he* was the only one, showed up at the same time. That's stress!"

These comments were made by students who were asked to describe their most stressful experience in the last year. They illustrate the fact that there are a great diversity of circumstances that may create stress in our lives. Stress comes in all sorts of packages: large and small, pretty and ugly, simple and complex. All too often, the package is a surprise. In this chapter, I will try to sort out these packages for you. I will describe the nature of stress, outline the major types of stress, and discuss how people respond to stressful events at several levels.

In a sense, stress is what a course on adjustment is all about. Recall from Chapter 1 that adjustment essentially deals with how people manage to cope with various demands and pressures. These demands or pressures that require adjustment represent the core of stressful experience. Thus, the central theme in a course such as this is: how do people adjust to stress, and how might they adjust more effectively?

Interest in stress as a topic has intensified markedly in the last decade. The gradual realization that stress exerts an enormous impact on physical and psychological health has led to an explosive growth in scientific research on stress. This expansion of research interest has been accompanied by a corresponding increase in the general public's thirst for information on the subject.

The Nature of Stress

TRANSACTIONAL MODEL OF STRESS. *A theory that proposes that the experience of stress depends on one's subjective appraisal of events. Thus, stress is neither a stimulus nor a response but a stimulus-response transaction.*

The term *stress* has been used in different ways by different researchers. Some (for example, Holmes & Rahe, 1967) define stress as a *stimulus* event that presents unusual demands; others (for example, Selye, 1976) define stress as the bodily *response* we make to the troublesome event. A point of view that lies between these extremes is gradually gaining dominance in psychology. That is the **transactional model of stress** championed by Richard Lazarus and his colleagues (Holroyd & Lazarus, 1982; Lazarus & Folkman, 1984). Lazarus emphasizes that the experience of stress is highly personal and subjective, depending on how people *appraise* the events they encounter. Indeed, there is ample evidence that two persons may view the same potentially stressful circumstances in altogether different ways. A particular event, let us say taking the national admissions test for medical school (the MCAT), may be overwhelmingly stressful for one person, while another person might eagerly look forward to the challenge. Thus, Lazarus concludes that stress involves stimulus-response transactions that require adaptation and tax the individual's resources.

STRESS. *Any circumstances or transactions with the environment that threaten or are perceived to threaten our well-being and thereby tax our adaptive capacities.*

In keeping with this transactional perspective, I will define **stress** as any circumstances that threaten or are perceived to threaten our well-being and thereby tax our adaptive capacities. In deference to the complexity of this concept, I will outline a number of additional points about the nature of stress. I will then sketch a model of the stress process that should give you an overview of how the various elements fit together and a preview of this chapter.

GENERAL PRINCIPLES

RICHARD LAZARUS

1. *Stress may be either physical or psychological.* Examples of physical stress include infections, exposure to excessive heat or cold, failure to get adequate sleep, and pain. Examples of psychological stress include arguing with your spouse, starting a new job, staring at a stack of bills you are unable to pay, and being lonely.

2. *Physical and psychological stress may overlap and interact.* Although it is convenient to distinguish between physical and psychological stress, you should not think of these two types of stress as being altogether independent. They may overlap in that a single event, such as being wounded in combat, can produce both physical and psychological stress. Furthermore, there is evidence (Friedman, Ader, & Glasgow, 1965) that physical and psychological stressors may function interactively. For example, the impact of the psychological stress typically experienced in starting a new job might be greatly exaggerated if the new jobholder is battling a nagging infection (physical stress). I will be focusing primarily on the effects of psychological stress. However, as I discuss the role of psychological stress in our lives, you should keep this potential for interaction in mind.

3. *The appraisal of stress is not necessarily objective.* When under threat, people respond emotionally and seem particularly prone to deviate from objective and rational modes of thought (Folkman, Schaefer, & Lazarus, 1979). Thus, it is clear that judgments about potentially stressful events may be decidedly irrational and unrealistic. For example, a study of hospital patients awaiting surgery (Janis, 1958) showed that there was only a slight relation between the objective seriousness of a patient's upcoming surgery and the amount of fear experienced by the patient. Although surgery is obviously an authentic source of threat, a serious problem for many people is their tendency to see harmless, everyday events as very threatening. For example, common events such as asking someone for a date or applying for a job generate great anxiety in some people.

4. *Stress may be self-imposed.* We tend to think of stress as something imposed on us from without by others and their demands. Surprisingly often, however, it would seem appropriate to characterize stress as self-imposed. For example, you might put pressure on yourself to get good grades or to climb the corporate ladder rapidly. Many people create stress by embracing unrealistically high expectations for themselves, which they are unlikely to fulfill. These overly high expectations often lead to perceptions of failure and feelings of disappointment.

5. *Our response to stress is complex and multidimensional.* Stress affects us at several levels. It tends to produce changes in our emotions, our physiology, and our behavior.

6. *The effects of stress may be cumulative or additive.* It has long been suspected that stress has *cumulative* effects along the lines of the fabled "straw that broke the camel's back." Recent evidence (Kanner, Coyne, Schaefer, & Lazarus, 1981) that little everyday "hassles" can add up to damage one's health appears to confirm that suspicion. For example, you might be experiencing stress of moderate intensity at home, at school, and at work. Coping with each source of stress singly, you might be able to handle things without great difficulty. But collectively, the stress in these three areas of your life might be over-

Tests and exams are a frequent source of stress in students' lives.

whelming. Moreover, it appears that the stressful events do not have to take place at the same time in order to have additive effects. The evidence suggests that a series of stressful events, following closely on one another, may also have cumulative effects.

A MODEL OF THE STRESS PROCESS

Figure 3.1, a diagrammatic model of the stress process, summarizes much of the preceding discussion. This model involves four phases. In the first phase, the stress process is initiated by the experience of some objective event that is potentially stressful. This event then leads to a subjective cognitive appraisal of the extent of the possible threat. If the experience *is* viewed as threatening, it will tend to trigger a multidimensional response that usually includes emotional, physiological, and behavioral components. A response at all three of these levels is typical but *not* inevitable. In cases of mild stress, the response at a particular level may be negligible. The emotional and physiological components of the stress response are frequently automatic, whereas we usually have more control over our behavioral response. The final phase of the model allows for the *possibility* that this sequence of events may have some lasting impact on the individual. Such effects, which are called **adaptational outcomes,** may or may not occur. They may be judged as positive/beneficial (such as learning a new skill) or negative/harmful (such as becoming ill). The model also allows for the fact that there are "moderating variables" that mediate the link between stress and adaptational outcomes by affecting our response to stressful events in phases 2 and 3 of the stress process.

ADAPTATIONAL OUTCOMES. *Used to refer to the effects of stress, or the consequences of efforts at coping and adaptation. These outcomes may be either favorable or unfavorable.*

If the model sounds complicated and the diagram looks too intricate, don't worry about it at this point. I will be talking about all these matters in detail in the remainder of this chapter. Once you have finished the chapter, I am confident that the diagram will allow you to fit the various topics together into a coherent whole—the pieces of the puzzle will fall into place. In the meantime, the diagram can provide you with a broad overview of the stress process.

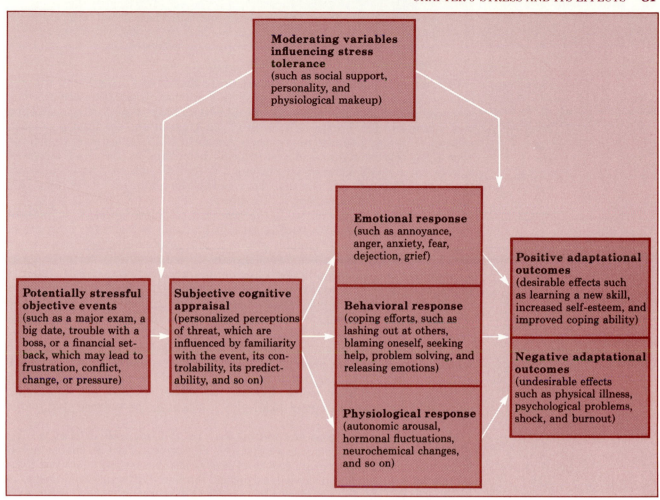

FIGURE 3.1 A model of the stress process.

Major Sources of Psychological Stress

There are an enormous variety of events that may be stressful for one person or another. To achieve a better understanding of stress, psychologists have tried to classify and organize the main sources of psychological stress in our lives. None of their organizational schemes has turned out to be altogether satisfactory because it has proved virtually impossible to classify stressful events into nonintersecting categories. Although this problem presents conceptual headaches for researchers, it need not prevent us from describing the main types of stressful situations you are likely to encounter. The classification system used here builds on a scheme developed by Coleman (1969).

Although they are not completely independent, it appears that the four fundamental sources of psychological stress are frustration, conflict, change, and pressure. As you read about each of these, you will surely recognize four very familiar adversaries.

FRUSTRATION

"It has been very frustrating to watch the rapid deterioration of my parents' relationship. Over the last year or two they have argued constantly and have refused to seek any professional help. I have tried to talk to them, but they kind of shut me and my brother out of their problem. I feel very helpless and sometimes even very angry, not at them, but at the whole situation."

FRUSTRATION. *The blocking of some motivated behavior; a situation resulting from unsuccessful pursuit of some goal.*

Psychologists use the term **frustration** to denote any situation in which a person cannot attain some desired goal. In a nutshell, frustration occurs when you want something and you can't have it. We all have to deal with frustration virtually every day. Fortunately, most of our frustrations are brief and insignificant. You may be quite angry when you go to a TV repair shop to pick up your ailing television and find that it hasn't been fixed as promised. However, a week later you'll have your precious TV, and all will be forgotten. Some frustrations, though, such as that described in the quotation above, may be a major source of chronic stress.

Failure and *losses* are probably the two most common sources of significant frustration in our lives. We tend to set high goals for ourselves in most of our endeavors. But for every person who gets into graduate school, there are a couple who do not. For every newly appointed vice-president, there are probably a dozen frustrated middle-level executives who see themselves as failures. Losses may be especially frustrating because we are deprived of something we are accustomed to having. The loss of one's spouse through death and the loss of one's physical capabilities through injury are examples of very frustrating losses that usually produce very severe stress.

In general, then, any time an obstacle prevents us from doing something or attaining some goal, we experience frustration. For example, an everyday obstacle in urban America is the traffic jam. In spite of the routine nature of this obstacle, one study (Novaco et al., 1979) found that subjects who had a difficult commute to work tended to display a relatively poor mood and higher blood pressure.

It should be noted that frustration may be self-imposed in that we frequently erect barriers to success ourselves. For instance, if you choose not to study adequately for an exam and then experience frustration when you flunk it, you have created your own frustration. Similarly, if your absenteeism at work prevents you from getting a promotion that you wanted badly, you have created the obstacle that blocks your path. Such self-defeating patterns of behavior are surprisingly common. For instance, chronic procrastination is a common source of self-imposed frustration.

CONFLICT

"Should I or shouldn't I? I became engaged at Christmas. My fiancé surprised me with a ring. I knew if I refused the ring he would be terribly hurt and our relationship would suffer. However, I don't really know whether or not I want to marry him. On the other hand, I don't want to lose him either."

CONFLICT. *The coexistence of incompatible motives, behavioral impulses, beliefs, or values.*

Like frustration, conflict is an unavoidable feature of everyday life. That perplexing question "Should I or shouldn't I?" comes up innumerable times in our lives. **Conflict** occurs whenever you have to decide between two or more incompatible motivational tendencies or struggle with incompatibility in beliefs or values. When behavioral impulses are competing, conflict can be differentiated into three basic types, which were researched thoroughly by Neal Miller (1959). These are approach/approach, avoidance/avoidance, and approach/avoidance (see Figure 3.2).

APPROACH/APPROACH CONFLICT. *A conflict wherein a choice must be made between two attractive or desirable goals.*

In an **approach/approach conflict,** you have approach tendencies toward two attractive goals, but you are limited to choosing only one of them. For example, you have a free afternoon; should you play tennis or racquetball? Do you want to order pizza or spaghetti? Shall you go to a movie Friday night or to a concert?

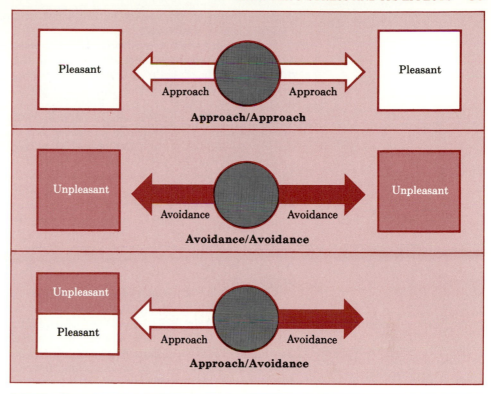

FIGURE 3.2   Types of conflict situations.

Among the three types of conflict, the approach/approach variety tends to be the least stressful. Whichever alternative you choose, you have a reasonably happy ending. Because of this pleasant reality, it is relatively easy to go ahead and make the choice. Nonetheless, approach/approach conflicts centering on important issues may sometimes be difficult to resolve. If you are torn between two appealing college majors or two attractive boyfriends, you may have a very tough time reaching a decision.

In an **avoidance/avoidance conflict,** you are caught between two repelling alternatives. You want to avoid both outcomes, but you must choose one. For example, you have very painful backaches; should you submit to surgery that you dread or should you continue to tolerate the pain? Do you want to study a boring textbook for an exam or do you want to risk failing the test? Should you continue to collect unemployment checks or should you take that degrading job in the car wash?

As you can readily see, this type of conflict is very unpleasant and therefore very stressful. Typically, people keep delaying the decision as long as possible, hoping that they will be able to escape the conflict situation. For example, you might delay the surgery to alleviate your backaches because you are hopeful that they will disappear on their own.

In an **approach/avoidance conflict,** you have both approach and avoidance tendencies toward a *single* goal that has both good and bad aspects. For example, you are offered a promotion and cannot decide whether to accept it; on the good side of the ledger, it will mean a large increase in pay; on the bad side, it will require a lot of travel, which you hate.

Many important decisions in life involve approach/avoidance conflicts. They are quite common, quite difficult to resolve, and potentially very stressful. Any time you have to take a risk in order to pursue some desirable outcome, you are likely to find yourself in an approach/avoidance conflict. Should you risk rejection in asking out that attractive woman in class? Should you risk your mar-

AVOIDANCE/AVOIDANCE CONFLICT. *A conflict wherein a choice must be made between two unattractive or undesirable goals.*

APPROACH/AVOIDANCE CONFLICT. *A conflict wherein a person is both attracted and repelled by a single goal.*

riage in order to pursue an extramarital affair? Should you risk failure by tackling a new challenge?

The typical behavior in approach/avoidance conflicts is *vacillation*. We tend to go back and forth; we decide to go ahead, then we decide not to, and then we decide to go ahead again. Miller's (1959) research suggested that in such situations avoidance tendencies tend to increase more rapidly than approach tendencies as one nears the goal. From this evidence, Miller concluded that, in trying to resolve an approach/avoidance conflict in which fear is preventing one from pursuing a desirable course of action, one should focus more on *reducing avoidance motivation* than on *increasing approach motivation*. For example, if you are vacillating over whether to ask someone out on a date, Miller would assert that you should work at downplaying the negative aspects of possible rejection rather than elevating your desire for the date by dwelling on how wonderful it would be. Later research has revealed that avoidance tendencies do not *always* increase more rapidly than approach tendencies (Epstein, 1978). In light of this new information, the best advice for resolving an approach/avoidance conflict would probably be to work on both features of it—in other words, try to lower avoidance motivation *and* raise approach motivation.

COGNITIVE DISSONANCE. *An unpleasant state of psychological tension that arises when thoughts are contradictory or inconsistent; a particular type of conflict.*

A fourth kind of conflict, sometimes called "conceptual conflict," exists when there is incompatibility between beliefs or values, as opposed to behavioral impulses (Epstein, 1982). This kind of conflict is more widely known as **cognitive dissonance,** a term coined by Leon Festinger (1957). According to Festinger, cognitive dissonance is an unpleasant state of psychological tension that occurs when two or more ideas are viewed as contradictory or inconsistent. For example, the belief "People should save money so that they always have a nest egg" would be inconsistent with the perception "I spend all my money on frivolous things" and would create cognitive dissonance. In a similar fashion, a belief such as "I am in love with Adam" would clash with a perception such as "Adam is lazy and undependable." Research on cognitive dissonance indicates that we deal with it by trying to alter one or both of the cognitions (for instance, you might shift your view, deciding that nest eggs are made worthless by inflation). While struggling with the dissonance, however, we tend to experience emotional arousal (Kiesler & Pallack, 1976). This link between dissonance and arousal suggests that dissonance is an important form of stress.

CHANGE

"The most stressful event I've experienced in the last year was going away to school, 2000 miles from my home. It wasn't that I didn't like it, but I was faced with many new challenges. It was difficult being away from home and not seeing a single familiar face. The classes were tough and I had to adapt to living in a tiny dormitory room. It got pretty tense and nerve-racking."

There is evidence that change, in and of itself, whether it is welcomed or not, may be stressful. Thomas Holmes and his colleagues (Holmes, 1979; Holmes & Rahe, 1967; Rahe, 1979) set out to explore the relation between stressful life events and the development of illness. Theorizing that stress might make people more susceptible to physical illness, they interviewed thousands of tuberculosis patients to find out what kinds of events preceded the onset of their disease. Surprisingly, the events that the TB patients cited frequently were *not* uniformly negative. There were plenty of the expected aversive events, such as death of one's spouse, personal injury, and loss of one's job, but there were also many neutral and seemingly positive events, such as marriage, gaining a new family member, and outstanding personal achievements.

Why would positive events such as getting married or taking a vacation produce stress? According to Holmes, it is because they produce change. His

TABLE 3.1 **Social Readjustment Rating Scale**

Life event	Mean value
Death of spouse	100
Divorce	73
Marital separation	65
Jail term	63
Death of close family member	63
Personal injury or illness	53
Marriage	50
Fired at work	47
Marital reconciliation	45
Retirement	45
Change in health of family member	44
Pregnancy	40
Sex difficulties	39
Gain of a new family member	39
Business readjustment	39
Change in financial state	38
Death of a close friend	37
Change to a different line of work	36
Change in number of arguments with spouse	35
Mortgage or loan for major purchase (home, etc.)	31
Foreclosure of mortgage or loan	30
Change in responsibilities at work	29
Son or daughter leaving home	29
Trouble with in-laws	29
Outstanding personal achievement	28
Wife begins or stops work	26
Begin or end school	26
Change in living conditions	25
Revision of personal habits	24
Trouble with boss	23
Change in work hours or conditions	20
Change in residence	20
Change in school	20
Change in recreation	19
Change in church activities	19
Change in social activities	18
Mortgage or loan for lesser purchase (car, TV, etc.)	17
Change in sleeping habits	16
Change in number of family get-togethers	15
Change in eating habits	15
Vacation	13
Christmas	12
Minor violations of the law	11

thesis is that any disruption of our daily routine causes stress. Thus, Holmes theorizes that changes in personal relationships, changes at work, changes in finances, and so forth can be stressful even when they are apparently changes for the better. This notion may initially seem surprising, but it is easy to see how welcome changes such as marriage or a promotion can subject a person to a variety of new demands.

On the basis of this analysis, Holmes and Rahe developed the Social Readjustment Rating Scale (SRRS) to measure the amount of change-related stress that people experience. The scale assigns to 43 common life events numerical values that are supposed to reflect the magnitude of the readjustment required by the change (see Table 3.1). These values were arrived at by asking subjects to rate the readjustment required by each event. Subjects were told to base their ratings on the assumption that marriage was worth 50 points on a 100-point scale. In taking the scale, respondents are asked to indicate how often they experienced any of these 43 events in a certain time period (usually one year). The person then adds up the numbers associated with each event checked. This sum is an index of how much change-related stress the person has recently experienced.

Holmes and Rahe and a great number of additional researchers all over the world have administered the SRRS to a variety of populations. In fact, Holmes (1979) has reported that over 1000 studies have been conducted with the SRRS. Overall, these studies have found SRRS scores to be related to an alarming array of negative adaptational outcomes (Barrett, Rose, & Klerman, 1979; Derogatis, 1982). They find that people with higher SRRS scores tend to be more vulnerable to many kinds of physical illness (see Chapter 4 for a more detailed discussion) and many types of psychological problems as well. This productive line of research and the attendant publicity have led to the widespread conclusion among both professionals and the public that change is inherently stressful.

More recently, however, experts have criticized this research, citing methodological shortcomings (Schroeder & Costa, 1984) and problems in interpreting the findings (Perkins, 1982). At this point, it is a key interpretive issue that concerns us. Many critics now assert that the SRRS does not assess *change* exclusively. The main problem is that the list of life changes is dominated by events that are clearly negative or undesirable (death of a spouse, jail term, fired at work, and so on) and probably generate great frustration. Although there are some positive events on the scale, it could be that these negative events create the bulk of the stress and are largely responsible for the negative adaptational outcomes experienced frequently by the subjects.

To sort out this confusion, more recent studies have taken into account how desirable/undesirable and controllable/uncontrollable the events are. When these factors are considered, the evidence suggests that change is *not* the crucial dimension tapped by the SRRS (Perkins, 1982; Zeiss, 1980). Instead, this research suggests that *the SRRS assesses a wide range of different kinds of stressful experience.*

So should we discard the notion that change is stressful? Not just yet. Although it is now clear that the SRRS and similar scales measure stress in a *general* sense, that does not mean that we can immediately write off change as a generally benign, nonstressful category of experience. There is considerable logical merit in the analysis that suggests that change creates significant adjustive demands. Moreover, there are entirely different lines of research, such as that relating geographic mobility to impaired mental and physical health (Brett, 1980), that bolster the theory that change may be an important form of stress. In conclusion, I would assert that while the SRRS measures more than mere change, the overall research picture *does* suggest that change tends to produce stress much of the time.

PRESSURE

> "I'm having problems with my boyfriend and parents. They both expect me to behave the way *they* want me to. My boyfriend is very jealous and tries to regulate who I go out with. My parents seem disapproving when I go out all the time. But I can't stand staying home with them. I don't know what to do. I sometimes feel very guilty."

At one time or another most of us have probably remarked that we were "under pressure." What does this mean? **Pressure** involves expectations and demands that we behave in a certain manner. Generally, there are two kinds of pressure: the pressure to *perform* and the pressure to *conform*.

Many of us are subjected to pressure that involves expectations for a high level of performance in some endeavor. For example, salespeople are under pressure to move merchandise, athletes to score touchdowns or hit home runs, professors to publish, and radio announcers to speak flawlessly. Although we usually think of *others* putting pressure on us, the pressure to perform is often self-imposed. Thus, you may put pressure on yourself to get better grades in school or work harder at your job.

PRESSURE. *Expectations and demands that one behave in a certain way; often a self-imposed form of stress.*

In addition to this pressure to perform, there is also a great deal of pressure to conform to others' expectations. Businessmen are expected to wear suits and ties, suburban homeowners are expected to keep their lawns well manicured, college students are expected to wear blue jeans, and adults are expected to get themselves married by the time they are 30. This pressure to conform often overlaps with or generates conflict. As is described in the quotation above, others' expectations often do not coincide with our own. We want to be ourselves; yet we want to be liked. Thus, we find ourselves in conflict about how to behave.

Although widely discussed by the general public, the concept of pressure has largely been ignored by researchers. When I wrote the first edition of this textbook, I was rather surprised to find that there were virtually no studies on pressure, except for a handful on *time* pressure. Noting a sizable gap in our knowledge of stress, I set out to develop a scale to measure pressure as a form of life stress in order to facilitate study of the phenomenon. Pilot studies yielded a 48-item scale (the Pressure Inventory) that assesses self-imposed pressure and pressure from others in five areas of life—family relationships, work relationships, school relationships, neighbor/peer relationships, and intimate relationships.

Although this research program is still in its infancy, the results thus far have been quite intriguing. In the first two studies (Weiten, Armstrong, & Dixon, 1984; Weiten & Dixon, 1984) we have used the Pressure Inventory (PI) to ascertain whether pressure is related to adaptational outcomes. In these studies, we have found a strong relationship between pressure and a variety of psychological symptoms and problems. In fact, pressure as measured by the PI turned out to be more strongly related to adaptational outcomes than widely used measures of change-related stress such as the SRRS. These findings suggest that pressure may be an important form of stress that merits more research attention.

Factors Influencing the Perception of Stress

You may recall that stress was defined as any circumstances that threaten or are *perceived* to threaten our well-being and thereby tax our adaptive capacities. The experience of feeling threatened depends on what events we notice and how we choose to appraise or interpret them. In this section I will discuss this perceptual process. I will describe both subjective and objective factors that influence our perception of threat.

PERSONALITY

REPRESSOR. *A personality type whose definitive characteristic is a tendency to be defensive and avoid facing up to threat.*

SENSITIZER. *A personality type whose definitive characteristic is a tendency to be overly sensitive to possible threat.*

I emphasized in Chapter 2 that one's personality inevitably influences one's patterns of adjustment. In regard to the perception of stress, *a key personality trait appears to be defensiveness, or the repression/sensitization dimension.* In dealing with stress, Goldstein (1959) found, some of us tend to be **repressors.** Such people try to deny the existence of threat and are oblivious to stress until it becomes overwhelming. At the opposite extreme, Goldstein found that some of us are **sensitizers.** These people tend to be more sensitive to threat and are willing to face up to it. Research by Mehrabian (1976) indicates that sensitizers become emotionally aroused by stress more quickly and more often than repressors. Thus, because of our personalities, some of us are more prone to feel threatened than others. Although it is a matter of some debate, most theorists feel that it is best to fall between the two extremes on this personality dimension (Krohne, 1978). Being an excessive sensitizer is undesirable because you may often feel threatened unnecessarily. Conversely, being a strong repressor is undesirable because you may fail to recognize significant stress until it is too late to deal with it easily or effectively.

COPING RESOURCES

A number of other personal factors govern individual differences in the perception of stress. A major factor is our belief about the extent of our resources for dealing with the stress (Walk, 1956). If the challenge lies in the academic area, and you have great confidence in your intellectual talents, you may not feel very threatened by an event that many other people would see as extremely stressful, such as an oral exam by the department chairperson in your major. However, if the challenge lies in the interpersonal realm, and you have little confidence in your social skills, you may feel very threatened by an event that many other people would see as relatively innocuous, such as joining a fraternity or sorority.

FAMILIARITY WITH THE STRESS

An important consideration in stress appraisal is your familiarity with the stressful situation. Although there are some important exceptions to this generalization, it appears that the more unfamiliar you are with a potentially stressful event, the more likely it is that you will find it threatening (McGrath, 1977). Thus, a person's first major job interview or surgery is usually more threatening than subsequent similar events. Familiarity and experience with a challenge can make yesterday's crisis today's routine.

IMMINENCE AND DURATION OF THE THREAT

The *imminence* of an anticipated threat clearly affects the amount of stress you experience (Lazarus, 1976). When a threat lies in the distant future, the stress may be seen as minimal. However, as a challenge looms near, the stress will generally become more severe. As you approach the day on which you have to submit to serious surgery or go away to college or speak at a convention or tell your spouse you want a divorce, you generally will find the stress increasing.

The impact of the *duration* of a problem is more complex. As a stressful problem continues for a period of time, you may become more familiar with it and view it as progressively *less* stressful. However, it appears that our resources for battling stress are limited (Selye, 1976). Thus, a long-running problem may "wear you down" and become progressively *more* stressful.

PERCEIVED CONTROL

Another factor that influences your appraisal of stress is your perception of how much *control* you can exert over the event in question. For example, if you are facing surgery and a lengthy rehabilitation period, your feelings might range from a sense of powerlessness to a firm belief that you will be able to speed up the recovery process if you act in certain ways. Stern, McCants, and Pettine (1982) found that when events are viewed as controllable, they tend to be seen as less stressful. *This finding that control reduces stress is fairly typical for this line of research, although Folkman (1984) points out it is not universal.* Some studies have found the perception of greater control to be associated with increased, rather than decreased, stressfulness. Folkman explains this exception to the general rule by pointing out that with control comes greater responsibility (to take charge and cope with the problem), which may be quite stressful to some people in some instances. Nonetheless, the general trend is for people to view more controllable events as less stressful.

PREDICTABILITY OF THE STRESS

There are a variety of logical reasons for expecting unpredictable stress to be more threatening than stress that can be anticipated. Unpredictable stress that "comes out of nowhere" is likely to be more traumatic, whereas predictable stress allows for preparation. Indeed, a substantial number of animal studies find that unpredictable shock creates more stress than predictable shock (Weinberg & Levine, 1980).

When the predictability of stress is studied with human subjects, the results tend to be similar but a bit more complicated (Lazarus & Folkman, 1984). In general, it appears that we prefer predictability over uncertainty. For instance, most students find it less stressful when exams are scheduled in advance than when they might occur at any time. Predictability is probably preferable when-

---

3.1   DELAYED STRESS RESPONSE SYNDROMES AMONG VIETNAM VETERANS

Although the Vietnam war came to an end over a decade ago, that controversial conflict continues to haunt some veterans who suffer from what has been labeled the "delayed stress response syndrome." We do not know just how many veterans are plagued by this affliction, but we do know that it is not rare. One report (Veterans Administration, 1981) estimated that as many as one-third of combat-experienced veterans might be victims.

Of particular interest is the *delayed* aspect of the Vietnam syndrome. Shatan (1978) estimates that the symptoms typically begin to surface anywhere from 9 to 60 months after a veteran's discharge. There were, of course, immediate stress reactions among soldiers as well—but these were expected. The delayed reactions were something of a surprise. Actually, however, they are quite understandable in retrospect. Many of the negative effects of stress discussed in this chapter often require an "incubation period" before they become apparent. Thus, the Vietnam syndrome is not unique in this regard.

Stress in Vietnam

In *any* war, stress is abundant and extremely intense. However, in the Vietnam war it was especially extraordinary. Blank (1982) has described this stress in some detail. I will summarize this description using our classification scheme for the common sources of stress: frustration, conflict, change, and pressure.

Frustration was inevitable in that our soldiers had to endure miserable living conditions that frequently fell far below the standards they were used to for food, water, and shelter. Because of the terroristic tactics employed in the war, there was no safe haven where soldiers could really relax their guard. This, of course, was extremely frustrating, as was the fact that American forces were restricted from using some offensive combat actions.

Conflict between behavioral impulses must have been commonplace in the risky environment of Vietnam. Soldiers probably debated whether to "cut corners" in their assignments to minimize their personal risk with great regularity. Moreover, because of the widespread opposition to the war in the United States, cognitive dissonance about the purpose and value of the war was frequent.

Change was also exorbitant for American soldiers in Vietnam. Young adults were torn from their usually comfortable and familiar lives at home and transported into the entirely foreign arena of international combat. Although such a transition is experienced in any war, in this one the combatants were transported to an exceptionally poor Third World country where the lifestyle, amenities, and customs were dramatically different from American norms.

Pressure to perform duties effectively was pervasive. People's lives (including one's own) depended on competent performance of one's responsibilities. That is about as intense as pressure gets.

Symptoms of the Delayed Stress Response Syndrome

In light of the incredible stress that was pervasive in the Vietnam conflict, it is not surprising that many veterans are experiencing adjustment problems. The range of problems is great and includes all the negative effects of stress discussed in this chapter. Among the problems observed most frequently are the following (Blank, 1982; Foy et al., 1984; Horowitz & Solomon, 1978; Shatan, 1978).

1. Diversified symptoms of emotional problems falling short of bona fide mental illness are common. Victims tend to be troubled by great guilt, dejection, paranoia, nightmares, and intrusive thoughts.
2. Full-fledged psychological disorders are also seen with regularity. Particularly prevalent are depression, anxiety disorders, paranoid disorders, and drug abuse disorders.
3. Many afflicted veterans are characterized by a sense of alienation—that is, they feel as if they don't "fit" into American society. These veterans tend to be exceedingly cynical, disgusted with life, and prone to underachievement relative to their abilities. They may adopt a "wandering" lifestyle and may turn to criminal activities.
4. Difficulties in interpersonal relationships also appear to be fairly common. Relations with family and friends become strained. Problems in expressing love and trust for others are typical.

ever we can engage in anticipatory coping to *prepare* for the stress. However, if there is little we can do to cope with the stress, it may not make much difference whether it is predictable or unpredictable.

Emotional Response to Stress

EMOTION. *A state in which feelings difficult to control are experienced. These feelings may be intense, are usually accompanied by internal bodily changes, and often affect overt behavior.*

Emotion has proved to be an elusive concept for psychologists. There is little consensus about how to define emotion, and there is a bewildering array of conflicting theories to explain emotion. Nonetheless, we all have extensive personal experience with emotion, and we all have a fairly good idea of what it means to be anxious, elated, gloomy, jealous, disgusted, excited, guilty, or nervous. Rather than pursue the technical debate about emotion, I will rely on your familiarity with the concept at a common-sense level and use a relatively simple definition: I will define emotion as *a powerful, largely uncontrollable feeling that is accompanied by physiological changes.* As you already know, these powerful feelings can have a tremendous impact on our behavior.

There is a great deal of evidence that when we are under stress, we tend to react emotionally. In fact, one influential theorist (Mason, 1975) has suggested that emotion is the one thing that all the diverse reactions to stress have in common. Many different emotions may be elicited by stressful events, although some are certainly more likely than others. Generally, stress tends to generate unpleasant rather than pleasant emotions.

EMOTIONS COMMONLY ELICITED BY STRESS

There are no simple one-to-one connections between certain kinds of stress and particular emotions. Nonetheless, it is possible to make some tentative statements about the link between stress and emotion. This section describes three dimensions of emotion that are often involved in our reactions to stress. This analysis borrows from discussion of the dynamics of stress by Woolfolk and Richardson (1978) and Davitz's (1969) effort to sort out the basic dimensions of emotion. Although this list is far from exhaustive, it should give you some insight about the kinds of emotion that are most commonly evoked by stress.

Annoyance, anger, and rage. Certain kinds of stress tend to produce feelings of anger, which may vary in intensity from mild annoyance to uncontrollable rage. In particular, stressful situations involving frustration seem most likely to generate anger. As you have surely noticed, many people are unable to tolerate even minor frustrations and fly into a rage over something as trivial as being delayed in a traffic jam. The type of stress discussed earlier as the pressure to conform also seems likely to provoke anger and resentment.

Apprehension, anxiety, and fear. This dimension of emotion is probably elicited by stress more often than any other. Anxiety is a key construct in psychology; in fact, the *Psychiatric Dictionary* (Hinsie & Campbell, 1970) contains 45 entries referring to various kinds of anxiety! For our purposes, it is sufficient to distinguish between **state anxiety,** which is a temporary emotional state, involving feelings of worry and dread, that we all experience in certain situations, and **trait anxiety,** which involves a consistent tendency to be anxious much of the time.

STATE ANXIETY. *The temporary experience of an unpleasant emotional state characterized by worry and tension; often accompanied by somatic symptoms.*

TRAIT ANXIETY. *A personality trait wherein the person has a general, enduring tendency to experience anxiety with great frequency in a variety of situations.*

State anxiety is a common and normal reaction to *all* the kinds of stress discussed earlier. Whereas Freud emphasized the link between conflict and anxiety, it is clear that pressure and the threat of impending frustration may also make one anxious. Furthermore, evidence that feelings of uncertainty can create anxiety (Epstein & Roupenian, 1970) suggests that change is also likely to lead to this emotion.

© 1968 UNITED FEATURE SYNDICATE, INC.

As Freud originally pointed out, anxiety and fear play a central role in adjustment processes. Because the experience of anxiety is unpleasant, we tend to resort to defensive behaviors to ward off these unwanted feelings. As I shall discuss later, this defensive approach to coping with stress often tends to prolong and aggravate the problem.

Dejection, sorrow, and grief. These are the emotions associated with depression. We all experience varying levels of depression at one time or another. The events that produce these feelings usually involve some form of frustration. Losses of various kinds, such as being jilted by a boyfriend or girlfriend, are particularly likely to cause feelings of dejection.

EFFECTS OF EMOTIONAL AROUSAL

The experience of emotion is usually accompanied by physiological arousal. Among the more obvious internal physical events associated with emotion are increases in heart rate, blood pressure, perspiration, and the rapidity of breathing. This emotional arousal is neither inherently good nor inherently bad. Its adaptive value depends on the situation. However, you should be aware that *a high level of emotional arousal may be disruptive and hamper your efforts to cope with a stressful situation.*

There is extensive evidence (for example, Berkun et al., 1962) that emotional arousal tends to temporarily impair one's mental efficiency. Specifically, high arousal has been shown to produce a narrowing of attention, poorer judgment, and a reduction in the effectiveness of one's memory.

An example of this tendency is the problem of "test anxiety." Students vary greatly in how anxious they get over classroom exams. Studies correlating students' test-related anxiety with their scores on the test have generally shown that the more nervous students tend to do more poorly on the exam (Gaudry & Spielberger, 1971). It appears that high anxiety has this negative impact by virtue of disrupting one's attention to the test (Sarason, 1984). For example, many anxious students seem to waste too much time worrying about how they are doing and wondering whether other students are having any problems with the test.

Although it is clear that emotional arousal *may* be disruptive, this is not *necessarily* true. The effects of emotional arousal depend on the difficulty and complexity of the task at hand. Many years ago, research led to the formulation of the Yerkes-Dodson principle (Yerkes & Dodson, 1908), which theorizes that as the task becomes more complex, the optimal level of arousal becomes lower. As you can see in Figure 3.3, the relation between arousal and performance is curvilinear, and performance peaks at a lower level of arousal on the more difficult task. Thus, if the task is simple—let us say, driving cross-country to comfort a friend—high arousal may have beneficial effects. If the task at hand is complex (for example, making a big decision in which you have to weigh many factors), high arousal may have harmful effects.

For coping with stress, it seems likely that emotional arousal will tend to have disruptive effects in the most critical situations. If there is a simple solu-

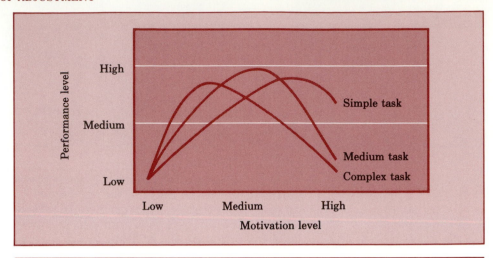

FIGURE 3.3 The Yerkes-Dodson principle. High levels of motivation yield the highest performance with easy tasks, but with difficult tasks low levels of motivation yield the highest levels of performance.

tion for a stressful situation, the situation is not likely to be all that stressful. Greater stress is likely in situations in which the solution is *not* obvious, and in these more difficult situations, emotional arousal is more likely to fog our thinking. Consequently, as you will see later, effective coping efforts often involve learning either to inhibit emotional arousal or to release it in some harmless way.

Physiological Response to Stress

As discussed in the previous section, stress generally elicits an emotional response accompanied by dramatic physiological changes. I will now describe some of the details of these physiological changes.

THE GENERAL ADAPTATION SYNDROME

GENERAL ADAPTATION SYNDROME. *As described by Selye, the nonspecific response of the body to stress. It consists of three stages: alarm, resistance, and exhaustion.*

A Canadian scientist named Hans Selye (1936, 1956, 1974) gets much of the credit for working out the details of how our bodies react to stress. In addition to his pioneering physiological research, Selye formulated the most widely used theoretical model of stress reactions, called the **general adaptation syndrome** (G.A.S.). I will use his three-phase theoretical model to summarize the findings of a great many researchers who have contributed to our understanding of how we respond to stress at the physiological level.

THE ALARM REACTION

ENDOCRINE SYSTEM. *Consists of a number of ductless glands located in various parts of the body, which synthesize chemicals called hormones and release them into the bloodstream.*

In the first stage of the general adaptation syndrome, your body musters its resources to combat the stress, leading to a multitude of physiological reactions. Some of these reactions are subtle, while others may be quite obvious. For example, even in cases of moderate stress, you may notice that your heart has started beating faster, you have begun to breathe harder, and you are perspiring more than usual.

HORMONES. *Chemical substances, produced by endocrine glands, that regulate a variety of physiological processes.*

How does all this happen? Well, it appears that there are two pathways along which the brain sends signals to the **endocrine system.** The endocrine system consists of certain glands located at various sites in the body (see Figure 3.4) that produce and secrete chemicals called **hormones.** These hormones are released into the bloodstream, so that they travel throughout the

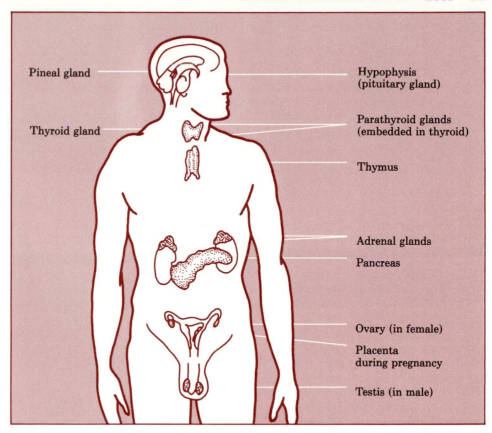

FIGURE 3.4   The glands of the endocrine system are located in various parts of the body.

AUTONOMIC NERVOUS SYSTEM (ANS). *The portion of the peripheral nervous system that controls the involuntary action of the glands, smooth muscles, heart, and blood vessels. It is divided into the* parasympathetic division, *which conserves bodily resources (by slowing heart rate, facilitating digestion, and so on), and the* sympathetic division, *which mobilizes the body for emergencies (by increasing heart rate, dilating blood vessels, inhibiting digestion, and so on).*

CATECHOLAMINES. *A group of similar chemicals that function as both neurotransmitters and hormones in the human body. The principal catecholamines released by the endocrine system are epinephrine (adrenaline) and norepinephrine (noradrenaline).*

body and regulate a great variety of physiological functions. The hypothalamus is the part of the brain that appears to initiate action along the two pathways to the endocrine system.

The first pathway is mediated by the **autonomic nervous system (ANS),** which controls involuntary visceral functions in the body (see Figure 3.5). The hypothalamus activates the *sympathetic division* of the ANS. A key part of this activation involves stimulating the central part of the adrenal glands (the adrenal medulla) to release large amounts of **catecholamines** into the bloodstream. These hormones radiate throughout the body, producing many important changes in physiological functioning. The net result of catecholamine elevation is that the body is mobilized for action: heart rate and blood flow increase, respiration rate and oxygen consumption escalate, perspiration increases, digestive processes are inhibited, and so forth.

The second pathway, which may be activated at the same time, involves more direct communication between the brain and the endocrine system. The hypothalamus sends signals to the so-called master gland of the endocrine system, the pituitary gland. The pituitary secretes a hormone (ACTH) that serves as a chemical messenger, activating the outer part of the adrenal glands (the adrenal cortex), which release into the bloodstream another important set of hormones—the **corticosteroids.** These hormones serve relatively subtle purposes, functioning to enhance the body's use of its energy stores and to inhibit tissue inflammation in certain organs.

Thus, your alarm reaction involves a complicated series of physiological changes, largely mediated by two sets of hormones—catecholamines and

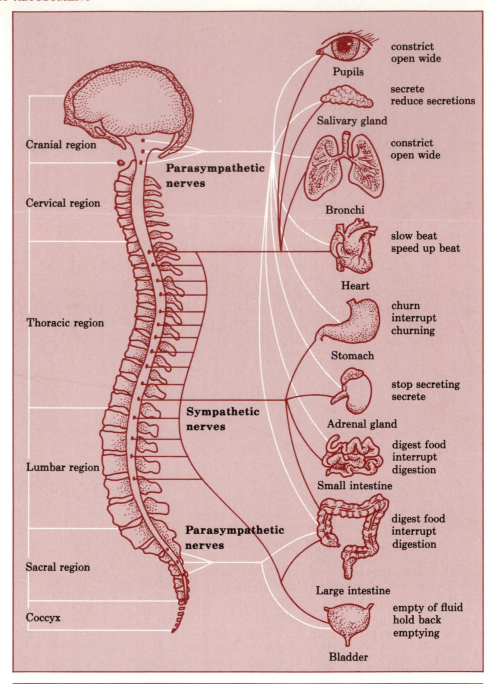

constrict
open wide
Pupils

secrete
reduce secretions
Salivary gland

constrict
open wide
Bronchi

slow beat
speed up beat
Heart

churn
interrupt
churning
Stomach

stop secreting
secrete
Adrenal gland

digest food
interrupt
digestion
Small intestine

digest food
interrupt
digestion
Large intestine

empty of fluid
hold back
emptying
Bladder

Cranial region

**Parasympathetic
nerves**

Cervical region

Thoracic region

**Sympathetic
nerves**

Lumbar region

**Parasympathetic
nerves**

Sacral region

Coccyx

FIGURE 3.5   The autonomic nervous system.

CORTICOSTEROIDS. *A
group of steroid hormones
produced by the adrenal
cortex.*

corticosteroids—that are designed to help you confront the challenges of stress
(see Figure 3.6).

STAGE OF RESISTANCE

If the stress continues over a sustained period, you may progress to this second
stage, in which the body attempts to *adapt* to the stress. Your autonomic and
endocrine systems continue to work overtime but not to the extent seen in the
first stage. Basically, your bodily reactions stabilize at a diminished level as
you become accustomed to the stress that is troubling you.

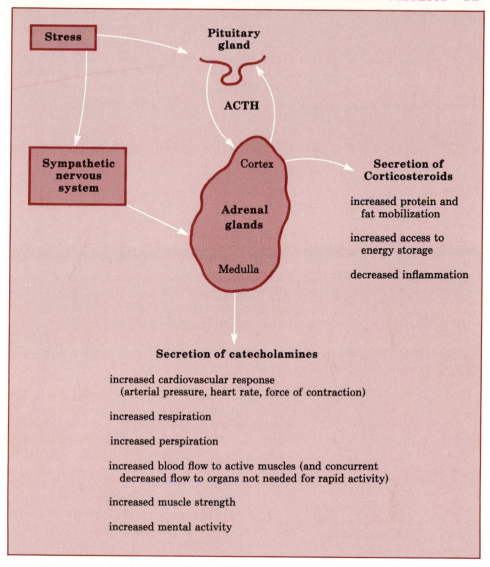

FIGURE 3.6 Activities of adrenal glands in response to stress.

STAGE OF EXHAUSTION

In most cases, the stress is conquered or escaped before you reach this ominous third stage. However, if the stress is long-lasting, there may be various kinds of unfortunate consequences. The principal problem is that some of the bodily chemicals summoned to combat the stress may be damaging to certain internal organs if they remain at high levels for too long. Selye describes how a prolonged struggle with stress may lead to "diseases of adaptation," involving damage to crucial organs such as the heart and the kidneys. Another potential problem arises because the body's resources for fighting stress are limited. The supply of certain important chemicals may be exhausted, and the *parasympathetic division* of the ANS may be forced to take over to conserve the remaining bodily resources. Furthermore, the parasympathetic shutdown of your stress response may be so traumatic that it produces a literal collapse from exhaustion.

The pioneering work of Selye and others focused on activity along the hypothalamic/autonomic/endocrine axes. Although some of Selye's (1975) theoretical assumptions have been questioned by various critics (Mason, 1975),

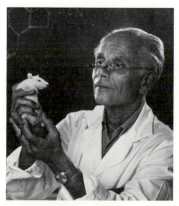

HANS SELYE

CARDIOVASCULAR.
Pertaining to the heart and blood vessels.

GASTROINTESTINAL.
Pertaining to the stomach and the intestine.

one cannot deny that this line of research shed considerable light on how stress can elicit physiological changes that can reverberate throughout the body, with potentially detrimental consequences. In particular, this work pinpointed some of the pathways that link stress to alterations in **cardiovascular** functioning (involving heart rate, blood flow, blood pressure, and so on) and **gastrointestinal** functioning (involving stomach secretions, intestinal movement of food, digestion, and so on). These pathways turn out to be very important in explaining some of the long-range effects of stress that I will soon be discussing.

OTHER ASPECTS OF OUR PHYSIOLOGICAL RESPONSE

Some new dimensions of the physiological response to stress have been discovered since Selye's formative work. In fact, it is now believed that *all* parts of the body and all organ systems have the potential to be activated by stressful experience (Zegans, 1982). Among the newer findings, two stand out as especially significant. First, we now know that stress can trigger neurochemical changes in the brain that can affect behavior in diverse ways (Anisman, 1978). Second, it is now clear that stress can disrupt the normal functioning of the immune system, which resists invasions by infectious organisms and other disease agents (Solomon & Amkraut, 1981). These exciting new findings show that our physiological reactions to stress may reach into every corner of our bodies in subtle ways that may be of the utmost importance.

Behavioral Response to Stress

Although we react to stress at several levels, it is clear that our *behavior* is the crucial dimension of our reaction. As you have seen, stress tends to elicit emotional responses accompanied by a variety of physiological changes, many of which may be less than desirable. These emotional and physiological responses to stress *tend* to be largely *automatic*. Shutting them off hinges on the behavioral responses we make to the stressful situation. Thus, the challenge that we face is to deal effectively with stress at the behavioral level, so as to short-circuit the potentially harmful emotional and physiological responses.

COPING. *Efforts to master, reduce, or tolerate the demands created by stress.*

We have a special name for the behavioral maneuvers that people make in response to stress. They are called *coping* responses. **Coping** refers to behavioral efforts to master, reduce, or tolerate the demands created by a stressful

---

3.2

RECOMMENDED READING
Life Stress
by Rosalind Forbes (Doubleday & Co., 1979)

This is a very *practical* book on the dynamics of stress. The author, who has developed stress management programs for various large corporations, draws nicely from her knowledge of research in the area, her actual experience, and her intuitive analysis in order to put together some down-to-earth advice about how to deal with stress. A sampling of subtitles will give you a clear picture of the book's purpose and content. Among other things, Forbes covers (1) things you can do to reduce the stress and strain of commuting, (2) how to tell whether you are a stress-prone personality, (3) ways to keep change within bounds, (4) steps to make your home more tranquil, and (5) how to make your move (relocation) less stressful.

But does watching television really relax our cares away? Not according to Dr. Clancy McKenzie, a therapist who claims that most television viewers experience a faster heartbeat, more perspiration, and a general jumpy feeling caused by increased adrenalin flow while watching their selected programs.

Watching television is actually a continual stress situation. The evening news is filled with stories of murder, violence, and other calamities. Prime-time shows portray the world deceptively in terms of sex and violence.

Daytime shows are equally guilty of broadcasting a stress-inducing unreality. Soap operas focus on infidelity, promiscuity, and perversion and, by so doing, continually hammer away at a spouse's confidence [pp. 21–22].

transaction (Folkman & Lazarus, 1980). The construct of coping includes no assumptions about whether the coping efforts will be "successful." Unfortunately, there are no coping strategies that can *ensure* success in dealing with stress. The concept of coping is also neutral with regard to whether the behavior should be judged to be healthy or ill advised. Coping efforts may range from decidedly healthy to grossly maladaptive. The coping responses made at the behavioral level are crucial in determining how stress affects us.

There are a great diversity of coping strategies that one might use in grappling with stress. Because of this diversity and the importance of the topic, I will defer a detailed review of coping processes until Chapter 5.

Effects of Stress

In this fourth phase of the stress process, we focus on the possible outcomes of our struggles with stress. These effects are often called "adaptational outcomes." They are relatively durable (though not necessarily permanent) consequences of the stress process. Some of these effects involve alterations in behavior (such as reduced mental efficiency), and you may have difficulty separating them from the *behavioral response* to stress. The distinction is a subtle one which resembles that between *actions* and *occurrences* (Kruglanski, 1975). Actions are voluntary and are determined by the actor's will, such as running in a race or cheating on an exam; occurrences are outcomes that are beyond the actor's control, such as finishing fourth in the race or getting caught cheating. Thus, the behavioral response of coping involves actions, while the behavioral effects of stress involve occurrences that are beyond one's control.

Most stressful experiences probably do not have any long-range impact. We struggle with innumerable minor stresses every day. Most of these probably come and go without leaving any enduring imprint on us. Sometimes, however, presumably when the stress is severe or when many stressful demands begin to pile up, we may begin to experience some "strain" that may have long-range consequences for us.

Because the research in this area has focused mainly on negative adaptational outcomes, you will find my coverage slanted in that direction. I do want to emphasize, though, that stress *can* have beneficial effects. It would be unfortunate and inaccurate to conclude that stress is a universally negative experience.

IMPAIRMENT OF COGNITIVE FUNCTIONING

A moderately common effect of stress is impairment of one's mental functioning. In discussing the emotional response to stress, I mentioned that a high level of arousal may disrupt thought processes. In some people, stress may lead to a narrowed focus of attention, reduced flexibility in thinking, poor concentration, and less effective memory storage. Such effects are far from inevitable (Mandler, 1979). When they do occur, however, they can produce a substantial impairment of one's problem-solving ability. As discussed earlier, this is why test-anxious students who find exams very threatening often "lose their cool" and are unable to perform effectively.

SHOCK AND DISORIENTATION

Severe stress can leave people dazed and confused (Horowitz, 1979). In these states, people tend to feel emotionally numb, and they respond in a flat, apathetic fashion to events around them. They often stare off into space and have difficulty maintaining a coherent train of thought. Their behavior frequently

Shock and disorientation are common effects of very severe stress.

has an automatic, rigid, stereotyped quality. Fortunately, this kind of disorientation is usually found only in extreme situations involving overwhelming stress. For instance, you will often see shock among people who have just been through a major disaster, such as a fire, a flood, or a tornado.

BURNOUT

BURNOUT. *A stress-related syndrome wherein one's behavior comes to be dominated by feelings of physical, mental, and emotional exhaustion.*

Burnout is a buzzword for the eighties. Although the term is probably overused, the syndrome has been described in a sensible fashion by Pines, Aronson, and Kafry (1981). They maintain that burnout constitutes a state of physical, emotional, and mental exhaustion. The physical exhaustion includes chronic fatigue, weakness, and low energy. The emotional exhaustion refers to feeling hopeless, helpless, trapped, and emotionally drained. The mental exhaustion is manifested in highly negative attitudes toward oneself, one's work, and life in general. Considerable debate exists about the exact causes of the burnout syndrome, but there is plenty of agreement that it is a consequence of chronic stress.

DISRUPTION OF SOCIAL RELATIONS

DELAYED STRESS RESPONSE SYNDROME. *Dysfunctional behavior attributed to exposure to significant stress, which emerges only after the stress has been alleviated. Although the concept is widely associated with the experiences of Vietnam veterans, it can occur in response to any severe stress.*

There is some evidence that stress can lead to a deterioration in one's normal social relations. Although this effect has a great deal of intuitive plausibility, we don't actually have much research data on it. In general, the effect of stress on interpersonal behavior has not attracted much attention. However, researchers working with Vietnam veterans suffering from the **delayed stress response syndrome** (also called "posttraumatic stress disorder") have observed disruptions in social functioning with some regularity (Blank, 1982; Shatan, 1978). These disruptions include feelings of alienation, difficulties in relating to spouses and friends, and impairments in the capacity to love and trust others (see Box 3.1).

PSYCHOLOGICAL PROBLEMS AND DISORDERS

On the basis of clinical impressions, psychologists have long believed that stress might be a key factor in the causation of many kinds of psychological problems and mental illness. In the last couple of decades, advances in the measurement of stress have allowed us to verify these suspicions repeatedly in empirical research (Barrett, Rose, & Klerman, 1979). In the domain of common psychological problems, it is clear that stress may contribute to poor academic performance, insomnia, sexual difficulties, drug abuse, excessive anxiety, nervousness, dejection, and depression. Above and beyond these "everyday" problems, we have evidence that stress frequently plays a role in the onset of full-fledged psychological disorders. We now believe that stress may contribute to the development of "neurotic" disorders, depressive disorders, personality disorders, schizophrenic disorders, and suicide attempts (see Chapter 13 for a description of these disorders). While stress is only one of a number of factors that may contribute to psychological problems and disorders, it is nonetheless sobering to realize that stress *can* have a dramatic impact on our psychological health.

PHYSICAL PROBLEMS AND ILLNESSES

The existence of a connection between stress and certain kinds of physical illnesses has long been recognized. Examples of illnesses that have long been viewed as stress-related are asthma, hypertension, migraine headaches, and ulcers. However, only a handful of insightful theorists anticipated the discovery in the 1970s that stress may play a role in the development of a wide range of diseases previously thought to be purely organic in origin. We now have evidence that *suggests* (there is still some debate) that stress may be related to the onset of tuberculosis, arthritis, diabetes, leukemia, and even cancer, not to mention minor problems such as colds, stomachaches, and backaches (Holmes & Masuda, 1974; Rahe & Arthur, 1978). Of course, stress is only one of several factors operating in a complex developmental process. Nonetheless, we once again find that stress can have a rather intimidating impact on the quality of our lives. We will explore this connection between stress and physical illness in much greater detail in the next chapter.

POSITIVE EFFECTS

The beneficial effects of stress are more difficult to pinpoint than the harmful effects because they tend to be more subtle. Although research data are sparse, I will describe three ways in which stress can exert positive effects.

First, we would probably experience a suffocating level of boredom if we lived a stress-free existence. Life would be very dull indeed if it were altogether devoid of challenge. There is evidence (Suedfeld, 1979) that an intermediate level of stimulation and challenge tends to be optimal for most people. Although most of us think of stress in terms of stimulus overload, it is clear that underload can be extremely unpleasant as well. Research on "restricted environments" in which challenge is decidedly absent indicates that this tends to be an aversive state. Thus, we seem to have a fundamental need to be challenged to some extent. In line with this analysis, research indicates that some people, called "sensation seekers," actively pursue stressful challenges (see Box 3.3). Such individuals may even be drawn to certain occupations that promise a steady diet of challenge. For instance, Kobasa (1982) discusses both folklore and data supporting the widespread belief that lawyers thrive on stress. In a sense, then, stress fulfills a basic need of the human organism.

Second, stress may frequently promote personal growth. Basically, *personal growth* refers to movement toward greater psychological health. Stress must sometimes force us to develop new skills, learn new insights, and acquire new strengths. In other words, the adaptation process initiated by stress may often lead to personal changes that are changes for the better. Confronting and conquering a stressful challenge may lead to improvement in specific coping abilities and to favorable alterations in one's self-concept. For example, a breakup with a boyfriend or a girlfriend frequently leads individuals to change aspects of their behavior that they find unsatisfactory. Moreover, even if we do not "conquer" the stresses, we may be able to learn from our mistakes.

Third, today's stress can "inoculate" us so that we are less affected by tomorrow's stress. If stressful experience is moderate in intensity and does not overwhelm us, it may increase our subsequent stress tolerance (Epstein, 1983; Janis, 1983). Thus, a fellow who has previously endured business setbacks may be much better prepared than most people to deal with the fact that the bank is about to foreclose on his home. In light of the negative effects that stress can have, improved stress tolerance is a desirable outcome.

Factors Influencing Stress Tolerance

In describing the entire four-phase stress process—the nature of stress, how we appraise threats to our well-being, how we respond to stress, and the long-range effects that stress may have—I have mentioned repeatedly that there are great individual differences among people in how they are affected by stressful events. I will now try to shed some light on these individual differences. This entails looking at "moderator variables"—that is, variables that moderate the causal link between stress and its potential effects. These are the variables that appear to influence how resistant people are to the stress they encounter.

STRESS TOLERANCE.
One's capacity to resist stress; the degree to which one can experience stress without showing ill effects.

The term **stress tolerance** is used to describe a person's ability to withstand the ravages of stress. Although a person's stress tolerance probably fluctuates somewhat with time, it appears to be a reasonably stable personal characteristic. You might expect that we would try to learn about stress tolerance

---

3.3   *SENSATION SEEKING: LIFE IN THE FAST LANE*

The highly personal, subjective quality of stress and the potentially important role of one's physical constitution are aptly illustrated by Marvin Zuckerman's (1974, 1978) work on "sensation seekers," who thrive on experiences that many people would consider very stressful. According to Zuckerman, some people have a strong need for a high level of stimulation. They satisfy this need by experimenting with drugs, numerous sexual partners, novel experiences (such as hypnosis), and risky adventures (such as skydiving), as well as less exotic things such as driving fast, traveling frequently, gambling, and partying. People who are high in sensation seeking are easily bored and continually need to be challenged. They enjoy change in their lives and often find the pressure to perform exhilarating.

Obviously, high sensation seekers actively *pursue* experiences that many people would find very stressful. However, now that you are aware of the great individual differences that exist in the perception of stress, it should come as no surprise that there is some evidence that sensation seekers see these experiences as *less threatening* than other people would. Hence, it is not clear whether sensation seekers are really search-

ing for stress. They may just have a higher threshold for the *perception* of stress. Or it may be a combination of both factors.

Zuckerman believes that there is a biological basis for this interesting behavioral disposition. In support of this assertion, he cites a study comparing fraternal with identical twins in regard to sensation seeking, which suggests that genetic inheritance influences this personality dimension. These findings support Eysenck's (1960) notion that constitutional factors influence one's stress tolerance.

In regard to adjustment processes, Zuckerman makes a couple of intriguing points. First, he suggests that persons very high and very low in sensation seeking may have difficulty understanding each other. If they are spouses or business partners, this gap in understanding can, obviously, create problems. Second, he expresses concern that high and low sensation seekers may be mismatched occupationally. It seems likely that a high sensation seeker would be particularly frustrated by routine, monotonous work, while a low sensation seeker might easily be overwhelmed by stress in a high-pressure job.

by studying people who appear to have outstanding or relatively strong resistance to stress. In reality, this approach has been used only a little. Until the recent advent of scales to measure stress, it was difficult to identify people with *high* tolerance. People with diagnosed psychological disorders provided a more readily identifiable pool of subjects who appeared to have relatively *low* stress tolerance. Hence, much of our evidence on individual differences in stress tolerance comes from studies that approach the issue by focusing on people who are assumed to have poor resistance to stress. I will draw from both these approaches as I outline the main determinants of stress tolerance.

SOCIAL SUPPORT

Recent studies (LaRocco, House, & French, 1980; Wilcox, 1981) suggest that social support can serve as a sort of protective buffer to minimize the wear and tear of stress. This research indicates that the amount and quality of socioemotional support available from significant others is a key moderating variable that accounts for some of the variation in how people are affected by stress.

Researchers are presently trying to figure out just *how* social support serves to ease the impact of stressful events. House (1981) has proposed that social support fulfills four important functions that can help to protect us from the deleterious effects of stress:

1. *Emotional support* involves expressions of affection, interest, and concern that tell recipients that they are appreciated. It also includes a willingness to listen to their problems. The expression of affection presumably bolsters recipients' self-esteem.
2. *Appraisal support* involves helping people to evaluate and make sense of their troubles and problems. It includes efforts to clarify the problem and provide the recipient with feedback about the significance of the stress.
3. *Informational support* involves the provision of advice about how to handle the problem. This includes suggesting possible solutions and discussing alternative coping strategies.
4. *Instrumental support* involves the provision of material aid and services. This may include a wide range of activities, such as providing recipients with a place to stay, lending money, going to a social service agency with them, or assuming some of their work or family responsibilities.

House's analysis of social support functions indicates that such support works in a variety of ways to increase a person's stress tolerance. It also indicates that love, friendship, and caring are valuable to us in subtle ways that may not be readily recognized.

PERSONALITY

Some clever research by Suzanne Kobasa (1979) has provided one of the few studies that focus on subjects who appear to have *high* resistance to stress. Kobasa used a slightly modified version of the Holmes and Rahe (1967) stress scale (SRRS) to evaluate the amount of stress experienced by a group of executives. As in previous studies, she found a link between heavy stress and a relatively high incidence of illness. However, she noted that the correlation between stress scores and illness was relatively weak (.24) and decided to carry her investigation one step further than other studies, *focusing on the executives who experienced heavy stress but did not get sick*. Specifically, she compared the high-stress executives who reported the expected high incidence of illness against the high-stress executives who reported *little* illness, to see whether they showed any systematic differences in personality. She administered a battery of psychological tests, comparing the executives along some 18 dimensions of personality. In this way, she isolated a small number of personality traits that were related to strong stress tolerance, or what she labeled "hardiness." These personality factors, which have surfaced in subsequent studies (Kobasa, Maddi, & Kahn, 1982; Kobasa & Pucetti, 1983), are described below.

1. *A sense of commitment.* The "hardy" executives tended to have a clear sense of values and a solid belief in their meaningfulness. They had well-defined goals and a commitment to their importance. In contrast, the less hardy executives were characterized as "alienated."

2. *A vigorous approach to life.* The stress-resistant executives tended to seek out and actively confront challenges. They viewed change, rather than stability, as a normal feature of life. They welcomed change rather than clinging to the past. In contrast, the less resistant executives were more passive in response to change and more likely to view change as alarming.

3. *Internal locus of control.* Locus of control is a personality dimension (Rotter, 1966) centering on the degree to which people believe that their successes and failures are governed by external factors (fate, luck, chance) as opposed to internal factors (their own actions and behavior). People with an *internal* **locus of control** tend to believe that people (including themselves) are responsible for their successes and failures. Conversely, people with a relatively *external* locus of control tend to attribute both individuals' successes and failures to luck, chance, or fate. Kobasa found that the high-tolerance executives had a strong belief in their ability to control their own destiny. In contrast, the low-tolerance executives displayed more external locus of control and reported more feelings of powerlessness.

LOCUS OF CONTROL. *A personality trait involving a generalized expectancy that people hold regarding the degree to which they control their fate. People with an internal locus of control feel that they have a reasonable amount of control over their outcomes. People with an external locus of control feel that their fate is largely beyond their control.*

PHYSIOLOGICAL FACTORS

In view of the fact that we respond to stress physiologically, it is not surprising that there has been extensive speculation about how certain constitutional factors might be related to stress tolerance. I will briefly discuss one such theory about the possible relation between physiological makeup and resistance to stress.

Some people thrive on challenges that most of us would find very stressful.

Hans Eysenck (1960), a prominent British psychologist, has proposed that differences between people in their reaction to stress may be due largely to differences in the sensitivity of their autonomic nervous system (ANS). Eysenck suggests that genetic inheritance may give some people a highly excitable ANS, while other people inherit a relatively placid or less sensitive ANS. This notion is supported by a few studies (for example, Richmond & Lustman, 1955) showing that infants display noticeable differences in ANS reactivity when only a few days old. Since the autonomic nervous system plays a central role in our physiological response to stress, such differences in ANS reactivity could have a critical influence on our ability to tolerate stress.

According to Eysenck, those of us who have a relatively placid ANS ought to be less affected by stress than those equipped with a highly reactive ANS. Eysenck's theory has been supported by new research on autonomically regulated cardiovascular reactivity in response to stress. Recent studies indicate that subjects exposed to stressful laboratory tasks show *consistent* individual differences in cardiovascular reactivity over a one-year period (Manuck & Garland, 1980) and across different types of stressful tasks (Lawler, 1980). These findings clearly support Eysenck's hypothesis that there are physiological differences in reactivity to stress. All that remains is to relate these differences to variations in long-range stress tolerance (see Box 3.4).

EXPERIENTIAL HISTORY

Much research has also been devoted to identifying the kinds of early experiences that might make a person particularly vulnerable to stress. Various kinds of experiences in childhood, such as love deprivation, parental overprotection, inconsistent discipline, and parental marital instability have been related to the likelihood of developing a variety of specific psychological disorders. Chapter 13 will review some of this evidence. At this point I will focus on one experiential factor that seems related to a *general* reduction in a person's capacity to tolerate stress. That factor is early psychological trauma.

Early psychological trauma generally refers to extremely stressful events occurring before adolescence that generate severe emotional distress. Examples of such traumatic events include the death of a parent, serious illness, accidents leading to severe injuries, beatings and generally brutal treatment, and incestual exploitation and other types of sexual molestation. The occurrence of these kinds of very dreadful and painful experiences during childhood has been shown to be statistically related to the probability of developing

3.4   HOT REACTORS

Hans Eysenck's (1960) idea that individual differences in autonomic reactivity might influence stress tolerance did not attract much attention for a long time. Recently, however, the idea has "come of age" as Robert Eliot has focused attention on what he calls "hot reactors" (Eliot & Breo, 1984). What are hot reactors? They are people who consistently show extreme cardiovascular reactions when confronted by stress. Such people may display perfectly normal blood pressure most of the time, including checkups in a doctor's office. What sets them apart from others is that their blood pressure tends to skyrocket when they encounter the stresses of everyday life. According to Eliot's preliminary estimates, about one of every five persons is a hot reactor. Part of the problem with this syndrome is that many hot reactors do not have any idea that they have a problem, because their blood pressure usually appears fine. Unfortunately, appearances may be deceiving. On the basis of his clinical observations as a cardiologist (physician specializing in heart disease), Eliot is convinced that hot reactors are much more vulnerable to heart attacks than the general populace. At present we have no precise estimates of the increase in cardiac risk associated with hot reacting, but Eliot and other researchers are beginning to gather the systematic data needed to pinpoint just how significant this physiological propensity might be.

many kinds of psychological disorders later in life (Coleman, Butcher, & Carson, 1980). Of course, these kinds of experiences tend to be quite threatening at any age, but they are likely to be particularly devastating to a young child, who is relatively helpless and defenseless. Although it is true that some people manage to survive such traumatic events without severe, permanent damage, it appears that early psychic trauma has a strong tendency to undermine our resistance to stress.

Early traumatic events tend to decrease stress tolerance for a number of reasons. First, they provide a dramatic demonstration of our human frailty. Although we all share a certain sense of vulnerability, some of us are more painfully aware of it than others. Early traumatic events lead many people to see the world around them as a particularly hostile, threatening, dangerous place. Second, childhood trauma may sometimes disrupt the normal developmental processes that usually lead to emotional maturity. Thus, the important process of acquiring adequate coping skills may be sabotaged, yielding a psychologically crippled adult. Third, these traumas may leave one with specific emotional wounds that are easily reopened by stressful events during adulthood. For example, a few insignificant but nasty remarks by one's spouse might reactivate all the emotional pain suffered decades ago when one experienced parental rejection. Fourth, traumatic events may trigger a chain of reactions that produce psychological damage. The traumatic event itself may not be as crucial as the aftermath of the event. For instance, after a divorce, the adjustment of the custodial parent has a great impact on how much the divorce affects the children (Pett, 1982). This complexity illustrates why the link between trauma and decreased stress tolerance is *not* automatic or inevitable. Many factors govern the impact of a particular event on a particular child.

You should not conclude from this evidence on the detrimental effects of childhood trauma that a totally stress-free environment is ideal during one's youth. This evidence indicates only that *early* and *severe* stress *may* undermine one's subsequent resistance to stress. However, being forced to deal with stress, particularly less severe stress occurring later in childhood, may have *beneficial* effects. It seems likely that confronting and conquering stress may improve our coping ability. Furthermore, even if we do not "conquer" the stress, we may be able to learn from our mistakes and failures. As noted earlier, sometimes exposure to stressful events can "inoculate" us against the effects of future stress.

Summary

The transactional model of stress proposes that stress involves circumstances that threaten or are perceived to threaten our well-being and tax our adaptive capacities. Stress may be either physical or psychological, and these kinds of stress may interact. Because the appraisal of stress is subjective, it may not be rational, and stress may often be self-imposed. Our response to stress is multidimensional. Stress may have a long-range impact, either positive or negative, on adaptational outcomes.

Most stress falls into one of four categories: frustration, conflict, change, or pressure. Frustration occurs when any obstacle prevents us from attaining a goal. Failures and losses are common frustrations. There are four types of conflict: approach/approach, avoidance/avoidance, approach/avoidance, and cognitive dissonance. Present evidence suggests that approach/avoidance may be particularly stressful. A large number of studies with the SRRS suggest that change may be stressful. Although this may be a reasonable conclusion, it is now clear that the SRRS is a measure of general stress rather than just change-related stress. Two kinds of pressure (to perform and to conform) appear to be related to adaptational outcomes. Because the perception of stress is subjective, it will be influenced by one's personality, one's coping resources, one's familiarity with the stress, the imminence of the threat, and perceptions of controllability.

Our reactions to stress are multidimensional, involving emotional, physiological, and behavioral responses. Particularly common among emotional reactions to stress are anger, anxiety, and dejection. Emotional arousal may interfere with our coping, especially when the task at hand is complex.

Selye's general adaptation syndrome describes three stages in our physiological reaction to stress. The G.A.S. sheds some light on how stress affects our cardiovascular and gastrointestinal functioning. Recent evidence suggests that stress may also lead to neurochemical changes in the brain and alterations in our immunal response.

Our behavioral response to stress involves coping—efforts to master, reduce, or tolerate the adjustive demands. The concept of coping includes efforts that are unhealthy and those that are unlikely to be successful.

Research on the effects of stress has concentrated on negative adaptational outcomes. Negative effects include impairments in cognitive functioning, disorientation, burnout, poor social relations, psychological problems and disorders, and physical problems and illnesses. On the positive side, stress seems to fulfill a basic human need for challenge and stimulation, may promote personal growth, and may inoculate one against the harmful effects of future stress.

There are great individual differences in how much stress people can tolerate. It appears that stress tolerance can be increased by the buffering effects of social support. The personality factors associated with hardiness can also serve to improve stress tolerance. Physiological factors, such as ANS reactivity, and experiential factors, such as exposure to early trauma, may also be related to stress tolerance.

In the upcoming application section, I will discuss the importance of monitoring the stress in your life. I will describe a relatively new scale for the assessment of stress and show you how to estimate the amount of stress in your life.

Monitoring the Stress in Your Life

Rank the following five events in terms of how stressful they would be for you (1 = most stressful, 5 = least stressful).

_____ 1. Trouble with in-laws.
_____ 2. Fired at work.
_____ 3. Marital separation.
_____ 4. Change in financial state.
_____ 5. Jail term.

All five events appear on the Social Readjustment Rating Scale (SRRS), developed by Holmes and Rahe (1967). If you ranked them in the same order as Holmes and Rahe's subjects, the rankings would be 5, 3, 1, 4, and 2. If you didn't rank them in that order, don't worry about it; that merely shows that the perception of stress is very personal and subjective. Unfortunately, the SRRS fails to take that reality into account. That is just one of a number of basic problems that are characteristic of the SRRS. What concerns me is that the SRRS and the research associated with it have received a great deal of publicity. The scale has been reprinted in many popular newspapers and magazines. In these articles, readers have been encouraged to attribute great significance to their scores. They have sometimes been told that they should reduce or minimize change in their lives if their scores are high (Cohen, 1979). Such bold advice could be counterproductive and needs to be quite cautiously qualified. Although there is much to be said for estimating the amount of stress in one's life, people have been led to attribute far too much significance to their scores on the SRRS. Therefore, in this application section I will elaborate on some of the problems with the SRRS as a measurement scale, introduce you to a newer and much improved scale for the measurement of stress, and explain why your scores on any such scale should be interpreted with caution.

PROBLEMS WITH THE SOCIAL READJUSTMENT RATING SCALE

As you learned earlier in this chapter, the SRRS was developed in the early 1960s by Holmes and Rahe (1967) to measure the amount of change-related stress that people experience. The scale assigns normative values to 43 life events that are supposed to indicate how stressful those events are. You respond to the scale by checking off those events that have happened to you in a recent time period and adding up the values of the events checked to arrive at your score. In a host of studies, these scores have been found to be related to the likelihood of developing an intimidating array of physical illnesses and psychological problems (Barrett, Rose, & Klerman, 1979; Perkins, 1982).

Now, before I start pointing out a variety of flaws in the SRRS, let me emphasize that Holmes and Rahe deserve enormous credit for having the imagination to tackle the difficult task of measuring life stress over two decades ago. They had the insight to recognize the potential importance of stress and the ingenuity to develop a scale that would permit its measurement. They pioneered a new area of research that has turned out to be extremely productive, and thus they made a major contribution to the fields of psychology and medicine. However, their ground-breaking foray into the assessment of stress was not without its flaws, and their scale has been improved on. So, borrowing from the analyses of a number of critics (notably Cleary, 1980; Derogatis, 1982; Perkins, 1982; Rabkin & Streuning, 1976), let me outline some of the *major* problems with the SRRS—not to discredit the SRRS but, rather, to illustrate the "self-correcting" nature of the scientific enterprise by giving you some idea of how our understanding of a research issue often evolves forward in a gradual fashion. Although this list is not exhaustive, the key problems with the SRRS are as follows.

First, as already discussed, the related assumptions that change is the core of stress and that the SRRS measures change exclusively have been shown to be inaccurate. We now have ample evidence (Perkins, 1982) that the desirability/undesirability of the events experienced affects adaptational outcomes more than the amount of change that they require. In terms of the key concepts in testing that you learned about in the application section of Chapter 2, it boils down to this—the construct *validity* of the scale appears questionable. Thus, it seems prudent to view the SRRS as a measure of diverse forms of stress, or stress in a general sense.

The second problem is that the SRRS fails to take into account differences among people in their perception of how stressful an event is. For instance, while divorce may deserve a stress value of 73 for *most* people, a particular person's divorce might generate much less stress and merit a value of only 25. Hurst, Jenkins, and Rose (1978) have suggested that it might be better to have respondents rate how *personally* stressful events were, rather than using the standardized, average weights. Research by Sarason, Johnson, and Siegel (1978) indicates that such an approach *can* provide better prediction. Thus, the normative weights assigned to events on the SRRS may not capture the true impact of an event on a particular person. The crucial flaw here is that the SRRS ignores the appraisal phase of the stress process, which has been shown to be of the utmost importance (Lazarus & Folkman, 1984).

A third problem involves the ambiguity that is inherent in many of the events listed on the SRRS. For instance, what qualifies as "trouble with boss"? Should you check that because you're sick and tired of your supervisor? What constitutes a "change in living conditions"? Does your purchase of a great new stereo system qualify? How should the "pregnancy" item be interpreted? Should a man who has a pregnant wife check that item? As you can see, then, the SRRS includes many "events" that are described inadequately, producing considerable ambiguity about how one should respond. In terms of psychological testing, this shortcoming undermines the scale's *reliability*.

A fourth problem with the SRRS is the failure to sample from the domain of stressful events more thoroughly. Could the 43 events listed on the SRRS exhaust all the stressful changes that one might encounter in life? Intuitively, looking the list over, one would be tempted to guess that there are some important omissions. Indeed, a study designed to explore that possibility (Dohrenwend et al., 1978) found many omissions that were thought to be significant. In fact, that study led to the development of an expanded variation on the SRRS that lists 102 life events.

THE LIFE EXPERIENCES SURVEY

In light of the problems outlined above, it is not surprising that a number of researchers (for instance, Dohrenwend et al., 1978; Paykel, 1974; Sarason, Johnson, & Siegel, 1978) have endeavored to develop improved versions of the SRRS. The scale that seems to be gaining the greatest usage in this area is the Life Experiences Survey (LES), assembled by Irwin Sarason and colleagues (Sarason et al., 1978; Sarason, Levine, & Sarason, 1982). The LES (see Table 3.2) revises and builds on the SRRS in a variety of ways that correct, at least in part, most of the problems discussed above.

TABLE 3.2 **The Life Experiences Survey**

Listed below are a number of events which sometimes bring about change in the lives of those who experience them and which necessitate social readjustment. *Please check those events which you have experienced in the recent past and indicate the time during which you have experienced each event.* Be sure that all check marks are directly across from the items they correspond to.

Also, for each item checked below, *please indicate the extent to which you viewed the event as having either a positive or negative impact on your life* at the time the event occurred. That is, *indicate the type and extent of impact that the event had.* A rating of −3 would indicate an extremely negative impact. A rating of 0 suggests no impact, either positive or negative. A rating of +3 would indicate an extremely positive impact.

	0 to 6 mo	7 mo to 1 yr	Extremely negative	Moderately negative	Somewhat negative	No impact	Slightly positive	Moderately positive	Extremely positive
Section 1									
1. Marriage			−3	−2	−1	0	+1	+2	+3
2. Detention in jail or comparable institution			−3	−2	−1	0	+1	+2	+3
3. Death of spouse			−3	−2	−1	0	+1	+2	+3
4. Major change in sleeping habits (much more or much less sleep)			−3	−2	−1	0	+1	+2	+3
5. Death of a close family member:									
a. mother			−3	−2	−1	0	+1	+2	+3
b. father			−3	−2	−1	0	+1	+2	+3
c. brother			−3	−2	−1	0	+1	+2	+3
d. sister			−3	−2	−1	0	+1	+2	+3
e. grandmother			−3	−2	−1	0	+1	+2	+3
f. grandfather			−3	−2	−1	0	+1	+2	+3
g. other (specify)			−3	−2	−1	0	+1	+2	+3
6. Major change in eating habits (much more or much less food intake)			−3	−2	−1	0	+1	+2	+3
7. Foreclosure on mortgage or loan			−3	−2	−1	0	+1	+2	+3
8. Death of close friend			−3	−2	−1	0	+1	+2	+3
9. Outstanding personal achievement			−3	−2	−1	0	+1	+2	+3
10. Minor law violations (traffic tickets, disturbing the peace, etc.)			−3	−2	−1	0	+1	+2	+3
11. *Male:* Wife/girlfriend's pregnancy			−3	−2	−1	0	+1	+2	+3
12. *Female:* Pregnancy			−3	−2	−1	0	+1	+2	+3

(continued)

TABLE 3.2 **The Life Experiences Survey** *(continued)*

	0 to 6 mo	7 mo to 1 yr	Extremely negative	Moderately negative	Somewhat negative	No impact	Slightly positive	Moderately positive	Extremely positive
13. Changed work situation (different work responsibility, major change in working conditions, working hours, etc.)			−3	−2	−1	0	+1	+2	+3
14. New job			−3	−2	−1	0	+1	+2	+3
15. Serious illness or injury of close family member:									
a. father			−3	−2	−1	0	+1	+2	+3
b. mother			−3	−2	−1	0	+1	+2	+3
c. sister			−3	−2	−1	0	+1	+2	+3
d. brother			−3	−2	−1	0	+1	+2	+3
e. grandfather			−3	−2	−1	0	+1	+2	+3
f. grandmother			−3	−2	−1	0	+1	+2	+3
g. spouse			−3	−2	−1	0	+1	+2	+3
h. other (specify)			−3	−2	−1	0	+1	+2	+3
16. Sexual difficulties			−3	−2	−1	0	+1	+2	+3
17. Trouble with employer (in danger of losing job, being suspended, demoted, etc.)			−3	−2	−1	0	+1	+2	+3
18. Trouble with in-laws			−3	−2	−1	0	+1	+2	+3
19. Major change in financial status (a lot better off or a lot worse off)			−3	−2	−1	0	+1	+2	+3
20. Major change in closeness of family members (increased or decreased closeness)			−3	−2	−1	0	+1	+2	+3
21. Gaining a new family member (through birth, adoption, family member moving in, etc.)			−3	−2	−1	0	+1	+2	+3
22. Change of residence			−3	−2	−1	0	+1	+2	+3
23. Marital separation from mate (due to conflict)			−3	−2	−1	0	+1	+2	+3
24. Major change in church activities (increased or decreased attendance)			−3	−2	−1	0	+1	+2	+3
25. Marital reconciliation with mate			−3	−2	−1	0	+1	+2	+3
26. Major change in number of arguments with spouse (a lot more or a lot less arguments)			−3	−2	−1	0	+1	+2	+3
27. *Married male:* Change in wife's work outside the home (beginning work, ceasing work, changing to a new job, etc.)			−3	−2	−1	0	+1	+2	+3
28. *Married female:* Change in husband's work (loss of job, beginning new job, retirement, etc.)			−3	−2	−1	0	+1	+2	+3
29. Major change in usual type and/or amount of recreation			−3	−2	−1	0	+1	+2	+3

(continued)

TABLE 3.2 **The Life Experiences Survey** (continued)

	0 to 6 mo	7 mo to 1 yr	Extremely negative	Moderately negative	Somewhat negative	No impact	Slightly positive	Moderately positive	Extremely positive
30. Borrowing more than $10,000 (buying home, business, etc.)			−3	−2	−1	0	+1	+2	+3
31. Borrowing less than $10,000 (buying car, TV, getting school loan, etc.)			−3	−2	−1	0	+1	+2	+3
32. Being fired from job			−3	−2	−1	0	+1	+2	+3
33. *Male:* Wife/girlfriend having abortion			−3	−2	−1	0	+1	+2	+3
34. *Female:* Having abortion			−3	−2	−1	0	+1	+2	+3
35. Major personal illness or injury			−3	−2	−1	0	+1	+2	+3
36. Major change in social activities, e.g., parties, movies, visiting (increased or decreased participation)			−3	−2	−1	0	+1	+2	+3
37. Major change in living conditions of family (building new home, remodeling, deterioration of home, neighborhood, etc.)			−3	−2	−1	0	+1	+2	+3
38. Divorce			−3	−2	−1	0	+1	+2	+3
39. Serious injury or illness of close friend			−3	−2	−1	0	+1	+2	+3
40. Retirement from work			−3	−2	−1	0	+1	+2	+3
41. Son or daughter leaving home (due to marriage, college, etc.)			−3	−2	−1	0	+1	+2	+3
42. Ending of formal schooling			−3	−2	−1	0	+1	+2	+3
43. Separation from spouse (due to work, travel, etc.)			−3	−2	−1	0	+1	+2	+3
44. Engagement			−3	−2	−1	0	+1	+2	+3
45. Breaking up with boyfriend/girlfriend			−3	−2	−1	0	+1	+2	+3
46. Leaving home for the first time			−3	−2	−1	0	+1	+2	+3
47. Reconciliation with boyfriend/girlfriend			−3	−2	−1	0	+1	+2	+3
Other recent experiences which have had an impact on your life. List and rate.									
48. _____			−3	−2	−1	0	+1	+2	+3
49. _____			−3	−2	−1	0	+1	+2	+3
50. _____			−3	−2	−1	0	+1	+2	+3
Section 2: Students only									
51. Beginning a new school experience at a higher academic level (college, graduate school, professional school, etc.)			−3	−2	−1	0	+1	+2	+3
52. Changing to a new school at same academic level (undergraduate, graduate, etc.)			−3	−2	−1	0	+1	+2	+3
53. Academic probation			−3	−2	−1	0	+1	+2	+3

(continued)

TABLE 3.2   **The Life Experiences Survey** (continued)

	0 to 6 mo	7 mo to 1 yr	Extremely negative	Moderately negative	Somewhat negative	No impact	Slightly positive	Moderately positive	Extremely positive
54. Being dismissed from dormitory or other residence			−3	−2	−1	0	+1	+2	+3
55. Failing an important exam			−3	−2	−1	0	+1	+2	+3
56. Changing a major			−3	−2	−1	0	+1	+2	+3
57. Failing a course			−3	−2	−1	0	+1	+2	+3
58. Dropping a course			−3	−2	−1	0	+1	+2	+3
59. Joining a fraternity/sorority			−3	−2	−1	0	+1	+2	+3
60. Financial problems concerning school (in danger of not having sufficient money to continue)			−3	−2	−1	0	+1	+2	+3

Specifically, the LES has the following characteristics. It recognizes that stress involves more than mere change and asks respondents to indicate whether events had a positive or negative impact on them. This strategy taps the very important dimension of *desirability* and permits the computation of positive change, negative change, and total change scores, which helps researchers to gain much more insight into which facets of stress are most crucial. The LES also takes into consideration differences among people in the *appraisal* of stress. It accomplishes this by dropping the normative weights and replacing them with personally assigned weightings of the impact of relevant events. Ambiguity in items is decreased by providing more elaborate descriptions of many items so as to clarify their meaning. There are still some ambiguous items, but there is probably no complete solution for this problem. The failure of the SRRS to sample the domain of stressful events fully is dealt with in several ways. First, some significant omissions from the SRRS were added to the LES. Second, the LES allows the respondent to write in personally important events that are not included on the scale. Third, the LES reprinted here has an extra section just for students. Sarason et al. (1978) suggest that special, tailored sections of this sort be added for specific populations whenever it appears useful.

I suggest that you respond to the LES, reprinted in Table 3.2. Although I have been critical of overinterpretation of SRRS scores, I do believe that there is much to be said for making an estimate of how much stress one has been under recently. Arriving at your scores on the scale is very simple. Just add up all the positive impact ratings on the right side. That sum is your *positive change score*. Your *negative change score* is simply the sum of all of the negative impact ratings that you made on the left. Adding these two values yields your *total change score*. Approximate norms for all three of these scores are listed in Table 3.3, so that you can get some idea of what your score means.

Research to date suggests that your negative change score is the crucial one. Positive change has not been found to be much of a predictor of adaptational outcomes. Total change is, but probably only because it includes the impact of negative change. In direct comparisons with the SRRS, the negative change score *has* turned out to be a better predictor of adaptational outcomes (Sarason et al., 1978). Although research with the LES has just begun, there is evidence that negative change scores are related to a variety of adaptational outcomes, including menstrual discomfort, nonconformity, job dissatisfaction, athletic injuries, vaginal infections, anxiety, psychological discomfort, depression, and coronary disease (Passer & Seese, 1983; Sarason et al., 1982; Williams & Deffenbacher, 1983).

TABLE 3.3   Approximate norms for college students on the Life Experiences Survey

Score category	Negative change	Positive change	Total change
High	14 and above	16 and above	28 and above
Medium	4–13	7–15	12–27
Low	0–3	0–6	0–11

Note: These norms should be regarded as approximate. They are adapted from data on 345 undergraduate subjects as reported in Sarason, Johnson, and Siegel (1978). Low scores are those that fall 0.5 standard deviations below the mean. Medium scores are those that fall within −0.5 and +1.0 standard deviations of the mean. High scores are those that fall more than 1.0 standard deviations above the mean. Data for males and females were combined, as sex differences were negligible.

QUALIFICATIONS

Although there is some merit in getting an estimate of how much stress you have experienced lately, scores on the LES or *any* measure of stress should be interpreted with caution. You need not panic if you add up your negative change score and find that it falls in the "high" category. Although it is clear that there is some sort of causal connection between psychological stress and a variety of undesirable adaptational outcomes, many people endure high levels of stress without significant problems resulting. Let me elaborate on why you should not be terribly worried if you scored high on either the SRRS or the LES.

First, the *strength* of the association between stress and adaptational problems is modest. Most of the correlations observed between stress scores and illness have been relatively low, often less than .30 (Kobasa, 1979). Even though it is theoretically very interesting to find any relationship at all, it has become clear that the association between stress and adaptational problems is moderate in strength.

Second, regardless of how strong the link is between stress and various maladies, you must bear in mind that stress is only one of a multitude of variables that affect your susceptibility to those maladies. For instance, in the next chapter we will describe how stress interacts with factors such as lifestyle, genetic inheritance, and exposure to pathogens in influencing whether you develop physical illnesses. Thus, stress is only one actor on a crowded stage.

Third, recent research has highlighted the fact that the impact of stress is mediated by a number of "moderator variables." Toward the end of this chapter, I discussed how moderator variables such as personality, social support, and experiential history influence stress tolerance. Stress scales do not take these factors into account. Thus, the potential impact of these mediating factors means that it is difficult to say just how a certain amount of stress will affect a particular person.

In light of these considerations, then, one should evaluate the potential meaning of SRRS or LES scores with caution. A high score should be food for thought but not reason for alarm.

CHAPTER 3 REVIEW

IDEAS: REVIEW OF LEARNING OBJECTIVES

When you have mastered the material in this chapter, you should be able to do the following.

1. Describe the key facets of the transactional model of stress.
2. List six general principles regarding the nature of stress.
3. Draw a diagram that provides an overview of the stress process.
4. List four principal sources of stress.
5. Discuss two common sources of frustration and the determinants of the intensity of frustration.
6. Describe four types of conflict.
7. Summarize ideas about resolving approach/avoidance conflicts.
8. Discuss the factors that determine the intensity of conflicts.
9. Describe the SRRS and research done with it.
10. Discuss whether change, in and of itself, is stressful.
11. Describe two kinds of pressure.
12. Describe how repressors and sensitizers react differently to stress.
13. Explain how the severity of stress is affected by one's resources for coping with the stress and one's familiarity with the stress.
14. Explain how the imminence and duration of stress affect its severity.
15. Explain how predictability and perceived control affect the perception of stress severity.
16. List three dimensions of emotion commonly elicited by stress.
17. Discuss the possible effects of emotional arousal on intellectual functioning and coping efforts.
18. Describe the three stages of Selye's general adaptation syndrome.
19. Summarize physiological changes that often take place in response to stress.
20. List six negative adaptational outcomes that are frequently a product of stress.
21. Discuss three ways in which stress might lead to positive adaptational outcomes.
22. Describe how social support tends to moderate the impact of stress.
23. List the four functions of social support identified by House.
24. Describe the characteristics of the "hardy personality" and how this personality moderates the impact of stress.
25. Describe how physiological factors may moderate the impact of stress.
26. Describe the relationship that is frequently observed between early trauma and stress tolerance.
27. Explain several reasons that early trauma tends to undermine stress tolerance.
28. List four problems with the SRRS that were described in the application section.
29. Summarize how the LES corrects problems that are characteristic of the SRRS.
30. Summarize three reasons that one should be cautious in interpreting the apparent link between scores on stress scales and adaptational outcomes.

TERMS: REVIEW OF NEW VOCABULARY

When you have mastered the material in this chapter, you should be able to define the following terms.

Adaptational outcomes	Burnout	Emotion	Repressor
Approach/approach conflict	Cardiovascular	Endocrine system	Sensitizer
Approach/avoidance conflict	Catecholamines	Frustration	State anxiety
Autonomic nervous system (ANS)	Cognitive dissonance	Gastrointestinal	Stress
Avoidance/avoidance conflict	Conflict	General adaptation syndrome	Stress tolerance
	Coping	Hormones	Trait anxiety
	Corticosteroids	Locus of control	Transactional model of stress
	Delayed stress response syndrome	Pressure	

PEOPLE: REVIEW OF MAJOR THEORISTS AND RESEARCHERS

When you have mastered the material in this chapter, you should be able to summarize the principal contributions and/or ideas of the following people.

Hans Eysenck	Suzanne Kobasa	Neal Miller	Hans Selye
Leon Festinger	Richard Lazarus	Irwin Sarason	Yerkes and Dodson
Holmes and Rahe			

4

BEHAVIORAL FACTORS AND PHYSICAL HEALTH

(with Beth A. Traylor, M.D.)

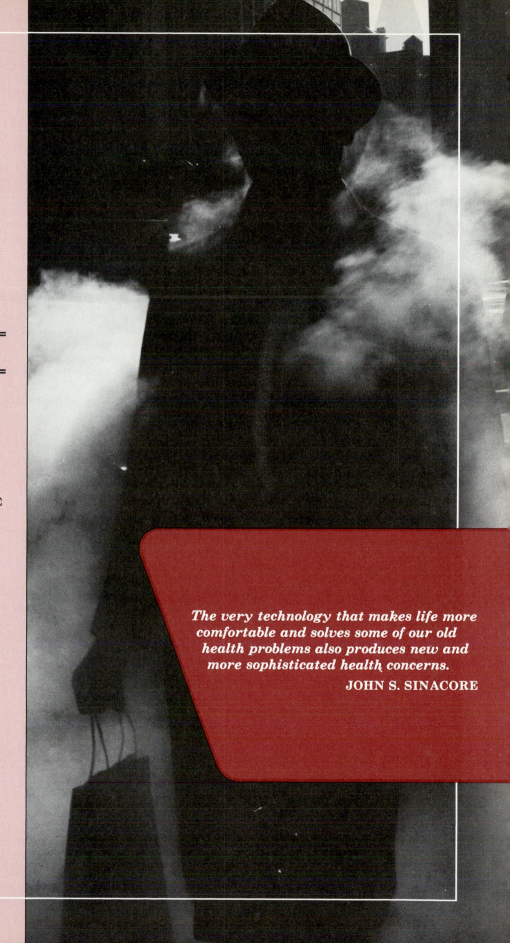

Summary

Applying Psychology to Your Life: Being Intelligent about Drugs

DRUG-RELATED CONCEPTS
- DRUG
- TOLERANCE
- PHYSICAL DEPENDENCE
- PSYCHOLOGICAL DEPENDENCE
- OVERDOSE

EFFECTS AND RISKS OF VARIOUS DRUGS
- NARCOTICS
- SEDATIVES
- STIMULANTS
- HALLUCINOGENS
- CANNABIS DERIVATIVES
- ALCOHOL

The very technology that makes life more comfortable and solves some of our old health problems also produces new and more sophisticated health concerns.

JOHN S. SINACORE

Let's take a trip back in time, to a period long, long ago before the dawn of what we today choose to call "civilization." Imagine that you're part of a small tribe that derives its subsistence from primitive hunting and gathering techniques. It is midday, and you have briefly halted your foraging activities to rest by yourself on a wooded hillside. Your relaxation is abruptly interrupted when you hear movement in the underbrush nearby. Your hand reaches for a knife, and your muscles tense in anticipation. Your heartbeat quickens, your breathing changes rhythm, and your pupils dilate as you vigilantly focus your gaze on the now threatening underbrush. What lurks there? A mountain lion? A wild boar? A warrior from an enemy tribe? Or is it merely some harmless animal? You glance around to consider possible escape routes. You are prepared for *a fight or a flight*. Which will it be? Fortunately, neither. A harmless-looking goat emerges from the shrubs, takes one look at you, and scampers off in the opposite direction. You breathe a sigh of relief. Your muscles relax and your racing heart slows to a trot. The threat has passed and the stress is over.

Now, let's return to today and our modern, civilized way of life. You're in your car heading home from work on the expressway. Traffic is barely moving. A radio report indicates that the traffic jam is only going to get worse. You groan audibly to a co-worker riding with you as your blood pressure escalates. Some moronic motorist nearly takes your fender off trying to cut into your lane. Your pulse quickens as you shout insults at someone who cannot even hear you. You ponder the marketing projections that you have to work on at home that evening. Will you be able to finish them on time? Your stomach knots up as you realize that it is going to be a close race. Suddenly, you remember that you promised your spouse that the two of you would go out to dinner tonight. Your muscles tense as you realize you're going to have to deal with one very unhappy spouse. The co-worker with you starts to discuss office politics and brings up the recent rumor that your entire division might be sold off and dismantled. Your heartbeat quickens as you contemplate your huge house mortgage and the prospect of being unemployed. You feel wired with tension as you realize that the stress in your life never seems to let up.

Changing Nature of Modern Stress

We have just sketched two prototype scenarios involving stress. Though thousands of years apart in time and lifestyle, they share common features. In both cases, you have reacted strongly to stress at a physiological level, with what has been labeled the "fight or flight" response (see Figure 4.1). The key difference between the two scenarios lies in the *adaptive value* of those physiological responses. In the first instance, your automatic physiological response had some utility. It increased your sensory vigilance and prepared you for your two basic options—fight or flight. In the second instance, your automatic physiological response was of little or no value. Your body was still preparing you for fight or flight, but these generally are not realistic options in confronting most modern stress. Sure, you might experience an urge to ram the car that just cut you off or slug the vice-president who might dismantle your division, but these are not acceptable behaviors in modern society. Similarly, you might think wistfully about heading for the airport, boarding a plane for Tahiti, and never returning—but such thoughts of flight rarely get beyond the fantasy stage. Thus, in the second instance, your built-in biological response to stress is an antiquated relic of the past that readies you for options you no longer have in most cases.

Why has our physiological response to stress become largely antiquated? Because the character or nature of stress has changed in a couple of ways. First, in a more primitive era, stress tended to involve direct threats to physical well-being that had to be confronted swiftly, making an *automatic* response of fight or flight quite adaptive. In our modern society, direct threats to

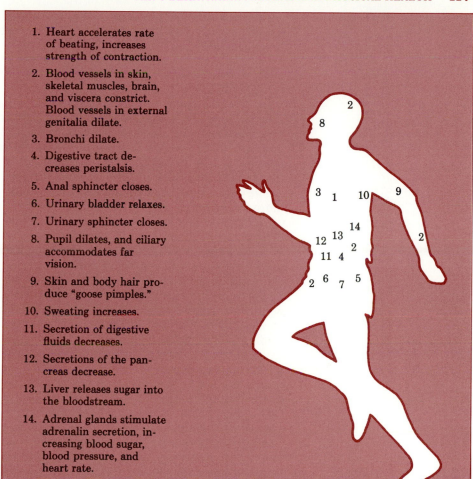

1. Heart accelerates rate of beating, increases strength of contraction.
2. Blood vessels in skin, skeletal muscles, brain, and viscera constrict. Blood vessels in external genitalia dilate.
3. Bronchi dilate.
4. Digestive tract decreases peristalsis.
5. Anal sphincter closes.
6. Urinary bladder relaxes.
7. Urinary sphincter closes.
8. Pupil dilates, and ciliary accommodates far vision.
9. Skin and body hair produce "goose pimples."
10. Sweating increases.
11. Secretion of digestive fluids decreases.
12. Secretions of the pancreas decrease.
13. Liver releases sugar into the bloodstream.
14. Adrenal glands stimulate adrenalin secretion, increasing blood sugar, blood pressure, and heart rate.

FIGURE 4.1 The body's response to stress.

our physical well-being are relatively uncommon. Instead we are confronted with a multitude of more subtle threats to our psychological well-being for which an automatic response is unnecessary and for which fight and flight are improbable solutions. Second, our ancestors' confrontations with predators and enemies were frequently brief—if they survived, the stress tended to be short-lived. In contrast, the modern landscape of life seems to be strewn with a great many stressors that tend to linger on for lengthy periods. Work pressures, marital problems, financial difficulties, and the like often drag on indefinitely. This is unfortunate in that the physiological component of our fight-or-flight response is poorly designed for dealing with prolonged stress. This was the key insight that several decades ago led Hans Selye to begin to explore the link between stress and "diseases of adaptation." His pioneering work showed how physiological arousal can backfire on us when it continues at length. His work eventually led to the description of the general adaptation syndrome (see Chapter 3), which set the stage for the current interest in the effects of stress on health.

Thus, it is the altered character of modern stress and the largely obsolete quality of our response to stress that have led to dramatic changes in the dynamics of health and illness in contemporary society. It is now widely recognized that psychological or behavioral factors play an extremely important role in governing our physical health (Smith & Kleinman, 1983). Therein lies the reason for the present chapter. In this chapter we will examine changing patterns and conceptions of illness in modern society. We will elaborate substantially on the link between stress and physical illness, discussed briefly in Chapter 3. We will also look at how a variety of other psychological considerations besides our reactions to stress influence health and illness. In the application section we will look at a very specific topic that falls in this area, the use of "recreational drugs."

Changing Patterns of Illness

EPIDEMIOLOGY. *The study of the distribution of physical and psychological disorders in a population, mainly for the purpose of gaining a better understanding of the causes of such disorders.*

The patterns of illness found in a society tend to fluctuate over time, and there have been some interesting trends in our society during the last century or so that are worthy of our attention. These shifting trends are monitored and investigated by epidemiologists. **Epidemiology** is the study of the distribution of both mental and physical illness in a population.

The most significant epidemiological trends in the last century have been the decreasing prevalence of contagious diseases and the rapidly escalating prevalence of stress-related illnesses. Before the 20th century, the principal threats to one's health were contagious diseases caused by an invasion of the body by a specific infectious agent. Because such diseases can be readily transmitted from one person to another, people used to live in fear of epidemics. The leading causes of death were diseases such as the plague, smallpox, typhoid fever, influenza, diphtheria, yellow fever, malaria, cholera, tuberculosis, polio, and scarlet fever. Today, the prevalence and dangerousness of these diseases have declined to the point that none of them ranks among the ten leading killers in the United States (Shank, 1983).

What led to the neutralization of these dreaded diseases? A number of trends contributed to it. The general public tends to attribute the conquest of these diseases to advances in medical treatment. Although progress in medicine certainly has played an important role, Grob (1983) marshals evidence that suggests the significance of such progress has been overrated. Of greater significance, according to Grob, are trends such as (1) improvement in nutrition, (2) improvements in public hygiene and sanitation (water filtration, treatment of sewage, and so forth), and (3) evolutionary changes in our immunal resistance to the diseases. Whatever the causes, it is clear that infectious diseases are no longer the preeminent threat to physical health in the industrialized nations of the world (many remain quite prevalent and dangerous in Third World countries).

Unfortunately, the void left by infectious diseases has been filled all too quickly and fully by various kinds of noncontagious illness. Foremost among these are heart diseases and cancer, which together account for nearly 60% of the deaths in the United States. In Table 4.1, which lists the ten illnesses with the highest mortality rates in the United States, only one is an infectious

TABLE 4.1 Diseases with the highest mortality rates in the United States

Disease	Death rate per 100,000	Percentage of deaths in year
Heart diseases	330.6	38.16
Cancer (all types)	184.3	21.27
Stroke	71.7	8.28
Pneumonia	22.3	2.57
Diabetes	15.2	1.75
Cirrhosis of the liver	12.9	1.48
Atherosclerosis	12.5	1.44
Miscellaneous cardiovascular diseases	8.4	0.96
Nephritic (kidney) diseases	7.6	0.87
Emphysema	5.9	0.68

Note: This table lists diseases only. The death rates for accidents (44.5 per 100,000), suicide (12.3), and homicide (10.7) exceed the rates for some of the diseases cited. Figures are estimates for the 1981 calendar year.
Source: National Center for Health Statistics.

disease (pneumonia). Moreover, although the evidence is just beginning to accumulate in some instances, there is at least some reason to believe that *every* one of those illnesses is influenced in part by stress or some other behavioral consideration. And these data on mortality rates allow us to view only the tip of the iceberg. Many other largely nonlethal kinds of illness (such as headaches, backaches, skin disorders, asthma, and ulcers) are thought to be greatly influenced by psychological factors. Thus, it seems fair to conclude that stress-related diseases are the preeminent threat to physical health in our modern society.

Changing Conceptions of Illness

In light of these dramatic epidemiological trends, it is not surprising that the way we think about illness is changing. Traditionally, illness has been thought of as a purely biological phenomenon produced by an infectious agent or some internal physical breakdown. In other words, the causation of illness was assumed to be entirely a matter of biological malfunctioning. However, the shifting patterns of disease in America and new findings relating stress to physical illness have rocked the foundation of this biological model.

BIOPSYCHOSOCIAL MODEL OF ILLNESS

In its place a new model is gradually emerging and gaining influence. Called the "biopsychosocial model" by Smith and Kleinman (1983), it rejects the notion that illness is exclusively a function of organic factors. Instead, the biopsychosocial model proposes that illness is caused by a complex interaction of biological, psychological, and sociocultural variables. This new model does not suggest that physiological factors are insignificant; rather, it simply asserts that these physiological factors operate in a psychosocial context, which also can be very influential and ought not to be ignored.

EMERGENCE OF HEALTH PSYCHOLOGY

HEALTH PSYCHOLOGY.
An area in psychology concerned with how psychosocial factors relate to the promotion and maintenance of health, the prevention and treatment of illness, and the causes of health and illness.

The growing recognition that psychological factors play a more important role in governing our physical health than previously realized has led to the emergence of a new specialty area in the field of psychology, called "health psychology." **Health psychology** is concerned with how psychosocial factors relate to the promotion and maintenance of health, the prevention and treatment of illness, and the causation of health and illness (Matarazzo, 1980). This specialty is very youthful—the Health Psychology division of the American Psychological Association was founded only in 1978. Our focus in most of the remainder of this chapter will be on this exciting new domain of health psychology.

Physiological Basis of Health and Illness

Before we plunge into a discussion of how psychological considerations influence health and illness, we need to sketch for you a brief overview of the role of physiological factors. Although we will be emphasizing behavioral factors in this chapter, you cannot fully appreciate the role of these factors unless you have some knowledge of the biological variables with which they interact.

HEREDITARY FACTORS

Even the most casual observer has probably noticed that many types of illness seem to run in families. Experts have long been aware that some diseases are transmitted from parent to child. In the last half century we have made considerable progress in understanding the details of this process.

The biochemical messengers that are passed on from one generation to another are called **genes.** The reason we are not all alike is that we inherit different collections of genes. Conversely, the reason you see a lot of similarity in traits within a family is that relatives share more genes than unrelated persons. Thousands of these genes are found on each of the 46 **chromosomes** that lie within the nucleus of every cell in your body. The chromosomes operate in 23 pairs, one member of each pair being contributed by each of the parents. The specific genes also pair off, and it is the nature of this pairing that determines one's traits. However, this pairing can get very complex because some genes exert dominance over one another, while others "blend" together. *Thus, genetic transmission is a complicated process in which all outcomes are a matter of probability.* Because a multitude of complex combinations of genes are possible, we cannot say for sure whether a child will inherit a particular trait from a parent.

The hereditary process is further complicated by the fact that many traits appear to be governed by more than one pair of genes. Traits such as eye color, hair color, or blood type are determined by a single gene pair, but many other characteristics are a product of tangled interactions among several or more gene pairs. For example, skin color appears to be determined by the interaction of three to five gene pairs. More complex personal qualities, such as autonomic reactivity or emotional temperament, may depend on the blended action of a great many gene pairs. Traits governed by more than a single pair of genes are said to involve **polygenic inheritance.**

GENES. *Specialized molecular structures, made up of DNA, that govern the process of hereditary transmission from one generation to another.*

CHROMOSOME. *A strand of DNA and protein found in the nucleus of a cell that carries genetic information.*

POLYGENIC INHERITANCE. *The hereditary process wherein a multiplicity of genes (at least more than one pair) collectively and interactively influence the expression of a trait.*

DIRECT INHERITANCE OF DISEASES

There are many diseases that are purely a matter of simple, direct genetic inheritance. Such diseases have been traced back to the operation of a single gene pair or chromosomal aberration. For example, *Huntington's disease* involves a progressive deterioration of the nervous system that leads to spastic muscle control, respiratory distress, seizures, and gradual loss of one's mental faculties. This disease usually does not manifest itself until around age 30. This terribly disabling disease is carried on a single dominant gene, so the probability that an affected parent will pass on the disease to a child is 50%.

Medical research has identified over 100 diseases like Huntington's disease that are the product of direct inheritance involving the operation of a single gene pair or chromosome. Some of the better known of these diseases are hemophilia, muscular dystrophy, sickle-cell anemia, cystic fibrosis, and Down's syndrome.

POLYGENIC INHERITANCE OF VULNERABILITY TO DISEASE

Although many diseases may be inherited directly, many more are influenced in much more subtle and complex ways by one's genetic endowment. *In these cases, it is not the disease itself that is inherited but, rather, an elevated vulnerability to the disease.* The most common form of diabetes, diabetes mellitus, provides an example of this more subtle genetic inheritance. Diabetes is a metabolic disorder, involving inadequate production or use of insulin in the body.

How do we know that genetic factors are involved in the development of diabetes? Because certain kinds of studies can be conducted to ascertain whether hereditary factors influence a characteristic. The most illuminating kind of research is the **twin study,** in which we compare *identical* against *fraternal* twins to see how similar they are on a particular trait. Since identical twins are genetically alike, while fraternal twins share a more modest number of genes (like any pair of siblings), greater similarity in personal qualities between identical twins can be attributed (with certain qualifications) to their

TWIN STUDY. *A research design for investigating the extent to which heredity governs a particular trait, characteristic, or disorder; involves a comparison between identical and fraternal twins to see how similar they are with respect to the trait in question.*

genetic uniformity. When both twins manifest a particular disease or disorder, they are said to be **concordant** for that disorder. When concordance rates are higher for identical than for fraternal twins, this indicates that genetic factors are playing a role in the acquisition of that disorder. For diabetes mellitus, the concordance rates hover around 65% for identical twins but are only about 18% for fraternal twins (Strickberger, 1976), suggesting a strong genetic predisposition for this disease. The issue of whether a disease has a genetic component can also be approached by examining parent/child resemblances. Using this approach, researchers find that while the overall prevalence of diabetes is well under 1%, children with one diabetic parent have about a 10% chance of developing the disease, and children with two diabetic parents have over a 20% chance (Nora & Fraser, 1974).

These and other lines of research clearly indicate that genetic factors influence one's vulnerability to diabetes. However, the pattern of inheritance does not resemble that which would be seen if a single gene were in control. We can therefore infer that polygenic inheritance is the mechanism of action and that what is passed on is an elevated predisposition to the disease. Thus, all people are not equally likely to develop various diseases. Their varying levels of vulnerability to a wide range of common diseases are determined in complex ways through polygenic inheritance. These genetic predispositions appear to play a role in the development of hypertension, asthma, skin disorders, rheumatoid arthritis, ulcers, heart disease, and cancer, as well as other types of illness. The *strength* of the genetic influence on vulnerability to these diseases varies. The genetic component is very large for some of them and only marginal for others.

CONCORDANCE. *When a pair of related persons display the same disorder, they are said to be concordant. They are said to be discordant if one displays the disorder and the other does not. A concordance rate is an index of what percentage of the relatives both manifest the disorder under study.*

PATHOGENIC AGENTS

PATHOGENIC. *Disease-producing. Usually limited to living organisms, but we are using the term more broadly to refer to any disease-producing agent, including environmental toxins.*

Our bodies are frequently subjected to an assault by unfriendly forces from the outside. These invaders that are capable of producing disease are called **pathogenic** agents. In this section we describe the principal sources of **infection,** outline the body's response to these invasions, and discuss the potential dangers of environmental toxins.

INFECTIOUS AGENTS

INFECTION. *The successful invasion, establishment, and growth of microorganisms in the tissues of the host, resulting in disruption of normal functioning.*

A great variety of illnesses are caused by infections. An infection involves the successful invasion of a host organism by a microorganism that establishes itself and multiplies. A number of kinds of microorganisms are capable of these invasions in humans. We will describe the two most frequent sources of infections in humans.

BACTERIA. *A diverse group of simple, single-celled microorganisms that can reproduce within the body. Some are pathogenic to humans, while others contribute to normal functioning.*

The most common invaders are **bacteria.** Fortunately, most bacteria are not disease-producing. Some, however, can lead to serious diseases, such as tuberculosis, syphilis, typhoid, ancient enemies such as the plague, and new enemies such as Legionnaire's disease. More common bacterial afflictions include strepthroat and tonsillitis.

VIRUS. *A primitive, microscopic life form whose survival and replication are dependent on a normal cell. It multiplies by taking over the reproductive process of a normal cell and is often pathogenic in humans.*

The other major source of infection in modern society is the **virus.** Viruses have highly varied effects on our physiological functioning. They often linger in our bodies in a dormant state with no ill effects unless they are later activated by some sort of "trigger," such as a hormonal or nutritional imbalance. Other viruses, however, may flare up quickly and have devastating effects on particular organs. Viral afflictions include polio, smallpox, hepatitis, herpes, the common cold, mumps, flu, and mononucleosis.

Infections are transmitted in a variety of ways. The most common is probably the inhalation of airborne microbes that may have been released through coughing or sneezing by an infected individual. Infections may also be spread by sharing food or drink or through direct contact with an infected person. Insects are also prime carriers of infectious agents.

RESISTANCE TO INFECTION

IMMUNE RESPONSE. *The multifaceted defensive reaction of the body to an invasion, usually initiated by a foreign substance.*

ANTIGEN. *A substance that stimulates the immune system to manufacture antibodies.*

ANTIBODIES. *Protein substances produced by the body, usually in response to an antigen. They function in a variety of ways to inactivate a particular antigen.*

IMMUNITY. *A state of relative resistance to a given source of infection.*

You may not immediately notice the invasion of your body by an infectious agent. Often there is an incubation period of a few days before the attack is launched. Once the invasion is recognized, your body responds automatically with a number of defensive reactions that constitute your **immune response.** At the site of the infection, inflammation may work to curtail the spread of the pathogenic agent. More important, specialized blood cells are dispatched to the area, where they attempt to engulf and destroy the bacterial cells or viral-commandeered cells.

If the pathogenic intruder slips through local defenses, your body will roll out bigger defensive guns. The invader will be recognized as a foreign substance, or **antigen,** and will stimulate the production of **antibodies**—specialized proteins that combat the spread of the antigens. There are several kinds of antibodies that collectively trigger a series of elaborate defensive maneuvers that work to neutralize and then destroy the pathogenic invaders. Antibodies are *specific* to the antigens that produce them, and they remain in the bloodstream after the battle has been won. The presence of these antibodies then provides **immunity** to future invasions by that particular antigen. That is why people are immune to mumps or a particular brand of measles after they have had the disease once.

TOXIC AGENTS IN THE ENVIRONMENT

A great many manufactured substances in our modern environment can be toxic—that is, poisonous or harmful to our health. These human-created pathogens seem to lurk everywhere and to be exerting an ever-increasing impact on our collective health. We will cite just a few examples to highlight the importance of this class of pathogenic agents. The *air pollution* in the larger cities in the United States has been linked to the prevalence of respiratory disorders, allergic disorders, cancer, and heart disease (Ensor, Henkel, & Means, 1977). *Pesticides* used to kill insects have greatly reduced the amount of insect-carried infections and improved agricultural yields, but they are now showing up as poisons in some of our food and water supplies. *Radiation,* which has clearly been linked to the prevalence of cancer, may soon produce similar contamination problems as we try to dispose of more and more radioactive waste (Combs, Hales, & Williams, 1980).

Thus, you should be aware that your health can be influenced profoundly by exposure to a startling diversity of toxic substances in your environment. It is ironic indeed that most of these environmental toxins are unintentional by-products of the modern technological progress that we cherish so much.

Overview of the Psychological Basis of Health and Illness

Having briefly discussed the physiological factors involved in the maintenance of health and illness, we can turn to our main topic and try to explain the lesser-known role of behavioral factors. It appears that there are at least three very different ways in which behavioral factors can influence our health (Krantz et al., 1981). These behavioral mechanisms are described briefly below.

1. *Direct effects of stress.* The most basic way in which psychological functioning can affect physical health is through the direct effects of stress on physiological processes. As we have already discussed, stress tends to elicit wide-ranging physiological arousal, which can lead to bodily changes that may be damaging in the long run.

2. *Health-impairing habits.* There are many habitual patterns of behavior that can have a direct negative impact on one's health or, acting more subtly, increase one's vulnerability to various kinds of illnesses. For instance, there is

ample evidence that the likelihood of developing heart disease is influenced by various aspects of lifestyle, including cigarette smoking, physical activity, and diet (Kaplan & Kimball, 1982).

3. *Reactions to illness.* One's behavioral response to illness can frequently have a decided impact on one's future health. A surprisingly great number of people ignore their doctors' advice or are unable to comply successfully with their doctors' instructions (Sackett & Snow, 1979). Some people find that they like certain aspects of being sick (such as all the attention they get), and they work in subtle ways to prolong their illness (Kinsman, Dirks, & Jones, 1982).

Links between Stress and Illness
CORONARY HEART DISEASE

CORONARY HEART DISEASE. *Heart pathology caused by a reduction in coronary blood flow; this type of heart disease accounts for about 90% of cardiac mortality. Also called ischemic heart disease.*

ATHEROSCLEROSIS. *A disease process in which fatty deposits and other debris line the inner walls of the arteries, narrowing the arterial channel. A common form of arteriosclerosis, a broader term referring to any degeneration of arterial blood flow.*

Coronary heart disease is far and away the number one killer in North America, accounting for nearly 40% of deaths every year (Shank, 1983). The coronary arteries are the blood vessels that supply the heart with blood. The principal cause of coronary disease is the process of **atherosclerosis,** which involves a gradual narrowing of the coronary arteries. This narrowing is most frequently caused by the buildup of deposits on the inner walls of the arterial channels (see Figure 4.2). Atherosclerosis progresses slowly over periods of years. This narrowing of the coronary arteries may eventually lead to situations in which the heart is temporarily deprived of adequate blood and oxygen flow, causing brief chest pain, a condition known as *angina pectoris.* If a coronary artery is blocked completely, an abrupt and severe deprivation of blood flow to the heart may produce a full-fledged heart attack, known as a *myocardial infarction.*

The evidence connecting stress to coronary heart disease is impressive. We will review two lines of research that suggest that stress plays a significant role in both the development and recurrence of heart problems.

STRESS AS MEASURED BY THE SRRS

Many studies have measured stress with some version of the Social Readjustment Rating Scale (SRRS) (see Chapter 3) and have found a relationship between stress and coronary disease. For example, Rahe and Lind (1971) interviewed relatives of heart-attack victims to assess the amount of life change the victims had experienced during the three years preceding their coronary deaths. They found that the amount of stress during the six months prior to the heart attack was more than *triple* the baseline levels of the preceding two and one-half years. In other words, the heart attacks tended to follow periods of heavy stress. Many other studies (for example, Orth-Gomer & Ahlbom, 1980; Theorell, 1974) have yielded similar findings.

TYPE A BEHAVIOR

A pair of cardiologists, Meyer Friedman and Ray Rosenman (1974), have identified a personality syndrome, labeled the "Type A personality," that they believe is associated with a high probability of heart disease. Originally, Friedman and Rosenman were interested in the usual factors that were thought to

FIGURE 4.2 Clogging of the arteries. **A,** Normal artery. **B,** Atherosclerosis: the inner lining of the artery is thickened and roughened by fatty deposits partially impeding blood flow. **C,** Atherosclerosis and thrombosis: a blood clot (thrombus) develops on the roughened wall and further blocks the flow of blood.

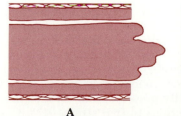
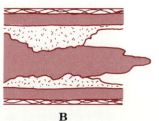
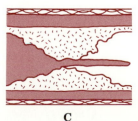

A   B   C

produce a high risk of heart attack: smoking, obesity, physical inactivity, and so forth. Although they found these factors to be important, they eventually recognized that a piece of the puzzle was missing. Many people would smoke constantly, get little exercise, and be severely overweight, yet remain immune to the ravages of heart disease. At the same time, other people who seemed to be in much better shape regarding these risk factors experienced the misfortune of a heart attack. Gradually, Friedman and Rosenman unraveled the riddle. What was their explanation for these perplexing discrepancies? Stress! Specifically, they found that people who were especially vulnerable to heart disease displayed a personality syndrome (Type A behavior) that involved exposure to a great deal of pressure and intense reactions to stress.

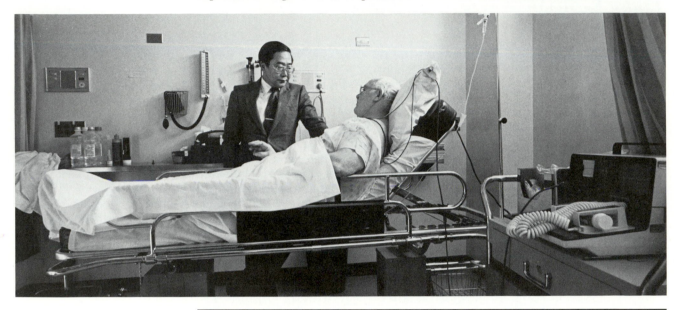

Stress probably contributed to this patient's heart attack. Unless that stress is reduced, the patient will be back—if he is lucky.

TYPE A PERSONALITY. *A personality syndrome marked by aggressiveness, competitiveness, and strong consciousness of time; differentiated from the more relaxed Type B personality syndrome. It is thought to be associated with a predisposition toward coronary disease and is sometimes called the coronary-prone personality.*

Elements.   How does the **Type A personality** behave? Type A's tend to be assertive, aggressive, competitive, and ambitious. They often are workaholics who want desperately to improve their social status. They are exceedingly time-conscious. This is perhaps their most definitive characteristic. They often try to do several things at once and fidget frantically over the briefest delay. They are so impatient that they frequently finish others' sentences for them. They are constantly trying to accomplish more and more in less and less time. To do this, they drive themselves with a multitude of deadlines. They speak rapidly and emphatically, and they are quick to anger and display hostility. (Of course, not every Type A personality will display all the characteristics in this constellation of traits.) In contrast, Type B's tend to be more relaxed, more patient, and more emotionally placid. They are less hurried, less competitive, and less time-conscious.

According to Glass (1978), the central feature of the Type A behavior pattern is a very strong need to *control* situations in general and one's outcomes in particular. This need for control leads Type A's to put themselves under an immense amount of self-imposed pressure and leads to strong reactions when that control is threatened. In terms of the model of the stress process that we constructed in Chapter 3, the Type A personality syndrome involves (1) a lifestyle that exposes people to an excessive amount of unnecessary or avoidable stress (primarily pressure) and (2) a style of coping that produces explosive emotional reactions to that stress.

Magnitude of risk. Considerable effort has been devoted to estimating the strength of the link between Type A behavior and the risk of coronary disease. Working with preliminary data, Friedman and associates originally estimated that Type A's were *six* times as prone to heart attack as Type B's (Friedman et al., 1968). More recent and more thorough data suggest that the elevation in coronary risk for Type A's is "only" about *double* that of Type B's. Actually, such ratios may be somewhat misleading anyway, in that they are based on the assumption that people can be divided clearly into the A and B categories. It seems likely that Type A and Type B personalities are better thought of as end points on a continuum, with many people falling between the extremes. If that is the case, the elevation in risk probably depends on the strength of one's Type A propensities.

Although the *strength* of the association between Type A behavior and coronary risk may be debatable, the *existence* of the link is not. The data are exceptionally clear and convincing. Particularly impressive is a recent study (Powell et al., 1984) indicating that the risk of a second heart attack in coronary patients can be reduced by therapeutic programs that decrease subjects' Type A propensities. Such programs train Type A persons to talk and move more slowly, to do only one thing at a time, to take life less seriously, to stop interrupting others, to allow themselves to lose in competitive endeavors, to wait in lines patiently, and so forth.

Unfortunately, however, Type A patterns of behavior turn out to be quite resistant to modification (Rosenman & Chesney, 1982). Our competitive Western culture values and rewards Type A behavior. Type A habits that are developed over a lifetime are deeply entrenched and are given up only very reluctantly, in spite of their dire consequences. Thus, it is a formidable challenge to get Type A's to alter their behavior.

HYPERTENSION

Taking a person's blood pressure is a routine part of virtually any kind of medical screening because high blood pressure is a very common and poten-

---

4.1 ARE YOU A TYPE A PERSONALITY?

As discussed in the text, there appears to be an association between susceptibility to heart disease and the Type A personality syndrome. Hence, you're probably wondering whether you're a Type A or Type B personality. You can use the checklist below to *estimate* the likelihood that you might be a Type A personality. However, note two precautionary points before you go through the checklist. First, it is an oversimplification to present this question as an either/or proposition. There are *degrees* of being Type A or Type B, which represent end points on a continuum. Second, the checklist should be regarded as only a rough estimate, because Friedman and Rosenman (1974) emphasize that *how* you can answer certain questions in their interview is often more significant than the answers themselves. Nonetheless, if you answer yes to a majority of the items below, you should seriously consider reading *Type A Behavior and Your Heart.*

_____ 1. Do you find it difficult to restrain yourself from hurrying others' speech (finishing their sentences for them)?

_____ 2. Do you often try to do more than one thing at a time (such as eat and read simultaneously)?

_____ 3. Do you often feel guilty if you use extra time to relax?

_____ 4. Do you tend to get involved in a multiplicity of projects at once?

_____ 5. Do you find yourself racing through yellow lights when you drive?

_____ 6. Do you need to win in order to derive enjoyment from games and sports?

_____ 7. Do you generally move, walk, and eat rapidly?

_____ 8. Do you agree to take on too many responsibilities?

_____ 9. Do you detest waiting in lines?

_____ 10. Do you have an intense desire to better your position in life and impress others?

HYPERTENSION. *A condition characterized by chronic display of abnormally high blood pressure.*

tially serious health problem. **Hypertension** is the name for the condition in which one displays a chronic elevation in blood pressure. It is estimated that over 40 million people in the United States may have hypertension, which is associated with an increased risk of premature death by virtue of several of its effects (Wing & Manton, 1983). Hypertension has been called a "silent disease" because its symptoms are mild and hardly noticeable. However, hypertension can cause or aggravate coronary problems and can cause kidney and visual disorders.

There is substantial evidence that hypertension is often stress-related. For instance, one study (Cobb & Rose, 1973) found that air traffic controllers under greater stress tended to have higher blood pressure than controllers under lesser stress. Another study (Kasl & Cobb, 1970) discovered a relationship between the stress of job loss and increased blood pressure. Researchers who have assessed stress with the SRRS and similar scales have frequently found the predicted association between high stress and hypertension in different cultures such as India (Lal, Ahuja, & Madhukar, 1982), Sweden (Svensson & Theorell, 1983), Italy (Osti, Trombini, & Magnani, 1980), and the United States (Egan et al., 1983). Thus, it seems reasonable to conclude that stress quite often makes a significant contribution to the development of hypertension.

CANCER

CANCER. *A general term that refers to malignant cell growth, which may occur in many parts of the body, leading to disruption of normal functioning in the system involved.*

If there is a single word that can strike terror into most of our hearts, it is probably *cancer.* We generally view cancer as the most menacing, lethal, sinister, tragic, loathsome, and unbearable of diseases. **Cancer** is actually a *collection* of closely related diseases. The core problem in these diseases is that cells begin to reproduce in a rapid, disorganized, and wild fashion. As this reproduction process lurches out of control, the teeming new cells clump together to form tumors. If this wild growth continues unabated, the spreading tumors create tissue damage and begin to interfere with normal physiological functioning. The causes of cancer are not well understood. It appears that a com-

---

4.2

RECOMMENDED READING

Is It Worth Dying For?

by Robert S. Eliot and Dennis L. Breo (Bantam Books, 1984)

Robert S. Eliot is the cardiologist whose recent work on "hot reactors" has been attracting attention. As you may recall (see Box 3.4), Eliot believes that some people are overly prone to heart attacks because they have an overly reactive cardiovascular response to stress. Hot reactors may or may not be Type A personalities. Hot reacting involves a *physiological propensity* that is probably greatly affected by one's genetic inheritance. Type A behavior involves *behavioral propensities* that are presumably acquired through learning over a lifetime. A person might be a hot reactor only, a Type A personality only, or both (or neither, of course). Those who are both a hot reactor and a Type A personality probably

have a *very* elevated risk of coronary problems. Eliot and Breo explain all this and much more in their highly readable book, which focuses on the connection between stress and cardiac risk. In addition to explaining how stress, hot reacting, and Type A behavior influence coronary risk, they discuss the significance of health-impairing habits such as physical inactivity, eating poorly, and smoking. They construct a nice overview of how a diverse array of factors govern cardiac vulnerability and then offer a great deal of useful advice on how to minimize your susceptibility to a heart attack.

Jeff was a living demonstration of the difference between Type A behavior

and hot reacting. He was *psychologically intense* most of the time, but he was not *physiologically intense.* His blood pressure rose a little under mental stress, as everyone's does, but it did not rise very much.

Jeff was like a person driving without a muffler—the car may make plenty of noise, but that has nothing to do with how the engine is working. It could be in great shape or it could be burning up; you can't tell from the revved-up sound. At the same time, driving without a muffler isn't a good idea—the noise is a strain on everybody else, if not on the engine. Extreme Type A behavior is worth modifying for that reason alone. Jeff's psychological overreactions kept him in enough hot water to harm the overall quality of his life [p. 53].

plex multiplicity of factors are involved. Many experts believe that there is at least a modest genetic component and that deficiencies in immune response contribute, but the evidence supporting these hypotheses is far from clear (Barofsky, 1981).

The research linking stress to cancer should probably be characterized as "thought-provoking" but hardly definitive. Taken as a whole, the evidence is not even remotely as strong as that which exists for coronary disease and hypertension. Some studies have found a connection between high stress as measured by the SRRS and the onset of cancer (for example, Jacobs & Charles, 1980), but generally the results have been very inconsistent in these kinds of investigations (Cooper, 1984). Although there is ample evidence that experimentally induced stress can affect the development of cancer in laboratory animals, the relevance of such research to humans is difficult to judge (Sklar & Anisman, 1981).

Many studies have attempted to ascertain whether there is a cancer-prone personality, which might be reflective of unsuccessful patterns of coping with stress. These studies (Kissen, 1963; LeShan, 1966) have yielded some intriguing threads of consistency, suggesting that lonely, isolated, alienated people who have difficulty expressing their feelings may have an elevated risk for cancer. However, these studies must be viewed with extreme caution in light of the very real possibility that one's personality may *change* dramatically after the discovery that one has the dreaded disease of cancer.

In conclusion, there *is* evidence linking stress to cancer, but it is weak and ambiguous. This weakness may simply reflect our general inability to pin down the causes of this very complicated and mysterious ailment. Or it may mean that the contribution of stress to the development of cancer is only a very small, marginal one. We can only hope that future research will shed more light on the matter.

PEPTIC ULCERS

PEPTIC ULCERS. *Sores, or lesions, in parts of the digestive tract exposed to gastric secretions, usually the stomach or duodenum.*

Peptic ulcers are sores that develop in the lining of the stomach or duodenum (a part of the small intestine). This very common and very painful affliction can be fatal if severe internal bleeding occurs. Although the evidence is less clear-cut than is generally believed, the preponderance of evidence does

Although the popular stereotype of the ulcer-prone executive may be misleading, there is no doubt that ulcers are related to stress.

suggest that stress often contributes to the precipitation of peptic ulcers. For instance, a recent study (Christodoulou, Alevizos, & Konstantakakis, 1983) comparing ulcer patients against control subjects found that the ulcer victims experienced more stressful life events and displayed more guilt and anxiety (emotions presumably elicited by stress) than controls.

Suggestive evidence on the link between stress and peptic ulcers has also been obtained in studies of occupational stress. One study of air traffic controllers, who perform under immense pressure (Grayson, 1972), found that an unusually high proportion (32.5%) of them suffered from ulcers. Moreover, Cobb and Rose (1973) found that ulcers were more frequent among air traffic controllers who worked in high-stress than in low-stress towers. In another study, Dunn and Cobb (1962) found a relation between stress associated with supervisory responsibility and the prevalence of peptic ulcers. Interestingly, it appears that the popular stereotype of the ulcer-prone executive may be inaccurate. In their study comparing executives, craftsmen, and foremen, Dunn and Cobb found that foremen had the most ulcers, while executives had the *fewest*. Such studies, in conjunction with animal research showing that experimentally induced stress can produce ulcers in monkeys (Brady, 1958) and rats (Weiss, 1970), suggest that peptic ulcers are frequently a stress-related condition.

ASTHMA

ASTHMA. *A disease characterized by a sudden narrowing of the bronchial airways, creating respiratory distress.*

Asthma is a common disorder involving constriction of the bronchial airways, leading to wheezing and difficulty in breathing. Asthmatic reactions can be caused by a host of factors, including infections and exposure to allergens. It has been estimated that stress may play little or no role for two-thirds of asthmatics (Williams et al., 1958). It is clear, however, that stress contributes to the condition of at least some asthmatics. This conclusion is based on demonstrations that experimentally induced stress can trigger asthmatic reactions in some subjects (Miklich et al., 1973). Other studies have found relations between asthmatic symptomatology and measures of life stress (Plutchik et al., 1978).

ILLNESS OF ANY KIND

Many studies have examined the relationship between stress and illness of *any* kind. In other words, the outcome variable is not a particular disease but, rather, any negative change in health. Holmes and Masuda (1974) summarize quite a number of studies that link high scores on the SRRS with a high incidence of physical illness in general. Figure 4.3 shows the data from one such study. As you can see, 51% of the people experiencing "moderate" stress and 79% of the people experiencing "major" stress suffered an illness of some kind. This link between stress and illness in general has been replicated by other researchers (for example, Garrity, Marx, & Somes, 1978; Rahe, 1972) with reasonable consistency. Moreover, Wyler, Masuda, and Holmes (1971) report that SRRS scores predict the *seriousness* of the subsequent illness as well as the probability of illness.

The evidence linking stress to illness in general raises the possibility that stress may influence susceptibility to virtually any illness—and, in fact, we are rapidly accumulating a large collection of studies linking stress to an incredibly wide range of health problems. Table 4.2 lists some of these. The sheer length of the list is rather intimidating. Admittedly, many of these stress/illness links must be regarded as very tentative, in that they are based on only one or two preliminary studies or a handful of contradictory studies. However, the evidence is fairly substantial for some of the health problems listed in Table 4.2 (for example, headaches, skin disorders, insomnia, and herpes).

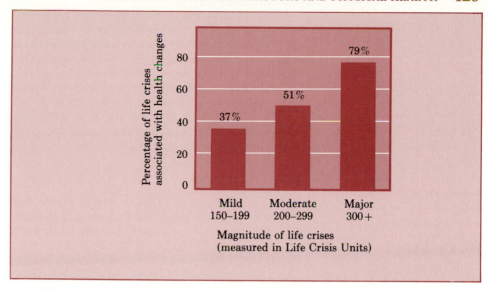

FIGURE 4.3   Percentage of life crises (as measured by the Social Readjustment Rating Scale) associated with health changes.

The apparent link between stress and illness in general raises the possibility that stress may undermine one's immune response. The research that addresses this possibility suggests that it is quite plausible. A wealth of research *on animals* indicates that experimentally induced stress can impair the immunal response (Ader, 1980). For example, crowding and shock have been found to reduce antibody production in rats (Solomon, Amkraut, & Kasper, 1974). Of course, the relevance of animal research to human physiological functioning is difficult to judge.

However, recent studies using *human* subjects *have* supported the hypothesis that stress may affect one's immune response (Gottschalk, Welch, & Weiss, 1983; Kiecolt-Glaser et al., 1984). The latter study was particularly intriguing in that it looked at the effect of an obvious, natural stressor as well as a self-

TABLE 4.2   Additional health problems that may be linked to stress

Health problem	Representative evidence
Common cold	Totman et al. (1980)
Insomnia	Healey et al. (1981)
Headaches	Featherstone and Beitman (1984)
Menstrual discomfort	Siegel, Johnson, and Sarason (1979)
Vaginal infections	Williams and Deffenbacher (1983)
Herpes	Robbins and Cotran (1979)
Skin disorders	Brown (1972)
Rheumatoid arthritis	Baker (1982)
Chronic back pain	Holmes (1979)
Female reproductive problems	Fries, Nillius, and Petersson (1974)
Complications of pregnancy	Georgas et al. (1984)
Diabetes	Bradley (1979)
Hernias	Rahe and Holmes (1965)
Glaucoma	Cohen and Hajioff (1972)
Hyperthyroidism	Weiner (1978)
Hemophilia	Buxton et al. (1981)
Tuberculosis	Wolf and Goodell (1968)
Leukemia	Greene and Swisher (1969)
Stroke	Stevens et al. (1984)

report measure of stress. In that study, medical students provided blood samples that allowed the researchers to evaluate certain components of their immune response. They provided the baseline sample a month before final exams and the high-stress sample on the first day of their finals. Lower levels of immune activity were found during the extremely stressful finals week. Reduced immune activity was also associated with higher scores on the SRRS in this population. Thus, we are beginning to accumulate some impressive evidence that stress may indeed lead to temporary impairments in our immunal functioning. This finding may shed considerable light on why stress seems to have such wide-ranging effects on physical health.

ACCIDENTS AND INJURIES

The role of stress in contributing to accidents has not attracted much publicity. However, research on this issue is remarkably consistent: nearly all the studies find that high stress is associated with an increased incidence of personal accidents. All the studies have measured stress with the SRRS or a scale patterned after it and have found some kind of link between stress and accident proneness. Thus, stress has been shown to be related to the likelihood of industrial accidents (Levenson et al., 1983), automobile accidents (Isherwood, Adam, & Hornblow, 1982), football injuries (Bramwell et al., 1975; Passer & Seese, 1983), and accidents in general (Stuart & Brown, 1981).

Although the relations between stress and accidents have been quite modest in strength, the consistency of the evidence suggests that stress elevates the probability of an accident for at least a portion of the population. There has been little speculation about the mechanisms that may underlie this apparent relationship. However, our analysis of the effects of stress in Chapter 3 suggests some possible explanations. The emotional arousal generated by stress may lead people to drive their cars aggressively (and dangerously), work too fast on the job, become reckless on the football field, and so forth. Emotional arousal can also impair cognitive functioning, leading to narrowed attention, distractibility, or poor judgment. Any of these effects could increase accident proneness in a variety of settings. Finally, when stress elicits either anger or dejection, one may simply become more careless.

CONCLUSIONS

In summary, it is clear that there is a link between stress and physical illness. However, you should not leap to the conclusion that *all* health problems are stress-related. There are still hundreds of diseases for which we have no idea whether stress might play a role, and the role of stress in the acquisition of some of the diseases discussed above is still open to argument. Nonetheless, it would seem reasonable to conclude that *stress can sometimes affect the vulnerability of some people to a great variety of health problems.* But there are qualifications to keep in mind.

- Most of the research suggests that the *strength* of the relationship between stress and health is moderate. It is clear that there are plenty of people who experience exorbitant levels of stress without becoming ill (Kobasa, 1979). There is nothing inevitable about the stress/illness connection.
- The impact of stress on physical health is influenced by many "moderator variables." In the last chapter we discussed how constitutional, experiential, personality, and social factors modulate the relationship between stress and its effects. The most crucial moderator—how you *cope* with the stress—will be discussed in the next chapter.
- Stress is only one of a number of factors that affect health and illness. It is but a single factor operating in a highly complex network that includes the person's genetic endowment, exposure to pathogens and toxins, current health status, attitudes, personal habits, and culture.

Health-Impairing Habits

Some people seem determined to dig an early grave for themselves. They do precisely those things that they have been warned are particularly bad for their health. For example, they consume liquor when they are well aware that they are corroding their liver, or they eat all the wrong foods when they know they are at risk for a second heart attack. Behavior that is downright *self-destructive* is much more common than most people realize. In fact, recent research (Kelley et al., 1984) reveals that chronic self-destructiveness is a measurable personality trait that is related to a variety of potentially harmful behaviors ranging from driving recklessly (as reflected by traffic tickets) to postponing important medical tests.

It may seem puzzling that people frequently behave in self-destructive ways. However, many of these health-impairing habits creep up on people ever so slowly. They often involve habits that initially are essentially harmless but gradually become problematic when taken to an extreme. Additionally, it appears that people have a tendency to *unrealistically underestimate the risks associated with their own health-impairing habits,* while viewing the risks associated with others' self-destructive behaviors much more accurately (Weinstein, 1984). In other words, people tend to be aware of the dangers associated with certain habits, but they often engage in *denial* when it is time to apply the information to themselves. In this section we will discuss the genesis of health-impairing habits and focus specifically on smoking, overeating, poor nutritional patterns, lack of exercise, and poor sleep habits.

SMOKING

Risks. The smoking of tobacco is widespread in our culture, with current consumption running around 4000 cigarettes a year per adult in the United States. The statistical evidence indicates quite clearly that smokers face a much greater risk of premature death than nonsmokers (Hammond & Horn, 1984). For example, a 30-year-old male who smokes two packs a day must confront an estimated life expectancy that is *eight years shorter* than that of a similar-aged nonsmoker. The overall risk is positively related to the number of cigarettes smoked and their tar and nicotine content. Cigar and pipe smoking are also associated with elevated health risks, although they are less hazardous than cigarette smoking.

Why are mortality rates higher for smokers? Because smoking increases the likelihood of developing a surprisingly large range of particular diseases, many of which are highly lethal (see Figure 4.4). These diseases include heart disease, cancer, ulcers, bronchitis, emphysema, and stroke (Insel & Roth, 1976).

Why do people smoke? A great variety of factors influence whether people acquire the habit of smoking. Tobacco companies spend millions of dollars to convince us that it is the thing to do. Parents, friends, and co-workers provide an abundance of role models who smoke. Many people find the pharmacological effects of nicotine to be quite pleasant; thus, the act of smoking is reinforced on a very regular basis. Although most people have been warned about the dangers of smoking, it is sometimes easy to ignore risks that typically lie 10, 20, or 30 years down the road.

Although acquisition of the smoking habit is complicated, the difficulty people have in giving up smoking is easy to explain. *Nicotine use gradually leads to a bona fide physical dependence,* commonly called an addiction (Jones-Witters & Witters, 1983). As discussed in our upcoming application section on drugs, it is extremely difficult to overcome physical dependence on a drug. Although it certainly is not impossible to "beat" a physical dependence, the immense difficulty in giving up cigarette smoking is illustrated by the fact that the long-term success rates are only around 25% (Hunt & Matarazzo, 1982).

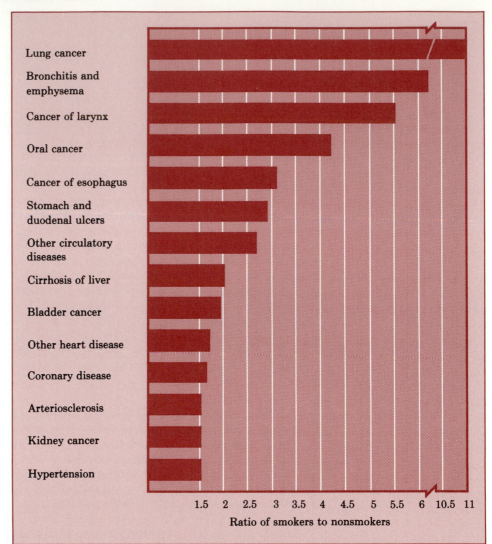

Lung cancer
Bronchitis and emphysema
Cancer of larynx
Oral cancer
Cancer of esophagus
Stomach and duodenal ulcers
Other circulatory diseases
Cirrhosis of liver
Bladder cancer
Other heart disease
Coronary disease
Arteriosclerosis
Kidney cancer
Hypertension

1.5 2 2.5 3 3.5 4 4.5 5 5.5 6 10.5 11
Ratio of smokers to nonsmokers

FIGURE 4.4 Increased ratio of smoker deaths from 14 kinds of disorders. For example, a smoker is more than 11 times as likely to develop lung cancer as a nonsmoker. (Data are from the U.S. Department of Health, Education, and Welfare, *The Health Consequences of Smoking,* 1973.)

OVEREATING AND OBESITY

OBESITY. *The condition of being overweight.*

Like smoking, **obesity** is a very common health problem, affecting as many as 70 million people in the United States. Obesity is also similar to smoking in that it exerts a relatively subtle impact on health that is easy for many people to ignore. Though subtle, the long-range effects of obesity can be quite dangerous. The evidence indicates that overweight people have an increased risk of heart disease, hypertension, stroke, respiratory problems, arthritis, diabetes, gall bladder disease, and back problems (Jeffrey & Lemnitzer, 1981).

Of course, overeating is not the sole cause of obesity. Many factors may contribute. It appears that obesity runs in families (Johnson, Burke, & Mayer, 1956), thereby raising the possibility of a genetic predisposition to the problem. Of course, there are other possible explanations; it may be that obese parents simply overfeed their children and expose them to excessive eating habits. The children are quite likely to copy their parents and thereby acquire poor eating habits of their own. Hence, because it is difficult to separate hereditary and environmental factors, we are not sure whether there is a genetically transmitted susceptibility to obesity.

ADIPOCYTES. *Specialized cells that store body fat in the form of fatty acids.*

There is also evidence (Boshell, 1974) that obese people have both a greater number of **adipocytes** (cells used to store fat) and larger adipocytes than normal people. Since the sheer number of fat cells in a human stops increasing sometime in adolescence, there is speculation that excessive eating during childhood may lead to an overabundance of oversized fat cells in adulthood. Speculation along this line further suggests that the affected adults may find it particularly difficult to lose weight later in life. It is also true that people vary in their **basal metabolic rate** (Whitney & Hamilton, 1977), so that some people "burn off" calories faster than others. Thus, it is clear that many physiological factors may influence the development of obesity.

BASAL METABOLIC RATE. *The rate of energy output of a body at rest after a 12-hour fast.*

While a variety of physiological factors may influence vulnerability to obesity, eating and exercise habits appear to be the crucial determinants. In particular, chronic overeating plays a very prominent role. Why is overeating such a routine habit for so many people? Stanley Schachter (1971) has advanced the hypothesis that obese people are overly sensitive to *external cues* that affect their hunger while being relatively insensitive to internal physiological cues that signal the true need for food. According to this notion, fat people pay little attention to messages from their stomachs, while responding to external cues such as the availability of food, the attractiveness of the food, and the time of day. This formulation suggests that obese people overeat because they cannot ignore environmental cues that trigger "hunger." For example, people who are not really hungry may be stimulated to pursue food simply by seeing a delicious-looking commercial on TV or by driving by the infamous golden arches. Such people often walk into a restaurant intending to eat very little but then have their hunger inflated by reading the menu or by seeing others' appetizing meals. Although Schachter's theory is still being refined (see Rodin, 1981), the notion that hypersensitivity to external eating cues plays a key role in the development of obesity continues to be a worthwhile insight. It provides the theoretical basis for a variety of useful strategies in weight-loss programs, which we will discuss in the application section of Chapter 5.

POOR NUTRITIONAL PATTERNS

NUTRITION AND HEALTH

NUTRITION. *A collection of processes (mainly food consumption) through which an organism receives and utilizes the materials (nutrients) required for survival and growth. Also refers to the study of these processes.*

Evidence is accumulating that patterns of **nutrition** influence susceptibility to a variety of diseases and health problems above and beyond the risks associated with obesity. An illustrative list of possible connections between food consumption patterns and particular diseases would include the following.

1. Heavy consumption of foods that elevate serum cholesterol level (eggs, cheeses, butter, shellfish, sausage, pizza, and the like) appears to increase the risk of heart disease (Luke, 1984).
2. High salt intake has long been thought to be a contributing factor to the development of hypertension (Friedewald, 1982), although there is still some debate about its role.
3. General malnutrition appears to undermine some aspects of our immune response (Law, Dudrick, & Abdou, 1973).
4. Diets high in fats have been implicated as possible contributors to some forms of cancer (Armstrong & Doll, 1975; Modan, 1977).
5. Certain *patterns* of sugar consumption (not sugar itself) may hasten the onset of diabetes in some people (Mayer, 1980).
6. Certain vitamin deficiencies can definitely cause a variety of diseases, although these afflictions are not seen in North America as often as in "underdeveloped" countries (Whitney & Cataldo, 1983).
7. Caffeine consumption may produce restlessness, nervousness, and insomnia in some individuals, and there is some very tentative evidence linking caffeine to pancreatic cancer (Jones-Witters & Witters, 1983).

In all these examples, the potentially problematic nutritional habits operate in conjunction with other factors to determine whether one develops a particular illness, making it difficult to estimate just how important nutritional factors may be. Nonetheless, the potential negative impact of our eating habits on our health certainly merits concern.

NUTRITIONAL FADS

The evidence just summarized clearly indicates that nutritional habits can increase one's susceptibility to certain diseases. However, many popular books and articles suggest that this nutrition/health link can be taken one step further and that large doses of vitamins or heavy reliance on particular foods can *raise* one's resistance to exceptionally high levels, conveying virtual immunity to some forms of illness. A prime example of this line of thought would be Pauling's (1970, 1980) assertion that vitamin C can prevent both cancer and the common cold. Rather extravagant claims have also been made for the benefits of vitamin E, the B vitamins, high-fiber diets, and some minerals and vegetables. The last couple of decades have seen the emergence of quite a number of nutritional fads based on such claims.

What is the current thinking of nutritional experts on this issue? Can "meganutrition" provide "super-resistance" to disease? According to Whitney and Cataldo (1983), *probably not*. In their excellent nutrition text, they review the evidence for many such claims and conclude that the findings do not support such claims in most instances and are inconclusive at best. There is little evidence that highly touted nutritional extremes can prevent disease.

Whitney and Cataldo note that books promoting all sorts of miraculous nutritional formulas are legion. Unfortunately, a great many of them are scientifically unsound and misleading. In fact, Whitney and Cataldo list 74 popular books about nutrition that they characterize as "not recommended." Although most of these offer groundless but harmless advice, it is important to realize that extreme nutritional patterns can sometimes be dangerous. For example, there is evidence that megadoses of vitamin E can actually be physically damaging (Prasad, 1980).

In conclusion, it appears that one's health can best be served by following well-moderated food consumption strategies that simply ensure nutritional adequacy while limiting the intake of certain substances that can be counterproductive. In Chapter 5 we will offer some general guidelines for achieving these goals.

LACK OF EXERCISE

Recently, James Fixx, the noted author of several books touting the great benefits of running, died from a heart attack *while out jogging*. All over the country, people who rarely exercise probably nodded their heads knowingly and made comments about exercise having little real value, so as to rationalize their own lack of exercise. It will be extremely unfortunate if Fixx's death becomes a widespread excuse for complacency about fitness, because there is considerable evidence that there is a link between exercise and health. Admittedly, the relationship appears to be more modest than suggested by many fitness proponents. It is true that you can be a fitness and nutritional "saint" and still not be immune to disease. Nonetheless, it is clear that a lack of exercise is *not* in your best interests in the long run.

The relationship between physical inactivity and increased risk of heart disease is extremely well documented (Peters et al., 1983). There is little doubt that lack of exercise heightens vulnerability to coronary problems. Additionally, insofar as physical inactivity promotes obesity, it is related indirectly to increased risk for a variety of health problems, including diabetes, respiratory difficulties, hypertension, and stroke. In particular, though, lack of exercise is most strongly related to the very serious health problems that originate in the cardiovascular system (heart attack, hypertension, and stroke).

In contrast, the potential benefits of regular exercise are substantial. First, regular exercise can increase your physical endurance (Johnson et al., 1975). Improved endurance should mean that you become fatigued less easily, and this reduction in fatigue should keep you closer to your maximal coping abili-

CATHY

ties. Moreover, insofar as fatigue affects your immune response, greater endurance *may* improve your resistance to infection (Zimkin, 1961). Second, an appropriate exercise program can enhance your cardiovascular fitness and thereby reduce your susceptibility to deadly cardiovascular diseases (Froelicher et al., 1984). Third, participation in a successful exercise program can have positive effects on your self-concept. There is evidence that systematic exercise can produce personality change. A recent review of relevant research (Folkins & Sime, 1981) concludes that fitness training can lead to improved mood, a more favorable self-concept, and greater work efficiency. Another recent study (McCann & Holmes, 1984) suggests that a systematic aerobic exercise program can help to elevate one out of feelings of depression.

It is important to note, however, that exercise programs have their own hazards. For example, jogging clearly elevates one's risk of muscular and skeletal injuries (it's especially hard on the knees) and can elicit heat stroke and possibly even a heart attack (Koplan et al., 1982). The fact that exercise can both improve cardiovascular health and cause a heart attack may seem paradoxical. However, the contradiction was easily explained in a recent study (Siscovick et al., 1984). It was found that men who participated in regular, *habitual* exercise activity lowered their cardiac risk. However, vigorous exercise itself does temporarily (during the exercise) increase cardiac risk—but almost exclusively among those who do not exercise habitually. Although James Fixx's death appears inconsistent with the assertion that exercise decreases cardiac risk, it should be pointed out that Fixx took up jogging because he knew there was a history of heart problems in his family. In other words, he may have carried a hereditary vulnerability to heart attack that might have killed him 20 years earlier if it weren't for his regular exercise (his father had had his first heart attack at age 35). Furthermore, a physician friend of Fixx's asserts that he failed to heed medical advice that might have averted the heart attack (Wallis, 1984), so that noncompliance with professional advice, a health-impairing habit that we will discuss momentarily, may have contributed to his controversial death. In any case, it is critical that one's exercise program be carefully planned so as to minimize the risks and maximize the benefits. We will discuss how to achieve these goals in Chapter 5.

POOR SLEEP HABITS

Sleep is an element in our lives whose importance should not be underestimated. On one occasion or another, you have probably had to try to function on an inadequate amount of sleep. If at such times you suffered from fatigue, headaches, and poor concentration, you know from personal experience just how damaging a lack of sleep can be to you.

The scientific evidence on sleep deprivation confirms that adequate sleep is necessary for most of us to function effectively. Research has shown that total or even partial sleep deprivation may produce difficulty in concentration, childish behavior, poor reality contact, aggressiveness, reduced interpersonal effectiveness, poor performance on various kinds of laboratory tasks, reduced motivation, hallucinations, and severe psychological disturbance (Webb, 1973). However, the impact of sleep deprivation is highly variable. Some people can handle lengthy periods without sleep and show relatively few ill effects (Ross, 1965). Furthermore, there is evidence that too *much* sleep may lead to fatigue and inept performance on tasks requiring alertness (Taub & Burger, 1969). The link between lack of sleep and physical health is only modestly problematic because sleep deprivation has a self-limiting quality. Generally, people can go only so long without sleep, so that massive sleep deprivation is relatively unusual. Nonetheless, there is evidence (Palmblad, 1981) to support the notion that sleep deprivation reduces the effectiveness of our immune response, making us more vulnerable to infectious agents.

REM sleep.   The sheer amount of sleep that you get is not the only important consideration. It appears that the *kind* of sleep that you get may also be relevant. Scientists have discovered that after we fall asleep, we go through a series of stages, during which the quality of our sleep changes. Typically, sleep is divided into five stages, which most of us revolve through in a cyclical fashion about four times each night. A rather special, deep stage of sleep (that is, a stage from which it is difficult to awaken you) is commonly called **REM sleep.** REM is an abbreviation for "rapid eye movements." One of the more noticeable signs of this stage of sleep is rapid, lateral eye movements that take place beneath the closed eyelids. This stage of sleep is also accompanied by relatively little muscular activity and large fluctuations in autonomic functions. Interestingly, it appears that *most* dreaming occurs during this stage, and your brain activity, as measured by an **electroencephalograph,** is surprisingly similar to that displayed while awake (Webb, 1973).

REM deprivation.   Of interest to us is the evidence that a lack of REM sleep may have detrimental effects similar to those of *total* sleep deprivation. Dement (1960) monitored sleep activity and prevented subjects from getting any REM sleep by awakening them just as they went into the REM stage. These subjects were able to get a reasonable amount of sleep (in other stages) but were deprived of REM sleep. Surprisingly, the REM deprivation led to negative effects such as heightened irritability, anxiety, and fatigue. This evidence suggests that not only do we need sleep, we also need "good quality" sleep, including a certain amount of REM sleep. Most adults spend about 20% of their total sleep time in the REM stage (Webb & Agnew, 1968). Although this exact proportion is not essential for everyone, it is clear that the task of getting proper sleep is more complex than most people realize. We will discuss this task in more detail in Chapter 5.

REM SLEEP. *A deep stage of sleep, during which there are rapid lateral eye movements beneath the closed eyelids; the stage of sleep during which most dreaming occurs.*

ELECTROENCEPHALO-GRAPH (EEG). *An elaborate electronic device used to record the electrical activity of the brain. Electrodes are attached to the scalp, and the recorded electrical activity is translated into line tracings, which are commonly called brain waves.*

Reactions to Illness
THE PERCEPTION OF PAIN

We tend to think of pain as a purely organic sensation resulting from some sort of tissue damage in the body. However, research in recent years has made it clear that the organic model of pain is much too simple. It fails to account for the fact that a host of psychological variables can affect the experience of pain (Steger & Fordyce, 1982). These include the individual's expectations, anxiety or tension level, personality, and previous conditioning. Pain is not a simple sensory effect. It is a complex, multifaceted perceptual experience that is very

The experience of pain is ultimately psychological. Some people learn to live with it.

much affected by subjective psychological factors. This reality is easy to illustrate. Let's say you're working in your basement at home and you hit your thumb with a hammer. Several hours later your thumb is still throbbing with excruciating pain, when your mother screams from the kitchen that there's a fire in the oven. As you race to her assistance to combat this emergency, your perception of pain in your thumb will almost certainly dwindle dramatically. Your experience of pain will have been altered substantially, even though the organic basis for the pain remains constant. If you doubt the subjective basis of pain, just ask a nurse who routinely gives the same shots to many patients. You will surely be told that different patients display an exceptionally wide range of pain reactions to essentially the same stimulus.

The above examples involve *acute* pain from specific sources of tissue damage. The evidence indicates that *chronic,* long-lasting pain of unclear origin (such as lower back pain) is even more affected by psychological considerations. The highly psychological nature of many chronic pain problems helps to account for the only modest success of medical treatment of chronic pain, with improvement rates typically ranging between 30% and 60% (Gatchel & Baum, 1983). The increasing recognition of the psychological basis of pain has led to the development of behavioral treatment programs for pain management. These new treatment regimens involve a variety of intervention procedures discussed in subsequent sections of this book, including relaxation training, behavior modification, cognitive restructuring, hypnosis, and biofeedback.

THE DECISION TO SEEK TREATMENT

It follows logically from our discussion of pain perception that judgments of health in general are quite subjective and that the distinction between health and illness is often quite blurred. Physical sensations that *could* be labeled "symptoms" are experienced by nearly everyone with much greater regularity than most people realize (Mechanic, 1972). Whether they are actually viewed as symptoms is a matter of interpretation that depends on the individual. If two persons experience exactly the same symptoms, one might shrug them off as a minor nuisance, while the other might rush to a physician. Thus, there are great differences among people in their readiness to seek treatment.

In regard to treatment seeking, the biggest problem is the tendency of many people to delay the pursuit of needed professional consultation. This consideration is of crucial importance because early diagnosis can facilitate more effective treatment of many health problems. A number of factors are associated with delaying professional consultation. Sex is one of these, as males are more prone than females to put off the act of seeking treatment (Mechanic, 1972). There is a weak tendency for lower education and socioeconomic status to be associated with greater delay (Rosenstock & Kirscht, 1979). This may be because it is more costly for people from the lower socioeconomic strata to seek care, as they often have less insurance, fewer sick days, and so forth. In terms of personality, locus of control seems to affect treatment seeking in complicated ways (Gatchel & Baum, 1983). People with an internal locus of control appear to be more likely to actively confront illness. However, this may lead to delay in utilization of professional services as the person engages in some self-diagnosis and self-treatment activities.

THE SICK ROLE

Some people are positively eager to seek professional care. These are people who have learned that once they are designated as "sick," they have a legitimate exemption from various responsibilities and obligations. Such people learn that the "sick role" can produce benefits that sometimes outweigh its negative aspects (Parsons, 1979). Fewer demands are placed on sick people, who often can selectively decide which to ignore. In conjunction with the reduction in demands, sick people often find themselves the center of attention. This increase in attention from others can be very rewarding to many people. Moreover, much of the attention is positive, in that the sick person is showered with affection, concern, and sympathy. As you can readily understand, some people find that they like the sick role (often unconsciously). Such people tend to behave in subtle ways that are likely to prolong their illness.

NONCOMPLIANCE WITH PROFESSIONAL ADVICE

Extent of the problem.   A problem that surfaces surprisingly often is that many patients fail to cooperate with the instructions of health care professionals. It is difficult to estimate precisely the extent of this problem, as many patients are not eager to admit their failure to comply with instructions. None-

---

4.3 CHOOSING A PHYSICIAN

Selection of a physician is a very important decision. In spite of its importance, however, many people merely make a random selection out of the Yellow Pages or leave the matter to fate, taking whomever they get when a problem forces them to head for an emergency room. It is ironic indeed that many people put more thought and effort into the selection of a painter, mechanic, or house cleaner.

One reason people leave this matter to fate is that they assume that since they know nothing about medicine, they cannot make any judgments about the quality of a physician's services. Although it is undeniably true that a physician has special expertise that you lack, you can still tell whether a doctor is sensitive, thorough, well organized, and so forth. People who know nothing about automobiles still evaluate the apparent competence of mechanics when they inquire about getting their car fixed. You do not have to be an expert in order to evaluate one. (You're probably not hesitant to evaluate your professors, although they too have great expertise that you lack.)

The other reason that people do not take a more active role in choosing a physician is that they assume, in light of physicians' extensive and demanding training, that physicians must all be superbly talented and competent in all facets and areas of medicine. Unfortunately, that is an unreasonable assumption. Incompetence exists in all fields. Consider the incompetent plumbers, porters, professors, photographers, pastors, and police officers that you have encountered in the past—and you should realize that medicine has not been spared. It is important to understand that there are some physicians who are not as competent as we would like to believe. When you assume that all physicians are competent, you are accepting what has been called the "medical mystique" (Belsky & Gross, 1975), the image of physicians as brilliant, omniscient, infallible, godlike masters of a nearly mystical craft who must be revered, deferred to, and held in awe. It would be nice if all that were true, but alas, M.D.s are only human.

So what should you look for in a physician? A large, fancy office? Lots of diplomas and certificates on the walls? Degrees from prestigious schools? Spellbinding mastery of medical jargon? No, all these are superficial symbols that provide no assurance of good care. The qualities you should look for are more subtle. The following characteristics are highly desirable:

1. A good physician should treat you with respect and show a genuine interest in you. Try to avoid physicians who take an adult/child approach to the doctor/patient relationship and those who practice "assembly line" medicine.

2. A good physician must be thorough. One simply cannot practice medicine effectively without a complete history and physical for a patient. If your physician strikes you as methodical, that's a good sign.

3. It is reasonable to expect a physician to run a well-organized, businesslike office. It is not inconceivable that quality care might emerge from chaos and disarray, but it is relatively unlikely.

4. A talented physician will respect your right to ask questions. The "assembly line" mentality, personal insecurity, and disrespect for patients lead many physicians to actively discourage questions. Such discouragement hampers effective communication and deprives you of your right to self-determination in your medical care.

5. A considerate physician will talk to you in everyday language for the most part. Discussion of technical matters may require the use of some technical terms. However, beware of doctors who try to intimidate you with unintelligible jargon. It is crucial that you understand what your doctor says. If you don't—ASK! A thorough understanding of your illness and recommended treatment is important, both to your recovery and to your satisfaction as a patient.

Quality medical care depends on more than finding a good doctor; it is also facilitated if you are a good patient. It is extremely important that you cooperate with advice and instructions. If you have doubts about the advice, speak up; do not passively resist by ignoring the advice while pretending to go along with it. Disguised noncompliance is not in your best interests.

theless, studies suggest that noncompliance occurs somewhere between one-third and one-half of the time (DiMatteo & Friedman, 1982). Such estimates indicate that noncompliance is a significant barrier to the provision of effective medical care. The consequences of noncompliance can reverberate beyond the obvious to hinder treatment in complicated ways. If a physician sees no improvement in a patient because of well-camouflaged noncompliance, the physician may reassess and abandon an accurate diagnosis in favor of a new, inaccurate one. An inappropriate approach to treatment might result.

Reasons for noncompliance. Why don't people adhere to the advice and instructions that they have sought out from highly regarded physicians? There are many possible reasons (DiMatteo & Friedman, 1982; Gatchel & Baum, 1983). Among the more prominent are the following.

- Some people probably have uncooperative personalities that lead them to ignore advice and instructions from a wide range of authority figures. Their noncompliance is deeply rooted in their personalities and not unique to the medical context.
- A key factor centers on how aversive or difficult the instructions are. If a prescribed drug has unpleasant side effects, this increases the probability of noncompliance. If a prescribed regimen is difficult to follow (such as giving up cigarettes), noncompliance is likely. The more that following instructions interferes with routine behavior, the less probable it is that the patient will cooperate successfully.
- Frequently, noncompliance is attributable to a failure by the patient to fully understand the instructions as given. Highly trained professionals often forget that what seems obvious and simple to them may be obscure and complex for many of their patients.
- If a patient has a negative attitude toward a physician, this will tend to increase the probability of noncompliance. When patients are dissatisfied with their interactions with the doctor, they are more likely to ignore the medical advice.

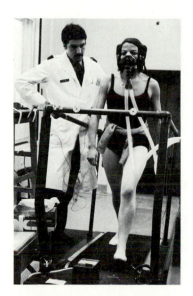

Signs of physical illness should not be ignored. When in doubt, one should seek appropriate diagnostic testing and treatment and comply with the physician's instructions.

Summary

The changing nature of modern stress has made our built-in fight-or-flight response to stress largely obsolete. This reality, coupled with the gradual conquest of contagious diseases, has made stress-related diseases the premier threat to health in our modern society. These trends have led us to adopt a biopsychosocial model of illness, which rejects the premise that disease is purely organic in origin.

Of course, biological factors continue to influence our health. Foremost among these are genetic factors. Also influential is exposure to pathogens such as bacteria or viruses. The probability of infection hinges on the quality of our immune resistance to such agents. Toxic substances in the environment may also damage our health through direct physiological processes.

Physical health may be affected by three behavioral mechanisms: the direct effects of stress, health-impairing habits, and reactions to illness. The link between stress and illness is most firmly established with regard to coronary heart disease. In particular, Type A behavior appears to double one's risk of heart disease.

It is also clear that hypertension is often stress-related. In contrast, the connection between stress and cancer is not well documented and may be relatively weak. There is ample evidence that many cases of peptic ulcers and asthma are stress-related. Research on whether stress contributes to accidents is in its infancy, but the findings to date are quite consistent in suggesting that there is at least a modest connection.

Studies also indicate that stress is related to the onset of illness in general. Although it is beginning to appear that nearly all types of illness may have the potential to be stress-related, the stress/illness relationship is probably moderate in strength, and stress is but one factor in a complex network of determinants that govern our health.

Health-impairing habits often seem harmless initially but can become very problematic. Smoking, which is related to a wide range of specific diseases, is difficult to give up because nicotine can produce physical dependence. Obesity, which creates similar health risks, appears to be due mainly to overeating and lack of exercise. However, a variety of physiological factors may influence one's susceptibility to being overweight. A variety of poor nutritional patterns have been shown to influence one's risk for many physical maladies. Unfortunately, nutritional fads do not provide the kind of protection against disease that their proponents suggest. Lack of exercise is linked most strongly to cardiovascular risk, although it may affect other health problems as well. Poor sleep habits have largely temporary effects on health because of the self-limiting nature of sleep deprivation.

The perception of pain is highly subjective, as are reactions to possible symptoms of illness. The most crucial problem is that many people delay seeking the professional treatment that they need. At the other end of the continuum, many people find the rewards of the sick role rather attractive and work to prolong their illnesses. Noncompliance with professional instructions represents a widespread problem that complicates and hinders effective medical care.

Our upcoming application section will discuss a very hazardous health-impairing habit that has become widespread: recreational drug use. We will try in this section to objectively summarize the risks associated with the use of various recreational drugs in order to promote more informed and intelligent decisions about drug use.

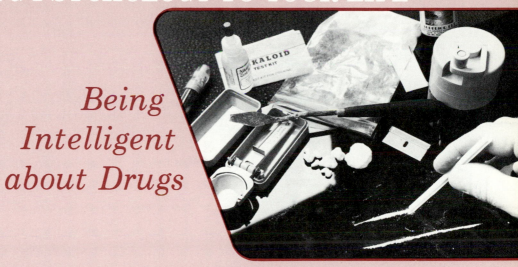

Being Intelligent about Drugs

True or false?

_____ 1. The most dangerous form of withdrawal is that associated with heroin use.

_____ 2. Overdose is a serious danger with LSD.

_____ 3. Amphetamines are physically addictive.

_____ 4. It is well documented that LSD causes chromosome damage.

_____ 5. Marijuana is a harmless drug.

The statements above are common myths about drugs. You will learn in this application section that all the above assertions are more false than true. If you answered all the questions accurately, you may already be very intelligent about drugs. If not, you *should* be. Regulating drug intake is a major health issue for many people in our modern society. Actually, the issue is not new. Although many people believe that controversy about drugs is a modern phenomenon, the reality is that many ancient cultures had ferocious debates about drug use. Nonetheless, technology has created a new era as far as drugs are concerned. Never before have so many drugs, of such great potency, been so widely available. Thus, the issue of drug use is uniquely important in our modern world.

The exact prevalence of drug use in our society is difficult to estimate. Since the use of many drugs is illegal, people tend to be less than candid about their drug habits. It is instructive, however, to examine a recent survey (Pope, Ionescu-Pioggia, & Cole, 1981) of a collegiate population. The results of that survey can be seen in Figure 4.5. It is readily apparent that alcohol and marijuana are used extensively by college students. Moreover, over 30% of the respondents report trying cocaine, and over 20% have experimented with hallucinogens and amphetamines. Although drug use by college students gets the lion's share of publicity, there is reason to believe that problematic drug use extends into every corner of our society. Illustrative of this reality is the fact that Valium, a drug usually obtained legitimately by prescription, generates far more hospital emergency-room visits per year than heroin and Quaaludes combined (McKinley, 1978).

Most discussions of drugs center on the concept of **drug abuse;** this one will not. *Drug abuse* refers to any drug use that is not approved of by one's

DRUG ABUSE. *Drug use that is not condoned by one's society or relevant reference group. This concept is different from "substance-use disorder," which is a more precise and less value-laden concept.*

SALLY FORTH

BY GREG HOWARD

© BY AND PERMISSION OF NEWS AMERICA SYNDICATE.

society or reference group. This is a value judgment that varies greatly from one culture to another, and even within a particular society there may be considerable disagreement. In our society, most nonmedical drug use is officially considered wrong. However, sizable segments of our society have embraced "recreational" drug use. It appears highly unlikely that this reality will be altered in the foreseeable future.

This discussion will assume that whether we like it or not, recreational drug use is here to stay. Without a doubt, recreational drug use is a potentially health-impairing habit, just like smoking, overeating, and so on. In fact, as health-impairing habits go, it ranks as a very, very dangerous one. Dangerous as it may be, however, its perils are often exaggerated by ardent opponents of recreational drug use. Such people, who are quite reasonably and understandably concerned about the drug problem in modern Western society, tend to overstate the case against recreational drugs. Thus, we frequently find researchers, writers, and educators suspending their critical thinking skills as they naively accept and perpetuate many drug myths in order to mount a devastating attack on recreational drugs. For instance, a former president of the American Medical Association garnered widespread headlines in 1971 when he declared that marijuana "makes a man of 35 sexually like a man of 70." As you will learn in this application section, there is no basis for such an assertion.

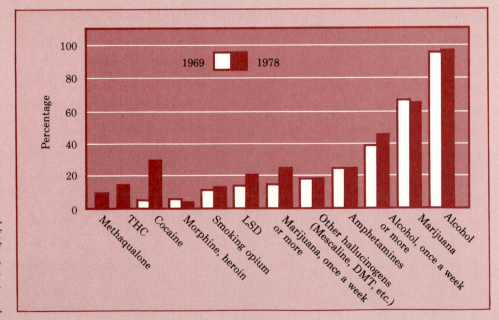

FIGURE 4.5 Percentage of respondents reporting use of various drugs in 1969 and in 1978 (THC, tetrahydrocannabinol; DMT, dimethyltryptamine).

This influential physician acknowledged that reality later when he retracted the statement, admitting that he said it simply to campaign against marijuana use (Leavitt, 1982). Unfortunately, such "scare tactics" often backfire because their heavy-handed, unrealistic, and one-sided nature undermine the source's credibility. Listeners then dismiss everything that such a person has to say, even though many of the other statements about drug risks may be quite accurate.

Cognizant of the credibility problems inherent in these moralistic, one-sided indictments of recreational drugs, we will endeavor to provide a nonjudgmental, objective, realistic review of the risks associated with recreational drug use. When evidence on an issue is lacking, ambiguous, or widely misconstrued, we will be candid about that reality. Our intent is simply to make you more knowledgeable about drugs so that you can make intelligent decisions on your own. In other words, we will try to educate you rather than scare you. This approach will differ substantially from the traditional approach centered on the concept of drug abuse. The traditional approach assumes that drug abuse is pathological and devotes much attention to *why* people misuse drugs. Undoubtedly, drug use *can* be pathological, and we will discuss **substance-use disorders** in Chapter 13. However, research evidence does not support the assumption that illicit drug use is inherently pathological. Studies such as that by Pope et al. (1981) find no differences between drug users and nonusers in regard to grades, college activities, career plans, and so forth. If users and nonusers are largely indistinguishable, it is difficult to defend the assumption that drug use is a sign of sickness and weakness.

Hence, we will take the following position: There is really little mystery about *why* people use drugs. They use them to get "high." These substances are ingested in order to produce a pleasant state of consciousness. Even rats, who presumably are not concerned about peer-group pressure, rebellion, or alienation, will voluntarily consume morphine, barbiturates, and amphetamines (Pickens, Meisch, & Thompson, 1978). Thus, the crucial question is not "Why do people use drugs?" but, rather, "What are the risks involved in drug use?" To provide you with an answer to that question, we will describe the various recreational drugs and their effects and then summarize the evidence on how hazardous they may be to one's physical and mental health.

SUBSTANCE-USE DISORDERS. *Pathological patterns of drug use marked by frequent intoxication, noticeable impairment of functioning, and psychological and/or physiological dependence.*

DRUG-RELATED CONCEPTS

Many drug-related terms, such as *addiction,* are used in a variety of ways, thereby creating confusion. Consequently, before discussing drug effects and risks, we need to define certain key concepts.

DRUG

DRUG. *A chemical substance (other than food) that alters psychological and physiological processes.*

A **drug** is simply any chemical substance, other than food, that modifies a person's physiological and/or psychological functioning when ingested. This includes preparations available over the counter, medically useful drugs requiring a prescription, and illicitly produced drugs acquired through the "black market." This definition also encompasses alcoholic beverages.

TOLERANCE

TOLERANCE. *A gradual reduction in an organism's responsiveness to a drug with repeated use.*

Tolerance refers to a progressive decrease in a person's responsiveness to a drug. With continued use, a person's body often comes to "tolerate" the presence of a drug. Because of this tendency, larger and larger doses of the drug are needed to attain the same effect.

PHYSICAL DEPENDENCE

PHYSICAL DEPENDENCE. *Condition brought on by repeated drug use in which termination of drug use leads to extreme physical distress.*

Physical dependence occurs when a person's body comes to depend on the presence of a drug in order to function normally. This is what was originally

ADDICTION. *Condition resulting from repetitive use of a drug in which physical dependence is established.*

meant by the term **addiction;** however, in popular usage *addiction* gradually came to encompass psychological dependence as well. To avoid confusion, we will use the terms *physical* and *psychological dependence.* The definitive feature of physical dependence is the occurrence of a **withdrawal syndrome** when use of the drug is stopped. The symptoms of withdrawal vary depending on the drug, but they commonly include fever, chills, vomiting, cramps, diarrhea, and aches and pains. The great physical distress associated with withdrawal virtually compels a person who is physically dependent on a drug to continue using it.

WITHDRAWAL SYNDROME. *Physical distress resulting from the cessation of use of a particular drug. This is the definitive sign that physical dependence on the drug has been established.*

PSYCHOLOGICAL DEPENDENCE

PSYCHOLOGICAL DEPENDENCE. *Mental and emotional dependence on a drug.*

Psychological dependence occurs when a person comes to depend mentally and emotionally on the presence of a drug in order to feel satisfied. In psychological dependence, a person experiences emotional rather than physical distress when the drug is unavailable. This condition is much more subtle than physical dependence. It can vary in intensity from a keen appetite for the drug to an insatiable craving.

OVERDOSE

OVERDOSE. *Excessive dose of a drug that will seriously threaten one's health.*

We will use the term **overdose** to refer to drug consumption sufficiently excessive to seriously threaten one's physical health. In other words, we are talking about a physically damaging dosage of a drug or combination of drugs. Used narrowly in this way, the term *overdose* does not include severe mental distress, such as a "bad trip," caused by ingesting some drug. This is not included under *overdose* because such psychological distress is not very strongly related to dosage. It can occur at low dose levels.

EFFECTS AND RISKS OF VARIOUS DRUGS

Now that our basic vocabulary is spelled out, we can examine the effects of various popular recreational drugs. We will, of course, be describing the typical, or modal, effects of each drug. Please bear in mind that the effects of any drug depend on the dosage, the user's unique physiology, the manner of ingestion, the expectations of the user, and the setting in which the drug is taken.

The discussion will draw extensively from two excellent texts on drugs (Dusek & Girdano, 1980; Julien, 1975). For potentially controversial points, however, we will cite specific sources.

RECOMMENDED READING

4.4

Drugs: A Factual Account

by Dorothy Dusek and Daniel A. Girdano (Addison-Wesley, 1980)

Although rather slender in size, this book provides a thorough and well-documented introduction to the topic of drug use. It is intended primarily for undergraduate students and is highly readable. A nice feature is that the authors place drugs in their social context. Historical and legal issues are discussed, along with the effects of various drugs. The book begins with a discussion of why people use drugs. Then, after providing a brief introduction to physiology, the authors examine specific categories of drugs. The coverage includes legal as well as illegal drugs.

Cocaine is one of the oldest drugs known with recorded use dating back hundreds of years. Coca's oldest use was in religious ceremonies as an inducer of meditative trance and as an aid for communicating with nature. The Incas reserved coca use for the nobility and priests, and those who were granted permission to use it were in extreme imperial favor. The leaves were offered in sacrifice to the gods, chewed during worship, and placed into the mouths of the dead to ensure a favorable welcome in the next life. For a while after the Spanish conquest of Peru, coca use was forbidden, until the Spanish discovered that the Indians could perform more work on less food while using the drug. A daily ration was then provided for the laborers. That practice became a habit that has never been relinquished [p. 127].

NARCOTICS

NARCOTICS. *A class of drugs that have both sedative and analgesic effects. The principal narcotic drugs are opiate derivatives, such as morphine, heroin, and codeine.*

The term **narcotic** has a variety of meanings. Pharmacologically, a narcotic is usually defined as a drug that has both a sedative (sleep-inducing) *and* an analgesic (pain-relieving) effect. The narcotic drugs are also called *opiates* because they are derived from the opium plant. This plant is grown in hot, arid regions of the world where there is plenty of land and cheap labor available (such as Turkey and Mexico).

The principal narcotics are morphine, heroin, codeine, and synthetic copies such as methadone. Morphine and codeine can be extracted directly from the opium plant. Heroin is manufactured by chemically treating the morphine in a manner that greatly increases its potency. Opiates can also be synthesized in the laboratory, prime examples being methadone and Demerol. These drugs have a variety of medical uses, although their primary value lies in their ability to relieve pain.

INTRAVENOUS INJECTION. *Injection into a blood vein.*

Most nonmedical use of narcotics involves heroin. The most effective mode of ingestion is **intravenous injection** through a hypodermic needle, but the drug can be snorted, smoked, or consumed orally. The more efficient injection approach is almost universally preferred in our society because of the great cost of the drug.

Effects. The main effect of heroin is to induce an overwhelming sense of euphoria. This peaceful, dreamlike, contented euphoric effect is the reason for the drug's popularity. Some experienced users feel a very intense spasm of ecstasy immediately after the injection. In any case, the period of euphoria typically lasts four to six hours.

The euphoric effect has a sort of "Who cares?" quality to it. This aspect means that heroin can provide an escape from unpleasant reality. Principal side effects include nausea, lethargy, drowsiness, slowed respiration, constriction of the pupils, and constipation.

Risks. Although opiates can produce a tremendous sense of euphoria, the narcotics user incurs some very substantial risks.

1. *Psychological dependence.* The highly pleasant quality of the drug often leads quickly to psychological dependence. Although this is certainly not inevitable, the seductiveness of the drug is demonstrated by the fact that many medical personnel, who are sophisticated about the drug's dangers, still get hooked on morphine that they steal from hospital and clinic supplies.

2. *Physical dependence.* Regular use brings about a tolerance effect that leads the user to require larger and larger doses. This eventually leads to physical dependence in a great many users. Heroin withdrawal can produce exquisite agony, including nausea, vomiting, diarrhea, cramps, hot flashes, cold sweats, fever, tremors, headaches, and delirium for up to ten days. Unlike barbiturate withdrawal, however, heroin withdrawal is usually not life-threatening (Gay & Way, 1972).

3. *Overdose.* Overdose is an exaggerated but real danger with heroin. The drug has additive effects when combined with sedatives or alcohol. Most heroin-related overdoses result from such combinations (Brecher et al., 1972). In an opiate overdose, the respiratory system slowly grinds to a halt. This can lead to coma, brain damage, and death within a very brief period.

4. *Infectious disease.* Although it is largely avoidable, heroin users, or "junkies," often contract a variety of infectious diseases, usually because they are sloppy about sterilizing their hypodermic needles. The most common of these diseases is hepatitis.

5. *Drug-centered lifestyle.* Once physical dependence is entrenched, a person's lifestyle comes to be centered on procuring heroin. This happens because the drug is very expensive and has to be acquired through highly undependable black-market channels. Because of the tremendous expense of heroin (of-

ten up to $200 a day), junkies frequently resort to crime to support their habit (*Nepenthe,* 1978). Obviously, it is very difficult to lead a well-adjusted life when one's existence is dominated by a desperate need to procure heroin. Junkies, by the way, tend to make lousy friends, because eventually a desperate need for money to support their habit forces them to steal from even their closest friends.

In summary, narcotics use involves some significant perils. It is *possible* to successfully evade all the dangers outlined above, but only a tiny handful of narcotics users have the self-discipline necessary to avoid the trap of psychological and then physical dependence.

SEDATIVES

SEDATIVES. *A class of drugs that have depressant and sleep-inducing effects.*

Sedatives are defined by their sleep-inducing and behavioral depression effects. Several groups of drugs have such effects. The first to be used medically were the *barbiturates,* drugs derived from barbituric acid. There are many barbiturate compounds, and they have a variety of medical uses, including treatment of insomnia, epilepsy, and anxiety. In the 1950s, some powerful *nonbarbiturate sedatives* were introduced. Today, the most popular of these for illicit use is methaqualone (Quaaludes). In fact, the illicit use of Quaaludes reached such an excessive level that the manufacturer felt compelled to discontinue their production (illicitly produced copies are still available on the black market). Many nonbarbiturate sedatives are actually quite similar to barbiturates in chemical structure, and their effects are essentially the same. Less similar and somewhat less potent are the *tranquilizers,* such as Valium and Librium, which are used to combat anxiety. Although they differ chemically from the barbiturates, they have similar effects and are included in the sedative category.

Effects. People using sedatives illicitly generally consume larger doses than are usually prescribed for medical purposes. These overly large doses have a euphoric effect very similar to that produced by drinking large amounts of alcohol. Feelings of tension, anxiety, and depression temporarily melt away. They are supplanted by a very relaxed, pleasant state of intoxication, in which inhibitions may be loosened.

Sedative drugs carry a truckload of side effects. Most obvious is the impact on motor coordination; one's body feels like rubber, and one tends to stagger about in something of a daze. Motor responses are slowed down, senses are dulled, and intellectual functioning is sluggish. Speech tends to be slurred, judgment is routinely impaired, and emotional tone becomes unstable as brief feelings of dejection and despair often intrude on the intended euphoric mood. Whereas these immediate effects are readily apparent, there are other, longer-lasting side effects that are more subtle. Although sedatives promote sleep, most of them *reduce* the amount of time spent in the valuable REM stage of the sleep cycle. Sedatives also tend to produce something of a "hangover" the next day. This hangover may include moderate impairment of motor and intellectual functioning, increased irritability, and an increased tendency to feel depressed.

Risks. A number of risks are associated with either licit or illicit use of sedatives.

1. *Psychological dependence.* Psychological dependence on sedatives is common. Although these drugs are probably less seductive than the narcotics, they do produce a very appealing state of bliss that has captured the heart of many a user.

2. *Physical dependence.* The barbiturates and the nonbarbiturate sedatives that are similar to them in chemical structure may induce physical dependence. Like the opiates, these drugs have a tolerance effect, which leads the

regular user to employ larger and larger doses. At the lower dosage levels, the withdrawal syndrome following the termination of steady use is relatively mild. However, at higher dosages the barbiturate withdrawal syndrome tends to be even more severe than heroin withdrawal. The physical distress is tremendous, and withdrawal-induced convulsions are often life-threatening. Thus, although physical dependence develops more easily with heroin than with barbiturates, the physical dependence associated with barbiturates may be more dangerous. Physical dependence on tranquilizers, such as Valium, is a far less frequent problem but appears to be moderately common.

3. *Overdose.* Of all the recreational drugs, barbiturates are the most dangerous when it comes to overdose. This is true for several reasons. First, tolerance of barbiturates' intoxicating effects increases more rapidly than tolerance of their respiratory depression effects. In other words, with prolonged use the dose needed to feel "high" increases quickly, and the dose that the body can handle without an overdose increases more slowly (see Figure 4.6). Thus, with steady use a person's preferred dose tends to get closer and closer to his or her lethal limit, increasing the risk of an accidental overdose. Second, the way sedatives impair mental judgment promotes overdose. Typically, people will gobble a handful of "downers" and experience considerable euphoria. In their ensuing mental fog, they then reason, quite foolishly, "If I feel this good on five, I'll feel twice as good on five more." They then gobble another handful and possibly exceed their lethal limit. Thus, their drug-induced daze leads them to take a dose that they would ordinarily recognize as dangerous. Third, the sedatives have additive effects with alcohol. A great many overdoses occur because people combine too many downers with too much alcohol.

4. *Personal injury.* We have already commented on how sedatives produce a tremendous deterioration of one's motor coordination. This lack of coordination leads many users to injure themselves by falling off barstools, tripping down steps, and so forth. This decrease in motor skills also plays a contributing role in a great many automobile accidents.

STIMULANTS

STIMULANTS. *A class of drugs that tend to increase behavioral activity.*

The principal central nervous system **stimulants** used for recreational purposes are the amphetamines and cocaine. The *amphetamines* ("speed") were developed in the 1920s. Originally it was thought that they would have a wide variety of medical uses, but they now appear to have limited medical value. Currently they are used in the treatment of narcolepsy, Parkinson's disease, and some cases of childhood hyperactivity, this last use being controversial.

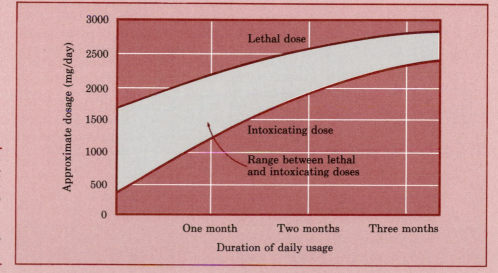

FIGURE 4.6 Relations between lethal and intoxicating doses of short-acting barbiturates in the blood as tolerance develops. (Dosages are only approximate because of individual differences in tolerance to the drug and patterns of use.)

Nonmedical use is fueled by theft of legally manufactured amphetamines, as well as illicit manufacture. The drug is usually consumed orally in a tablet or capsule form but is also sold in a crystalline powder form, which may be snorted or injected intravenously.

Cocaine is an organic substance extracted from the coca shrub, which grows most prominently in certain regions of South America. It has been used recreationally for centuries, and until 1906 it was an ingredient in Coca-Cola. Medically, it is used as a vasoconstrictor and local anesthetic. It is usually smuggled into the United States in a crystalline powder form that is diluted to varying degrees. Typically, the drug is snorted, but occasionally it is injected intravenously. An increasing number of users are "freebasing" cocaine. This is an elaborate (and dangerous) process in which the cocaine is treated with an ether base in order to purify the drug and thereby enhance its impact. The recreational use of cocaine enjoyed a surge of popularity in the mid-1970s. Its recreational use would probably be even more widespread if it were not extremely expensive.

Although there is little resemblance in chemical structure, the amphetamines and cocaine have fairly similar effects. This is because they both appear to exert their effects by moderating the action of norepinephrine, a **neurotransmitter** in the brain. However, the drugs do *not* have identical effects; they modify neural transmission somewhat differently. Generally, I will discuss the two drugs together, while occasionally highlighting some dissimilarities.

NEUROTRANSMITTER. *A chemical substance involved in transmission of nerve impulses. It carries information from one neuron to another across a gap called a synaptic cleft.*

Effects. Stimulants have a euphoric effect very different from that of narcotics or sedatives. They elevate mood by giving one a sense of energy and optimism. The high creates a feeling that "I can conquer the world." Typically, a person feels buoyant, elated, fearless, enthusiastic, and talkative. Stimulants also increase alertness and can ward off fatigue. They improve mental concentration for many people. Although they have proved largely ineffective in the treatment of obesity, they do suppress appetite temporarily. Many athletes use stimulants to improve their performance. Stimulants don't actually increase a person's speed or strength, but they may enhance some athletes' performance by boosting subjective feelings of energy and endurance. Unfortunately, this leads some athletes to push themselves to dangerous levels of exhaustion.

In addition to these effects desired by most users, stimulants also have a variety of incidental side effects. Physically, stimulants tend to increase blood pressure, heart rate, muscle tension, and sweating. They also tend to produce pupillary dilation, "cotton mouth," and nausea in some people. Psychological side effects include a sense of restlessness, difficulty in concentration, irritability, and, for some people, distressing anxiety. At higher dosage levels, this anxiety may escalate into intense **paranoia.** Insomnia is also a common side effect.

PARANOIA. *Feelings of being persecuted; the dominant symptom in several psychological disorders.*

The effects of cocaine and the amphetamines differ in two ways. First, there is a major disparity in duration of effect, due to differences in how the drugs are metabolized. Cocaine produces a very brief high, often lasting only 15–20 minutes, although it may extend for about an hour with larger and purer doses. The amphetamines may continue to work for up to 10 or 20 hours. Second, people develop tolerance to amphetamines fairly quickly and therefore need to escalate their dosage levels. In contrast, the findings on cocaine tolerance are very inconsistent; some research suggests that tolerance to the drug is relatively meager (Leavitt, 1982).

Risks. Overall, the stimulants seem less dangerous than either the narcotics or the sedatives. Primarily, this is because they do not produce the particularly problematic affliction of *physical* dependence. If steady, long-term use of stimulants is terminated abruptly, the user's body does go through a readjustment period often characterized by exhaustion and depression. However, this physical distress is nothing in comparison with that associated with barbiturate or heroin withdrawal. More important, it does not produce the same kind of compulsion to pursue the drug in order to avoid withdrawal.

Stimulants also carry relatively little risk of overdose. It *is* possible to consume a dose so excessive as to cause seizures and respiratory arrest. However, this requires an exorbitant dose far beyond what one normally ingests in order to produce the desired high. Hence, accidental overdoses are relatively infrequent (Kalant & Kalant, 1979), although they *are* increasing as cocaine gains wider use (Mittleman & Wetli, 1984).

Nonetheless, stimulants are far from harmless. The principal risks associated with stimulant use are outlined below.

1. *Psychological dependence.* A good number of people who use stimulants become psychologically dependent on them. Both cocaine and the amphetamines produce a captivating sense of euphoria. People come to depend on the drugs for feeling good and to provide them with energy. In particular, cocaine can create an exceptionally powerful form of psychological dependence, which compels the user to pursue the drug with a fervor normally seen only when physical dependence exists. The prevalence of such dependence appears to be increasing dramatically. These serious problems with psychological dependence have led to the curtailment of most legitimate medical use of amphetamines.

2. *Deterioration of physical health.* Regular use of stimulants often has a detrimental effect on one's physical health. This deterioration of health occurs mainly with heavy use. The problem is that both cocaine and the amphetamines suppress appetite and disrupt normal sleep patterns. Consequently, many heavy users do not eat properly and do not get adequate sleep. Over a long period, poor sleep and poor eating are quite likely to lead to poor health. Because of their longer-lasting pharmacologic action, amphetamines are more likely to damage one's health than cocaine. Additionally, there is some very tentative evidence linking heavy stimulant use to an increased incidence of stroke, liver disease, and kidney disease (Jones-Witters & Witters, 1983).

PSYCHOSIS. *A generic term referring to any disturbance so severe as to produce impaired contact with reality.*

3. *Psychosis.* **Psychosis** is a general term referring to a variety of severe psychological disorders involving significant impairment of one's contact with reality. Stimulant use occasionally leads to the onset of a psychosis that roughly resembles paranoid schizophrenia (Snyder, 1979). Although this is not a common effect of the drug, it certainly represents a very serious risk.

4. *Nasal damage.* Cocaine is usually ingested by snorting it through the nasal passages. Although this is the most effective mode of ingestion, it may damage the nasal tissues (Eiswirth, Smith, & Wesson, 1973). The mucous membranes lining the nose are often harmed, leading to soreness, nosebleeds, and a frequent "runny" nose. Extensive use can produce even more serious damage, such as a perforated septum.

HALLUCINOGENS

HALLUCINOGENS. *A class of drugs with powerful effects on perceptual, mental, and emotional functioning, hallucinatory effects being among the more prominent.*

HALLUCINATION. *A sensory perception in the absence of a real external stimulus; a sensory distortion. It may occur in any of the senses, but auditory and visual hallucinations are most commonly reported.*

The **hallucinogens** are a diverse group of drugs that share the capacity to produce dramatic alterations in perception called **hallucinations.** Actually, the term *hallucinogen* fails to convey the full range of effects produced by these drugs. They are very powerful substances that also alter emotional, intellectual, and motor functioning.

The principal hallucinogens are mescaline, psilocybin, and LSD. *Mescaline* is the key ingredient in the peyote cactus, which grows in Mexico and the Southwestern United States. The crown of this plant is cut off and consumed, yielding a hallucinogenic effect. Many Native American tribes have used peyote for centuries, particularly in religious ceremonies. Today, mescaline can also be produced synthetically in the laboratory. *Psilocybin* is derived from a relatively rare mushroom that grows in Mexico and Central America. Like peyote, it has a long history of use in religious rites. *LSD* is a largely synthetic drug discovered in 1938 by Albert Hoffman, who stumbled onto its hallucinogenic properties about five years later.

CROSS-TOLERANCE.
Tolerance to one drug produced by use of another, related drug.

These three drugs have very similar subjective effects, and they even display **cross-tolerance.** This means that use of one produces a tolerance effect for all three. However, they vary tremendously in potency; it has been estimated that LSD is 5000 times as potent as mescaline and 200 times as potent as psilocybin. This means that LSD works in doses much smaller than those necessary with the other two drugs. In fact, LSD works in incredibly minuscule doses. All three drugs appear to exert their effects by modifying neural transmission in the brain.

The three drugs can be discussed collectively because of their similarity and because most of the mescaline and psilocybin sold "on the street" is really LSD anyway. In a study conducted by the University of Maryland School of Pharmacy (see Dusek & Girdano, 1980), only one of 57 samples of "mescaline" purchased on the street actually contained mescaline. Most (43) of the samples actually contained LSD. This was found to be true for "psilocybin" as well. The substitution of LSD for these other drugs is probably done because LSD is easier to synthesize, and only a chemist can tell the difference.

Effects.   Ingested orally, in tablets, capsules, and other forms, these drugs are operative for 4 to 12 hours, depending on the dose (psilocybin is shorter-acting). Their operation is paradoxical in that they can produce spectacular psychological effects while causing only very meager and insignificant physical effects. LSD, for instance, has only a very slight impact on heart rate, blood pressure, body temperature, and pupillary dilation.

Some of the psychological effects of hallucinogens are such a great departure from the norm that they are difficult to describe. Perception is both intensified and altered qualitatively. In visual perception, colors appear radiant, scenes appear more beautiful, objects appear to change shape, and components of intricate patterns appear to move. One's sense of time may be greatly distorted; five minutes may seem like five hours, or vice versa.

LSD may have overpowering effects on one's emotional functioning. On the pleasant side, the drug can induce an awesome feeling of euphoria. For many people it includes a profound sense of oneness with the human race that has a mystical quality to it. It is this ability of hallucinogens to produce a seemingly mystical state of bliss that has led to their use in religious ceremonies in various cultures. Unfortunately, at the other end of the spectrum, hallucinogens can also produce an overwhelming, nightmarish feeling of emotional distress. One's entire being may be consumed by feelings of anxiety, fear, and paranoia. It is this experience that is referred to as a "bad trip." It can be a very terrifying ordeal.

The ingestion of hallucinogens usually produces significant impairment of intellectual functioning (Hollister, 1978). Memory and problem-solving ability usually suffer badly. Thought processes are meteoric but jumbled. Attention span usually becomes pathetically short as multiple trains of thought careen along wildly. People also tend to become highly suggestible. The impact of hallucinogens on motor functioning is less clear and more unpredictable but generally appears to be negative.

Risks.   The dangers of hallucinogens received much publicity during the 1960s and 1970s. Actually, the risks associated with the use of these drugs have probably been exaggerated. There is no potential whatsoever for physical dependence. It is extremely difficult to overdose on hallucinogens, and no deaths attributable to overdose are known to have occurred. Psychological dependence has been reported but appears to be very rare. The most typical pattern of use for these drugs is to experiment with them for a few months to a few years and then abandon them. Research reports that LSD increases chromosome breakage appear to be based on poor methodology, and chromosome damage is probably not a significant problem (Dishotsky et al., 1971). However, it should be emphasized that hallucinogens, like many other drugs, may be harmful to a fetus if taken by a pregnant woman. Although many dangers associated with hallucinogen use have been overstated, there are some significant risks, which we will describe below.

1. *Acute panic in a bad trip.* When a hallucinogenic trip goes bad, it can go very, very bad. A pleasant setting and a good attitude decrease the likelihood of a bad trip, but emotion is highly volatile with these drugs. Users can never be sure they won't experience a bad trip. It can happen to anyone, and when it does, it is very scary. People often panic, become incoherent, and believe that they are "losing their mind." Generally, a bad segment of a trip subsides in a few hours and usually does not leave permanent emotional scars. However, in such a severe state of disorientation, accidents and even suicide are possible.

FLASHBACK. *Spontaneous recurrence of a drug-induced experience from the past.*

2. *Flashbacks.* A **flashback** involves reliving a portion of a hallucinogenic experience months or even years after the original experience. We do not know how many users are bothered by these unpredictable flashbacks. They are bothersome because they suggest that the person does not have full control over his or her consciousness and because people have a tendency to relive traumatic trips more than pleasant ones (Shick & Smith, 1970). The basis for flashbacks is not presently understood but is thought to be psychological rather than physiological.

3. *Precipitation of psychological disorders.* A small minority of people who use hallucinogens subsequently develop a variety of psychological disorders that appear partially attributable to the use of the drug (Hollister, 1978). In these cases, the hallucinogens probably do not directly cause the disorders themselves. Rather, they seem to uncover latent disorders that may have been lurking beneath the surface all along. In any case, the use of hallucinogens appears particularly risky for people characterized by an unstable personality.

Although the three dangers outlined above are the principal risks incurred with these drugs, it should be emphasized that we do not really know very much about the hallucinogens. Relatively little research is done on them because they do not have any demonstrated medical value (and seem to have little potential) and because they exert such powerful effects. Hence, there may be additional dangers yet to be discovered.

CANNABIS DERIVATIVES

CANNABIS. *The hemp plant, from which marijuana, hashish, and THC are derived.*

Cannabis is a plant that grows readily in many regions of the world. Cannabis derivatives include marijuana, hashish, and THC. *Marijuana* is a mixture of dried leaves, flowers, stems, and seeds taken from the plant. It is usually ingested by smoking the substance in a pipe or a cigarette (commonly called a "joint"). *Hashish* comes from a sticky resin produced by the plant. It tends to be more potent than marijuana and is also usually ingested by smoking. *THC,* or tetrahydrocannabinol, is the principal active ingredient in cannabis. It can be synthesized in a lab, but doing so is very expensive. For the most part, it is not available on the black market. The various preparations sold as THC are almost inevitably something else (often PCP; see Box 4.5).

The use of cannabis as an intoxicant has a long history in a diverse array of cultures. In the United States, usage of the drug was very limited until the 1960s. Before that time, the media had portrayed marijuana as a very dangerous drug, linked to crime and acts of violence. A substantial portion of the nation's youth began experimenting with the drug in the 1960s, and by the 1970s marijuana use was widespread. Today, it is estimated that about 60% of the collegiate population has tried the drug (Pope et al., 1981).

Cannabis does not fit into any of the traditional classes of drugs. It is often classified *legally* as a narcotic, but in reality it has little or nothing in common with the narcotic drugs. It shares some effects with the hallucinogens and with the sedatives, but it does not really fit into either of these categories. Thus, it merits its own unique category, and we will discuss it as such.

Marijuana is still a widely used and highly controversial drug.

Effects. When smoked, marijuana has an almost immediate impact that may last several hours. The effects of the drug vary greatly, depending on the setting, the user's expectations and experience with the drug, the potency of the drug, and the quantity ingested.

Physiologically, the effects of the drug are very moderate. It accelerates heart rate, dries out the mouth, and gives one bloodshot eyes. There are some modest, nonpathological changes in EEG activity. Total time spent sleeping tends to increase, but there is a reduction in REM-stage sleep (Jones, 1978).

Marijuana is used for its psychological effects, which are also relatively moderate. The drug seems to have subtle effects on emotion, perception, and cognition. The subjective psychological effects of the drug can be seen in Figure 4.7, which summarizes common reasons for using marijuana. Emotionally, the drug seems to elevate mood by creating a mild sense of euphoria and by reducing feelings of tension. Cognitively, it distorts one's sense of time, enhances one's sense of humor, intensifies one's concentration, and leads one to see profundity in everyday observations. Perceptually, it seems to increase one's enjoyment of both sights and sounds. The mechanism by which this is accomplished is a mystery, since studies show that the drug does not make people more sensitive to incoming stimulation (Jones, 1978).

Subjectively, it is reported that marijuana increases one's interest in both food and sexual activity. Insofar as this tends to be true, the mechanism of action appears to be psychological rather than physiological. People *may* learn from past experience that food tastes better and sex feels better and therefore display an elevated interest in both. This explanation is an admittedly speculative one that exists in the absence of clear evidence on these issues.

The effects of marijuana on intellectual and motor functioning vary greatly from one person to another. The dosage and the nature of the task are also important. Marijuana may improve some people's performance on some tasks. Generally, however, cannabis tends to impair memory, learning, reaction time, and perceptual-motor coordination (Jones, 1978). These negative effects typically lead to a moderate impairment in ability to drive an automobile (Klonoff, 1974).

4.5 PCP

PCP (phencyclidine hydrochloride) is a perplexing drug that has gained considerable popularity in recent years. It is known on the street as "angel dust." It was originally developed in the 1950s as an anesthetic for use with humans. Because of its undesirable side effects, it was eventually limited to use as an animal tranquilizer.

The drug defies classification in that it has stimulant, hallucinogenic, and sedative effects (Vourakis & Bennett, 1979). At lower doses, the sedative effects seem to dominate; at higher doses, the hallucinogenic effects become more pronounced. In any case, the bizarre combination of effects produces a unique euphoria that often includes a feeling of depersonalization.

The drug's popularity is due in part to its ready availability. It can be synthesized easily by an illicit chemist. Unfortunately, these illicit preparations often include toxic by-products that may produce physical distress.

Although little is known about long-term use of PCP, it is clear that there are many risks associated with the use of this powerful drug. Because of its sedative properties, overdose through respiratory depression is a significant problem. Although it is a less potent hallucinogen than LSD, PCP seems to produce a higher proportion of "bad trips," wherein feelings of fear and agitation become dominant. It is very difficult to reverse this state of agitation (Vourakis & Bennett, 1979). Like the amphetamines, PCP has the potential to trigger a schizophrenialike psychosis in some users (Cohen, 1977). In addition to these problems, PCP can produce a severe state of confusion and disorientation that has been linked to automobile accidents, drownings, and suicides. In fact, one study of 16 PCP-related deaths in the Los Angeles area (Noguchi & Nakamura, 1978) found that a majority were attributable to *disordered behavior* rather than to fatal doses of the drug. The 11 cases involving nonfatal concentrations of PCP in the blood were caused by suicide, homicide, and accidents. Thus, the principal risk associated with the use of PCP may be exceedingly high-risk behavior undertaken in a state of disorientation.

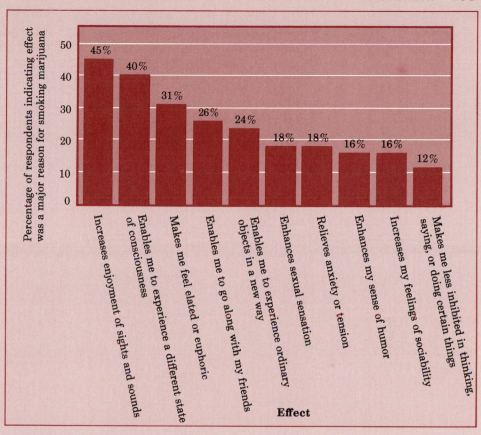

Percentage of respondents indicating effect was a major reason for smoking marijuana

- Increases enjoyment of sights and sounds — 45%
- Enables me to experience a different state of consciousness — 40%
- Makes me feel elated or euphoric — 31%
- Enables me to go along with my friends — 26%
- Enables me to experience ordinary objects in a new way — 24%
- Enhances sexual sensation — 18%
- Relieves anxiety or tension — 18%
- Enhances my sense of humor — 16%
- Increases my feelings of sociability — 16%
- Makes me less inhibited in thinking, saying, or doing certain things — 12%

Effect

FIGURE 4.7 Reasons for smoking marijuana.

Tolerance effects with cannabis are more complex than with most drugs. Because the psychological effects of the drug are subtle, many people report a *reverse tolerance* effect. In other words, as they learn to use the drug, they need progressively *less* to attain their customary high. However, conventional tolerance effects tend to emerge with regular use and relatively high doses (Cohen et al., 1976).

Risks. A great number of studies have been conducted to determine whether marijuana has any harmful effects. Given the enormous volume of such studies, it is not surprising that some appear to suggest that such harmful effects exist. Those studies that find dangers associated with marijuana use inevitably receive a great deal of publicity. In contrast, those that *fail* to find dangers usually languish in obscurity. Thus, the popular media often provide a very biased and inaccurate picture of the research on cannabis.

The reality of the situation is quite complex. In regard to nearly every alleged danger involving marijuana, there is contradictory evidence! Hence, depending on one's bias, it is very easy to cite evidence proving either that marijuana is very harmful or that it is absolutely harmless. We will try to sort through this evidence in order to give you an idea about which dangers are exaggerated and which are reason for authentic concern.

Let us begin with the myths and exaggerations. First, it should be emphasized that one does not develop physical dependence on marijuana, and the drug is nonlethal—people do not overdose on it. Furthermore, reports of brain damage (Campbell et al., 1971) have been shown to be methodologically unsound, and more sophisticated studies (Kuehnle et al., 1977) find no such effects. Concerns about chromosome damage from smoking marijuana also appear to be greatly exaggerated. There is some disturbing evidence (Nahas et al., 1974) that marijuana may impair some of the body's natural immune responses, thereby lowering resistance to infectious disease. Although this evidence cannot readily be dismissed, statistical evidence does *not* suggest that regular smokers are exceptionally vulnerable to infection (Braude & Szara, 1976).

Many dangers of marijuana use have been exaggerated, but it would be premature at this point to give cannabis a clean bill of health and characterize it as a harmless drug. Although the evidence is ambiguous, there is reason for concern about the following potential risks.

1. *Psychological dependence.* Like almost any other drug that produces pleasant feelings, marijuana has the potential to produce psychological dependence. A portion of habitual users would be very hard-pressed to live without it.

2. *Acute anxiety.* Cannabis appears to have the potential to intensify negative as well as positive emotions. While high, some users experience transient feelings of anxiety and/or depression. There is also some concern that regular cannabis use might make some people more vulnerable to chronic psychological disorders. At present, the evidence is very ambiguous (Meyer, 1975).

3. *Endocrine changes.* Evidence suggests that one's endocrine system may be affected by smoking marijuana. Studies have found that male smokers show a lowered level of an important hormone (testosterone) and a depressed sperm count (Kolodny et al., 1974). The popular press has implied that such findings mean that marijuana might render male smokers impotent and sterile. Such dramatic conclusions do not follow from the findings in these studies, and other evidence makes such conclusions highly improbable. The researchers themselves have been very cautious about the implications of these findings. Nonetheless, there is some reason for concern about how marijuana may affect one's endocrine functioning.

4. *Respiratory and cardiovascular problems.* Evidence on the effects of marijuana on pulmonary (lung) function is paradoxical. On a short-term basis, cannabis may produce dilation of the bronchial tubes, which temporarily *improves* pulmonary function for some people. However, marijuana is loaded with tar content and impurities that are taken into the lungs. Over the long run, marijuana seems to have a negative effect on pulmonary and respiratory function (Mendelson, Rossi, & Meyer, 1974). Just *how* negative remains to be determined. It seems likely (although we do not yet have data) that smoking marijuana ought to elevate one's risk of lung cancer in a manner similar to smoking tobacco, although the strength of that link may be constrained by the fact that most people smoke far less marijuana than tobacco. It also appears plausible that cannabis smoking (like cigarette smoking) may increase one's vulnerability to cardiovascular problems, but again we do not yet have adequate data to evaluate this possibility.

5. *Lethargy.* One of the oldest dangers thought to be associated with marijuana is the "amotivational syndrome," wherein a chronic smoker's behavior comes to be dominated by feelings of lethargy and a general lack of motivation. There *is* some evidence to support this theory (Sharma, 1975), but it is very difficult to separate cause and effect in this alleged relationship. If, in fact, there is an excess of lethargic marijuana smokers (a highly debatable premise), one cannot simply conclude that marijuana causes chronic lethargy. It may be that lethargic people are drawn to marijuana. Evidence presently available is very ambiguous. The fact that marijuana smokers perform as well as nonsmokers in college (Brill & Christie, 1974) suggests that lethargy may not be as problematic as previously believed.

ALCOHOL

The most widely used drug in our society is alcohol. Since its use is socially approved, many people use it very casually without even thinking of it as a drug. "Booze" is a dear friend to many; however, it is potentially a very dangerous friend. It is estimated that about one in three people who use alcohol has a drinking problem.

Effects. The effects of alcohol are mediated by the user's experience, expectancy, motivation, and mood, just as with any other drug. Additionally, factors that influence the body's absorption of alcohol govern the effects achieved. These include the presence of food in the stomach, the concentration of alcohol in the blood, the proof of the beverage, and the rate of drinking. Thus, there is great variability in how alcohol affects different people on different occasions.

Basically, alcohol is a central nervous system depressant whose effects are very similar to those of the sedative drugs. The central effect is a "Who cares?" brand of euphoria that temporarily boosts self-esteem as one's problems melt away into insignificance. Negative emotions such as tension, worry, anxiety, and depression are dulled. In this relaxed, euphoric state, inhibitions may be loosened, so that people tend to socialize more spontaneously.

The side effects of alcohol are numerous. In substantial amounts alcohol has a decidedly negative effect on intellectual functioning. In particular, judgment and memory may be impaired. Serious deterioration of perceptual-motor coordination is typical. With their inhibitions released, some people become argumentative and prone to aggression. Others become more sexually oriented than usual, but alcohol ultimately diminishes sexual arousal. Finally, of course, there is that infamous source of regret, the "hangover," which may include headaches, dizziness, nausea, and vomiting.

Risks. Though socially sanctioned, alcohol appears to be even more dangerous than some of the illegal drugs. Major risks include the following.

1. *Dependence.* Both psychological and physical dependence are possible with alcohol. The psychologically dependent person needs to drink almost daily in order to feel good and alleviate tension or anxiety. With frequent and heavy use, tolerance to alcohol develops and the drinking escalates. Eventually, physical dependence may be established, and the person becomes an *alcoholic.* The withdrawal syndrome associated with alcohol can be quite severe and even lethal. Aware of this, alcoholics come to orient their lives around drinking, much to the detriment of their adjustment.

2. *Overdose.* It takes a lot of hard drinking, but it *is* possible to consume lethal amounts of alcohol. A more frequent problem is overdosing on *combinations* of alcohol and other drugs, particularly the sedatives.

3. *Deterioration of physical health.* There is considerable debate about whether the negative effect of alcohol on health is direct or indirect. In either case, it is clear that excessive alcohol consumption is associated with a wide range of very serious health risks. It has long been known that heavy use of alcohol can cause liver disease, gastrointestinal problems such as ulcers, complications of pregnancy, fetal abnormalities, and malnutrition. More recently, it has become clear that chronic alcohol use is related to an elevated risk of heart disease, cancer, neurological disorders, impaired immune response, and bleeding problems (Jones-Witters & Witters, 1983; Mello & Mendelson, 1978).

4. *Drunk driving.* Although individuals vary somewhat in how quickly or easily they are affected, it is an indisputable fact that alcohol impairs one's ability to drive. It is estimated that alcohol contributes to about half of the traffic fatalities in the United States.

5. *Psychological disorders.* There is no doubt that a drinking problem tends to undermine the quality of one's adjustment. Above and beyond this, however, it is clear that **alcoholism** often leads to any of several severe psychotic states (Coleman, Butcher, & Carson, 1984). For instance, some alcoholics develop *Korsakoff's psychosis,* a condition characterized by serious memory losses for recent events that individuals often try to cover up with bumbling falsifications. Afflicted individuals may also experience delirium, disorientation, and hallucinations.

ALCOHOLISM. *A disorder marked by chronic and excessive drinking of alcoholic beverages, dependence on alcohol, and resulting impairment of normal functioning.*

Social costs.   In this application section we have focused on the *personal* risks associated with the use of recreational drugs. In the case of alcohol, however, one cannot help mentioning the enormous costs to our society as a whole. According to the National Institute on Alcohol Abuse and Alcoholism (1980), alcohol appears to cause or play a major contributing role in a very substantial portion of automobile accidents, aviation accidents, drownings, fire fatalities, homicides, suicides, rapes, assaults, robberies, and incidents of child abuse. Alcohol-related absenteeism from work is monumental and, in conjunction with reduced efficiency on the job, may cost American industry something in the vicinity of $20 billion annually. The cost of medical care for alcohol-related health problems is believed to be similarly staggering and may approach 20% of all health care expenditures in the United States.

Equally lamentable and tragic are the more subtle costs incurred by the *families* of people with drinking problems. Alcoholics tend to go through many changes that create havoc and dreadful suffering for their families (Milam & Ketcham, 1981). Homes of alcoholics tend to become tense battlegrounds as family members try to cope with the problem drinker's self-destructive behavior. Alcoholics often become moody, high-strung, and easily irritated as their self-esteem plummets. Temperamental outbursts produce increasing discord with one's spouse and children. As an alcoholic's behavior deteriorates, family members experience feelings of anger, fear, concern, disgust, pity, and bitter resentment. These conflicting and confusing feelings lead them to go through their own emotional crises. There is no way to put a price on the extraordinary anguish suffered in watching the relentless degeneration of someone you love.

In summary, the social and personal costs of alcoholic problems are so inordinate as to be virtually incalculable. Though legal (maybe *because* it is legal), alcohol is far and away the most problematic and costly of the recreational drugs.

CHAPTER 4 REVIEW

IDEAS: REVIEW OF LEARNING OBJECTIVES

When you have mastered the material in this chapter, you should be able to do the following.

1. Explain why our fight-or-flight response to stress has become antiquated and maladaptive.
2. Summarize how patterns of disease have changed in modern society.
3. Explain how conceptions of illness have changed in modern society.
4. Explain and give an example of the direct inheritance of disease.
5. Explain and give an example of the polygenic inheritance of vulnerability to disease.
6. List two kinds of infectious agents.
7. Describe the body's immune response to invasion by infectious agents.
8. Provide several examples of toxic agents in the environment.
9. List three behavioral mechanisms that influence health and illness.
10. Explain the principal cause of coronary heart disease.
11. Summarize three lines of evidence that suggest stress affects vulnerability to heart disease.
12. Describe the elements of the Type A personality.
13. Discuss the strength of the relationship between the Type A personality and coronary risk.
14. Discuss physiological mechanisms that may underlie the link between Type A behavior and elevated coronary risk.
15. Summarize evidence that hypertension is stress-related.
16. Summarize evidence that cancer is stress-related.
17. Discuss whether peptic ulcers or asthma appears to be stress-related.
18. Summarize evidence that illness of any kind may be stress-related.
19. Discuss whether accidents and injuries appear to be stress-related.
20. Give some reasons that many people display self-destructive, health-impairing habits.
21. Discuss the risks associated with smoking and why people smoke.
22. Summarize ideas about the physiological and behavioral basis for obesity.
23. Provide a few examples of links between nutrition and health, and discuss the merits of nutritional fads.
24. Discuss whether physical activity and fitness are related to cardiovascular risk.
25. Summarize the potential benefits of regular exercise.
26. Summarize the effects of sleep deprivation and the importance of REM sleep.
27. Discuss the role of psychological factors in pain perception.
28. Specify the crucial problem in treatment-seeking behavior and discuss correlates of treatment seeking.
29. Discuss the appeal of the "sick role."
30. Discuss the prevalence of noncompliance with professional advice and its causes.
31. Explain why "scare tactics" in drug education programs may be counterproductive.
32. Distinguish between physical and psychological dependence.
33. List the principal narcotics and describe their effects.
34. List the risks associated with the use of narcotics.
35. List the principal sedatives and describe their effects.
36. List the risks associated with the use of sedatives.
37. List the principal stimulants and describe their effects.
38. List the risks associated with the use of stimulants.
39. List the principal hallucinogens and describe their effects.
40. List the risks associated with the use of hallucinogens.
41. List the principal cannabis derivatives and their effects.
42. List the risks associated with the use of cannabis derivatives.
43. Describe the effects of alcohol.
44. List the risks associated with the use of alcohol.

TERMS: REVIEW OF NEW VOCABULARY

When you have mastered the material in this chapter, you should be able to define the following terms.

Addiction
Adipocyte
Alcoholism
Antibodies
Antigen
Asthma
Atherosclerosis
Bacteria
Basal metabolic rate
Cancer
Cannabis
Chromosome
Concordance

Coronary heart disease
Cross-tolerance
Drug
Drug abuse
Electroencephalograph
Epidemiology
Flashback
Genes
Hallucinations
Hallucinogens
Health psychology
Hypertension
Immune response

Immunity
Infection
Intravenous injection
Narcotics
Neurotransmitter
Nutrition
Obesity
Overdose
Paranoia
Pathogenic
Peptic ulcers
Physical dependence

Polygenic inheritance
Psychological dependence
Psychosis
REM sleep
Sedatives
Stimulants
Substance-use disorders
Tolerance
Twin study
Type A personality
Virus
Withdrawal syndrome

PEOPLE: REVIEW OF MAJOR THEORISTS AND RESEARCHERS

When you have mastered the material in this chapter, you should be able to summarize the principal contributions and/or ideas of the following people.

Meyer Friedman and Ray Rosenman

Stanley Schachter

CONFRONTING STRESS: COPING PROCESSES

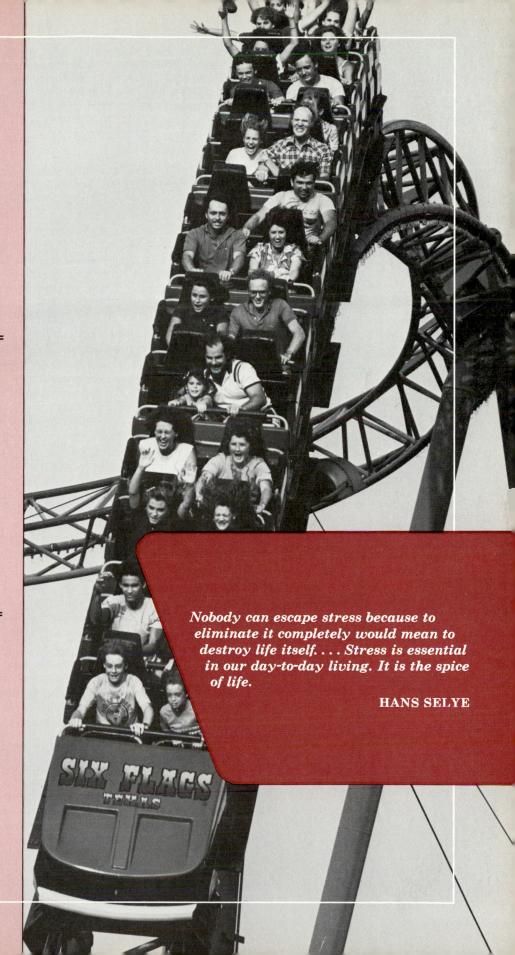

Applying Psychology to Your Life: Achieving Self-Control through Behavior Modification (Using Weight Control as an Example)

Nobody can escape stress because to eliminate it completely would mean to destroy life itself. . . . Stress is essential in our day-to-day living. It is the spice of life.

HANS SELYE

"I have begun to believe that I have intellectually and emotionally outgrown my husband. However, I'm not really sure what this means or what I should do. Maybe this feeling is normal and I should ignore it and continue my present relationship. This seems to be the safest route. Maybe I should seek a lover while continuing with my husband. Then again, maybe I should start anew and hope for a beautiful ending with or without a better mate."

The woman quoted above is obviously in the throes of a thorny conflict. Although it is hard to tell just how much emotional turmoil she is experiencing, it is clear that she is under substantial stress. What should she do? Is it psychologically healthy to remain in an emotionally hollow marriage? Is seeking a secret lover a reasonable way to cope with this unfortunate situation? Should she just strike out on her own and let the chips fall where they may? There are no simple answers to these questions, and the answers that could be offered would definitely reflect value judgments.

This chapter focuses on how we *cope* with stress. In the previous two chapters we have described the nature of stress and talked extensively about its potential negative effects. Although stress can be a challenging, exciting stimulus to personal growth, the "bottom line" is that, more often than not, stress has an unpleasant and ominous quality. All too often, stress can prove damaging to our psychological and physical health because it tends to trigger emotional responses accompanied by a variety of physiological changes, many of which may be harmful. These emotional and physiological responses to stress tend to be largely automatic. Controlling them depends on the coping responses that we make to the stressful situation. Thus, the preservation of our mental and physical health depends, in part, on coping effectively with stress, so as to neutralize these potentially injurious emotional and physiological reactions. To put it bluntly, our coping strategies and styles are of the utmost importance.

My plan of attack in the present chapter is as follows. I will first elaborate on the concept of coping and then briefly describe some common coping patterns that *tend* to be counterproductive or of minimal value. I will then devote the bulk of the chapter to discussing more desirable coping tactics that you might be able to use in dealing with stress in the future. The intent is to equip you with an improved repertoire of coping strategies for encounters with the inevitable stresses of modern life.

The Concept of Coping

COPING. *Efforts to master, reduce, or tolerate the demands created by stress.*

On the basis of work by Folkman and Lazarus (1980), I defined **coping** as behavioral efforts to master, reduce, or tolerate the demands that are created by stressful transactions (see Chapter 3). In other words, coping encompasses our behavioral efforts to deal with the stress in our lives. Borrowing liberally from more recent work by Lazarus and Folkman (1984), I will now elaborate on this important concept.

First, when I say that coping involves *behavioral* efforts to deal with stress, I am using the term in a broad sense, which includes purely cognitive efforts— that is, internal mental maneuvers. Second, please note that coping involves *active efforts* to manage the demands of stress. This means that not all behavioral responses to stress constitute coping. Stress often triggers largely automatic, almost "mechanical" behavior that does not represent coping. For instance, a major setback might send you into "shock" and leave you wandering the streets aimlessly. Lesser frustrations might provoke reflexive temper tantrums. Aimless wandering and temperamental outbursts are behavioral in nature, but they generally do not qualify as coping. Third, you should be aware that coping is an *ongoing process*. Efforts to manage stress are not static or fixed. They change and evolve with the passage of time. Coping often involves a trial-and-error process. As we struggle with a particular source of stress, we may try out different strategies, sometimes discarding those that seem ineffective. Fourth, at least some people display certain consistent *styles* of coping (Gorzynski et al., 1980). Although I have emphasized that coping is an ever-changing process, this should not be interpreted to mean that coping is wholly capricious and erratic. Coping is not a random activity. There are styles of coping, some of which are less than optimal. Thus, it may be fruitful for you to examine your personal style of coping and, in light of what you are about to learn in this chapter, to consider whether you might be able to improve on your characteristic patterns of coping. Fifth, our definition is neutral with regard to whether coping efforts are healthy or maladaptive. Often it is assumed that coping is inherently healthy (see, for instance, Vaillant, 1977). Indeed, our popular use of the term reflects this implicit value judgment. When we say that someone "coped with his problems," we imply that he handled them effectively. In reality, however, it is clear that coping processes may be healthy or unhealthy. Quite frequently, coping strategies are clearly ill advised and sometimes downright pathological. For example, if you were to cope with the disappointment of not getting a desired job promotion by carefully plotting the sabotage of your company's computer system, there would be little argument that this was a rather immature way of coping.

Although the concept of coping itself includes no assumptions about the adaptive value of the behavior, I most certainly will offer value judgments about the relative merits of different coping tactics. On the basis of extensive research and plenty of expert opinion and theory, I will try to distinguish between those coping patterns that *tend* to be adaptive and those that *tend* to be maladaptive. Please bear in mind, however, that evaluations of the adaptive value of various coping strategies are based on trends or tendencies. No coping strategy can ensure a desirable or successful outcome. The adaptive value of a coping pattern depends on the exact nature of the situation.

Common Patterns of Coping That Tend to Be of Limited Value

In this section I will describe some relatively common coping patterns that, more often than not, are less than optimal, of marginal or little adaptive value, and perhaps even decidedly counterproductive. In general, you should try to avoid relying on these strategies, although some may have value in certain circumstances.

STRIKING OUT AT OTHERS

AGGRESSION. *Behavior that is intended to hurt someone; may involve either a physical or a verbal attack.*

Aggression is an intentional effort to harm or injure another (Berkowitz, 1969). An act of aggression may be either physical (attack) or verbal (making nasty remarks). This formal concept of aggression does not include some everyday uses of the term—for example, as in describing an "aggressive" salesperson. Psychologists prefer to use the term *assertive* to denote bold, forceful, but nonharmful interpersonal behavior. In contrast, aggression involves striking out at others with the intent to hurt them.

THE FRUSTRATION/AGGRESSION HYPOTHESIS

As I pointed out in discussing emotional reactions to stress, anger and rage are common responses to frustration. It has long been known that this frustration-induced anger tends to lead to acts of aggression (see Box 5.1). Many years ago, a team of psychologists (Dollard et al., 1939) described this relationship in the frustration/aggression hypothesis, which generated decades of controversial research. Since then, a great number of studies (for example, Rule & Percival,

1971; Sears, Hovland, & Miller, 1940) have verified that there is a causal link between frustration and aggression. However, Berkowitz (1969) notes that this research has also shown (1) that frustration does not *necessarily* lead to aggression, (2) that many factors other than frustration (including one's personality) affect the likelihood of aggression, and (3) that frustration may produce responses other than aggression (for example, apathy). Hence, Berkowitz theorizes that frustration serves to arouse anger, which lowers the threshold for aggressive actions. In any case, it is clear that when we become frustrated, we tend to strike out at the people around us.

It should be emphasized that this sort of aggressive response is often directed at an irrelevant person who had nothing to do with the frustration. In many situations, it is risky or unwise to vent our anger at the real source of our frustration, but we may lash out later at an irrelevant target. For example, you might be reluctant to express your anger toward a police officer who has just ticketed you for a minor speeding violation. Twenty minutes later, however, you might be downright brutal in rudely rebuking a harmless service station attendant who fails to wipe your windshield thoroughly.

ADAPTIVE VALUE OF AGGRESSION

The adaptive value of aggressive behavior tends to be minimal. Hurting someone, especially an "irrelevant" someone, is not likely to alleviate frustration or rid one of stress. Moreover, the interpersonal conflicts and crises that may emerge from aggressive behavior will typically produce *additional* sources of stress. Let's say you are under extreme pressure at work. Your boss expects you to accomplish the impossible. If you respond to that pressure by unfairly bawling out a subordinate at work, you may undermine the motivation of someone you need to depend on in order to run your department effectively. If you then go home and pick a fight with your spouse, you will create a new source of current stress and will probably lose the valuable empathy and social support that might have been forthcoming from your spouse.

There is evidence, however, that behaving aggressively after frustration may serve to release unwanted emotional tension. Hokanson and Burgess (1962) found that the opportunity to aggress physically or verbally after frustration led to a decrease in subjects' blood pressure and heart rate. In view of the negative effects of emotional arousal already discussed, this release could be quite beneficial. Recall that arousal often impairs intellectual functioning. Worchel (1957) has shown that allowing frustrated subjects to aggress (verbally) can lead to improved performance on a cognitive task. However, it is obvious that we cannot, in good conscience, strike out at people just to release our pent-up emotions. Later I shall discuss how to express and release anger in healthy and socially acceptable ways.

5.1 *STRIKING OUT AT OTHERS: HOSTILITY ON THE HIGHWAY*

As if highways weren't dangerous enough, an article in *Time* magazine (August 14, 1978) says that frustrated motorists are attacking each other more and more frequently. For example, one California motorist shot and killed another driver in an argument about a lane change! Such incidents of violence, triggered by fender benders and differences of opinion about right-of-way, appear to be on the upswing. Not only are motorists attacking one another, they're also assaulting the police officers who pull them over for violations. The California Highway Patrol recorded 413 such acts of aggression in 1977 (up 69% from 1973)!

The exact causes of this increase in highway violence are obscure. Whatever the causes underlying the increase, it is clear that driving an automobile can be a highly stressful, tension-packed, often frustrating activity. These incidents of aggression vividly illustrate our tendency to strike out at others in response to even minor frustrations.

GIVING UP

Some people, when confronted with stress, will simply give up and withdraw from the battle. This behavioral pattern of apathy and inaction tends to be associated with the emotional reactions of dejection, sorrow, and grief. Bettelheim (1943) observed this kind of behavioral reaction among some prisoners in the Nazi concentration camps of World War II. While many prisoners aggressed against their captors through acts of sabotage and worked valiantly to maintain their will to live, many others sank into total apathy and exerted no effort toward adaptation and survival.

LEARNED HELPLESSNESS

LEARNED HELPLESSNESS. *A syndrome described by Seligman involving passive behavior produced by prolonged exposure to unavoidable aversive events; used as a model to explain depression in humans.*

Martin Seligman (1974) has described a laboratory analog of this withdrawal syndrome, which may shed some light on the conditions that cause it. In Seligman's research, animals are subjected to electrical shocks that they are helpless to escape. The animals are then given an opportunity to learn a response that will allow them to avoid the shock. However, they tend to display what Seligman calls **learned helplessness,** which means that they become so apathetic and listless that they make little, if any, effort to learn the avoidance response. Other research (Hiroto, 1974) suggests that *humans* also tend to display this learned helplessness after being subjected to uncontrollable aversive events. Thus, it appears that encounters with stress that we are powerless to overcome (for example, death of one's spouse) may lead to motivational deficits that promote withdrawal tendencies. Unfortunately, this tendency to give up may be transferred to situations in which we are not really helpless. Thus, we find some people who routinely repond to stress with fatalism and resignation. Setbacks that could be dealt with effectively are simply accepted passively.

ADAPTIVE VALUE OF WITHDRAWAL

MARTIN SELIGMAN

The appeal of giving up as a coping strategy lies in the fact that your subjective distress tends to diminish once you decide to "throw in the towel." As you can surely anticipate, however, surrender is not highly regarded as a mode of coping. Obviously, giving up precludes the possibility of resolving a problem in a favorable manner. More important, there is reason to believe that learned helplessness in humans may contribute to serious emotional disorders, such as depression (Seligman, 1974). This suggests that giving up is generally a rather counterproductive pattern of coping.

However, withdrawal from a stressful situation *could* be adaptive in some instances. For example, if you were thrown into a job that you simply were not equipped to handle effectively, it might be better to quit rather than face constant pressure and diminishing self-esteem. There is something to be said for recognizing one's limitations. There may also be occasions when we need to recognize that our goals are unrealistic or ultimately unimportant. The highly competitive nature of American society leads many of us to push ourselves toward heights that are very difficult to achieve and to pursue goals that really represent *others'* notions of what we should accomplish. Goals such as making a college basketball team, gaining admission to medical school, or earning enough money to afford a Mercedes may be better discarded if they are not realistic or if they are really the goals that our parents and friends desire for us. It is important to understand that the adaptive value of any coping response depends on the situation. Even a coping strategy such as giving up, which sounds terribly "un-American," may be highly adaptive. As you will see again and again, there are no simple rules regarding the best ways to cope with life's challenges.

BLAMING ONESELF

Once my favorite football team absorbed a tough defeat in a game that it just as easily could have won. In the postgame interviews, the head coach was brutally critical of himself. He said that he was outcoached, that he had made poor decisions, and that his game plan was faulty. He almost eagerly assumed all the blame for the loss himself. In reality, he had taken some reasonable chances that didn't go his way and had suffered the effects of poor execution by his players. The loss was really attributable to the collective failures of 50 or so players and coaches. The head coach's unrealistically negative self-evaluation was a fairly typical response to stressful frustration. When confronted by stress (especially frustration and pressure), people have a tendency to become highly self-critical.

NEGATIVE SELF-TALK

This tendency to engage in highly negative, exceedingly critical self-talk in response to stress has been noted by quite a number of influential theorists. Meichenbaum and Turk (1982) have described how stress can elicit such pervasively negative inner dialogues. Ellis (1973) calls this cognitive phenomenon "catastrophic thinking" and focuses on how it is rooted in irrational assumptions. Aaron Beck (1972) analyzes this negative self-talk into *three* tendencies, noting that people often (1) unreasonably attribute their failures to personal shortcomings, (2) focus on negative feedback from others while ignoring favorable feedback, and (3) make unduly pessimistic projections about the future. Thus, if you performed poorly on an exam, you might blame it on your woeful stupidity, dismiss comments from a classmate that the test was inaccurate, and hysterically predict that you would surely flunk the course.

ADAPTIVE VALUE OF NEGATIVE SELF-TALK

Although there is something to be said for recognizing one's frailties, all the theorists mentioned above agree that negative self-talk tends to be counterproductive. According to Ellis (1973), catastrophic thinking simply acts to cause, aggravate, and perpetuate emotional reactions to stress that are often problematic. Along even more serious lines, Beck (1972) marshals evidence that negative self-talk can contribute to the development of serious depression. There certainly are occasions when getting tough with oneself is a mature, adaptive response; however, in general it appears that self-blame and self-criticism are not very healthy ways to cope with stress.

INDULGING ONESELF

Our discussion would not be complete without mentioning that stress sometimes leads to excesses in self-indulgence. What exactly do I mean by "indulging oneself"? Basically, I am referring to a seemingly common tendency to engage in excessive consummatory behavior when troubled by stress. I can illustrate this point with personal examples. When I have an exceptionally stressful day, a frequent coping response on my part is to head for the refrigerator, the grocery store, or a restaurant—usually in pursuit of something chocolate. In other words, I sometimes deal with life's hassles by stuffing myself with all of my favorite foods. In a similar vein, I have a close friend who copes with stress by making a beeline for the nearest shopping mall for a wild spending spree. Thus, when I speak of excesses in consummatory behavior, I am referring to injudicious patterns of eating, drinking, smoking, using drugs, spending money, and so forth.

Although much of the evidence relating stress to self-indulgence is anecdotal, it does not appear that my friend and I are so unusual. In their classification of coping processes, Moos and Billings (1982) list *developing alternative rewards* as a common response to stress. It makes sense that when things are going poorly in one area of a person's life, he or she might try to compen-

CATHY

sate by pursuing substitute forms or sources of satisfaction. Consummatory responses probably rank high when this happens, because they are relatively easy to execute and they tend to be very pleasurable. Thus, it is not surprising that there is evidence relating stress to increases in eating (Slochower, 1976), smoking (Tomkins, 1966), consumption of alcohol (Marlatt & Rose, 1980), and some types of drug use (Krueger, 1981).

There is nothing inherently maladaptive about indulging oneself as a way of coping with life's stresses. This pursuit of alternative rewards is a very simple, readily available coping strategy that seems to have some merit if kept under control. However, *if one consistently responds to stress with chronic and excessive consummatory behavior, obvious problems are likely to develop.* Excesses in eating may produce obesity, excesses in drinking may pave the way to alcoholism, excesses in drug use may lead to drug dependence, and excesses in spending may create havoc in one's personal finances. In light of the fact that indulging oneself is not likely to be a very productive mode of coping (in terms of problem solving), the risks associated with chronic use of this strategy suggest that it has rather marginal adaptive value.

DEFENSIVE COPING

Defensive coping is a very common approach to dealing with stress. Quite a number of diverse coping tactics fall into this category. As noted earlier, Sigmund Freud (1959) gets credit for developing the important concept of the defense mechanism. Though rooted in the psychoanalytic tradition, this concept has enjoyed widespread acceptance among psychologists of all persuasions. Building on Freud's original insight, modern psychologists have broadened the scope of the concept and added profusely to the list of specific defense mechanisms.

THE NATURE OF DEFENSE MECHANISMS

DEFENSE MECHANISM. *A largely cognitive procedure used to defend against unpleasant emotions through self-deception and the distortion of reality.*

Defense mechanisms are descriptions of certain behavioral patterns that people tend to exhibit, particularly when they are struggling with stress. More specifically, defense mechanisms are coping procedures that serve to protect a person from the threatening aspect of stressful events. You probably already have some general familiarity with the notion of defense mechanisms, since they are often mentioned in popular books, magazines, movies, and TV shows. Unfortunately, this popular treatment in the media has created many misconceptions. To clear up any such misunderstandings, I will use a question/answer format to acquaint you with the general nature of defense mechanisms.

What exactly do they defend against? Above all else, they function to shield a person from the *emotional discomfort* that is so often elicited by stress. Their main purpose is to reduce the intensity of these unpleasant emotions. Sometimes they may even ward off unwelcome emotions *before* such emotions can be experienced. Foremost among the emotions that are guarded against is *anxiety*. We tend to be especially protective when the anxiety is due to some threat to our self-concept or self-esteem. Defenses are also used to suppress dangerous feelings of anger so that they do not explode into acts of aggression, which we often regret. Guilt and grief are two other emotions that we often try to evade through defensive maneuvers.

How do they work? Through *deception*. They accomplish their goals by distorting reality so that it does not *appear* so threatening. For example, let us say that you are doing very poorly in school and are in danger of flunking out, in spite of the fact that you desperately want to succeed. You might reduce the anxiety brought about by this threat of frustration in several ways. Initially, you might *deny* the obvious danger, refusing to even think about such a possibility. If it becomes impossible to deny the obvious, you might defend your self-esteem through *rationalization,* saying "It's not my fault. The crummy teachers here don't grade fairly." You might also *fantasize* about how you will salvage adequate grades by performing spectacularly well on the upcoming final exams, when the objective fact is that you are hopelessly behind in your studies. In this case, each of these three defense mechanisms—denial, rationalization, and fantasy—would bend or distort reality so as to reduce your feelings of anxiety. Thus, defense mechanisms usually operate at a cognitive level and essentially involve self-deception.

Are they conscious or unconscious? Probably *both*. It is extremely difficult to do research on this question of awareness. Freud originally believed that the defense mechanisms operated at an unconscious level. It now appears that, *some* of the time, we are at least dimly aware of their operation. For the most part, however, we seem to use defense mechanisms unconsciously.

Are they normal? Yes. We all use defense mechanisms on a fairly regular basis. They are perfectly normal behavioral patterns that are acquired through learning. Although many people equate the presence of defense mechanisms with neurosis, this is definitely an error.

Are they healthy? This is a much more complex question, and I will return to it after describing the specific defense mechanisms in some detail. More often than not, the answer is *no*. Defensive behavior tends to be self-defeating. Distorting reality rarely solves a problem. On the contrary, it tends to put off dealing with the problem, often until it is too late to deal with it effectively. Nonetheless, defensive behavior is sometimes adaptive.

How many defense mechanisms are there? Too many. Because of their fascination with the concept, theorists in the 1930s and 1940s got a little carried away, identifying and naming hordes of new defense mechanisms that were only slight variations from already existing ones. Some books (for example, Freedman, Kaplan, & Sadock, 1976) list as many as 30 mechanisms of defense! No two books have exactly the same list, although there is a small core of defense mechanisms that appear on virtually every list. The problem with the lengthy lists is that they have too much redundancy. I will use a list of moderate length (nine items) that will give you a sound understanding of defensive coping without making you learn fine distinctions between defenses that are only superficially different. Even with this relatively short list, you will notice some conceptual overlap between certain defense mechanisms.

REPRESENTATIVE DEFENSE MECHANISMS

REPRESSION. *An effort to keep anxiety-arousing thoughts in the unconscious.*

1. **Repression** involves pushing into the unconscious any thoughts or feelings that are distressing or painful. We tend to repress wishes that are unlikely to be fulfilled, desires that make us feel guilty, conflicts that make us anxious, and the memory of events that were traumatic. "Battle amnesia" is a clear example of repression at work. In this syndrome, a soldier is usually trauma-

tized by the death of a comrade or by his own close brush with death in combat. However, he is unable to remember anything about the event itself.

Repression is probably used more than any other defense mechanism. As you will see, it often works in conjunction with one or more other defense mechanisms. By definition, repression works unconsciously. The notion of "consciously" pushing thoughts into the unconscious would be self-contradictory.

DENIAL. *A conscious refusal to acknowledge the truth.*

2. **Denial** involves a *conscious* effort to suppress unpleasant thoughts. In denial, the threatening thoughts surface at a conscious level, but you refuse to believe them and try to avoid thinking about them. Denial is usually deployed to deal with various kinds of frustration. For example, in spite of overwhelming evidence, you might deny that your spouse appears to be having an extramarital affair or that you have unintentionally become pregnant.

PROJECTION. *Attribution of one's own unacceptable thoughts or feelings to another.*

3. **Projection** consists in attributing your own unacceptable thoughts, feelings, or motives to another person in your social sphere. Usually we project onto others feelings of our own that would make us feel guilty. For example, if you felt hostile to someone because of your envy of her success, you might project this hostility onto her and believe that there was animosity between the two of you because *she* did not like *you*. Similarly, if you felt guilty about your erotic infatuation with a co-worker, you might attribute any latent sexual tension between the two of you to the *other person's* desire to seduce you. In addition to feelings of hostility and lust, people often project their own dishonesty and untrustworthiness onto other people.

DISPLACEMENT. *Redirection of anger (or another emotion) toward an irrelevant person rather than the original target.*

4. **Displacement** involves redirecting emotional impulses (usually anger) from the real source to a substitute person or object. As we have already seen, frustration tends to generate feelings of anger and aggressive impulses. Certain social realities, however, make most of us cautious about actually expressing these aggressive impulses. Rather than lash out at someone who wields some power over us (for example, our supervisor at work), we often shift our anger to a harmless recipient (perhaps a subordinate at work). As we go through a particularly frustrating day, social etiquette leads most of us to "bite the bullet" and suppress our anger. A most unfortunate outcome of this necessary deference to social decorum is that we often come home after a tough day and lash out at the very people we love the most.

REACTION FORMATION. *An exaggerated effort to behave in a manner that is exactly opposite to one's true feelings.*

5. **Reaction formation** involves behaving in a manner that is opposite to your real feelings. Like displacement, it is often used to cope with feelings of anger and hostility. Instead of shifting the hostility to an irrelevant target, we convert the resentment into exaggerated displays of affection. We tend to use reaction formation when we feel hostility toward someone whom we really should like or even love, such as a family member. The hallmark of reaction formation is the *excessive* quality of the affection. Some parents, who resent their children deep down inside, react against these guilt-producing feelings by being excessively tolerant of their children's misbehavior. Guilt about sexual desires may also generate reaction formation. Freud theorized that many males who go out of their way to portray themselves as tough, rugged "macho" men may be defending against latent homosexual impulses. Similarly, people who crusade against allegedly "loose" sexual morals may be working desperately to battle back their own powerful desires for sexual promiscuity.

REGRESSION. *Reversion to less mature, sometimes childish ways of coping.*

6. **Regression** consists in a return to less mature behavioral patterns. Probably the most common example of regression is when a supposedly mature adult throws a "temper tantrum." This sort of behavior is a very direct but very immature way of getting rid of feelings of hostility and anger. Some adults react to frustration with childish boasting and bragging. Although anyone is likely to make self-serving statements about his or her capabilities and accomplishments, the regressive version of this behavior involves ridiculous overstatements that virtually anyone can see through. For example, a discharged executive having difficulty finding a new position might start making preposterous statements about his incomparable talent and his invaluable contributions to his previous company.

RATIONALIZATION. *Creation of false but plausible excuses to justify unacceptable behavior.*

7. **Rationalization** involves creating superficially plausible excuses to justify unacceptable behavior or to minimize the severity of disappointment. After behaving unscrupulously in a business transaction—for example, selling an auto without mentioning some crucial flaw—you might alleviate your guilt by assuring yourself that "everyone does it." To deal with your disappointment over not getting into law school, you might convince yourself that you really would have hated being an attorney anyway. When we are unable to control our desires for immediate gratification in the way that we feel we should, we often resort to rationalization. For example, when you quit studying for an exam in order to watch TV, you may tell yourself that additional study "wouldn't do any good anyway." After sleeping in instead of going to classes, you might say "My body was telling me it needed more sleep."

IDENTIFICATION. *The perception of oneself as essentially similar to another person; also, a defense mechanism wherein feelings of self-esteem are enhanced by forming a real or imaginary alliance with an admired person or group. In either case, it tends to lead to some imitation of the target of identification.*

8. **Identification** involves enhancing your feelings of self-esteem by forming a real or imaginary alliance with some admired person or group. Usually, this defense mechanism serves to reduce anxiety when you are experiencing some doubt about your self-worth. For example, adolescents tend to identify with their television and rock-star heroes in order to shore up their often precarious feelings of self-esteem. Many people assure themselves of their worth and importance by joining various kinds of groups, including cliques, gangs, fraternities, sororities, clubs, civic organizations, and church-related societies (obviously, there are also many other reasons for joining some of these groups). Ego enhancement through identification may take place without formally joining a group. People may augment their self-esteem by simply embracing the ideals and lifestyles of rather informal "groups," such as the jet set, the disco crowd, intellectuals, liberals, conservatives, hippies, or soldiers of fortune.

FANTASY. *Internal focus on imagination of satisfactions that are not actually attained.*

9. **Fantasy** involves imaginary thoughts about satisfactions that are not attained in actual experience. We all engage in a certain amount of daydreaming, much of which is highly unrealistic. As a defense, fantasy helps us to cope with our feelings of inadequacy and our personal setbacks. We also tend to act out our hostile feelings in daydreams. Fantasies in which we see ourselves as a conquering hero or a martyr are particularly common. Defense through fantasy may also be manifested in the form of an addiction to novels, TV shows, and movies that portray heroic figures who overcome tremendous adversity to attain great achievements and satisfactions.

ADAPTIVE VALUE OF DEFENSE MECHANISMS

Is defensive behavior psychologically healthful? This question is very difficult to answer. As you learned in Chapter 2, there is much debate about the value-laden concept of psychological health. In addition to this fundamental problem, we have to face the complex reality that the adaptive value of a defense mechanism depends on various situational and personal factors that are unique to each instance of defensive behavior. Hence, we cannot make any sweeping, across-the-board generalizations about the value of defensive behavior. What we *can* do is discuss some of the problems that *tend* to be associated with defensive behavior.

Before addressing these problems, I should emphasize that occasionally there *are* situations in which defensive behavior *clearly* represents a healthful response. For example, displacement sometimes allows us to channel aggressive energy into socially acceptable outlets. If you worked in a job in which a lot of frustration was inevitable, you might start playing vicious racquetball matches in the evenings to release your smoldering aggressive urges in a harmless way. Identification is often a very healthful way to alleviate doubts about one's worth as a person. Identification could lead you to emulate an exceptionally good role model or to affiliate with, and contribute to, a very worthwhile social organization. Creative use of fantasy is sometimes the key to dealing effectively with temporary periods of frustration, such as a stint in the military service or a period of recovery in the hospital.

In addition to situations such as these, in which the positive value of defensive behavior is readily evident, there are many situations in which its value is ambiguous. In many cases, calling defensive behavior healthful or unhealthful is a matter of opinion or personal taste. For instance, denial is a common reaction to the imminent death of a loved one. Some people deny until the last minute that their spouse or parent or child is inexorably approaching death. In a negative vein, one could argue that such denial grossly distorts reality and delays coming to grips with a frustrating event that has to be faced sooner or later. However, if this denial allows one to suppress overwhelmingly powerful emotions that would severely disrupt everyday functioning, one could argue that it has some positive value. Thus, the adaptive value of defensive behavior is often ambiguous and open to question or debate.

Now that I have stressed that defensive behavior is not inherently bad, let me discuss some of its typical shortcomings. First, defense mechanisms often produce pseudo solutions to our problems by reducing the threat of stressful circumstances in our minds but not in reality. Thus, the biggest problem with defensive behavior is simply that it rarely provides an authentic solution to our problems. Second, these defensive pseudo solutions often preclude more constructive efforts to find a satisfactory solution for a problem. Instead of focusing our resources on the problem, to deal with it as effectively as possible, we avoid facing up to it through evasive tactics. These defensive tactics use up energy that might have been expended more wisely by tackling the problem systematically. Thus, defense mechanisms may prevent the use of healthier coping patterns until it is too late for them to be effective. A third flaw of defensive behavior is that it usually is only partly successful in warding off unwelcome emotions. This partial success tends to make defense mechanisms self-perpetuating: defensive behavior often breeds still more defensive behavior. A fourth flaw of defensive behavior is that it often puts us out of touch with our true feelings. Although this may occasionally have some merit, generally speaking it is healthier to have an accurate awareness of one's own emotions.

In summary, there are a number of reasons that defensive behavior is usually less than optimal. Nonetheless, defensive behavior is universal and is not altogether without some positive value. In judging the adaptive value of defense mechanisms, two factors appear crucial: the degree to which they distort reality and the degree to which they prevent more constructive coping efforts. The more defensive behavior leads to either of these two outcomes, the more it tends to be regarded as unhealthful and maladaptive.

Constructive Coping Patterns

Thus far, our discussion of coping processes has had a rather negative theme. Although I have emphasized that the adaptive value of any response depends on the overall situation, I have concentrated on coping strategies that usually are less than ideal. However, I have not intended to be discouraging, and I have not meant to imply that stress always, or even usually, leads to negative outcomes. On the contrary, this entire book is based on the firm conviction that increased knowledge about the principles of behavior can help you to develop more effective coping skills. Please be assured that stressful events *can* be dealt with successfully!

Shifting to a more positive perspective, I will borrow the term *constructive coping* from Torrance (1965) to describe behavioral reactions to stress that *tend* to be relatively healthful or adaptive. Some adjustment texts discuss these behavioral patterns under terms such as *effective coping* (Coleman, 1979) or *competent coping* (Nikelly, 1977); however, terms such as *effective* or *competent* seem to suggest (inaccurately) that certain coping procedures consistently lead to positive outcomes. Unfortunately, even the healthiest and most optimal coping strategies may turn out to be ineffective. No strategy of coping can guarantee a successful outcome. In contrast, the term *constructive coping* seems preferable because it clearly conveys a positive, healthy connotation, without promising success.

ASSUMPTIONS ABOUT THE NATURE OF CONSTRUCTIVE COPING

CONSTRUCTIVE COPING
Efforts to deal with stressful events that are judged to be relatively healthy and adaptive.

In labeling certain coping procedures "constructive," I am making value judgments about whether those behavior patterns should be regarded as psychologically healthy. In light of that reality, I must spell out explicitly my assumptions about the nature of **constructive coping.** In spite of the diverse views that exist about the healthy personality, I believe that most theorists would agree with the assumptions listed below. They are not particularly unusual or controversial.

1. Constructive coping involves confronting problems directly. It is task-relevant and action-oriented. It involves a conscious effort to rationally evaluate one's options in order to try to solve one's problems.
2. Constructive coping requires staying in tune with reality. It is based on realistic appraisal of stress and one's resources, rather than defensive self-deception or catastrophic thinking.
3. Constructive coping involves learning to recognize, and in some cases inhibit, disruptive and potentially harmful emotional reactions to stress. It requires the acquisition of some emotional self-control.
4. Constructive coping involves learning to exert some control over potentially harmful or destructive habitual behaviors. It requires the acquisition of some behavioral self-control.
5. Constructive coping includes making efforts to ensure that one's body is not exceptionally vulnerable to the possible damaging effects of stress. It requires taking reasonable care of one's body.

The description above should give you a general idea of what I mean by "constructive coping." These assumptions will guide our discourse in the remainder of this chapter, as we go into more detail on how to cope constructively with stressful events.

CLASSIFICATION OF COPING RESPONSES

Many theorists have tried to develop a classification scheme for organizing the diverse array of coping efforts that we make in response to stress. As you learned in Chapter 1, this is important because the clear *description* of a phenomenon is the first goal of scientific investigation. The great diversity of coping responses has made this task difficult, and at present there is no universally accepted taxonomy of coping mechanisms. To facilitate our analysis, I will use and build on a classification scheme proposed by Rudolph Moos and Andrew Billings (1982). I will add one mode of coping to the three basic types of coping identified by Moos and Billings. Thus, I will discuss four domains, or types, of coping strategies that are classified according to their focus, or goal:

- *Appraisal-focused coping* involves efforts to reevaluate the apparent demands and/or redefine the apparent meaning of stressful transactions. Its goal is to alter the appraisal of threat in the situation.
- *Problem-focused coping* involves efforts to circumvent, modify, remedy, or conquer the problem and its consequences. Its goal is to directly master the threat or problem itself.
- *Emotion-focused coping* involves efforts to control and usually reduce the emotional reactions aroused by stress. Its goal is to reestablish a healthy emotional equilibrium.
- *Physiologic-focused coping* involves efforts to diminish the impact of the

physical demands placed on the body by stressful encounters. Its goal is to minimize the susceptibility of one's body to the possible damaging effects of stress.

Of course, like most efforts to classify complex behavior, this scheme is not totally satisfactory. There are coping tactics that fall between the cracks or are difficult to categorize because they have more than one goal or because they have an impact at more than one point in the stress process.

Appraisal-Focused Constructive Coping

People tend to underestimate the importance of the appraisal phase in the stress process. They tend to think of stress in terms of objective events and fail to appreciate the highly subjective feelings that color the perception of threat to one's well-being.

MINIMIZING DEFENSIVE DISTORTION

There is a reasonable consensus among theorists in psychology that effective coping is facilitated by *accurate* appraisal of potentially stressful events (Cameron & Meichenbaum, 1982). That is one of several reasons that defensive coping tends to be less than optimal. Overdependence on defense mechanisms usually leads to distortion of reality. Of particular concern is the fact that defensive coping often leads people to underestimate or ignore problems, allowing them to worsen and grow more deeply entrenched. Thus, constructive coping requires that one attempt to minimize defensive self-deception. The first step toward minimizing one's use of defense mechanisms is to develop a certain vigilance by accepting the fact that they exist and that we all use them. The next step is simply to familiarize oneself with the various defense mechanisms in order to become more skilled at spotting them.

ELLIS'S APPROACH TO COMBATING NEGATIVE SELF-TALK

RATIONAL-EMOTIVE THERAPY. *An approach to therapy, developed by Albert Ellis, that emphasizes changing irrational assumptions and thinking that produce maladaptive emotions and behaviors.*

Albert Ellis (1973; Ellis & Harper, 1975) is a prominent theorist who was the architect of **rational-emotive therapy,** an approach to psychotherapy that focuses mainly on changing clients' appraisals of situations in order to reduce negative self-talk. According to Ellis, our negative emotional reactions to events are caused not by the events themselves but rather by our interpretation of these events.

CATASTROPHIC THINKING AND EMOTION

Ellis maintains that *you feel the way you think.* Specifically, he argues that maladaptive emotional reactions are caused by negative self-talk, which he calls **catastrophic thinking.** Let us elaborate on his theory. He uses a simple A-B-C sequence to explain his analysis.

CATASTROPHIC THINKING. *Ellis's term for exceedingly negative self-talk that is unrealistically pessimistic and greatly exaggerates the magnitude of one's problems.*

A—Activating event.   The *A* in Ellis's system stands for the activating event that produces the stress. The activating event is simply something unfortunate that happens to you. Examples might include an automobile accident, a delay while waiting in line at the bank, the cancellation of a date, failure to get a promotion you were expecting, or being beaten in a handball match.

B—Belief system.   *B* stands for your belief about the activating event. It is your mental reaction to, or appraisal of, the event. According to Ellis, this often involves seeing the event as some sort of disaster or catastrophe. Thus, we think negative thoughts: "How awful this is! I can't stand it. Things never turn out fairly for me. I'll be in this line forever! I'll never get a promotion."

ALBERT ELLIS

C — Consequence. *C* stands for the emotional upset that appears to be a consequence of the unfortunate event. Thus, in reaction to the event, we feel angry, outraged, anxious, panic-stricken, gloomy, disgusted, or dejected. The actual emotional reaction is viewed as the third stage in a three-phase sequence.

According to Ellis, most of us do not understand the importance of phase B in this three-stage process. We unwittingly believe that the activating event (A) directly causes the consequent emotional turmoil (C). *However, Ellis maintains that A does not cause C!* It only *appears* to do so. Instead, Ellis asserts that C is really caused by B! Our emotional reaction is actually brought on by our unrealistic appraisal (B) of the event.

Ellis contends that during phase B we can choose to think rationally or irrationally about the event. *He further contends that it is catastrophic thinking during phase B that causes most unpleasant emotions.* Instead of viewing the unfortunate event realistically, we irrationally "make a mountain out of a molehill." We turn inconvenience into disaster. Let's say someone "stands you up" on a date you were looking forward to with eager anticipation. You might think as follows. "Oh, this is *terrible!* Now I'll have a *rotten,* boring weekend. People *always* treat me unfairly. I'll *never* find anyone to fall in love with. *Nobody* likes me. I must be a *crummy, worthless* person!" Ellis would argue that such thoughts are irrational. He would point out that just because you were stood up by an inconsiderate person, it does *not* follow logically that you (1) must have a lousy weekend, (2) will never fall in love, and (3) are a worthless person. These are irrational thoughts and beliefs that will cause you to feel angry, anxious, and dejected. According to Ellis, you can avoid such distressing emotions if you evaluate the event rationally, thinking "Gee, this is a disappointment. What can I do to salvage the weekend?"

Ellis suggests that catastrophic thinking is derived from irrational assumptions that we hold. He points out that we often reason from a logically indefensible premise, such as "I must have approval from everyone" or "I must do well in all endeavors." These faulty assumptions, which we often hold unconsciously, generate our catastrophic thinking. Ellis proposes that to reduce our negative self-talk and unwarranted emotional reactions, we must root out these faulty assumptions.

IRRATIONAL ASSUMPTIONS THAT PROMOTE CATASTROPHIC THINKING

To facilitate emotional self-control, it is important to learn to spot irrational assumptions and the unhealthy patterns of thought that they generate. Woolfolk and Richardson (1978; see Box 5.2) discuss five common, emotion-arousing, irrational assumptions. A lengthier list can be found in Box 5.3.

1. *I must have love and affection from certain people.* We all want to be liked and loved. There is nothing wrong with that. However, many of us foolishly believe that we should be liked by everyone we come into contact with. This obviously is unrealistic. Once we fall in love, we tend to believe that our future happiness and gratification depend absolutely on the perpetual continuation of that one, special relationship. Many of us erroneously believe that if our current love relationship were to end, we would never again be able to achieve a comparable one. This is an unrealistic view of the future. Such views make us anxious during a relationship and severely depressed if it is terminated.

2. *I must perform well in all endeavors.* We live in a supercompetitive society. We are indoctrinated to believe that victory brings happiness. Consequently, we feel that we must always win. For example, many sports enthusiasts are never satisfied unless they perform at their *best* level. However, by definition, their best level is not their typical level, and they therefore set themselves up for inevitable frustration.

3. *Other people should always behave competently and be considerate of*

me. We are often angered by others' stupidity and selfishness. For example, you may become outraged when a mechanic fails to fix your car properly or when a salesperson treats you rudely. It would be nice if people were always competent and considerate, but you know better—they are not! Yet, many of us go through life counting unrealistically on others' efficiency and kindness.

4. *Everyone I identify with should have pleasant experiences.* Many of us extend our personal boundaries so that we become very upset when unfortunate events happen to others. When a friend's wife walks out on him, we become furious and depressed *for* him. The broader your personal boundaries are, the more likely it is that you will vicariously experience some negative event. A classic example is the sports fan who goes berserk when a referee or umpire makes a bad call that goes against his or her team.

5. *Events should always go the way I like.* Some people simply won't tolerate any kind of setback. They seem to believe that things should always go their way. For example, some people become very tense and angry each time they get stuck in a rush-hour traffic jam. They seem to believe that they are entitled to coast home easily every day, even though they know from past experience that only very rarely is the rush hour a breeze. Such expectations are clearly unrealistic and doomed to be violated. Yet, few people recognize the obvious irrationality of the assumption that underlies their anger, unless it is pointed out to them.

REDUCING CATASTROPHIC THINKING

To reduce your catastrophic thinking and unnecessary emotional reactions, you need to learn to do two things. You must learn how to (1) detect your irrational beliefs and (2) dispute them.

Detection involves acquiring the ability to quickly identify emotion-generating, irrational modes of thought. This requires, first of all, that you become tuned in to your emotional fluctuations. You need to be sensitive to the fact that tension is creeping up on you or anger is beginning to smolder within. Second, in addition to this vigilance, you need to become adept at spotting catastrophic thinking. Ask yourself why you're getting upset. Force yourself to verbalize your concerns, covertly or out loud. Examine this self-talk closely. Ask yourself whether you are exaggerating the seriousness of the problem. Look for key words that often show up in catastrophic thinking, such as *should, ought, never,* and *must.*

Disputing your irrational beliefs involves subjecting them to a tough, skep-

---

tical scrutiny. Basically, you need to *argue* with yourself about your thinking. Try to root out the premise from which your conclusions are derived. As Ellis has pointed out, many of us are unaware of the assumptions that form the basis for our catastrophic analyses. Does your premise make sense? In making this evaluation, it is helpful to become familiar with the many faulty assumptions that commonly underlie our evaluations of situations. If your assumption seems reasonable, ask yourself whether your conclusions follow logically from this premise. Systematically trace your trains of thought and challenge any irrationality. Then work at replacing your irrational beliefs with more low-key, rational views.

ADDITIONAL APPRAISAL-FOCUSED COGNITIVE TACTICS

Ellis has a comprehensive theory that focuses on how we appraise stress. Some additional specific tactics along the same lines have emerged from other theorists. All these additional suggestions are consistent with Ellis's approach.

5.3 IRRATIONAL IDEAS THAT CAUSE AND SUSTAIN EMOTIONAL DISTURBANCE

1. *The idea that it is a dire necessity for an adult to be loved or approved by everyone for everything one does*—instead of the idea that it would be better for one to concentrate on one's own self-respect, on winning approval for practical purposes, and on loving rather than being loved.

2. *The idea that one should be thoroughly competent, adequate, and achieving in all possible respects if one is to consider oneself worthwhile*—instead of the idea that one would do better to accept oneself as a quite imperfect creature, who has limitations and fallibilities like anyone else.

3. *The idea that certain acts are awful or wicked and that people who perform such acts should be severely blamed and punished*—instead of the idea that certain acts are inappropriate or antisocial and that people who perform such acts are behaving stupidly, ignorantly, or neurotically and had better be helped to change.

4. *The idea that it is horrible when things are not the way one would like them to be*—instead of the idea that it is too bad, that one had better try to change or control conditions so that they become more satisfactory, and if that is not possible, one had better temporarily accept their existence.

5. *The idea that human unhappiness is externally caused and that people have little or no ability to control their sorrows and disturbances*—instead of the idea that emotional disturbance is caused by the view that one takes of conditions.

6. *The idea that if something is or may be dangerous or fearsome, one should be terribly upset about it and should keep dwelling on the possibility of its occurring*—instead of the idea that one had better frankly face it and render it nondangerous and, when that is not possible, accept the inevitable.

7. *The idea that it is easier to avoid than to face life's difficulties and responsibilities*—instead of the idea that the so-called easy way is invariably the much harder in the long run.

8. *The idea that one should be dependent on others and need someone stronger than oneself on whom to rely*—instead of the idea that it is better to take the risk of thinking and acting independently.

9. *The idea that because something once strongly affected one's life, it should indefinitely have a similar effect*—instead of the idea that one can learn from one's past experiences but not be overly attached to or prejudiced by them.

10. *The idea that one should become quite upset over other people's problems and disturbances*—instead of the idea that one would do much better to help them to change and if that is not possible, to resign oneself to making the best of a bad situation.

11. *The idea that there is invariably a right, precise, and perfect solution to human problems and that it is catastrophic if this perfect solution is not found*—instead of the idea that the world is full of probability and chance and that one can still enjoy life despite this.

12. *The idea that one has virtually no control over one's emotions and that one cannot help feeling certain things*—instead of the idea that one has enormous control over one's destructive emotions if one chooses to work at changing the bigoted and unscientific hypotheses that one employs to create them.

13. *The idea that the world (and especially other people) should be fair and that justice (or mercy) must triumph*—instead of the idea that one can realistically continue to prefer and seek more fair behavior and give up the notion of absolutes.

14. *The idea that beliefs held by respected authorities or society must be correct and should not be questioned*—instead of the idea that it would be better to think clearly about what is being offered and to do so solely on the value of the belief, not on who holds it.

Adapted by a colleague (Dr. Basil Najjar) from *Reason and Emotion in Psychotherapy* (Ellis, 1977).

Making positive comparisons. When you are feeling overwhelmed by life's difficulties, there is some merit in the common-sense strategy of focusing on the fact that "things could be worse." No matter how severe our problems get, most of us know a number of people who have even bigger troubles. That is not to say that you should derive satisfaction from others' misfortune; however, comparing your own plight with others' even tougher struggles can help you put things in perspective. This strategy of making positive comparisons with others is called *cognitive redefinition* by Moos and Billings (1982). Research by McCrae (1984) suggests that it is a very commonly employed coping mechanism. It seems to be a relatively healthy one, in that it can facilitate calming reappraisals of stress without the necessity of distorting reality.

Humor as a stress reducer. When the going gets tough, it may pay to just laugh about it. McCrae's (1984) study of coping suggests that this strategy is used less frequently than making positive comparisons, but its use is far from rare. When asked to check off those coping tactics that they used to deal with a particular source of stress, roughly 40% of McCrae's subjects reported using humor.

In analyzing the stress-reducing effects of humor, Dixon (1980) emphasizes its impact on appraisal. Finding a humorous aspect in a stressful situation redefines the situation in a less threatening way, producing a positive reappraisal. However, Dixon also notes that humor can function as an emotion-focused coping mechanism, in that laughter and mirth may serve to discharge pent-up emotions. These dual functions of humor may make joking about life's difficulties a particularly useful coping strategy. While psychologists have long suspected that humor might be a worthwhile coping response, empirical evidence to that effect has emerged only recently. Martin and Lefcourt (1983) measured sense of humor in a variety of ways and found that a good sense of humor functioned as a buffer to lessen the link between stress and mood disturbance.

Problem-Focused Constructive Coping

As noted earlier, problem-focused coping involves efforts to circumvent, modify, remedy, or conquer the stress-producing problem itself. In this category, I will discuss (1) systematic problem solving, (2) the importance of seeking help, (3) developing alternative rewards, and (4) achieving behavioral self-control.

SYSTEMATIC PROBLEM SOLVING

I am now ready to discuss how to attack the problems that produce stress in your life. Unfortunately, since every problem situation is unique, and there are an infinite number of problems that may arise, I can only sketch a very *general* outline of how to systematically approach life's difficulties. I cannot spell out pat solutions; there are none. All I can do is give you some advice about how to efficiently go about the business of confronting your problems. Such a general outline is necessarily abstract, and you may find it a little disappointing. However, it sets the stage for the remainder of the book, in which I will tackle, in a more concrete and detailed fashion, specific problems that emerge in particular areas of life.

The problem-solving plan to be described is a synthesis of observations by various experts, including Mahoney (1979) and Miller (1978). It involves four steps: (1) clarify the problem, (2) generate alternative courses of action, (3) evaluate your alternatives and select a course of action, and (4) take action while maintaining flexibility.

STEP 1: CLARIFY THE PROBLEM

You can't tackle a problem head on if you're not sure what the problem is. Therefore, *the first step in any systematic problem-solving effort is to clarify the nature of the problem.* Sometimes the problem will be all too obvious; at other times it may be quite difficult to pin down the source of trouble. In any case, you need to arrive at a *specific* and *concrete* definition of your problem. Two common tendencies typically hinder people's efforts to get a clear picture of their problem. First, we tend to describe our problems in vague generalities (for example, "My life isn't going anywhere" or "I never have enough time"). Second, we tend to focus too much on negative feelings, thus confusing the consequences of problems with the problems themselves ("I'm so depressed all the time" or "I'm so nervous I can't concentrate").

To overcome these tendencies and develop a clear specification of your problem, it may be helpful to think in terms of the four types of stress discussed in Chapter 3. Most problems can be conceived of in terms of frustration, conflict, pressure, and change. In the case of frustration, you need to identify the motive being thwarted and the barrier preventing goal attainment. In the case of pressure, it helps to pinpoint the source of the pressure. Once you start thinking in these terms, you may be surprised how often your problem boils down to a simple matter of conflict. Whatever your troubles are, it is crucial that you dig beneath the superficial appearances to arrive at a specific and concrete definition of your problem.

STEP 2: GENERATE ALTERNATIVE COURSES OF ACTION

The second step in systematic problem solving is to generate alternative courses of action. Notice that I did not call these alternative *solutions*. Many problems do not have a readily available "solution" or course of action that will *completely* resolve and terminate the problem. If you think in terms of searching for complete solutions, you may prevent yourself from considering many worthwhile courses of action. Instead, it is more realistic to search for alternatives that might produce some kind of *improvement* in your situation.

BRAINSTORMING. *A technique for fostering creative problem solving that involves free expression of ideas while withholding criticism and evaluation.*

In addition to avoiding this tendency to look for solutions, you need to avoid the temptation to go with the first alternative that comes to mind. Many of us are a little "trigger happy," and we thoughtlessly try to follow through on the first response that occurs to us. *Various lines of evidence suggest that it is wiser to engage in brainstorming about a problem.* **Brainstorming** involves generating as many alternatives as possible without initially paying any attention to their apparent practicality. This requires that you temporarily defer evaluation of alternatives.

STEP 3: EVALUATE YOUR ALTERNATIVES AND SELECT A COURSE OF ACTION

Once you generate every imaginable alternative you can, you need to start evaluating the possibilities. There are no simple criteria for judging the relative merits of your alternatives. However, there are three general issues you will probably want to address. *First, ask yourself whether each alternative is a realistic plan.* In other words, what is the probability that you can successfully execute the intended course of action? Try to think of any obstacles you may have failed to anticipate. In making this assessment, it is important to try to avoid both foolish optimism and unnecessary pessimism. *Second, consider whether any costs or risks are involved in each alternative.* The "solution" to a problem is sometimes worse than the problem itself. Assuming you can successfully implement your intended course of action, what are the possible negative consequences? *Finally, compare the desirability of the probable outcomes of each alternative.* After eliminating the unrealistic possibilities, list the probable consequences (both good and bad) associated with each alternative. Then review and compare the desirability of these potential outcomes. In making this decision, you have to ask yourself, "What is important to me? Which outcomes do I value the most?"

STEP 4: TAKE ACTION WHILE MAINTAINING FLEXIBILITY

Once you have chosen your course of action, you should follow through and try to implement your plan. In so doing, try to maintain flexibility. Do not get "locked into" a particular course of action. Few choices are truly irreversible. You need to monitor results closely and be willing to revise your strategy.

Being flexible does *not* mean that you should execute your plan halfheartedly. To be able to evaluate your plan accurately, you must enact it with vigor and confidence and give it time to succeed. In evaluating your course of action, try to avoid the overly simplistic success/failure dichotomy. You should simply look for any improvement of any kind. If the plan doesn't work out too well, consider whether it was undermined by any unforeseen circumstances that you could not possibly have anticipated. Finally, remember that you can learn from your "failures." Even if things did not work out so well, you may now have new information that will facilitate a new attack on the problem.

SEEKING HELP

In your efforts to solve problems systematically, please bear in mind that it is entirely reasonable to solicit assistance from friends, family, colleagues, and so forth. It is unfortunate that, because of potential embarrassment, many people are reluctant to acknowledge their problems and seek help from others that could prove very useful. What makes this reality so lamentable is that others can provide a great deal of help in many ways and at many levels. Two of the four functions of social support discussed in Chapter 3, informational support and instrumental support, may aid problem-focused coping. In proceeding

---

5.4 RECOMMENDED READING
How to Get Control of Your Time and Your Life
by Alan Lakein (Peter H. Wyden, 1973)

Many of us whine constantly about not having enough time to do everything we want to do. We feel overwhelmed by the tasks that confront us and frustrated by our inability to tackle all of them. If you're locked in a perennial struggle with time, and if you're losing the battle—this may be the book for you.

Alan Lakein is an expert on time management who has served as a consultant for numerous corporations. Although his book is slanted toward improving time use in the business world, its basic ideas may be useful to anyone. He emphasizes that he is *not* an "efficiency expert" who tries to reduce wasted motion. Instead, he see himself as an "effectiveness expert" who has a system that can aid you in making the right decisions about how to allocate your time. At the core of the system is the idea that *you have to decide what is important to you.* Lakein suggests that you closely examine your goals and make a list of both long-term and more short-term priorities. Then, each day, review the tasks at hand and tackle those that will contribute the most to achieving your life goals. Lakein points out that many of us tend to tackle simple, routine tasks first, while saving the important tasks for later, when we supposedly will have more time. He mercilessly crucifies the "logic" underlying this tendency and describes in detail how to reverse it.

The book has plenty of advice that will warm the heart (somewhat literally) of any ultra-time-conscious, Type A personality. However, it does not encourage as much Type A behavior as one might expect. Lakein focuses more on time *allocation* than on time *saving.* Nonetheless, he offers a wealth of tips on how to get organized and save time.

The 80/20 rule says, "If all items are arranged in order of value, 80 percent of the value would come from only 20 percent of the items, while the remaining 20 percent of the value would come from 80 percent of the items." Sometimes it's a little more, sometimes a little less, but 80 percent of the time I think you will find the 80/20 rule is correct [pp. 83–84].

80 percent of sales come from 20 percent of customers

80 percent of production is in 20 percent of the product line

80 percent of dinners repeat 20 percent of recipes

80 percent of TV time is spent on 20 percent of programs most popular with the family

80 percent of telephone calls come from 20 percent of all callers [p. 84].

The support of a friend can be invaluable in dealing with stress.

through the first three steps of systematic problem solving as just described, *informational support* in the form of advice can be of immense value. It can really help to be able to bounce ideas off someone as you try to clarify your problem, generate alternative strategies, and evaluate those alternatives. When you finally decide on a course of action, *instrumental support* in the form of material aid may make all the difference in the world.

Not only can help from others assist in problem-solving efforts, but seeking social support is one of those coping tactics that can have impact in other coping domains as well. According to House's (1981) functional analysis of social support, others may often provide *emotional support* in the form of affection that may aid emotion-focused coping and *appraisal support* in the form of helping one to make sense out of life's difficulties that may aid appraisal-focused coping. Thus, seeking help from others is a strategy that has enormous potential in that social support may facilitate coping in several ways.

DEVELOPING ALTERNATIVE REWARDS

Much to our dismay, life often confronts us with problems that we cannot conquer. Frustration, in the form of failures and losses, is the type of stress that most frequently produces these irreversible problems. For instance, there may be nothing you can do to reverse the fact that your boyfriend has dumped you, or you have been cut from the football team, or your parents have divorced, or "your" promotion was given to someone else. *When there is nothing that you can do to alter frustrating circumstances, one option (in terms of problem-focused coping) is to seek new, alternative sources of satisfaction* (Moos & Billings, 1982). Let's take the example of the jilted girlfriend mentioned above. If she has to endure for many months without having a regular male companion, it would be unwise to simply sit at home, dwelling on the past. Instead, refocusing her energies, developing new interests, and exploring new activities in order to substitute for the fun that she used to enjoy with her old boyfriend would be a much more constructive response than moping about all the sources of gratification that she lost with his departure.

ACHIEVING BEHAVIORAL SELF-CONTROL

The conquest of many of life's problems requires behavioral self-control. All four of the forms of stress described in Chapter 3 can create challenges to your self-control. Whether you're struggling with the *frustration* of poor grades in school, constant *conflicts* about your overeating, *pressure* to do well in sports, or downhill *changes* in finances that require readjustment, you will need reasonable self-control if you expect to make much progress. It is an inescapable fact that to live life effectively and successfully, one has to develop some behavioral self-control.

For most of us, however, satisfactory self-control is very difficult to achieve. Fortunately, the last several decades have produced major advances in the psychotechnology of self-control. These advances have emerged from psychological research on *behavior modification,* a relatively new approach to controlling behavior that utilizes the principles of learning and conditioning. In this chapter's application section I will explain how you can use behavior modification to improve self-control.

Emotion-Focused Constructive Coping

Let's be realistic: there are going to be numerous occasions when a person's appraisal-focused and problem-focused coping efforts are not going to be successful in warding off emotional turmoil as a response to stress. Even well-chosen and well-executed coping strategies may take quite a while to work before emotional tensions begin to subside. Consequently, it is helpful to have some coping mechanisms that are useful in reducing and controlling emotional arousal. I will discuss the merits of three such coping mechanisms in this section: releasing pent-up emotions, distracting oneself, and learning to relax.

RELEASING PENT-UP EMOTIONS

Virtually all of us are going to experience periods in our lives when emotion-induced tension will become excessive. When this happens, there is some merit in the old common-sense notion that you should try to release or discharge the emotions that may be welling up inside you. In view of the potentially problematic physiological arousal that accompanies emotions, it does *not* appear to be a good idea to let unconquered emotions seethe within you for a long time. Although there is no guarantee, there is evidence (Hokanson & Burgess, 1962) that you can sometimes reduce your physical arousal by *expressing* your emotions.

The key, of course, is to express your emotions in a mature and socially acceptable manner. For example, if you have good reason to be angry, it may be best to go ahead and vent that anger verbally. Speak up and tell your boss (or spouse or parent) that you feel you have been treated unfairly. This verbalization of anger should not involve aggressive efforts to hurt the other person's feelings. Such efforts will typically lead to escalating conflict and further emotional arousal. However, it *is* possible to express anger in a calm, reasonable manner. Psychologists call such a style "assertiveness" (see Chapter 8).

Verbalization also has some value in releasing anxiety. Sometimes it helps to "talk it out." If you can find a good listener, you may be able to discharge some of your anxiety by letting your secret fears, misgivings, and suspicions spill out in a session of candid conversation. Freud used the term **catharsis** for this

CATHARSIS. *A release of emotional tension.*

Crying is a natural coping response that can release pent-up emotions.

release of emotional tension through talking it out. Many approaches to psychotherapy depend on this principle. The key to doing this in a socially acceptable manner is to find someone who is really willing to listen. You shouldn't unload your problems on just anyone.

In dejection and grief, it may be worthwhile to go ahead and "cry your heart out." We have a natural inclination to use this simple response; unfortunately, many of us (especially men) are taught that it is inappropriate behavior for an adult. However, there is nothing wrong with crying if the situation merits it. The problem to be avoided here is the tendency to constantly use crying as a device to go fishing for sympathy.

DISTRACTING ONESELF

Distraction is a fairly simple coping tactic that involves diverting your attention away from a problem by thinking about other things or engaging in other activities. Substantial reliance on this strategy was observed in a study of coping efforts made by 60 married couples (Stone & Neale, 1984). If your blood is boiling and your stomach is churning over some snafu at work, it may be a good idea to go out to a movie or play, take in a ball game, or head for the bowling alley, depending on your preferences. Activities that really require some attention are probably best when using this strategy.

One could argue endlessly about the adaptive merits of distracting oneself. On the one hand, it probably does tend to be inferior to appraisal-focused or problem-focused tactics that might yield longer-lasting solutions. These other kinds of tactics probably should be given priority. On the other hand, distracting oneself certainly seems like a better idea than lashing out at others, getting bogged down in negative self-talk, or making wholesale distortions of reality with defensive coping efforts. Thus, it appears to be a strategy that has modest, short-term value when more direct tactics have failed to produce progress.

LEARNING TO RELAX

One very useful way to neutralize problematic emotions is to learn how to use some systematic relaxation procedure. Such procedures may help you to suppress and control emotional turmoil. Moreover, relaxing oneself is a versatile strategy in that it can function as a physiologic-focused coping tactic also.

There are many worthwhile approaches to achieving beneficial relaxation. It is up to you to select the approach most suitable for your unique personality and problems. Some approaches can be very effective but have the disadvantage of requiring elaborate professional training, assistance, or apparatus. I will discuss some of these more elaborate approaches, such as systematic desensitization, meditation, or biofeedback, in later chapters. One of the simpler approaches that virtually anyone can learn and use on an everyday basis is Benson's "relaxation response."

After studying various approaches to meditation, Herbert Benson, a Harvard Medical School cardiologist, concluded that it is the *relaxation* induced by meditation that makes it beneficial. Benson decided that elaborate religious rituals and beliefs were not necessary in order to profit from meditation. After "demystifying" meditation, Benson (1975) set out to devise a simple, nonreligious procedure that could provide similar benefits. He calls his procedure the *relaxation response.*

REQUIREMENTS FOR BENSON'S RELAXATION RESPONSE

On the basis of his study of various sorts of meditation, autogenic training, and progressive relaxation, Benson believes that the following four factors promote the relaxation response.

1. *A quiet environment.* It is easiest to induce the relaxation response in a distraction-free environment. After you become skilled at the relaxation response, you may be able to accomplish it in spite of various distractions; initially, however, you should practice it in a quiet, calm place.

2. *A mental device.* To shift attention inward and keep it there, you need to focus your attention on some constant stimulus, such as a sound or word that is recited repetitively. You may also choose to gaze fixedly at some bland object, such as a vase. Whatever the case, you need to focus your attention on something.

3. *A passive attitude.* It is important not to get upset when your attention strays to distracting thoughts. You must realize that such distractions are inevitable. Whenever your mind wanders from your attentional focus, *calmly* redirect attention to your mental device.

4. *A comfortable position.* Reasonable body comfort is essential to avoid a major source of potential distraction. Simply sitting up straight works well for most people. Some people can practice the relaxation response lying down, but such a position is too conducive to sleep for most people.

THE PROCEDURE

Benson's (1975, pp. 114–115) actual procedure for inducing the relaxation response is deceptively simple. For full benefit, it should be practiced daily.

1. Sit quietly in a comfortable position.
2. Close your eyes.
3. Deeply relax all your muscles, beginning at your feet and progressing up to your face. Keep them relaxed.
4. Breathe through your nose. Become aware of your breathing. As you breathe out, say the word, "ONE," silently to yourself. For example, breathe IN . . . OUT, "ONE"; IN . . . OUT, "ONE"; etc. Breathe easily and naturally.
5. Continue for 10 to 20 minutes. You may open your eyes to check the time, but do not use an alarm. When you finish, sit quietly for several

minutes, at first with your eyes closed and later with your eyes opened. Do not stand up for a few minutes.

6. Do not worry about whether you are successful in achieving a deep level of relaxation. Maintain a passive attitude and permit relaxation to occur at its own pace. When distracting thoughts occur, try to ignore them by not dwelling upon them and return to repeating "ONE." With practice, the response should come with little effort. Practice the technique once or twice daily, but not within two hours after any meal, since the digestive processes seem to interfere with the elicitation of the Relaxation Response.

Physiologic-Focused Constructive Coping

Our bodies are intimately involved in our response to stress. As I have emphasized repeatedly, it has clearly been documented that the wear and tear of stress may be injurious to our health. To combat this potential problem, it helps to keep your body in relatively sound shape. You don't have to be a physical fitness fanatic, but it *is* a good idea to consume a nutritionally balanced diet, get adequate sleep, engage in at least a moderate amount of exercise, and learn how to control overeating and use of tobacco, alcohol, and other drugs. Doing these things will not make you immune to the corrosive effects of stress. However, failure to do them may increase your vulnerability to stress-related physical disorders.

In this section on physiologic-focused coping, I will offer advice on proper nutrition, sleep, and exercise. The challenge of controlling one's overeating and use of tobacco, alcohol, and other drugs is ultimately a question of self-control. As mentioned earlier, I will discuss how to improve self-control in the upcoming application section.

NUTRITION

In the previous chapter, I reviewed research suggesting that your food consumption patterns may affect your ability to withstand the ravages of stress. Moreover, you should realize that the *energy* that you need to tackle the challenges of life is derived from the essential nutrients found in your food. Hence, it is very important that your food intake be nutritionally sound. Unfortunately, in our modern era, the cunning mass marketing of a multitude of nutritionally worthless foods makes it more and more difficult to achieve nutritional adequacy.

PSYCHOLOGICAL BASIS OF POOR NUTRITION

Let me begin by emphasizing that, in the developed countries of the world, poor nutrition is largely a function of psychological considerations rather than lack of access to adequate food. Evidence indicates that nutritional deficiency is more widespread in the United States than one might expect but that it is not particularly a function of low income or inability to afford appropriate foods. Instead, Ensor, Henkel, and Means (1977) assert that most malnutrition in America is attributable to lack of knowledge about nutrition and lack of effort to ensure good nutrition.

In other words, our nutritional shortcomings are due to *ignorance* and *poor motivation*. Collectively, we are remarkably naive about the basic facts and principles of nutrition. Our schools tend to provide very little education in this area, so that we readily fall for nutritional fads and foolishly believe nutritional myths. Our monumental ignorance is matched by our cavalier disregard for the importance of good nutritional habits. Most of us are not highly motivated to make sure our food consumption is nutritionally sound. Instead, we approach our eating very casually, guided not by nutritional needs but by convenience, palatability, and clever advertising.

For most people, then, the first steps toward improved nutrition involve changing attitudes and acquiring information. First and foremost, one has to recognize the importance of nutrition and commit oneself to making a real effort to regulate eating patterns. Second, one should try to acquire a basic education in regard to nutritional principles. In executing this step, bear in mind that an alarming number of popular books on nutrition are riddled with inaccuracies (see Chapter 4). Thus, the safest route may be to take a full-fledged college course on nutrition.

GENERAL NUTRITIONAL GOALS

Nutrition is an immensely complicated topic. A typical book providing a basic undergraduate introduction to the field of nutrition tends to be at least as large as this entire text. In light of the reality that this is a *psychology* text, I can digress only briefly to offer some very general advice about sound nutritional habits, based on suggestions by a panel of experts assembled by the U.S. Senate, as summarized in Luke's (1984) nutrition text.

1. *Do not consistently consume more calories than you expend.* As you surely know, food consumption can be measured in *calories*. This difficult-to-picture unit of measurement indicates how much energy has to be expended to "burn up" the food consumed. As most of us are painfully aware, the tastiest foods tend to have high caloric values. Table 5.1 gives you a general idea of how many of these calories you burn up in various kinds of daily activities. If you routinely take in more calories than you use up in your daily activities, you are going to gain weight. Eventually this pattern of eating will lead to obesity. As obesity is related to a wide range of serious health risks, not to mention poor self-image, it is important that you avoid constant overeating and try to maintain an "ideal" body weight, based on your age, height, and sex.

TABLE 5.1 Calories expended in various types of activities

Type of activity	Calories per hour
Sedentary activities, such as reading; writing; eating; watching television or movies; listening to the radio; sewing; playing cards; and typing, office work, and other activities done while sitting that require little or no arm movement.	80 to 100
Light activities, such as preparing and cooking food; doing dishes; dusting; handwashing small articles of clothing; ironing; walking slowly; personal care; office work and other activities done while standing that require some arm movement; and rapid typing and other activities done while sitting that are more strenuous.	110 to 160
Moderate activities, such as making beds; mopping and scrubbing; sweeping; light polishing and waxing; laundering by machine; light gardening and carpentry work; walking moderately fast; other activities done while standing that require moderate arm movement; and activities done while sitting that require more vigorous arm movement.	170 to 240
Vigorous activities, such as heavy scrubbing and waxing; handwashing large articles of clothing; hanging out clothes; stripping beds; walking fast; bowling; golfing; and gardening.	250 to 350
Strenuous activities, such as swimming; playing tennis; running; bicycling; dancing; skiing; and playing football.	350 or more

2. *Consume a balanced variety of foods.* Food is made up of a variety of components, six of which are essential to your physical well-being. These six *essential nutrients* are proteins, fats, carbohydrates, vitamins, minerals, and fiber. Proteins, fats, and carbohydrates supply the body with its energy. Vitamins and minerals help to release that energy and serve other important functions as well. Fiber provides roughage that facilitates the digestion process. It

is probably a bit unrealistic to expect most people to keep track of which nutrients are found in which foods. However, it is fairly easy to promote adequate intake of all essential nutrients. All you have to do is to consume a balanced diet in terms of the *four basic food groups,* which are easy to remember: (1) milk and milk products, (2) meats or other protein sources, (3) fruits and vegetables, and (4) breads and cereals. Table 5.2 includes some recommendations for balanced consumption of these four basic food groups.

TABLE 5.2 Four basic food groups

Food group	Amount suggested and foods included	Nutrients provided
1. Milk or milk products	Children: 3 or more glasses; smaller glasses for children under 9 Teenagers: 4 or more glasses (low-fat) Adults: 2 or more glasses (low-fat) 1 cup milk = 1 cup yogurt = 1⅓ oz processed cheddar cheese = 1½ cups cottage cheese = 2 cups ice cream	Protein, fat, carbohydrate Minerals: calcium, phosphorus, magnesium Vitamins: riboflavin, pyridoxine, D and A (if fortified)
2. Meat	2 or more servings (1 serving = 2 to 3 oz cooked lean meat) Meat, poultry, fish, legumes	Protein, fat Minerals: iron, magnesium, phosphorus, zinc Vitamins: B vitamins (cobalamin, folic acid, niacin, pyridoxine, thiamin)
3. Fruits and vegetables	4 or more servings (1 serving = ½ cup raw or cooked) All fruits and vegetables (include one citrus fruit for vitamin C and one dark green or yellow vegetable for carotene)	Carbohydrate Minerals: calcium and iron (some greens) Vitamins: A (as carotene), B vitamins (folic acid, thiamin), C, E, K
4. Breads[a] and cereals[a]	4 or more servings (1 serving = 1 slice fortified or whole grain bread = 1 oz fortified or whole grain dry cereal = 1 corn tortilla = ½–¾ cup cooked fortified or whole grain cereal, rice, grits, macaroni, etc.)	Carbohydrate, protein Minerals: iron, magnesium, phosphorus, zinc Vitamins: B vitamins (niacin, pyridoxine, thiamin), E

[a]Bran, whole grain breads and cereals, and, to a lesser degree, raw and dried fruits and raw vegetables will increase the amount of unabsorbable fiber in the diet.

3. *Avoid excessive consumption of fats, cholesterol, sugar, and salt.* These are all commodities that are overrepresented in the typical American diet. They are not inherently bad but can become problematic when consumed in excess. Among fats, it is particularly prudent to limit the intake of saturated fats by reducing one's eating of beef, pork, ham, hot dogs, sausage, lunch meats, nonskim milk, and fried foods. Consumption of many of the same foods should be limited in order to reduce cholesterol intake. In particular, beef, pork, lamb, sausage, cheese, butter, and eggs are high in cholesterol. Refined (processed) sugar is believed to be grossly overconsumed. Hence, one should limit one's dependence on soft drinks, chocolate, candies, pies, cakes, and jams. Finally, it is thought that most people should cut down on their salt intake. This may require more than ignoring your salt shaker, as many prepackaged foods are loaded with salt.

4. *Increase consumption of complex carbohydrates, polyunsaturated fats, natural sugars, and foods with fiber.* If you have typical American eating habits, you may be groaning in disbelief and wondering what is left to eat if you have to avoid all the foods mentioned in the preceding paragraph. Well, first of all, please note that the experts suggest only that you *limit or reduce* the

consumption of those foods. It is only the excessive consumption of these items that is viewed as problematic. Second, as you cut down on these undesirable foods, the experts recommend that you increase consumption in other areas. In particular, fruits, vegetables, and whole grains are highly touted because they contain complex carbohydrates, natural sugars, and ample fiber. Additionally, in order to substitute polyunsaturated fats for saturated ones, it is suggested that we should eat more fish, chicken, turkey, and veal, trim our meats of fat more thoroughly, use skim (nonfat) milk, and switch to vegetable oils that are high in polyunsaturated fats.

SLEEP

REM SLEEP. *A deep stage of sleep, during which there are rapid lateral eye movements beneath the closed eyelids; the stage of sleep during which most dreaming occurs.*

As discussed in Chapter 4, your sleep may vary in quality as well as quantity. It is essential that you get adequate sleep overall, and in particular it appears important that you obtain enough **REM sleep.** Researchers who have studied the sleep process have uncovered some clues about how to maximize the beneficial effects of your sleep and how to minimize problems associated with insomnia. The main source on which this practical advice is based is an interview with Julius Segal in the December 28, 1970, issue of *U.S. News and World Report.*

DETERMINING YOUR SLEEP NEEDS

Sleep needs vary greatly from person to person, and it is possible to get either too little or too much sleep. You can get some idea of your personal sleep needs in the following way. During a relatively stress-free vacation, retire at your usual time each night and allow yourself to sleep through until you awaken naturally. During this period of a week or so, avoid any excessive alcohol consumption or drug use. If you average your sleeping times over this period, you should have a good idea of how much sleep *your* body needs.

MAXIMIZING THE QUALITY OF YOUR SLEEP

1. *Try to establish a regular pattern for sleeping.* Going to bed at about the same time each night promotes good sleep. Your body has a 24-hour rhythmic cycle involving consistent fluctuations in many physiological functions, such as body temperature and hormonal secretions. Highly irregular sleep patterns may disrupt this rhythm and lead to lighter sleep. Conversely, if you follow a regular pattern, your body may become primed for falling asleep quickly and easily at your usual bedtime.

2. *Try to get sustained sleep rather than naps.* Although some of us can profit from napping (McCoy & Mewaldt, 1984), most people benefit more from sustained sleep. For example, if you have a choice between (1) sleeping seven hours straight and (2) taking a two-hour catnap now and sleeping only five hours later, the seven hours of straight sleep will probably be more beneficial to you. The reason may be that the longer you sleep, the longer your REM periods get.

3. *Avoid excessive liquor and drug consumption.* Alcohol in large amounts and many drugs may affect your sleep negatively. They may disrupt your normal sleep pattern and depress your REM sleep. Even drugs intended to make you sleep may reduce the quality of your sleep.

INSOMNIA. *Condition characterized by problems with falling or staying asleep. There are three chronic patterns: difficulty in falling asleep initially, difficulty in remaining asleep, and persistent early morning awakening.*

BATTLING INSOMNIA

1. *Don't initiate chemical warfare.* Sedatives are a poor long-range solution for **insomnia** for a number of reasons. You can become physically dependent on them, and as your body develops tolerance to them, you will need to increase the dosage. It is also possible to overdose quite accidentally on such drugs. Furthermore, they may have carryover effects to the next day, including making you sluggish and prone to depression. Sedatives may be a reasonable

solution if your sleep is being disrupted by a *short-term* crisis. However, if you have perennial sleep difficulties, you will have to find some other solution.

2. *Don't panic.* Some people will experience a few nights of sleep difficulties, which may be due to unrecognized stress, and then jump to the conclusion that they have become insomniacs. Once they become fearful about their sleep, they approach nighttime with anxiety, and this aggravates the problem. You should be aware that all of us are likely to experience sleep difficulties occasionally. If you don't panic, the problem may soon clear up on its own.

3. *Try "daydreaming" yourself to sleep.* If you lie in bed thinking how terrible you'll feel tomorrow if you don't fall asleep, you'll just get more upset and less likely to drift off. The harder you "work" at falling asleep, the less success you'll have. Instead, it's a good idea to launch yourself into a pleasant daydream. This is a normal presleep process that can take your mind off the fact that you're not sleeping.

4. *Learn to relax.* Insomnia in many people is due to excessive tension. If you have persistent sleep problems, you may simply need to learn to relax more effectively. Try practicing Benson's (1975) relaxation response or some other relaxation exercise.

EXERCISE

Putting together a good exercise program is difficult for many people. Exercise is time-consuming, and if you're out of shape, your initial attempts may be painful, aversive, and discouraging. To circumvent these problems, it is wise to heed the following advice (Greenberg, 1983; Mirkin & Hoffman, 1978).

Regular exercise can do wonders for one's self-concept—not to mention one's physical health.

1. *Look for an activity that you will find enjoyable.* There are a great many physical activities in which you can participate (see Box 5.5). Shop around and try to choose one that you find intrinsically enjoyable. This will make it much easier for you to follow through and exercise regularly.

2. *Increase your participation gradually.* Don't try to do too much too quickly. This can lead to frustration, not to mention injury. An exercise regimen should be built up gradually. If you *do* experience injuries, avoid the common tendency to ignore them. Consult your physician to see whether continuing your exercise program is advisable.

3. *Exercise regularly but without overdoing it.* Sporadic exercise will not

---

5.5 WHICH EXERCISE IS FOR YOU?

If you want to experience the various benefits that can be derived from regular exercise, your first decision concerns what kind of activity to engage in. Should it be calisthenics? Isometrics? Yoga? Weightlifting? Swimming? Softball? The list of options is virtually endless. In making your decision, you should consider a number of things.

- *What are your goals?* As you can see from the table in this box, some sports are better than others for promoting weight loss, muscular strength, or cardiovascular fitness. You need to ask yourself "What do I want out of exercise?" and then figure out which activities can best achieve your goals.
- *What are your time constraints?* Some activities are more time-consuming than others. Since it is crucial that you get *regular* exercise, it is essential that you choose activities that you will be able to fit into your schedule consistently.

- *What is your level of fitness?* Not everyone can engage in every sport. Your age and current physical condition may limit your choices. Most experts recommend that you get a physical checkup before you embark on any strenuous new sporting activities.

The table below shows experts' ratings of how much 14 sports can contribute to various aspects of physical fitness (Conrad, 1976). If that information is not adequate, you might want to consult an excellent book entitled *Rating the Exercises* (Kuntzleman et al., 1980). It reviews the advantages and disadvantages of numerous activities. It is quite thorough and includes ratings of such esoteric sports as bobsledding, cricket, jai alai, karate, scuba diving, lacrosse, polo, and surfing.

A quick scorecard on 14 sports and exercises

	Jogging	Bicycling	Swimming	Skating (ice or roller)	Handball/Squash	Skiing–Nordic	Skiing–Alpine	Basketball	Tennis	Calisthenics	Walking	Golf[a]	Softball	Bowling
Physical fitness														
Cardiorespiratory endurance (stamina)	21	19	21	18	19	19	16	19	16	10	13	8	6	5
Muscular endurance	20	18	20	17	18	19	18	17	16	13	14	8	8	5
Muscular strength	17	16	14	15	15	15	15	15	14	16	11	9	7	5
Flexibility	9	9	15	13	16	14	14	13	14	19	7	9	9	7
Balance	17	18	12	20	17	16	21	16	16	15	8	8	7	6
General well-being														
Weight control	21	20	15	17	19	17	15	19	16	12	13	6	7	5
Muscle definition	14	15	14	14	11	12	14	13	13	18	11	6	5	5
Digestion	13	12	13	11	13	12	9	10	12	11	11	7	8	7
Sleep	16	15	16	15	12	15	12	12	11	12	14	6	7	6
Total	148	142	140	140	140	139	134	134	128	126	102	66[a]	64	51

Here's a summary of how seven experts rated various sports and exercises. Ratings are on a scale of 0 to 3; a rating of 21 indicates maximum benefit (a score of 3 by all seven panelists). Ratings were made on the basis of regular (minimum of four times per week), vigorous (duration of 30 minutes to one hour per session) participation in each activity.

[a]Ratings for golf are based on the fact that many Americans use a golf cart and/or caddy. If you walk the links, the physical fitness value moves up appreciably.

improve your fitness. A widely cited rule of thumb is that you should plan on exercising vigorously for a minimum of 30 minutes three times a week, or you will gain little from your efforts. At the other extreme, do not try to become fit overnight by working out too vigorously and too frequently. Even highly trained athletes intersperse days off or days of light training in their schedules. These off days are necessary to allow muscles to recover from their hard work.

4. *Reinforce yourself for your participation.* To offset the inconvenience or pain that may be associated with exercise, it is a good idea to reinforce yourself for your participation. The behavior modification procedures discussed in the upcoming application section can be very helpful in shaping up a viable exercise program.

5. *Avoid the competition trap.* If you choose a competitive sport for your physical activity (for example, baseball, basketball, tennis), try to avoid becoming obsessed with victory. It is easy to get overly concerned with winning at games. When this happens, you put yourself under pressure. This is obviously self-defeating, in that it *adds* another source of stress to your life. Support for this point comes from a recent study (France, 1984) of competitive versus noncompetitive attitudes during exercise. France reports that workouts characterized by competitive thinking led to a greater elevation of norepinephrine (one of the key catecholamines) than similar workouts in which subjects were instructed to think noncompetitively. Although this evidence should be regarded as very preliminary (there were only five subjects), France asserts that competitive thinking may contribute to the temporary increase in cardiac risk that may occur during vigorous exercise.

Summary

Coping involves behavioral efforts to master, reduce, or tolerate the demands created by stress. Coping is an ongoing process involving active efforts. Although the concept itself is neutral in regard to adaptive value, we reviewed a variety of coping strategies that *tend* to be maladaptive. One of these is striking out at others with acts of aggression. Frequently caused by frustration, aggression tends to be counterproductive because it often creates new sources of stress. Giving up, possibly best understood in terms of learned helplessness, is another common coping pattern that tends to be of limited value. Blaming oneself with pervasively negative self-talk and indulging oneself are other relatively nonadaptive coping patterns. Particularly common is defensive coping, which may involve any of a number of defense mechanisms. Although the adaptive value of defensive coping tends to be less than optimal, it depends on the situation.

Coping responses can be classified into four domains: appraisal-focused, problem-focused, emotion-focused, and physiologic-focused. Appraisal-focused constructive coping is facilitated by Ellis's suggestions on how to recognize catastrophic thinking and reduce such thinking by digging out the irrational assumptions on which it is based. Other valuable strategies are minimizing defensive distortion of reality, making positive comparisons with others, and using humor to deal with stress.

In problem-focused constructive coping, one makes a systematic effort to solve problems. I described a four-step process for doing so: (1) clarify the problem, (2) generate alternative courses of action, (3) evaluate your alternatives and then select a course of action, and (4) take action while maintaining flexibility. Other approaches with immense potential value include seeking help or social support, developing alternative sources of reward to alleviate frustration, and having strategies to maintain behavioral self-control.

The discussion of emotion-focused constructive coping noted the possible value of releasing pent-up emotions in socially acceptable ways and the occasional efficacy of distracting oneself. Primarily, though, I stressed the merits of learning to relax effectively. Of the many worthwhile procedures for achieving beneficial relaxation, I described one that is fairly simple—Benson's "relaxation response."

Physiologic-focused constructive coping includes giving attention to nutrition, sleep, and exercise.

In the application section, I will return to the issue of problem-focused coping and talk about how to improve behavioral self-control. Specifically, I will describe the essential principles of behavior modification and provide you with a step-by-step program for using self-modification procedures.

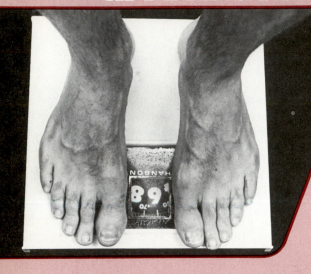

Achieving Self-Control through Behavior Modification

(Using Weight Control as an Example)

DAVID WATSON

ROLAND THARP

Answer the following questions yes or no.

_____ 1. Do you have a hard time passing up food even when you're not hungry?

_____ 2. Do you experience difficulty in getting yourself to exercise regularly?

_____ 3. Do you wish you studied more often?

_____ 4. Would you like to reduce your smoking or drinking?

_____ 5. Do you wish you had more "willpower"?

If you answered yes to any of these questions, you have struggled with the challenge of self-control. This chapter discusses how you can use the techniques of behavior modification to improve your self-control. The nice thing about behavior modification, besides the fact that it works so well (see Wolpe, 1981), is that anyone can learn to use it, with only a moderate amount of training. *Moreover, you can use behavior modification on yourself in order to promote greater self-control.* Self-control—or, actually, a lack of it—underlies many of the personal problems that we struggle with in everyday life. Problems such as losing weight, increasing studying, decreasing drinking or drug use, giving up smoking, and diminishing anxiety can be tackled very effectively with behavior modification strategies.

This chapter spells out detailed procedures for engaging in "self-modification." These procedures are based largely on analyses by David Watson and Roland Tharp (1985), who have put together a superb book (see Box 5.6) on self-modification. To provide concrete illustrations of how these procedures can be used, I will focus on the problem of weight control. Behavior modification can be used fruitfully with numerous other problems, many of which I will mention. However, I will use weight control as my main illustration because it is a significant problem for so many of us in the diet-crazed, thin-thinking 1980s. I will begin by discussing the underlying philosophy (assumptions) of behavior modification and giving some general information on weight control. Then I will outline step-by-step procedures for designing a behavior modification program.

ASSUMPTIONS OF THE BEHAVIOR MODIFICATION APPROACH

BEHAVIOR MODIFICATION. *An approach to changing behavior that relies on the principles of learning.*

Behavior modification consists in *the application of the principles of learning in direct efforts to change behavior.* More specifically, it involves using the principles of respondent conditioning, operant conditioning, and observational learning in systematic ways to modify future behavior. In other words, the principles and concepts that you learned about in Chapter 2 when I discussed the behavioristic model (reinforcement, extinction, generalization, discrimination, and so on) are put to work outside the research laboratory in an effort to control behavior. This approach to self-control is predicated on a number of simple assumptions, which are listed below.

ADJUSTMENT IS SITUATIONALLY SPECIFIC

I have already discussed some of the pitfalls involved in making judgments about adjustment as an achievement. In addition to the problems associated with the value-laden nature of such judgments, the behaviorists point out that *the quality of one's adjustment may vary tremendously from one situation to another.* Most of us are well adjusted in some areas of our lives and very poorly adjusted in other areas. For example, you might be quite competent in the academic sphere of your life but terribly inept in the social sphere. Because adjustment is situationally specific, the behaviorist maintains that efforts to solve problems by changing one's entire personality are unnecessary, not to mention unlikely to succeed. Instead, we need to identify specific adjustment problems and work on them individually.

BEHAVIOR IS LEARNED

It is assumed that your behavior is a product of your experience, or learning history. The behaviorist believes that whether you are happy or unhappy with your behavior, it is the result of your past conditioning. Furthermore, your behavior is controlled by the environment in that your tendency to make various responses is influenced greatly by external, situational stimuli.

WHAT IS LEARNED CAN BE UNLEARNED

The same processes that led to the acquisition of your current response tendencies can also be used to change your future response tendencies. In other words, bad habits that have been acquired through conditioning can be dislodged through reconditioning.

5.6   *RECOMMENDED READING*
Self-Directed Behavior: Self-Modification for Personal Adjustment
by David L. Watson & Roland G. Tharp (Brooks/Cole, 1985)

Behavior modification procedures are powerful tools that can help you gain greater control over your behavior. Numerous books are available that purport to explain how the average person can use behavioral techniques. I have examined most of them, and *this is the book.* It is solidly based on scientific research, admirably systematic, and yet very practical. It is written in an engaging, nonpatronizing manner with ample use of anecdotal evidence. Not only has your author used it as a textbook in the classroom, he also regularly lends it out to friends. The section on behavior modification that you are presently reading borrows liberally from this excellent book.

If you have difficulty with self-control, behavior modification is your best bet for ameliorating the problem. Watson and Tharp provide a detailed, step-by-step analysis of how to achieve self-control through self-modification.

Casual opinions about ourselves are often inaccurate. . . . A group of people who wanted to lose weight were asked by an experimenter how much they ate. Many assured themselves and the researcher that they "really didn't eat very much." Then they were asked to remember and write down everything they had eaten in the preceding two days. Their lists were checked, and it appeared that the people were *not* overeating. The researcher then put them all on a diet consisting of the foods they had reported eating. Every one of them began to lose weight [p. 55].

cathy®

BACKGROUND INFORMATION ON WEIGHT CONTROL

Although the criteria for obesity vary, it is clear that more and more adults are struggling with the problem of being overweight. Obesity is widespread, affecting people of all ages and from all walks of life. As I have mentioned repeatedly, obesity is a significant health problem; overweight people are more likely than slender people to develop cardiovascular disease, diabetes, hypertension, and pulmonary disorders, among other things (Stare, 1974).

Whether it is due to concern about their health or to good, old-fashioned vanity, an ever-increasing number of people are trying to lose weight. Our preoccupation with losing weight is evidenced by the spectacular proliferation of books on dieting. One book (Berland, 1980) reviewed over 70 different diet regimens! This epidemic of diet books has been accompanied by the appearance of numerous gimmicks that are alleged to produce easy weight reduction, including rubber sweat suits, special body wraps, massage, mechanical vibrators, steam rooms, diet pills, and special preparations such as liquid protein. The success enjoyed in marketing these largely worthless gimmicks, some of which border on the ludicrous, shows that we have become obsessed with losing weight.

Unfortunately, our obsession with weight loss can sometimes become dangerous. According to medical and nutritional experts, many of the popular "fad" diets promising dramatic weight reductions can be perilous to one's health. For instance, a recent article in the *Journal of the American Medical Association* (Wadden et al., 1983) discussed major concerns about the popular "Cambridge diet." The authors reviewed a number of reasons that the diet might be hazardous to health and reported that the U.S. Food and Drug Administration had received 138 complaints of illness (including six deaths) in people using the Cambridge diet by the end of 1982. In their discussion of extremist diets, they also mention that the liquid protein diets that were widely used in 1976–1977 were thought to be associated with some 58 deaths before they faded from view. So let me reemphasize the point made in Chapter 4: faddish, extreme nutritional programs are simply money-making ventures for their developers that usually have little genuine merit and may even be dangerous. What, by the way, do Wadden et al. (1983) recommend in order to achieve durable and safe weight loss? Exactly what I am discussing in this chapter—"behavior modification, nutrition counseling and exercise" (p. 2834).

As discussed in Chapter 4, numerous factors may contribute to the development of obesity, but one's *eating habits* are ultimately the most crucial consideration in the vast majority of cases. Whatever the developmental causes of obesity are, there is ultimately only one way to lose weight: to change your ratio of energy intake (through food consumption) to energy output (accomplished largely through exercise). All the popular fads and gimmicks notwithstanding, to lose weight you *must* expend more energy than you take in. To be quite specific, you need to burn up 3500 more calories than you consume in order to lose one pound. For example, if you expend 3000 calories a day while consuming 2500 calories a day, you'll burn off an extra 500 calories each day and rid yourself of one pound in about a week. You have three options in trying to change your ratio of energy input to energy output: (1) you can *sharply* reduce your food consumption, (2) you can *sharply* increase your exercise output, or (3) you can simultaneously decrease your food intake *and* step up your exercise output in more *moderate* ways. Most experts (for example, Stuart & Davis, 1972) recommend the third option. Accordingly, as I describe a step-by-step procedure for executing a behavior modification program, I will illustrate the principles involved by discussing how you can change both your eating and exercising habits.

Self-Modification Procedures

I am now prepared to explain to you how to go about developing and executing a self-modification program. The description will proceed step by step. Five steps are involved in this process:

Step 1: Specifying your target behavior.
Step 2: Gathering baseline data.
Step 3: Designing your program.
Step 4: Executing and evaluating your program.
Step 5: Ending your program.

SPECIFYING THE TARGET BEHAVIOR

The first step in any systematic effort at behavior modification is to specify the target behavior or behaviors. These are the behaviors that you will try to change in some way. This step may sound simple and trivial; however, it is a crucial step and is often complex and difficult. A behavior modification program can be applied only to a clearly defined, discrete behavioral response. However, many of us tend to be vague in describing our problems, and we are hard-pressed to identify the exact nature of the behavior that needs to be changed. For example, it is not adequate for an introverted person to say simply "I'm too shy." That may very well be an accurate statement, but a behavioral approach to the problem requires that the person precisely specify the patterns of social responding that have led to dissatisfaction. The "ultimate" goal of a behavior modification program may be nonbehavioral (for example, weighing less or being in better physical condition), but the program itself can be designed only with reference to specific target behaviors.

The basic problem in completing this first step is that we tend to think in terms of *traits* rather than *behavior*. In other words, we describe our problems in terms of negative personality traits instead of listing undesirable behaviors. To correct this problem, you must learn how to translate ambiguous statements about an undesirable trait into clear descriptions of the specific behaviors that lead you to conclude that you have this trait. The best way to do this is to thoughtfully ponder past behavior or closely observe future behavior in order to dredge up specific *examples* of responses that lead to the trait description. For instance, a man who describes himself as "too irritable" might decide, after listing some examples, that the problem boils down to only two common responses: arguing with his wife and snapping at his young children. These are specific responses for which a behavior modification program could be designed.

BEHAVIORAL EXCESS. *A response that is judged to occur too frequently.*

BEHAVIORAL DEFICIT. *A response that is judged to occur too infrequently.*

Most problems can be characterized as either behavioral excesses or behavioral deficits (Martin & Poland, 1980). A **behavioral excess** involves a response that is problematic because it occurs too often. For example, people who overeat, drink too much, or smoke constantly are troubled by behavioral excesses. A **behavioral deficit** involves a response that is problematic because it doesn't occur often enough. For example, people who exercise only occasionally or students who study infrequently might decide that they have a behavioral deficit. In either case, the decision that some response is emitted too frequently or too infrequently is a personal judgment based on your own value system.

In many instances, the problem may be characterized as either an excess or a deficit, depending on the perspective you choose to take. For example, a problem with shyness might be described in terms of socially withdrawing too often (an excess) or in terms of making social overtures too rarely (a deficit). *When you have a choice about whether to describe your problem behavior as an excess or a deficit, it is usually better to define it as a deficit.* Generally, designing a program to *increase* some deficit behavior is preferable to designing a program to *decrease* some excess behavior. The reason is that programs intended to decrease the frequency of a response typically depend on the use of punishment, and it is often difficult to punish oneself.

In regard to weight control, the target behaviors obviously would involve consuming less than a certain number of calories per day or consuming fewer snacks or not consuming certain foods. For exercise, the target might consist of jogging a certain distance each day, bicycling a certain number of miles each week, or doing certain calisthenics on a regular schedule. The particular target behaviors will depend on each person's unique problem, history, habits, and tastes. What is crucial is that the target behaviors involve specific responses that can be measured.

GATHERING BASELINE DATA

BASELINE PERIOD. *In behavior modification, a time interval, before the actual intervention, during which you carefully observe your target behavior.*

The second step in your behavior modification effort is to gather the baseline data. The **baseline period** is a span of time, before the actual beginning of your program, during which you systematically observe your target behavior. People are often tempted to skip this step and plunge ahead into the design of their program. It is imperative that you overcome this temptation. In gathering your baseline data, you need to monitor three things: the initial response level of the target behavior, the typical antecedents of the target behavior, and the typical consequences of the target behavior.

INITIAL RESPONSE LEVEL

You need to know the preprogram response level of the target behavior in order to evaluate the effectiveness of your program later. Obviously, you cannot judge whether your program is successfully increasing or decreasing the frequency of a target response unless you know what the initial baseline rate of occurrence was.

In most cases you will simply need to keep track of how often the target behavior occurs in a predetermined time interval. Thus, you might count the daily frequency of snapping at your children, smoking cigarettes, or biting your fingernails. In some cases, the *duration* of responding is a more meaningful measure than simple frequency. For instance, if you were monitoring study behavior or tennis practice, it would make more sense to keep track of the time spent engaging in those activities. The appropriate unit of measurement will depend on the exact nature of the target behavior. In a weight-control program it is probably best to estimate the daily *amount* of consumption by counting calories.

It is crucial that you have accurate data about the initial response level of the target behavior. Therefore, it is important that you be honest with yourself and work hard at counting *all* instances of the target response. It may be necessary to carry some kind of portable device for recording your behavior. This device might be something as simple as an index card on which you write down everything you eat (see Figure 5.1). These daily tabulations should then be transferred to a permanent, written record or score sheet. In the long run, it is usually best to portray your records graphically (see Figure 5.2).

There are no simple guidelines about how long you should gather information on the baseline rate of the response. If you're sure the baseline rate is zero, you *may* be able to skip this step. Generally, it is necessary to gather data on the initial level of response for a minimum of one week. If the response level fluctuates a great deal from day to day, the baseline period may need to be two or three weeks. Basically, you need to gather baseline data until you discern a recognizable pattern of responding.

ANTECEDENTS

ANTECEDENTS. *In behavior modification, events that precede the target behavior.*

Antecedents are situations or events that typically precede the occurrence of your target behavior. You need to analyze antecedents because they often play a major role in governing your target response. Sometimes a target behavior that represents an excess, let us say nail biting, occurs only in certain situations. In a sense, these situations may "trigger," or bring on, the undesirable response. *Recognizing such links between situations and behaviors can be very helpful in designing your program.* For example, if your target was overeating, you might discover during your collection of baseline data that the bulk of your overeating takes place at suppertime, with lunch and breakfast presenting no problems. You might further discover that your excessive eating is almost always preceded by the consumption of a couple of martinis, which undermine your self-control. Once you discern these connections between antecedents and your target behavior, you can set up a program that specifically attacks and attempts to break down these connections.

In discussing how to pinpoint antecedents, Watson and Tharp (1972, p. 148) recommend that you ask yourself four questions.

1. What were the physical circumstances of the last few minutes?
2. What was the social setting?
3. What behavior of other people occurred?
4. What did I think or say to myself?

Date			
Food eaten	Time	Where eaten	Mood when eaten
3-egg omelette w/ ham +cheese	7:30 AM	home	normal
2 pc. bacon	7:30 AM	home	normal
Candy bar	10:30 AM	work	tired
tunafish sand.	12:15 PM	work	bored
1oz bag potato chips	12:15 PM	work	bored
large salad	7:00 PM	restaurant	anxious
3 enchiladas, beans + rice	7:00 PM	restaurant	anxious
2 cones	7:00 PM	restaurant	anxious

FIGURE 5.1 Form for monitoring daily consumption of food.

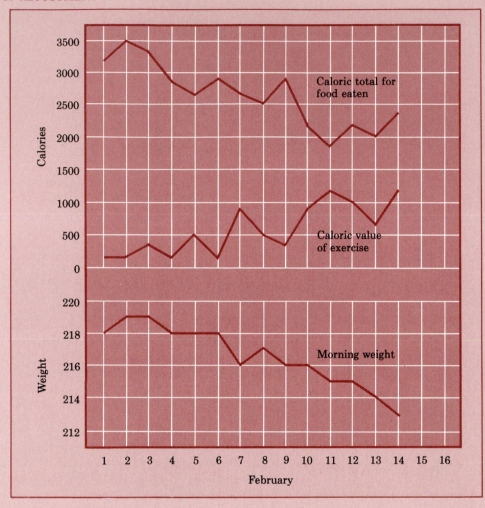

FIGURE 5.2 Graphic record of daily food consumption, exercise, and weight.

CONSEQUENCES

If your problem involves a behavioral excess, it is important that you understand the consequences that are reinforcing the response. Once the **reinforcement** is identified, you may be able to cut it off and extinguish your undesirable response. In trying to figure out what the reinforcement is, you need to ask yourself some fairly simple questions. These are: What do I get out of the response, or what is the payoff?

Generally, this is a simple matter, but there are several points worth noting that may help you identify the consequences that maintain your problem behavior. *First, you should be aware that sometimes the response itself is the reinforcement.* In particular, this is true of consummatory responses, such as eating, drinking, and smoking. Such responses are inherently reinforcing and therefore present special challenges in developing a behavior modification program. *Second, you should keep in mind the concept of negative reinforcement* (see Chapter 2), wherein a response leads to the removal of some aversive situation. Many troublesome "avoidance responses" are maintained by negative reinforcement. For example, let's say that you find big parties a little scary and tend to skip them, thereby missing a good opportunity to meet new people. Since these parties make you anxious, the reinforcement for the response of not going is the removal or reduction of this internal anxiety. This sort of negatively reinforcing anxiety reduction is often at work in supporting self-defeating avoidance behavior. *Third, you should be aware that some responses are reinforced only occasionally.* Such **intermittent reinforce-**

ment can maintain a response at a high level while making it difficult to pinpoint the reinforcer at work. You can avoid unnecessary confusion in your search for reinforcers by remembering that each and every response may *not* be reinforced.

DESIGNING THE PROGRAM

Once you have selected a target behavior and gathered adequate baseline data, it is time to put together a program intended to change your behavior. Generally speaking, a program will be designed either to increase the frequency of your target response or to decrease its frequency. Since these are two very different tasks, I will discuss each separately.

INCREASING RESPONSE STRENGTH THROUGH REINFORCEMENT

Efforts to increase the frequency of some deficit response depend largely on the use of positive reinforcement. In other words, you reward yourself for behaving appropriately. Although the basic strategy of rewarding yourself is uncommonly simple, a number of considerations are involved in doing it skillfully and successfully.

Selecting a reinforcer.   If you intend to reward yourself for engaging in a particular response, you need to find an effective reinforcer. Your choice will depend on your unique personality and situation. Reinforcement is subjective; something that is reinforcing for someone else may not work for you. For instance, I have designed programs in which my primary reinforcer was reading the morning newspaper. This wouldn't be a very potent reinforcer for most people, but it works great for that handful of people who are "newspaper junkies." *Therefore, you have to think about what kinds of activities give you pleasure.* Watson and Tharp (1985, p. 182) list a number of questions you can ask yourself in order to ascertain what your personal reinforcers are:

1. What will be the rewards of achieving your goal?
2. What kind of praise do you like to receive, from yourself and others?
3. What kinds of things do you like to have?
4. What are your major interests?
5. What are your hobbies?
6. What people do you like to be with?
7. What do you like to do with those people?
8. What do you do for fun?
9. What do you do to relax?
10. What do you do to get away from it all?
11. What makes you feel good?
12. What would be a nice present to receive?
13. What kinds of things are important to you?
14. What would you buy if you had an extra $20? $50? $100?
15. On what do you spend your money each week?
16. What behaviors do you perform every day? (Don't overlook the obvious or the commonplace.)
17. Are there any behaviors that you usually perform instead of the target behavior?
18. What would you hate to lose?
19. Of the things you do every day, which would you hate to give up?
20. What are your favorite daydreams and fantasies?
21. What are the most relaxing scenes you can imagine?

Additionally, it is important that you be realistic and choose a reinforcer that is *available* to you. For example, you might like to reinforce yourself for eating less by awarding yourself a trip to Tahiti when you have lost 15 pounds. However, if you can't afford a trip to Tahiti, this is obviously out of the question.

It should be emphasized that you do not have to invent spectacular, new reinforcers that you have never or only rarely experienced. *You can use reinforcers that you are already getting!* However, you have to restructure the contingencies so that you get them only if you behave appropriately. For example, buying new clothes may be a very rewarding event for you, which you already experience on a semiregular basis. You can use this event of purchasing clothes as a reinforcer by making it contingent on certain kinds of responding.

You want to choose a reinforcer that is relatively potent. *A stronger or more desirable reinforcer will usually have a greater effect on your behavior.* This is particularly important in trying to control overeating. Since eating is a consummatory response, it reinforces itself. Eating good food is a powerful reinforcer for most people with weight problems. Thus, the challenge in this case is to find a reinforcer for eating less that is comparable in strength to the reinforcement derived from eating. This requires a fairly potent reinforcer, which may not be easy to find. You should also be aware, however, that it is possible to select a reinforcer that is *too strong!* Remember that you may have to go without your reinforcer; you may not earn it. Hence, it is important that your reinforcer be something that you *could* live without.

REINFORCEMENT CONTINGENCIES. *The circumstances or rules that govern whether reinforcement is received.*

Arranging the contingencies.   Once you have chosen your reinforcer, you then have to set up **reinforcement contingencies.** These are statements of the conditions that you have to meet in order to earn the reinforcers. A reinforcement contingency describes the exact nature of the target behavior that must be emitted and the reinforcement that may then be awarded. For example, in a program to increase exercise, you might make spending $15 on clothes each week (the reinforcement) contingent on jogging 15 miles during that week (the target behavior). In a program to increase study behavior, you might make having a couple of beers contingent on studying three hours. In a program to decrease overeating, you might make listening to your stereo in the evening contingent on consuming less than 1200 calories. As you can see, reinforcement contingencies simply spell out what has to be done in order to earn a particular reinforcer.

5.7   *RECOMMENDED READING*
Slim Chance in a Fat World: Behavior Control of Obesity
by Richard B. Stuart and Barbara Davis (Research Press, 1972)

If you want to lose weight, read this book! It is a truly outstanding guide to weight reduction. It knits together three of the themes emphasized in this chapter: the utility of behavioral control of overeating, the importance of having some rudimentary knowledge of nutrition, and the value of adequate exercise. The collaboration between Stuart, who is trained in the behavioral sciences, and Davis, who is trained in the nutritional sciences, produces a very comprehensive approach to weight-reduction efforts.

The authors begin with a sophisticated discussion of the scientific evidence on the causes of obesity. They then cover, in a detailed but readable way, how to set up a behavior modification program to conquer overeating. This is followed by a brief but informative introduction to basic principles of nutrition. This presentation succeeds in explaining why it is crucial to monitor *what* you eat as well as *how much.* Moreover, simple strategies for ensuring nutritionally sound food intake are discussed. The authors then explain why the significance of exercise is often underestimated. After convincing you of the potential value of exercise, they illustrate how behavioral techniques can be used to promote an increase in exercise. Finally, a highly valuable appendix includes numerous tables on weight distribution, recommended dietary allowances, nutritional values, and energy expenditure norms. Charts are also provided for graphing eating, exercise, and weight loss.

Rather than relying upon eccentric foods, fasting or dietary aids, it is generally recognized that education in sound dietary practice is an essential in durable weight control programs....

In a recent study which carefully monitored the food intake of dieting adults, for example, successful dieters consumed 1,511 calories and 68 percent of their minimum daily food requirements, while unsuccessful dieters averaged 1,748 calories per day. The margin of difference between effective and ineffective diets, therefore, can be found for some people to be as little as a single rich dessert [p. 30].

In arranging your contingencies, try to set a behavioral target that is both challenging and realistic. You want your goal to be challenging so that it represents an improvement in your behavior. But you need to be wary of setting your goals too high. If you set them unrealistically high, you may consistently fail to achieve your goals and therefore fail to earn your reinforcers. Such discouraging failures may lead you to abandon the program.

In addition to worrying about getting too little reinforcement, you also need to be concerned about doling out too much. If you earn too much reinforcement too quickly, you may become *satiated,* and the reinforcer may lose its potency. For example, I once used the purchase of two record albums each week to increase a deficit response. This worked fine for a while, until the albums I wanted the most were salted away. Soon there weren't enough albums that I wanted badly enough to make them potent reinforcers.

Thus, the reinforcement contingencies have to be arranged carefully and thoughtfully. Many considerations have to be balanced in order to maximize their effectiveness. You may have to experiment a little and make revisions as your program progresses.

Shaping. In some cases, you may want to reinforce a response that you are not presently capable of making, such as speaking in front of a large group, smoking no cigarettes whatsoever, or jogging five miles a day. In such cases, you have to build up to your ultimate target behavior gradually. This is usually accomplished through a process called **shaping,** which involves reinforcing closer and closer approximations of your ultimately desired response. For instance, if you were taking up jogging with a terminal goal of five miles a day, you might start at only one mile a day and increase that goal by a half mile each week. Thus, the target behavior required to earn reinforcement would change from week to week, gradually getting closer and closer to the final goal.

In shaping yourself, you should set up a schedule spelling out how and when your target behaviors and reinforcement contingencies should change. Try to adhere to this schedule, but be flexible. Generally, it is a good idea to move forward very gradually. The scheduled improvements in your target behavior should be fairly small.

SHAPING. *In operant conditioning, the reinforcement of closer and closer approximations to the desired response; used to gradually develop a response that the person is initially incapable of emitting.*

The token economy. A **token economy** is a system for doling out symbolic reinforcers, which can be redeemed later for real reinforcers. This kind of system is particularly useful when you have *several* related target behaviors that would be difficult to reinforce on a daily basis. For example, let's say you wanted to put together a comprehensive program to improve your health and physical condition. You might have four related target behaviors for each day: (1) consuming less than 1600 calories, (2) doing a half hour of calisthenics, (3) taking several vitamins, and (4) drinking no liquor. It would be difficult to reward each of these daily without getting buried in reinforcers, which would then lose their potency. Instead, it would probably be wise to set up a point system, so that you could earn so many points each day for appropriate behavior. Then, at the end of the week, the points could be converted into real reinforcement. You can see an example of a token economy in Table 5.3.

Another advantage of the token economy is that it permits you to reinforce yourself (symbolically) every time you engage in appropriate behavior. Without the token economy you might have to wait until the end of the day or the end of the week before you received any reinforcement. Such delays make a reinforcer less effective.

Generally, rapid reinforcement works better than delayed reinforcement. In fact, this is the heart of the problem in trying to control overeating. The reinforcement for the response of eating, your enjoyment of the food, is immediate. In contrast, the reinforcement for *not* eating (a slimmer, better-looking, healthier you) is typically several months in the distance. It's not a fair contest. The more rapid reinforcement will win out most of the time. This is why

TOKEN ECONOMY. *In behavior therapy or behavior modification, a system employing symbolic reinforcers, which can be converted into authentic reinforcement.*

behavior modification can be so valuable in combating overeating. If you use a behavior modification program, you can set up your contingencies so that you earn *rapid* reinforcement for not eating. Decreasing the delay between the response of not eating and the reinforcement for that behavior improves the likelihood that you will choose not to eat.

TABLE 5.3   **Example of a token economy designed to reinforce exercise**

Responses earning tokens		
Response	*Amount*	*Number of tokens*
Jogging	½ mile	4
Jogging	1 mile	8
Jogging	2 miles	12
Tennis	1 hour	4
Tennis	2 hours	8
Sit-ups	25	1
Sit-ups	50	2

Redemption value of tokens	
Reinforcer	*Tokens required*
Purchase one record album of choice	30
Go to a movie	50
Go to a nice restaurant	100
Special weekend trip	500

DECREASING RESPONSE STRENGTH

You have a number of options open to you in trying to decrease the frequency of a response. Often you will want to use a combination of several strategies in order to rid yourself of undesirable behavior.

Reinforcement.   Reinforcement can be used to *decrease* as well as to increase response frequency. In this case you simply reinforce yourself for *not* emitting some target response. As mentioned earlier, many problem behaviors can be characterized as either an excess or a deficit, depending on the perspective you choose to take. For example, in the case of overeating you might define your behavioral target as eating more than 1600 calories (a behavioral excess that needs to be decreased in frequency) or as eating less than 1600 calories (a behavioral deficit that needs to be increased in frequency). Thus, one way to tackle the problem of decreasing some undesirable response is to work at increasing the opposite response. This allows you to use reinforcement (for not responding) to reduce the frequency of an unwanted behavior.

Control of antecedents.   For many behavioral excesses there are various antecedent factors that increase the likelihood that the unwanted response will occur. *A worthwhile strategy for decreasing the occurrence of an undesirable response may be to identify these antecedents and avoid exposure to them.* This strategy is especially useful when you are trying to decrease the frequency of a consummatory response, such as overeating. Excessive eating is much more likely to occur when there is a great deal of delicious food readily available. The easiest way to resist temptation is to avoid being confronted by the temptation.

A good behavioral program to reduce overeating will generally include some effort to control antecedents that promote extravagant food consumption. One obvious strategy is to not stock your home with tasty foods that require little preparation. Instead, you should load up on healthful, nonfattening foods that require considerable work to prepare. Then, when hunger strikes and you mentally review the contents of your kitchen, you'll find nothing to lure you into deviating from your diet. Another obvious tactic for controlling antecedents is to avoid going into your favorite restaurants. Many people diet successfully during the week but then go berserk as soon as they set foot in a restaurant on the weekend. The solution to such a problem is quite simple: avoid the restaurant altogether. If social obligations require that you go out to eat, suggest a restaurant where you don't like the food very much. This does not mean that you have to eat at a "seedy" restaurant. It merely means that if you love Chinese food and don't like Mexican food, you should suggest going to a Mexican, not a Chinese, restaurant. There are numerous things you can do to control the antecedents of overeating. You will find an illustrative list in Box 5.8.

Control of antecedents can also be helpful in a program to improve study behavior. Let's say you have a problem in that you socialize and loaf too much when you are supposed to be studying. Such a problem can often be corrected by changing *where* you study. Excessive socializing can be reduced by studying in an area devoid of people. Excessive loafing can often be decreased by studying someplace where there are no distractions (such as TV, stereo, food, phone). Thus, by manipulating the antecedent conditions, you can minimize

---

5.8 *CONTROLLING THE ANTECEDENTS OF OVEREATING*

An important behavioral strategy for promoting weight reduction involves controlling the antecedent variables that tend to trigger overeating. At the core of this strategy is the notion that the best way to overcome temptation is to avoid it altogether. Below you will find a host of tips that have proved useful to some people.

A. Shopping for food
  1. Do not purchase problematic foods. These include:
     a. very fattening, high-calorie foods
     b. your favorite foods, unless they have very low caloric values (you will be tempted to overconsume favorite foods)
     c. foods requiring little preparation (they make it too easy to eat)
  2. To facilitate the above, you should:
     a. use a shopping list from which you do not deviate
     b. shop just *after* eating (your willpower is reduced to jelly when you're hungry)
     c. carry only enough money to pay for items on your list
B. In your kitchen
  1. Don't use your kitchen for anything other than food preparation and consumption. If you study or socialize there, you'll be tempted to eat.
  2. Keep food stock stored out of sight.
  3. If you have problematic foods in your kitchen (for other household members, of course), arrange cupboards and the refrigerator so that these foods are out of reach or in the rear.
  4. Don't hover over cooking food. It will cook itself.
  5. Prepare only enough food for immediate consumption.

C. While eating
  1. Don't do anything besides eating. Watching TV or reading promotes mindless consumption.
  2. Leave serving dishes on the kitchen counter or stove. Don't set them right in front of yourself.
  3. Eat from a smaller dish. It will make the quantity of food appear greater.
  4. Slow the pace of eating. Relax and enjoy your food.
D. After eating
  1. Quickly put away or dispose of leftover foods.
  2. Leave the kitchen as soon as you are through.
E. In regard to restaurants
  1. Insofar as possible, do not patronize restaurants. Menus are written in a much too seductive style.
  2. If social obligations require that you eat out, go to a restaurant that you don't particularly like.
  3. When in restaurants, don't linger over the menu, and don't gawk at the food on other tables.
  4. Avoid driving down streets and going to shopping centers that are loaded with alluring fast-food enterprises.
F. In general
  1. Try to avoid boredom. Keep yourself busy.
  2. Try to avoid excessive sleep loss and fatigue. Your self-control diminishes when you are tired.
  3. Avoid excessive fasting. Skipping meals often leads to overeating later.

study problems. As with overeating, it is largely a matter of avoiding as much temptation as possible.

Developing an incompatible response.   Martin and Poland (1980) note that in trying to get rid of an undesirable behavior it sometimes helps to find a replacement to fill the gap. The replacement should be incompatible with the target response that you want to decrease. In other words, you shouldn't be able to make both responses at the same time. For example, if you're giving up smoking cigarettes, it might help to replace this response by giving yourself some lemon drops when you feel like smoking. This procedure certainly won't eliminate smoking by itself, but it can be very helpful in conjunction with reinforcement and the control of antecedents.

Developing an incompatible response can also be helpful with overeating. For example, whenever hunger strikes at home, you may want to play the piano. In eating, obese people tend to gulp their food down while focusing their attention on something else, such as reading or watching TV. Often they shovel in an enormous volume of food without being aware of it. This behavior can sometimes be corrected by having the person count the times he or she chews each bite. This strategy makes it difficult to divert attention to reading or TV and thus prevents a person from inhaling a great deal of food without even registering it.

Extinction.   When you cut off the customary reinforcement for a response, you are using the procedure of **extinction**. This termination of reinforcement generally leads to a gradual reduction in the frequency of the affected response. Although extinction is often at work in governing our everyday responding, it is difficult to use in a self-modification program, because many of the problems that people have with self-control involve undesirable behaviors that are inherently reinforcing (overeating, not studying, sleeping too much, and so on). When a response is inherently reinforcing, it is impossible to cut off the reinforcement. In such cases, extinction is not one of the available options.

EXTINCTION. *In both respondent and operant conditioning, the weakening of a tendency to make a response. In operant conditioning, also used to denote the procedure wherein reinforcement for a response is terminated (thus weakening the response tendency).*

Occasionally, you may want to decrease an undesirable behavior that is maintained by social reinforcement from others. In such cases, extinction might be a worthwhile strategy. For example, let's say that you notice that you talk too much at parties in order to be the center of attention. You decide that this behavior is somewhat obnoxious, and you would like to reduce its frequency. You further recognize that it has been reinforced in the past by polite attention from your friends, who have been reluctant to insult you by ignoring your excessive talking. In this situation you could talk to the friends with whom you party regularly and ask them to stop reinforcing you (with attention) for your verbal excesses. If you can get them to cut off your social reinforcement, you may be able to simply extinguish the undesirable behavior.

Punishment.   The strategy of decreasing unwanted behavior by punishing yourself for such behavior is an obvious option that is probably overused. There are a number of problems with **punishment** that make it a relatively poor alternative to positive reinforcement. The biggest problem in a self-modification program is that it is quite difficult to punish oneself. Moreover, if you manage to follow through and punish yourself when the contingencies require it, there may be unfortunate emotional side effects, such as anger and depression. For these and other reasons, you should virtually never design a program that depends exclusively on punishment.

PUNISHMENT. *In operant conditioning, the presentation of an unpleasant, or noxious, stimulus. Responses that are followed by punishment tend to be weakened.*

If you're going to use punishment, you should keep two guidelines in mind. First, do not use punishment alone; use it in conjunction with positive reinforcement. If you set up a program wherein you can *only* earn *negative* consequences, you probably won't stick to the program. If you're going to use punishment, make sure you can also earn some positive outcomes. Second, use a reasonably mild punishment. This increases the likelihood that you will actually be able to administer the punishment to yourself. Often, the best way to punish yourself in a mild way is to deny yourself some positive reinforcer.

Nurnberger and Zimmerman (1970) developed a very useful method of self-punishment. They had subjects set up a punishment for themselves by writing out a check to their most hated organization (the Ku Klux Klan, the American Nazi Party, or whatever group a subject detested). Then if the subject did not behave properly, someone else actually mailed the check to the specified organization. Such a punishment is relatively harmless to the person but provides a strong motivation for many people.

EXECUTING AND EVALUATING YOUR PROGRAM

Once you have designed your program, the next step is to put it to work. You have to start enforcing the contingencies that you have carefully planned. During the actual intervention period, you must continue to accurately record the frequency of the target behavior. You hope that the frequency of your target response will gradually increase or decrease in accordance with your plan.

BEHAVIORAL CONTRACT.
In behavior modification, a written agreement involving a promise to adhere to the contingencies of the program.

A device that is often used to solidify your commitment to your program is a **behavioral contract.** A contract is exactly what it sounds like. It is a written agreement that you sign, in which you promise to adhere to the contingencies spelled out in your program (see Figure 5.3). Obviously, such a contract will not ensure that you comply with your plan. However, the formality of signing such a contract seems to make some people take their program more seriously. It is also a good idea to have friends or family witness the signing of your contract. This sort of public commitment can further intensify your determination to stick to your program.

The success of your intervention plan depends on your not "cheating." The most common form of cheating is to reward yourself when you have not actually earned the reinforcer. An occasional cheating incident in a self-modification program is not unusual and does not constitute a reason for dumping the program. However, if you find yourself engaging in wholesale cheating, it is a sign that you need to revise your program.

I, _____ , do hereby agree to initiate my self-change strategy as of (date)_____ and to continue it for a minimum period of _____ weeks—that is, until (date)_____ .
My specific self-change strategy is to _____
_____
_____
_____ .

I will do my best to execute this strategy to my utmost ability and to evaluate its effectiveness only after it has been honestly tried for the specified period of time.

Optional Self-Reward Clause: For every_____ day(s) that I successfully comply with my self-change contract, I will reward myself with _____
_____

In addition, at the end of my minimum period of personal experimentation, I will reward myself for having persisted in my self-change efforts. My reward at that time will be

I hereby request that the witnesses who have signed below support me in my self-change efforts and encourage my compliance with the specifics of this contract. Their cooperation and encouragement throughout the project will be appreciated.

Signed _____
Date _____

Witness:
Witness:

FIGURE 5.3 Self-change contract.

One way to reduce the likelihood of cheating is to have someone other than yourself dole out the reinforcers and punishment. When a spouse or friend is monitoring the program contingencies, it is harder to cheat than when you do everything yourself.

If your program does not work successfully, you should not conclude that behavior modification is a worthless approach. In view of the well-documented evidence that behavior modification procedures can be very effective, it would seem more reasonable to conclude that you did a poor job of designing *your* program. Rather than abandoning the effort, you should think about revising the program. Often, a small revision or two can turn a program around and make it a success. In particular, if you are inexperienced with behavior modification procedures, you should probably *expect* to have to do a little fine-tuning after your program is initiated.

Several flaws are particularly common in poorly devised behavior modification plans. Among the things you should look out for are (1) dependence on a reinforcer that is not really very potent, (2) permitting lengthy delays between appropriate behavior and the actual reinforcement, and (3) trying to do too much too quickly by setting your behavioral goals unrealistically high.

ENDING YOUR PROGRAM

If your behavioral intervention is very successful, it may fade into oblivion without a conscious decision on your part. Often, your new behavior patterns become self-maintaining. Responses such as eating right, exercising regularly, studying, or not smoking may become habitual and then no longer need to be supported by an elaborate program. In many cases, the new behaviors become intrinsically reinforcing. In other words, you come to enjoy jogging or the good grades that you get through additional study. In these cases, the formal program helps you bridge the delay between developing the appropriate behavior and experiencing the intrinsic reward, which often lies in the distant future. Once you have bridged that delay, the program itself may become unnecessary.

However, some programs will need to go on indefinitely. Some people just aren't very good about controlling their behavior without a formal program. There is no reason a program *must* come to an end. *Sometimes it is a good idea to phase your program out gradually, to see whether you can get by without it.* In order to phase it out, you may systematically reduce the potency of your reinforcers or gradually decrease the frequency of your reinforcement.

Whether your program is faded out spontaneously or phased out intentionally, you should always be prepared to reinstitute the program if it becomes necessary. You should be vigilant about slipping back to your old patterns of behavior. If you find this happening, it is a simple matter to reactivate the program to rebuild your good habits.

CHAPTER 5 REVIEW

IDEAS: REVIEW OF LEARNING OBJECTIVES

When you have mastered the material in this chapter, you should be able to do the following.

1. Discuss the five points made about the nature of coping at the beginning of the chapter.
2. Describe the relation between frustration and aggression.
3. Discuss the adaptive value of aggression as a response to stress.
4. Describe the learned-helplessness syndrome and its apparent cause.
5. Discuss the adaptive value of withdrawal/giving up as a response to stress.
6. List the three negative self-talk tendencies identified by Beck.
7. Discuss the adaptive value of negative self-talk.
8. Provide some examples of indulging oneself and discuss its adaptive value.
9. Specify what defense mechanisms defend against and how they work.
10. Discuss whether defense mechanisms are unconscious and normal.
11. List the nine defense mechanisms described in the text.
12. Discuss the adaptive value of defense mechanisms.
13. Summarize the five assumptions made about the nature of constructive coping.
14. List the four types of constructive coping strategies.
15. Discuss how to minimize defensive distortion.
16. Describe Ellis's A-B-C analysis of how catastrophic thinking causes maladaptive emotions.
17. Describe five common irrational assumptions that promote catastrophic thinking.
18. Summarize how one can work to reduce catastrophic thinking.
19. Discuss the merits of making positive comparisons and humor as coping strategies.
20. List four steps in systematic problem-solving efforts.
21. Describe two tendencies that hinder people in their efforts to clarify their problems.
22. Describe three criteria that should be considered in evaluating alternative courses of action.
23. Discuss the adaptive value of seeking help, developing alternative rewards, and achieving behavioral self-control.
24. Discuss the adaptive value of releasing pent-up emotions, distracting oneself, and learning to relax.
25. Describe the requirements and procedure for Benson's relaxation response.
26. Explain the psychological basis for poor nutrition.
27. List four general nutritional goals discussed in the text.
28. Summarize advice on how to improve the quality of your sleep.
29. Summarize advice on how to combat insomnia.
30. List five guidelines for embarking on a successful exercise program.
31. List three assumptions underlying the behavioral approach to solving problems.
32. Explain the "recipe" for weight loss and describe the best way to go about it.
33. List the five steps involved in developing and executing a self-modification program.
34. Explain why traits cannot be target behaviors.
35. Explain the concepts of behavioral excess and deficit. Which concept is better when you have a choice?
36. List three kinds of information you should pursue in gathering your baseline data.
37. Explain why it may be useful to know about the common antecedents of your target behavior.
38. Discuss some advice about identifying the consequences of your target behavior.
39. Discuss how to select a reinforcer for your program.
40. Discuss how to set up reinforcement contingencies.
41. Define shaping and explain when you would use it.
42. Describe a token economy and some of its advantages.
43. Describe four strategies for decreasing the strength of an unwanted response.
44. Describe two problems in the use of punishment and two guidelines for its use.
45. Discuss the value of a behavioral contract.
46. Discuss how you should react if your program is not a success.
47. Describe the ways in which your program may come to an end.

TERMS: REVIEW OF NEW VOCABULARY

When you have mastered the material in this chapter, you should be able to define the following terms.

Aggression	Catharsis	Insomnia	Regression
Antecedents	Constructive coping	Intermittent reinforcement	Reinforcement
Baseline period	Coping	Learned helplessness	Reinforcement
Behavioral contract	Defense mechanism	Projection	contingencies
Behavioral deficit	Denial	Punishment	REM sleep
Behavioral excess	Displacement	Rationalization	Repression
Behavior modification	Extinction	Rational-emotive therapy	Shaping
Brainstorming	Fantasy	Reaction formation	Token economy
Catastrophic thinking	Identification		

PEOPLE: REVIEW OF MAJOR THEORISTS AND RESEARCHERS

When you have mastered the material in this chapter, you should be able to summarize the principal contributions and/or ideas of the following people.

Aaron Beck	Albert Ellis	Moos and Billings	Martin Seligman
Herbert Benson	Sigmund Freud	Julius Segal	Watson and Tharp

The Interpersonal Realm

6

PERSON PERCEPTION: HOW WE SEE OURSELVES AND OTHERS

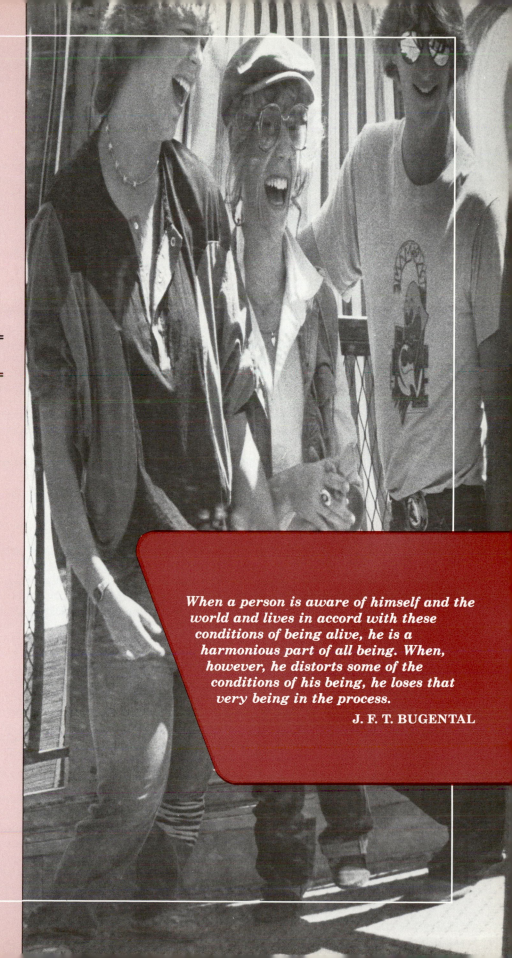

Summary

Applying Psychology to Your Life: Building Self-Esteem

1. RECOGNIZE THAT YOU CONTROL YOUR SELF-IMAGE
2. DON'T LET OTHERS SET YOUR STANDARDS
3. RECOGNIZE UNREALISTIC GOALS
4. MODIFY NEGATIVE SELF-TALK
5. EMPHASIZE YOUR STRENGTHS
6. WORK TO IMPROVE YOURSELF
7. APPROACH OTHERS WITH A POSITIVE OUTLOOK

When a person is aware of himself and the world and lives in accord with these conditions of being alive, he is a harmonious part of all being. When, however, he distorts some of the conditions of his being, he loses that very being in the process.

J. F. T. BUGENTAL

It's Friday night and you're bored. The menu of TV shows for the evening looks terribly tedious, and the thought of studying on a Friday night is positively revolting. You call a couple of friends to see whether they want to go out to a movie. Both friends tell you that they would "love" to go, but they have other commitments. One is going to study, and the other has to pick up someone at the airport. In both cases, you feel that their reasons for not going out with you are rather flimsy. It seems that if they really wanted to go, they could have worked it in. To what do you attribute these rejections? Do the friends really have other commitments? Are they simply too lazy; are they apathetic about going out? Are they being sincere when they say that they would love to go out with you? Is it possible that they really don't enjoy spending time with you? Could it be that they find you boring? Are you boring?

These questions illustrate a basic process that we are engaged in constantly. That process is the *interpretation of behavior.* We have a fundamental need to understand both our own behavior and the behavior of others. We are continually expending effort to explain behavior. In this effort, we create and rely on images, or pictures, of ourselves and others. These pictures have an enormous impact on how we feel about ourselves and how we relate to other people. This chapter discusses how we develop these pictures of ourselves and others. The first portion of the chapter will cover self-perception and talk about how our self-concepts are shaped by our interactions with others. The second portion will discuss how we see *other* people. In particular, it will focus on why we are often inaccurate in our perceptions of others.

Basic Principles of Social Perception

Before tackling the topic of self-perception, we need to examine a few basic aspects of social perception.

THE ATTRIBUTION PROCESS

NATURE OF ATTRIBUTIONS

ATTRIBUTION. *An inference drawn about the causes of behavior.*

In our efforts to understand behavior, we regularly draw inferences about the apparent cause of a person's behavior. *Psychologists refer to these inferences about the causation of behavior as* **attributions.** For example, let's say that someone compliments you on your clothing. To what should you *attribute* that compliment? Was this person truly impressed by your mode of dress? Or was the compliment merely part of everyday social routine? Could the compliment be part of a systematic effort to "butter you up"? Or suppose that your boss bawls you out for doing a sloppy job on some insignificant project. To what do you *attribute* this tonguelashing? Was your boss just in a grouchy mood? Is your boss under too much pressure? Was your work really that sloppy? These two everyday examples illustrate the nature of the attribution process. This process is exceedingly complex. At this point you should simply be aware of two things: (1) that we constantly make attributions in order to understand the causation of behavior and (2) that these attributions involve *inferences* that ultimately represent *guesswork* on our part.

INTERNAL VERSUS EXTERNAL ATTRIBUTIONS

Psychologists have developed several theories (Heider, 1958; Jones & Davis, 1965; Kelley, 1967) to explain the laws governing our attributions. A thorough review of these complex theories and the voluminous research that they have generated is beyond the scope of our present concern. However, I should mention the principal dimension along which attributions can be analyzed. This is the internal versus external dimension. *In trying to understand the causation of behavior, we generally may choose to attribute it either to internal, personal factors or to external, situational factors.* For example, if you do well on a test, you can choose to attribute it to your hard work and great intelligence (an internal attribution) *or* to the fact that the test was ridiculously easy (external attribution). Similarly, when a friend drops out of school, you may attribute it to a lack of motivation (internal) or to financial difficulties (external). When another friend cheats on her husband, you may attribute it to that friend's lack of character (internal) or to overwhelming temptation (external). The point is that there is a fundamental difference between attributing behavior to one's abilities or personality traits (internal) and attributing it to situational factors (external). These attributions have a tremendous impact on how we see others, as well as ourselves. In fact, we now have evidence that some patterns of attribution may even contribute to serious depressive disorders (Lewinsohn et al., 1980). This evidence suggests that people who attribute their failures to internal, personal causes while discounting external, situational explanations may be more prone to depression than people who display opposite tendencies. Thus, the roots of depression may sometimes lie in excessive self-blame, which is a function of a particular attributional style.

ACTOR/OBSERVER DIFFERENCES IN ATTRIBUTIONS

Some theorists (for example, Bem, 1965; Kelley, 1971) maintain that the processes involved in self-perception and one's perception of others are essentially the same. Although it may indeed be true that the perceptual *processes* are quite similar, there is evidence that an actor and an outside observer have different perspectives. For example, Jones and Nisbett (1971) argue that *actors tend to attribute their behavior to situational requirements, while observers tend to attribute those same actions to the actors' personalities.* Thus, if you fly into a rage when the bank makes a small mistake on your account, *you* will probably attribute the rage to the frustrating situation, but an *observer* standing near you in line will be more apt to attribute the rage to your bad temper and surly personality. In a nutshell, then, actors seem to favor external attributions, while observers are more prone to make internal attributions.

Although there is a general tendency for actors to attribute their own behavior to external determinants while observers make internal attributions, these biases are greatly affected by the exact nature of the situation. For example, when we succeed or do well in some endeavor, these tendencies are reversed to some degree (Bradley, 1978). In explaining *success,* an actor tends to take personal credit, thus making an internal attribution, while an observer is more likely to attribute the success to favorable situational factors, thus making an external attribution. In explaining *failure,* the usual biases are at work; actors tend to attribute their failure to unfavorable situational factors, while observers blame the failure on the actors' personal shortcomings. A simple example of these tendencies can be drawn from the classroom. When a class does exceptionally well on a test (success), the students usually attribute their outstanding performance to their intelligence and diligent study (internal), while the teacher is more likely to attribute it to an excessively easy test (external). But if the class performs very poorly (failure), the students will probably blame it on an excessively difficult exam (external), while the teacher blames their poor performance on their stupidity and/or lack of work (internal).

Because of differences such as these, I will discuss self-perception and perception of others separately. Although the two topics have much in common, the crucial issues are somewhat different.

THE PREMIUM ON CONSISTENCY

In developing our pictures of ourselves and others, we strive for consistency. That is, we prefer that our attitudes and beliefs mesh together nicely rather than contradicting each other. A perceived inconsistency among our beliefs

COGNITIVE DISSONANCE.
An unpleasant state of psychological tension that arises when thoughts are contradictory or inconsistent. A specific type of conflict.

leads to what Leon Festinger (1957) calls **cognitive dissonance.** According to Festinger, the experience of such dissonance is unpleasant; therefore, we may try to rid ourselves of the dissonance by modifying our beliefs so that they at least appear to be internally consistent. Consider a simple example. Let's say that you consider yourself a hard-working, reliable person. However, at the moment you're sitting out at the ballpark taking in a baseball game after calling in sick at work. Obviously, the cognitions that "I'm reliable" and "I'm skipping work" are inconsistent, thereby creating dissonance. Festinger's theory suggests that you will feel some need to modify one of the cognitions in order to reduce the disturbing feeling of dissonance. Thus, you may admit to yourself that you're not all that reliable, or you may look for some way to rationalize skipping work so that it does not appear that you're being unreliable ("Even the best of us play hooky once in a while"). The first alternative would require modifying your self-concept. As I shall discuss later, you're more likely to choose the second, less drastic alternative. In either case, the crucial point is that we try to maintain consistency among our beliefs, even if we have to twist reality a little bit (or a lot) to achieve this consistency.

SELECTIVITY IN SOCIAL PERCEPTION

There is an old saying that "people see what they expect to see." This common-sense notion that expectations influence perceptions has been confirmed repeatedly by social scientists. For example, in a classic study, Harold Kelley (1950) showed how a person is preceded by his or her reputation. Kelley told students that their class would be taken over by a new lecturer whom they would be asked to evaluate later. Before the class, the students were given a short description of the incoming instructor, with one important variation. Half the students were led to expect a "warm" person, while the other half were led to expect a "cold" one (see Figure 6.1). Although all the subjects were exposed to the same 20 minutes of actual interaction with the new instructor, those who were led to expect a warm person rated the instructor as more considerate, sociable, humorous and good-natured, informal, and humane than those who were led to expect a cold person!

Thus, it is clear that our expectations color our social perceptions. This selectivity in perception probably explains why people may continue to believe in uncomplimentary racial stereotypes even if they are exposed to contradictory evidence. For purposes of illustration, let's create an imaginary racial group called the Nerdians. Let us further assume that you have always been led to believe that all Nerdians were loudmouths. Over a period of years, you

Mr. Blank is a graduate student in the Department of Economics and Social Science here at M.I.T. He has had three semesters of teaching experience in psychology at another college. This is his first semester teaching Ec. 70. He is 26 years old, a veteran, and married. People who know him consider him to be a rather cold person, industrious, critical, practical, and determined.

Mr. Blank is a graduate student in the Department of Economics and Social Science here at M.I.T. He has had three semesters of teaching experience in psychology at another college. This is his first semester teaching Ec. 70. He is 26 years old, a veteran, and married. People who know him consider him to be a very warm person, industrious, critical, practical, and determined.

FIGURE 6.1 Descriptions of the guest lecturer in Kelley's (1950) study of impression formation.

may work with ten Nerdians, only two of whom are actually loudmouths. However, because of selectivity in social perception, there is an excellent chance that you will take note of those two and ignore or forget about the other eight. Thus, in spite of contradictory evidence, you will believe that your personal experience confirms what you were always told about Nerdians. In summary, you should bear in mind that social perception is subjective and selective; there is no guarantee of accuracy. *We do have a tendency to see what we expect to see.*

Self-Perception

SELF-PERCEPTION THEORY. *The theory that we infer our attitudes, traits, and motives from our observations of our own overt behavior.*

According to Daryl Bem's (1972) **self-perception theory,** the reasons for our behavior are not always readily apparent even to ourselves. Bem further asserts that we try to understand ourselves by inferring our motives and attitudes from our behavior. Thus, he argues that often *we derive our attitudes from our behavior.* This analysis is a significant departure from the conventional wisdom that our attitudes determine our behavior. Typically, a person might explain his habits by saying "I don't like plays. Therefore, I don't go to them." However, Bem suggests that sometimes the reasoning proceeds in the opposite direction, so that a person says "Gee, I don't go to any plays. I guess I don't like them." In summary, Bem maintains that we are actively involved in efforts to understand our *own* behavior. I will focus now on that process of self-perception and related issues.

SELF-CONCEPT

SELF-CONCEPT. *A collection of beliefs and judgments about one's own nature, typical behavior, strengths, and weaknesses.*

Through the processes of social perception that I have been discussing, you develop a **self-concept,** which is your own subjective mental picture of yourself. It consists of *a collection of beliefs about what you are like* (Rosenberg, 1979). It might include beliefs such as "I am friendly" or "I am lazy" or "I am introverted" or "I am exceptionally bright" or "I am too skinny." As you can see from those examples of self-referent beliefs, the self-concept includes many aspects. Among other things, we all have a picture of our unique physical self, social self, emotional self, and intellectual self. *Cutting across all these components of the self, there is the crucial dimension of self-evaluation.* We generally look at ourselves in an approving or disapproving manner. These favorable or unfavorable self-evaluations determine our self-esteem. As we shall see later, self-esteem is probably the most important aspect of our self-concept.

A person's self-concept is *not* poured in concrete. However, it is not easily changed, either. Once it is established, we have a tendency to preserve and defend our self-concept. Therefore, our pictures of ourselves tend to be fairly stable. In the context of this stability, however, the self-concept has a certain dynamic quality. Although it rarely changes overnight, your self-concept may very well undergo gradual change over time.

Jourard (1974) argues that one's self-concept is both descriptive and prescriptive. Its descriptive nature is obvious in that it describes past patterns of behavior. Its prescriptive nature may be less apparent, but Jourard, like Rogers (1959), maintains that our self-concept influences *future* behavior because we try to act consistently with our self-concept. Jourard believes that we may feel uncomfortable when we act out of character; therefore, our personal perception of what we are like prescribes how we should behave in the future. Thus, we have a "two-way street." Our behavior influences our self-concept (through the process of self-perception), and our self-concept influences our behavior.

The key point here is that your self-concept is not merely some obscure abstraction of interest to psychologists. It governs your day-to-day behavior in significant ways. For instance, if you have been "eyeing" an attractive classmate recently, your self-esteem may be the crucial factor that determines whether you actually approach that person.

FACTORS SHAPING THE SELF-CONCEPT

ONE'S OWN OBSERVATIONS

Your own observations of your behavior are obviously a major source of information about what you are like. Early in childhood we begin observing our own behavior and drawing conclusions about ourselves. For example, young children will make statements about who is the tallest, who can run fastest, or who can swing the highest.

Social comparison. These observations do not take place in a social vacuum. Even in early childhood they involve comparisons with other children. **Social comparison theory** (Festinger, 1954; Goethals & Darley, 1977) proposes that people need to compare themselves with others in order to gain insight into their own behavior. The potential impact of such social comparisons was dramatically demonstrated in a study by Morse and Gergen (1970). Their subjects thought they were being interviewed for a job. Half the subjects met another applicant who appeared to be *very* impressive, while the other half were exposed to a competitor who appeared to be a clod. All subjects filled out measures of self-esteem both before and after the bogus job interviews. The self-esteem of subjects who encountered the impressive competitor became less favorable after the interview, while the self-esteem of those meeting the unimpressive competitor became more positive. Thus, our comparisons with others *may* have immediate effects on our self-concept.

Of course, we do not choose just anyone for a point of comparison. According to social comparison theory, we tend to compare ourselves with a **reference**

SOCIAL COMPARISON THEORY. *The theory that in order to understand themselves, people need to evaluate their opinions and abilities by comparing themselves with others. According to the theory, the more uncertain people are about something, the greater is their need for comparison. Generally, people seek similar others for their standard of comparison.*

RECOMMENDED READING

6.1 *Encounters with the Self*
by Don E. Hamachek (Holt, Rinehart & Winston, 1978)

This book is all about the many aspects of the self-concept. It describes how the contours of the self-concept are molded by our interactions with others, how the self-concept continues to undergo metamorphosis throughout life, and how the self-concept is expressed in our everyday behavior. Though reasonably compact in size, the book is quite broad in scope, and Hamachek manages to cover a sizable diversity of intriguing topics, including defense mechanisms, how we perceive others, the role of physical appearance in shaping self-concept, how child-rearing styles influence self-concept, how self-perceptions affect academic adjustment, feelings of inferiority, and how to pursue a more positive self-image.

This is one of those rare books that can provide satisfactory reading for both the sophisticated professional and the naive layperson. Academicians will appreciate the well-documented and thorough review of relevant research. At the same time, the uninitiated will find the book highly readable and brimming with practical insights and advice. Although the author disavows any intention of writing a "self-help" book, this volume is likely to be about as helpful to readers as any mere book can be.

Some individuals avoid finding out more about themselves for fear of having to give up a self with which they have grown comfortable or "satisfied." Most people have an initial inclination to resist personal change anyway, but this resistance is even stronger for a person who refuses to try new or changed behavior into his current concept of self. For example, a shy, timid, submissive person may not want to see his strengths and assets for fear that he might have to be more assertive and socially aggressive. If shyness has become a way of life designed to protect one from the risks of social disapproval (in this case, nothing ventured, nothing lost—in terms of self-esteem), then it may be difficult indeed for a shy person to give up his timidity. Other individuals are reluctant to find out more about themselves because of the threat of having to change in the direction of being more personally mature. Maturity implies many things, among which are a certain degree of independence and autonomy, capacity for self-discipline, certainty about goals and values, and motivation toward some level of personal achievement. Most of all, greater maturity means greater responsibility, and for some this is a frightening possibility [p. 18].

REFERENCE GROUP.
*According to social
comparison theory, the
particular group of people
against whom you compare
yourself in order to better
understand your attitudes,
values, beliefs, and behavior.*

group that includes people who are similar to us in certain key ways. The crucial dimensions of similarity depend on which aspects of our behavior we are trying to evaluate. If you want to judge the progress of your racquetball game, you will probably compare yourself against people who are similar in the length of time that they have been playing. If you want to evaluate your career progress, you'll compare yourself with people of roughly the same age who are in the same general occupational area. Consistent with this hypothesis, Zanna, Goethals, and Hill (1975) found that when subjects were led to believe that performance on a task was influenced by one's sex, males wanted to know how other men did, while females sought information about the performance of other women.

Distortive tendencies.   Another important point about our own observations is that they are not entirely objective; social perception may be very selective. As Carl Rogers (1959) has pointed out, we learn early in life about what is judged to be good and bad behavior. Then, in order to feel worthy of others' affection, we tend to distort our behavior in ways that permit positive self-evaluations. As noted in Chapter 2, this selectivity in self-perception means that *your self-concept may not be a particularly accurate reflection of your behavior.*

The general tendency is to distort reality in a *positive* direction. In other words, we tend to evaluate ourselves in a more positive light than is really merited. The great strength of this tendency was highlighted in a recent survey

How we see ourselves may be very different from how others see us. The pictures and text on the right illustrate the subjective quality of the self-concept and of our perception of others.

As she sees herself: Unchanged since age 22. Sociable, scintillating, sexy. Her hair styled like Jane Fonda's.

As the husband sees her: Older than her years. Someone more suited to suburban domesticity and PTA.

As he sees himself: Stylish haircut, rakish moustache; benevolent, generous, powerful. A smooth operator.

As the wife sees him: Slightly overweight, trying to look younger than his years. Not very decisive or strong.

responded to by some 829,000 high school students (Myers, 1980). In this survey, 70 percent of the students rated themselves above average in leadership ability, while a minuscule 2 percent rated themselves below average (obviously, by definition, 50 percent must be above average and 50 percent below). In regard to "ability to get along with others," over 99 percent saw themselves as above average, and 25 percent of the respondents thought they belonged in the top 1 percent!

Although the general tendency is to distort reality in a positive direction, this is clearly not a universal rule. A minority of people tend to do just the opposite; they constantly evaluate themselves in an unrealistically negative way. Moreover, most of us tend to make *both* negative and positive distortions, although the latter are more common. For example, you might overrate your social skill, emotional stability, and intellectual ability while underrating your physical attractiveness. Thus, the tendency to see ourselves in an overly favorable light is strong but not universal.

FEEDBACK FROM OTHERS

Our self-concept is also shaped by the feedback that we get about our behavior from other people. It should be readily apparent that not everyone is equally influential. Early in life our parents and other family members play a dominant role in providing us with feedback. As we grow older, feedback from a much wider array of people becomes significant.

Our parents give us a great deal of direct feedback. They constantly express approval or disapproval, making statements such as "You're cute as the dickens" or "You're a lazy bum like your Uncle Patrick." Most of us, especially when young, take this sort of feedback quite seriously. Consequently, it comes as no surprise that various empirical studies reveal a correspondence between parents' views of a child and the child's self-concept (Wylie, 1968).

Our parents may also sway *our own observations* of our behavior. In many ways, parents influence the standards we use to judge ourselves. Furthermore, Rogers (1959) asserts that our parents influence our tendency to distort our

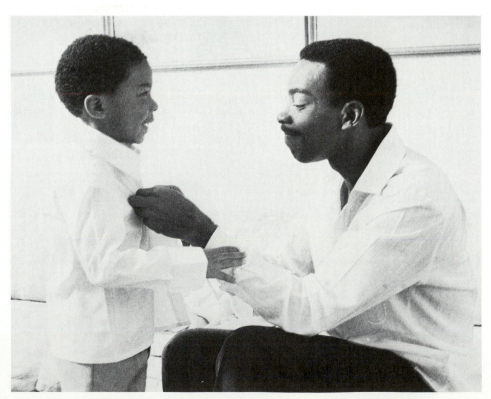

Feedback from parents has an enormous impact on a child's self-concept.

own behavior. According to Rogers, when parents provide unconditional love, the child has less need to make distortions in a positive direction in order to feel worthy of that love. In other words, Rogers believes that unconditional love promotes relatively accurate self-perception, while conditional love increases the likelihood of distortion.

Parents and family are not the only source of feedback from others. Teachers, Little League baseball coaches, Girl Scout leaders, and so forth also provide significant feedback. As adolescence approaches, one's peer group becomes progressively more influential (Monge, 1973).

The feedback that we receive from others has to filter through our social perception systems and therefore may be distorted just like our own observations. As you would logically expect, *most people tend to be more receptive to positive than to negative feedback* (Eagly & Whitehead, 1972). However, there are many qualifying conditions. For instance, there is evidence (Glenn & Janda, 1977) that people with relatively little self-esteem are quite amenable to accepting negative feedback, which "confirms" their beliefs about their lack of worth.

CULTURAL GUIDELINES

Our self-concept is also shaped, albeit indirectly, by our culture. The society where we are brought up defines what is good and bad in the way of personality and behavior. For example, American culture tends to put a high premium on competitive success, strength, skill, and individuality. These cultural guidelines about what is valued influence how we may distort our observations of our behavior. We are more likely to make distortions in areas that our culture considers important.

Our culture is also responsible for various stereotypes that may mold our self-perceptions. For instance, there is evidence (Donelson, 1973) that the sex-related stereotypes in American culture leave their stamp on how men and women see themselves. If a young female is led to believe that girls are silly, frivolous, and emotional, she is much more likely to see herself in that way than a boy who has been trained otherwise is to see himself. In a similar manner, uncomplimentary racial stereotypes may influence the self-concepts of people in certain ethnic groups.

SELF-ESTEEM

The term **self-esteem** refers to your global evaluation of your worth as a person (Hamachek, 1978). As mentioned earlier, this is a very important element of your self-concept.

Self-esteem is a somewhat messy concept to investigate, for a couple of reasons. First, there is some doubt about the validity of many measures of self-

---

6.2

RECOMMENDED READING

Why Am I Afraid to Tell You Who I Am?
by John Powell (Argus Communications, 1969)

This is a charming, easy to read, and very nontechnical book that has proved very popular over the years. It focuses on self-awareness and interpersonal relationships. The central theme is: Why don't we open up to others instead of using roles as barriers to authentic communication? Powell points out that there are many reasons, which largely grow out of our insecurity.

We are afraid that if we reveal our true selves, others might not like us. Powell conducts a fascinating review of a host of roles that people use as masks. He discusses "the body beautiful," "the braggart," "the clown," "the cynic," "the dreamer," "the flirt," "the hedonist," "the egghead," "the martyr," "the sex bomb," and "the predatory male," among others.

None of us wants to be a fraud or to live a lie; none of us wants to be a sham, a phony, but the fears that we experience and the risks that honest self-communication would involve seem so intense to us that seeking refuge in our roles, masks, and games becomes an almost natural reflex action [p. 13].

SELF-ESTEEM. *A person's overall assessment of his or her personal adequacy or worth. The evaluative component of the self-concept.*

esteem. We tend to rely on verbal reports from subjects, which may obviously be biased. Wells and Marwell (1976) point out that, for many people, the "real" self-esteem that they feel and the level of self-esteem that they report on a questionnaire may be quite different. Second, in probing self-esteem it is often quite difficult to separate cause from effect. We have a fairly large volume of correlational data that tell us that certain behavioral characteristics are associated with positive or negative self-esteem. However, it is hard to tell whether these behavioral tendencies are the cause or the effect of a particular level of self-esteem. For instance, we know that people with a favorable self-concept are less willing than people with little self-esteem to accept negative feedback about themselves from others (Glenn & Janda, 1977). Unfortunately, we are not sure whether this distortive tendency leads to high self-esteem or whether high self-esteem leads to this distortive tendency. This problem in pinpointing causation should be kept in mind as we look at the determinants and effects of self-esteem.

IMPORTANCE OF SELF-ESTEEM

The importance of developing a positive attitude toward oneself can hardly be overestimated. A host of unfortunate behavioral tendencies are associated with poor self-esteem. Although it is difficult to distinguish cause from effect, it is clear that self-esteem is a very significant aspect of one's personality. To illustrate the enormous importance of self-esteem, I will review some of the behavioral characteristics that often accompany *low* self-esteem.

1. People with unfavorable self-concepts tend to develop more emotional problems than people with good self-esteem (Fitts, 1972; Howard & Kubis, 1964; Rosenberg, 1965). Among other things, they are more likely to report that they are troubled by anxiety, nervousness, insomnia, unhappiness, and psychosomatic symptoms.

2. There is also a relation between low self-esteem and relatively poor achievement. For instance, there is a correlation between low self-esteem and low grades in school (O'Malley & Bachman, 1979). This relatively poor achievement is probably due to the fact that people with low self-esteem set low goals for themselves (Purkey, 1970). They lack confidence and assume that they would not succeed even if they tried.

3. In social interactions, people with low self-esteem are often awkward, self-conscious, and especially vulnerable to rejection (Rosenberg, 1965). They have a particularly great need for acceptance from others, but they are often unable to pursue that social acceptance vigorously. Thus, they end up becoming socially "invisible." They rarely join formal groups and do not participate very actively in social encounters.

4. Because of their great need to be liked, people with unfavorable self-concepts tend to be quite susceptible to social influence (Wells & Marwell, 1976). They tend to be conforming, agreeable, and highly persuasible. They are often afraid to behave independently or assertively because they feel it might endanger their acceptance by others.

5. People who have a negative self-concept are also less likely than most to authentically like other people (Baron, 1974; Wylie, 1961). They tend to look for flaws in others and "tear them down." They do this because it allows them to feel a little better about themselves when they make their inevitable social comparisons. However, this also gives them a bias toward disliking others. They therefore tend to relate to others in negative ways, thereby courting rejection and compounding their problems.

DETERMINANTS OF SELF-ESTEEM

The foundations for high or low self-esteem appear to be laid down very early in life. There is evidence (Wattenberg & Clifford, 1964) that some children enter the first grade already possessing an unfavorable self-image.

Such an unfortunate circumstance so early in life would almost have to be attributable to parental feedback. Indeed, there is ample evidence that *parents have a marked influence on their children's self-esteem.* This became apparent in an extensive study of the antecedents of self-esteem in young boys conducted by Stanley Coopersmith (1967). He compared the child-rearing styles of parents of high- and low-self-esteem boys and found that the former (1) expressed more affection to their children, (2) were more interested in their children's activities, (3) were more accepting of their children, (4) used sound, consistent disciplinary procedures, and (5) had relatively high self-esteem themselves. In particular, it was parents' sincere *interest* in their children that seemed most strongly related to the development of a positive self-concept.

While parental feedback may be the crucial childhood determinant of self-esteem, it is clear that *children (and adults) make their own judgments about themselves as well.* Here the paramount issue is how they view their *achievements* in comparison to others. A history of failure in school is typically associated with a negative self-image (Glasser, 1969). Yet, success in an endeavor as simple as learning to swim can lead to enhanced self-esteem (Koocher, 1971). Thus, it is clear that our self-esteem may be augmented or diminished by our own observations of our successes and failures.

Of course, it should be mentioned that our definitions of success and failure are greatly influenced by others, especially parents and teachers. Some overly demanding parents and teachers employ unrealistically high standards and are virtually never satisfied with children's performance. Sometimes these unrealistic standards are an unfortunate by-product of good intentions; the parents and teachers simply want to push the children to high levels of achievement. However, this push for excellence sometimes backfires and leads children to apply unrealistically high standards in evaluating themselves. These unrealistic standards then cause the children to make largely unfavorable self-appraisals of their performance, thus lowering their self-esteem.

Perceptions of success and failure will also be influenced by the nature of one's *reference group.* Marsh and Parker (1984) found that preadolescents' self-esteem was affected by the quality of competition they faced in school. Children from schools in higher-socioeconomic-class areas with "high quality" competition were compared against children from schools in lower-class areas with "low quality" competition. In other words, children from a high-ability reference group were contrasted with children from a low-ability reference group. Interestingly, the children in the low-quality schools tended to display greater self-esteem than children of similar academic ability who were enrolled in the high-quality schools. Thus, the authors conclude that it might be benefi-

---

6.3   ***Be the Person You Were Meant to Be***
by Jerry Greenwald (Simon & Schuster, 1973)

A disciple of Fritz Perls, Greenwald does an excellent job of presenting the Gestalt theory as it relates to everyday living. The Gestalt philosophy emphasizes taking responsibility for oneself, being very present-oriented, and freeing oneself of external regulation. The major strength of the book is its straightforward presentation of how we often let others' expectations bottle up our spontaneity. The forces that interfere with our natural function-ing are called "toxic" influences, and Greenwald offers a wealth of advice regarding antidotes to this toxic living.

The T person toxifies himself with his constant need to explain himself and justify his behavior to others. These explanations and justifications bog him down and hamper his freedom to act decisively. Explanationitis ranges from meek defensiveness to belligerent defiance. The victim tor-ments himself by seeking to justify or excuse his every action. The hook in this self-torture game is the importance the person places on other people's understanding and accepting the "whys" of his attitudes and actions. Since one rarely finishes explaining himself, this T pattern becomes an endless barrier to free-flowing self-expression and spontaneity of action [p. 79].

cial to one's self-esteem to be "a large fish in a small pond." This finding that kids with similar talents vary in self-esteem, depending on their reference group, demonstrates the immense importance of social comparison processes in governing self-concept.

PUBLIC SELVES

PUBLIC SELF. *An image or façade presented to others in public interactions.*

Whereas your self-concept involves how *you* see yourself, your **public self** involves how you want *others* to see you. As you are surely aware, we rarely behave in a totally spontaneous fashion. Let's face it, *most people see only an edited version of our behavior, which is usually calculated to present a certain image.* This may sound deceitful, but it is perfectly normal and all of us do it (Alexander & Knight, 1971; Goffman, 1959, 1971). Actually, most of us are not limited to a single public self; typically, we have a number of public selves that are tied to certain situations and certain groups of people with whom we interact. For instance, you may have one public self for your parents and another for your siblings. You may have still others for your spouse, your same-sex friends, your opposite-sex friends, your boss, your subordinates, your colleagues, your customers, and your neighbors.

SELF-PRESENTATION

Why do we behave in this way? Basically, it's a matter of necessity. Erving Goffman (1959) argues that societal norms are such that we are virtually *required* to engage in careful self-presentation. In other words, we are expected to portray ourselves in certain ways when interacting with our parents, peers, co-workers, and so forth. Goffman further points out that our social norms also support others' acceptance of these efforts at impression management. Although people may be skeptical, they rarely challenge these self-presentations. Unless your self-presentation is clearly and exorbitantly out of line with reality, people will keep their suspicions to themselves.

In interacting with others, we all engage in impression management as we try to present ourselves in a favorable light.

IMPRESSION MANAGEMENT. *Efforts to present oneself to others in a particular (usually socially desirable) way.*

MARK SNYDER

SELF-MONITORING. *The act of paying special attention to one's effect on others; also, a trait involving the degree to which one does this.*

In summary, we engage in **impression management** because it is expected of us. It is necessary if we want people to like us, respect us, hire us, buy products from us, and so forth. This basic reality was illustrated in a study of behavior in job interviews (Von Baeyer, Sherk, & Zanna, 1981). Female job applicants were led to believe that the man who would interview them held either very traditional, "chauvinistic" views of women or just the opposite. Applicants who expected a chauvinist presented themselves in a more "traditional feminine" manner than subjects in the other condition. Their self-presentation efforts affected both their communication style and their appearance (such as wearing more makeup). The bottom line is this: impression management is a normal feature of everyday social interactions. Although we certainly don't do it all the time, we probably do it a lot more than many of us realize.

Although we all engage in *some* self-presentation, we vary greatly in *how much* we edit our behavior. Some people are more concerned than others about portraying themselves "appropriately" for various audiences. Moreover, some people have many public selves, which are highly discrepant from one another, while other people have only a few public selves, which may overlap to a large degree (see Figure 6.2). As we shall see momentarily, the number and diversity of your public selves may influence your actual self-concept and even your psychological health.

SELF-MONITORING

According to Mark Snyder (1979; Snyder & Gangestad, 1982), people vary in how aware they are of how they are being perceived by others. People who are high in self-monitoring are very sensitive to their impact on others, while those who are low in self-monitoring are less concerned about this and behave more spontaneously. Basically, **self-monitoring** is a personality trait that affects the degree to which people consciously use impression management strategies in social interactions.

People who are high in self-monitoring display the following characteristics. They actively seek information about how they are expected to or ought to behave and try to tailor their actions accordingly. They are very sensitive to situational cues and relatively skilled at deciphering what others want to see.

FIGURE 6.2 Public selves and identity confusion. Person 1 has very disparate public selves with relatively little overlap among them. He or she is more likely to develop identity confusion than Person 2, whose public selves are relatively similar.

Public selves for (a) spouse, (b) parents, (c) neighbors, (d) boss, (e) colleagues.

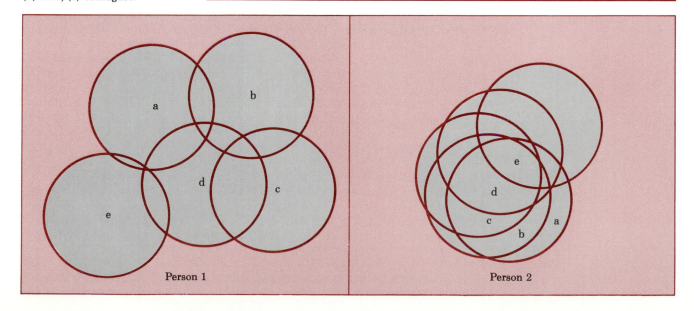

Person 1

Person 2

Their behavior is guided more by situational expectations than by their true feelings. Moreover, because they really *work* at it, they are relatively talented at self-presentation. They control their emotions well and deliberately regulate nonverbal signals that are more spontaneous in others. They tend to be good actors, playing their roles with cunning effectiveness. Additionally, their earnest attention to the process of self-presentation makes them particularly adept at spotting deceptive impression management *in others.*

INGRATIATION

INGRATIATION. *A conscious effort to solicit someone's liking by using a variety of self-presentation strategies.*

A special form of self-presentation called ingratiation has been described by E. E. Jones (1964). **Ingratiation** is a conscious, systematic effort to gain liking from another person. Jones outlines four techniques that are commonly used in shrewd efforts to pursue others' affection.

- *Compliments.* Good old-fashioned flattery is far from obsolete. The key is to make the compliments appear spontaneous and believable.
- *Conformity.* Conforming to others' opinions tends to promote liking. As with compliments, it must be judiciously done in order to maintain credibility.
- *Favors.* It doesn't hurt to do favors for those whose liking you wish to win. However, the favors shouldn't be too spectacular, or they may leave the target person with an irritating feeling of social indebtedness.
- *Presentation of a favorable self-image.* If you expect to procure another's liking, it certainly helps to portray yourself as likable. Depending on the situation, some false modesty may be useful.

Obviously, successful ingratiation requires a certain amount of social skill. It therefore comes as no surprise that Snyder (1981) concludes that ingratiation is most effective when people are able to hide their manipulative intentions. Nonetheless, Snyder points out that human vanity is such that ingratiation may pay off even when the duplicity of the ingratiation is apparent.

THE SEARCH FOR THE "AUTHENTIC" SELF

Although we may be aware of the dubious accuracy of our self-presentations, Goffman (1959) has argued that *we sometimes come to believe in our fabrications.* In other words, if you present yourself in a certain way often enough, you may begin to actually see yourself in that way. For example, if you were really quite conceited but incorporated false humility into many of your public selves, you might begin to view yourself as a very humble person. There is empirical evidence (Jones, Gergen, & Davis, 1962) to support Goffman's assertion that our self-presentations may affect our actual self-concept.

When this happens, it blurs the distinction between the real self and the various public selves. *If this blurring effect takes place with respect to many fundamental aspects of your self-concept, you could become confused about the "real you."* Jourard (1964, 1971) maintains that constant misrepresentation for purposes of impression management may lead people to lose touch with their "authentic" selves. Jourard also believes that this kind of confusion is very dangerous, and he suggests that it may be the cause of much psychological distress.

It is this identity-related confusion that leads many people to be concerned about "finding" themselves. This search for the real self became something of a fad in the 1970s, and many people used the concept to rationalize their "rudderless" lives. It has since become more common to ridicule people who say they are "looking for the real me," but this search for the authentic self may often be a genuine effort to come to grips with a self-concept that is in disarray.

Two practical points can be derived from this line of discourse. First, it is probably a good idea to avoid going overboard on self-presentation efforts.

Taken to an excess, impression management may be harmful to one's sense of identity. Second, there is some merit in seeking knowledge about oneself. Accurate self-knowledge may facilitate development of a well-defined self-concept.

Perception of Others: Sources of Error

We are now ready to shift gears and move from self-perception to how we perceive *others*. Here, the main issue is why we may see each other inaccurately. Mistakes in person perception appear to be quite common. In one study (Kremers, 1960) only *14%* of the subjects were judged to be highly accurate in their perceptions of others.

I focus on this particular issue because I believe that effective interpersonal relations are facilitated by accuracy in social perception. Becoming aware of sources of error in person perception may help you improve the accuracy of your social perceptions. A multitude of factors may contribute to inaccuracy in person perception. I have already mentioned the most obvious source of error—the pervasive tendency of people to create false impressions for each other. It is clear that others' efforts at impression management may give us erroneous pictures of them. In this section, however, I will review *our own perceptual tendencies* that often lead us to create inaccurate pictures of other people.

EXCESSIVE FOCUS ON PHYSICAL APPEARANCE

We quite regularly draw inferences about people's personality and behavior from their physical appearance. Unfortunately, there is little basis in fact for most of the conclusions we draw. Instead, this focus on physical appearance often sways our judgments in ways that may be unfair to the person involved.

Attractiveness. The most influential aspect of physical appearance is probably the person's overall attractiveness. *There is plenty of evidence that we attribute desirable characteristics to good-looking people.* For example, Dion, Berscheid, and Walster (1972) found that we believe that attractive people are especially sensitive and we assume that they lead particularly interesting lives. We also believe that beautiful people are more intelligent (Clifford & Walster, 1973) and more pleasant (Adams & Huston, 1975) than others. Essays allegedly written by attractive women are rated higher than those supposedly written by unattractive women (Landy & Sigall, 1974), suggesting that we also see a link between good looks and competence. Furthermore, studies simulating jury trials have found that physically attractive defendants are better liked by the "juror" subjects and punished less severely than unattractive defendants (Efran, 1974).

There may be a few negative characteristics that are associated with attractiveness. Dermer and Thiel (1975) found that attractive people were believed to be relatively vain and egotistical. Nonetheless, the overall tendency is to see beautiful people in a very favorable light. If these biases applied only to attractive people, it wouldn't be such a terrible thing. Unfortunately, however, these biases can all be inverted; *thus, we unjustifiably see ugly people in a very unfavorable light.* We tend to perceive unattractive people as less sensitive, less interesting, less intelligent, less pleasant, and less competent than others. This deplorable prejudice against the plain and homely is clearly unfair and tragic.

Other features. Our social perceptions are also affected by other aspects of physical appearance. For example, Lawson (1971) found that dark-haired men are viewed as more masculine and more intelligent than light-haired men. Greater virility, confidence, maturity, and courage are attributed to bearded than to clean-shaven men (Verinis & Roll, 1970). For women, the "dumb blonde" stereotype is not entirely mythical: Lawson (1971) found that blondes were seen as more beautiful and feminine but less intelligent and dependable. We also judge people differently when they wear glasses. People with eyeglasses are assumed to be relatively intelligent and reliable (Manz & Lueck, 1968).

Clothing is also a powerful determinant of our perceptions of others. Gibbins (1969) found that female subjects were willing to draw conclusions about a person's shyness, snobbishness, and morality on the basis of her or his mode of dress. There is also evidence (Bickman, 1971) that people may be treated more honestly when they are well dressed. In Bickman's clever study, a dime was repeatedly left in an obvious place in a public phone booth. When unsuspecting subjects pocketed the dime, an experimental confederate went into action. The confederate approached the subject and asked whether she or he had found the dime that the confederate claimed to have forgotten in the booth. The confederate's mode of dress was varied to convey either high social status (suit and tie) or low status (work clothes, lunch pail). Bickman found that when the confederates were well dressed, they got the dime back about twice as often as when they were more poorly dressed.

Actually, clothing may have some legitimacy as a determinant of our social perceptions. People have relatively little to say about such features of appearance as their attractiveness and hair color, but they *do* freely choose their clothes. Moreover, these choices may indeed reflect personality. For instance, Aiken (1963) found that women whose interest in clothing focused on decoration were relatively sociable, conforming, and nonintellectual. The fact is that people do use clothing to communicate to others how they wish to be seen. Hurlock (1974) points out that people may convey their sense of independence, their identification with some group, and their feelings of maturity or success by dressing in certain ways. Thus, clothing *may* be a legitimate source of information about a person; however, one should be cautious in interpreting these cues.

STEREOTYPES

STEREOTYPE. *A popular, usually oversimplified belief about some group of people; involves inaccurate overgeneralization.*

A **stereotype** is a widely shared, oversimplified belief about some group of people (Berkowitz, 1980). When we use stereotypes, we assume that people have certain characteristics because of their membership in some group. For example, we assume that Jews are shrewd or ambitious, that Blacks have athletic or musical ability, that Germans are methodical and efficient, that women are passive and conceited about their appearance, and that men are unemotional and domineering. Stereotyping is very similar (in a sense, identical) to the processes involved when we react to people on the basis of their physical appearance. In stereotyping, however, the reaction is based on membership in some group rather than physical qualities.

The most prevalent kinds of stereotypes are those based on sex and on membership in ethnic or occupational groups. Sex-role stereotypes, though in transition, remain pervasive in our society and are learned quite early in life (Williams, Bennett, & Best, 1975). Because of their great significance, I will focus on sex-role stereotypes in detail in a later chapter. Ethnic and racial stereotypes have also undergone some change but remain quite common (Karling, Coffman, & Walters, 1969). I shall discuss the contribution of stereotyping to racial prejudice in an upcoming portion of this chapter. Occupational stereotypes also exist, although they are obviously much less of a social problem. For example, people believe that accountants are conforming, executives are conservative, lawyers are manipulative, physicians are calm, artists are moody, and professors are radical (Beardslee & O'Dowd, 1962).

Although a kernel of truth may underlie some stereotypes (Triandis & Vassiliou, 1967), it should be readily apparent that not all Jews, business executives, women, and so forth behave alike. There is enormous diversity in behavior within any group. Thus, stereotyping involves a process of gross overgeneralization and thereby forms the basis for a great deal of inaccuracy in social perception.

Although stereotypes generate much inaccuracy in person perception, they persist because of the selectivity in social perception discussed earlier: Because we tend to see what we expect to see, we twist and distort the behavior of others until it fits our stereotypes. We thereby confirm and perpetuate our stereotypes. The truly unfortunate part of this process is that our stereotypes often lead to *discrimination* against others. In particular, women and certain ethnic minorities are quite regularly treated unfairly.

THE FUNDAMENTAL ATTRIBUTION ERROR

FUNDAMENTAL ATTRIBUTION ERROR. *The tendency of an observer to overestimate the role of personal factors and underestimate the role of situational factors in explaining an actor's behavior.*

As I mentioned, observers tend to attribute behavior to a person's dispositional tendencies while discounting the importance of situational determinants. Although this tendency is *not* universal (Harvey, Town, & Yarkin, 1981), it is strong enough to have been labeled the *fundamental* attribution error by Ross (1977). Thus, the **fundamental attribution error** involves observers' bias in favor of internal, as opposed to external, attributions. This bias leads them to leap to conclusions about others' personal qualities.

The fundamental attribution error is different from stereotyping or focusing on physical appearance in that the inferences *are* based on behavior. However, the crucial point for us is that those inferences may still be inaccurate. Because we underestimate the importance of external, situational factors, we often may attribute to people motives and traits that they do not actually have. For instance, recall the example of the person who flies into a rage over an error made by the bank on his account. Observers will probably infer that this person is temperamental, moody, quarrelsome. That *could* be true. However, this person may be a generally calm, quiet, easygoing person who happens to be running very late for an important appointment, has waited in line for a preposterous 45 minutes, just straightened out a similar error by the same bank last week, and is being treated rudely by sarcastic and discourteous tellers. Thus, you never know. A person's behavior may or may not be reflective of his or her personality. However, we often tend to assume erroneously that behavior *does* reflect internal personality dispositions.

IMPLICIT THEORIES OF PERSONALITY

IMPLICIT THEORIES OF PERSONALITY. *Assumptions about what personality traits go together, based on common sense or casual observation.*

Implicit theories of personality consist of *our personal notions about what personality traits go together* (Schneider, 1973). For example, if you believe that warm people are usually cooperative, that uninhibited people are also irresponsible, or that socially skilled people are exploitive, you are using implicit theories of personality. While some implicit theories of personality are more popular (commonly shared) than others, all such theories tend to be somewhat individualized, based on one's unique experiences with people. Of interest to us is that these personal theories are typically based on very casual and inadequate observation. They may have no basis in reality, and they may lead us to inaccurate conclusions about the characteristics of others.

THE POWER OF FIRST IMPRESSIONS: PRIMACY EFFECTS

Although the evidence is not overwhelming, some studies (Asch, 1946; Friedman, 1983) suggest that first impressions have a particularly powerful influence on our perceptions of others. *When initial information carries more*

PRIMACY EFFECT. *The tendency for information acquired early in a sequence to be more influential than information acquired later.*

weight than subsequent information, psychologists speak of a **primacy effect.** There are a couple of reasons that first impressions tend to be particularly potent. In part, this tendency is caused by the previously discussed fact that people see what they expect to see. Once the initial impression creates a particular expectation, we may be equipped with a somewhat distortive perceptual set. Moreover, our preference for consistency in social perception may lead us to discount later information that contradicts our initial impression. In either case, it is clear that primacy effects may undermine our accuracy in forming impressions of other people.

Of course, it *is* possible to override a primacy effect. First impressions are not likely to last forever if most subsequent interactions contradict them. Interestingly, one study (Briscoe, Woodyard, & Shaw, 1967) suggests that *it may be easier to override positive than negative first impressions.* It appears that when the initial impression is negative, it may be especially difficult to change. Thus, "getting off on the wrong foot" may be particularly damaging to a person.

MOTIVATIONAL ERROR

At various points I have discussed the fact that people tend to see what they expect to see. Although the distinction is a fine one, it is also true that *we sometimes see what we want to see.* This sort of "wishful thinking" may produce perceptual errors that are attributable to our motivation.

MOTIVATIONAL ERROR. *Inaccurate perceptions or beliefs attributable to letting one's wants, needs, and desires undermine one's objectivity.*

This **motivational error** probably explains the well-known phenomenon wherein "love is blind." People in love, especially people who have recently fallen in love, want very much to believe that the object of their love is a wonderful person. Their needs get in the way of objective perception, and they

---

6.4   "A ROSE BY ANY OTHER NAME..."

What's in a name? Quite a bit. Advertisers have long recognized that a clever name can make all the difference in the world when they try to sell their products. It also appears that people's efforts to sell themselves in the interpersonal marketplace are affected by their names. Television and movie stars are well aware of this, and many have discarded names that they thought might handicap their careers. Although it's hard to believe that the talented actor Alphonso D'Abruzzo would not have become a star without changing his name (to Alan Alda), there is scientific evidence that names do make a difference.

Generally speaking, you're better off with a common name. Using grade-school children as subjects, McDavid and Harari (1966) found that frequently used first names (for example, John, Michael, David) were evaluated more positively than unusual names (for example, Ivan, Bernard, Edmond). They likewise found that relatively uncommon names were rated lower in social desirability. More significantly, they found that the children with the socially desirable names were more popular with their classmates! Most disconcerting of all, Harari and McDavid (1973) discovered that names may affect teachers' grades. They asked teachers to judge fifth-grade essays supposedly written by children with either desirable or undesirable names (as determined by their earlier research). The essays allegedly written by children with desirable

names (David, Michael, Karen, Lisa) received higher grades than those written by children with undesirable names (Elmer, Hubert, Bertha, Adelle).

How do we acquire the stereotypes that we associate with certain names? Probably in several ways. First, the fame or notoriety acquired by certain people may promote or undermine the popularity of their names. For instance, Bruning and Albott (1974) report that attitudes toward the female names Bridget, Sophia, and Ursula have improved in recent years. Second, advertisers use certain names in ways that promote stereotyping. Illustrative of this is the fact that, back in 1965, a fellow by the name of Harvey Edwards got so tired of seeing Harveys portrayed as bumbling clods in commercials that he organized a protest! Finally, our personal experiences with people bearing particular names probably influence our attitudes toward those names. If you truly detested the only Andy you ever knew, that could color your attitude toward that name indefinitely.

Just how influential are names? In everyday interactions they probably constitute only a very tiny handicap or advantage. If your name is Matilda or Percival, you need not go into a severe depression. If Hubert Horatio Humphrey could garner great success in the political arena, *any* name can be overcome by actual behavior and talent.

see only the good aspects of their lover's personality, ignoring the bad.

A similar motivational error is probably responsible for the tendency to perceive political candidates inaccurately. Sherrod (1971) showed that voters often erroneously believe that on various issues their favorite candidates hold positions similar to their own, when in fact they are quite different. This inaccuracy may be due to the voters' need to believe that their candidate adheres to the "right" positions on important issues (of course, their own positions are the "right" ones).

DEFENSIVE ATTRIBUTION

DEFENSIVE ATTRIBUTION. *A bias in the attribution process wherein people derogate the victims of misfortune so that they feel less likely to be similarly victimized.*

Motivational bias also appears to form the basis for an interesting phenomenon called **defensive attribution** (Thornton, 1984). Let's say that a friend of yours gets mugged and severely beaten. If you attribute this unfortunate event to chance, then you have to face the ugly reality that it could just as easily happen to you. To avoid distressing thoughts like these, we often tend to attribute such mishaps to the victim's stupidity, foolishness, and negligence. By blaming and derogating the victim, we can downplay the likelihood that we will encounter a similar disaster. Thus, *we tend to see victims of calamitous events in an unfairly negative light* because we want to maintain our belief that we live in a "just world" where we are unlikely to experience similar adversity (Lerner, 1970). Recent evidence (Howard, 1984) suggests that this tendency to blame victims may be particularly strong when the victims are females, providing us with an example of sex-role stereotyping in action.

FALSE CONSENSUS

FALSE CONSENSUS. *A bias in person perception wherein people overestimate the degree to which others are like them.*

There is evidence (Ross, Greene, & House, 1977) that we tend to assume that other people are just like us. *This belief that the rest of the world generally behaves much as we do* is called the **false consensus** effect. This bias provides yet another source of error in social perception. For example, let's say you know a fellow who "cheats" on his wife every chance he gets. When this person spots friends dining out with members of the other sex who are not their spouses, he is likely to assume that they too are engaging in marital infidelity, even though their socializing is probably entirely innocent. Essentially, he attributes his own behavioral tendencies to others.

Though quite common, this false-consensus assumption is not made with reference to all of one's qualities. For instance, while we tend to overestimate the extent to which others share our opinions, we underestimate the likelihood that others have *abilities* similar to ours (Marks, 1984). In regard to abilities, we like to think of ourselves as unique.

An Example of Perceptual Inaccuracy in Action: Racial Prejudice

To further illustrate how inaccuracy in social perception develops and to show how it may affect our interpersonal behavior, I will digress briefly to consider the serious social problem of racial prejudice. My main purpose will be to show how distortions in the process of person perception contribute to ethnic or racial prejudice. My secondary purpose will be to discuss how this prejudice is costly both to its victims and to society as a whole.

First, I need to clarify certain interrelated terms that are tossed around with great abandon and often mixed up. According to Pettigrew (1973), **prejudice** refers to a negative attitude that people hold toward certain human groups that leads to rigid prejudgments and unfair misjudgments of group members. Pettigrew distinguishes **racial discrimination** from prejudice by asserting that the former involves overt behavior whereas the latter is simply a cognitive

PREJUDICE. *A negative attitude held toward members of some group, usually racial or ethnic. The negative attitude leads one to unfairly prejudge group members.*

RACIAL DISCRIMINATION.
Behaving differently (usually negatively) toward someone because of his or her membership in a racial group.

RACISM. *An effort to subjugate some racial group; usually used to describe institutional discrimination that promotes the subordination of an ethnic group.*

set. Thus, discrimination involves behaving differently toward a person (generally in a rejecting way) than one otherwise would because that person is a member of a certain racial group. As you can see, prejudice and discrimination are closely linked, but there is no one-to-one correspondence. For example, a salesman might be quite prejudiced against Chicanos and yet treat them like anyone else in his store, thus behaving in a nondiscriminatory manner. Of course, that same salesman might later behave in a very discriminatory fashion when Chicanos try to join his country club. Finally, I should define the term **racism,** which usually refers to discrimination at an institutional or societal level for the purpose of subordinating and controlling a racial group (Carmichael & Hamilton, 1967).

PERSON PERCEPTION AND PREJUDICE

With our definitions out of the way, we can now turn to a discussion of person perception as it relates to prejudice. Inaccuracy in social perception is both a cause and an effect of prejudice. At least five of the eight sources of inaccuracy just described contribute to racial prejudice in major ways.

STEREOTYPING

The most apparent source of inaccuracy in racial prejudice is stereotyping, of which members of racial minorities are obvious victims. Although there is evidence that our ethnic stereotypes have undergone change over the years, Table 6.1 makes it clear that many people still subscribe to derogatory racial stereotypes (Karling et al., 1969). Moreover, as previously discussed, belief in such stereotypes often ensures that, in actual face-to-face interaction, people see what they expect to see and thereby confirm and strengthen their stereotypes.

TABLE 6.1 **Three generations of ethnic stereotypes**

	Percentage of respondents attributing traits to various ethnic groups		
	1933	*1951*	*1967*
Americans			
Industrious	48	30	23
Intelligent	47	32	20
Materialistic	33	37	67
Ambitious	33	21	42
Germans			
Stolid	44	10	9
Aggressive	—	27	30
Irish			
Pugnacious	45	24	13
Extremely nationalistic	21	20	41
Italians			
Artistic	53	28	30
Passionate	37	25	44
Japanese			
Sly	20	21	3
Industrious	43	12	57
Jews			
Shrewd	79	47	30
Mercenary	49	28	15
Ambitious	21	28	48
Blacks			
Superstitious	83	41	13
Lazy	75	31	26
Musical	26	33	47

THE FUNDAMENTAL ATTRIBUTION ERROR

Recall that the fundamental attribution error is a bias toward explaining events by pointing to the internal, personal characteristics of the actors as causes. Pettigrew (1979) argues that we are particularly prone to this bias when explaining the failures of out-group members. For example, when people take note of ethnic neighborhoods that are dominated by crime, poverty, and squalor, the personal qualities of the residents are blamed for these problems, while plausible alternative explanations centering on situational factors (job discrimination, poor police services, and so on) are ignored or downplayed. The fundamental attribution error is clearly seen in such statements as "They should be able to pull themselves up by their own bootstraps." Such assertions are a blanket dismissal of numerous situational factors that militate against minorities in their efforts to achieve upward mobility. The strength of this attributional bias is such that even minority-group members themselves may exhibit it (Gurin et al., 1969).

PRIMACY EFFECTS

Another problem emerges from the aforementioned power of first impressions. The problem is that many people's first impressions of racial minorities are derived not from actual interaction but from disparaging and abusive remarks about the minorities made by prejudiced parents, peers, neighbors, and so forth. Many highly impressionable youngsters are exposed to prejudicial attitudes throughout their childhood. Consequently, many children develop an unfavorable picture of racial groups before they have any opportunity for rewarding interactions with members of those groups. These negative first impressions *may* eventually be overridden by subsequent contradictory experiences, but primacy effects probably contribute to prejudicial attitudes in many people.

MOTIVATIONAL ERROR

As Roberts (1971) points out, prejudiced people may often be motivated to see minorities in a negative light so as to reduce their feelings of guilt about being prejudiced. Most of us like to think of ourselves as "fair-minded." However, if you become aware of your prejudice, this conflicts with your belief in your fair-mindedness and creates cognitive dissonance. You can reduce this dissonance if you can convince yourself that minority-group members are terrible people who deserve their ill fortune and humiliations. Thus, to minimize their guilt feelings, many prejudiced people *want* to view minorities in unfavorable ways. As discussed earlier, these people may then tend to see what they want to see.

DEFENSIVE ATTRIBUTION

You have already seen that we sometimes derogate victims of adversity unfairly in order to reassure ourselves that we are unlikely to experience a similar fate. There is evidence that many of us engage in this defensive attribution when we encounter people who have been victimized by prejudice and racism. For example, Hallie (1971) asserts that many Germans who lived through the era of Nazi persecutions somehow convinced themselves that those sent to concentration camps deserved their fate.

THE COSTS OF PREJUDICE

PSYCHOLOGICAL COSTS TO THE VICTIMS

It seems inevitable that prejudice and discrimination must impose special adjustive demands on the victimized racial minorities (Douglass, 1967; Kramer, Rosen, & Willis, 1973). These additional demands tend to lead to various negative consequences, which will be discussed momentarily. Interestingly, the negative psychological consequences of prejudice and racism do not appear to be as severe as one might expect, given the prevalence and intensity of prejudice in the world around us. In view of the extra stress they experience, one might expect racial minorities to show a greater-than-average incidence of at least some forms of psychopathology. Although we do not have nearly as much epidemiological data on the issue as we would like (Kramer et al., 1973), this does *not* appear to be the case. For instance, Black Americans, who have certainly been the victims of a great deal of racism, do not display more overt psychological disorders than other groups, when researchers control for socioeconomic class in their comparisons (Nathan & Harris, 1975). Nonetheless, there are some psychological costs associated with prejudice, summarized below.

1. *Negative self-concepts*. It appears that some members of minority groups acquire unfavorable self-concepts because of the prejudice of others. Actually, there is a great deal of conflicting data about whether minority groups collectively show lower self-esteem than the general population (Rosenberg, 1979). Nonetheless, we have plenty of clinical, experimental, and anecdotal evidence that many minority-group members have their self-concepts battered by racial prejudice (Barnes, 1972). Fortunately, there is some evidence (Dansby, 1972) that this tendency may be counteracted by minority groups' recent emphasis on racial pride.

2. *Limited horizons*. It seems logical to expect that victims of discrimination would come to believe that there is little to be gained by working hard in order

---

6.5 ENCOUNTERS WITH PREJUDICE AND RACISM: EXCERPTS FROM THE AUTOBIOGRAPHY OF MALCOLM X

The impact of prejudice is difficult to convey. It's one of those things that you have to experience in order to understand. The following excerpts are taken from *The Autobiography of Malcolm X* (1965), an eloquent and moving story. As you probably know, Malcolm X was one of several truly outstanding Black leaders whose careers were ended by a fusillade of assassins' bullets. These excerpts focus on events in his childhood, events that communicated to Malcolm X the extent of his "inferior" status in White-dominated America.

They all liked my attitude, and it was out of their liking for me that I soon became accepted by them—as a mascot, I know now. They would talk about anything and everything with me standing right there hearing them, the same way people would talk freely in front of a pet canary. They would even talk about me, or about "niggers," as though I wasn't there, as if I wouldn't understand what the word meant. A hundred times a day, they used the word "nigger." I suppose that in their own minds, they meant no harm; in fact they probably meant well. It was the same with the cook, Lucille, and her husband, Duane. I remember one day when Mr. Swerlin, as nice as he was, came in from Lansing, where he had been through the Negro section, and said to Mrs. Swerlin right in front of me, "I just can't see how those niggers can be so happy and be so poor." He talked about how they lived in shacks, but had those big, shining cars out front [p. 26].

What I am trying to say is that it just never dawned upon them that I could understand, that I wasn't a pet, but a human being. They didn't give me credit for having the same sensitivity, intellect, and understanding that they would have been ready and willing to recognize in a white boy in my position. But it has historically been the case with white people, in their regard for black people, that even though we might be with them, we weren't considered of them. Even though they appeared to have opened the door, it was still closed. Thus they never did really see me [p. 27].

I know that he probably meant well in what he happened to advise me that day. I doubt that he meant any harm. It was just his nature as an American white man. I was one of his top students, one of the school's top students—but all he could see for me was the kind of future "in your place" that almost all white people see for black people.

He told me, "Malcolm, you ought to be thinking about a career. Have you been giving it thought?"

The truth is, I hadn't. I never have figured out why I told him, "Well, yes, sir, I've been thinking I'd like to be a lawyer." Lansing certainly had no Negro lawyers—or doctors either—in those days, to hold up an image I might have aspired to. All I really knew for certain was that a lawyer didn't wash dishes, as I was doing.

Mr. Ostrowski looked surprised, I remember, and leaned back in his chair and clasped his hands behind his head. He kind of half-smiled and said, "Malcolm, one of life's first needs is for us to be realistic. Don't misunderstand me, now. We all here like you, you know that. But you've got to be realistic about being a nigger. A lawyer—that's no realistic goal for a nigger. You need to think about something you can be. You're good with your hands—making things. Everybody admires your carpentry shop work. Why don't you plan on carpentry? People like you as a person—you'd get all kinds of work" [p. 36].

to "make good." Indeed, empirical studies have found below-average achievement motivation in American Blacks (for example, Rosen, 1959).

3. *Stereotype fulfillment.* When racial minorities allow the dominant group to define their image, they sometimes begin to believe the stereotypes fostered by others and may begin to act accordingly. Carmichael and Hamilton (1967) have described this insidious process of stereotype fulfillment in Blacks, and Trimble (1974) has observed it among Native Americans. This self-fulfilling prophecy may be the saddest consequence of prejudice.

COSTS TO SOCIETY

In thinking about the costs of prejudice, we tend to focus on the negative consequences experienced by the victims themselves. However, the costs of prejudice are more widespread than that. The purveyors of prejudice also suffer, in that they force themselves into rigid patterns of behavior, which often require that they engage in defensive mental gymnastics in order to justify their unfairness. Furthermore, we *all* suffer as a society, in that there is a loss of human potential when a person's hopes and aspirations are snuffed out by demeaning oppression. Likewise, we all suffer because prejudice and discrimination act to perpetuate racial strife in our world. The last thing we need is an unnecessary source of conflict and tension.

Summary

Social perception requires drawing inferences about the causes of behavior. Generally, we tend to attribute behavior either to internal dispositions or to external situational factors. We usually try to maintain consistency among our beliefs, and this, along with other factors, may lead to selectivity in social perception. Self-perception may be somewhat different from the perception of others in that we may display differing biases.

The self-concept is a collection of beliefs about what you are like. It is both descriptive and prescriptive. It is shaped greatly by your own observations, which involve comparisons with other people (usually similar others). Of course, these observations may involve distortions of reality. Feedback from others is very influential in shaping your self-concept, and it too may be distorted. Finally, cultural guidelines may also sway how we see ourselves.

Self-esteem is your global evaluation of your worth. Low self-esteem tends to be associated with emotional problems, poor achievement, great vulnerability to rejection, conformity, and efforts to find fault with others. Parents are especially important in determining our self-esteem. They provide direct feedback and influence the standards we use to evaluate ourselves.

Public selves are the various images we portray to others. A certain amount of self-presentation is expected, although some of us edit our behavior more than others. Ingratiation is a systematic self-presentation effort aimed at winning others' regard. Some people get so wrapped up in their public selves that they lose contact with their authentic self.

Numerous factors lead us to see others inaccurately. We may be swayed by physical attractiveness, hair color, clothes, and so forth. In stereotyping, we assume that people have certain characteristics because of their membership in some group. Inaccuracy in social perception is also produced by the fundamental attribution error, implicit theories of personality, primacy effects, motivational error, defensive attribution, and the false-consensus effect.

Racial prejudice provides a particularly unfortunate example of how we often see others inaccurately. Most of the usual sources of error in person perception contribute to prejudicial beliefs about minority groups. This prejudice is tragic in that it may lead to a number of psychological costs for the victims. It is also costly to our society as a whole.

Because of the enormous importance of self-esteem, the upcoming application section will discuss how to build a more favorable self-concept, outlining seven steps for promoting high self-esteem.

Building Self-Esteem

Answer the following yes or no.

_____ 1. I am very sensitive to criticism.
_____ 2. I tend to have a hard time accepting praise or flattery.
_____ 3. I have very little confidence in my abilities.
_____ 4. I often feel awkward in social situations and just don't know how to take charge.
_____ 5. I tend to be highly critical of other people.

INFERIORITY COMPLEX. *A personality syndrome dominated by low self-esteem and an overly critical attitude toward oneself.*

If you answered yes to several of the above questions, you may be suffering from what Hamachek (1978) calls an **inferiority complex.** This syndrome, which is dominated by low self-esteem, is quite common. It is also quite unfortunate. As noted earlier in the chapter, people with exceptionally low self-esteem tend to develop more emotional problems than others, set low goals for themselves, become socially invisible, conform against their better judgment, and court rejection by putting down others.

"I don't suppose it's much compared with other inferiority complexes."

As you can see, self-esteem is a very important component of your self-concept. It appears that an overly negative self-image can contribute to many kinds of behavioral problems. An overly *positive* image can also cause problems, but people characterized by excessive conceit do not suffer in the same way that self-critical people do.

In this application section, I will describe some guidelines for building higher self-esteem. These guidelines are based on my own distillation of the advice of many theorists, including Rogers (1977), Ellis (1977), Jourard (1974), Hamachek (1978), Mahoney (1971), and Zimbardo (1977).

1. RECOGNIZE THAT YOU CONTROL YOUR SELF-IMAGE

The first thing you must do is recognize that *you* ultimately control how you see yourself. You *do* have the power to change your self-image. True, I have discussed at length how feedback from others influences your self-concept. Yes, social comparison theory suggests that we need such feedback and that it would be unwise to ignore it completely. However, the final choice about whether to accept or reject such feedback rests with you. Your self-image resides in your mind and is a product of your thought processes. Although others may influence your self-concept, you are the final authority.

2. DON'T LET OTHERS SET YOUR STANDARDS

A common trap that many of us fall into involves letting others set the standards by which we evaluate ourselves. People around us are constantly telling us that we should do this or we ought to do that. Thus, we hear that we "should study computer science" or "ought to lose weight" or "must move to a better neighborhood," and so forth. Most of these people are well-intentioned, and many of them may have good ideas. However, people who are low in self-esteem are particularly susceptible to persuasion and too readily accept others' standards for their own. For example, consider a business executive in his early forties who sees himself in a negative light because he has not climbed very far in the corporate hierarchy. The crucial question is: Did he ever *really* want to make that arduous climb? It could be that he has misgivings about the value of such an effort. Perhaps he has gone through life thinking he should pursue that kind of success only because that standard was imposed on him by society. You should think about the source of and basis for your personal standards. Do they really represent goals and ideals that you value? Or are they goals and ideals that you passively accepted from others without thinking?

3. RECOGNIZE UNREALISTIC GOALS

Even if you truly value certain ideals and sincerely want to achieve certain goals, another question remains. Are those goals realistic? Many people get in the habit of demanding too much of themselves. They *always* want to perform at their best, which is obviously impossible. For instance, you may have a burning desire to achieve international stardom as an actress. Such a goal is admirable and is well worth working on diligently. However, the odds against such an achievement are enormous. It is important to recognize this reality so that you do not condemn yourself for failure. Some overly demanding people pervert the social comparison process by always comparing themselves against the *best,* rather than similar others. They assess their looks by comparing themselves with famous models, and they judge their finances by comparing themselves with the wealthiest people they know. Such comparisons are unrealistic and almost inevitably undermine self-esteem.

4. MODIFY NEGATIVE SELF-TALK

The way you analyze your life influences how you see yourself (and vice versa). People who are low in self-esteem tend to engage in various counterproductive modes of thinking. For example, when they succeed, they may attribute it to good luck, and when they fail, they may blame themselves. Quite to the contrary, you should take credit for your successes and consider the possibility that your failures may not be your fault. As discussed earlier, Ellis has pointed out that we often think irrationally and draw unwarranted negative conclusions about ourselves. For example, if you apply for a job and are rejected, you might think "They didn't hire me. I must be a crummy, inept person." The conclusion that you are a "crummy person" does *not* follow logically from the fact that you were not hired. Such irrational thinking and negative self-talk breed poor self-esteem. It is important to recognize the irrationality of such negative self-talk and bring it to a halt.

5. EMPHASIZE YOUR STRENGTHS

This advice may seem trite, but it has some merit. People with low self-esteem often derive little satisfaction from their accomplishments and virtues. They dismiss compliments as foolish, unwarranted, or insincere. They pay little heed to their good qualities while harping constantly about their defeats and frailties. The fact is that we all have our strengths and weaknesses. You should accept those personal shortcomings that you are powerless to change and work on those that are changeable, without becoming obsessed about it. At the same time, you should take stock of your strengths and learn to appreciate them.

6. WORK TO IMPROVE YOURSELF

As just mentioned, some personal shortcomings *can* be conquered. Although it is important to reassess your goals and discard those that are imposed by others or are unrealistic, this advice is not intended to provide a convenient rationalization for personal complacency. There is much to be said for setting out to conquer personal problems. In a sense, this entire text is based on a firm belief in the value of self-control and self-improvement. There is ample evidence that efforts at self-improvement can pay off by boosting self-esteem.

7. APPROACH OTHERS WITH A POSITIVE OUTLOOK

People who are low in self-esteem often try to cut others down to their (subjective) size through constant criticism. As you can readily imagine, this fault-finding and generally negative approach to interpersonal transactions does not go over well with other people. Instead, it leads to tension, bitter exchanges, and rejection. This rejection lowers self-esteem still further. Efforts to build self-esteem can be facilitated by recognizing and reversing this self-defeating tendency. If you approach people with a positive, supportive outlook, it will promote rewarding interactions and help to earn their acceptance. There is probably nothing that enhances self-esteem more than acceptance and genuine affection from others.

6.6 RECOMMENDED READING
Like Yourself* and others will too
by Abraham J. Twerski (Prentice-Hall, 1978)

I have emphasized repeatedly in this chapter that a negative self-concept can be a personal tragedy. Twerski explores this problem in much greater depth. Using numerous case studies, he shows how low self-esteem causes or contributes to a vast array of personal problems. Half the battle in reversing a negative self-image consists in *recognizing* the sources of negativity. Twerski's book can be very useful in helping you pinpoint these sources in your life.

Many faulty behavior patterns are the outcome of a negative self-image. The cases to be described are actual, true-life stories of persons treated or observed in the practice of psychiatry. These cases are only examples of maladaptation and by no means exhaust the legion of possible complications consequent to the negative self-image. Some of the cases cited depict a very intense behavioral consequence of the negative self-image. It is important to realize that, although very intense reactions are by no means infrequent, milder forms of such reactions are very common. To whatever extent a person reacts to a distorted self-concept, to that same extent he suffers the consequences of a maladaptation [pp. 7–8].

CHAPTER 6 REVIEW

IDEAS: REVIEW OF LEARNING OBJECTIVES

When you have mastered the material in this chapter, you should be able to do the following.

1. Describe the attribution process, including the principal dimension along which we make attributions.
2. Discuss how patterns of attribution may be related to the development of depression.
3. Describe how actors and observers are different in their attributional biases (including success/failure situations).
4. Use the concept of cognitive dissonance to explain why we strive for consistency in our beliefs.
5. Explain what selectivity in social perception involves.
6. Explain Bem's notion that we may derive our attitudes from our behavior.
7. Define self-concept and explain its prescriptive nature.
8. Summarize social comparison theory and its relation to one's self-concept.
9. Describe distortive tendencies in the formation of one's self-concept.
10. Discuss how other people may shape one's self-concept.
11. Discuss how cultural guidelines may shape one's self-concept.
12. Define self-esteem and describe some problems in its investigation.
13. List five behavioral characteristics that tend to be associated with low self-esteem.
14. Discuss the determinants of self-esteem.
15. Define and give examples of public selves.
16. Describe Goffman's view of why we engage in self-presentation.
17. Summarize how people who are high in self-monitoring tend to behave.
18. Describe ingratiation techniques.
19. Explain why some people are involved in a search for their authentic self.
20. List some characteristics commonly attributed to physically attractive people.
21. List some aspects of physical appearance besides attractiveness that influence our perception of others.
22. Define *stereotype* and list the three types of groups most commonly stereotyped.
23. Describe the fundamental attribution error.
24. Explain what implicit theories of personality involve.
25. Describe primacy effects and explain how they may promote inaccuracy in person perception.
26. Explain what is meant by motivational error in person perception.
27. Explain the concept of defensive attribution.
28. Explain false consensus and its role in producing errors in person perception.
29. List five sources of error in person perception that commonly contribute to racial prejudice.
30. List three common costs to the victims of racial prejudice.
31. Discuss how prejudice is costly at the societal level.
32. Briefly describe seven steps that are suggested for building high self-esteem.

TERMS: REVIEW OF NEW VOCABULARY

When you have mastered the material in this chapter, you should be able to define the following terms.

Attribution	Implicit theories of personality	Prejudice	Self-concept
Cognitive dissonance	Impression management	Primacy effect	Self-esteem
Defensive attribution	Inferiority complex	Public self	Self-monitoring
False consensus	Ingratiation	Racial discrimination	Self-perception theory
Fundamental attribution error	Motivational error	Racism	Social comparison theory
		Reference group	Stereotype

PEOPLE: REVIEW OF MAJOR THEORISTS AND RESEARCHERS

When you have mastered the material in this chapter, you should be able to summarize the principal contributions and/or ideas of the following people.

Daryl Bem	Erving Goffman	Carl Rogers	Mark Snyder
Leon Festinger	E. E. Jones		

7 INTERPERSONAL COMMUNICATION

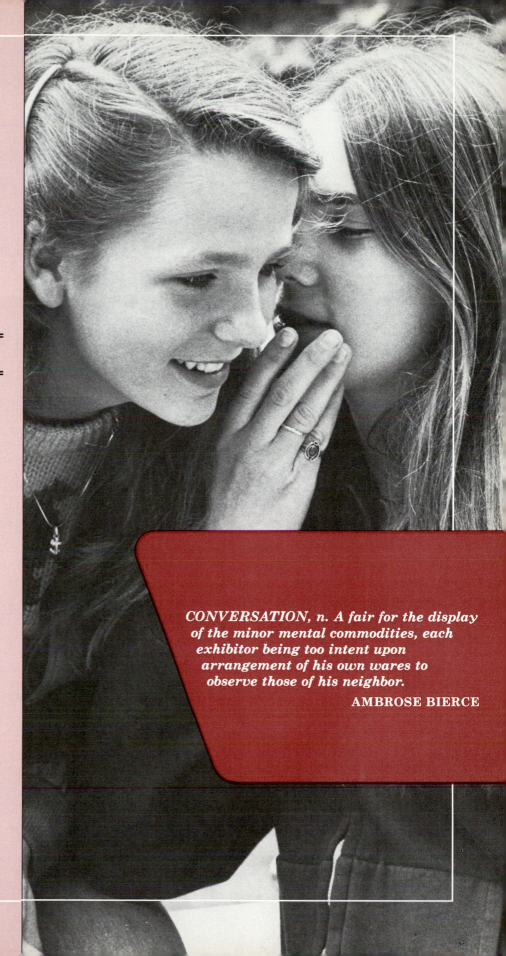

Summary

Applying Psychology to Your Life: Dealing Constructively with Interpersonal Conflict

THE NATURE AND VALUE OF INTERPERSONAL CONFLICT

PERSONAL STYLES OF DEALING WITH CONFLICT

GUIDELINES FOR CONSTRUCTIVE CONFLICT RESOLUTION

CONVERSATION, n. A fair for the display of the minor mental commodities, each exhibitor being too intent upon arrangement of his own wares to observe those of his neighbor.

AMBROSE BIERCE

Have you ever raced home eager to tell someone about something that happened that day, only to find everyone gone, so that you were left with no one to listen to your story? It may not have been a spectacular or earthshaking story—maybe you simply picked up an intriguing bit of gossip or met someone who was a little unusual—but it was something you wanted to share with others. Chances are you had rehearsed your eloquent description all the way home. You probably had already pictured how people would react to your story. On finding no receptive ears for your tale, how did you feel? It was probably quite a letdown. You may have paced around the house impatiently waiting for an audience. The refrains of your story may have continued to echo through your mind. If you were particularly excited, you may have felt as if you were going to burst if you didn't get an opportunity soon to let the story spill out.

Such a predicament illustrates the strength of the human imperative to communicate. The experience that you wanted to share with another person probably seemed incomplete without someone else to appreciate it. In a sense, we need to share our experiences with others in order to validate their significance. In fact, the interest we expect others to show may be what gives certain events their significance. In any case, it is clear that we have a powerful need to reach out to others through interpersonal communication.

The present chapter describes and analyzes this process of interpersonal communication. I begin by outlining the basic elements in the communication process. I then look at the sometimes mysterious dynamics of nonverbal communication. After examining the nonverbal channel, I shift to the verbal channel and discuss how to maximize the effectiveness of speaking and listening. I then turn to a special topic: self-disclosure and achieving intimacy with others. In the application section I talk about how people tend to deal with interpersonal conflict and how such conflict can be dealt with constructively.

The Process of Interpersonal Communication
DEFINITION

INTERPERSONAL COMMUNICATION. *A process wherein one person sends a message to another person. The communication may be either one-way or two-way, but at least two persons must be involved.*

Communication is typically defined as the transmission of meaning. Our personal thoughts have meaning, of course, and when we "talk to ourselves," we are engaging in *intrapersonal communication.* **Interpersonal communication,** in contrast, consists of *the transmission of meaning from one person to another* (Shuter, 1979). In a nutshell, then, interpersonal communication is a process wherein people send and receive messages.

When we mention the process of communication, we generally think of words, language, and vocalization. However, it is important to note that words are not the only means by which we transmit messages. As you are surely aware, people communicate with gestures, facial expressions, touch, and so forth. We will explore both verbal and nonverbal interpersonal communication in this chapter.

ELEMENTS IN THE COMMUNICATION PROCESS

Various models of the interpersonal communication process have been developed over the years. I will use a popular model proposed by David Berlo (1960), which is notable for its elegance and simplicity. As you can see in Figure 7.1, this model decomposes the communication process into four basic elements: the source, the message, the channel, and the receiver. I will briefly describe each of these components.

SOURCE. *In interpersonal communication, the person who sends or transmits the message; also known as the sender or originating communicator.*

Source. The **source** is simply *the person who originates, or sends, the message.* In a typical two-way conversation, both persons involved serve as sources of messages (as well as receivers). Each source person brings a unique

The need to communicate—to share with others what we think, how we feel, and who we are—is a powerful human imperative.

combination of attitudes, knowledge, experiences, and skills to the communication effort. Research in persuasion shows that various characteristics of the source may influence the communication process (McGuire, 1969). Among other things, the source's credibility, competence, attractiveness, status, and power may affect the communication effort.

MESSAGE. *In interpersonal communication, the information, or meaning, transmitted from one person to another.*

Message. The **message** is *the meaning that is transmitted from one person to another.* The message is the content of the communication. It consists of the ideas or feelings that are sent and received. A message inevitably requires the use of *symbols* that stand for the meanings conveyed by the source. Generally, we use language as the symbols by which we transmit our meaning. It should be noted, however, that it is an oversimplification to regard the message as simply a string of words, phrases, and sentences. A shrug or facial expression may also be used to symbolically transmit some idea or feeling. Moreover, a particular string of words may be used to deliver two or more completely different messages, depending on vocal inflections that indicate

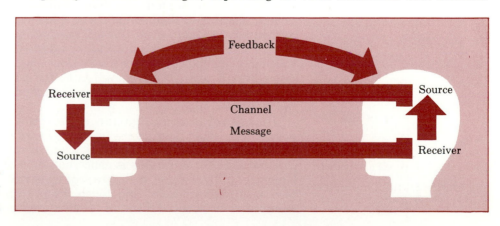

FIGURE 7.1 A model of interpersonal communication.

sincerity or sarcasm. Surely you have heard people say "That's just great," intending to convey either sincere pleasure or sarcastic displeasure.

CHANNEL. *In a communication effort, the medium through which the message is sent.*

Channel. The **channel** is *the method used to transmit the message*. The principal channel, or conduit, in human communication consists of sounds transmitted via air waves. When you talk to someone over a phone, this is the only channel available to you. However, in face-to-face interaction much information may be sent through the visual modality (for example, a wink) or through touching (for example, putting your arm around someone). For our purposes, I will simply differentiate between two basic channels: (1) the verbal, or linguistic, channel and (2) the nonverbal channel. I will discuss these separately.

RECEIVER. *In interpersonal communication, the person to whom the message is sent.*

Receiver. The **receiver** is, obviously, *the person(s) for whom the message is targeted*. As noted a moment ago, in two-way interactions each participant functions as both a source and a receiver. Each source/receiver has a unique history and frame of reference that affect the communication process. Research (Applbaum & Anatol, 1974) indicates that message reception may be influenced by many qualities of the receiver, including intelligence, motivation, and personality.

IMPORTANCE OF INTERPERSONAL COMMUNICATION

Let's take a second to stress the monumental importance of interpersonal communication in our lives. Think about it. In our waking hours we are almost constantly engaged in interpersonal communication. A tremendous number of the satisfactions we gain are derived from our interactions with others, interactions that depend on communication. Whether it's a matter of ordering a pizza or making new friends, it all hinges on interpersonal communication. Some theorists believe that the human race is set apart from other species mainly by its much greater capacity for complex communication. It seems virtually impossible to overemphasize the importance of developing sound skills in interpersonal communication.

Nonverbal Communication

You're standing at the bar in your favorite lounge, gazing across a dark, smoky room filled with people drinking, dancing, and talking. You motion to the bartender that you're ready for another martini. Your companion comments on the loudness of the music, and you simply nod your head in agreement. You spot an attractive stranger across the bar. Your eyes meet for a moment and you smile.

In a matter of seconds you have sent three messages without uttering a syllable. Most of us don't think about it much, but a substantial portion of our communication takes place through the nonverbal channel. Although we tend to take nonverbal communication for granted, one expert (Mehrabian, 1971) maintains that in face-to-face interactions about *90%* of the message transmission occurs at the nonverbal level! Although it is difficult to judge the accuracy of such an estimate, it is clear that a great deal of information is exchanged in the nonverbal channel.

NONVERBAL COMMUNICATION. *Interpersonal communication that does not depend on the use of words as symbols.*

KINESICS. *The study of communication through bodily movement.*

Nonverbal communication is *the transmission of meaning from one person to another through the use of nonword symbols* (Heun & Heun, 1975). The study of nonverbal communication involves three branches of inquiry (Swensen, 1973): **Kinesics** is concerned with what is popularly called "body language." This includes messages sent by gestures, facial expressions, eye contact, postural variations, and touch. **Proxemics** deals with communicative manipulations of social distance or territoriality. **Paralanguage** involves the

PROXEMICS. *The study of communicative use of personal space and distance.*

PARALANGUAGE. *The study of communication through manipulation of sound productions that are vocal but not verbal.*

various aspects of vocalizations that are not verbal, such as inflections or tone. I will examine each of these after discussing the functions of nonverbal communication and outlining some general principles.

Although most of us do not devote much thought to nonverbal communication, it plays an important role in our lives. A couple of recent studies illustrate the significance of nonverbal communication. One of them (Noller, 1980) examined the importance of nonverbal communication in marital relationships. Husbands and wives were instructed to send ambiguous messages to each other in the nonverbal channel. This permitted the evaluation of each couple's skill and success in nonverbal communication. These measures of couples' talent in nonverbal communication were then correlated with measures of marital adjustment. *A positive correlation between nonverbal transmission success and marital adjustment was found, suggesting that effective nonverbal communication may contribute to marital satisfaction.* The other study (Friedman et al., 1980) also looked at differences between people in nonverbal talent. Specifically, it focused on individual differences in nonverbal expressiveness—ability to use facial expressions, gestures, body movements, and so forth to enhance the impact of one's verbal statements. The main conclusion emerging from this study was that high expressiveness may be the key element of what we often vaguely label "charisma." *Charisma* usually refers to a special ability to move, lead, inspire, or captivate others. *Thus, there is some reason to believe that nonverbal talent may be the crucial consideration that makes some people charismatic leaders.*

FUNCTIONS OF NONVERBAL COMMUNICATION

What purposes does nonverbal communication serve? Many, according to experts such as Mahl (1968) and Ekman and Friesen (1969). I will highlight five of the functions of nonverbal communication described by these theorists.

1. *Nonverbal signals may serve as substitutes for verbal expressions.* In some cases, gestures, eye movements, and facial expressions may simply take the place of verbal transmissions. For instance, you may use nonverbal signals to order a drink at a noisy bar where hearing is difficult. Certain signals, such as nodding one's head (agreement), shaking one's head (disagreement), or

Nonverbal signals sometimes can be more effective than words.

shrugging one's shoulders ("I don't know"), are commonly accepted substitutes for verbal expressions

2. *Nonverbal signals may serve to accent concurrent verbal transmissions.* Often nonverbal signals are used to emphasize certain words or verbally expressed thoughts. A football coach may smack his fist into his palm as he tells his players that they have to "hit harder." A scolding mother may shake her finger at her child to emphasize how naughty the child has been.

3. *Nonverbal signals may supplement the verbal transmission.* When used for emphasis, nonverbal signals are redundant with the verbal message. Sometimes, however, the nonverbal transmission may supplement speech by adding a second message. For instance, you might be having a ferocious disagreement with a close friend. While arguing at a verbal level, you might use posture and eye contact to communicate the continuing strength of your friendship.

4. *Nonverbal signals may regulate the flow of conversation.* When talking with people, we only very rarely say something like "OK, I'm through, now what's your response?" Most of the time, such messages are delivered through the nonverbal channel. We use eye contact, facial expressions, and gestures to indicate when we are ready to speak, when we have finished speaking, when we are bored, when we are interested, and so forth.

5. *Nonverbal signals may be used to communicate emotions.* In many respects, words are inadequate when we are trying to convey our internal emotions. Hence, we often rely on nonverbal cues to successfully express our feelings. Much of this is *unintentional.* A variety of nonverbal actions seem to accompany certain emotions naturally or automatically. For example, we tend to grimace, gaze downward, and slump our shoulders when we feel unhappy.

GENERAL PRINCIPLES OF NONVERBAL COMMUNICATION

In discussing the nature of nonverbal communication, I will start with a general overview and then proceed to describe some particular kinds of nonverbal communication.

1. *Nonverbal communication is multichanneled.* I have chosen to differentiate between two broad channels of communication: verbal and nonverbal. However, it should be noted that nonverbal communication typically involves simultaneous transmissions through a number of modalities, or subchannels (Verderber & Verderber, 1977). For instance, at the same time, messages may be sent through gestures, facial expressions, eye contact, and vocal tone. In contrast, verbal communication is limited to a single channel: words. If you have ever tried to follow two persons speaking at once, you are aware of how difficult it is to handle multiple inputs. The multichannel nature of nonverbal communication is one of the reasons many nonverbal transmissions sail by the receiver unnoticed.

2. *Nonverbal communication is relatively spontaneous.* In comparison with verbal communication, nonverbal transmissions tend to be more spontaneous (Verderber & Verderber, 1977). In other words, you often send nonverbal messages without thinking about them. Although it is certainly not unheard of for people to speak thoughtlessly, speech is usually under more conscious control than most nonverbal communication. It is this less guarded quality of nonverbal communication that often makes it a more accurate index of people's true feelings.

3. *Nonverbal communication is relatively ambiguous.* Nonverbal signals tend to be less clear than spoken words. Although there is certainly room for ambiguity in speech, there generally is more consensus about the meaning of words than the meaning of nonverbal signs. A shrug or a raised eyebrow is more likely to mean different things to different people. Although some popular books on body language imply otherwise, it appears that few, if any, nonverbal signals carry universally accepted meanings (Swensen, 1973). Hence,

nonverbal signals should be interpreted with great caution.

4. *Nonverbal communication is very culture-bound.* Like language, nonverbal signals are quite different in different cultures (Hall, 1959). For instance, Americans and people of Northern European heritage tend to engage in less physical contact and keep a greater distance between themselves than people of Latin or Middle Eastern heritage. Thus, an Englishman might be quite upset when a well-meaning Brazilian "trespasses" on his personal space. Sometimes the cultural differences are quite dramatic. For example, in Tibet people greet their friends by sticking out their tongue at them (Ekman, 1975).

5. *Nonverbal communication may contradict what is said.* We have all seen people who proclaim "I'm not angry" while their bodies clearly convey that they are positively furious. Thus, it is well known that verbal and nonverbal messages may be quite inconsistent. When confronted with such inconsistency, which should you believe? Well, there are no absolute rules, but you're probably better off betting on the nonverbal signals, because of their greater spontaneity. Indeed, there *is* evidence indicating that deception by someone instructed to tell a lie is more readily detected in the nonverbal channel of communication (DePaulo, Lanier, & Davis, 1983). In line with this finding, research (Mehrabian & Ferris, 1967) indicates that people do tend to give more credence to nonverbal cues when there is inconsistency between verbal and nonverbal messages. Studies by Ekman and Friesen (1974, 1975) suggest that you should pay particular attention to the lower part of the body. Ekman and Friesen found that when subjects tried to deceive someone, they were more successful in controlling their head and face than their trunk and legs. Apparently, deceitful people are quite concerned about giving themselves away through eye and facial signals, but they may neglect to control their shuffling feet or their nervously tapping fingers.

KINESICS: THE LANGUAGE OF THE BODY

UNMASKING THE FACE

The face may be the major source of nonverbal messages. We are capable of literally thousands of slightly different facial expressions. After extensive research, Albert Mehrabian (1971) has derived a formula for face-to-face interactions that suggests that the face accounts for more than half of the message transmission. According to his formula, total impact = 7% verbal + 38% vocal emphasis + 55% facial expression.

Above all else, the face is involved in the transmission of emotion. This is true for animals as well as humans, and there is evidence that some facial expressions, broadly defined at least, may be innate (Eibl-Eibesfeldt, 1975).

Most people are capable of distinguishing among a variety of basic emotions displayed in others' faces. Ekman and Friesen (1975) asked subjects to identify what emotion a person was experiencing on the basis of facial cues provided in photographs. Their subjects were generally successful in discerning fundamental emotions, such as happiness, sadness, anger, fear, surprise, and disgust. Moreover, although there is some cultural variation, these facial signals tend to be pretty similar across highly divergent cultures. Ekman and Friesen took their photographs to New Guinea and showed them to natives living in rural areas who had had no contact with Western culture. The natives were nonetheless able to do a fair job of identifying the emotions portrayed in the stimulus photos.

As noted earlier, *people can send deceptive messages better with their faces than with other areas of their bodies* (Ekman & Friesen, 1974). As you may know, a successful bluff in poker involves careful control of the expression of emotion through the face. Facial deceit may take two common forms: modulation or outright falsification. In **modulation,** people consciously control their facial expressions to display either more or less of the underlying emotion than they are actually experiencing. **Falsification** involves complete suppression

MODULATION. *In nonverbal communication, the intentional control of facial expression to emphasize or downplay an emotional feeling.*

FALSIFICATION. *In nonverbal communication, the use of facial expression to mislead an observer about emotions being experienced.*

of a felt emotion or faking an emotion that is not actually experienced.

How can you detect facial deceit? It's not easy, but there are a couple of things you can look for. First, since we control the lower parts of our bodies less effectively than the upper parts, you might want to watch out for inconsistencies between facial expressions and messages from the trunk of the body. For example, a friendly smile might be accompanied by an unfriendly bodily posture. Second, because of the spontaneity of nonverbal expression, you may want to focus on timing or immediacy. People tend to hesitate more before mustering their deceptive nonverbal signals. Consequently, a certain hesitancy or lack of spontaneity *may* indicate that a person is being less than totally honest (DePaulo et al., 1983).

THE EYES HAVE IT

Eye contact is another major means of nonverbal communication. Above all else, it is the *duration* of eye contact between people that is most meaningful. A great deal of research has been done on communication through the eyes, and I will briefly summarize some of the more interesting findings.

Various factors influence the amount of eye contact between people.

- As you might expect, people maintain more eye contact with another person when they are listening than when speaking (Argyle, 1975).

7.1 CAN YOU IDENTIFY THESE EMOTIONS?

What emotions are being expressed by the woman in the four pictures below? The chances are excellent that you will be able to identify the emotions correctly. As you can see from the percentages to the right (based on research by Ekman & Friesen, 1975), people in highly disparate cultures show a fair amount of agreement about the emotions portrayed by the young woman. This cross-cultural consensus suggests that the facial expressions that so often accompany certain emotions may have a genetic or biological basis. In any case, it is clear that the face provides important clues about a person's emotional state.

Percentage agreement in judging the photos				
United States	85%	92%	97%	67%
Brazil	67%	97%	95%	90%
Chile	68%	92%	95%	94%
Argentina	54%	92%	98%	90%
Japan	66%	90%	100%	90%
New Guinea	54%	44%	82%	50%

Answers: fear, disgust, happiness, anger.

- Generally, women tend to engage in a bit more eye contact than men (Exline, 1963).
- A speaker trying to deceive his or her listener is likely to engage in relatively little eye contact. Moreover, people are aware of this tendency and interpret a lack of eye contact as an indication of possible lying (Hemsley & Doob, 1978).
- Eye contact will also be reduced when an interaction is unpleasant or embarrassing and when people feel that their personal space is being invaded (Argyle & Dean, 1965).

Eye contact is closely attuned to feelings of interpersonal attraction.

- The amount of eye contact is greater in friendly than in unfriendly encounters (Efran & Broughton, 1966).
- Taking things a step further, it appears that couples who are in love spend an inordinate amount of time gazing into each other's eyes (Rubin, 1970).
- Given these realities, it comes as no surprise that people interpret the duration of eye contact as an index of liking. We generally interpret a great deal of eye contact from someone as an indication that he or she likes us (Kleinke, Meeker, & LaFong, 1974).
- The eyes may also be used extensively in flirting (see Figure 7.2). When a strange male enters a room, a *second* glance from a woman may indicate that a conversational overture would be welcomed (Cary, 1978). Additionally, intentionally letting someone see you looking over his or her body is a gambit that may be used to signal sexual interest (Fast, 1977).

Eye contact may also be used to transmit specific messages that are unrelated to attraction. For example, staring in certain ways can be used to convey feelings of dominance and to induce anxiety in others (Argyle, 1975). In particular, a lengthy stare wherein you "look down your nose" at someone can produce feelings of inferiority in the other person. A stare can also be used to make someone feel obligated to interact with you. Furthermore, the appropriate kind of staring may be helpful in getting someone to comply with a request on your part (Kleinke, 1977). Conversely, you might use a *reduction* in eye contact in an ongoing conversation to signal boredom, a desire to change the subject, or a wish to escape the exchange altogether.

FIGURE 7.2 Eye contact is a good indicator of interpersonal attraction.

POSTURE

Bodily posture can provide information about a person's level of tension or relaxation (Swensen, 1973). When relaxed, a seated person tends to lean back and arrange his or her arms and legs in an "open" array. In a more general vein, a casual posture intended to maximize comfort appears to be associated with feeling relaxed in a situation. For instance, Goffman (1956) noticed that in hospital staff meetings the relatively high-status doctors tended to assume careless and comfortable positions while lower-status personnel, such as nurses and social workers (who presumably would be more tense), were more likely to display less casual posture.

A person's posture may also be indicative of his or her attitude toward you (Mehrabian, 1969). A forward lean communicates interest and a positive attitude. When people angle their bodies away from you instead of facing you squarely, they may be conveying more negative attitudes.

HAND GESTURES

Hand gestures are used a great deal in regulating conversations and supplementing speech. Scheflen and Scheflen (1972) have described a variety of ges-

---

7.2   THE BODY LANGUAGE OF "COURTING" BEHAVIOR

One of the big selling points for the various popular books on nonverbal communication (Fast, 1970, 1977; Nierenberg & Calero, 1971) has been their emphasis on the body language of sex. Apparently, people are eager to know about the subtle signals that indicate whether a member of the other sex is "receptive" to them. Fortunately, you do not have to read an entire book to learn about these signals; I can summarize them in a few paragraphs, and you will find that many of them are already familiar to you. First, however, I need to clarify just what "courting" signals indicate—or, more important, what they do *not* indicate.

It is important to understand that the presence of courtship signals does *not* usually mean that a person wants to "come on" to you sexually. Scheflen (1965), who has done the most thorough research on courtship behavior, was surprised to find that courtship signals permeate many kinds of interactions, most of which have little possibility of leading to a sexual encounter. Scheflen observed courtshiplike behavior in clearly nonsexual transactions, such as business meetings and therapy sessions. In a nutshell, Scheflen found that people often give off sexual signals, both intentionally and unintentionally, even when they have absolutely no interest in an actual sexual overture. Why? There are probably many reasons. To some extent, courting signals may be a *natural* reaction when an attractive member of the other sex is present. In some cases, people send off these signals in order to elicit similar quasi-flirtatious signals from another, thereby reconfirming their attractiveness. A third explanation is simply that such signals are a good attention-getting device. In any case, courtship signals do *not* necessarily indicate an interest in courtship. More often than not, they mean only that a person wants you to recognize his or her attractiveness as a member of the other sex.

So, what are the nonverbal signals associated with courting behavior? Well, eye contact is important. In a room full of strangers, holding a direct gaze a bit longer than usual, taking a lengthy second glance, and letting a person observe you looking over his or her body may indicate some sexual interest. Preening behavior is an easily observed signal. People will check out their reflection in a mirror or window, stroke their hair, or adjust their clothing. In terms of body posture, men may cock their head and thrust their hips forward a bit; women may cross and recross their legs to expose them advantageously; both sexes tend to maintain erect posture and high muscle tonus. If a conversation ensues, the attentional orientation will be good; courting couples tend to face each other directly, lean forward, and use their bodies to screen out other people nearby. In terms of paralanguage, the vocalization will often be soft and hushed. Touch may also be a key signal. Courting people often rub their own bodies unconsciously. They may also brush against the other person "accidentally" or, if the situation permits, touch the person quite intentionally.

How do you distinguish authentic courting behavior from what Scheflen calls quasi-courtship behavior? It may not be easy, but Scheflen asserts that we often send "qualifying" signals to indicate the limited intentions underlying our quasi-courtship behavior. The signal may be something as simple as mentioning one's husband or wife affectionately. In terms of nonverbal communication, the main thing to look for is *inconsistency* in the bodily signals. For instance, if postural orientation or vocal tones do not jibe with the seemingly flirtatious eye contact, it is unlikely that anything more than quasi-courting is taking place.

BORN LOSER CARTOON © 1974 NEWSPAPER ENTERPRISE ASSOCIATION, INC.

tures that are used in conjunction with speech. The *referencing gesture* is used in referring to an object or person who is the subject of the conversation (see Figure 7.3). For instance, you might point at a car that you're commenting on. The *gesture of emphasis* is used to stress a point that is made verbally (see Figure 7.3). Thus, you might slam your fist onto a desk to emphasize the importance of your statement. *Demonstrative gestures* mimic what is being said. For example, in discussing a cutoff of someone's financial support, you might make chopping motions with your hand.

FIGURE 7.3 *(Left)* GESTURES OF EMPHASIS. Frequently, gestures are used to emphasize or bolster a point that is being made verbally. *(Right)* THE REFERENCING GESTURE. A speaker's gestures may refer to objects or persons about whom she is speaking.

PROXEMICS: THE DYNAMICS OF CLOSE ENCOUNTERS

PERSONAL SPACE

TERRITORIALITY. *A pattern of behavior wherein people or animals mark off and defend a certain area against intrusion by other members of their own species.*

Most people are aware that animals display **territoriality;** that is, they mark off and defend certain areas as their own. It is less well known that humans exhibit very similar tendencies. Sommer (1969) has investigated the maintenance of personal space in humans. **Personal space** is *the immediate area around people, which they feel "belongs" to them.* Basically, we're talking

PERSONAL SPACE. *A zone of space surrounding a person that is felt to "belong" to that person. It is portable and ultimately imaginary, although it may be marked off in tangible ways under some conditions.*

about a sort of invisible "bubble" that people carry around with them in their social interactions. The size of this mobile zone is related to one's cultural background, social status, personality, age, and sex. For example, Sommer (1967) reports that introverts tend to have larger buffer zones than extroverts.

DISTANCE AND RELATIONSHIPS

The nature of a social encounter greatly influences the amount of distance people put between themselves. For instance, people of similar social status maintain less distance between themselves than people who have a status discrepancy (Lott & Sommer, 1967). As you might expect, people who like each other tend to come closer than people who are not fond of each other (Mehrabian, 1969).

Edward Hall (1966) has described four distance zones that are appropriate for particular kinds of social encounters in American culture.

- *Intimate distance (0–18 inches).* This obviously represents tight quarters and is appropriate only for very intimate relationships, such as those between parents and children or between lovers.
- *Personal distance (1½–4 feet).* This is the minimum distance maintained in most encounters between friends. In appropriate situations, such as a cocktail party, strangers may venture into this zone.
- *Social distance (4–12 feet).* Most social interactions in America are transacted from this zone. It is a nice intermediate distance that makes most of us feel comfortable.
- *Public distance (12 feet and beyond).* Interpersonal interactions can take place at distances beyond 12 feet, but they tend to be quite impersonal. People often prefer to maintain this distance because it gives them the option of choosing to ignore someone without appearing rude.

The key point emerging from Hall's analysis is that there is an appropriate distance between people, which depends on their relationship and the situation. When someone approaches you more closely than the situation and your relationship warrant, this act is an invasion of your personal space. Such an invasion may make you feel quite uncomfortable.

INVASIONS OF PERSONAL SPACE

Generally, people don't like it when their personal space is invaded by another person. A number of reactions are common in such a situation (Heun & Heun, 1975; Sommer, 1969). To illustrate, let's say that you have parceled out some territory for yourself at a table in the library. Although there are study carrels available, a stranger sits down at "your" table and forces you to share it. How might you react? Well, you might begin by expressing your disapproval

FIGURE 7.4 Territoriality is not characteristic of animals alone—humans exhibit it, too.

nonverbally through a hostile stare or frown. You might also experience some tension, which could be betrayed by nonverbal signals such as bodily rigidity, a shuffling of position, or a lack of eye contact. If other tables are free, you might move away in order to reestablish a satisfactory distance. If moving away is not practical, you will probably reorient your body away from the intruder. Another common response is to place some barrier (for example, books, a package) between yourself and the invader (see Figure 7.4). Whatever response you choose, the point is that invasions of personal space rarely go unnoticed; they may elicit quite a variety of reactions.

PARALANGUAGE: IT'S ALL IN HOW YOU SAY IT

Paralanguage deals with *how* something is said rather than *what* is said. It is concerned with all aspects of vocalization other than the verbal message itself. Vocalizations vary in loudness, pitch, rate, rhythm, and quality (Keltner, 1973). All these features of vocalization may be manipulated in ways that affect the message being transmitted.

The key point is that *variations in vocal emphasis can give a particular string of words different meanings* (Mehrabian, 1972). Consider the sentence "I really enjoyed myself." By varying the word accented, it could be spoken in three ways with three slightly different meanings.

I really enjoyed myself.
(Although others may not have enjoyed themselves, I did.)

I *really* enjoyed myself.
(My enjoyment was exceptional or greater than expected.)

I really *enjoyed* myself.
(Much to my surprise, I had a good time.)

As you can see above, the way you say something can make a considerable difference in its meaning. Variations in vocal emphasis constitute a language within a language.

The great importance of paralanguage can best be emphasized by pointing out that vocal emphasis can actually *reverse* the literal meaning of a verbal message. For example, with the appropriate inflection to indicate sarcasm, a statement such as "That's wonderful" may actually transmit exactly the opposite message.

Features of vocalization may also betray emotions. For example, rapid and loud vocalization with distinct punctuation may be a sign of anger and annoyance. A relatively high pitch may indicate anxiety. Slow speech, low volume, and low pitch are often associated with sadness. Thus, vocal quality is yet another clue that you can use to discern someone's true inner feelings.

Verbal Communication

Having analyzed the dynamics of nonverbal communication, I will now turn to the intricacies of communication in the verbal channel. I begin by pointing out some common problems that often act as barriers to effective communication. Then I tackle the question of how you can improve your communication. I discuss some broad guidelines about how to promote a positive climate for communication, how to speak effectively, and how to listen effectively.

BARRIERS TO EFFECTIVE COMMUNICATION

Misunderstandings between people are commonplace. They happen all the time. In fact, effective communication may be the exception rather than the rule. Heun and Heun (1975) define a **communication barrier** as *anything*

COMMUNICATION BARRIER. *Any problem in the communication process that interferes with the communication effort or reduces its effectiveness.*

that inhibits or blocks effective communication. There are many such barriers, and an exhaustive review is beyond the scope of this chapter. Rather than focusing on very specific problems, such as excessive intensity in speaking or poor timing, I will describe four barriers of a general sort: carelessness, motivational distortion, self-preoccupation, and defensiveness. The discussion will be based largely on the analyses of Giffin and Patton (1971), Heun and Heun (1975), and Gibb (1961).

CARELESSNESS

An extremely common problem in communication is simple carelessness. Nonchalance and carelessness, whether by the source or by the receiver, can create misunderstandings. In the case of the source, it is usually a matter of speaking without thinking. Most of us probably know someone who often "speaks off the top of his head," without adequate forethought. This person will often insult someone accidentally by saying something he really didn't mean. Virtually all of us are guilty of this kind of carelessness on occasion. Probably even more common is careless listening on the part of the receiver. It's easy for the receiver to get careless, because we can process speech reception at up to about 600 words per minute, while most people speak at a rate of only 100 to 140 words per minute (Adler & Towne, 1975). With all that spare time, it's not surprising that people get distracted, bored, and inattentive. As we shall see later, effective listening requires active effort. It is important to learn how to overcome the temptation to listen in an apathetic and perfunctory manner.

MOTIVATIONAL DISTORTION

In the previous chapter I talked at length about how our wishes and desires lead us to see what we want to see. Exactly the same thing commonly takes place in communication. To put it simply, *we often hear what we want to hear.* As listeners, we each have our own unique frame of reference. This includes certain attitudes and prejudices. Because of our aversion to cognitive dissonance, we often attend selectively to information that supports our beliefs and ignore information that contradicts them. We may read meanings into statements that were not intended, and we may jump to conclusions based on superficial listening. These tendencies often show up most obviously in heated debates of political issues. People often deliver what they believe to be an eloquent and clear defense of their position, only to hear their opponent respond to a twisted and distorted version of their message.

SELF-PREOCCUPATION

Some people are too self-centered to communicate effectively. They tend to ramble on and on about themselves. They want to listen only to themselves. They thrive on hearing themselves talk, as long as they have an audience. These egocentric people have little concern for the welfare of others and therefore have little interest in hearing what others have to say. When the other person is talking in a conversation, they are wrapped up in rehearsing what they are going to say as soon as they get a chance. Some use conversation as a vehicle to show off; their primary concern is to impress you and thereby impress themselves. Others may be bogged down in self-pity and are busily searching for sympathy. Whatever the case, they can't relate well to others and generally communicate rather ineffectively.

DEFENSIVENESS

The most basic barrier to effective communication is probably defensiveness—an excessive concern with protecting oneself from being hurt. People react defensively when they feel threatened. Although the threat may be more imagined than real, it will still elicit defensive behavior. Defensiveness in communication has been studied in depth by Jack Gibb (1961), who delineated a number of communication behaviors that trigger defensiveness. I will briefly describe four of these.

- *Evaluation.* We tend to be defensive when we feel that someone is going to pass judgment on us. When we feel that we are being evaluated as good or bad, we become cautious in our communication.
- *Control.* When people engage in efforts to manipulate or control us, we often react defensively.
- *Superiority.* When another person works to communicate his or her superiority to us, this tends to produce defensiveness. People who overemphasize their status, wealth, brilliance, or power may make us feel less than adequate and therefore put us on the defensive.
- *Certainty.* The dogmatic person who communicates that "I'm always right" breeds defensiveness. "Know-it-all" types force us to defend our beliefs more than we otherwise would.

ACHIEVING EFFECTIVE COMMUNICATION

This section will pursue a more positive line of thought and discuss how you can enhance the effectiveness of your communication. First, I describe a general attitudinal orientation that can promote an open, nondefensive climate for communication. Next, I list some general guidelines for effective speaking. Finally, I provide some advice about listening effectively.

PROMOTING A POSITIVE CLIMATE

A positive climate makes people feel that they can be open rather than defensive. You can promote such a climate by behaving in ways that are basically the opposite of those that lead to defensive behavior (Gibb, 1961). The following communication behaviors can promote an open, supportive climate characterized by interpersonal trust.

EMPATHY. *Putting oneself into the psychological frame of reference of another so that one can truly understand the other person's thoughts and feelings.*

1. *Empathy.* **Empathy** involves showing your respect for the other person and your ability to understand his or her point of view. When you empathize with others, you are able to appreciate their feelings and understand their problems. This is sometimes called being *sensitive* to others. It may be the most important factor in promoting a positive climate.

2. *Withholding judgment.* An open climate is more likely if you try to be nonjudgmental. This does not mean that you have to give up your right to have opinions and make judgments. It merely means that you should approach people in a way that does not make them feel they are being put on the spot.

3. *Honesty.* It also helps if you are candid and honest. So-called hidden agendas often don't stay hidden very long. Even if the other person doesn't know exactly what your underlying motives are, he or she can often sense that you're not being entirely honest. An open climate is facilitated by avoiding deception and manipulation.

4. *Equality.* People do not like to be reminded of another's higher status or greater ability. Communication will be more open and effective if such differences are disregarded. It is better to approach people on equal terms.

5. *Provisionalism.* This is the opposite of dogmatism. Rather than communicating that you alone know the answer, you should convey that your beliefs and attitudes are flexible and subject to revision. It is often better to express thoughts with an air of tentativeness rather than finality. This can be done by slipping in a "qualifying" phrase. For instance, instead of saying "This is how we should do it . . . ," you might say "There are several possible approaches; the one that *seems* best to me is . . . ."

GUIDELINES FOR EFFECTIVE SPEAKING

Speaking is an art that is cultivated over a lifetime. Obviously, then, I am not going to produce any spectacular changes in your speaking skills with a couple

cathy

of paragraphs of advice. Nonetheless, it may prove helpful to remind you of a few general guidelines that you have probably encountered before. For more thorough coverage you might want to consult two excellent communication texts: Heun and Heun (1975) and Verderber and Verderber (1977).

1. *Be specific and concrete.* Communication is hampered when you speak in vague generalities. If you're vague, it is possible to speak at great length without succeeding in communicating anything! Unless you're a politician, this is not something you want to do.

2. *Consider your listener's frame of reference.* In a majority of situations, you are likely to be familiar with, and have some knowledge about, your listener. It is a good idea to consider your listener's background, intelligence, attitudes, and so forth, so that you can put the message in terms that he or she can understand. In particular, you want to avoid "talking over the heads of your audience," and steer clear of jargon or special terminology that is foreign to them. You should try to illustrate your ideas with examples that your listener will be able to relate to on the basis of his or her experience.

7.3

RECOMMENDED READING
Contact: The First Four Minutes
by Leonard Zunin with Natalie Zunin (Ballantine Books, 1972)

I talked in Chapter 6 about primacy effects, or the power of first impressions. The Zunins are convinced that when strangers encounter each other for the first time, the first four minutes are crucial to the impressions made. Actually, they offer little empirical evidence to support their assertion that *four* minutes (not, say, three or six) is the critical time interval. Nonetheless, they have a great deal of worthwhile advice to offer that might help you improve your interpersonal communication.

The book is much broader in scope than its title suggests. The Zunins discuss a wide range of topics besides how to handle initial encounters. Among other things,

they offer insights on nonverbal communication, self-concept, and how to cope with rejection. The outstanding feature of the book, however, is its wealth of advice on how to make social overtures toward others. In one chapter alone, there are 19 down-to-earth suggestions about conversational openers.

Let us look in at a typical party. The hostess is introducing two strangers, after which she excuses herself to circulate. The two become locked in contact according to unwritten rules of social congeniality. They tend to respond to each other, perhaps automatically, guided by conditioned cultural traditions—but for a minimum

period of time (again an average of four minutes). One of them may then say, "A pleasure meeting you. I'm going for a refill," and he walks away. He has been cordial enough and socially appropriate, but most probably the two have not made an effective or favorable contact.

The average person shrugs off such a routine rejection and moves on to new contacts, which continue to range from three to five minutes, averaging four minutes. It is hardly an interval guaranteed to change your life, but what is communicated can determine whether or not strangers become acquaintances, friends, lovers, life-time mates—or remain strangers [p. 11].

3. *Avoid "loaded" words.* Certain words are "loaded" in the sense that they tend to trigger emotional reactions from your listener. In the interests of effective discourse, it is usually best to avoid using such words, which are unnecessarily derogatory. Politics can be discussed without using terms such as "right-winger" and "knee-jerk liberal." Labels such as "male chauvinist pig" and "women's libber" need not come up in discussions of sex roles. You can remind children of chores left undone without calling them "lazy," you can ask a clerk to correct an error without referring to it as a "ridiculous blunder," and you can disagree with people older than yourself without calling them "senile."

4. *Make your verbal and nonverbal messages congruent.* Now that you are aware of the great amount of message transmission that takes place at the nonverbal level, you should be able to appreciate the importance of being consistent verbally and nonverbally. Inconsistency may generate confusion in your listener. The relative spontaneity of nonverbal communication makes it somewhat difficult to control. Nonetheless, you can work at being more aware of your nonverbal signals.

GUIDELINES FOR EFFECTIVE LISTENING

Listening is a vastly underappreciated art. It is every bit as important to effective communication as speaking, but it gets far less attention. This is particularly unfortunate because evidence suggests that we spend far more time listening than speaking (Verderber & Verderber, 1977).

Although you are not likely to produce a dramatic change in your speaking skills overnight, you *may* be able to substantially improve your listening quite quickly. Effective listening hinges largely on your attitude. If you're willing to *work* at it, you can be a good listener.

The key to effective listening is simply to engage in active effort. We tend to think of listening as something we do with our ears, but to do it right, you

7.4   IS ANYONE LISTENING?

America has better means of communication than any nation on earth. We are constantly developing splendid new techniques for the dissemination of sound, pictures, and print. The only problem is that on the most basic level of communication—person-to-person, live, mouth-to-ear, low-frequency conversation—we're still in the dark ages; for everyone sends well enough, but very few of us are receiving.

Last week in the elevator of my mother's apartment house, a man asked her, "How are you?"

Since Mother had just spent three hours with a tax collector, she smiled graciously and said, "Lousy, thank you."

The man returned the smile and said, "That's nice."

Mother suspected that he either had misunderstood her or was simply a sadist. However, later the same day, she passed a woman who said, "How are you?"

"Suicidally distraught," said Mother.

"Fine," said the woman. "Hope the family's well, too."

This second exchange gave Mother the kind of revelation that only scientists have known when discovering great truths. Because that man and woman weren't people who would have wanted to see Mother out of the way (neither is in her will), she reached a profound conclusion: if you are well enough to be talking, people consider your condition superb, even if you colorfully describe an internal hemorrhage.

Mother's pioneering experimentation in the amenities has so inspired me that I have dedicated myself to continuing her work. Yesterday, I made real progress.

"How are you?" asked a man in front of my house.

"I'll be dead in a week," I said.

"Glad to hear it. Take care now."

There is no known way to shake the composure of the man who makes a perfunctory inquiry about your health; he loves his lines so well that the grimmest truth can't make him revise them. Never is human communication so defeated as when someone asks casually about your condition.

Some day, perhaps when I'm under a bus getting the last rites, I expect such a man to throw me a breezy, "How are you?"

"As well as can be expected," I'll say.

"Good. And the kids?"

"The older one goes to the chair tomorrow. The little one was lost on a Scout hike."

"Swell. The wife okay?"

"She just ran off with the milkman."

"Glad to hear it. You'll have to bring the whole family over one night soon."

From *Time Lurches On* by Ralph Schoenstein.

have to use what lies *between* your ears. Successful listening requires that you actively process the incoming information. Some general guidelines are provided below.

1. *Attend physically to the speaker.* The first step in active listening is to send a clear nonverbal message to the speaker that you are truly interested. You can do this by displaying physical involvement. Egan (1986) suggests facing the person squarely, maintaining good eye contact, and adopting an "open" posture, leaning forward if you are seated.

2. *Actively process the verbal message.* We have already seen that a listener can receive information faster than the speaker can send it, leaving extra time for the listener. The trick to effective listening is to devote this extra time to the incoming train of thought rather than irrelevant lines of thought. Huseman, Lahiff, and Hatfield (1976) suggest (a) reviewing points already made, (b) trying to anticipate what the speaker will say next, and (c) searching for "deeper" meanings that may underlie the surface message.

3. *Pay attention to nonverbal signals.* As you know, much of the message transmission takes place in the nonverbal channel. Hence, Egan (1986) emphasizes that it is very important that you focus on nonverbal signals in order to achieve a full understanding of the message.

4. *Check your understanding of the message.* It is often a good idea to check to make sure you understood the message properly. There are a variety of ways to accomplish this. The simplest way is to ask a direct question to clarify a point. Another way is to briefly summarize what has just been said and see whether there are any objections from the speaker. If you think there was a deeper meaning underlying the words themselves, a simple summary may not be sufficient. Instead, you may want to translate the ideas (including the underlying ones) into your own words to see whether the speaker agrees with your interpretation of his or her message.

Revealing Ourselves to Others: Self-Disclosure

SELF-DISCLOSURE. *The act of revealing private information about yourself to another person. It is a voluntary act of verbal communication.*

In discussing public selves in Chapter 6, I noted that people do not behave in an altogether spontaneous fashion. On the contrary, most people carefully edit their behavior and monitor what they reveal about themselves to others. This act of revealing oneself to another is called self-disclosure; it is a very important kind of interpersonal communication. I shall define **self-disclosure** as *the voluntary act of verbally communicating private information about yourself to another person.* By "private" I mean information that would not otherwise be readily available to the other party. It doesn't have to be a deeply hidden secret, but it may be. In general terms, self-disclosure involves opening up about yourself to others. It means engaging in deep, personal, and meaningful communication, as opposed to superficial and perfunctory communication.

Self-disclosure is an important element in our lives. It is a crucial factor in the development of friendship, as well as more intimate relationships. It is a valuable outlet for venting our feelings. But it's a risky proposition. When we open ourselves up to others, we become more vulnerable. Consequently, we often struggle with decisions about whether we should reveal certain things to certain people. In this section I will try to shed some light on the dynamics and implications of this struggle.

WHY DO WE ENGAGE IN SELF-DISCLOSURE?

Self-disclosure is inherently hazardous in that we make ourselves vulnerable to rejection, not to mention possible ridicule. Given these dangers, why do we take the gamble? Because the potential payoffs are great. Self-disclosure has considerable functional value.

What are the functions of self-disclosure? Derlega and Grezlak (1979) have addressed this question in an excellent theoretical article, and it is worthwhile looking at some of their answers. Among other things, they believe that self-disclosure serves the following functions. Their analysis will give you some ideas about why it is so important for us to engage in self-disclosure.

1. *Expression.* Letting things spill out may sometimes have a cathartic value. It may help to release tensions and emotions.

2. *Clarification.* We all get confused about problems in our lives. Talking about things may help us sort them out. Just *thinking* about disclosing some problem may lead us to further analyze the problem and clarify our feelings.

3. *Social comparison.* As noted earlier, Festinger (1954) believes that we need to compare ourselves with others in order to better understand ourselves. We often need to engage in self-disclosure in order to gain this comparative information that we seek. For instance, if you wanted to know whether your anxieties about a particular course were realistic, you would probably have to divulge those anxieties to other students to obtain the kind of feedback you needed.

4. *Relationship development.* Self-disclosure is crucial in building new interpersonal relationships. If you want to get to know someone, you generally will have to let her or him get to know you. This requires mutual self-disclosure. Your willingness to disclose to others indicates that you trust them. This is an important message to send to someone with whom you want to develop a relationship.

SELF-DISCLOSURE AND PSYCHOLOGICAL HEALTH

As you can see above, self-disclosure serves many important purposes. Sidney Jourard (1964), a pioneer investigator in this area, felt that the value of self-disclosure was so great that it appeared crucial to psychological health. He believed that many people who sought therapy were troubled primarily by their inability to open up to others. *Thus, Jourard theorized that self-disclosure was a cornerstone element of the healthy personality.* He implied that the more open people were, the healthier they were.

More recently, other theorists have modified this formulation slightly. Derlega and Chaikin (1975) point out that self-disclosure can be unhealthy. *It*

7.5

RECOMMENDED READING

The Transparent Self

by Sidney M. Jourard (Van Nostrand Reinhold, 1964; second edition, 1971)

This is a classic humanistic manifesto extolling the importance and value of self-disclosure. Jourard argues convincingly that many of us are troubled by an inability to open up to others. He explains the roots of this problem and discusses how self-disclosure can promote psychological health.

Jourard was a rare animal—an authentic humanist who backed up his ideas with hard-nosed research. Although he was research-oriented, the book is skillfully written in everyday language. Jourard provides eloquent discourse on how self-disclosure plays a key role in love, marriage, family, education, health care, and therapy.

Jourard was a pioneer researcher working in previously unexplored territory. Consequently, as discussed in the text proper, some of his ideas have turned out to be a bit oversimplified. Nonetheless, the book has some timeless advice about relationships and interpersonal communication.

> Now I think unhealthy personality has a similar root cause, one which is related to Selye's concept of stress. Every maladjusted person is a person who has not made himself known to another human being and in consequence does not know himself. Nor can he be himself. More than that, he struggles actively to avoid becoming known by another human being. He works at it ceaselessly, twenty-four hours daily, and it is work! In the effort to avoid becoming known, a person provides for himself a cancerous kind of stress which is subtle and unrecognized, but nonetheless effective in producing not only the assorted patterns of unhealthy personality which psychiatry talks about, but also the wide array of physical ills that have come to be recognized as the province of psychosomatic medicine [pp. 32–33].

is possible to engage in inappropriate self-disclosure. For example, some people tend to divulge too much to the wrong people at inappropriate times. Surely you have encountered one or more of these people, who, although you barely know them, bore you with their life story or embarrass you by blurting out their innermost secrets. Thus, Derlega and Chaikin argue that it is quite possible to be *too* open.

Given these considerations, Derlega and Chaikin (1975) theorize that *a moderate amount of selective self-disclosure is probably most healthy.* To be more specific, they assert that there is a curvilinear relationship between self-disclosure and psychological health, as illustrated in Figure 7.5. According to their theory, either too little or too much self-disclosure may be associated with relatively poor adjustment. Thus, they agree with Jourard in saying that an inability to be open is unhealthy. However, they maintain that being an "overdiscloser" is also unhealthy. According to their theory, the healthy personality engages in discriminating self-disclosure, revealing the right things to the right people at the right times.

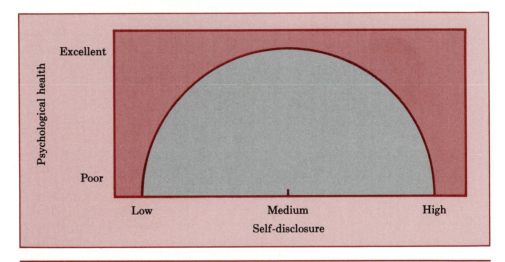

FIGURE 7.5 Hypothesized relationship between self-disclosure and psychological health according to Derlega and Chaikin (1975).

WHO REVEALS WHAT TO WHOM UNDER WHAT CIRCUMSTANCES?

There has been a substantial amount of research on the factors that govern self-disclosure. I will briefly review some of that research.

WHO?

It is clear that some people are more open and willing to engage in self-disclosure than others (Jourard, 1971). However, this inclination toward self-disclosure does not appear to be closely related to other personal characteristics. Research that has attempted to relate self-disclosure tendencies to personality has generally yielded weak and inconsistent findings, which suggest that personality interacts in complex ways with situational factors (Archer, 1979).

There are some sex differences in self-disclosure, but these too depend on complex situational determinants. *Jourard (1964, 1971) consistently found that females tended to be more openly self-disclosing than males.* He attributed this difference to sex-role socialization in our culture. Because of his firm belief in the importance of self-disclosure, he thought it was rather tragic that men were trained to be inexpressive.

A considerable number of studies have supported Jourard's findings on sex differences, and it has become widely accepted that men are less "open" than women. However, there is also some contradictory evidence, and it appears that in some situations, at least, men may be *more* prone to self-disclosure than women. For example, there is evidence (Rosenfeld, Civikly, & Herron, 1979) that *in dealing with strangers (as opposed to friends), males tend to be more self-disclosing than females.* Thus, it appears to be an oversimplification to say that women are more open than men.

WHAT?

Obviously, people are willing to open up more readily on some topics than on others. Jourard (1964) noted that we are more likely to discuss our hobbies, interests, work, and political attitudes than our sex life or financial affairs. Altman and Taylor (1973) point out that we quickly give biographical information (for example, where we live, age, education) but are understandably reluctant to divulge inner fears (for example, insecurity about our job). They also assert that we are generally willing to reveal socially desirable things about ourselves, such as our membership in the Jaycees, while we tend to be reticent about socially undesirable things, such as our history of convictions for tax evasion.

TO WHOM?

A crucial factor in self-disclosure is the target person who will receive the information. Some people are particularly skilled at getting others to "open up" and engage in self-disclosure. Sociability, self-esteem, empathy, and lack of shyness are associated with this ability to elicit self-disclosure from others (Miller, Berg, & Archer, 1983). There is a trend in favor of disclosing more readily to females than to males, but it is moderated by the exact nature of the topic (Cunningham, 1981). As you might expect, we tend to disclose more to people we like (Taylor, Altman, & Sorrentino, 1969) and to people we know relatively well (Jourard & Landsman, 1960). The social status of the target person is also important (Slobin, Miller, & Porter, 1968). Self-disclosure is most common when people are of similar status. When there is a status discrepancy, we are more likely to reveal ourselves to people of higher status than to people of subordinate status. According to research by Jourard (1961), as we get older, we tend to disclose less to our parents and same-sex friends and more to our opposite-sex friends. Generally speaking, we tend to disclose more to our spouse than to anyone else (Jourard, 1964). Interestingly, recent research (Hendrick, 1981) suggests that spouses who engage in a good deal of self-disclosure report relatively high levels of marital satisfaction.

UNDER WHAT CIRCUMSTANCES?

The question of circumstances has not been addressed adequately in self-disclosure research (Chelune, 1979). Nonetheless, it is clear that the circumstances have an enormous impact on self-disclosure. Consider a simple example. If you want to tell someone that you have fallen in love or that you want to discontinue a relationship, you will wait for the appropriate time and place. You don't reveal these things at the ballpark, as you're casually walking out the door, or as you wait in line to register for classes. Thus, *there are appropriate situations for certain kinds of self-disclosure.* Generally, we value privacy when we want to engage in significant self-disclosure.

There *is* one situational variable that we know figures prominently in self-disclosure. It is *reciprocity.* It has repeatedly been shown that *we disclose more when people reciprocate by making disclosures to us* (Cozby, 1973). In other words, self-disclosure breeds self-disclosure. When one person becomes brave enough to divulge some inner secret, the other person often will communicate his or her interest, and the acceptability of the disclosure, by sharing some similarly intimate information. Thus, in a cyclical manner, one self-disclosure elicits another. This reciprocity norm is probably the most influential determinant governing self-disclosure.

WHEN IS SELF-DISCLOSURE APPROPRIATE?

To disclose or not to disclose—that is the question. By now you should be able to appreciate the complexity of this question. The crucial issue in regard to self-disclosure is: When is it appropriate?

The answer to this question is both simple and complex. I'll give you the simple part first. *Self-disclosure is appropriate when your target recipient is sincerely interested and willing to listen.* But how do you know whether your target person is interested? This is where the answer gets complex. In trying to avoid inappropriate self-disclosure, it helps to go slowly and pay close attention to the other person's reaction. It's something like testing the water to see whether it's warm. Instead of jumping in full force, you tentatively stick in a toe or two.

In assessing the other person's reaction, you should pay close attention to both verbal and nonverbal transmissions. In the verbal channel, the things to look for are empathy and reciprocity. These are good signs. In particular, if the other person reciprocates with self-disclosure, this generally indicates a willingness on his or her part to proceed to a more intimate level of communication. Of course, some people aren't very comfortable engaging in self-disclosure themselves but are sincerely willing to listen to you anyway. Hence, you cannot depend on reciprocity alone as an indicator of the other person's interest. You therefore have to tune in to nonverbal signals. When people are uncomfortable with your self-disclosure, they will often try to send you a nonverbal message to that effect, so as to avoid embarrassing you with a more obvious verbal putdown. This message is often delivered by reducing eye contact and by displaying a puzzled, apprehensive, or pained facial expression. The other person may also angle his or her body away from you (if seated) or increase the distance between the two of you and shuffle his or her feet impatiently (if standing). In contrast, if your target person faces you squarely, leans forward, appears relaxed, and maintains good eye contact, you can be fairly certain that he or she is willing to listen to you unburden yourself.

Summary

Interpersonal communication—the transmission of meaning from one person to another—takes place when a source sends a message to a receiver through either the verbal or the nonverbal channel.

Nonverbal signals may function (1) as substitutes for verbal expressions, (2) to accent or supplement verbal transmissions, (3) to regulate the flow of conversation, and (4) to communicate emotions. Nonverbal communication tends to be more spontaneous and ambiguous than verbal communication, and it may appear to contradict what is said. It is often multichanneled, and like language, it is culturally bound.

Facial expressions often convey internal emotional states. However, the face is relatively easy to use in efforts to send deceptive signals. The duration of eye contact is an important cue and is influenced by a variety of factors. Above all else, eye contact is a function of the amount of liking between two persons. Bodily posture may be indicative of a person's relaxation and his or her attitude toward you. Hand gestures are used primarily to regulate and supplement speech.

Proxemics deals with the use of personal space. Hall has described how certain distances are maintained in certain kinds of social relationships. When these norms are violated and personal space is invaded, people tend to react negatively. Paralanguage is concerned with the use of vocal emphasis in speaking. Slight variations in vocal emphasis can reverse the literal meaning of a message.

Effective communication may be blocked by barriers such as carelessness, motivational distortion, self-preoccupation, and defensiveness. To promote effective communication, it helps to treat people as equals, withhold judgment, and be sensitive, honest, and provisional. In speaking, it helps to consider your listener's frame of reference, be specific and concrete, avoid loaded words, and keep your verbal and nonverbal messages consistent. Effective listening depends on physical attending, active listening, focusing on nonverbal signals, and checking your perceptions.

Self-disclosure involves revealing ourselves to others. We take this risk because self-disclosure serves many important functions. The likelihood of self-disclosure depends on who is revealing what to whom under what circumstances. It appears that learning to engage in appropriate self-disclosure may be important to psychological health.

The application section of this chapter will discuss a sensitive communication issue—interpersonal conflict. It will provide some guidelines about how to cope constructively with interpersonal discord.

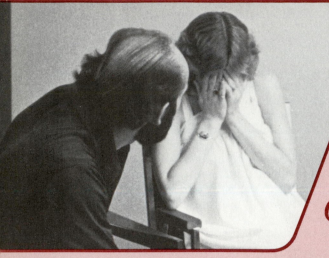

Dealing Constructively with Interpersonal Conflict

Check those that apply to you.

When I have a conflict with another person:

_____ 1. I *have* to be the winner.
_____ 2. I always begin by overstating my case.
_____ 3. I play on the other party's weaknesses.
_____ 4. I use threats to force the other person into submission.
_____ 5. I will use deceit if necessary.

If you checked several items, you take a very negative and short-sighted approach to dealing with interpersonal conflict. The characteristics listed above are associated with a strategy of *domination*—a strategy which may pay off with victory but which almost always leads to hard feelings. Conflict itself is inevitable, but hard feelings afterward are not. Conflict *can* be dealt with in positive ways and can produce positive outcomes for *both* parties. This application section will discuss how to deal with conflict constructively.

THE NATURE AND VALUE OF INTERPERSONAL CONFLICT

INTERPERSONAL CONFLICT. *A situation wherein two or more persons disagree. The disharmony may be a product of incompatible goals, values, attitudes, or ideas.*

Conflict is an inevitable feature of interpersonal interaction. People do not have to be enemies to be in conflict, and being in conflict does not make people enemies. Conflict is a natural element of life. According to Johnson (1972), an **interpersonal conflict** exists *whenever an action by one person obstructs or interferes with the intended actions of another*. This will occur between friends and lovers, as well as competitors and enemies.

Many people have the impression that conflict is inherently bad and that it should be avoided or suppressed if at all possible. In reality, conflict is neither inherently bad nor inherently good. It is simply a natural phenomenon that may lead to either good or bad outcomes, depending on how people deal with it. Avoidance tends to be one of the *worst* ways of coping with conflict. Interpersonal discord that is suppressed usually affects a relationship in spite of the suppressive effort, and the effects tend to be negative.

When dealt with in an open and constructive manner, interpersonal conflict can lead to a variety of valuable outcomes (Johnson & Johnson, 1975; Thomas, 1976). Among other things, constructive confrontation may (1) bring

problems out into the open where they can be solved, (2) put an end to chronic sources of discontent in a relationship, (3) stimulate personal change and the further evolution of a relationship, and (4) lead to new insights through the clashing of divergent views.

PERSONAL STYLES OF DEALING WITH CONFLICT

How do you react to conflict? Most people have a certain personal style in dealing with conflict (Sternberg & Soriano, 1984). I will describe five common styles in this section, so that you can see where you fit in. These descriptions of modes of dealing with conflict are adapted from theoretical models pioneered by Blake and Mouton (1964) and Thomas (1976).

Avoidance. Some people simply do not like to face up to the existence of conflict. They operate under the unrealistic hope that if they ignore the problem, maybe it will go away. When a conflict emerges, the avoider will change the subject, make a hasty exit, or pretend to be preoccupied with something else. This person finds conflict extremely unpleasant and distasteful and will go to great lengths to avoid being drawn into a fight. Of course, most problems will not go away while you pretend they don't exist. This style generally just delays the inevitable clash. Suppression is not an adequate means of dealing with conflict.

Accommodation. Like the avoider, the accommodating person feels uncomfortable with conflict. However, instead of ignoring the disagreement, this person brings the conflict to a quick end by giving in easily. This style grows out of basic feelings of insecurity. People who are overly worried about acceptance and approval from others are likely to use this strategy of surrender. It is a poor way of dealing with conflict because it does not generate creative thinking and bona fide solutions. Moreover, feelings of discontent may continue because the accommodating person often likes to play the role of a "martyr."

Domination. The dominator turns every conflict into a black and white, win/lose situation. This person will do virtually anything to emerge victorious from the confrontation. The dominator tends to be aggressive and deceitful. This person rigidly adheres to one position and will use threats and coercion to force submission by the other party. Giving no quarter, the dominator will often get personal and "hit below the belt." This style is undesirable because, like accommodation, it does not generate creative thinking aimed at mutual problem solving. Moreover, this approach is particularly likely to lead to postconflict tension, resentment, and hostility.

Compromise. Compromise is a pragmatic approach to conflict, wherein the divergent needs of both parties are acknowledged. A compromise approach involves negotiation and a willingness to "meet the other person halfway." While trying to be reasonable, the compromiser nonetheless works hard to maximize the satisfaction of his or her own needs. Thus, the compromise approach may involve some manipulation and misrepresentation. Compromise is a fairly constructive approach to conflict, but its manipulative aspects make it somewhat inferior to the final approach, which is integration.

Integration. Integration involves a *mutual* effort to maximize the satisfaction of *both* parties. When this approach is used, the conflict is viewed as a mutual problem to be solved as effectively as possible. Integration encourages open expression and honesty. When you disagree, you attack the other person's *ideas* rather than the other *person*. Much effort goes into clarifying differences *and* similarities in positions, so that you can build on the similarities. While compromise simply entails "splitting the difference" between positions, inte-

gration involves a sincere effort to find a solution that will be truly satisfactory for both parties. Generally, this is the best approach to dealing with conflict. Instead of yielding a postconflict residue of tension and resentment, this approach tends to produce a climate of trust.

GUIDELINES FOR CONSTRUCTIVE CONFLICT RESOLUTION

The preceding section was meant to convey to you the desirability of integration as an approach to conflict resolution. I will now spell out some explicit guidelines on how to achieve an integrative, problem-solving style of dealing with interpersonal conflict. In general, Johnson and Johnson (1975) suggest that you should do the following in order to promote constructive conflict resolution.

1. To begin with, you should acknowledge the existence of a conflict and the legitimacy of the other person's needs and goals.
2. The conflict should be defined as a mutual problem to be solved cooperatively, rather than as a win/lose proposition.
3. You should choose a mutually acceptable time to actually sit down and work on resolving the conflict. It is not always best to tackle the conflict when and where it first appears.
4. You should show respect for the other person's position. Try to empathize with, and fully understand, the other person's frame of reference.
5. Communication should be honest and open. You should not withhold information or misrepresent your position. Deceit and manipulation must be avoided.
6. When disagreements surface, be critical of the other person's ideas without making disparaging remarks about the other person's stupidity or foolishness.
7. Approach the conflict as equals, with a balance of power between the two of you. If you have a higher status or more power, these considerations should be ignored.
8. A great deal of effort should go into clarifying your respective positions. It is imperative that each of you understand the exact nature of your disagreements.
9. Communicate your flexibility and willingness to modify your position.
10. Emphasize the similarities in your positions rather than the differences. Try to use those similarities to build toward a mutually satisfactory solution.

RECOMMENDED READING

7.6

The Intimate Enemy: How to Fight Fair in Love and Marriage
by George R. Bach and Peter Wyden (William Morrow, 1969)

Most of us are not fond of conflict. However, it has its value and it is a fact of life. In particular, some conflict is virtually inevitable in intimate relationships. In deference to this reality, Bach (a psychologist) and Wyden (a writer) have put together a guide about how to fight fairly and productively. A sampling of some chapter titles can probably best convey the content of the book. Among other things, Bach and Wyden cover "Why Intimates Must Fight," "Training Lovers to Be Fighters," "Male and Female Fight Styles," "Bad Fighters and How to Reform Them," "Fighting over Trivia," and "Fighting before, during and after Sex."

The book is somewhat repetitive and rather lengthy, but its size is swelled by some interesting excerpts from actual fights. It is clearly written and quite provocative.

We have entered a psychological ice age. Except for occasional bursts of warmth, often fueled by sex after a few cocktails, truly intimate encounter has begun to disappear from civilized Western life. Closeness has become a paradox: longed for, but increasingly intolerable.

We believe that the inability to manage personal conflicts is at the root of the crisis that threatens the structure of the American family. Communications between children and parents are breaking down. More and more young people are "tuning out" by escaping into the world of drugs and other short-lived emotional kicks. One out of every three marriages ends in divorce [p. 17].

CHAPTER 7 REVIEW

IDEAS: REVIEW OF LEARNING OBJECTIVES

When you have mastered the material in this chapter, you should be able to do the following.

1. List the four elements in the communication process.
2. List five functions of nonverbal communication.
3. Explain five general principles of nonverbal communication.
4. Discuss what can be discerned from facial cues.
5. Describe two forms of facial deceit and discuss how such deceit may be detected.
6. List four factors that influence the amount of eye contact between people.
7. Discuss the relation between eye contact and attraction.
8. Discuss what can be discerned from postural cues.
9. Discuss the use of hand gestures in communication.
10. Describe Hall's four distance zones.
11. Discuss how people may react to invasions of personal space.
12. Explain why variations in vocal emphasis may be important.
13. List four barriers to effective communication.
14. Describe four communication behaviors that tend to elicit defensiveness.
15. Describe five communication behaviors that tend to produce a supportive, trusting climate.
16. List four guidelines for effective speaking.
17. List four guidelines for effective listening.
18. List four reasons that we need to engage in self-disclosure.
19. Discuss the relation between self-disclosure and psychological health.
20. Discuss sex differences in self-disclosure.
21. Discuss to whom we are likely to disclose personal information.
22. Describe the crucial situational variable that influences self-disclosure.
23. Describe a simple guideline regarding when self-disclosure is appropriate.
24. Discuss the potential value of interpersonal conflict.
25. List and describe five personal styles of dealing with conflict.
26. List ten guidelines for constructive conflict resolution.

TERMS: REVIEW OF NEW VOCABULARY

When you have mastered the material in this chapter, you should be able to define the following terms.

Channel
Communication barrier
Empathy
Falsification
Interpersonal communication
Interpersonal conflict
Kinesics
Message
Modulation
Nonverbal communication
Paralanguage
Personal space
Proxemics
Receiver
Self-disclosure
Source
Territoriality

PEOPLE: REVIEW OF MAJOR THEORISTS AND RESEARCHERS

When you have mastered the material in this chapter, you should be able to summarize the principal contributions and/or ideas of the following people.

Ekman and Friesen
Jack Gibb
E. T. Hall
Sidney Jourard
Albert Mehrabian

8

WOMEN AND MEN RELATING TO EACH OTHER: SEX DIFFERENCES AND SEX ROLES

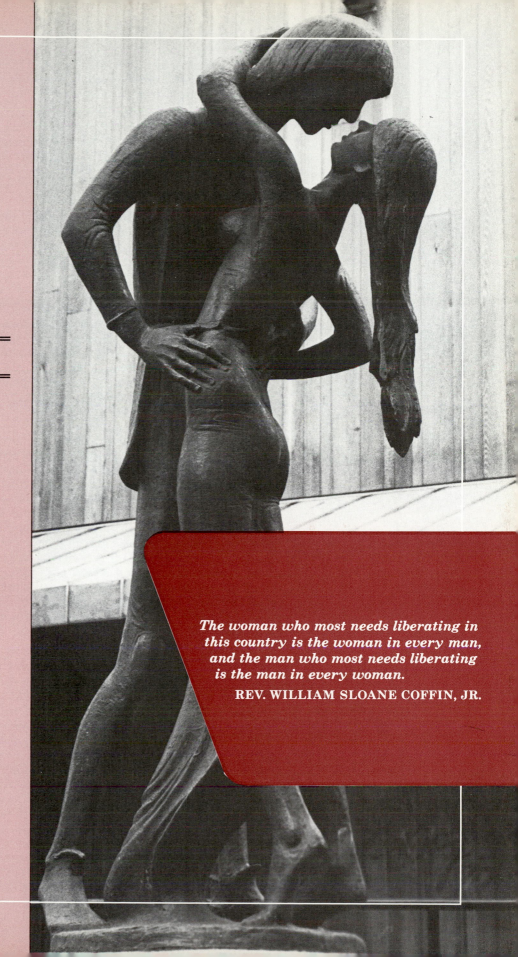

Summary

Applying Psychology to Your Life: Learning to Be Assertive

DEFINING ASSERTIVENESS

ASSERTIVENESS TRAINING

The woman who most needs liberating in this country is the woman in every man, and the man who most needs liberating is the man in every woman.

REV. WILLIAM SLOANE COFFIN, JR.

"I wanted to be a doctor, but I was told in direct and indirect ways that my ultimate ambition should be marrying a doctor and raising a family. I gave up my dream."

"For me the evidence of my mental competence was unavoidable, and I never had any trouble defending or voicing my opinion with men, because I beat them in all the tests. Consequently, none of them would come near me in my first seventeen years of life."

—Two women quoted in *Our Bodies, Ourselves* (Boston Women's Health Book Collective, 1973, p. 7)

"I could have made her feel better," said the young man, "if I'd told her that I had trouble speaking in class because I was very self-conscious. But instead of telling her (which would have helped me too), I didn't say anything. Trivial as it was, I couldn't bring myself to say that I, at twenty-one, a man who hoped to be a great writer, couldn't raise my hand in class."

"I play the reassuring, protective father. She is my faithful, dependent child. Her faith and dependency are a form of reassurance and support for me. But there are days when I would like to come to her, as she comes to me, as a child, to tell her that I was hurt when my roommate didn't think my seminar professor liked me anymore—but I could never bring myself to talk about such sentimental drivel even though I wanted to."

—Two men quoted in *Dilemmas of Masculinity* (Komarovsky, 1976, p. 165)

The women and men quoted above feel "boxed in" by sex roles. They all are struggling with limitations placed on their behavior by virtue of their sex. They are not unique or even unusual. All of us have to face up to the dilemmas of being masculine or feminine. Surely you have had occasions when you did or did not do something because it was considered appropriate or inappropriate for your sex. You may not think about it much, and you may not resent it like the people quoted above, but it is an undeniable fact that your **gender** has a pervasive impact on your behavior. In particular, it influences how you relate to others of both sexes. In this chapter, I will examine the role of gender in our lives; I will focus on how it affects our interpersonal relationships and adjustment. To be more specific, I will discuss sex-related stereotypes, the actual evidence on sex differences, the acquisition of sex roles, the costs of traditional sex roles, and the future influence of gender in our lives.

GENDER. *A classificatory term that has other uses but generally refers to a person's biological sex.*

Sex Differences

SEX DIFFERENCES. *Usually used to refer to disparities between the sexes in behavior.*

The term **sex differences** is generally used to refer to *behavioral* rather than biological disparities between the sexes. Obviously, women and men are biologically different. Besides the readily apparent anatomical dissimilarities, there are many subtler differences in physiological functioning. For the most part, I will not concern myself with these physical disparities (except as they relate to behavioral differences). Instead, I am going to review research on how and why the sexes differ in ability, personality, and social behavior. I will begin by examining popular stereotypes about sex differences. I will then briefly summarize the scientific evidence on sex differences.

STEREOTYPES ABOUT SEX DIFFERENCES

You may recall from Chapter 6 that **stereotypes** are widely shared beliefs that people have certain characteristics because of their membership in some group. Stereotypes based on sex are very prevalent in our society. Research

STEREOTYPE. *A popular, usually oversimplified belief about some group of people; involves inaccurate overgeneralization.*

(Broverman et al., 1972) indicates that there is a great deal of consensus on supposed behavioral differences between men and women. In fact, this consensus seems to transcend age, sex, marital status, and educational background.

These sex-related stereotypes are too numerous to summarize here. Instead, you can examine Table 8.1, which lists 41 behavioral characteristics thought to be associated with femininity or masculinity. This list is based on a study (Broverman et al., 1972) in which subjects were asked to indicate the extent to which various traits were characteristic of each sex. The traits listed are those for which there was at least 75% agreement among respondents of *both* sexes. Although the list may contain a few surprises, you have probably encountered most of these stereotypes before. After all, we all know that women are more passive, dependent, emotional, irrational, submissive, persuasible, insecure,

**TABLE 8.1   Stereotypic sex-role items
(responses from 74 college men and 80 college women)**

Competency cluster: Masculine pole is more desirable	
Feminine	*Masculine*
Not at all aggressive	Very aggressive
Not at all independent	Very independent
Very emotional	Not at all emotional
Does not hide emotions at all	Almost always hides emotions
Very subjective	Very objective
Very easily influenced	Not at all easily influenced
Very submissive	Very dominant
Dislikes math and science very much	Likes math and science very much
Very excitable in a minor crisis	Not at all excitable in a minor crisis
Very passive	Very active
Not at all competitive	Very competitive
Very illogical	Very logical
Very home-oriented	Very worldly
Not at all skilled in business	Very skilled in business
Very sneaky	Very direct
Does not know the way of the world	Knows the way of the world
Feelings easily hurt	Feelings not easily hurt
Not at all adventurous	Very adventurous
Has difficulty making decisions	Can make decisions easily
Cries very easily	Never cries
Almost never acts as a leader	Almost always acts as a leader
Not at all self-confident	Very self-confident
Very uncomfortable about being aggressive	Not at all uncomfortable about being aggressive
Not at all ambitious	Very ambitious
Unable to separate feelings from ideas	Easily able to separate feelings from ideas
Very dependent	Not at all dependent
Very conceited about appearance	Never conceited about appearance
Thinks women are always superior to men	Thinks men are always superior to women
Does not talk freely about sex with men	Talks freely about sex with men

Warmth-expressiveness cluster: Feminine pole is more desirable	
Feminine	*Masculine*
Doesn't use harsh language at all	Uses very harsh language
Very talkative	Not at all talkative
Very tactful	Very blunt
Very gentle	Very rough
Very aware of feelings of others	Not at all aware of feelings of others
Very religious	Not at all religious
Very interested in own appearance	Not at all interested in own appearance
Very neat in habits	Very sloppy in habits
Very quiet	Very loud
Very strong need for security	Very little need for security
Enjoys art and literature	Does not enjoy art and literature at all
Easily expresses tender feelings	Does not express tender feelings at all easily

talkative, and conceited than men. Or do we? We'll examine the reality of the situation in a moment.

Before I review the actual evidence on sex differences, one other point should be emphasized. In sex-related stereotypes, women definitely get the short end of the stick. The popular male stereotype is far more complimentary than the conventional female stereotype. The list in Table 8.1 blatantly suggests that men have cornered the market on competence and rationality. In contrast, the female stereotype is highly negative and sometimes downright demeaning.

CURRENT EVIDENCE ABOUT SEX DIFFERENCES

Now that I have set the stage by reviewing popular stereotypes about sex differences, it is time to examine the actual evidence. The research in this area is not easy to summarize, because there is an enormous volume of studies, many of which report conflicting findings. Moreover, it is a very active research area, with new evidence pouring in constantly. The task is further complicated by the fact that the meaning of research findings in this area is often hotly debated. Nonetheless, I will try to give you a coherent and up-to-date overview of the empirical evidence on sex differences.

A few other preliminary points are in order. First, as you read about the behavioral differences between the sexes, you should not jump to the conclusion that these are biologically built in. I will address this question later. Second, it should be stressed that we will be looking at sex differences only in modern Western culture. The story is quite different for many other cultures. Third, the fact that there are indeed some behavioral differences between the sexes does not in any way justify the widespread discrimination that takes place against women. I will pursue this point in some detail later.

Finally, in examining sex differences it is crucial that you understand that these are mean *group* differences, which tell us nothing about individuals. Essentially, we are comparing the "average man" against the "average woman." The problem is that every individual is unique; the average female and male are ultimately figments of our imagination, existing only in theory. Figure 8.1 illustrates this point. It shows how scores on some trait might be distributed differently for men and women. You can see that the *average* scores for the two sexes are somewhat discrepant, indicating the existence of a group sex difference. Let's assume that the trait in question is empathy, with women scoring a bit higher, on the average, than men. Note that even when there is a bona fide difference between the group averages, there is still a great deal of overlap between the two group distributions. *Thus, although men may be less empathic than women on the average, there are nonetheless plenty of men who are more empathic than plenty of women.* This graphic illustration should drive home the point that group differences, although they may be interesting and instructive, tell us little about individuals. With this in mind, let us look at the evidence on some of these group differences.

COGNITIVE ABILITIES

There are some differences between the sexes in specific cognitive skills. In their massive review of research on sex differences, Eleanor Maccoby and Carol Jacklin (1974) report that three such disparities appear fairly well documented. First, women are superior to men in *verbal ability*. Females perform somewhat better than males on a variety of verbal tests, with the gap opening up during early adolescence. Second, on tests of *mathematical ability*, males show an advantage. This advantage first surfaces with consistency after the age of 12 or 13. Third, males also display better *visual-spatial ability* (see Figure 8.2) than females. Like the other differences in cognitive abilities, this disparity emerges during adolescence. It should be emphasized that these sex differences in mental abilities are quite small (Sherman, 1978).

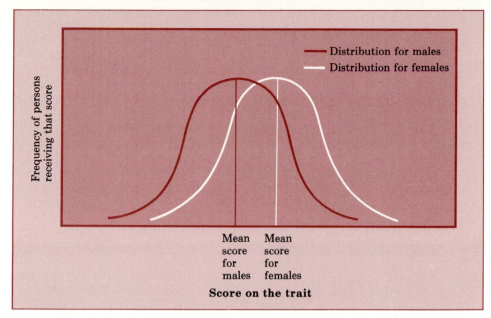

FIGURE 8.1 Examples of distribution of scores for each sex that might lead to statistically significant sex differences in a trait. Note that the distributions overlap considerably.

FIELD DEPENDENCE. *A cognitive style, measured by perceptual tests, that involves the degree to which one's perceptions are influenced by the surrounding visual field or context.*

It is also commonly reported that women and men differ in cognitive style. This conclusion is based on research by Herman Witkin (1964) indicating that women are relatively field-dependent and men are more field-independent. **Field dependence** is the degree to which an individual's perceptions are influenced by the visual field surrounding the object to be perceived. This cognitive style can be measured with several perceptual devices, of which the most commonly used is the Embedded Figures Test (see Figure 8.3). People who are field-independent are relatively good at spotting the embedded figures and are characterized as "analytic." Field-dependent subjects, who have a tougher time sorting out the contextual cues, aren't as good at recognizing the embedded figures and are characterized as "global." It is this sex difference in field dependence that has led to the often-voiced belief that men are analytic while women are global in cognitive style. *However, these broad generalizations about sex differences in cognitive style do not appear to be justified.* Sherman (1967) has argued convincingly that males' greater field independence is due simply to their superior visual-spatial ability and that it does not reflect a far-reaching difference between the sexes in cognitive style.

PERSONALITY

A great number of personality traits have been examined in research on sex differences. I will discuss those that have attracted the most attention.

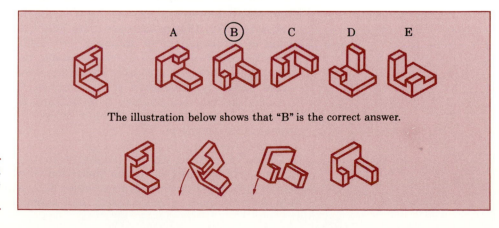

The illustration below shows that "B" is the correct answer.

FIGURE 8.2 Sample item and solution from a test of spatial ability.

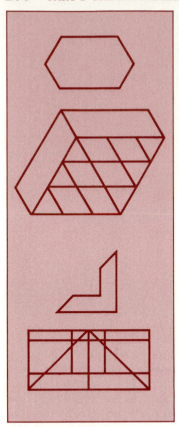

FIGURE 8.3 Examples of drawings used in the Embedded Figures Test. The object is to identify the simple figures in the more complex ones.

Aggressiveness. Men do tend to be more aggressive than women (Maccoby & Jacklin, 1974). This is true for both physical and verbal aggression. This disparity shows up early in childhood. Its continuation through adulthood is verified by the fact that men account for a grossly disproportionate amount of violent crime. There may be a few circumstances in which the sexes are equally prone to aggression (Frodi, Macaulay, & Thome, 1977), but generally males are more combative than females.

Influenceability and conformity. It is commonly believed that females are highly susceptible to persuasion, conforming, and compliant. The empirical evidence does *not* support this belief. Although it is true that young girls comply with adults' requests more readily than young boys (Maccoby & Jacklin, 1974), there is little support for the notion that women are more easily influenced and more conforming than men (Eagly, 1978).

Emotionality. Popular stereotypes suggest that men react to stressful events with less emotion than women. Supposedly, men are more likely to remain cool and calm. The empirical evidence on this issue is sparse, but the meager data available do *not* support the stereotype. In fact, Maccoby and Jacklin (1974) note that in reacting to frustration males are more emotionally volatile than females. The belief in females' emotional reactivity is probably due to the fact that they *are* more willing than men to openly acknowledge their emotions. However, this does not mean that women are more emotional than men; it merely means that men are trained to hide their emotions while women are not.

Passivity. Like many of the personality traits studied in this area, passivity has different meanings for different investigators. I will define passivity as a lack of assertiveness. In regard to this dimension, it is widely believed that women are relatively passive while men are more assertive and domineering. Though not entirely consistent, the empirical evidence appears to support this stereotype. For example, O'Leary (1977) cites various studies showing that in mixed-sex groups women talk less than men and are less likely to influence group processes or assume leadership roles. Similarly, after reviewing the evidence, Block (1976) concludes that males make more efforts at dominance than females. It is this relative passivity that has led to the increasing popularity of assertiveness training for women (see the application section of this chapter).

SOCIAL ORIENTATION AND SKILLS

Sociability. It is commonly believed that women have a stronger social orientation than men. According to this notion, women are interested in people, while men are more interested in objects. One kind of evidence that is often cited to support this assertion is the finding (for example, Angrist & Almquist, 1975) that women are more likely than men to put family concerns ahead of career demands. However, this difference in priorities seems to be virtually forced on women by requirements inherent in the traditional homemaker role, and it relates only in a very distant way to sociability. In their review, Maccoby and Jacklin (1974) conclude that women and men are similar in social interest, time devoted to socializing, and responsiveness to social reinforcement. Thus, the sex difference between men and women in sociability appears to be mythical.

Love. According to conventional stereotypes, women are more dependent on love relationships with men than vice versa. However, the empirical data suggest just the opposite! For example, Hill, Rubin, and Peplau (1976) found that men fall *in* love more easily than women, while women fall *out* of love more readily. They also observed that men tended to be more despondent than women after the breakup of a relationship. Along the same lines, Kanin, Davidson, and Scheck (1970) found that men were more romantic than women. Furthermore, in Chapter 11 I will review evidence that suggests that marriage is more important to men than to women. Thus, if there are any sex differences in regard to the importance attributed to intimate relationships, it appears that men are more concerned about love than women are.

Empathy.   Some research *does* support the stereotype that women are more sensitive to the feelings of others than men. Although the difference appears small, females do indeed score higher than males on various measures of empathy (Hoffman, 1977). It remains to be seen whether this difference might simply be due to females' greater willingness to *express* empathy because it is more consistent with their sex role.

Sensitivity to nonverbal communication.   Although it is not part of the conventional package of stereotypes, it appears that there may be a sex difference in sensitivity to nonverbal cues in communication. In a review of 75 studies, Hall (1978) concludes that women are more accurate than men in decoding nonverbal signals. The superiority of women in this area fits in neatly with their greater empathy. As usual, the difference is small in magnitude.

Nurturance.   Nurturance consists in the provision of help, physical care, and emotional support to others. Usually, the term is used in reference to caring for children. In this regard, it is widely assumed that women are predisposed to be nurturant, whereas men are not. In other words, women are thought to have "maternal instincts." The fact is that we do not have adequate evidence about whether women are more nurturant than men (Maccoby & Jacklin, 1974). The assumption about maternal instincts is so deeply rooted that only a handful of studies have been conducted. The evidence from these studies is ambiguous and certainly does not provide solid support for the existence of maternal instincts. It is clear that women are assigned more responsibility for nurturance in our society, but it is an open question whether women are predisposed to be more nurturant than men.

8.1   ARE MALES THE "SECOND" SEX?

The male is a biological accident: the Y (male) gene is an incomplete X (female) gene, that is, has an incomplete set of chromosomes. In other words, the male is an incomplete female, a walking abortion, aborted at the gene stage.

–Valerie Solanis (quoted in Cox, 1976, p. 29)

Although the quotation above is something of a strident overstatement, it *is* based on a little-known biological fact. Contrary to Biblical legend, which suggests that women were derived from men, biological evidence indicates that it would be more appropriate to regard males as a derivative of females. Although the entire question is rather nonsensical, the contrast between folklore and reality is interesting.

A child's sex is determined by the father's contribution to the twenty-third pair of chromosomes. If pop provides an X chromosome, the resulting XX configuration should eventually yield a female. If he provides a Y chromosome, the resulting XY pairing should yield a male. However, during the first six weeks of fetal development, the embryo actually has the potential to go either way in terms of anatomical sex differentiation. This flexibility is illustrated by the fact that occasionally aberrations in prenatal development lead to reversals of the genetic coding.

Of interest to us presently is the finding (Money & Ehrhardt, 1972) that during those first six weeks the fundamental structure of the embryo is female. In order for a male to develop, the Y chromosome must do its job and trigger male gonadal differentiation while suppressing the possible female gonadal differentiation. Insofar as it makes sense to regard one sex as more "basic" than the other, it appears that females earn this distinction. Hence, it would seem more appropriate to regard males as the "second" sex.

SEXUALITY

There *are* some important differences between the sexes in their expression of sexuality. I will discuss most of these differences in Chapter 12. At the moment, I will confine myself to a consideration of the popular stereotype that men are more interested in sex, and have a stronger sex drive, than women.

It is true that men are more sexually active than women, engaging in more masturbation, more premarital sex, and more extramarital sex and preferring more marital sex (Hunt, 1974). These disparities, which appear attributable to differences in upbringing rather than biology, would seem to support the idea that men are conditioned to have a stronger sex drive. However, as attitudes about sex have changed in recent years, the gap between women and men in sexual activity has narrowed (Curran, 1975). Moreover, in recent experiments studying subjects' response to erotic stimuli (for example, Fisher & Byrne, 1978; Heiman, 1975), women have displayed every bit as much lust as men.

In summary, it is probably still true today that men, as a group, pursue sex more actively than women do. However, recent research findings suggest that this gap may be much smaller than commonly believed, may be shrinking rapidly with changing attitudes, and may even be nonexistent in younger age groups.

PSYCHOLOGICAL HEALTH

Statistics on mental illness and its treatment show that there are substantially more female patients than male patients in psychotherapy (Al-Issa, 1982). It has been estimated that women patients outnumber men by about two to one (Gove & Tudor, 1973). It should be emphasized, however, that these figures do *not* prove that men generally enjoy better psychological health than women. It may be simply that women are more willing than men to acknowledge their problems and pursue professional help. Men *may* have just as many adjustment problems, but their reluctance to seek help may obscure this reality. This interpretation is supported by a study (Srole et al., 1962) in which researchers fanned out over Manhattan one day, interviewing people in their homes in order to assess their mental health. This approach nullified the possible sex difference in willingness to seek therapy. The researchers found *no* relationship between sex and their estimates of subjects' mental health.

Another possible factor contributing to the excess of women in psychotherapy may be a sex bias in diagnosis. Phyllis Chesler (1972) argues, with some merit, that the male-dominated psychiatric establishment is overly eager to label women as "crazy," "neurotic," and "depressed." She views this alleged bias as a device to keep women "in line" by coercing them into adhering to traditional roles. This bias in labeling may be even stronger in laypersons than in mental-health professionals. Thus, many women may be propelled into therapy by their husbands' derogatory remarks about their "neurotic" qualities. Although it is doubtful that this sex bias alone accounts for the higher number of female patients (Scarf, 1979), it probably contributes to the inequality.

It is possible, however, that women actually do suffer through more psychological problems than men. As I shall discuss later in this chapter, women have probably had their psychological growth blunted by sex-role restrictions more than men. Traditionally, women have been assigned inferior roles and status that would appear to carry with them special sources of frustration and discontent (Marecek, 1978). Therefore, we presently are not sure just how to interpret the fact that women end up in therapy considerably more often than men.

It should also be noted that the sexes differ in what *kinds* of disorders they are most likely to develop (Marecek, 1978). Women are most vulnerable to problems centering on excessive anxiety and to depression. They are much more likely than men to *attempt* suicide. However, men are more prone to antisocial behavior, alcoholism, and drug abuse.

SUMMARY

Overall, *the empirical evidence does not support the popular stereotypes about women and men.* In a few areas the stereotypes are consistent with the evidence, but for the most part, the stereotypes bear little relation to reality. Instead, they promote errors in social perception. They lead many people to view themselves and others inaccurately. Moreover, this inaccuracy may often be detrimental to one's psychological health and social relationships.

Another point worth making is that although there *are* some bona fide behavioral differences between the sexes, they are merely *group* differences with a great deal of overlap between the groups. Moreover, the differences appear to be smaller and fewer than commonly believed. In other words, in regard to personality, ability, and social behavior, men and women are not nearly as different as conventional wisdom suggests. *Ultimately, the similarities greatly outweigh the differences.*

EXPLAINING SEX DIFFERENCES: NATURE VERSUS NURTURE

SOCIALIZATION. *The process of rearing children in such a way that they learn the norms of a particular society.*

Are the sex differences that do exist acquired through learning, or are they biologically built in? Until now, I have deferred tackling this sensitive and controversial question. Essentially, it represents the age-old "nature versus nurture" issue, which pits heredity against the environment as the prime determinant of behavior. The "nature" theorists concentrate on how biological differences between the sexes may contribute to behavioral dissimilarities. The "nurture" theorists focus on how disparities in the **socialization** of women and men may account for behavioral differences. Today, virtually all theorists recognize the validity of the *interactionist* viewpoint and acknowledge that *both* biology and socialization play a significant role in governing behavior. *However, a great debate still rages over the relative contributions of biology and socialization to the development of sex differences.*

HISTORICAL OVERVIEW OF THE CONTROVERSY

The popularity of biologically based explanations for sex differences has had a curious history. The "anatomy is destiny" doctrine was widely accepted during the first half of the 20th century, dropped dramatically in popularity during the 1960s and 1970s, and is now making something of a comeback. During the early part of the century, researchers simply *assumed* that of course sex differ-

---

8.2   ARE WOMEN VICTIMS OF PENIS ENVY?

The concept of "penis envy" plays a pivotal role in psychoanalytic theories of sex-role development. According to Freud, when little girls discover that little boys are built differently, they feel shocked, cheated, and envious. Furthermore, Freud felt that this envy of males' anatomical features provided the basis for allegedly feminine characteristics such as inferiority feelings, vanity, and passivity.

The construct of penis envy has been attacked on a variety of theoretical grounds (for example, Horney, 1922/1973). Critics point out that insofar as women may envy men, this can easily be explained by the fact that women have been saddled with inferior roles and status in Western society.

More significantly, there is little evidence to suggest that such envy actually exists in women (Sherman, 1971). Illustrative of this reality is the reaction of a female classmate of mine during our undergraduate days. We were listening to a lecture on Freudian theory in which the professor was expounding eloquently and emphatically on the crucial role of penis envy. My friend Terry was quite skeptical and replied to the professor that *she* had *not* experienced envy when she discovered that boys and girls have different genitalia. On the contrary, she recalled that her feelings went something like this: "When I discovered that little boys were built different, I *was* surprised. However, I don't remember feeling cheated or jealous. Rather, I recall feeling *sorry* for them, because they had to carry all that *extra garbage* around with them." So much for penis envy!

FRONTAL LOBES. *One of four divisions of each cerebral hemisphere. This area is located toward the front of the skull and is involved in fine motor activity and speech.*

PARIETAL LOBES. *One of four divisions of each cerebral hemisphere. This area is located toward the upper rear area of the cerebrum and is involved in the detection of body position.*

CEREBRAL HEMISPHERES. *The cerebrum, the largest and most prominent structural division of the human brain, is located in the upper area of the cranium and is covered by the cerebral cortex. It is involved in higher mental processes and consists of a right and a left hemisphere, which are connected by the corpus callosum.*

LATERALIZATION. *Functional specialization in the cerebral hemispheres. The more a person appears to depend on a particular hemisphere to handle a task, the more lateralized the person is said to be for that task.*

ences were due largely to biological factors (Shields, 1975). The bias of the male-dominated scientific community was so strong that scholars managed to find "proof" that the **frontal lobes** of the brain, thought to be the seat of reason, were larger in men than in women! However, Shields (1975) notes that when evidence surfaced to suggest that the **parietal lobes** rather than the frontal lobes were crucial to complex cognition, the scientific community suddenly found that males had a size advantage in the parietal area instead! It is now clear that there are no meaningful size differences between male and female brains. *The story simply illustrates how sex bias can contaminate scientific research on sex differences.*

As it became clear that early research linking sex differences to biology was marred by severe methodological flaws, the pendulum swung the other way. Buoyed by the growing popularity of behaviorism and by egalitarian concerns stimulated by the feminist movement, the environmental viewpoint became dominant. During the 1960s and 1970s, the scientific consensus was that sex differences were produced almost entirely by sex-related differences in child rearing and socialization.

RECENT RESEARCH ON BRAIN ORGANIZATION

In the latter part of the 1970s, the momentum shifted yet again. Goleman (1978) reported on a host of studies purporting to show a biological basis for certain sex differences. *Generating the greatest interest was research that suggested that male and female brains may differ in hemispheric organization.* As you may know, the human brain is divided into two **cerebral hemispheres.** There is evidence (for example, Ornstein, 1972; Weiten & Etaugh, 1974) that the right and left hemispheres are "specialized" to handle different cognitive tasks (see Figure 8.4). For example, it appears that in most people the *left hemisphere* is more actively involved in *verbal processing,* while the *right hemisphere* is specialized to handle *spatial problems.*

Through a number of complex procedures it is possible to estimate the *degree* to which a person shows hemispheric specialization on a particular task. This trend toward specialization is often called **lateralization.** As evidence began to suggest that verbal and spatial processing were two of the most strongly lateralized cognitive functions, investigators began to wonder whether there might be a connection between neurological organization and the well-known sex differences in these areas. Consequently, they began looking for sex disparities in brain lateralization. According to McGlone (1980), a number of researchers appear to have found such disparities. Basically, what has been observed is that men seem to be more highly specialized than women. *Men seem to be lateralized more strongly to the left for verbal processing, and more strongly to the right for spatial processing, than women.*

These findings are provocative, but we have a long way to go before we can explain sex differences in verbal and spatial ability neurologically. The first problem is that the data indicating men are more strongly lateralized than women have been challenged and are the source of much controversy (Harris, 1980; Kinsbourne, 1980). Moreover, even if men *do* have stronger brain lateralization than women, *no one is really sure just how that would account for the observed sex differences in cognitive abilities.* It seems peculiar that strong lateralization would produce for males an advantage on one kind of task (spatial) and a disadvantage on another kind of task (verbal). Thus, the theory linking cerebral lateralization to sex differences in cognition remains highly speculative.

THE CASE FOR SOCIALIZATION

Although recent years have witnessed a resurgence of interest in linking sex differences to biology, it would seem fair to say that most experts still believe that socialization is the key to understanding the development of sex differences. The "bottom line" is that efforts to explain sex differences through

HOW THE BRAIN DIVIDES ITS WORK

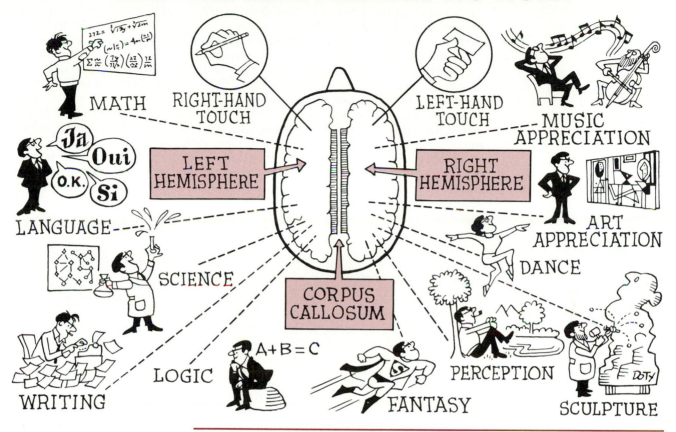

FIGURE 8.4 A cartoonist's conception of the two hemispheres of the cerebrum and how they divide their work.

biology simply haven't been very successful (Frieze et al., 1978).

After decades of research, we still do not have any solid evidence linking obvious hormonal differences between the sexes to behavioral differences in a clear way. For example, even the assumed link between hormonal fluctuations and the legendary **premenstrual syndrome** in women has been seriously questioned. The premenstrual syndrome involves an alleged negative shift in mood, including increased anxiety, depression, irritability, and hostility, just before a menstrual period. Although some researchers believe that it is a by-product of hormonal changes (for example, Bardwick, 1971), the evidence for this thesis has been effectively criticized as methodologically unsound (Parlee, 1973). The purported link between hormones and the premenstrual syndrome has been further undermined by evidence suggesting (1) that the syndrome emerges at least partly out of social training (Paige, 1973) and (2) that the syndrome is less common than popularly believed (Moos, 1968). Most scientists (for example, Diamond, 1977) remain convinced that hormonal disparities contribute to sex differences, but the overall evidence suggests that they probably play a relatively minor role (Money & Ehrhardt, 1972). In contrast, researchers pursuing evidence connecting sex differences with disparities in the way males and females are socialized have had greater success. They have accumulated considerable evidence showing how differences in upbringing are logically related to differences in behavior.

Finally, cross-cultural studies by anthropologists seem more consistent with environmental than with biological explanations of sex differences. There is a

PREMENSTRUAL SYNDROME. *Negative shift in mood believed to occur in women a few days before menstruation.*

cross-cultural consistency in sex differences, but there is some rather dramatic variability as well (Munroe & Munroe, 1975). For instance, Margaret Mead (1950) studied three tribes in New Guinea and found one in which *both* sexes were similar to our masculine stereotype (the Mundugumor), one in which *both* sexes approximated our feminine role (the Arapesh), and one in which the male and female roles were roughly the *reverse* of our own (the Tchambuli; see Box 8.3). If biology exerted a very strong influence over sex differences, one would not expect to see such remarkable discrepancies between cultures that existed within 100 miles of one another.

In conclusion, the preponderance of scientific evidence suggests that sex differences are largely acquired through learning. The physiological differences between the sexes may very well contribute in subtle ways to development of sex differences, but it appears that their contribution is small in relation to the contribution of the environment. Therefore, I will turn in the next section to a more detailed analysis of how sex-role socialization differentially shapes males and females.

Socialization of Sex Roles

Let's begin this section with a brief riddle.

> A boy and his father are in an automobile accident. The father is killed, and the boy is seriously injured. The boy is rushed to the hospital and taken into the operating room. A few minutes later, the surgeon comes out of the operating room and says "I cannot operate on this boy; he is my son." Justify this set of facts.

In view of the topic at hand (sex roles), you probably had little difficulty with the above riddle. The answer is really quite simple: the surgeon is the boy's mother. A surprisingly high number of people fail to recognize this when the riddle isn't placed in the middle of a chapter on sex roles. Many people have a hard time conceiving of a female surgeon; in their minds "it just doesn't compute." Such attitudes, by the way, are *not* a thing of the past. I know a young woman who began medical school recently. When that fact surfaces among casual acquaintances, an astonishing number of apparently intelligent people inquire about how she likes studying *nursing*. After all, we all know that, in the medical field, doctors are *men;* women are nurses. These are the *roles* traditionally prescribed for men and women in our society.

ROLE. *The behavior expected of a person in a particular social position and situation.*

A **role** involves a set of behaviors that are considered appropriate for someone in a particular social position (Shaw & Costanzo, 1970). Roles are products

---

8.3 *CULTURE AND SEX ROLES: THE STARTLING EXAMPLE OF THE TCHAMBULI*

In the early part of this century, the anthropologist Margaret Mead (1950) conducted some fascinating research on sex differences in three primitive cultures that coexisted within 100 miles of one another in New Guinea. Most interesting were the Tchambuli, who showed sex roles and sex differences that were almost exactly the *opposite* of those believed to exist in Western culture.

Consider these descriptions. The females were the dominant sex; they were practical, took care of economic matters, and "brought home the bacon" through fishing. In terms of personality, they were character-

ized as assertive, aggressive, impersonal, and self-reliant. In contrast, the men stayed home and made trinkets to adorn themselves and gossiped with one another. In terms of personality, the males were described as dependent, timid, suspicious, skittish, and sensitive.

Although the role reversal was not complete (the men were still the warriors), the transposition was quite dramatic and led Mead to conclude that culture (that is, the environment) is the major determinant of sex-related differences in behavior.

SEX ROLES. *Expectations for someone's behavior based simply on his or her gender.*

of societal norms, and they consist basically of *expectations* that certain people should behave in certain ways. **Sex roles** involve expectations about a person's behavior that are based on that person's sex. For example, we expect women to sew, do laundry, and cook meals, while we expect men to watch football, tinker with cars, and be the family "breadwinner."

Sex roles, as well as other roles, are acquired through the mechanism of socialization. *Socialization* is a far-reaching term that refers to all the efforts made by society to ensure that its children learn to behave in a manner that is considered appropriate. It includes all the techniques used by a society to put its unique imprint on its children. In this section I will talk about this socialization process as it applies to sex roles. More specifically, I will try to explain how our society trains children about sex roles and how these roles account for the previously discussed behavioral differences between the sexes. I will then discuss how the limitations inherent in sex roles may be psychologically costly to both women and men.

PROCESSES INVOLVED IN SEX-ROLE SOCIALIZATION

Sex-role socialization takes place through several key learning processes. These include differential imitation, differential reinforcement, and self-socialization.

DIFFERENTIAL IMITATION

According to observational-learning theory (Mischel, 1970), young children develop a tendency to imitate same-sex models more than opposite-sex models. Young girls imitate mommy's behavior, playing with dolls, dollhouses, toy stoves, and so forth. Young boys tinker with toy trucks and cars, miniature gas stations, and so forth. Experts believe that differential imitation takes place for two reasons. First, children are thought to be more likely to imitate someone whom they perceive to be similar to themselves. Second, it is believed that

Sex-role socialization begins early in life, as boys learn to tinker with cars and girls learn to do household chores.

boys get more exposure to male models than girls and that girls get more exposure to female models than boys. According to this notion, dad is likely to take Johnny with him to the auto-parts store, while Mary goes grocery shopping with mom. Similarly, girls and boys spend more time with same-sex peers, who serve as each other's models.

This intuitively appealing theory of differential imitation was severely undermined when Maccoby and Jacklin (1974) published their classic review and reported that the evidence did *not* support the theory. However, Perry and Bussey (1979) point out that most of the studies examined by Maccoby and Jacklin used highly unrealistic and artificial laboratory situations (unfamiliar models performing unfamiliar tasks), which could hardly be expected to generate sex-typed imitation. Perry and Bussey (1979) further reported on more-recent studies that *have* provided support for the hypothesis that differential imitation promotes the acquisition of sex roles.

DIFFERENTIAL REINFORCEMENT

It is also believed (Mischel, 1970) that parents, teachers, and peers reinforce "sex-appropriate" behavior while responding negatively to "sex-inappropriate" behavior. For example, a young boy who has just hurt himself may be told by his dad that "men don't cry." If the child succeeds in inhibiting his crying, he may get a pat on the back, a warm smile, or even an ice-cream cone. Actually, the evidence suggests that parents may use differential *punishment* more than differential reward and that they pay more attention to shaping behavior in boys than in girls (O'Leary, 1977). Thus, if a young boy wants to play with a dollhouse, he probably will elicit a negative response from his parents.

SELF-SOCIALIZATION

According to Kohlberg (1966), once children recognize their gender and the fact that it is a permanent feature, they actively pursue information about how males and females are supposed to behave. Thus, children may be more than passive receptors of socialization through modeling and reinforcement. Rather, they may get actively involved in their own socialization, working diligently to discover the "rules" that are supposed to govern their behavior.

SOURCES OF SEX-ROLE SOCIALIZATION

There are three *main* sources of sex-role socialization. These can be thought of as the locales in which the processes just described operate. These three major sources of socialization are the home, the school, and the media.

THE HOME

Obviously, a great deal of sex-role socialization occurs in the home. Although there is no sensible reason for it, parents usually dress infants in different colors from the very beginning. When a child is a mere *three weeks* old, mothers have been observed playing more roughly with boys than with girls (Moss, 1967). As children grow, the parents typically buy quite different toys and clothes for girls and for boys. When the kids are old enough to help with household chores, the assignments are very dependent on sex—laundry and dishes for the girls, mowing the lawn and sweeping the garage for the boys. Likewise, the leisure activities that children are encouraged to engage in vary by sex—Johnny is shipped off to Little League practice, while Mary gets piano lessons. In light of these patterns, it is not surprising that parents' attitudes about sex roles have been shown to influence the acquisition of sex roles in their children (Repetti, 1984).

THE SCHOOL

Schools also make a major contribution to the socialization of sex roles (Etaugh, Collins, & Gerson, 1975). In the early years, many grade-school readers provide a very thorough and remarkably sexist indoctrination regarding the characteristics of males and females. One survey of some 134 books (Women on Words and Images, 1972) found that boy-centered stories outnumbered girl-centered stories 5 to 2! In these stories, boys got to display cleverness 131 times, while girls were clever only 33 times. Girls were shown doing domestic chores more than three times as often as boys (see Box 8.4 for more information). As youngsters progress through the school system, they are quite intentionally channeled in different directions. Boys are told to take mathematics, while girls are told to take home economics. Males are encouraged to be doctors, lawyers, and engineers, while females are encouraged to be nurses, secretaries, and homemakers.

THE MEDIA

Television is still another significant source of sex-role indoctrination (Morgan, 1982). Youngsters in the United States watch an awful lot of TV—about 25 to 30 hours a week (Singer & Singer, 1981). Although there has been a *little* improvement in recent years, women on TV have typically been portrayed as loving mothers and dedicated homemakers, while men get dynamic, exciting roles as cool, competent leaders. When scriptwriters finally give a heroic role to a woman, they very likely have men coming to her aid at the last minute. Moreover, the commercials are even worse than the show. Women are shown worrying about the ring around their husbands' collars, how shiny their dishes are, and how to use expensive cosmetics to "snare" a man. Even when women are shown in their alleged domain of expertise—the kitchen—they are often portrayed as incompetent, requiring advice from a male repairman on how to get their dishes cleaner or their laundry whiter. A recent finding demonstrates strikingly just how influential television can be in sex-role socialization. As you may have noticed, children's shows on public/educational TV often work systematically to promote nontraditional sex roles. Repetti (1984) found that children who watch a great deal of educational TV tend to be much less traditional in their sex-role stereotyping than other children. Thus, there appears to be a clear link between media content and the acquisition of sex roles.

8.4   *DICK AND JANE AS VICTIMS OF SEX-ROLE STEREOTYPING*

As I mention in the text proper, grade-school readers are a major source of sex-role socialization. In itself, this is not particularly surprising. However, the sheer *size* of the gap between the male and female portrayals is quite startling. Statistics compiled in a survey of some 134 readers (Women on Words and Images, 1972) show that the sex-related disparities are enormous. In a total of 2760 stories, the following trends were found.

1. Boy-centered stories outnumbered girl-centered stories by a ratio of 5 to 2.
2. As *adult* main characters, men appeared three times as often as women.
3. Biographies, which may be inspirational to children, showed a 6-to-1 ratio in favor of males. A total of 88 men were profiled in 119 stories, while only 17 women were similarly honored in 27 stories.
4. Boys were found to display clever resourcefulness in 131 stories, while girls got to appear clever only 33 times.
5. Heroic themes were common, but boys virtually cornered the market on heroism, with a tally of 143 to 36.
6. Similarly, adventures were largely awarded to the boys, with the comparative score stacking up at 216 to 68.
7. In spite of the 5:2 ratio in favor of boy-centered stories, girls managed to get involved in domestic chores 166 times, while boys were shown in similar activities only 50 times.
8. Also defying the 5:2 ratio, girls were portrayed as passive and docile 119 times, whereas boys displayed docility on only 19 occasions.
9. Adult males were invariably awarded breadwinner roles, while women were portrayed as traditional homemakers. A mere *3* working mothers showed up in the 2760 stories reviewed!

Costs of Traditional Sex Roles

SANDRA BEM

Many psychologists are arriving at the conclusion that some unfortunate costs are associated with traditional sex roles, at least in our modern society. *The basic problem, in a nutshell, is that the traditional roles are too narrow; they constitute a sort of "psychological straitjacket."* Sandra Bem (1975), for instance, has argued that conventional sex roles are unnecessarily restrictive and that they prevent people from expressing themselves spontaneously.

A rather common misconception is that it is only women who suffer from narrow sex roles. There are probably two reasons for this misconception. First, women clearly *have* been saddled with a subservient role, and the negative aspects of this lower-status role are more obvious than those associated with the male role. Second, because of this subservience, the initial concerns about sex roles surfaced in the feminist movement, which generated some compelling analyses of the oppressive nature of the female role (for example, Friedan, 1964; Millett, 1970). Only more recently have similar discerning analyses (Fasteau, 1974; Goldberg, 1976) focused public attention on the costs inherent in the *male* role.

COSTS ASSOCIATED WITH THE FEMALE ROLE

MATINA HORNER

Fear of success. In a very influential study, Matina Horner (1968) showed that *some women have their drive for achievement dulled by an underlying fear of success.* Using a procedure resembling a projective test, she asked subjects of both sexes to complete a story that began, "After first-term finals, Anne [or John, depending on the subject's sex] finds herself [himself] at the top of her [his] medical school class." A surprisingly high number (65%) of Horner's female subjects proceeded to write stories with very negative themes, suggesting that they believed that such success would lead to unfortunate consequences for Anne. Samples from some of these stories can be seen below (from Horner, 1969, p. 38).

> "Although Anne is happy with her success she fears what will happen to her social life. The male med students don't seem to think very highly of a female who has beaten them in their field. . . . She will be a proud and successful but alas, a very lonely doctor."
>
> "Anne is pretty darn proud of herself, but everyone hates and envies her."
>
> "Anne feels guilty. . . . She will finally have a nervous breakdown and quit medical school and marry a successful young doctor."

Among other things, Horner found that her female subjects expressed fear of social rejection and concern that such achievement might be unfeminine. In contrast, Horner's *male* subjects generally wrote fairly positive stories; only 10% showed comparable fear-of-success imagery. On the basis of this evidence, Horner suggested that many women do not fulfill their intellectual and career potentials because they fear that such success might have a negative effect on their social lives.

Horner's research generated many follow-up studies, which collectively have suggested some qualifications to the original findings and added some further information. Recent reviews of this research (Baker, 1980; O'Leary, 1977) suggest (1) that the percentage of women who fear success is smaller than the original figure of 65%, (2) that more *men* fear success than originally reported, (3) that it is success in *competition against men,* rather than any kind of success, that women fear, and (4) that apprehension about *social rejection* is the prime force behind women's fear of success.

The housewife syndrome.   The second problem has been christened the "housewife syndrome" by Tavris and Offir (1977). *What they are referring to is the frustration experienced by many (certainly not all) women whose sole identity is that of a housewife.* The housewife syndrome is best understood by comparing the feelings of wives who work with those who serve exclusively as housewives. Compared with working wives, housewives feel lonelier and more anxious and have a lower sense of worth (Shaver & Freedman, 1976). Even when the baseline for comparison is working women in relatively dull nonprofessional jobs (waitresses, department-store clerks, and so on), the housewives still report being less satisfied than the employed wives (Ferree, 1976).

Why is housework so unrewarding? For a number of reasons. First, the work *does* tend to involve a lot of drudgery. But so do many jobs outside the home. *The heart of the problem appears to lie in the housewife's relative isolation from other adults and the lack of recognition for the work done.* Ferree (1976) points out that, years ago, housewives were more likely to be part of a supportive social network, consisting of other housewives and relatives living nearby. Today, in our more mobile society, fewer people live near their relatives or in close-knit neighborhoods, and many of the other wives are too busy working. Thus, many modern housewives spend their day in a desolate social desert, yearning for adult conversation. The other problem, according to Ferree, is that housewives are taken for granted. They rarely get much overt appreciation from their families. Moreover, their work is endless—it is *never* really done; hence, it is difficult to experience a sense of accomplishment.

Suppressed sexuality.   Both women and men may have sexual problems that stem, in part, from their sex-role socialization. For females, the problem is that many young girls are brought up in ways that generate guilt about sex (Victor, 1980). This is not unheard of for males, but young girls are much more likely to be led to believe that sex is disgusting, dirty, and sinful—that it is an unpleasant *duty* associated with marriage. As the following comment illustrates (Boston Women's Health Book Collective, 1973, p. 25), this kind of upbringing makes it difficult for many women to really express and enjoy their sexuality: "It has been very hard for me to allow myself to feel good sexual energy in my body. 'You mean it's okay, it's not dirty, it's not loose?' I can hear one little voice saying to another little voice inside me. The other voice an-

---

8.5   RECOMMENDED READING

The Feminine Mystique by Betty Friedan (Dell, 1964) and *The New Our Bodies, Ourselves: A Book by and for Women* by the Boston Women's Health Book Collective (Simon & Schuster, 1984)

Because the feminist movement has generated many outstanding books on the oppressive nature of women's sex roles, selecting one to recommend is quite difficult. However, Friedan's classic, in spite of its age, still does an outstanding job of showing how women are coaxed and coerced into accepting a subservient role. Moreover, the book has historical significance in that it was a major force in stimulating the women's movement in the United States.

It is my thesis that the core of the problem for women today is not sexual but a problem of identity—a stunting or evasion of growth that is perpetuated by the feminine mystique. It is my thesis that as the Victorian culture did not permit women to accept or gratify their basic sexual needs, our culture does not permit women to accept or gratify their basic need to grow and fulfill their potentialities as human beings, a need which is not solely defined by their sexual role [p. 69].

The New Our Bodies, Ourselves is a revised and greatly expanded version of a remarkably popular and worthwhile book. As its title suggests, it is primarily about the female body and how it works. However, it goes beyond this and talks about self-concept and interpersonal relationships with men and with women. The book grew spontaneously out of a women's discussion group that began meeting in Boston in 1969. Part of its charm lies in its unique mixture of information drawn from technical sources and information drawn from personal experiences. These two disparate sources of insight are interwoven nicely through the use of numerous quotations. The book is illustrated where necessary, and it provides many suggestions for additional reading. Rarest of all, it is grossly *underpriced*.

swers: 'Sure, it's fine, that's what you feel.'" *Thus, more women than men have to struggle with overcoming the suppression of their sexual feelings and desires.* The uphill nature of this struggle is attested to by the fact that far more women than men have difficulty reaching orgasm (Masters & Johnson, 1970).

COSTS ASSOCIATED WITH THE MALE ROLE

Pressure to succeed. Whereas many women are trained to be inhibited about pursuing success, our society tends to go too far to the other extreme with males. Men are socialized to believe that success is everything. They are trained to engage in cutthroat competition. As Gould (1976) points out, they are taught that a man's masculinity is measured by the size of his paycheck. *Small wonder, then, that they pursue success with a fervor that is sometimes dangerous to their health.* The extent of this danger is illustrated by the fact that males' life expectancy is eight years shorter than females' (Goldberg, 1976). Although factors other than sex roles are at work, you can see in Figure 8.5 that death rates for males exceed those for females at most ages.

Obviously, the majority of men who have internalized this success ethic are unable to realize their dreams. How does this affect them? Well, many are able to adjust to it; but many are not. The latter group are likely to suffer from poor self-esteem and a diminished sense of virility (Gould, 1976). Males' obsession with success creates further problems for women. It contributes to economic discrimination against women. Many men want to "keep women in their place" because their masculinity is *especially* threatened when a *woman* earns more than they do.

The inexpressive male. Young boys are trained to believe that men should be strong, tough, cool, and detached. *Males are socialized in a way that leads many of them to work overtime trying to hide their feelings.* Public displays of emotion are taboo. A number of years ago, a presidential candidate, Edmund Muskie, made the mistake of shedding a few tears on the campaign trail. That incident—so antagonistic to the American male ideal—destroyed his campaign with an abruptness that was truly amazing.

As noted earlier, there is little evidence to suggest that men are really less emotional than women. The difference is that men have to expend a lot of energy covering up their emotion. This is tragic on two counts. First, it makes it difficult for many men to express feelings of affection for their loved ones. Many a male can barely stutter through "I love you." Second, as you saw in

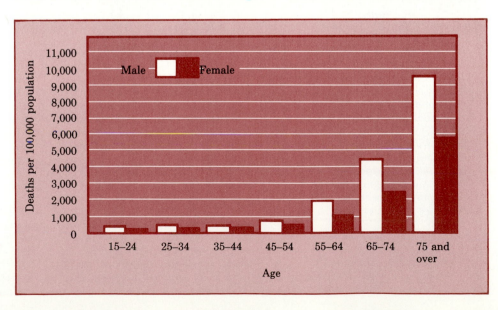

FIGURE 8.5 Death rates in the United States by age and sex, 1978.

CATHY

Chapter 3, some dangers are inherent in bottling up emotions. Suppressed emotions are at the root of many stress-related disorders. Hence, it is unfortunate that a preponderance of males feel compelled to stifle and conceal their emotions.

Sexual problems. Like women, men have certain sexual problems that derive partly from their sex-role socialization. For men, the problem is that they have a "macho" sexual image that they feel they must live up to. Thus, there are few things that most men fear more than a sexual encounter in which they are unable to achieve an erection (Litewka, 1977). Unfortunately, these very fears often *cause* the impotence that men dread so much. The upshot is that *males' obsession with sexual performance produces self-imposed pressure that ultimately may interfere with their sexual responsiveness.*

HOMOPHOBIA. *A behavioral syndrome involving intense fear, hatred, and intolerance of homosexual behavior.*

A related problem involves a phenomenon called **homophobia** (Lehne, 1976). Homophobia is an irrational fear of homosexuality which manifests itself in intolerance of homosexuals and abhorrence of any behavior that has even the most remote homosexual overtones. It is much more common in men than in women, because there is much more pressure on males to avoid any behavior characteristic of the other sex. Parents will tolerate "tomboyism" in girls, but they are highly intolerant of any "sissy" behavior exhibited by their sons. If you watch three adolescent males try to share the back seat of a car, you have an excellent chance of seeing homophobia in action. Typically, they

---

8.6 | *RECOMMENDED READING*
The Male Machine
by Marc Feigen Fasteau (McGraw-Hill, 1974)

In this book, Fasteau, an attorney, outlines some of the problems associated with the traditional male sex role. He maintains that society programs men in such a way as to extract the maximum work from them. Thus, they become competitive, hard-driven success machines, unable to enjoy life spontaneously. According to Fasteau, males' socialization undermines their capacities for true intimacy in relationships with other men as well as with women. He further laments how

men are estranged from their own families, how they have difficulty expressing affection to their own children, and how they are robbed of much of the gratification that child rearing can provide.

Men tend to camouflage their tender feelings toward children, to express them in roughhousing: a mock punch instead of a hug; telling a six-year-old boy on his way to a birthday party to "give 'em hell" when that isn't what is meant at all [p. 96].

Somewhere in me a voice was still saying, even though I haven't been in a fight since high school, if you were a real man, if you had any guts, you'd get out and knock him on his ass, instead of trading insults from the safety of the car [p. 155].

Another book in this genre that might prove useful is *Men and Masculinity* by Joseph H. Pleck and Jack Sawyer (Prentice-Hall, 1974).

will "scrunch up" in highly uncomfortable positions in order to avoid any physical contact with one another. Their body language is just shouting "I'm not queer." This touching phobia is merely a symptom of a much more deep-seated problem. Most homophobics are probably troubled by doubts about their own masculinity. It is unfortunate that these seeds of doubt are sown by society's unnecessary derogation of, and paranoia about, homosexuality.

SEXISM: A SPECIAL PROBLEM FOR WOMEN

SEXISM. *Discrimination against a person based on his or her sex. Often used to refer to economic subjugation of women.*

Intimately intertwined with the topics of sex differences and sex roles is the issue of sexism. **Sexism** is defined as discrimination against someone on the basis of sex (Hyde & Rosenberg, 1980). Generally, it is used to describe discrimination by men against women. However, it should be pointed out that sometimes *women* discriminate against other women, and occasionally *men* are the victims of sex-based discrimination.

In the broadest sense of the term, I have been discussing sexism throughout this chapter, in that I have talked extensively about how men and women are treated differently on the basis of their sex. In this section, however, I am going to focus briefly on the problem that the term *sexism* is most commonly associated with: economic discrimination against women.

Women are the victims of widespread economic discrimination. Levitin, Quinn, and Staines (1971) distinguish between two kinds of discrimination: (1) that involving differential *access* to jobs and (2) that involving differential *treatment* once on the job.

In regard to job access, it is clear that women do not have the same employment opportunities as men. Many occupations—from garage mechanic to chemist—are traditionally considered men's jobs. Women are breaking into these male-dominated fields only very slowly. Moreover, even when a job is considered "suitable" for a female, she may often be the victim of sexism. For example, Fidell (1970) varied the applicant's sex (and nothing else) in distributing bogus academic résumés to the heads of psychology departments across the United States. The department heads were asked to assess the quality or desirability of the job applicants. Although only their sex was different, the female applicants received lower ratings than the male applicants!

Once women have obtained a traditionally masculine job, they are often treated differently at work. They are likely to be assigned relatively routine and unchallenging tasks (Terborg & Ilgen, 1975). When performing the same work as men, they usually are paid less. Moreover, the earnings gap is sizable: the average woman receives about 58% of the pay given to men in comparable jobs (Rytina, 1981). Furthermore, since many men and a fair number of women feel uneasy about having a female boss (Tavris & Offir, 1977), opportunities for promotion are scant for women.

Finally, one other problem for working women is that *they still have to do virtually all the housework when they get home.* You might expect that working women would be relieved of part of their responsibility for housework. Unfortunately, the evidence (Vanek, 1974) indicates that their husbands only rarely step up their participation in household chores.

In summary, although there may be some costs associated with traditional sex roles for *both* sexes, it is clear that sexism is a very special and very significant problem for women. It seems particularly unfair that those women who manage to overcome their fear-of-success socialization may often have the doors of opportunity slammed in their faces.

Gender in the Past and in the Future

Up until now I have focused largely on *traditional* sex roles and the sex differences they tend to generate. I have not addressed the fact that in Western society, at least, sex roles are very much in a state of transition (see, for example, Dambrot, Papp, & Whitmore, 1984). In this section I will discuss *why* sex roles are changing and what the future might hold.

WHY ARE SEX ROLES CHANGING?

Many people are baffled about why sex roles are changing. They cannot understand why age-old traditions are being flouted and discarded. There are a number of theories about why sex roles are in transition. Basically, they look at the past in order to explain the present and the future. What you need to understand is that, *above all else, sex roles have always constituted a division of labor.* Although some ardent feminists would argue the point, in more "primitive" societies the division of labor along sexual lines was a natural outgrowth of some simple realities. In most hunting-and-gathering societies, as well as most agricultural societies, an economic premium was put on *physical strength.* Before the invention of tractors, directing a plow was heavy work. Generally, men tend to be stronger physically than women. Hence, men were deemed better equipped to handle such jobs as hunting and farming, and in most societies they got those assignments while the women were left with home maintenance and child rearing (Nielsen, 1978). Another factor was that, in these more primitive societies, women not only bore the children, but they also had to assume responsibility for nursing them (no baby bottles). In summary, although people might have worked out other ways of doing things (and some cultures did), there were a couple of basic reasons for dividing labor according to sex in earlier, more primitive societies.

Essentially, our traditional sex roles today are a carryover from our ancestral past. Once traditions are established, they have a way of perpetuating themselves. Moreover, males have had a vested interest in perpetuating these traditions, since the arrangements made them something of a privileged class.

During the last century or so in Western society, these divisions of labor have become increasingly antiquated and out of touch with economic reality. Therein lies the prime reason for changes in sex roles, according to many theorists (Holter, 1975). *Traditional sex roles no longer make economic sense!* In our industrial economy, the number of jobs for which physical strength is important has become fewer and fewer. Moreover, many experts believe that we are moving into more of a "service economy" in which physical strength will become almost completely irrelevant. Furthermore, although women still have to bear the children, the traditional nursing responsibilities are now optional. *Thus, the principal cause of shifts in sex roles appears to be economic change that has rendered these roles obsolete and unnecessary.*

Another factor seems to be adding momentum to the movement toward nontraditional sex roles. Sex roles used to be taken for granted and to be considered a "God-given" fact of life. However, this significant source of inertia has largely been negated by the fact that sex roles are now an issue of hot debate.

In conclusion, sex roles are likely to remain in flux for quite some time to come. Barring some unanticipated catastrophe, this appears to be a virtually inevitable outcome of fundamental changes in our economic system. The traditionalists who yearn for a return to simpler days are likely to be frustrated. However, in deference to those traditionalists, it should be pointed out that they should be allowed to retain their right to self-determination. *People who feel comfortable with traditional sex roles ought to be free to live their lives as they please without being subject to unnecessary derogation.* In other words, women who are happy in the homemaker role should not be coerced into making difficult readjustments. Furthermore, they should get the same respect accorded women who work outside the home. Child rearing is an important task. The lower status accorded to the domestic role is really very arbitrary and, ultimately, sexist.

IS ANDROGYNY THE ANSWER?

ANDROGYNY. *A behavioral pattern wherein a person displays both masculine and feminine characteristics.*

Recently, some theorists (Bem, 1975; Spence & Helmreich, 1978) have argued that people might be better off if they displayed *both* feminine and masculine characteristics. Such a coexistence of personality traits traditionally considered to be masculine or feminine is called **androgyny.** The androgynous person is a male or female who scores higher than average on measures of *both* masculinity and femininity. Androgyny is not the same thing as being a "masculine" woman or a "feminine" man. Males who score high on femininity but low on masculinity, and females who score high on masculinity but low on femininity, are called "cross-sex-typed" rather than androgynous.

Sandra Bem (1975) argues that traditionally masculine men and feminine women feel compelled to adhere to rigid and narrow sex-role expectations that unnecessarily restrict their behavior. She asserts that such people are not as flexible in their behavior as androgynous people. *She further suggests that flexibility is desirable and adaptive and that, therefore, androgynous people tend to be psychologically healthier than conventionally sex-typed people.* Essentially, she proposes that androgynous people combine the best of masculinity and femininity. Finally, noting that old sex-role patterns are falling by the wayside, Bem expresses a hope that androgyny will come to set the future standard for ideal socialization.

What of Bem's analyses and projections? Is androgyny healthy? Will it be the role model of the future? There is great controversy on the first point and little but speculation on the second. In regard to the first point, Bem (1975) *has* mustered some data that suggest an association between androgyny and psychological health. However, her technique for measuring androgyny and her evidence linking it to superior adjustment have both been harshly criticized (Locksley & Colten, 1979; Pedhazur & Tetenbaum, 1979).

Overall, there is probably more evidence to support a connection between traditional *masculinity* (in either sex) and psychological health (Locksley & Colten, 1979). However, the problem in all this research is that psychological health is such a value-laden concept and is quite difficult to measure objectively. For instance, the evidence linking masculinity to sound adjustment *could* reflect a sexist bias in the definition and measurement of psychological health. Recognizing the ambiguity inherent in the concept of psychological health, a recent analysis focused instead on the relationship between androgyny and *self-esteem*. Whitley (1983) chose to examine the variable of self-esteem because it was thought to be a key feature of psychological health that was relatively noncontroversial and easier to measure objectively than health in a global sense. Once again, however, the evidence indicated that masculinity is more strongly related to self-esteem than either androgyny or femininity. At the present, then, we have little evidence to support Bem's proposal that androgyny is particularly healthy.

As for the *future* of androgyny, only time will tell. Casual observation suggests that more and more children are being socialized in an androgynous manner, but there is really no substantive evidence on this point. There *is* evidence that androgyny has a fairly favorable image, at least among college students. Major, Deaux, and Carnevale (1981) found that androgynous persons of either sex were perceived (rated) by college students as more likable and better adjusted than traditionally masculine or feminine persons. Whether such perceptions will translate into more androgynous behavior in the future is difficult to say.

It should be emphasized that although many social scientists find the concept of androgyny appealing, there are those who are concerned about the decline of traditional sex roles. Bardwick (1973) has pointed out that the period of transition is apt to be quite stressful and has argued that an egalitarian society might present some new problems. In a more heated and polemical analysis, Gilder (1973) has argued that the demise of traditional sex roles could have disastrous consequences for our society. Gilder maintains that conventional sex roles provide a fundamental underpinning for our economic and social order. He asserts that changes in these sex roles will damage intimate relationships between women and men and that the changes will have a devastating impact on the quality of family life. Gilder argues that women are needed in the home in their traditional homemaker role in order to provide for the socialization of the next generation. Without this traditional socialization, Gilder suggests, our moral fabric will decay, leading to an increase in crime, violence, and drug abuse. Given the very different projections of Gilder and Bem, it should prove most interesting to see what unfolds during the next few decades.

Some theorists believe that androgyny will be the wave of the future.

Summary

There are innumerable stereotypes about behavioral differences between the sexes. In reality, the evidence is complicated, and the nature of group differences is often misunderstood. It appears that males are superior in mathematical and visual-spatial ability, while women excel in verbal ability, and purported differences in cognitive style are largely mythical.

In regard to personality, there is some evidence to suggest that men are relatively aggressive while women tend to be more passive. However, research has *not* supported alleged differences in influenceability and emotionality. Similarly, evidence for differences in sociability, the importance attributed to love, and nurturance is scant. Women do appear, though, to have a slight advantage in regard to empathy and sensitivity to nonverbal communication. Differences in sexual interest do not appear to be attributable to biology and may be shrinking. Although more women than men do seek psychotherapy, there are a number of reasons to doubt whether men really enjoy greater psychological health.

The "nature versus nurture" controversy has raged for a long time, and the pendulum has swung back and forth. In spite of recent excitement about a possible link between lateralization and sex differences, most experts still believe that socialization is more important than biology in producing behavioral disparities between the sexes. The main reason is that extensive biological research has not paid off with clear-cut explanations.

The socialization of sex roles appears to take place through (1) differential imitation of same-sex models, (2) differential reinforcement of sex-appropriate behavior, and (3) self-socialization by inquisitive children. These processes operate in many locales, but the home, the school, and the media appear to be the three primary sources of sex-role socialization.

Many theorists believe that traditional sex roles are too narrow and restrict people's behavior. Among the principal costs for women are (1) problems in competing with men, (2) frustration associated with the housewife role, and (3) suppressed sexuality. For males, the principal costs involve (1) excessive pressure to succeed, (2) inability to express emotions, and (3) sexual difficulties. In addition to these psychological problems, women face uniquely sexist hurdles in the economic domain.

Sex roles have always represented a division of labor. They are changing today, and seem likely to continue changing, because they no longer jibe with economic reality. As sex roles shift, some theorists have proposed that androgyny may be the answer in the future. Although the idea is intriguing, it has its critics, and only time will tell what the future holds.

In the upcoming application section, I will talk about how to pursue a more assertive lifestyle. Assertiveness training has proved particularly popular among women, but it can be beneficial to members of either sex.

Learning to Be Assertive

Answer the following questions yes or no.

_____ 1. When someone says something that you consider foolish, do you have difficulty voicing your disagreement?

_____ 2. When a salesperson pressures you to buy something you don't want, do you have a hard time expressing your lack of interest?

_____ 3. When someone asks you for an unreasonable favor, do you have difficulty saying no?

_____ 4. Do you feel timid about returning flawed merchandise?

_____ 5. Do you have a hard time requesting even small favors from others?

_____ 6. When you're in a group that is hotly debating some issue, are you shy about speaking up?

If you answered yes to several of the above questions, you may have difficulty being assertive. Many people have a hard time being properly assertive. In particular, women in our society often resort to passive rather than assertive behavior. Although the problem is definitely not confined to women, females are socialized to be more passive and submissive than males, and assertiveness training has become especially popular among women. Regardless of your sex, it is important to understand the differences among assertive, submissive, and aggressive behavior. In this application section, I will elaborate on those differences and discuss some of the procedures used to increase assertiveness.

DEFINING ASSERTIVENESS

ASSERTIVE BEHAVIOR. *A behavioral pattern wherein a person stands up for his or her rights by speaking up in an honest and direct manner.*

Assertive behavior is that which enables people to act in their own best interests by expressing their thoughts and feelings directly and honestly (Alberti & Emmons, 1974; Lange & Jakubowski, 1976). Essentially, assertiveness involves standing up for your rights when someone else is about to infringe on them. This is done by speaking out openly rather than "pulling punches."

The nature of assertive behavior can best be clarified by contrasting it with submissive behavior, on the one hand, and aggressive behavior, on the other. *Submissive, or passive, behavior involves consistently giving in to others on possible points of contention.* Submissive people tend to let others take advantage of them. Typically, their biggest problem is that they cannot say no to requests that they consider unreasonable. They have difficulty voicing disagreement with others and making requests themselves. To put it into traditional trait terminology, they are too meek, timid, diffident, bashful, restrained, and retiring. Although the roots of nonassertiveness have not been investigated

---

8.7 *RECOMMENDED READING*
Asserting Yourself: A Practical Guide for Positive Change
by Sharon Anthony Bower and Gordon H. Bower (Addison-Wesley, 1976)

There are over 20 books on assertiveness training, and many of them are fairly good, making it difficult to decide on a recommendation. However, the Bowers' book is considered especially strong because it is very specific, detailed, and concrete. Bower and Bower put the problem of nonassertiveness into perspective, relating it to self-esteem and anxiety. They then lay out a very systematic program for increasing assertive behavior. They make extensive use of probing questions so that you can work out a plan of attack that is personally relevant. They also provide sample verbal scripts for numerous common situations that typically call for assertive behavior. The book is smoothly written in a nonpatronizing tone. The table reprinted below (from p. 100) illustrates the explicit guidelines for assertive verbal behavior that are explained by the Bowers.

There are, of course, other books on assertiveness that can be recommended highly. In particular, it is worth noting one of the very first entries in this area, *Your Perfect Right* by Robert E. Alberti and Michael L. Emmons (Impact Publishers, 1974). Many of the books are put together with women in mind and focus on the unique problems encountered by women. Of these, *The Assertive Woman* by Stanlee Phelps and Nancy Austin (Impact Publishers, 1975) appears particularly useful.

Rules for assertive DESC scripts

	Number	Do	Don't
Describe	D1	Describe the other person's behavior objectively.	Describe your emotional reaction to it.
	D2	Use concrete terms.	Use abstract, vague terms.
	D3	Describe a specified time, place, and frequency of the action.	Generalize for "all time."
	D4	Describe the action, not the "motive."	Guess at your Downer's motives or goals.
Express	E1	Express your feelings.	Deny your feelings.
	E2	Express them calmly.	Unleash emotional outbursts.
	E3	State feelings in a positive manner, as relating to a goal to be achieved.	State feelings negatively, making putdown or attack.
	E4	Direct yourself to the specific offending behavior, not to the whole person.	Attack the entire character of the person.
Specify	S1	Ask explicitly for change in your Downer's behavior.	Merely imply that you'd like a change.
	S2	Request a small change.	Ask for too large a change.
	S3	Request only one or two changes at one time.	Ask for too many changes.
	S4	Specify the concrete actions you want to see stopped and those you want to see performed.	Ask for changes in nebulous traits or qualities.
	S5	Take account of whether your Downer can meet your request without suffering large losses.	Ignore your Downer's needs or ask only for your satisfaction.
	S6	Specify (if appropriate) what behavior you are willing to change to make the agreement.	Consider that only your Downer has to change.
Consequences	C1	Make the consequences explicit.	Be ashamed to talk about rewards and penalties.
	C2	Give a positive reward for change in the desired direction.	Give only punishments for lack of change.
	C3	Select something that is desirable and reinforcing to your Downer.	Select something that only you might find rewarding.
	C4	Select a reward that is big enough to maintain the behavior change.	Offer a reward you can't or won't deliver.
	C5	Select a punishment of a magnitude that "fits the crime" of refusing to change behavior.	Make exaggerated threats.
	C6	Select a punishment that you are actually willing to carry out.	Use unrealistic threats or self-defeating punishment.

fully, they appear to lie in excessive concern about gaining the social approval of others. However, this strategy of "not making waves" is more likely to garner others' contempt than their approval (Jakubowski-Spector, 1973).

It is sometimes difficult to differentiate between assertive behavior and aggressive behavior. In principle, the distinction is fairly simple. You may recall that aggressive behavior involves an intention to hurt or harm another. Assertive behavior includes no such intention to inflict harm. The problem in real life is that assertive and aggressive behavior *may* overlap. When someone is about to infringe on their rights, people often lash out at the other party (aggression) while defending their rights (assertion). The challenge, then, is to learn to be firm and assertive, without going a step too far and becoming unnecessarily aggressive.

Advocates of assertiveness maintain that assertive behavior is much more adaptive than either submissive or aggressive behavior (Dawley & Wenrich, 1976). They maintain that submissive behavior leads to poor self-esteem, self-denial, emotional suppression, and strained interpersonal relationships while aggressive behavior tends to promote guilt, alienation, and disharmony. In contrast, assertive behavior purportedly fosters higher self-esteem and more satisfactory interpersonal relationships.

ASSERTIVENESS TRAINING

Numerous assertiveness training programs are available in book form or through seminars. Some recommendations about books appear in Box 8.7. Most of the programs are behavioral in nature and emphasize gradual improvement and reinforcement of appropriate behavior. The key elements in most programs include the following.

Clarifying the nature of assertive behavior. Most programs begin, as I already have, by trying to make clear the nature of assertive behavior. *Obviously, you need to understand what assertive behavior looks and sounds like in order to produce such behavior.* This demonstration of the nature of assertive behavior is usually accomplished by looking at numerous situations calling for assertive behavior and comparing hypothetical submissive, assertive, and aggressive responses. One such comparison can be seen below. In this example, a woman is asking her partner, who is functioning as a "downer," to help plan a garden (excerpted from Bower & Bower, 1976, pp. 8, 9, 11).

The Passive Scene
- *She:* Uh, excuse me but I wonder if you would be willing to take the time to decide about the garden?
- *Downer:* (looking at paper) Not now, I'm busy.
- *She:* Oh, okay.

The Aggressive Scene
- *She:* Listen, I'm sick and tired of you putting off deciding about this damn garden. Are you going to help?
- *Downer:* (looking at paper) Not now, I'm busy.
- *She:* Why can't you look at me when you're turning me down? You don't give a damn about the garden or the house or me! You just care about yourself!
- *Downer:* That's not true. I do care.
- *She:* No, you don't. You never pay any attention to your household or to me. I have to do everything around here myself!

The Assertive Scene
- *She:* It's spring and time to make plans for our garden.
- *Downer:* (looking at paper) Oh, c'mon—not now! It's only April.
- *She:* I feel that the garden is more enjoyable if we've planned it carefully together in advance.

> *Downer:*   I'm not sure I'm going to have the time for that.
> *She:*   I've already drawn up and budgeted two alternative plans—will you look at them? I'd like to get your decisions about them, say, tonight after supper.

For people to whom assertive behavior is foreign, this clarification process can be critical. In such cases, it may be a good idea to read two or three books on assertiveness in order to get a good picture of assertive behavior. The differences may best be conceptualized in terms of how people deal with their own rights and the rights of others. Passive people sacrifice their own rights. Aggressive people tend to ignore the rights of others. Assertive people consider both their own rights and the rights of others.

Monitoring your assertive behavior.   For most people, assertiveness varies from one situation to another. In other words, they may be quite assertive in some social contexts and quite timid in others. Consequently, once you understand the nature of assertive behavior, *you should monitor yourself and identify when you are nonassertive.* In particular, you should figure out *who* intimidates you, on *what topics,* and in *which situations.*

Modeling assertive behavior.   *Once you have identified the situations in which you are nonassertive, it is often a good idea to find someone who does behave assertively in those situations and observe that person's behavior closely.* In other words, find someone to model yourself after. By doing this, you should (1) learn better how to behave assertively in situations crucial to you and (2) see the *payoff* for behaving assertively, which should vicariously reinforce your own assertive tendencies.

Practicing assertive behavior.   Ultimately, the key to achieving assertive behavior is to practice it *and work toward gradual improvement.* Your practice may take several forms. In *covert rehearsal,* you may dream up a certain situation and then imagine the dialogue that you would engage in. In *role playing,* you might get a therapist or friend to play the role of some antagonist, and you would act out your new assertive behaviors in this artificial situation. Eventually, you will have to transfer your assertiveness skills to real-life situations. Most experts recommend that you shape up your behavior gradually, setting realistic goals for yourself and rewarding yourself when you achieve them.

Adopting an assertive attitude.   Most assertiveness training programs are highly behavioral and focus on shaping up specific responses for specific situations. However, some experts (Shoemaker & Satterfield, 1977) have pointed out that, unfortunately, real-life situations are only rarely just like those portrayed in the books. Hence, they maintain that acquiring a repertoire of verbal responses for certain situations is not as important as developing a new attitude that you're not going to let people push you around anymore. Although most programs don't talk explicitly about attitudes, they appear to instill a new attitude indirectly, and this attitude is probably crucial to achieving flexible assertive behavior.

CHAPTER 8 REVIEW

IDEAS: REVIEW OF LEARNING OBJECTIVES

When you have mastered the material in this chapter, you should be able to do the following.

1. Explain why group sex differences tell us little about individuals.
2. List three cognitive abilities on which the sexes differ (and the nature of the difference).
3. Explain why the often cited sex difference in cognitive style appears inaccurate.
4. Indicate whether there really are sex differences on the personality dimensions of aggressiveness, influenceability, emotionality, and passivity.
5. Summarize the evidence on alleged sex differences in regard to five aspects of social orientation and skills.
6. Summarize evidence about whether men have a stronger sex drive than women.
7. Discuss three explanations for the excess of women (over men) in psychotherapy.
8. Explain the nature/nurture controversy and the interactionist position as they relate to the development of sex differences.
9. Review evidence relating sex differences to brain organization.
10. List some of the reasons that biological explanations of sex differences appear less plausible than environmental explanations.
11. List and describe three processes implicated in sex-role socialization.
12. List three sources of sex-role socialization.
13. Review evidence on fear of success in women.
14. Describe two other common problems among women that appear to stem partly from their sex-role socialization.
15. List three common problems among men that appear to stem partly from their sex-role socialization.
16. Describe two ways in which women are victimized by economic discrimination.
17. Explain the basis for sex roles in more primitive societies.
18. Explain why sex roles are currently in transition.
19. Describe Bem's views on androgyny.
20. Discuss the actual evidence on androgyny.
21. Define assertive behavior and contrast it with passive behavior.
22. Differentiate between assertive and aggressive behavior.
23. Explain why assertive behavior is believed to be more adaptive than passive or aggressive behavior.
24. Describe five steps in developing and increasing assertive behavior.

TERMS: REVIEW OF NEW VOCABULARY

When you have mastered the material in this chapter, you should be able to define the following terms.

Androgyny	Frontal lobes	Parietal lobes	Sexism
Assertive behavior	Gender	Premenstrual syndrome	Sex roles
Cerebral hemispheres	Homophobia	Role	Socialization
Field dependence	Lateralization	Sex differences	Stereotype

PEOPLE: REVIEW OF MAJOR THEORISTS AND RESEARCHERS

When you have mastered the material in this chapter, you should be able to summarize the principal contributions and/or ideas of the following people.

Sandra Bem	Phyllis Chesler	Matina Horner	Maccoby & Jacklin

9

INTERPERSONAL ATTRACTION: FRIENDSHIP AND LOVE

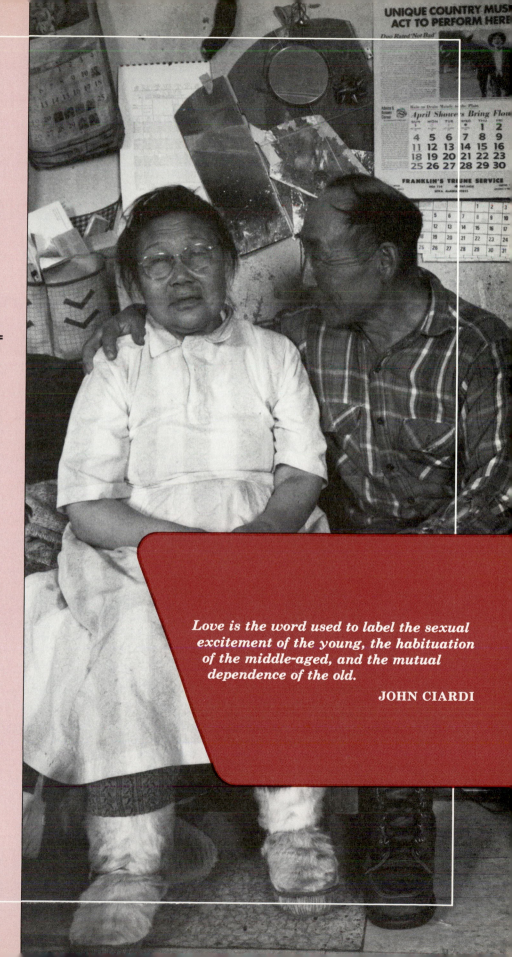

Love is the word used to label the sexual excitement of the young, the habituation of the middle-aged, and the mutual dependence of the old.

JOHN CIARDI

The column reprinted in Box 9.1 gives us three very different viewpoints about the vagaries of extramarital love affairs. The first two women certainly do not

9.1 *"HOW IT REALLY IS" ON MISTRESS FRONT*
THREE WOMEN: one a mistress, one a wife, one both.

All three read the interview with Melissa Sands that appeared here. Miss Sands has started a group called Mistresses Anonymous, to take the side of the "other woman" in extramarital affairs.

All three read the same words, yet each reacted differently. That happens sometimes. Here they are:

BOB GREENE

"Melissa Sands wants people to think that a mistress' life is very glamorous. That's a joke. I ought to know.

"I suppose I'm a mistress, although I don't like that word. That's just one of the things wrong with what Melissa Sands says. 'Mistress.' It sounds so . . . fancy. Like a woman sitting in a high-rise apartment waiting for her man to visit her.

"That's not how it is. I'm 34. I live on the Near North Side. I have been going with a married man for seven years. I met him at work. It was very exciting at first. It made me feel special, knowing that I could attract a man who belonged to somebody else.

"It's not so exciting any more. Do you know what the most important part of my day is? Waiting by the telephone to see if he'll call. That's what a mistress is: someone waiting for a phone to ring.

"And holidays. Those are very nice. Every year it's the same thing. He'll come to see me Christmas Eve, and we'll exchange presents, and then he'll hurry on home to the suburbs to be with his family while I lie awake all night waiting for Christmas to come.

"I'm not asking anyone to feel sorry for me. I got myself into this, and I was an adult at the time. I have no excuses. I've learned by now that he's never going to get a divorce, no matter what he says, and that I'll have to be satisfied with what I have.

"I could break off with him, but I'm not going to. I happen to be in love with him, so I'll take him when I can have him. What I really object to, though, is this Melissa Sands giving the picture of mistresses as a bunch of adventurous, sophisticated, beautiful women who are supposed to band together for their common good. I know that I'm destined to lose, and that's what mistresses are, in the end—losers."

"I WAS SO ANGRY when I read about Melissa Sands. I wish I could talk to her.

"She says that 'a mistress can't break up a marriage. Only a husband and a wife can do that.' Very cute.

"My husband has been having affairs for years. It started right after we got married, and I found out about it and confronted him with it, and it almost ended our marriage. Now he thinks I don't know what he's doing, but I've just gotten smart. I've learned to keep my mouth shut.

"Melissa Sands wants mistresses to get a fair deal, does she? I realize that I'm probably dumb to get mad about what she said—she's just trying to sell her book, and this is probably the reaction she wants people to have. But I wish she'd tell me what a fair deal is.

"Is it a fair deal to love a man and know that all he really wants to do is get out of the house to be with whomever he's seeing? Is it a fair deal to try to raise your children at the same time you don't know whether their father is ready to leave you? Is it a fair deal to feel guilty because you're starting to look a little old?

"I'm so sick of picking up the phone late in the afternoon to hear one of his excuses about why he has to stay downtown and 'work late.' I'm so sick of sounding cheerful and making him think that I believe him. I'm trying to save my marriage, but sometimes I forget what it is that's so worth saving.

"I'm sure that for Melissa Sands and women like her, it's all a very exciting game to play. She told you that she never thought about the wives—she said that there are enough people to think about the wives, and she just wants to think about the mistresses.

"I'd like her to tell me who it is she thinks is caring about the wives. She said that her man is going to get a divorce and marry her. If he does it, I hope it happens to her some day. I hope she wakes up one morning and finds out that her new husband is having an affair. I can't help it, she makes me sick."

I'M A MISTRESS. I'm a wife, too.

"I thought that the article about Melissa Sands was funny. Unintentionally so.

"She takes everything so seriously, and apparently you went along with her, because you wrote the article that way.

"She makes it seem like mistresses are some exotic species that people should examine like jungle animals. 'Mistresses Anonymous.' What a laugh.

"Do you know what a mistress is? It's a woman who is seeing a man who's married. No more, no less. That makes me a mistress. I'm married and I'm staying married, but I see a man who's also married, and I'm not going to let it disrupt my life.

"It's no big deal. People get bored, and they see other people. I don't really believe that this Melissa Sands was ever a mistress herself. She gets too excited about the whole thing for any of it to ring true. If she had been through it, she wouldn't talk about it.

"I was just kidding when I said I was a mistress. I really am married and I really do see a married man, but I don't feel like any mistress. That's what was so funny about the article. There are no mistresses in this world. There are just people who are doing things to get themselves through from day to day. None of it really matters."

paint a very pretty picture. One is a mistress, the other a wife whose husband is "cheating" on her. They are at opposite corners of the proverbial love triangle, with radically different social roles. In spite of their disparate roles, they tell the same story. It is a common story, a story laced with tears, anguish, and depression. It is the story of frustration in love. It is a story *you* may have experienced. Furthermore, it is a story that you cannot fully appreciate unless you *have* experienced the knot in your stomach, the lying awake at night, the thoughts of your loved one in the arms of another. Mere words fail when one seeks to convey the essence of this extraordinary agony. What is this thing called love, that it can cause such pain?

The first two women are clearly unhappy. What are they doing about it? Nothing! They are bogged down in self-despair; yet they choose not to expend any effort to extricate themselves. Are they adjusting to their situations in a healthy manner? The second woman says "I've just gotten smart. I've learned to keep my mouth shut." Is it really "smart" for her to keep her mouth shut? You should be aware by now that the answer to this question represents a value judgment. Some people would agree with the second woman's course of action and argue that she is making the best of a bad situation. Others would argue that she is following a course of *inaction,* that she is passively accepting a thoroughly unsatisfactory situation. Given the philosophical stance of this book, that one should actively try to "take charge" of one's own life, the author would argue that *both* women are displaying rather feeble coping efforts. In any event, the crucial point that I wish to stress is the enormous significance of love in our lives. There may be no more important area of adjustment.

The great prominence of this need for love and belongingness is illustrated by the pervasiveness of love-oriented themes in our literature and music. Wander through a bookstore and you will see an endless array of titles such as *How to Make It with Another Person* (Austin, 1976), *Making Contact* (Wassmer, 1978), *Friends* (Gillies, 1976), *How to Be Loved* (Broadbent, 1976), *Love Can Be Found* (Arieti & Arieti, 1977), and *How to Survive the Loss of a Love* (Colgrove, Bloomfield, & McWilliams, 1976). Turn up your radio and you will hear the refrains of "All You Need Is Love," "All in Love Is Fair," "Only Love Can Break Your Heart," "Love Has No Pride," "Love the One You're With," and "50 Ways to Leave Your Lover."

Although interpersonal attraction is an exceptionally important topic, this may be the most tentatively written chapter in the text, because we understand so little about the great enigmas of friendship and love. As Rubin (1973) points out, interest in the mystery of interpersonal attraction has existed throughout history; however, the *scientific* study of this topic has a relatively short past, encompassing only the last 15 years or so. This startling lack of research is probably due in part to the monumental complexity of the phenomenon. As Marlowe and Gergen (1969) note, psychologists have been hard-pressed to *define* the multifaceted phenomenon of attraction, let alone *understand* it. Another roadblock has been the widespread belief that the very personal experience of attraction cannot or should not be investigated by the impersonal scientific approach. Illustrative of this attitude is Senator William Proxmire of Wisconsin, who bestowed his Golden Fleece Award for excessive waste of taxpayers' money on social psychologists Ellen Berscheid and Elaine Walster for the study of romantic love (see Box 9.2)

Nonetheless, recognizing the enormous significance of friendship and love in our lives, psychologists and other social scientists are pushing ahead in their investigation of the magnetic forces that govern interpersonal relationships. In this chapter I will review and discuss this research. I will begin with an analysis of the basis for our affiliation needs. This will lead to a summary of the empirical data on the dynamics of who is attracted to whom. I will then make some specific comments on friendship and love. Finally, I will consider the problem of loneliness. In the application section I will focus on shyness, a problem closely related to loneliness.

The Affiliation Drive

AFFILIATION. *The human need to interact with other people.*

Affiliation is the term psychologists use to denote our very basic need to associate with other people. Affiliation encompasses our need to simply enjoy the company of other people, to have friends, to develop intimate relationships, and to fall in love. It is a very fundamental drive, and when it is thwarted, people often experience enormous frustration.

There are many reasons that we pursue affiliation so ardently. Some theorists (for example, Bowlby, 1958; Harlow, 1958, 1959) have argued convincingly that affiliation may have a *biological* foundation. More important, it is clear that there are many *psychological* benefits that can be derived from communion with one's fellow human beings.

Stanley Schachter (1959) conducted a pioneering study that demonstrated that *the experience of stress increases the drive to affiliate.* Undergraduate females recruited to participate in an experiment were exposed to one of two conditions. In both conditions, an official-looking man was introduced as a member of the medical school faculty, and subjects were told that the study would require that they be subjected to a series of electrical shocks. In the *high-stress* condition, the experimenter told the subjects that the shocks would be very painful. The realism of this intimidation effort was enhanced by placing a sizable collection of electronic equipment on display in the room. In the *low-stress* condition, the alarming array of equipment was absent, and subjects were told they would receive a series of mild, painless shocks. These procedures were an elaborate deception designed to arouse different levels of fear, and none of the subjects was actually shocked. Instead, the experimenter indicated (in both conditions) that there would be a delay while the shock apparatus was prepared for use, and the subjects were allowed to choose whether they would like to wait alone or in the company of others. The percentage of subjects wanting to wait with others was nearly twice as great in the high-stress as in the low-stress condition (see Figure 9.1).

Schachter's experiment indicates that stress increases our desire to affiliate with others. In light of what we learned in Chapter 3, it appears that this pursuit of affiliation is a well-chosen strategy for coping with stress. As you may recall, there is considerable evidence that *social support can serve as a sort of "protective buffer" to diminish the potential wear and tear of stress* (LaRocco, House, & French, 1980). Thus, it appears that the drive to affiliate

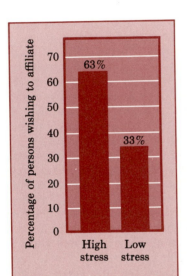

FIGURE 9.1 The effects of stress on affiliation tendencies.

9.2 CONTROVERSY OVER THE SCIENTIFIC STUDY OF LOVE

Scientific research on love has a brief but controversial history. Pioneering studies by social psychologists such as Ellen Berscheid at the University of Minnesota and Elaine Hatfield (formerly Walster) at the University of Wisconsin have come under heavy fire from Senator William Proxmire, a Wisconsin Democrat. Proxmire periodically gains media attention by announcing his selections of the most wasteful expenditures of federal tax dollars. In 1975 he bestowed what he calls his "Golden Fleece Award" on Drs. Berscheid and Hatfield for their use of a National Science Foundation grant to underwrite the study of love. Proxmire asserted that "200 million Americans want to leave some things in life a mystery, and right at the top of things we don't want to know is why a man falls in love with a woman and vice versa."

Proxmire raised several provocative issues in his critique of this research. Do people really want to see the mysteries of love unraveled? Is love such a subjective experience that we cannot hope to achieve an understanding of it? Should taxpayers provide financial support for this "frivolous" research? These questions are not easily answered. The fact that there have been so many best-selling books about love suggests that people *are* interested in understanding this confusing human emotion. Whether such an understanding can be achieved through empirical research can be ascertained only by encouraging such research to see what sorts of results emerge. Whether taxpayers should foot the bill is a purely political question that each of us must grapple with individually.

has important functional value in dealing with the stresses of modern life.

While affiliation is an important drive in and of itself, a full appreciation of its significance requires consideration of all the other drives that depend on affiliation as a precondition for their fulfillment. Table 9.1 is a well-known and often used list of psychological needs developed by Henry Murray (1938). If you glance at this list of needs, you will find very few that could be satisfied in a social vacuum. For example, we need friends to praise our accomplishments (achievement), to be impressed by our wit (exhibition), to sympathize with our failures (succorance), and to join in our games and parties (play). It should be clear that affiliation with others is essential to the satisfaction of many important drives. Thus, the psychological profits of affiliation are many and varied.

TABLE 9.1 Illustrative list of Murray's needs

Need	Brief definition
Abasement	To submit passively to external force. To accept injury, blame, criticism, punishment. To admit inferiority, error, wrongdoing, or defeat.
Achievement	To accomplish something difficult. To master, manipulate, or organize physical objects, human beings, or ideas. To overcome obstacles and attain a high standard. To excel oneself. To rival and surpass others.
Affiliation	To draw near and enjoyably cooperate or reciprocate with an allied other. To please and win affection of another. To adhere and remain loyal to a friend.
Aggression	To overcome opposition forcefully. To fight. To revenge an injury. To attack or injure another. To oppose forcefully or punish another.
Autonomy	To get free, shake off restraint, break out of confinement. To resist coercion and restriction. To avoid or quit activities prescribed by domineering authorities. To be independent.
Counteraction	To master or make up for a failure by restriving. To obliterate a humiliation by resumed action. To overcome weaknesses, to repress fear.
Defendance	To defend the self against assault, criticism, and blame. To conceal or justify a misdeed, failure, or humiliation.
Deference	To admire and support a superior. To praise, honor, or eulogize. To yield eagerly to the influence of an allied other.
Dominance	To control one's human environment. To influence or direct the behavior of others by suggestion, seduction, persuasion, or command.
Exhibition	To make an impression. To be seen and heard. To excite, amaze, fascinate, entertain, shock, intrigue, amuse, or entice others.
Harmavoidance	To avoid pain, physical injury, illness, and death. To escape from a dangerous situation. To take precautionary measures.
Infavoidance	To avoid humiliation. To quit embarrassing situations or to avoid conditions that may lead to belittlement.
Nurturance	To give sympathy and gratify the needs of a helpless object: an infant or any object that is weak.
Order	To put things in order. To achieve arrangement, organization, neatness, tidiness, and precision.
Play	To act for "fun" without further purpose. To seek enjoyable relaxation. To participate in games and sports.
Rejection	To separate oneself from a negatively cathected object. To exclude, abandon, snub, or jilt an object.
Sentience	To seek and enjoy sensuous impressions.
Sex	To form and further an erotic relationship. To have sexual encounters.
Succorance	To have one's needs gratified by the sympathetic aid of an allied object. To be supported, sustained, protected, loved.
Understanding	To ask or answer general questions. To be interested in theory. To speculate, formulate, analyze, and generalize.

The Many Facets of Attraction

INTERPERSONAL ATTRACTION. *A person's attitudinal orientation to evaluate another person in a positive manner.*

Now that we have seen *why* people need to affiliate with each other, we shall try to gain some insight into the nature of certain types of affiliatory relationships. Walster and Walster (1976) have defined **interpersonal attraction** as an individual's tendency to evaluate another person in a positive way. This definition conceives of attraction as an *attitude* that one holds toward another person. This definition is broad in scope, including a great variety of experiences, such as comradeship, respect, lust, and parental love, to name but a few. As you can see, there are many kinds of affiliatory relationships. We will be focusing on two in particular: liking and loving.

Definitions of liking and loving proposed by social scientists do not seem to do justice to these highly personal phenomena. Therefore, I will not introduce any additional formal definitions. Rather, I will provide a simple description of the types of experience I intend to discuss under these terms. The term *liking* will be used interchangeably with *friendship* and will denote the affection and fondness one feels for casual acquaintances as well as more intimate companions of either sex. The term *loving* will be used to denote the less common and more intense feeling of romantic affection that one often develops for a very special member of the other sex (usually). My use of the term *love* will be somewhat narrow, excluding parental love (unless specifically noted otherwise) and "platonic" love. In summary, *liking* will refer to friendship, and *loving* will refer to the sexually oriented, romantic variety of love.

Obviously, there is some conceptual overlay between the descriptions of liking and loving provided above. There is considerable continuity between these two types of interpersonal attraction. Data collected in a recent survey of friendship (Parlee et al., 1979) illustrate this fact. A startling 92% of the respondents indicated that they saw friendship as a form of love, and 77% reported that they would be willing to tell a friend that they loved her or him. Thus, the similarities between friendship and love are sufficient to permit a single, unified discussion (in the next section of this chapter) of the factors that influence both types of attraction.

However, while there are similarities between liking and loving, there are also differences. Love involves much more than just very intense liking. Therefore, after a unified discussion of the dynamics of attraction (who is attracted to whom and why), I will focus on special issues related to friendship and love individually.

Factors Influencing Interpersonal Attraction

"I just don't know what she sees in him. She could do so much better for herself. I suppose he's a nice guy, but they're just not right for each other." How many times have you heard comments such as these? Probably quite often. These comments illustrate the great interest we have in analyzing the dynamics of interpersonal attraction. They further illustrate the fact that we are often perplexed by the profound mysteries of attraction. *Who is attracted to whom* is an exceedingly complex topic. A bewildering multitude of factors influence your assessment of a person's attractiveness. Adding to the complexity of the situation is the fact that attraction is a two-way street, thus producing intricate interactions between factors.

My review of research in this area will deal with *both* friendship and love. Although liking and loving represent two very different levels and types of attraction, the *dynamics* are sufficiently similar to justify a unified treatment of the topic. In some cases, a particular factor, such as physical attractiveness, may play a more influential role in love than in friendship, or vice versa. However, all the factors to be discussed in this section appear to enter into both types of attraction. To simplify this very complex issue, I shall divide the coverage into three segments. In the first segment, I will review the characteristics of people that tend to make them attractive to us. In the second, I will analyze interaction factors, which do not reside in either person alone but emerge out of a pair's particular relationship to each other. In the third, I will discuss how *your* characteristics influence your assessment of others' attractiveness.

CHARACTERISTICS OF THE OTHER PERSON

PHYSICAL ATTRACTIVENESS

Various old sayings warn us about putting too much emphasis on physical attractiveness. Statements such as "Beauty is only skin deep" or "Don't judge a book by its cover" imply that we should be cautious about being seduced by the superficiality of physical beauty. However, the empirical evidence suggests that we do not pay much heed to this advice.

The importance of physical attractiveness was dramatically demonstrated in a study (Walster et al., 1966) in which male and female freshmen were invited to a dance where their dates had supposedly been selected by a computer. Actually, the couples had been paired randomly, but the computer cover story provided a good rationale for interrupting the dance midway and asking participants to rate the degree to which they would like to go out with their dates again. These ratings were then correlated with a wealth of data collected on the participants, including their level of physical attractiveness (as assessed by impartial judges), their intelligence, their social skill, and various personality characteristics. Out of this host of variables, *only one* was predictive of a subject's desire to see her or his date again. That single variable of significance was physical attractiveness. *For both sexes, more attractive partners were rated as more desirable for future dates.* Obviously, the demonstration that beauty is an influential determinant of heterosexual attraction is hardly an exciting new discovery. However, the fact that physical appearance was the *only* significant determinant of attraction in the Walster et al. (1966) study certainly underscores the prominence of this factor.

This great premium on physical attractiveness presents something of a problem because, obviously, we cannot all be beautiful (see Box 9.3). However, the emphasis on beauty *may* not be as great as the evidence reviewed thus far suggests. Table 9.2 summarizes some of the results of a large-scale survey on people's perceptions of the ideal man and woman. You will notice that although men do place more emphasis on physical appearance than women do, *for both sexes many other personal qualities, such as intelligence, confidence, and warmth, are rated as essential to the ideal more often than physical attractiveness.* These results are somewhat reassuring. We have seen earlier, however, that verbal reports such as these are not necessarily an accurate reflection of how people actually behave. Even if these results are accurate, the fact remains that we are brainwashed by the media into placing a great deal of emphasis on physical beauty. It seems inevitable that this indoctrination must have a corrosive effect on the self-concepts of those of us who do not correspond to the unrealistic Madison Avenue standards of physical beauty.

9.3 THE "FARRAH FACTOR"

The constant parade of remarkably attractive men and women that we see in the media may be producing an effect that *Human Behavior* magazine christened "The Farrah Factor." A study by Kenrick and Gutierres (1980) suggests that our standards of physical attractiveness may be raised by overexposure to the dazzling beauties who decorate our film and print media. Kenrick and Gutierres asked two groups of subjects to rate the attractiveness of average men and women who were portrayed in photographs. One group made these ratings immediately after viewing a series of advertisements featuring splendid-looking models. This group rated the appearance of the normal people significantly lower than the other group did.

In a second study, males living in a college dormitory were asked to look at a photo of a prospective date and give advice to a fellow student about whether to go out with the woman. When this advice was solicited while the subjects were watching *Charlie's Angels*, the woman's desirability was rated lower than in a control condition in which subjects were not watching this popular TV show starring three dazzling actresses.

TABLE 9.2   Perceptions of the ideal man and ideal woman

How important or unimportant is each of the following traits to your concept of the ideal man and the ideal woman?	Ideal man		Ideal woman	
	Men	Women	Men	Women
	Percentage saying trait is "very important" or "essential" to ideal			
Intelligent	71	84	70	83
Self-confident	86	86	76	87
Physically strong	19	21	4	7
Tall	7	11	4	2
Physically attractive	26	29	47	32
Successful at work	54	66	41	60
Competitive	38	27	18	22
Aggressive	30	28	16	21
Takes risks	34	25	21	26
Stands up for beliefs	87	92	82	90
Fights to protect family	77	72	72	70
Able to love	88	96	92	97
Warm	68	89	83	88
Gentle	64	86	79	86
Soft	28	48	63	62
Romantic	48	66	64	67
Able to cry	40	51	50	58
Skilled lover	38	48	41	44
Many sexual conquests	5	4	4	5
Sexually faithful	42	67	56	66

MATCHING HYPOTHESIS. *The principle of attraction that postulates that males and females of approximately equal physical attractiveness are likely to select each other as partners.*

The matching hypothesis.   It is important to emphasize that one does *not* have to be spectacularly good-looking in order to enjoy a rewarding social life. In spite of the common preference for attractive others, people have to realistically take into consideration their own level of attractiveness. The **matching hypothesis** suggests that *people of similar levels of physical attractiveness gravitate toward each other.* Berscheid and Walster (1974) have reviewed a considerable body of evidence that suggests that the ever-present possibility of rejection leads people to use reasonable standards in judging others' appearance. In addition to drawing people together, this matching on the dimension of physical attractiveness may make relationships evolve more smoothly. Thus, a study of dating couples (White, 1980b) found that similarity in attractiveness was related to courtship progress. Specifically, greater progress toward a more serious relationship (over a nine-month period) was observed for dating partners who were relatively similar to each other in level of physical attractiveness. Moreover, Murstein's (1972) finding that married couples tend to be quite similar in attractiveness provides further support for this trend and for the validity of the matching hypothesis.

The bulk of the research on the influence of physical attractiveness has zeroed in on its role in heterosexual dating rather than friendship formation. However, there is some evidence that *physical appearance may also play an influential role in the development of same-sex friendships.* Two studies (Cash & Derlega, 1978; Riedel & McKillip, 1979) have found that friends of the same sex are more similar in level of physical attractiveness than would be expected by chance. Thus, it appears that the matching hypothesis may apply to friendship formation as well as dating.

HALO EFFECT. *An error in social perception, in which an individual's rating of some characteristic of another person is influenced by other characteristics of that person.*

Why is attractiveness so important?   There are probably a number of reasons that we are drawn to physically attractive people. I have already discussed one of the more important reasons in talking about errors in person perception (see Chapter 6). There appears to be a sort of **halo effect** wherein *we attribute desirable characteristics to good-looking people.* I noted earlier that attractive people tend to be seen as more sensitive, interesting, intelligent,

People of similar levels of attractiveness tend to gravitate toward each other.

competent, and pleasant than unattractive people. Thus, our assessment of people's personality and behavior is swayed by our perception of their physical attractiveness in a manner that is advantageous to those who are attractive.

A second reason for our being drawn to good-looking men and women is that *their companionship may enhance our status in the eyes of others.* Sigall and Landy (1973) found that men were regarded more favorably by others when they were accompanied by a beautiful woman. Thus, attractive people may be seen as status symbols. This tendency may work to the advantage of attractive people, but it may also create some problems for them. Since many people like to "use" attractive companions as status symbols, persons who are especially attractive may have difficulty discerning whether they are liked sincerely or for the prestige they convey.

In addition to these somewhat "artificial" advantages, attractive people may have some more "authentic" advantages over those who are less attractive. Probably because we treat them so favorably, attractive people *tend* to acquire relatively good social skills (Goldman & Lewis, 1977). Their greater social abilities would then make them relatively likable. A recent study (Reis et al., 1982) found support for this line of reasoning for males but not for females. Among the women subjects greater physical attractiveness was associated with a lack of assertiveness and greater distrust of men. Additional research focusing on a more diverse array of social skills and attributes will be needed to resolve this interesting issue.

What makes someone attractive?   Although the advertising business has fostered a rather narrow conception of physical attractiveness, it appears that there is a fair amount of variability among people in regard to what they find attractive. Wiggins, Wiggins, and Conger (1968) studied male preferences for female body types and found that men with different kinds of personalities showed a diversity of preferences in regard to the ideal shape of women's breasts, buttocks, and legs. Moreover, Murstein (1971) has argued that analyzing attractiveness into specific components is hopeless because what is crucial is the total picture. The key point, then, is that one does *not* have to match up perfectly with the Madison Avenue ideals of good looks. *The range of what is considered attractive is probably wider than commonly believed.*

In view of the great emphasis placed on physical appearance, it is intriguing to find that there are some great misconceptions about the *male* ideal. A study of female preferences regarding male body types (Lavrakas, 1975) found that the alleged male ideal of a brawny and muscular fellow was *not* the most popular among women. Instead, it appears that females' strongest preference is for small buttocks in men (Beck, 1979). Although not derived from a scientific study, the data in Table 9.3 also indicate that men are quite misled about what women admire in the male physique.

TABLE 9.3 What's sexiest about men?

Howard Smith, a reporter for the *Village Voice,* asked 100 men to see themselves as "sex objects" and imagine what would most turn on women sexually. Then he asked 100 women what parts of the male physique really turned them on. The results suggest a gap in male awareness.

What men imagine *women admire*	*Percentage*	*What women* really *admire*	*Percentage*
Muscular chest and shoulders	21	Buttocks (usually described as "small and sexy")	39
Muscular arms	18	Slimness	15
Penis (as suggested by tight pants and jeans)	15	Flat stomach	13
Tallness	13	Eyes	11
Flat stomach	9	Long legs	6
Slimness	7	Tallness	5
Hair (texture, not length)	4	Hair	5
Buttocks	4	Neck	3
Eyes	4	Penis	2
Long legs	3	Muscular chest and shoulders	1
Neck	2	Muscular arms	0

DESIRABLE PERSONALITY CHARACTERISTICS

Personality characteristics are another rather obvious factor influencing interpersonal attraction. It should come as no surprise that Norman Anderson (1968) found subjects' ratings of a hypothetical person's likability to be much higher when the person was described as sincere, honest, and dependable rather than loudmouthed, deceitful, and obnoxious. Table 9.4 displays some of the findings from Anderson's research on the likableness of 555 different personality-trait descriptions. These ratings give us some insight into what personal qualities we value in others. The previously discussed data on the ideal man and woman (see Table 9.2) also provide information on the personality characteristics we value. A glance back at that table will show that we look for qualities such as confidence, integrity, warmth, gentleness, and the ability to love.

TABLE 9.4 Likability of personality traits

Norman H. Anderson (1968) and his colleagues have obtained likableness ratings for 555 words that can be used to describe personality. Although these normative data were collected to facilitate further research on impression formation, the findings provide us with some empirical indication of what personality traits people value in others. The 20 most highly rated personality traits are listed below.

Rank	Trait	Rank	Trait	Rank	Trait
1.	Sincere	8.	Dependable	15.	Mature
2.	Honest	9.	Open-minded	16.	Warm
3.	Understanding	10.	Thoughtful	17.	Earnest
4.	Loyal	11.	Wise	18.	Kind
5.	Trustful	12.	Considerate	19.	Friendly
6.	Trustworthy	13.	Good-natured	20.	Kind-hearted
7.	Intelligent	14.	Reliable		

ELWOOD CARTOON REPRINTED BY PERMISSION: TRIBUNE MEDIA SERVICES, INC.

INTELLIGENCE AND COMPETENCE

Generally we prefer people who are bright and competent over those who are not (Iverson, 1964). The survey data on Table 9.2 support this notion: a high proportion of people stressed intelligence and success in work as essential features of their ideal mate. Yet, extremely competent people are sometimes threatening to us, and we may occasionally dislike them. The legendary student who turns in his perfectly prepared term paper six weeks before the due date is not likely to win a class popularity contest. Given this reality, it is not surprising that a substantial number of people of both sexes report that they "play dumb" occasionally (Hughes & Gove, 1981).

Apparently, many extremely competent people have learned the advantage of keeping a low profile or showing a fallible side of themselves. There is experimental evidence that this strategy may work well. In a study by Aronson, Willerman, and Floyd (1966), students listened to a tape recording of another student who was portrayed either as unusually competent or as somewhat inept. As one might expect, the subjects liked the competent student slightly more than the incompetent one. In another experimental condition, the two stimulus figures on tape made a clumsy blunder, spilling coffee on themselves. While this blunder slightly *reduced* the liking of the inept person, it dramatically *increased* the liking of the competent person, making him substantially better liked than his incompetent counterpart. Although Deaux (1972) found similar results only for males evaluating males, it appears that extremely competent people may seem more human, and therefore more appealing, if they masquerade as a clown occasionally.

STATUS

Social status is also an important determinant of a person's appeal. Even at the grade-school level, youngsters show a decided preference for associating with popular classmates. Among adults, this factor may be more important for the interpersonal marketability of males than for that of females. College women were asked to rate the acceptability of men from various occupations as dates (VanGorp, Stempfle, & Olson, 1969). The women indicated a preference for men in high-status occupations (such as lawyer or doctor), as opposed to men in low-status occupations (such as janitor or bartender). Interestingly, the women's physical attractiveness influenced their standards about acceptable social status. More attractive women were more likely to demand high status in their prospective dates than were less attractive women.

It is often remarked, with considerable insight, that "fame is a powerful aphrodisiac." Illustrative of this principle is the "groupie" phenomenon, in which fans of both sexes zealously pursue any sort of contact, even if it is sometimes very demeaning, with their rock-star heroes. Although this is an extreme example, it is clear that status in all its forms (power, prestige, renown, and so forth) tends to substantially enhance one's interpersonal appeal.

INTERACTION FACTORS

Some factors in the dynamics of attraction lie neither in you nor in the other party. Instead, they emerge out of your unique relationship to each other. These include proximity, similarity, complementarity, and reciprocity.

PROXIMITY

It would be most difficult for you to develop a friendship with someone you never met. Obviously, physical proximity influences the likelihood of two persons' being attracted to each other. Evidence to this effect was collected in a study (Festinger, Schachter, & Back, 1950) of friendship patterns among married graduate students in a pair of university housing projects. People whose apartment entrances were close together were found to be friends more often than those whose dwellings were more distant, even though everyone really lived in fairly close proximity. The significant impact of spatial arrangements was dramatically highlighted by the finding that those whose homes faced the central court area had more than twice as many friends in the complex as those whose homes faced outward toward the street. Apparently, the centralized nature of the court area increased the likelihood that people would meet and become friends.

In addition to these findings on friendship patterns, there is evidence that *marriage* patterns are greatly influenced by **propinquity effects.** In a rather old study, Bossard (1931) found that one-quarter of the couples applying for marriage licenses in Philadelphia lived within *two blocks* of each other. Although the increasing geographic mobility in our society may be diminishing the importance of proximity, there is also relatively recent evidence (Ineichen, 1979) that you are likely to marry someone who grew up quite close to you.

PROPINQUITY EFFECTS. *The tendency for people who live near each other to become acquainted with, and attracted to, each other.*

Admittedly, this research is another example of social scientists documenting the obvious. However, when you consider the diverse array of variables that people supposedly consider in friendship selection and dating, it is rather disconcerting to realize that "a marriage can be the end result of an instructor's arbitrary seating chart" (Baron & Byrne, 1977, p. 220). A variety of hypotheses have been advanced as explanations of proximity effects in interpersonal attraction. Among these are the following.

1. Increased contact provides you with more information about someone, who thus becomes differentiated into a unique person. In essence, a "nonperson" in your life becomes converted into a person. This represents a first step toward attraction.
2. There is evidence (Zajonc, 1968) that mere exposure to a stimulus makes it more pleasant. Thus, regular contact with certain people may make them more familiar to us and lead us to have more positive feelings toward them (even without actual interaction).
3. The norms of social interaction promote pleasant encounters. In other words, our society expects us to treat people nicely when we meet them. If we treat each other well, friendship may evolve out of a chance encounter. Furthermore, the social pressure to be nice to others is even greater when they happen to be our neighbors or classmates.

SIMILARITY

Over the years, considerable evidence (see Rubin, 1973, for a review) has accumulated that indicates that married and dating couples tend to be similar in age, race, religion, social status, education, intelligence, physical attractiveness, and attitudes. This tendency for relatively similar people to marry each other is called **homogamy.** As you might expect, similarity also appears to play a role in friendship formation. A study of adolescent best friends (Kandel, 1978) found great similarity in regard to demographic factors such as age, grade, sex, and ethnicity. More interestingly, these best-friend pairs also showed consider-

HOMOGAMY. *The tendency for people who are similar in attitudes, social class, and other dimensions to marry each other; marriage between people who have similar personal characteristics.*

able similarity in educational goals and performance, participation in political or religious activities, and both licit and illicit drug use.

Although the existence of similarity effects is well documented, the underlying dynamics still require some clarification. If you are alert to methodological problems, you may have already realized that propinquity and homogamy effects are **confounded.** Since our cities tend to be segregated along social class and racial lines, which are often mirrored by attitudinal differences, our tendency to develop friendships with our neighbors may be a function of similarity as well as proximity. Inversely, similarity effects may be due in part to the proximity factor. Furthermore, the evidence on homogamy is correlational, and correlations give us only suggestive information about the direction of the underlying causal sequence. Thus, it may be that similarity makes people more attractive to each other, or it may be that mutual attraction makes people behave more similarly.

Experimental, as opposed to *correlational,* studies of this question suggest that, at least in part, *similarity causes attraction.* Donn Byrne (1971) has done extensive research on the role of attitudinal similarity, using an experimental paradigm that usually involves the following. Students in a class fill out a questionnaire about their attitudes on certain issues, such as belief in God. Later they are recruited to participate in a study in which they are asked to judge the likability of a stranger on the basis of information provided by the experimenter. This information is manipulated so that the stranger is portrayed as very similar or very dissimilar to the subject in regard to attitudes. Subjects' attraction to the stranger consistently turns out to be a direct linear function of the proportion of similar attitudes that they share (see Figure 9.2). Additionally, similar strangers are rated as more intelligent, better adjusted, and more desirable as work partners than dissimilar strangers are.

Although this experimental procedure has been criticized for its artificial nature, Byrne has collected data that are more naturalistic with similar results. Byrne, Ervin, and Lamberth (1970) matched up 44 pairs of college students for a brief date on the basis of a questionnaire filled out early in the semester. Some were matched to be very similar in attitudes, whereas others were matched so as to be quite dissimilar. Consistent with Byrne's other studies,

CONFOUNDED. *Variables are said to be confounded when they covary together in a way that makes it difficult to sort out their independent effects.*

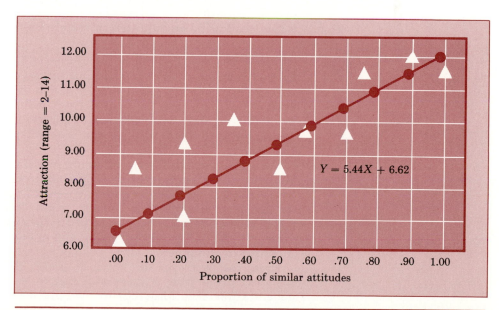

FIGURE 9.2 Attraction toward a stranger is a positive linear function of proportion of similar attitudes. Attraction as measured by the Interpersonal Judgment Scale can be predicted by multiplying the proportion of similar attitudes by 5.44 and adding 6.62.

there was a tendency for similar pairs of students to be more attracted to each other than dissimilar pairs.

The similarity/attraction effect appears to be quite potent in regard to both friendship and love. A host of explanations have been offered for these similarity effects. I will briefly mention two of the less technical and more plausible theories advanced.

1. Agreeing with someone about something is usually a pleasant, reinforcing experience. The probability of such reinforcing experiences is greater if we associate with people similar to ourselves. Thus, relationships between similar people may be facilitated by the greater mutual reinforcement they provide for each party.
2. We generally desire acceptance from others. Many people are probably drawn to similar others because they *expect* that they will be well received and that there is less likelihood of rejection.

COMPLEMENTARITY

COMPLEMENTARY NEEDS. *A principle of attraction according to which two persons are drawn together because they are uniquely well suited to satisfy each other's emotional needs.*

There is an old saying that "opposites attract." This folklore has been refined by Winch (1958), who argues that people with **complementary needs** will be drawn to each other. The principal example used to propagate this theory consists of the proverbial domineering husband paired with a submissive wife. According to the formulation, the husband has a need to dominate and the wife has a need to submit. The complementary meshing of their needs is supposed to make them a good match.

It may occur to you that the notion that opposites attract seems incompatible with similarity effects in attraction. Actually, the apparent contradiction is a superficial one, and complementarity and similarity tendencies *could* be simultaneously operative in a single relationship. For instance, the dominant and submissive mates described above, while being opposites in personality, might nonetheless be very similar in religion, socioeconomic class, political attitudes, and recreational tastes.

Although the complementary-needs hypothesis has some logical merit, Nias (1979) stresses that there is little empirical evidence to support the assertion that complementarity *draws* people together. Rubin (1973) speculates that the complementarity we often see in couples may *emerge as the relationship grows* rather than being an important precondition of the pairing.

RECIPROCITY

RECIPROCITY. *The tendency for liking and loving to stimulate a mutual interchange of affection.*

In his book *How to Win Friends and Influence People,* Dale Carnegie (1936) suggests that one can gain liking by ample use of praise and flattery. In contrast, we have all been told that "flattery will get you nowhere." Which advice is right? Well, the research evidence indicates that there is no simple answer. It appears that flattery *will* get you somewhere, with some people, some of the time.

Carnegie's formula for success would seem to be supported by the **reciprocity** principle. The evidence on reciprocity indicates that we tend to like those who show that they like us *and* that we tend to see others as liking us more if we like them (Berscheid & Walster, 1978). Thus, there does appear to be an interactive process in which liking promotes liking and loving promotes loving. However, this intuitively appealing and apparently simple principle must be qualified in a number of ways.

First, the *source* of the liking or praise influences its impact on us. For instance, praise from a high-status person, such as a popular classmate, will generate greater reciprocal liking than praise from a low-status person, such as an unpopular classmate. In a similar vein, Aronson and Linder (1965) showed that praise from an *unexpected* source is especially powerful. In their study, subjects were maneuvered into "overhearing" a series of conversations about themselves. Four different sequences of comments were made by an experi-

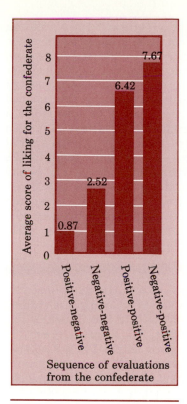

FIGURE 9.3 Liking of a confederate after different sequences of evaluations.

mental confederate. One-fourth of the subjects initially heard rather negative comments about themselves, which then gradually became positive. Another quarter of the subjects heard favorable comments at first, but these gave way to unfavorable evaluations. Still another quarter of the subjects heard consistently positive comments; the remaining subjects heard consistently negative remarks. Subsequently, the subjects were asked to rate their liking of the confederate who had made the comments they had overheard. Surprisingly, the subjects in the negative-positive condition returned the highest ratings of the confederate; these ratings were even higher than when consistently positive remarks were made (see Figure 9.3). Although efforts at replicating Aronson and Linder's experiment have not been consistent, the implications of the study are intriguing. The results suggest that there may be a law of diminishing returns in regard to positive behavior toward others. Consistently positive behavior from an old pal or spouse may come to be taken for granted, while positive reactions from someone who has previously displayed a negative attitude may be especially potent.

The second qualification centers on the level of self-esteem of the recipient of the praise. If the recipient is low in self-esteem and/or has an unusually high affiliation drive, flattery and praise will probably be soaked up eagerly and work very effectively. A person who is high in self-esteem may not be so easily swayed by positive treatment. This analysis has received suggestive support in a couple of experiments (Jacobs, Berscheid, & Walster, 1971; Walster, 1965).

You might expect that another qualification to the reciprocity principle would involve the old "playing hard to get" routine. This common-sense notion suggests that showing relatively little interest in the social overtures of a member of the other sex (nonreciprocity) may make the other person even more eager to pursue the relationship. *However, the empirical evidence suggests that "playing hard to get" may not be advisable.* Research by Walster et al. (1973) indicates that we prefer members of the other sex who appear hard for *others* to get but who eagerly accept *us*.

YOUR OWN CHARACTERISTICS

Thus far I have addressed how others' characteristics and factors residing in a relationship with another person affect interpersonal attraction. I am ready now to turn the spotlight on you.

SELF-PERCEPTION

You may recall that Daryl Bem (1972) has theorized that we attempt to better understand ourselves by inferring our motives and attitudes from our behavior (see Chapter 6). A couple of studies (Dutton & Aron, 1974; Valins, 1966) suggest that these self-perception efforts may play a key role in attraction.

In Valins's (1966) study, the experimental task for the male subjects was to view pictures of seminude females. A microphone was attached to the chest of each subject so that he could hear his heartbeat amplified. In reality, the experimenter controlled the auditory feedback about heart rate. The men were led to believe that slides of certain women triggered a dramatic change in their heartbeat. When later asked to rate their attraction to the various women seen in the slides, the men indicated that they were most attracted to the women who had apparently affected their heart rate.

Valins's findings illustrate our need to interpret our emotional states. Schachter (1964) has proposed that when we experience the physiological arousal usually associated with emotion (which was faked in this study by providing false feedback on heart rate), we try to explain it by looking at the characteristics of the environmental situation. In this particular situation, the most plausible explanation for the men was that they were really "turned on" by the women who apparently affected their heart rate.

Similar evidence was garnered in a more naturalistic study by Dutton and

Aron (1974). They arranged for young men crossing a footbridge to encounter a good-looking young woman. She stopped the men, asking them to fill out a questionnaire for a class project. When the men returned the questionnaire, she offered to explain the research at some future time and gave them her phone number. The key to the experiment was that this procedure was enacted on two very different bridges. One was a long suspension bridge that swayed precariously over a 230-foot dropoff; the other was a solid, safe structure a mere 10 feet above a small stream. The experimenters reasoned that men crossing the shaky, frightening bridge would be experiencing emotional arousal and that some of them might misinterpret that arousal as being caused by the woman rather than the bridge. If these men attributed their arousal to the woman, they would probably infer that they found her very attractive. What Dutton and Aron were looking for was how many men later called the woman to pursue a date. Consistent with the experimenters' hypothesis, the men who met the woman in an aroused state (on the precarious bridge) were more likely to call than those who met her in a normal emotional state.

What does all this mean? This and other studies (White, Fishbein, & Rutstein, 1981) suggest that the self-perception processes described by Bem may be particularly relevant to our efforts to understand the emotional turmoil triggered by heterosexual attraction. Many of us spend long hours mulling over whether a certain member of the other sex is "right" for us. Much of this thought involves self-perception efforts such as "Gee, I don't get very excited when Mary Ann calls to say she's coming over. I guess maybe I'm not all that crazy about her" or "Wow, I just glow when I'm around Bill. I can't stop smiling. He must be the one." Thus, it appears that interpersonal attraction may be influenced by the way we tend to interpret our behavior and emotions. In other words, self-perception processes may be of paramount importance.

While highlighting the importance of self-perception, it seems worthwhile to mention that *this propensity to misinterpret emotion may be the basis for the apparently common tendency to mistake lust for love.* If artificial manipulations of physical arousal in experiments can influence attraction, it is easy to imagine how genuine arousal that has really been elicited by the target person might "color" one's feelings for that person. Thus, it seems entirely plausible that sexual arousal attributable to a person might be misinterpreted and mislabeled as love. Although sexual arousal is an important aspect of romantic love, they are certainly not equivalent—love is more than mere lust. However, research on self-perception shows just how easy it may be for people to mix up sexual arousal and more profound feelings of love.

SELF-ESTEEM

SOCIAL EXCHANGE THEORY. *The view that interpersonal behavior is governed by expectation of rewards and costs. Interaction between people is thought to continue as long as participants feel that the benefits outweigh the costs.*

Social exchange theory postulates that interpersonal relationships are based on fair exchanges between participants. To illustrate, consider a pair of regular tennis partners who are very uneven in skill, so that one player consistently trounces the other. According to social exchange theory, the winner in this pairing probably gets ego enhancement out of the relationship, while the loser gets the benefit of practice against a superior opponent (which is more valuable to his tennis game than playing with a poor partner). Social exchange theory predicts that a relationship will continue as long as the participants view their outcomes favorably. In our example, if the winner continued to annihilate his opponent with complete regularity over a long period, he might reach a point at which he no longer derived any satisfaction from the victories. If this occurred, the exchange might not be viewed subjectively as "fair," and the winner would probably terminate the partnership. This theory of an "interpersonal marketplace" provides an excellent model for analyzing heterosexual interactions. For instance, the stereotyped example of the beautiful young woman dating the fat, homely, but very wealthy older man is readily understood by this model.

Social exchange theory also provides a good explanation for the fact that people's level of self-esteem has some influence on their tendency to be attracted to one person rather than another. *If you have relatively low self-esteem, you are likely to appraise yourself as having relatively little market value to the opposite sex.* This evaluation will influence the standards that you set for your potential dates as well as friends. Thus, Kiesler and Baral (1970) found that low-self-esteem subjects selected less attractive dates than high-self-esteem subjects. In summary, your level of self-esteem may influence whom you are attracted to. People with a favorable self-concept may see themselves as having a wider range of choices than people with an unfavorable self-concept.

Friendship

Friends play a very significant role in our lives. They may provide help in times of need, advice in times of confusion, sympathy in times of failure, and praise in times of achievement. The importance of friends was underscored in a survey study (Parlee et al., 1979) in which 51% of the respondents indicated that in times of crisis they were more likely to turn to friends than to family for help. This section will discuss what makes a good friend, how friendships develop, and how sex and marriage affect patterns of friendship.

WHAT MAKES A GOOD FRIEND?

The most intriguing aspect of the Parlee et al. (1979) survey on friendship was its probing into what it is that makes a "good friend." Over 40,000 respondents indicated what qualities they valued in a friend. Figure 9.4 lists the ten most frequently endorsed qualities. The results suggest that *loyalty* is the heart and

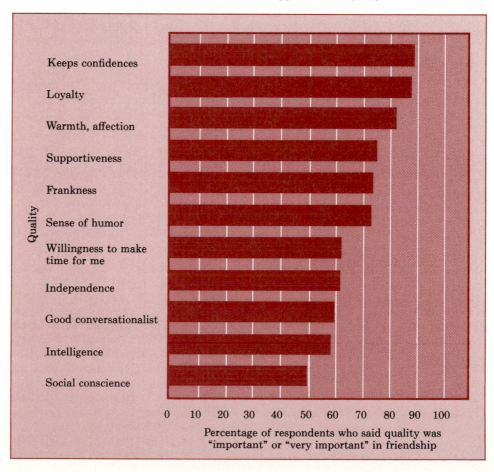

FIGURE 9.4 Important qualities in a friend.

Percentage of respondents who said quality was "important" or "very important" in friendship

Friends play a very significant role in our lives.

soul of friendship. As you can see, the top two qualities in Figure 9.4 are keeping confidences (an aspect of loyalty) and loyalty itself. As one might guess, the next most important ingredients of friendship are warmth/affection and supportiveness. The high premiums put on candor (frankness) and a sense of humor are interesting and well worth keeping in mind. These results generally coincide with those of another survey on friendship (Block, 1980), although one other crucial factor emerged in this second survey. That additional factor was a willingness to let people be themselves. Block (1980) points out that we often tend to put our friends under pressure to behave in ways that are consistent with *our* expectations. The respondents to his survey emphasized the importance of friends' accepting them in a relatively unconditional manner.

THE DEVELOPMENT OF FRIENDSHIP

The birth of a friendship evolves out of a curious combination of chance factors and specific intentions. George Levinger (1974) has put together an insightful theory of how interpersonal relationships develop. The model outlines three levels of human relatedness and identifies some of the factors that propel people toward each stage of involvement. The model is summarized briefly below.

Stage 1: Unilateral awareness. You are aware of another's existence but have no expectation of interaction and no idea whether the other person is aware of you. For example, you might recognize a person who is in one of your classes at school, but the two of you do not say hello in the hallway or interact in any way. This level of relatedness is facilitated by spatial and social proximity and depends, in part, on how much interest you take in other people.

Stage 2: Bilateral surface contact. You are aware of each other and acknowledge that fact, but interaction tends to be brief and is governed by stereotyped role expectations. Communication is superficial, maintenance of the relationship is not important to either of you, and you really know very little about each other. For example, you might exchange a casual hello and remarks about the weather with the attendant at a parking garage that you use regularly. This level of relatedness is facilitated by available time for verbal exchanges and your perception of the other person's social attractiveness and interest in you.

Stage 3: Mutuality. You respond to each other as unique individuals and share some real knowledge about each other. Communication may concern personal feelings, and maintenance of the relationship becomes important to both of you. For example, you might discuss difficulties you are having in school with a classmate who displays a genuine interest. This level of relatedness is facilitated by your satisfaction with the other person's role-regulated behavior in the previous stage, by circumstances that force the interaction beyond routine roles, and by your perception of the person's potential likability.

As you can see, in the first stage, chance factors such as enrollment in the same class or riding the same bus govern unilateral awareness. In contrast, the third stage, in which friendship may emerge, is governed by your intentions and the nature of previous interactions.

PATTERNS OF FRIENDSHIP

Marital status and sex are major determinants of adult friendship patterns. When a person marries, the freedom to develop friendships with members of the other sex is seriously curtailed by social norms. Cross-sex friendships may be seen as a threat by the other spouse. There is also a tendency for some people to assume that something must be missing in a marital relationship if one spouse (or both) is involved in a close cross-sex friendship. Married *women* are sometimes even discouraged from having many *same-sex* friends. It is more acceptable for husbands to have an extensive network of male companions with whom they share recreational interests, such as bowling or hunting. However, in spite of social pressure to the contrary, there is evidence (Blau, 1971) that wives are more likely than husbands to depend on a close friend rather than their spouse as their principal confidante.

These social constraints that limit the freedom of married people to pursue new friendships seem unfortunate. As I have already noted, friends are a valuable resource in times of stress. Moreover, with close-knit kinship networks becoming less common, it seems even more important for people to be free to develop worthwhile friendships outside their marriage. The increasing rate of marital dissolution provides yet another reason for encouraging people to seek nonmarital companionships. In times of marital distress it would seem especially important for a person to have friends to depend on for emotional support.

Irrespective of marital status, there are some interesting sex differences in friendship patterns. Friendships between women seem to involve more intimacy than friendships between men. There is some evidence (Block, 1980; Jourard, 1964, 1971) that female friends engage in more self-disclosure with each other than male friends do. In contrast, interactions between men are regulated more by role expectations. Men have a greater tendency to relate to each other in a narrow way, as business partners, as racquetball rivals, or as fellow baseball fans. Men are less likely than women to reveal inner secrets or insecurities to each other. As discussed earlier, this sex-typed socialization, which discourages males from confiding in each other, probably robs many men of an important source of psychological support and emotional sustenance.

Love

We turn now to the topic of romantic love. Back in 1958, Harry Harlow issued a scathing indictment of psychology, writing: "So far as love or affection is concerned, psychologists have failed in their mission. The little we know about love does not transcend simple observation, and the little we write about it has been written better by poets and novelists" (1958, p. 673). Unfortunately, the situation today is only moderately better. This important human emotion has proved an elusive target for investigation. However, researchers are devoting much more attention to this topic lately, and noticeable progress may be just around the corner. In this section I shall discuss some myths about love, the nature of love, the capacity for love, and sex differences regarding love.

MYTHS ABOUT LOVE

Love is a highly idealized concept, and some interesting myths have been nurtured by this idealism. Accordingly, our first task is to take a realistic look at love and dispel some of these problematic notions.

Myth No. 1: When you fall in love, you'll know it. People often spend a great deal of time agonizing over whether they are experiencing true love or mere infatuation. When these people consult others, they are often told that "if it were true love, you'd know it." This statement, which is tantamount to telling the person that he or she is *not* really in love, is simply not accurate. A minority of people may recognize love clearly and quickly, but most of us have to struggle with some confusion. There is no "bolt out of the sky" that clearly marks the beginning of love. On the contrary, love usually grows gradually, and doubts are quite normal.

Myth No. 2: Love is a purely positive experience. Our idealization of love sometimes creates unrealistic expectations that love should be an exclusively enjoyable experience. In reality, love may bring great pain and very intense negative feelings. Ambivalent feelings in love are quite common. In part, this may be because we tend to expect and demand a lot from someone we love. Recent research suggests that we tend to be more critical and less accepting and tolerant of lovers and spouses, in comparison with friends (Davis, 1985). Berscheid and Walster (1978) note that psychologists are often asked "Can you love and hate someone at the same time?" This common question illustrates the dilemma experienced by many people who find that their lover may stimulate indescribable anger and irritation as well as sublime joy. The passionate quality of love is such that a lover is capable of taking us to emotional peaks in *either* direction.

Myth No. 3: True love lasts forever. Love *may* last forever, but unfortunately, you can't count on it. People perpetuate this myth in an interesting way. If they have a love relationship that eventually disintegrates, many people conclude that they were never really in love, and they relegate the dissolved relationship to the inferior status of infatuation. This disavowal of love in the previous relationship allows the person to return to the search for the one, great, idealized lover who will supposedly provide complete happiness. A more realistic view of love would be to conceive of it as a sometimes frustrating experience that *might* be encountered on several occasions in one's life. Berscheid and Walster (1978) argue that love seems to peak early and then fight a difficult battle against the erosion of time. At first, love is "blind," and we usually develop a very idealized picture of our lover. However, as time passes, the intrusion of reality often undermines this idealized view. Additionally, the high level of passion experienced early in a love relationship is difficult to maintain over time. Although Berscheid and Walster may be unduly pessimistic, it is nonetheless clear that even very authentic and passionate love may come to an unpleasant end.

Myth No. 4: Love can conquer all problems. This myth is the basis for many doomed marriages. Numerous couples, fully cognizant of certain problems in their relationships (for example, poor communication, disagreement about sex roles, lack of financial resources), forge ahead blissfully into marriage anyway, thinking "As long as we love each other, we'll be able to work it out." Authentic love certainly helps in tackling marital problems, but it is no guarantee of success, as we shall see in Chapter 11, on marital relationships. In fact, there is some provocative evidence that suggests (tentatively) that how much you *like* your lover may be more important than how much you *love* your lover. Sternberg and Grajek (1984) correlated a host of variables with a measure of the "successfulness" of romantic relationships. Surprisingly, liking of one's partner was more highly correlated (.62) with relationship success than was love of one's partner (.50). Although a small difference such as this in just one study is hardly definitive, it raises the *possibility* that liking may conquer problems more effectively than love.

THE CAPACITY FOR LOVE

People vary in their capacity for experiencing and expressing love. These individual differences in the ability to give love are deeply rooted in our personality structure and therefore are greatly influenced by our upbringing.

Sidney Jourard (1974) provides an extensive discussion of the factors that appear to promote a sound capacity for love. Some of the more important factors include the following.

1. *Gratification of basic needs.* People whose basic needs have been satisfied can be more sensitive to someone else's needs. A history of nongratification will often lead one to focus exclusively on one's own needs.
2. *High frustration tolerance.* Because love sometimes requires one to put another's welfare ahead of one's own, some frustration must be inevitable. Ability to deal with this frustration is essential.

9.4   STYLES OF LOVING

In a thought-provoking analysis, a sociologist, John Alan Lee (1974), has argued that there are different varieties of love. Noting that disappointment in love is commonplace, Lee says "I think that part of the reason for this failure rate is that too often people are speaking different languages when they speak of love. The problem is not *how much* love they feel, but *which kind.* The way to have a mutually satisfying love affair is not to find a partner who loves 'in the right amount,' but one who shares the same approach to loving, the same definition of love" (p. 44).

Lee suggests that love is like color, with many varieties emerging out of the mixture of three basic emotional approaches, which he compares with the blending of the three primary colors. Using this analogy, Lee arrived at a typology of no fewer than *nine* kinds of love! Six of these (the most basic varieties) are described briefly below.

Eros.   This style is dominated by a fascination with beauty. The magnetism of powerful physical attraction greatly outweighs the importance of personality or intellectual qualities. Erotic lovers are confident, secure, and rarely possessive.

Ludus.   This style views love as a game. The ludic lover avoids getting too involved in an intimate relationship. The key to ludus is a casual, detached attitude, which often permits the ludic lover to enjoy juggling several relationships at once.

Storge.   In this type, love "grows on you" gradually. Storge is a "slow-burning," relatively nonintense version of love. Storgic lovers prefer stability over the hectic ups and downs of passionate love.

Mania.   This approach to love is characterized by feverish intensity, excessive need for attention, possessiveness, and quickly triggered jealousy. Manic lovers are consumed by passion and often feel that they are unable to control their emotions. They tend to lack confidence and often seem to fall in love with someone they don't particularly like.

Pragma.   This is the rational approach to love. The emphasis is on practical compatibility in interests and attitudes. If a relationship does not appear to be working out too well, the pragmatic lover will simply move on.

Agape.   This type of love is described as "deeply compassionate and utterly altruistic." The agapic lover is described as unselfish, undemanding, and giving. Lee suggests that this type of love is rare.

This taxonomy of the varieties of love is not as well grounded empirically as many social scientists would like, and Lee himself admits that it should be regarded as "preliminary" and tentative. Even if the typology does provide an accurate description of the basic kinds of love, one must recognize that love may often involve a *mixture* of several subtypes. Moreover, the question of which styles match up best for successful coalitions of love remains unresolved. Nonetheless, the analysis is provocative and illustrates the diversity and complexity of the phenomenon of love.

The attitudes of men and women toward love present some interesting differences. Several studies suggest that, contrary to traditional stereotypes, men may be more romantic than women.

3. *Self-love.* Many theorists believe that loving oneself (having a reasonably favorable self-concept) is a precondition for loving another. People low in self-esteem tend to have excessive dependency needs and often relate to others in negative ways.
4. *Reality contact.* Effective loving requires accurate perception of the partner's moods, desires, needs, and problems.
5. *Reasonable ideals.* Unrealistic expectations of perfection in one's partner lead to disappointment and unwarranted withdrawal of love.
6. *Emancipation from one's parents.* A mature adult relationship should be governed by the needs and wishes of the partners, not their parents. Excessive devotion to parental approval often undermines one's capacity to give freely to one's partner.

In an analysis related to this issue of differing capacities for love, some theorists have attempted to develop a *typology* of love. For example, Maslow (1970) has differentiated two kinds of love, "deficiency-love" and "being-love." He describes *deficiency-love* as that which we feel for someone who gratifies our deficiency needs (see Chapter 2) for security and belongingness. The key feature of this type of love is its *conditional* quality; it is contingent on continued gratification of our dependency needs. In contrast, Maslow describes what he believes to be a more mature form of love, called *being-love;* this type of love is less conditional. In being-love, the gratification that the partner provides is not all that important. According to Maslow, relatively few of us experience this higher form of love. Maslow's distinction between two types of love is not unique. Fromm (1956) describes a similar dichotomy, using the terms *symbiotic love* and *mature love*. In making these distinctions, both theorists are focusing on what they consider a major inadequacy in most love relationships. They both feel that most of us are too wrapped up in what we can *get* out of a relationship, rather than in what we *give* to it. *To put it bluntly, they feel that most of us are overly concerned about the "balance sheet" in a relationship.*

Their point is worthwhile, though probably overstated. It certainly seems reasonable to assert that many relationships would be more successful if the partners gave of themselves more unselfishly. However, the generalization that *most* coalitions of love are dominated by dependency needs seems excessively pessimistic. Moreover, the implicit suggestion that we should completely dis-

---

9.5

RECOMMENDED READING

A New Look at Love
by Elaine Walster and G. William Walster (Addison-Wesley, 1978)

This book represents a fine effort at combining empirical research with practical advice. As you may have noticed from the references to studies in this chapter, the Walsters have conducted a great deal of research on the mysteries of love. Moreover, they have been among the more innovative and down-to-earth investigators in this area. Although their own work is highlighted, their review of research is broad in scope. The book is smoothly written, with minimal dependence on technical jargon.

Unlike many psychologists from a theoretical research background, the Walsters are not timid about giving practical advice on ordinary questions. Drawing from scientific research, casual observation, and their obviously extensive and astute thoughts about the subject, they offer abundant advice on how to deal with the intricacies of romantic relationships. The book is loaded with fascinating case histories and intriguing questionnaires.

Critics of the Walsters appear to have derived some amusement from the fact that this husband-and-wife team was broken up by divorce soon after publication of the book (Ms. Walster now publishes under the name Elaine Hatfield). Though admittedly ironic, their parting of ways in no way undermines the quality of their contribution to our understanding of love. As they pointed out themselves, love is a beautiful but *fragile* flower.

Passionate love is characterized by fragility. Every lover always hopes that *this* love will last forever. But the rest of us, looking on, know that that's unlikely [p. 108].

card the balance sheet in favor of totally unconditional love seems unreasonable. Flanders (1976) argues convincingly that a mature love relationship *should* be characterized by a fair exchange of benefits: one partner should not be permitted to exploit the other. In summary, less emphasis on the balance sheet would probably be beneficial to many relationships, but the doctrine of fair exchange should not be thrown out altogether.

SEX DIFFERENCES REGARDING LOVE

As we already know, males and females are socialized quite differently in our society. It appears that this different socialization affects male and female attitudes toward love. The traditional stereotype suggests that love is primarily a feminine pursuit and that women are more romantic than men. However, much of the *research* evidence suggests the opposite, that men are more romantic than women! For example, Kanin, Davidson, and Scheck (1970) report that men score higher than women on romanticism scales, that men recognize love earlier than women do, and that females are more cautious and rational than males in their mate selection. Other research (Rubin, Peplau, & Hill, 1981) suggests that men tend to fall *in* love more readily than women, while women fall *out* of love more easily. Furthermore, Safilios-Rothschild (1977) argues that men are more likely than women to marry a person they love, while women are more likely to make a practical mate selection. Specifically, men are thought to base their marital choice on *their feelings* toward the potential partner, while women base their marital choice on their estimate of the intensity of *their suitor's feelings.*

Given the above evidence, one could argue with merit that men are more romantic than women. However, such a conclusion hinges on how one defines romanticism. In regard to *verbal expressions* of love, women seem more romantic than men (Balswick & Avertt, 1977). Women are more willing to verbalize and display their affection overtly. In conclusion, there are complex sex differences in this area that do *not* provide great support for the traditional belief that women are more romantic than men.

9.6

RECOMMENDED READING

How to Break Your Addiction to a Person

by Howard M. Halpern (McGraw-Hill, 1982)

As its title suggests, this book is about the termination of romantic relationships. In particular, it focuses on why some people have enormous difficulty in extracting themselves from relationships that are decidedly unsatisfactory. The book is predicated on the belief that substantial numbers of people linger in "romantic love" relationships even though they create more pain than happiness.

Using a psychoanalytic perspective, Halpern asserts that excessive affiliation needs rooted deeply in childhood make it difficult for some people to break away from counterproductive relationships. He compares their desperate interpersonal dependency to drug addiction to emphasize how powerful the compulsion to maintain a relationship can be. After analyzing the psychological basis for this problem, Halpern offers a great deal of advice about how to muster the courage to get out of "dead end" relationships.

The book is not without its flaws. The theoretical analysis regarding the causation of this problem is *highly* speculative, and the drug-addiction analogy is somewhat contrived. However, Halpern is a veteran psychotherapist who offers a lot of worthwhile advice on how to get out of interpersonal dependency traps. The book is loaded with thought-provoking case histories that propel the reader along at a fairly fast pace.

To break a relationship with someone on whom your sense of existence has depended means that you will have to, sooner or later, risk facing the terror of your own feelings of invisibility and nonexistence. Norma, a woman of forty, had ended her marriage, and several years later she was still so terrified of being alone that she never spent a weekend without the company of a man for at least a substantial part of the time, even if it meant remaining in relationships that were dreadful. And she went from one dreadful relationship to another because she would clutch onto someone new, with little regard for his suitability, to enable her to leave the last disastrous affair [p. 42].

Loneliness

LONELINESS. *An unpleasant emotion caused by dissatisfaction with one's interpersonal network, usually accompanied by a desire for greater intimacy with others.*

I began this chapter by discussing the importance of the affiliation drive. I shall now discuss what happens when this very fundamental drive is thwarted. **Loneliness** has been defined by Peplau and Perlman (1979) as a condition that exists to the extent that an individual's network of interpersonal relationships is smaller or less satisfying than desired.

DIMENSIONS OF LONELINESS

Young (1979) distinguishes among three kinds of loneliness. *Chronic loneliness* refers to people who have been unable over a period of years to acquire a satisfactory interpersonal network. *Transitional loneliness* refers to people who have had satisfying social relationships in the past but are currently lonely because of some specific disruption of their previous social network (examples include death of a loved one, divorce, and moving to a new locale). *Transient everyday loneliness* involves brief and sporadic feelings of loneliness, which many people may experience even when their social life is reasonably adequate.

Schmidt and Sermat (1983) point out that loneliness often may not occur "across the board" in all areas of one's life. They maintain that it is an oversimplification to think of loneliness as a unidimensional construct. For instance, you might be highly satisfied with your friendship network but feel very dissatisfied about your lack of a suitable romantic/sexual relationship. With this analysis as a backdrop, Schmidt and Sermat set out to identify the specific areas of life in which people experience relationship deficits that produce feelings of loneliness. Their research suggests that there are four such areas. They found that loneliness may be attributable to perceived deficits in (1) romantic/sexual relationships, (2) friendship relationships, (3) family relationships, and (4) community relationships. Thus, in trying to better understand one's loneliness, it may be useful to pinpoint the exact nature of the relational deficits that produce the feelings of loneliness.

PREVALENCE AND CONSEQUENCES OF LONELINESS

Survey studies designed to gain some insight into the prevalence of loneliness in our society have yielded notably disparate figures, depending on the nature of the sample interviewed and the shaping of the questions. In Seeman's (1971) survey of some 400 Los Angeles workers, the statement "I often feel lonely" was endorsed by 10% of respondents. In contrast, in the Parlee et al. (1979) survey on friendship, 67% of the respondents indicated that they felt lonely either "sometimes" or "often." Such startlingly high figures probably reflect the fact that most of us experience the pain of transient everyday loneliness at one time or another. The crucial question is how many people are *chronically tormented* by the more severe forms of loneliness. We currently do not have sound data for a precise estimate of the incidence of this affliction. We do know, however, from anecdotal evidence, that the number of people plagued by loneliness is substantial. Telephone hotlines for troubled people report that complaints of loneliness dominate their calls. The ever-increasing popularity of singles clubs, computer dating services, encounter groups, and so forth indicates that there are many lonely people eagerly searching for intimacy.

The personal consequences of the experience of loneliness may be overwhelming. Agonizing thoughts of one's lonely plight may come to dominate one's consciousness. Bradburn (1969) found a strong correlation (in the .70s for both men and women) between feelings of loneliness and feelings of depression. Shaver and Rubenstein (1979) found a relationship between loneliness and poor physical *and* psychological health. Thus, it is clear that the consequences of loneliness are quite serious.

CAUSES OF LONELINESS

Quite a number of factors may contribute to feelings of loneliness. Any event that ruptures the social fabric of one's life may lead to loneliness. Thus, no one is immune. In this section I will describe some social trends and personal qualities that are among the more prominent causes of loneliness.

Contributing social trends. A number of theorists (Fromm, 1941; Keyes, 1973; Packard, 1972; Riesman, 1950) have commented on various social trends that have undermined the sharing of intimacy in our culture. For instance, dramatic increases in residential mobility have played havoc with friendship networks. Families are becoming less effective sources of socioemotional security as divorce rates reach alarming levels and the extended family becomes a relic of the past. Urban environments seem to promote mere superficiality in social interactions, as we get our meals from drive-through fast-food franchises, make our financial transactions from our cars at drive-through bank facilities, and get our entertainment at drive-in theaters. Moreover, with the advent of personal computers, more and more people will fulfill their job responsibilities by working at terminals in their homes, *alone.*

Low self-esteem. A key personal factor that promotes loneliness is low self-esteem (Cutrona, 1982). People who have unfavorable opinions of themselves often do not feel worthy of others' affection and may make little effort to pursue such affection. This lack of confidence probably has a spiraling effect, as low self-esteem begets loneliness and loneliness begets still lower self-esteem.

Lack of social skills. Interpersonal skill, though not particularly difficult to develop, *does* have to be acquired. Social ineptitude probably prevents many people from experiencing rewarding social interactions. Thus, studies of conversational style find that lonely people tend to pay inadequate attention to someone they are talking with (Jones, Hobbs, & Hockenbury, 1982) and that they are relatively inhibited, speaking less than nonlonely people (Sloan & Solano, 1984).

Fear of intimacy. Some people with positive self-concepts and sound social skills seem overly wary of intimate interaction. They keep people at an emotional distance and (often unconsciously) limit their interactions to a relatively superficial level. Illustrative of this fear of intimacy is recent evidence that lonely people are relatively reluctant to take social risks (Schultz & Moore, 1984). The difficulty that lonely people tend to have in engaging in self-disclosure (Solano, Batten, & Parish, 1982) also demonstrates how this fear of intimacy undermines rewarding social interactions.

Irrational thinking. Ultimately, what underlies many of the factors listed above is *irrational thinking* about one's social skills, the likelihood of achieving intimacy, the probability of rejection, and so forth. Thus, there is evidence (Anderson, Horowitz, & French, 1983) that lonely people tend to *reverse* normal attributional propensities, attributing their interpersonal failures to basic personal defects in themselves (internal attribution). Taking a cognitive approach to the problem, Young (1979) points out that lonely people engage in a great deal of negative self-talk that prevents them from pursuing intimacy in an active and positive manner. He has identified some clusters of ideas that undermine or preclude productive interpersonal behavior (see Table 9.5), thus making loneliness a likely outcome.

TABLE 9.5 **Clusters of cognitions typical of lonely clients**

Clusters	Cognitions	Behaviors
A	1. I'm undesirable 2. I'm dull and boring	Avoidance of friendship
B	1. If I ever admitted this thought to anyone, he/she would reject me or ridicule me 2. Other people aren't interested in my thoughts and feelings	Low self-disclosure
C	1. I'm not a good lover in bed 2. I can't relax, be spontaneous, enjoy sex	Avoidance of sexual relationships
D	1. I can't seem to get what I want from this relationship 2. I can't say how I feel or he/she might leave me and I'd be alone	Lack of assertiveness in relationships
E	1. I won't risk being hurt again 2. There must be something wrong with me if he/she left me	Avoidance of potentially intimate relationships
F	1. I don't know how to act around other people 2. I'll make a fool of myself	Avoidance of any contact with people

COPING WITH LONELINESS

In view of the seriousness of the emotional deficit of loneliness, it is disheartening to report that there are no simple solutions. Weiss (1973) notes: "I can offer no method for ending loneliness other than the formation of new relationships that might repair the deficit responsible for the loneliness. And I think this solution ordinarily is not easy. If it were, there would be fewer lonely people" (p. 231).

A major reason that people have difficulty overcoming feelings of loneliness is that many of them tend to withdraw into a passive state of self-pity. For example, when Rubenstein and Shaver (1979) asked people what they do when they feel lonely, the top three responses were: read, watch television, and listen to music. Obviously, these activities are not going to help one acquire new friends. Thus, in a nutshell, the key to overcoming loneliness may be to avoid the temptation to withdraw, stay afloat socially, and try to maintain an optimistic outlook, recognizing that things can get better. The importance of staying socially active cannot be overestimated. As we learned earlier in this chapter, *proximity* is a surprisingly powerful determinant of interpersonal attraction. You have to be around people in order to expand your network of friends. A lonely person might respond to this advice by saying "If I had people to be around, I wouldn't be lonely." True, but the fact is that you can seek out many kinds of social interaction which initially may be superficial but which hold the potential for more intimate kinds of interaction. There are a vast array of organizations you can join (everything from the Young Republicans to the PTA). Get involved in activities that coincide with your interests and hobbies. Visit beaches, parks, museums, and bars. Go to church. But whatever you do, if you want to conquer loneliness, stay afloat socially.

Beyond this very general advice, there are many comments that one might make about overcoming loneliness, but they depend on the specific causes or constellation of causes producing the loneliness. Useful information and recommendations for further reading are sprinkled throughout this central part of your book on "The Interpersonal Realm." Each of the clusters of cognitions and behaviors inducing loneliness that are summarized in Table 9.5 is discussed at some point in this text. Clusters A (poor self-concept, Chapter 6), B (low self-disclosure, Chapter 7), and D (lack of assertiveness, Chapter 8) have already been discussed. Clusters E and F represent the core of shyness and will be addressed in the application section of this chapter. Finally, cluster C, sexual anxiety, will be treated in Chapter 12. The fact that the behavioral problems relevant to loneliness are distributed across *five* chapters should serve to dramatically demonstrate the complex causation of this unfortunate malady.

Summary

The psychological benefits associated with affiliation are many and varied. Schachter's study indicates that stress increases the drive to affiliate, and research on social support as a stress buffer suggests that this is a wise response. Individual differences in the affiliation drive may influence patterns of adjustment.

The dynamics of attraction are similar for friendship and love. Generally, we are attracted to people who are physically attractive, intelligent, competent, high in status, and equipped with a pleasant personality. Evidence also indicates that proximity, similarity, and reciprocity promote attraction. Evidence on complementarity effects in attraction is more ambiguous.

The key ingredients of friendship are keeping confidences, loyalty, warmth and affection, supportiveness, and candor. Levinger's model suggests that a combination of chance factors and intentions governs the development of friendship. Patterns of friendship are influenced primarily by marital status and sex.

A number of interesting myths have grown up around the concept of love. People vary greatly in their capacity to give love, and Jourard has identified some characteristics associated with a solid capacity for love. Sex differences regarding love are interesting in that they do not support the traditional stereotype that women are more romantic than men.

Loneliness involves discontent with the extent and quality of one's interpersonal network. Evidence suggests that a surprisingly great number of people in our society are troubled by loneliness. Although a number of social trends promote loneliness in our society, it appears to be due mainly to personal factors, such as low self-esteem, poor social skills, fear of intimacy, loss of loved ones, and irrational thinking. Coping with loneliness is difficult. The key appears to be staying active socially rather than withdrawing.

The application section that follows will discuss shyness, a problem that intersects with loneliness. Specifically, I focus on the prevalence and consequences of shyness and discuss how to cope with this problem.

Coping
with
Shyness

Answer the following yes or no.

_____ 1. When I am the focus of attention, I often become anxious.

_____ 2. In interacting with people, I tend to be very self-conscious.

_____ 3. I get embarrassed in social situations quite easily.

_____ 4. I wish that I could be more aggressive about pursuing social relationships.

_____ 5. I am often concerned about being rejected by others.

If you answered yes to several of the above questions, you may be hampered in your social life by a very common problem, shyness. Loneliness and shyness are intersecting problems. Although many lonely people are not shy, and many shy people are not lonely, it is nonetheless true that loneliness is a common consequence of shyness (Cheek & Busch, 1981). The concept of **shyness** is not easily defined, but basically it refers to excessive caution in interpersonal relations. Specifically, shy people tend (1) to be timid about expressing themselves, (2) to be overly self-conscious about how others are reacting to them, (3) to embarrass easily, and (4) to experience physiological symptoms of their anxiety, such as a racing pulse, blushing, or an upset stomach (Zimbardo, 1977).

SHYNESS. *Excessive caution in social interaction; may include timidity, self-consciousness, anxiety, and sensitivity to embarrassment.*

PREVALENCE AND CONSEQUENCES OF SHYNESS

Philip Zimbardo (1977) and his associates have recently done some admirable, pioneering research on shyness. Their survey data indicate that shyness may be more common than previously realized. Over 80% of the respondents to their survey reported being shy during some stage of their lives, and 40% reported being currently troubled by shyness.

The personal significance of shyness is generally quite negative. The vast majority of shy people report that they do not like being shy. This is understandable in view of the common consequences of shyness. Shy people tend to have difficulty making friends and are more likely than others to be sexually inhibited. They are often very lonely and prone to depression.

SITUATIONAL NATURE OF SHYNESS

Interestingly, the traditional stereotype of the shy person being consistently timid all the time appears to be largely inaccurate. In Zimbardo's original study, 60% of the shy people reported that their shyness was *situationally specific*. That is, they experienced shyness only in certain social contexts, such as asking someone for help, interacting with a member of the other sex, or attending large parties, for example. Table 9.6 lists the situations that most commonly elicited shyness in Zimbardo's subjects. The situational specificity of shyness has been reconfirmed in a more recent study by Jones (1984), who argues that it is misleading to think of shyness as primarily a personal disposition or personality trait. Instead it is probably more accurate to conceive of shyness as a fairly common *reaction* to certain situations.

COPING WITH SHYNESS

PHILIP ZIMBARDO

Shyness tends to be a deeply entrenched feature of an individual's personality, and it would be foolish to pretend that shyness can be overcome easily. However, it is important to emphasize that *shyness can be overcome successfully!* Think about it. If 40% of Zimbardo's survey respondents are *currently* shy and 80% *were* shy at some previous time, obviously half of the shy people feel that they have conquered their problem.

Much of Zimbardo's (1977) book is devoted to how to deal successfully with the problem of shyness. Basically, the three key steps in this process are (1) understanding your shyness, (2) building your self-esteem, and (3) improving your social skills.

UNDERSTANDING YOUR SHYNESS

The first step is the easiest. You should analyze your shyness and try to pinpoint exactly what social situations tend to elicit your shy behavior. You should further try to ascertain what *causes* your shyness in the identified situations.

Zimbardo's data indicate that most people are shy only in certain situations. To combat your problem effectively, you need to identify these situations. In order to identify them, you may want to use some of the behavior modification procedures discussed in Chapter 5 under the heading "Gathering Baseline Data." You might also benefit from scanning Table 9.6, which summarizes Zimbardo's findings on which people and situations tend to generate reticence in others.

There are a number of possible reasons or combinations of reasons for your shyness. In his survey, Zimbardo enumerated eight that seemed potentially

TABLE 9.6 What makes you shy?

Other people	Percentage of shy students	Situations	Percentage of shy students
Strangers	70	Where I am focus of attention—large group (as when giving a speech)	73
Opposite sex	64		
Authorities by virtue of their knowledge	55	Large groups	68
Authorities by virtue of their role	40	Of lower status	56
Relatives	21	Social situations in general	55
Elderly people	12	New situations in general	55
Friends	11	Requiring assertiveness	54
Children	10	Where I am being evaluated	53
Parents	8	Where I am focus of attention—small group	52
		Small social groups	48
		One-to-one different-sex interactions	48
		Of vulnerability (need help)	48
		Small task-oriented groups	28
		One-to-one same-sex interactions	14

relevant: (1) concern about negative evaluation, (2) fear of rejection, (3) lack of self-confidence, (4) lack of specific social skills, (5) fear of intimacy, (6) preference for being alone, (7) emphasis on and enjoyment of nonsocial activities, and (8) personal inadequacy or handicap. If you find this list too abstract, you might want to reexamine Table 9.5, which contains more-concrete statements that are largely manifestations of the problems listed above.

BUILDING YOUR SELF-ESTEEM

Zimbardo stresses that your shyness lies primarily within your own mental set. Poor self-esteem underlies most of the causes of shyness just listed. Hence, it is important to work on improving your self-confidence. In his book, Zimbardo spells out "fifteen steps to a more confident you." Many of these coincide with the suggestions made in the application section of Chapter 6.

IMPROVING YOUR SOCIAL SKILLS

The third step is the most difficult. As I have discussed repeatedly, it is not easy to change deeply ingrained habits. Zimbardo suggests using the behavior modification approach covered in Chapter 5. Specifically, he recommends specifying certain target social responses that you want to increase and then setting up a reward system to help you to follow through. He further emphasizes that you should be realistic and work toward *gradual* improvement. For example, he suggests that you start with relatively simple and nonthreatening social behaviors, such as anonymous conversations. These are conversations with strangers in public places such as a theater line, a bank, or a stadium. Other simple social responses that you might work on in the beginning include saying "hello" to people or giving compliments to others.

Zimbardo (1977) offers many other suggestions for improving social skills that are too numerous to detail here. However, I can mention a few other outstanding ideas. First, it's a good idea to select a nonshy role model to watch closely. Identify someone in your personal sphere who is quite extroverted. It's probably a good idea to use a same-sex model. Observe how your role model handles various kinds of social situations. In particular, pay attention to how he or she acts in the situations that trigger your shyness. Second, develop some "expertise" in some area so that you have something to contribute to conversations. In other words, become a movie buff or a sports buff or an amateur political analyst. Third, listen actively and attentively. People love to talk about themselves. Encourage them to do so. After going on and on about themselves, they'll probably compliment you on what an interesting and enjoyable "conversation" the two of you just had.

As you work on developing your social skills, bear in mind that progress will probably be gradual. Social skills are honed over a lifetime. Although they *can* be improved with practice, it normally takes a good bit of time, and your progress may seem barely perceptible. However, if you stick with it, shyness *can* be conquered.

9.7

RECOMMENDED READING
Shyness: What It Is, What to Do about It
by Philip G. Zimbardo (Addison-Wesley, 1977)

Zimbardo, an outstanding social psychologist, focuses his keen insight on the frustration of being shy. A lack of jargon and ample use of actual case histories make this book very readable. Zimbardo explores the roots of shyness in Part I and then addresses the question of "what to do about it" in Part II. The second part of the book is full of exercises and sound advice for tackling this problem head on.

Theories are like enormous vacuum cleaners, sucking up everything in their paths. Each of the theories outlined here has vigorous backers, hawkers of the best vacuum cleaner on the market. We shall borrow freely from any and all of them when we come to design programs for coping with shyness [p. 55].

IDEAS: REVIEW OF LEARNING OBJECTIVES

When you have mastered the material in this chapter, you should be able to do the following.

1. Describe Schachter's research on the relation between stress and affiliation.
2. Describe the relation between social support and the effects of stress.
3. Discuss how physical beauty affects interpersonal attraction.
4. Explain the matching hypothesis.
5. Discuss some reasons that physical attractiveness is so important in interpersonal relationships.
6. List some characteristics of others, besides physical beauty, that tend to influence a person's attraction to them.
7. Discuss the possible relations between intelligence/competence and attraction.
8. List the "interaction factors" that influence interpersonal attraction.
9. Discuss how and why proximity facilitates attraction.
10. Discuss how and why similarity affects attraction.
11. Summarize evidence on the complementary-needs hypothesis.
12. Explain the reciprocity effect and discuss some of the limitations of this principle.
13. Explain how Bem's self-perception theory relates to the findings of Dutton and Aron.
14. Explain how social exchange theory views the role of self-esteem in interpersonal attraction.
15. List the five most important ingredients of friendship according to the Parlee et al. survey.
16. Describe the stages of friendship formation proposed by Levinger.
17. Discuss how marital status and sex affect patterns of friendship.
18. List four myths about love.
19. List the six factors that, according to Jourard, enhance the capacity for love.
20. Describe the two types of love proposed by Maslow.
21. Summarize how men and women differ in their approach to love.
22. Describe three types of loneliness and four types of relationships that might be regarded as deficient.
23. Summarize evidence on the prevalence of loneliness.
24. Describe evidence on the personal consequences of loneliness.
25. List some social trends that contribute to increasing loneliness in our society.
26. List four personal factors that tend to be associated with loneliness.
27. Explain the key to coping successfully with loneliness.
28. Describe the symptoms of shyness and its situational nature.
29. Discuss the prevalence of shyness.
30. List three steps suggested by Zimbardo for coping with shyness.
31. Discuss some of Zimbardo's suggestions for improving social skills.

TERMS: REVIEW OF NEW VOCABULARY

When you have mastered the material in this chapter, you should be able to define the following terms.

Affiliation	Halo effect	Loneliness	Reciprocity
Complementary needs	Homogamy	Matching hypothesis	Shyness
Confounded	Interpersonal attraction	Propinquity effects	Social exchange theory

PEOPLE: REVIEW OF MAJOR THEORISTS AND RESEARCHERS

When you have mastered the material in this chapter, you should be able to summarize the principal contributions and/or ideas of the following people.

Daryl Bem	Donn Byrne	George Levinger	Philip Zimbardo
Berscheid and Walster (Hatfield)	Sidney Jourard	Stanley Schachter	

10

OVERVIEW OF ADULT DEVELOPMENT AND VOCATIONAL ADJUSTMENT

Summary

Applying Psychology to Your Life: Confronting Death and Dying

CULTURAL AND INDIVIDUAL
ATTITUDES ABOUT DEATH

CONTROVERSY OVER THE
"RIGHT TO DIE"

DYING A "GOOD" DEATH:
PLANNING AHEAD

THE PROCESS OF DYING

DEALING WITH THE
DYING PERSON

BEREAVEMENT, GRIEF,
AND MOURNING

DEALING WITH
BEREAVEMENT

The work of adult life is not easy. As in childhood, each step presents not only new tasks of development but requires a letting go of the techniques that worked before. With each passage some magic must be given up, some cherished illusion of safety and comfortably familiar sense of self must be cast off, to allow for the greater expansion of our own distinctiveness.

GAIL SHEEHY

AGE COHORT. *A group of people born in the same time period, who develop in the same historical context.*

I was part of that **age cohort** that originated the slogan "Never trust anyone over 30." Now that I am no longer on the sunny side of 30, I am thankful that the age cohorts that followed us didn't pay much attention to our advice. Looking back, I am amazed at the amount of change I have seen in myself and my friends since our undergraduate days (1968–1972). In 15 or so years I have seen introverts become extroverts, artists become bankers, radicals become conservatives, the lazy become industrious, the selfish become unselfish. In other words, we have continued to develop, change, and evolve throughout our adult lives thus far. Collectively, we provide crystal-clear evidence that *adults do develop.*

This observation may not startle you, but until fairly recently (the 1970s) psychologists showed relatively little interest in adult development, and it was widely assumed that developmental processes petered out as one crossed the threshold into adulthood. There were a handful of lonely theorists who contemplated the significance of adult development before the 1970s, but they mostly languished in obscurity while attention was focused almost exclusively on development in childhood and adolescence. In recent years, however, social scientists have begun to realize that important developmental changes continue throughout adult life, and we have started probing into these changes to identify crucial patterns and trends. This chapter focuses on this recently burgeoning research area and the closely related topic of vocational development. In the application section I consider the final scene in the drama of life—death. Like adult development, the topic of death and dying has recently begun to attract considerable attention from social scientists. Their findings are illuminating.

Key Developmental Concepts
DEVELOPMENT AND AGING

DEVELOPMENT. *The orderly sequence of age-related changes that occur as an organism progresses from conception to death.*

Development is a broad concept referring to the process of sequential change that occurs as an organism progresses in age. It encompasses both biological and behavioral changes that occur with increasing age. Thus, we can focus on physical development, cognitive development, social development, personality development, and emotional development, to name just a few of the key dimensions of human development. These topics fall within the province of **developmental psychology,** the branch of psychology that is concerned with conception, growth, and age-related changes in behavior.

DEVELOPMENTAL PSYCHOLOGY. *An area of specialization in psychology concerned with conception, growth, and age-related changes in behavior.*

A key insight derived from developmental psychology is that the pacing of development may be highly variable. Periods of rapid development may alternate with periods of slow or negligible development called "plateaus." Further, during a particular segment of one's life, development in one area (say, social relations) might be very rapid, while development in another area (say, cognitive abilities) might be very slow. Consequently, you cannot assume that development proceeds at a steady pace or that the pace is similar across different dimensions of development.

AGING. *As used herein, refers to the biological process of growing older. Some theorists restrict the concept to growing older, after maturity has been reached.*

The term *aging* is used in different ways by different theorists and researchers, reflecting the fact that adult development is a relatively young field of study. I will use the term **aging** to refer to the biological process of growing older. Thus, aging is an inevitable, inexorable aspect of development. It takes place every minute of every day. It may or may not be accompanied by other developmental changes during a particular period. For instance, an individual's personality might stabilize, so that there would be virtually no personality development during a particular period, in spite of the fact that aging must, of course, continue. Aging in the later years is the focus of **gerontology,** a multidisciplinary field concerned with the study of old age and the elderly.

GERONTOLOGY. *The scientific study of the elderly and old age.*

STAGES OF DEVELOPMENT

STAGE. *A period in human development during which (1) certain critical experiences must be dealt with, (2) certain characteristic patterns of behavior are exhibited, and (3) certain capacities become established or consolidated.*

Most theories of development are stage theories. Such theories propose that people evolve through a series of stages in a predictable, orderly sequence. A **stage** is a period during which certain critical experiences must be dealt with and certain characteristic patterns of behavior are exhibited. Stage theories focus on the *universals* in the developmental process, the *discontinuities* between stages, and the *transitions* that facilitate movement from one stage to another. We encountered an example of a stage theory in Chapter 2—Sigmund Freud's notions about psychosexual development.

Stage theories have been criticized in many quarters because they are built on assumptions that are open to question. These theories generally assume (1) that people must progress through stages in a particular order because each stage builds on the accomplishments of the previous stage, (2) that progress through this orderly sequence is strongly and universally related to age, and (3) that transitions from one stage to another involve fundamental changes or discontinuities in behavior. There is considerable evidence that human developmental patterns often do not coincide with these assumptions (Goodman & Feldman, 1975; Lacy & Hendricks, 1980). For instance, it is clear that people often display a "mixed bag" of behaviors that are characteristic of several stages of development. This blending of stages violates the third assumption, that there are fundamental discontinuities between stages.

The main problem with stage theories is that they fail to adequately consider and account for the *individual differences* in development that exist among people. Although there *are* consistent patterns of development that are worth noting, there are also great differences among people. Everyone does *not* develop at the same pace. Troll (1982) reviews how various factors such as sex, social class, ethnic background, and personal experience promote variability in developmental patterns. Thus, chronological age is only modestly related to developmental status in adulthood.

Although stage theories are troubled by questionable assumptions and inadequate attention to individual differences, most influential theories of adult development continue to use the stage construct. The concept does seem to have great descriptive utility. However, when I describe a number of important stage theories later in the chapter, you should bear in mind that *development is probably not quite as orderly, uniform, and predictable as these theories imply.* They are a bit too tidy to reflect the immense complexities of reality. Nonetheless, they provide worthwhile descriptions of certain consistencies in human development that can aid us in achieving a better understanding of the challenges we confront in adult life.

AGE ROLES AND SOCIAL CLOCKS

AGE ROLE. *Expectations for someone's behavior based exclusively on his or her chronological age.*

You may recall that a *role* involves the behavior expected of a person in a particular social position. **Age roles** consist of expectations that are based on one's chronological age. The frequently used expression "They should act their age" captures the essence of age roles. Our society has widely accepted norms about how someone of a particular age should act, think, dress, and so forth. For instance, it is age roles that make it easy for someone in her twenties to live with mom and dad without attracting negative comment, while someone in her thirties will be criticized more frequently.

AGEISM. *Discrimination against a person based on his or her age. Usually refers to discrimination against the elderly.*

Like the sex roles discussed in Chapter 8, age roles often place *constraints* on people that may prevent them from behaving in certain ways. Thus, some people decide that they are too old to go back to school, too young to start their own business, or too feeble to take care of themselves. Often these kinds of limitations are self-imposed by virtue of one's passive acceptance of traditional age roles. Constraints may also be imposed *by others* who discriminate against the elderly on the basis of their age. Such discrimination is called **ageism.** Like sexism, ageism often leads to economic subjugation.

SOCIAL CLOCK. *A mental agenda that spells out what one should have accomplished or experienced by the time one reaches various ages.*

Closely related to age roles and norms is the concept of a social clock. A **social clock** is a person's notion of a developmental schedule that specifies what one should have accomplished by certain points in one's life (Neugarten, 1968). For example, if you feel that you should be married by the time you're 30, that belief constitutes a marker on your social clock. Social clocks are personalized but are very much a product of socialization and age norms. They can exert considerable influence over decisions about career moves, marriage, parenting, and so forth.

There is reason to believe that important events or transitions in life that come too early or too late according to one's social clock produce more stress than transitions that occur "on time" (Neugarten & Hagestad, 1976). Indeed, it is easy to imagine how an early marriage, delayed career promotion, or premature retirement might be extra stressful. In particular, it seems likely that lagging behind one's personal schedule in regard to certain achievements would produce chronic frustration. Thus, many of us pay great heed to social clocks ticking in the background as we proceed through our adult life.

Developmental Trends in Adulthood

Now that I have outlined some basic developmental concepts, I will turn to the task of describing patterns of development during the adult years. I will summarize age-related trends in three broad areas: physical development, cognitive development, and personality development.

PHYSICAL DEVELOPMENT

It is readily apparent to anyone that many changes in physical functioning occur with increasing age. While some of the changes are quite obvious, others may be very subtle but important. My summary of the trends in physical development is based on more detailed reviews by Troll (1982) and Huyck and Hoyer (1982), except where noted otherwise.

Changes in appearance. Height is a rather stable characteristic in adulthood, although it does tend to decline by an inch or so after age 55, as the spinal column "settles." Weight is more variable and tends to increase in most adults up through the mid-50s, when a very gradual decline typically begins. Although overall weight often goes down late in life, the percentage of body weight that is fat tends to increase throughout adulthood, much to the chagrin of many people. Hair tends to thin out and become gray in both sexes, and many males have to confront receding hairlines and baldness.

The net impact of these and other changes often leads older people to view themselves as progressively less attractive. This unfortunate reality is probably aggravated by our society's media obsession with youthful attractiveness. These changes in physical appearance may often have a significant impact on older persons' self-concepts.

NEURON. *The basic unit of the nervous system, consisting of a cell body, nucleus, axon, and dendrites.*

Neurological changes. As you may have heard, the number of active **neurons** in the brain declines steadily during adulthood. Although the rate of loss is difficult to measure, the figures are shocking: estimates of the loss range as high as 100,000 brain cells *per day* after age 30. Startling as the estimates are, we are not sure whether this neuron loss has much functional significance. Our brains have about 10 billion brain cells, so these losses may be mere drops in a bucket. In fact, some theorists believe that this may be a healthy process involving selective decay of little-used or nonessential neurons (Dawkins, 1971). At present, there is little reason to suspect that this progressive neuronal loss contributes to the onset of **senile dementia,** which involves an abnormal decline in cognitive functioning that is observed in a small minority of people over 65.

SENILE DEMENTIA. *A disorder affecting about 5% of people over 65, involving a progressive, general deterioration of mental faculties.*

If they can rise above stereotypes, the elderly don't have to think of themselves as unattractive.

Sensory changes. The most important changes in sensory reception occur in the visual and auditory senses. Visual acuity is rather strongly related to age; the proportion of people with 20/20 vision declines steadily as age increases. Farsightedness, difficulty adapting to darkness, poor recovery from glare, and a yellowing of color perception are common among older people. Noticeable hearing losses usually do not show up until people reach their fifties. Only about one-third of older adults suffer hearing losses that require corrective treatment, whereas the vast majority of the elderly require some sort of treatment for visual losses. Small sensory losses in touch, taste, and smell have been detected (usually after age 50), but they generally have little impact on day-to-day functioning, although older people often complain that their food is somewhat tasteless. In contrast, the visual and hearing losses that occur often make interpersonal interaction more awkward and difficult, thus promoting social withdrawal in some older people.

Endocrine changes. There are age-related changes in hormonal functioning, but their significance is not well understood. They do *not* appear to be the chief cause of declining sexual activity during the later years (Solnick & Corby, 1983). Rather, this decline seems to be due mainly to acceptance of age roles that suggest that sexual activity in the elderly is "inappropriate." The vast majority of older adults remain physically capable of engaging in rewarding sexual encounters right on through their seventies, although arousal tends to be somewhat slower and less intense.

MENOPAUSE. *The time during middle age when a woman's menstrual periods cease entirely.*

Among women, **menopause** is a rather dramatic transition that typically occurs between the ages of 47 and 51. This ending of menstruation and the associated loss of fertility is an obvious landmark in adult development. Not so long ago it was thought that menopause was almost universally accompanied by severe psychological dislocation and distress. It is now clear that women are highly variable in their reactions to menopause. Episodes of moderate physical discomfort during the transitional period are fairly common (Goodman, Stewart, & Gilbert, 1977), but emotional problems appear to be much less common than is widely believed (Weg, 1978). In fact, a substantial percentage of women seem to welcome menopause with some relief.

Although there has been much discussion in recent years of "male menopause," there really is no equivalent experience among men. Significant endocrine changes do occur in males in their later years, but in the vast majority of cases they are very gradual and are largely unrelated to physical or psychological distress.

Changes in health status. Unfortunately, the quality of one's health does tend to diminish with increasing age (Siegler, Nowlin, & Blumenthal, 1980). There are many reasons for this trend. Vital organ systems lose some of their functional capacity. Vulnerability to some diseases (such as heart disease) increases with age. For other diseases (such as pneumonia), the vulnerability may remain unchanged, but the effects of the condition, if contracted, may be much more devastating. In any case, there is a clear trend in the direction of declining health, as you can see from Table 10.1, which highlights the fact that the proportion of people with a chronic health problem escalates to nearly 90% in the over-65 age category.

TABLE 10.1 **Percentage distribution of people by chronic condition and activity limitation status, according to age (United States, July 1965–June 1967)**

Age	Total population	With no chronic conditions	Total with chronic conditions	With no limitation of activity	With some limitation
All ages	100.0	50.5	49.5	38.0	11.4
Under 17	100.0	77.2	22.8	20.9	1.9
17–44	100.0	45.9	54.1	46.7	7.4
45–64	100.0	28.9	71.1	51.8	19.3
65 and over	100.0	14.4	85.6	39.6	46.0

COGNITIVE DEVELOPMENT

It seems entirely plausible that cognitive abilities might undergo significant change during adult life. Indeed, there are many widely held notions about intellectual decline during adulthood. It is commonly believed that intelligence drops during middle age and that memory lapses become frequent in the later years. In this section we will review the evidence that relates to these and other beliefs about cognitive processes in adulthood.

INTELLIGENCE

INTELLIGENCE. *General mental ability. Operationally, refers to one's ability to perform on IQ tests.*

Intelligence is an ill-defined concept that is the subject of considerable controversy. Although experts are unable to reach a consensus on just how to define intelligence, they paradoxically agree on how to *measure* it with so-called IQ tests. Thus, when psychologists discuss **intelligence,** the simple reality is that they are talking about the ability to score well on these tests. Intelligence testing is widespread in our society, and people tend to ascribe considerable importance (probably too much) to how well someone does on an IQ test. Given this cultural emphasis on intelligence testing, it is understandable that researchers have been interested in whether IQ remains stable throughout the adult years.

The early evidence on the stability of IQ was rather disconcerting. Wechsler (1958) reported that intelligence peaked in the twenties and began to decline already in the thirties, with gradual decline continuing across the remainder of the life span. We now understand, however, that this finding was largely the by-product of methodological shortcomings associated with Wechsler's approach to data collection. More recent studies (see Schaie, 1983) that have circumvented these methodological problems have yielded an entirely different picture. They suggest that IQ is fairly stable throughout adulthood until about age 60, when a relatively small decline often begins. They also indicate that, despite this general trend, there are rather large individual differences among people in IQ fluctuations. Although some people do experience a modest decline during middle age, many others actually show an *increase* in IQ, as late as their fifties. Overall, intelligence as measured by IQ tests seems to be a reasonably stable personal quality.

MEMORY

Numerous studies find age-related decreases in the efficiency of long-term memory (Walsh, 1983). This decline generally starts to become apparent around age 55. However, these post-55 deficits are very small when sensitive measures of retention are used or when the older subjects are instructed to use more efficient storage strategies. Moreover, most of these studies have investigated retention by asking subjects to memorize simple lists of words or associations. These artificial laboratory tasks bear little resemblance to memory challenges that we encounter in everyday life. At present there is relatively little evidence on age-related changes in the retention of more meaningful information, although the limited evidence on the retention of prose or discourse *does* suggest that there tends to be a modest impairment of memory among the elderly (Hartley, Harker, & Walsh, 1980).

It seems that older people often have very vivid recollections of events in the distant past while being very forgetful about recent events. This apparent paradox may not be all that perplexing. First, there is reason to believe that the vivid memories of events long ago may be "loose," embellished reconstructions that are less accurate and impressive than one might assume (Huyck & Hoyer, 1982). Second, the apparent forgetfulness about recent events may not reflect memory deficits as such. Such "memory lapses" may be due to lack of interest in or attention to the input, so that the person never really *stored* the event or information in long-term memory (Schaie & Geiwitz, 1982).

LEARNING AND PROBLEM SOLVING

Although overall intelligence and memory capacity may be more stable during adulthood than is widely believed, there *are* some significant age-related changes in cognitive functioning during the adult years. These changes show up most clearly when we look at specific aspects of learning and problem solving.

There is ample evidence that ability to narrow one's focus of attention diminishes somewhat with increasing age, as does ability to handle simultaneous multiple inputs (Hoyer & Plude, 1980). It is thought that these changes in attentional capacity may be due to decreased efficiency in filtering out irrelevant stimuli. Most of the studies in this area have simply compared extreme age groups (very young subjects against very old subjects), so that we have not yet pinpointed at what age these changes in attentional processes tend to emerge.

There are also plenty of studies that indicate that one's *speed* in learning, solving problems, retrieving memories, and processing information tends to decline with age (Birren, Woods, & Williams, 1980). Although additional data are needed, some evidence suggests that this trend may be a gradual, lengthy one commencing in middle adulthood. Birren et al. (1980) argue that the very general nature of this trend (across differing tasks) suggests that it may be due to age-related changes in neurological functioning.

Irrespective of speed, overall *success* on laboratory concept-formation and problem-solving tasks also appears to decrease as people grow older (Rabbitt, 1977). However, the findings in this area are far from consistent (Giambra & Arenberg, 1980), and the trend is certainly not as clear or as strong as that observed in regard to speed of processing. Evidence suggests that this reduction in learning effectiveness becomes significant only after about age 60. Before then, problem-solving ability is largely unimpaired, if the older person is given adequate time to compensate for the reduced speed in cognitive processing.

In spite of some negative trends noted in this section, it should be emphasized that *many people remain capable of great intellectual accomplishment well into their later years.* This reassuring reality was clearly verified in a study of scholarly, scientific, and artistic productivity that examined lifelong patterns of work among 738 men who lived at least through the age of 79 (Dennis, 1966). Table 10.2 summarizes the results of this study. As you can see, the forties were generally the most productive decade for most professions. However, productivity was remarkably stable through the sixties and even the seventies in many areas.

TABLE 10.2 Percentage of total works between ages 20 and 80 that were done in each decade

	N	N	Age decade					
			20s	*30s*	*40s*	*50s*	*60s*	*70s*
Scholarship	*Men*	*Works*						
Historians	46	615	3	19	19	22	*24*	20
Philosophers	42	225	3	17	20	18	*22*	20
Scholars	43	326	6	17	*21*	*21*	16	19
		Means	4	18	20	20	*21*	20
Sciences	*Men*	*Works*						
Biologists	32	3456	5	22	*24*	19	17	13
Botanists	49	1889	4	15	*22*	*22*	*22*	15
Chemists	24	2420	11	21	*24*	19	12	13
Geologists	40	2672	3	13	22	*28*	19	14
Inventors	44	646	2	10	17	18	*32*	21
Mathematicians	36	3104	8	*20*	*20*	18	19	15
		Means	6	17	22	21	20	15
Arts	*Men*	*Works*						
Architects	44	1148	7	24	*29*	25	10	4
Chamber musicians	35	109	15	*21*	17	20	18	9
Dramatists	25	803	10	27	*29*	21	9	3
Librettists	38	164	8	21	*30*	22	15	4
Novelists	32	494	5	19	18	*28*	23	7
Opera composers	176	476	8	30	*31*	16	10	5
Poets	46	402	11	21	*26*	16	16	10
		Means	9	23	26	21	14	6

Note: Maximum values for each group (row) are shown in italics.

PERSONALITY DEVELOPMENT

Overall, the evidence indicates that personality is relatively stable during adulthood. That is not to say that the contours of personality are chiseled in concrete. Significant changes may take place. Nonetheless, the general conclusion emerging from several major longitudinal studies (Block, 1981; Costa & McCrae, 1980; Neugarten & associates, 1964) is that personality traits are characterized by striking continuity, durability, and persistence. In regard to personality, stability tends to outweigh mutation and change. Personality in young adulthood is an excellent predictor of personality in late adulthood. Insofar as change occurs, it often involves a strengthening or intensification of traits that were present in earlier years.

Although stability in adult personality is striking, there are, of course, certain patterns of change that show up with some consistency. Among the more prominent of these is a shift away from traditional sex-role behaviors toward greater **androgyny** (see Chapter 8 for a discussion of androgyny). It seems that many males become less "masculine" and many females become less "feminine" as they grow older (Monge, 1975). In other words, people begin to discard the constraints imposed by traditional sex roles, and men and women move toward greater similarity in personality. Thus, personality gradually tends to become less sex-typed.

ANDROGYNY. *A behavioral pattern wherein a person displays both masculine and feminine characteristics.*

There also are some trends worth noting in regard to self-esteem. In general, self-esteem tends to increase modestly through middle age, when it becomes relatively stable. It then starts to decline gradually in the fifties (Lowenthal & Chiriboga, 1972). This decline tends to be minimized or avoided by people whose lifestyle remains largely unchanged and by those who maintain decent health and a reasonable income (Turner, 1981).

There are a handful of other personality traits for which age-related trends have been noted (Reedy, 1983). For instance, it appears that older adults often become more passive, conforming, and cautious during their later years. There also tends to be movement toward being more serious and sober. Finally, older adults often undergo a metamorphosis that leads them to be more inner-directed.

Phases of Adult Development: Major Theories

Human development is characterized by both continuity and discontinuity. The preceding section on developmental trends in adulthood emphasized the continuity. I turn now to the task of summarizing stage theories of adult development that highlight the discontinuities. There are many such stage theories, and I cannot describe all of them in detail. My plan of attack is as follows. First, I will focus on Erik Erikson's (1963) life-span theory of development, which stresses the psychosocial crises that must be dealt with successively. Second, I will describe Robert Havighurst's (1972) model, which elaborates on Erikson's work by seeking to identify the developmental tasks that must be confronted during each period of life. Third, after covering these older theories, first published in the 1950s, I will try to integrate the findings of two recent research projects that produced highly publicized new models of adult development in the 1970s. Specifically, I will attempt to summarize and interweave recently influential theories proposed by Roger Gould (1978) and Daniel Levinson (Levinson et al., 1978). All these theories provide very broad *overviews* of adult developmental patterns. They serve nicely as a point of departure for more detailed analyses of particular areas of adult development or adjustment that will follow.

ERIKSON'S THEORY OF PSYCHOSOCIAL CRISES

ERIK ERIKSON

As you may recall from Chapter 2, Erik Erikson (1963, 1968) is a prominent psychoanalytic theorist who proposed a rather sweeping revision of Freud's stage theory of psychosexual development. Of interest to us at this juncture is the fact that Erikson was one of the first theorists to recognize the importance of continued development during adulthood.

INNOVATIONS RELATIVE TO FREUD

Erikson's theory fits squarely in the psychoanalytic tradition. However, there are a number of innovations that I want to highlight. First, Erikson expanded the model to describe developmental events throughout the entire life span, reflecting his disagreement with Freud's belief that personality is fundamentally shaped during the first five to ten years of life. Erikson partitioned development across the life span into a series of eight stages extending into old age. Second, he reduced Freud's emphasis on sexual conflicts as the prime determinants of personality. Instead, Erikson stressed social and cultural influences on developmental processes.

Third, Erikson introduced the concept of *psychosocial crises,* which he viewed as the main considerations governing development. Like Freud, Erikson believed that certain events have crucial significance during each stage. However, Erikson's crucial events, the psychosocial crises, focus on coping with transitions in social relationships rather than on coping with one's sexuality. Each crisis is viewed as a potential "turning point" from which either growth or regression might result. Each stage is described in terms of the outcomes that are likely after grappling with the crisis at hand. In each case, the two proposed alternative outcomes represent a healthy and an unhealthy resolution of the crisis of that stage. Unhealthy crisis resolution at any stage is thought to hinder or undermine the quality of subsequent development. Ultimately, then, psychological health is predicated on successfully navigating one's way through this series of transitional challenges. The cumulative nature of the progression means that the *order* of stages must be fixed, although Erikson regarded his age norms as approximate. Table 10.3 spells out the life periods, psychosocial crises, and optimal outcomes for each of Erikson's eight stages and lists the comparable psychosexual stages proposed by Freud.

TABLE 10.3 **Erikson's eight stages of psychosocial development**

Life stage	Psychosocial crises	Optimal outcome	Psychosexual stages (Freudian)
1. Infancy (1st year of life)	Trust vs. mistrust	Basic trust, optimism, and hope	Oral
2. Early childhood (2nd year)	Autonomy vs. shame and doubt	Sense of control over oneself and the environment	Anal
3. Play age (3rd through 5th year)	Initiative vs. guilt	Goal-directedness and purpose	Phallic
4. School age (6th year to start of puberty)	Industry vs. inferiority	Competence	Latency
5. Adolescence	Identity vs. role confusion	Clear sense of identity	Puberty
6. Young adulthood	Intimacy vs. isolation	Capacity for commitment, closeness, and love	Genital
7. Adulthood	Generativity vs. self-absorption	Production and care for future generations	
8. Mature age	Integrity vs. despair	Satisfaction with one's past life, wisdom	

THE FIRST FOUR STAGES DURING CHILDHOOD

Erikson's first four stages correspond roughly to Freud's oral, anal, phallic, and latency phases of psychosexual development (see Chapter 2). I will summarize their significance briefly before describing the adult portion of Erikson's life-span model. Whereas Freud was concerned almost exclusively with feeding and weaning experiences during the first stage, Erikson's theory shows a broader concern with the overall care and attention given to the infant. If the infant's basic biological needs are well met, a healthy attitude of trust toward the world should be created. If, however, the child's basic needs are taken care of poorly or haphazardly, an attitude of mistrust is likely to develop. In the second stage, Freud's interest in toilet training is expanded into a broader interest in a variety of sources of parent/child conflict. The challenge is to acquire a sense of autonomy as an independent organism that is capable of self-regulation. Erikson's third stage is comparable to Freud's phallic stage, but the fact that children sometimes develop a "sexually" oriented preoccupation with the opposite-sex parent (Freud's Oedipal complex) is not considered to be of crucial importance. Rather, the crucial issue is whether children can learn to function socially in the family unit without having their sense of initiative crushed by parents or older siblings. In the fourth stage, this challenge of learning to function socially is extended beyond the family to the broader social realm of the neighborhood and school. A sense of industry or competence results if the child is able to function effectively in this less nurturant social sphere, where productivity, efficiency, and responsibility are highly valued.

STAGE 5: IDENTITY VERSUS ROLE CONFUSION

During the fifth stage, adolescents struggle with what Erikson called the *identity crisis*. They work to establish a clear and stable sense of who they are, what they stand for, and where or how they fit into society. They analyze and reevaluate various features of their self-concept, deciding which are central and which are more peripheral or incidental. They look for an ideology, or system of values and beliefs, that they can embrace as their own. During this crisis period, they often experiment in a tentative way with various identities as they grope for one that seems to "fit." One's identity crisis is resolved when one finally commits with some confidence to a particular self-concept and ideology. If a person is unable to make such a commitment and continues to struggle with this crisis, role confusion is thought to result. This identity confusion may lead to the fairly common problem described in Chapter 6, wherein a person searches indefinitely for the "authentic" or "real" self. As part of this search, the person experiments tentatively with varying public selves. This identity confusion and search for the real self often lasts well beyond adolescence in modern Western society. According to Erikson, when this happens, it may delay other important developmental processes.

STAGE 6: INTIMACY VERSUS ISOLATION

During the sixth stage, encompassing young adulthood, the psychosocial crisis centers on whether one can develop the capacity to share intimacy with others. Erikson is not concerned simply with the young adult's need to find a marriage partner. Rather, his concern penetrates much deeper, to the more subtle issues of whether one can learn to open up to others, truly commit to others, and give of oneself unselfishly. The person who can achieve these goals and thereby experience genuine intimacy is thought to be much more likely to develop a mature and successful marital relationship. This capacity for intimacy will also facilitate the development of stronger bonds of affection with one's friends. Failure to resolve this psychosocial crisis favorably leads one to have difficulties in relating to others in a genuine fashion. This sense of isolation promotes manipulative relations with friends and hollow, often troubled marriages.

STAGE 7: GENERATIVITY VERSUS STAGNATION

According to Erikson, developmental crises continue throughout adulthood. Next up, in middle adulthood, is the challenge of acquiring a profound concern for the welfare of future generations, which is called "generativity." This generativity is manifested in the provision of unselfish guidance to members of the next generation. The recipients of this benevolent guidance are often one's own children, but not necessarily. For a variety of reasons, some people bestow this altruistic direction on people other than their own offspring. For example, a 50-year-old female attorney might serve as a "mentor" for a younger woman in her law firm. Thus, generativity and its opposite, stagnation, do not hinge on whether one has children. Stagnation is characterized by self-absorption and a self-indulgent obsession with satisfying one's own needs and desires.

STAGE 8: INTEGRITY VERSUS DESPAIR

In Erikson's last stage, during old age, the challenge is to avoid the frequently seen tendency to dwell on the mistakes of the past, bemoan paths not chosen, gripe about opportunities lost, and bitterly contemplate one's imminent death. Rather than wallowing in sullen regret, resentment, and despair, one should accept one's choices and fates in a dignified manner. Achieving integrity involves finding meaning in one's life and looking back with a sense of satisfaction.

HAVIGHURST'S DESCRIPTION OF DEVELOPMENTAL TASKS

Erikson's overview of human development across the life span is provocative and inspirational. It is provocative in that it embraces value-laden positions about the nature of psychological health. It is inspirational in that it vividly describes the great heights to which the human spirit can soar. However, Erikson's analysis of adult development provides a rather general overview that sometimes lacks detail. This shortcoming is corrected to some extent by Robert Havighurst's developmental theory, which interfaces nicely with Erikson's model. Using a stage model similar to Erikson's, Havighurst (1972) endeavored to provide a more comprehensive and detailed description of the challenges confronted during successive periods of adult development.

DEVELOPMENTAL TASKS. *The age-related challenges that a person must master during certain life periods in order to facilitate healthy and full development.*

Havighurst's theory centers on the construct of developmental tasks. **Developmental tasks** are personal challenges that emerge predictably during certain life periods and need to be mastered. Examples of developmental tasks that emerge in childhood are easy to provide. For instance, children must learn to communicate, learn to distinguish right from wrong, and learn to get along with age-mates. According to Havighurst, it is important to deal successfully with developmental tasks during the appropriate time period. Such success leads to personal satisfaction as well as approval from society and paves the way for easier conquest of developmental tasks that emerge in subsequent life periods. Failure leads to dissatisfaction, disapproval from others, and trouble with subsequent developmental tasks.

Havighurst divided adulthood into three major periods that correspond closely to Erikson's last three stages. These three periods are early adulthood, encompassing ages 18 through 30; middle age, encompassing ages 30 through 60; and later maturity, encompassing the years after the age of 60. The major developmental tasks encountered in each of these three periods are outlined briefly below. These three lists (from Havighurst, 1972) provide a fairly comprehensive description of the key challenges that people face as they progress through adult life.

For early adulthood (roughly ages 18–30)
1. Getting started in an occupation
2. Selecting a mate
3. Learning to live with a marriage partner
4. Starting a family
5. Rearing children
6. Managing a home
7. Taking on civic responsibilities
8. Finding a congenial social group

For the middle years (roughly 30–60)
1. Assisting teenage children to become responsible and happy adults
2. Achieving adult social and civic responsibility
3. Reaching and maintaining satisfactory performance in one's occupational career
4. Developing adult leisure-time activities
5. Relating to one's spouse as a person
6. Accepting and adjusting to the physiological changes of middle age
7. Adjusting to aging parents

For later maturity (roughly 60–end of life)
1. Adjusting to decreasing physical strength and health
2. Adjusting to retirement and reduced income
3. Adjusting to death of one's spouse
4. Establishing an explicit affiliation with one's age group
5. Adopting and adapting social roles in a flexible way (such as expansion in family, community, or hobbies or a slowdown in all activities)
6. Establishing satisfactory physical living arrangements

Admittedly, Havighurst's theory is culture-bound, in that it describes the landmark developmental tasks that tend to occur in modern Western society. It also assumes that one will marry and have children—assumptions that cannot be taken for granted in the 1980s. Furthermore, it is merely descriptive in nature; it lacks the explanatory value of Erikson's theory. Nonetheless, it is a useful model and is more detailed and more specific than Erikson's. Moreover, the concept of developmental tasks has considerable utility in shedding light on the dynamic challenges of adult development.

RECENT RESEARCH BY GOULD AND LEVINSON ON PHASES OF ADULT DEVELOPMENT

There was a flurry of influential research on adult development during the 1970s. In particular, two studies garnered an enormous amount of attention. These two studies were summarized in a pair of widely read books: *Transformations* by Roger Gould (1978) and *The Seasons of a Man's Life* by Daniel Levinson and colleagues (1978). Both these studies focused on the central years of adulthood, from one's twenties through one's fifties. Whereas Erikson and Havighurst divided these four decades into only two stages, Gould and Levinson analyzed the transitions of early and middle adulthood in greater detail, yielding seven and eight stages, respectively (see Table 10.4).

Gould (1972, 1978) based his model on two samples that included both men and women. One was made up of psychotherapy outpatients for whom exten-

TABLE 10.4 **Summary of two stage theories of adult development**

Gould's (1978) seven stages	*Levinson's (1978) eight stages*
1. *Ages 16 to 18* People feel a strong desire to get away from parents, but autonomy is precarious	1. *Ages 17 to 22* Leave adolescence, make preliminary choices for adult life
2. *Ages 18 to 22* Feel halfway out of family and worry about being reclaimed; peer group important ally in cutting family ties	2. *Ages 22 to 28* Initial choices in love, occupation, friendship, values, lifestyle
3. *Ages 22 to 28* Feel established, autonomous, and separate from family; feel "now" is the time for living, growing, and building; peers still important, but self-reliance paramount	3. *Ages 28 to 33* Change in life structure; either a moderate change or, more often, a severe and stressful crisis
4. *Ages 29 to 34* Begin to question what they are doing; feel weary of being what they are supposed to be, but continue	4. *Ages 33 to 40* Establish a niche in society, progress on a timetable, both in family and in career accomplishments
5. *Ages 35 to 43* Feel that time seems to constrict for shaping the behavior of their adolescent children or "making it"; their own parents turn to them with muffled renewal of old conflicts	5. *Ages 40 to 45* Life structure comes into question, usually a time of crisis in the meaning, direction, and value of each person's life; neglected parts of the self (talents, desires, aspirations) seek expression
6. *Ages 43 to 53* Feel "die is cast" and view life with bitterness; blame parents and find fault with children but seek sympathy from spouse	6. *Ages 45 to 50* Choices must be made, a new life structure formed; person must commit to new tasks
7. *Ages 53 to 60* Feel less negative feelings than in the forties; relationships with selves, parents, children, and friends become warmer and more mellow; marital happiness and contentment increase	7. *Ages 50 to 55* Further questioning and modification of the life structure; men who did not have a crisis at age 40 are likely to have one now
	8. *Ages 55 to 60* Build a new life structure; can be time of great fulfillment

sive case-history data were available, and the other consisted of 524 White, middle-class persons who responded to a questionnaire. Using this data base, Gould concluded that adult development could be broken into seven phases. *In each phase, the crucial issue is whether the person can challenge and discard certain "false" assumptions about life that are left over from childhood.* There are a *major* false assumption and a number of subordinate *component* assumptions (derived from the major one) that must be reevaluated and repudiated during each stage. For example, in Gould's first phase, young adults between the ages of 17 and 22 are thought to grapple with the major assumption that "I'll always belong to my parents and believe in their world." During this phase young adults need to wrestle free of this false assumption, which functions as a barrier to achieving emotional independence from one's family. In a similar fashion, Gould's subsequent stages detail how people evolving through adulthood undergo major transitions by experiencing personal insights that permit them to get rid of counterproductive assumptions about life.

Levinson's theory is based on a much smaller sample of 40 subjects, all men (Levinson et al., 1974, 1978). Although Levinson's cross-sectional sample was exclusively male, it did include Blacks and blue-collar workers, who were not well represented in Gould's samples. These subjects were interviewed extensively over a 2–3-month period. On the basis of these interviews, Levinson mapped out eight developmental phases in early and middle adulthood. *He believes that phases of relative stability alternate with phases characterized by turmoil and transition.* In describing these phases, he traces changes in what he calls one's "life structure." A person's life structure encompasses the basic pattern or design of one's life at a particular time, which is revealed through the *choices* that one makes about marriage, career, child rearing, and so forth.

The overview of the phases of adult development that follows shortly is based primarily on the models proposed by Gould and Levinson. Although their findings were far from identical, their models are not all that incompatible. Some of the dissimilarities are a function of differing theoretical viewpoints, and they turn out to be more superficial than substantive. In Table 10.4 you can see that the age ranges for the stages are often similar, and many congruent or at least reconcilable themes are apparent. Therefore, I will attempt to integrate the observations of the two studies in an effort to provide you with a coherent overview of adult development. On the basis of this integration of their models, I will describe seven phases of development in early and middle adulthood and conclude with a brief look at late adulthood as an eighth stage. Occasionally, when relevant, I will mention the findings of a handful of other studies on adult development that have surfaced in recent years.

Before I sketch this overview, however, I should emphasize the limitations inherent in our current knowledge. The studies in this area are decidedly culture-bound. Moreover, even within the boundaries of modern Western culture they have focused rather narrowly on middle- to upper-middle-class subjects. We really have no idea whether impoverished people who struggle to keep a roof over their heads go through similar transitions. The data are also limited to a particular historical period and a relatively narrow range of age cohorts. The patterning of adult development in more recent age cohorts may be quite different. This seems especially likely to be true for women in light of alterations in sex roles during the last couple of decades. You should keep these limitations in mind as I describe the phases of adult development that have been identified in recent years.

LEAVING THE FAMILY AND BECOMING INDEPENDENT (EARLY TWENTIES)

Both Gould and Levinson emphasize that the key transition in one's late teens and early twenties is the movement out from under the safe shelter of the family umbrella. Emotionally, this transition requires confronting insecurity about the future as one attempts to break away and establish independence. According to Gould, the major false assumption that needs to be discarded is the idea that "I'll always belong to my parents and believe in their world." Component assumptions that illustrate the anxiety-provoking nature of this transformation include such ideas as "If I get any more independent, it will be a disaster" and "Only my parents can guarantee my safety." Levinson discusses how the young adult must scramble to achieve some financial independence while adapting to new roles, responsibilities, and living arrangements. Thus, the key challenge during this phase is to achieve psychological independence from one's parents while successfully mastering the many practical demands involved in learning to live on one's own. Both theorists believe that this is a period characterized by considerable agitation and change.

According to Levinson, it is during this phase that a young adult begins to shape a Dream—an imaginary vision of what she or he would like to become and would like to accomplish as an adult. Initially, this Dream may be vague and unrealistic. Simplistic visions of becoming a baseball star, rising to the presidency, or finding a cure for cancer are common. As young adults move through their twenties, they typically add definition, detail, and some realism to this vision of the future.

ENTERING THE ADULT WORLD (MID TO LATE TWENTIES)

The remainder of one's twenties is typically devoted to completing the transition into the adult world. This tends to be a relatively stable phase in comparison to the tumultuous change that is characteristic of the previous stage. Tentative decisions from the previous stage regarding marriage, family, and career are converted into deeper commitments that represent one's life structure. According to Levinson, the key conflict at this time centers on the contradictory urges to continue *exploring* various options and to make firm *commitments* to vocations, intimate relationships, and so forth. Thus, people in this phase find themselves struggling with doubts about whether they have committed themselves too quickly to an occupation or delayed too long in making a decision. Gould emphasizes that the struggle to become fully independent of one's parents continues during this phase. While direct dependence should have been ended in the previous stage, indirect dependence on one's parental value system lingers, so that the young adult must work free of the false assumption "Doing things my parents' way, with willpower and perseverance, will bring results."

Levinson believes that a very special and important relationship is often formed during this phase. This is the relationship with a "mentor"—an older, more experienced person who serves as a teacher, adviser, role model, and sponsor for the younger individual. Usually (but not always) the mentoring relationship emerges in a work setting with a senior colleague. Typically, the mentor is about a half-generation (8–15 years) older than the individual, and they interact with each other in a way that blends parent/child and equal/peer relations. The mentor's key function is to help define, support, and facilitate the younger person's Dream. The mentoring relationship is a transitional one, usually lasting from two to ten years. It may peter out gradually but often comes to an abrupt end when a bitter conflict surfaces. Although Levinson found a great deal of mentoring among his male subjects, currently available evidence (Hennig & Jardim, 1978) indicates that career women are less likely to enjoy the benefits of mentoring. Presumably, this is because there are fewer older women available in work settings to serve as mentors for the younger women who have recently been entering the world of work in greatly increased numbers. Besides, the mentoring relationship tends to be emotionally intense, and this makes it awkward for older males to serve as mentors for younger women because their relationship may be misunderstood by colleagues.

Another study (Vaillant, 1977) suggests that this phase may be the best time to establish and solidify intimate relationships. Vaillant assessed the adjustment of his male subjects at age 47 and divided them into "best and worst outcomes." He found that virtually all the "best outcome" men married before age 30 and stayed married to the same woman, while the "worst outcome" men married later and had less successful marital unions. Vaillant also found that the "best marriages" in his sample tended to be formed while the man was between the ages of 23 and 29. Thus, although it is difficult to separate cause from effect, it appears that delay in achieving a satisfactory intimate relationship may be associated in some modest way with relatively poor adjustment in middle adulthood.

AGE 30 TRANSITION: DOUBTS AND REEVALUATION

Around the age of 30, give or take a few years, both Gould and Levinson found signs of increased inner turmoil. Levinson estimated that over 60% of his male subjects experienced a moderate or severe crisis around this time. These crises centered on doubts about the commitments made in the previous stage. These doubts surface just as the person is feeling that choices are getting "locked in" to an extent that will make it difficult to alter one's life path later. Gould likewise sees this as a period of questioning one's decisions about marriage, family, and career. Thus, people struggle with the false assumption "Life is simple and controllable. There are no significant contradictory forces within me."

SETTLING DOWN AND BECOMING ONE'S OWN PERSON (THIRTIES DECADE)

According to Levinson, the vacillation found around age 30 is followed by a period of relative tranquility and consolidation. A solid commitment is made to the life structure that was reformulated around age 30. Men attempt to establish their niche in society and concentrate on climbing up their career ladders. This pursuit of career advancement may necessitate that they challenge their mentor in order to advance more rapidly. Thus, it is not uncommon for a man to give up his mentor in order to "become one's own man," as Levinson puts it.

The reasonable correspondence that we have seen in Levinson's and Gould's findings up until this point diminishes in the thirties decade. Unlike Levinson, Gould did not observe a distinct period of settling down in the thirties. Rather, he concluded that the period of questioning around age 30 lasted until the midthirties, at which time people begin to enter the midlife transition, which Levinson found to occur a bit later (around age 40). At this time it is impossible to say which model is more accurate. The discrepancy may be due to differences in the composition of Gould's and Levinson's samples (in particular, the lack of women in Levinson's sample). In any case, this issue will surely be the subject of additional research in the future.

THE MIDLIFE TRANSITION (AROUND AGE 40)

A major landmark of adult development is the midlife transitional period, which Gould found to occur between ages 35 and 45. Levinson found the modal age bracket for this transition to be 40 to 45. Since these age norms are mere approximations of averages, this discrepancy is not all that important. What *is* important is that both theorists view this period as a potentially turbulent time of reappraisal and restructuring.

Levinson found that men subjected their life structure to tough scrutiny and reevaluation. Most found that they had not fulfilled their Dream. Dismayed by this reality, they worked to alter their expectations to be more realistic or increased their efforts to achieve their goals. Even those men who *had* reached or exceeded their Dream experienced a crisis. Many found their success less satisfying than they had expected, and all had to confront the fact that success and acclaim do not arrest the inevitable process of aging.

This confrontation with the aging process during the midlife transition is also emphasized by Gould. He notes that many people are forced to acknowledge their mortality as they more and more frequently witness the deaths of parents, colleagues, and friends. Thus, they wrestle with the false assumption "There is no evil or death in the world." Women also tend to struggle with a component assumption that their husbands can serve effectively as "protectors." Those who succeed in outgrowing this assumption often become less dependent on their husbands and work harder to realize their own Dream, concentrating less on helping their husbands to realize theirs. Gould also emphasizes that during this period people feel pressed by time. They hear their social clocks ticking rather loudly as they frantically battle time limitations to accomplish what they had hoped to.

Vaillant (1977) did not find the midlife transition to be nearly as troublesome for his subjects as Levinson and Gould did. Nonetheless, he did see a lot of intergenerational conflict during this phase of life. People in their forties often find their parents trying to reestablish closer emotional ties, while their adolescent children are moving in the opposite direction, trying to achieve emotional independence. Thus, there may be tension and an opening (or reopening) of emotional wounds on both fronts.

Like Vaillant, Livson (1976) did not find that people universally experience a midlife "crisis." Her data suggest that such troublesome crises may be particularly infrequent in men and women who are firmly wed to traditional sex roles. In a study examining midlife transitions among women, Rubin (1979) found that many women *do* have problems grappling with the great variety of changes that tend to occur during this period. Foremost among these changes is the fact that children progressively depend less on their mother and often leave home. As a woman's nurturant role becomes less important, she may have to redefine her identity and decide whether to enter or reenter a career.

RESTABILIZATION (MID AND LATE FORTIES)

Both Gould and Levinson observed a period of relative calm after the convulsive instability frequently seen during the midlife transition. Although most people probably are not entirely satisfied with their lives, Gould notes that they feel that the die is cast and they begin to accept their fate with less resistance. Thus, this appears to be a period when people accommodate to the realities of their lives. Among his male subjects, Levinson found a tendency to shift some attention and energy away from career concerns in favor of family concerns. Some of the men who had rewarding relationships with their mentors now became mentors themselves.

CULMINATION OF MIDDLE ADULTHOOD (FIFTIES DECADE)

Information on developmental patterns after age 50 tapers off abruptly. Neither Gould nor Levinson has finished following his subjects through this decade. Although they lack concrete empirical data, both have made some theory-based projections. Gould suggests that the fifties are a period of "mellowing" as people continue to become more tolerant and accepting of their past. The limited data available (Lowenthal, Thurnher, Chiriboga, & associates, 1975) seem to support this idea. Levinson speculates that those people who do not have much of a midlife crisis around age 40 may experience a delayed transitional crisis near age 50. Otherwise, Levinson projects that the mid to late fifties may resemble the mid to late thirties, with people settling into the life structures that they have recently rearranged for themselves. He believes that the fifties *can* be a period of great fulfillment.

LATE ADULTHOOD (AFTER AGE 60): DISENGAGEMENT?

Levinson theorizes that another major transitional phase, comparable to the midlife transition, should occur sometime around age 60. Although that projection certainly seems plausible in light of all the changes that generally occur then, additional research data are needed.

Another prominent theory about late adulthood (Cumming, 1963) suggests

Elderly people who stay active tend to be happier than those who do not.

that a process of *disengagement* should ensue. According to this notion, older people gradually withdraw psychologically and socially from the world around them. Supposedly they reduce their emotional investment in current events and social issues and reduce their actual interactions with others as well. People are thought to gradually turn inward and disengage from society, as society likewise disengages from them. There is some evidence (Havighurst, Neugarten, & Tobin, 1968) supporting the idea that there is a trend toward disengagement during late adulthood. However, the theory is very controversial, and available evidence suggests that this disengagement process is not inevitable (Palmore, 1975). Some critics suggest that when disengagement does occur, it is imposed on older people by society, rather than being a matter of choice. In other words, society disengages from the elderly rather than the elderly disengaging from society.

Much of the opposition to disengagement theory is based on data that suggest that many people maintain a high level of activity during late adulthood (Palmore, 1975). Since the maintenance of a high activity level is inconsistent with the disengagement process, there is reason to doubt whether disengagement is a universal theme in the later years. Moreover, this research suggests that those who minimize disengagement may tend to be relatively satisfied and contented during late adulthood. How can we reconcile these contradictory findings? It may be that the developmental stream flows in the direction of disengagement, but a portion of older people with certain values and personality characteristics may resist this undercurrent successfully. In any case, it is clear that we need a great deal of additional research before we really understand the developmental dynamics of late adulthood.

Vocational Development across the Life Span

Now that we have examined the progression of adult development in a general way, we will focus our attention on a very important area of adjustment during the adult years—the world of work. The importance of work in our lives can hardly be overestimated. When adults meet for the first time and try to strike up a conversation, they will often begin with the question "What do you do for a living?" The popularity of this conversational opener illustrates the central role that work plays in adult life. To a large degree, your very sense of identity is determined by the kind of work you do. Many people define themselves in terms of their occupations.

A **vocation** is an urge or commitment to work in a particular occupational area. Research on vocational adjustment is concerned with such matters as how we arrive at vocational choices, the determinants of vocational success, factors relating to job satisfaction, and patterns of career development. I will discuss most of these topics in the remainder of this chapter, commencing with the subject of vocational development.

VOCATION. *A desire or commitment to seek work in a particular occupational area.*

The most influential theory of vocational development is that outlined by Donald Super (1957, 1972). He views vocational development as a process that unfolds gradually across most of the life span, beginning in childhood and ending with retirement. Super asserts that one's self-concept is the critical factor that governs this evolutionary process. Decisions about work and career commitments are thought to be expressions of one's personality. Table 10.5 provides a concise summary of Super's model of vocational development. As you can see, Super breaks the vocational life cycle into five major stages and a variety of substages. Although I will use his model to summarize what we know about patterns of vocational development, insights from other theorists (Ginzberg, 1972; Jordaan, 1974; Schein, 1978) will be integrated into my description of what tends to happen during each stage.

TABLE 10.5 **Stages of vocational development in Super's (1957) theory**

1. *Growth stage* (birth to 14 years):	A period of general physical and mental growth.
a. Prevocational substage (to 3):	No interest or concern with vocations.
b. Fantasy substage (4–10):	Fantasy is basis for vocational thinking.
c. Interest substage (11–12):	Vocational thought is based on individual's likes and dislikes.
d. Capacity substage (13–14):	Ability becomes the basis for vocational thought.
2. *Exploration stage* (15 to 24 years):	General exploration of work.
a. Tentative substage (15–17):	Needs, interests, capacities, values, and opportunities become bases for tentative occupational decisions.
b. Transition substage (18–21):	Reality increasingly becomes a basis for vocational thought and action.
c. Trial substage (22–24):	First trial job is entered after the individual has made an initial vocational commitment.
3. *Establishment stage* (25 to 44 years):	The individual seeks to enter a permanent occupation.
a. Trial (25–30):	A period of some occupational change due to unsatisfactory choices.
b. Stabilization (31–44):	A period of stable work in a given occupational field.
4. *Maintenance stage* (45 to 65 years):	Continuation in one's chosen occupation.
5. *Decline stage* (65 years to death):	
a. Deceleration (65–70):	Period of declining vocational activity.
b. Retirement (71 on):	A cessation of vocational activity.

GROWTH STAGE

The growth period encompasses childhood, a period during which youngsters fantasize about exotic jobs that they would find pleasurable. Generally, they imagine themselves as detectives, airline pilots, and brain surgeons, rather than plumbers, grocers, and bookkeepers. Until the very end of this period, they are largely oblivious to realistic considerations such as the abilities or education required for various jobs. Instead, they base their fantasies on their likes and dislikes.

EXPLORATION STAGE

The pressure to make a vocational decision begins to intensify as one progresses through high school. Pressure from parents, teachers, and peers leads one to think about narrowing the range of career possibilities. Typically, a tentative commitment to some occupational area is made, and the first steps are taken to pursue one's career goals. This may involve going to work as some kind of "apprentice" or pursuing a particular major in college. Whether it's a matter of studying or working, the person tries to get a real taste of the projected occupational area. The key transitions in the first part of this stage involve (1) becoming much more realistic about vocational opportunities and (2) beginning to "test out" various options.

During the latter part of the exploration stage, which typically encompasses one's early twenties, the person attempts to achieve full entry into the world of work. This typically involves finishing any necessary training and securing the crucial first job. The challenge at this time is to conquer insecurity and inexperience by developing a sense of confidence and by learning how to perform effectively in one's occupational role. Though fully moved into the adult world, many people in this phase are still only rather tentatively committed to their chosen occupational area. If their initial experiences are gratifying, their commitment will be strengthened. However, if their initiation is not rewarding, they may shift to another occupational area, where they will continue the process of exploration.

A frequently encountered problem during this stage is the "entry-level blues." Many people find that their first job is a letdown. This disappointment is a function of two considerations. First, most professions and companies tend to intentionally distort the nature of work in their occupational area. They try to create a very favorable picture in order to recruit talented people, thereby creating unrealistic expectations in those people. Second, many entry-level jobs are not particularly challenging or interesting. Newly hired workers usually wield little influence in an organization and often get stuck with the dullest and least important tasks. In light of these realities and the tentative nature of vocational commitment at this point, it is not surprising that many young people experience distress and doubt about their initial occupational choice.

ESTABLISHMENT STAGE

Vacillation continues to be moderately common during the first part of the establishment stage. For some people, this simply involves carrying earlier doubts into the next stage. For others, doubts may begin to surface for the first time, possibly as part of the reappraisal that occurs during the age-30 transition. In any case, some people continue the exploration process by changing careers during the "trial" portion of this stage.

If and when one's career choice turns out to be appropriately gratifying, the person moves into the heart of the establishment stage, where the principal themes are stabilization and consolidation. With the necessary skills and experience secured, the individual firmly commits to an occupational area. With few exceptions, future job moves will take place *within* this occupational area. During the remainder of this period, the person concentrates on advancing up the career ladder. Energy is focused on being very productive, demonstrating superior performance, achieving success, gaining recognition, and improving one's position and status.

MAINTENANCE STAGE

Eventually people reach a point (typically in their midforties) when they begin to feel that opportunities for further career advancement have been exhausted or greatly reduced. People then cross into the maintenance stage, during which they worry more about *retaining* their achieved status, rather than *improving* their status. Having to face competition from younger workers, they endeavor simply to maintain the security, power, advantages, benefits, and "perks" that they have earned. With the decreased emphasis on career advancement, many people shift energy and attention away from career concerns in favor of family concerns or leisure activities.

The realization that further career advancement is unlikely leads many people to take stock of what they have accomplished. This evaluation may lead to either satisfaction or disenchantment. Most of those who are disappointed learn to live with their frustration and discontent. Some, however, get bogged down in feeling sorry for themselves and may experience significant depression. More often than most people realize, this sort of discontent leads people to make career changes well into middle age (Kohen, 1975). These career shifts are made in spite of the fact that organizational arrangements such as accumulated seniority and pension investments conspire to make them costly. It appears that it is people who are willing to take risks who tend to gamble on these dramatic deviations from their original career path (Krantz, 1977).

DECLINE STAGE

Deceleration involves a decline in vocational activity during one's later years as retirement looms near. People redirect their energy and attention toward planning for this major transition. In his original formulation, which was based on research in the 1950s, Super projected that deceleration ought to begin around age 65. Since the 1970s, however, slowed economic growth and the entry of the large "baby boom" cohort into the work force have combined to create an oversupply of skilled labor and professional talent. This social change has created pressures that promote early retirement, so that today about three-quarters of retirees exit from the work force before age 65 (Kimmel, 1980). However, projected economic and demographic changes in the future may make early retirement a historical curiosity. Economic inflation, the trend toward people living longer, and the immense size of the "baby boom" cohort may make it virtually impossible for the United States to support its Social Security and pension programs by the early part of the 21st century (Kieffer, 1982). Recognition of these financial pressures in the 1990s may lead to a restructuring of retirement programs so that early retirement may become extremely expensive, if not nearly impossible.

Retirement brings vocational activity to a halt. People approach this transition with highly varied attitudes (Kimmel, 1980). Many look forward to it eagerly. Many others approach it with apprehension, unsure how they will occupy themselves and worried about their financial viability. Mixed feelings are also common—many people approach retirement with a combination of hopeful enthusiasm and anxious concern. Although concern about what lies ahead is not irrational, a major study of retirement (Streib & Schneider, 1971) found that few people presently experience the negative consequences (boredom, financial problems, feelings of uselessness) that are widely thought to be associated with retirement.

VARIATIONS AND QUALIFICATIONS

As mentioned earlier, stage theories tend to highlight general trends while ignoring the variability in developmental patterns. However, Super deserves credit for acknowledging that there is diversity in the patterning of vocational development. In fact, he identified some of the atypical patterns that do not coincide with the modal patterns described above. One of these is the *unstable pattern,* which finds people alternating between "trial" jobs (exploratory, entry-level positions) and "stable" jobs throughout life. These people get beyond entry-level jobs and earn positions with potential, but then they forsake their progress and move on to another occupational area, where they start the exploration sequence all over again. The *multiple-trial pattern* is another deviation identified by Super. People who follow this pattern move quickly through an endless series of briefly held trial jobs. They are occupational vagabonds who wander aimlessly from one career area to another.

It is also important to note that most of the research on vocational development has focused on *males'* careers. At this point, we are not sure whether the patterns of development are similar for women. There are many reasons to suspect that they might be quite different. Indeed, a recent study of career progress among men and women (Larwood & Gattiker, 1984) uncovered some significant differences. For the male subjects, it was possible to trace a clear, consistent path that led to vocational success. Among the women, however, success was much less predictable and was characterized as nearly "random." In other words, the researchers were unable to find a consistent path to success for women. Why was there no pattern for women? We are not yet sure, but it is easy to speculate. Vocational development among women may tend to be chaotic and unpredictable because women are more likely than men to experience career interruptions, wherein they leave the work force temporarily to concentrate on child rearing or some family crisis. Additionally, the fact that many women tend to subjugate their career goals to their husbands' probably helps to make vocational development among women less orderly than it is among men. In any case, we need more research on sex differences in vocational development.

Important Considerations in Vocational Choice

UNDEREMPLOYMENT. *A condition that exists when a person works (usually reluctantly) in a job that does not fully utilize his or her skills, abilities, potentials, and training.*

One of the biggest decisions that you'll face in your lifetime will be choosing a vocation. The importance of this decision is enormous. It may determine whether you are successful or unsuccessful, employed or unemployed, happy or unhappy. Thoughtful consideration about vocational choice is particularly crucial given the current economic context. As I mentioned in discussing the trend toward early retirement, there is presently an oversupply of skilled labor and talent because of the slowdown in economic growth and the entry of the sizable "baby boom" cohort into the work force. This oversupply does *not* spell doom for young people. The business and professional world is always looking for "new blood," and the fact that younger workers initially get paid less than more experienced workers makes them attractive. Nonetheless, the absorption of newly trained workers into the labor force is slower and more selective than it used to be. More and more frequently, young people are working hard to earn a college diploma, only to find that they can't get the kind of job they were trained for (Freeman, 1976). They end up taking jobs as taxi drivers and department-store clerks and are said to be **underemployed.** Most of these

TRAVELS WITH FARLEY BY PHIL FRANK. COPYRIGHT FIELD ENTERPRISES, INC. COURTESY OF FIELD NEWSPAPER SYNDICATE.

people find this situation exceedingly frustrating. These unpleasant economic realities make it more important than ever for people to think rationally and systematically about their vocational choices. To facilitate this end, I will discuss important considerations in vocational choice in this section.

GENERAL PRINCIPLES

1. *There are limits on your vocational options.* Entry into a particular occupation is not simply a matter of choosing what you want to do (Blau et al., 1956). It's a two-way street; you get to make choices, but you also have to persuade schools and employers to choose you. Your options may be limited by your personality, abilities, background, finances, and so forth.

2. *Chance may play a role in your vocational development.* Although vocational theorists such as Super (1957) do not like the word *chance,* the reality is that unplanned, accidental events do influence one's vocational evolution (Miller & Form, 1951). For example, your career plans might be changed by enrolling in a particular college course that you took only because the class you really wanted was full. This reality does not mean that you should leave career development to fate and fortune. Rather, your challenge is to minimize the role of chance in your vocational development.

3. *You have the potential for success in a variety of occupations.* Gilmer (1975) stresses that people have multiple potentials. It would be foolish to believe that there is only one career that would be right for you.

4. *Vocational choice is a developmental process that extends throughout life.* Vocational choice involves not a single decision but a series of decisions. Although this process was once believed to extend only from prepuberty through one's early twenties, it is now recognized that the process often continues throughout one's lifetime (Ginzberg, 1972). It is most unfortunate that middle-aged people tend to underestimate the options available to them and therefore miss various kinds of opportunities. Hence, it is important to emphasize that vocational choices are not limited to one's youth.

5. *Some vocational decisions are not easily undone.* Although it's never too late to strike out in new vocational directions, it is important to be realistic and realize that many decisions are not readily reversed. One influential theory of occupational choice in the 1950s (Ginzberg, 1952) went so far as to propose that vocational decisions are characterized by *irreversibility.* That has since been retracted as an overstatement (Ginzberg, 1972), but it is clear that once you invest time, money, and effort in moving along a particular career path, it may not be easy to change paths. This reality is illustrated by a recent survey (Renwick & Lawler, 1978) in which *44%* of the respondents indicated that they felt "locked into" their current job. This potential problem highlights why it is so important for you to devote a lot of systematic thought to the question of vocational choice.

6. *The perfect job does not exist.* Gilmer (1975) points out that no job is likely to provide total satisfaction for a person. As in other areas of life, it is important to have realistic expectations.

7. *Vocational choice is an expression of one's personality.* Various influential theories of vocational choice focus on how this process is related to one's ego functioning (Ginzberg, 1952), one's self-concept (Super, 1953), and one's psychological needs (Roe, 1956). Although these theories use different models of personality, they clearly agree that choosing a career is a very significant expression of one's personality.

8. *Vocational choice is influenced by a vast array of factors.* There is evidence that one's vocational choice tends to be influenced by one's sex, family, socioeconomic class, geographic location, school, peers, and community (Crites, 1969) and even one's hereditary endowment (Grotevant, Scarr, & Weinberg, 1978; see Box 10.1). You might want to think about how these sources of influence may have affected you. In particular, you might want to consider how

they may have limited your horizons and whether you really want to accept those limitations.

EXAMINING YOUR PERSONAL CHARACTERISTICS

The first step is self-analysis. In order to match yourself up with a job, you need to have a clear picture of yourself. In piecing together this picture, you will want to consider your personality, your abilities, and your interests (Shertzer, 1977). I will describe each of these issues below. Box 10.2 spotlights a book that can be very helpful in guiding you through this self-exploration.

Personality. Most vocational theorists agree that it is very important to choose an occupation that is compatible with your personality. One influential theorist (Holland, 1973) has identified six basic personality types that fit optimally with various career areas. In evaluating your personality, a crucial issue is how socially skilled you are. Some jobs require much more social dexterity than others. In assessing your personality, you should try to identify your dominant traits, your dominant needs, and your dominant values.

Aptitudes and abilities. It is important to realistically evaluate your aptitudes and abilities. Foremost among these is your general intelligence. Intelligence is clearly related to the academic success that is necessary to enter many fields. In many occupational areas, however, social skills or special aptitudes are more important than general intelligence. Specific aptitudes that might make a person particularly well suited for certain occupations include perceptual-motor coordination, creativity, artistic or musical talent, mechanical ability, clerical skill, mathematical ability, and persuasive talents.

10.1   IS THERE A BIOLOGICAL BASIS FOR CAREER INTERESTS?

It is well known that children often follow in their parents' career footsteps. Not always, of course, but more often than one would expect by chance. The fact that parents influence the career interests of their children has never been a source of surprise or mystery for psychologists. It made good sense. One would expect that children would acquire certain interests from their parents through the processes of exposure, modeling, and learning.

However, one study (Grotevant, Scarr, & Weinberg, 1978) suggests that this correspondence of interests may be due more to genetic inheritance than to social learning! Grotevant and his colleagues studied career-interest patterns in families that had at least two adopted children (between ages 16 and 22) as well as families with children who were biological offspring. The adopted children were placed in their homes at an average age of 2.6 months and therefore had plenty of time to acquire interests similar to their parents. Contrary to expectation, however, the adopted children showed little similarity to their parents in career interests as measured by the Strong-Campbell Interest Inventory. However, children and their *biological* parents showed moderate but statistically reliable similarity in career interests.

Although additional research is needed, these findings suggest that your genetic endowment may some-

Many children, such as Julian Lennon, follow in their parents' career footsteps. Some recent research suggests that this may be due more to genetic inheritance than to learning.

how influence your career interests. This does not mean that you carry a gene marked "lawyer" or "engineer." Instead, the mechanism appears indirect. Hereditary factors are known to influence your personality and temperament. Your personality, in turn, influences your career interests. Thus, through this indirect route your hereditary endowment apparently predisposes you to be interested in certain occupational areas.

Interests.   As you meander through life, you acquire interests in different kinds of activities. In making vocational decisions, you should consider your pattern of interests. Are you intrigued by the business world? The academic world? International affairs? Agriculture? The outdoors? Social sciences? Physical sciences? Arts and crafts? Drama? Music? Travel? Athletics? Human services? Marketing? The list of potential interests is virtually infinite. Although interests may change, they tend to be reasonably stable, and they definitely should be considered in developing a career orientation.

Utility of psychological tests.   Numerous psychological tests are available that can be quite valuable in helping you arrive at a good picture of your personality, abilities, and interests. If you are very much "up in the air" about what kind of occupation might intrigue you, you might want to take an *occupational interest inventory.* This is a special kind of psychological test that measures your interests as they relate to various jobs or careers. There are many such tests. Among the more widely used are the Strong-Campbell Interest Inventory (see Figure 10.1), the Kuder Occupational Interest Survey, the Minnesota Vocational Interest Inventory, the California Occupational Preference Survey, and the Hall Occupational Orientation Inventory.

It is important to understand the logic underlying these tests. They vary somewhat in how they're set up, but they share the same general strategy. They do *not* measure how well one would perform in an occupation; rather, they measure how relevant one's interests are to an occupation. They relate more to the likelihood of job *satisfaction* than job *success.* Indeed, there is evidence (Crites, 1969) that occupational interests as assessed by such scales show moderate positive correlations with measures of job satisfaction.

In developing these tests, the interests of people already in various occupations are measured. The test taker's interests are then compared with the interest profiles compiled for various occupational groups. For example, if you receive a high score on the "Accountant" scale of a test, this indicates that your interests are similar to those of a typical accountant. Although this correspondence in interests is interesting information, there is no *assurance* that you would find accounting enjoyable or rewarding. You have to decide that for yourself. These tests can merely give you food for thought. Typically, they'll give you a list of 10 or 15 occupational groups that have interests similar to yours. You may be able to dismiss some of them instantly. Others may provide you with worthwhile possibilities that you had never thought of before.

In summary, as long as you regard the results from these tests as thought-

10.2   *Coming Alive from Nine to Five: The Career Search Handbook*
by Betty Neville Michelozzi (Mayfield Publishing, 1980)

This is a brief but thorough book that takes you step by step through the process of making vocational decisions. This book is *very* strong on self-analysis. Numerous checklists, exercises, and questionnaires help you get a clear picture of your needs, values, interests, and abilities. One chapter allows you to assess your personality and then relate it to a host of job families. There is also some interesting speculation about future trends in the job market to aid you in thinking about vocational choices.

Michelozzi goes beyond the issue of vocational choice in a very practical chapter on hunting for a job. In this chapter she discusses researching companies, résumés, letters of application, and interviewing for a job. Michelozzi, a career counselor, writes clearly, and the book is very cleverly illustrated.

We are gathering information to match a special person—you—with satisfying positions in the world of work. In order to match your needs, wants, and values with job specifica-

tions, you should examine various dimensions of career choice, including some that are often overlooked. When you finally enter the workplace, you may have to make some compromises but the ideal is to minimize the compromises and maximize the match [p. 43].

Making a good career decision is a growth process, and growth takes patience. You can't make a flower grow by pulling on it [p. 87].

				Occupational scales						
Code	Scale	Sex norm.	Std. score	Very dissimilar	Dissimilar	Ave.	Similar	Very similar	Code	Scale
RC	Farmer	m							AE	Int. Dec
RC	Instrum. assembl.	f			✴				AE	Advertis
RCE	Voc. agric. tchr.	m							A	Languag
REC	Dietitian	m							A	Librarian
RES	Police officer	m							A	Librarian
RSE	Hwy. patrol off.	m							A	Reporter
RE	Army officer	f					✴		A	Reporter
RS	Phys. ed. teacher	f				✴			AS	English
R	Skilled crafts	m							AS	English
RI	Forester	m							SI	Nurse

IS	Speech pathol.	f						✴	ERC	Purchas
IS	Speech pathol.	m							ESR	Chiropr
IAS	Psychologist	f						✴	CE	Account
IAS	Psychologist	m		15	25	45	55		CE	Banker
IA	Language interpr.	f					✴		CE	Banker
ARI	Architect	m							CE	Credit
A	Advertising exec.	f				✴			CE	Dept. S
A	Artist	f				✴			CE	Busines
A	Artist	m							CES	Busines
A	Art Teacher	f				✴			CSE	Busines
A	Photographer	m							C	Account
A	Musician	f					✴		C	Secretar
A	Musician	m							CR	Dental
A	Entertainer	f					✴		CRI	Nurse,
AE	Int. decorator	f				✴			CRE	Beautic

FIGURE 10.1   Example of a score report on an occupational interest inventory. A portion of a score report from the Strong-Campbell Interest Inventory is reproduced here. It shows the kind of information that one gets through taking an occupational interest inventory. Such inventories tell you how similar your interests are to those of people in a wide variety of occupations.

provoking rather than definitive, they can be quite useful. Specifically, two precautions should be mentioned. First, if you score high on an occupation that you're sure you would hate, don't dismiss the rest of the results as worthless. Given the way the test is set up, this can easily happen. Second, don't let the test make career decisions for you. Some students naively believe that they should go into whatever occupation yields their highest score. This is not how the tests are meant to be used. Ultimately, you have to think things out for yourself.

RESEARCHING JOB CHARACTERISTICS

In order to match yourself up with an occupation, you have to pursue information on jobs. There are about 20,000 occupations (Michelozzi, 1980). Their sheer number is overwhelming. Obviously, you have to narrow down the scope of your search before you can seek extensive information.

Once you have selected some jobs that might interest you, the next question is: Where do you go to get information on them? This is not a simple matter. The first step is usually to read some occupational literature. A very general reference is the *Occupational Outlook Handbook,* available in most libraries. This rather sizable volume provides information for over 800 occupations. Another good book is *Careers Tomorrow* by Gene Hawes (1979). In addition to these very general books, you can often get more detailed information on particular occupations from government agencies, trade unions, and professional organizations. For example, if you were interested in psychology, you could obtain a number of pamphlets or books from the American Psychological Association (see Box 10.3).

If you're definitely interested in an occupation after reading the available literature, it's often a good idea to talk to some people working in that area. Occupational literature tends to be a little one-sided and usually paints a pretty positive picture. Talking to people in the field can provide you with more down-to-earth information.

In examining occupational literature and interviewing people, what kinds of information should you seek? Well, to some extent it depends on your unique values. However, there are some general things that should be of concern to virtually anyone (Shertzer, 1977; Weinrach, 1979). These include:

- *The nature of the work.* What are your duties and responsibilities on a day-to-day basis?
- *Working conditions.* Is the working environment pleasant or unpleasant, low-key or high-pressure?
- *Job-entry requirements.* What education and training are required to break into this occupational area?

10.3 IF YOU'RE THINKING ABOUT A CAREER IN PSYCHOLOGY . . .

Since you're reading this textbook, there is a reasonable chance that you might have some interest in a career in psychology. If so, the American Psychological Association (APA) publishes a number of books and pamphlets that could be useful to you. Many professional organizations such as the APA publish pamphlets on careers. If you're interested in some other field, you might want to contact the appropriate organization to inquire about occupational literature. Career-oriented books available from the APA are listed below. They can be ordered at the following address (prices are 1981 figures):

American Psychological Association
Order Department
1200 Seventeenth Street NW
Washington, D.C. 20036

Careers in Psychology. This is a brief pamphlet that introduces you to career opportunities in the field of psychology. It describes various specialties in psychology and the kinds of education required to enter them. Single copies can be ordered free.

The Psychology Major: Training and Employment Strategies, edited by Paul J. Woods (1979, $10). This book provides practical career advice for undergraduate psychology majors. It analyzes the job market in specific areas of psychology and provides information on programs and internships. The appendixes include information on where to go to pursue various kinds of jobs.

Preparing for Graduate Study in Psychology: Not for Seniors Only, by Bruce R. Fretz and David J. Stang (1980, $6.50). Many careers in psychology require some graduate-level education. Competition for admission to graduate programs in psychology is fierce. This book can help you play the admissions game successfully. As its title indicates, you should get this book long before your senior year if you're thinking about graduate school.

Graduate Study in Psychology (revised yearly, $7). This is a reference book that provides information on over 550 graduate psychology programs in the United States and Canada. Whereas the previous book helps you plot your admissions strategy, this book tells you about the schools. It includes data on application procedures, admission requirements, degree requirements, tuition, financial aids, and minority considerations.

Career Opportunities for Psychologists: Expanding and Emerging Areas, edited by Paul J. Woods (1976, $6). This book examines new career opportunities for psychologists in nontraditional areas such as health research, population and environment, industry, forensic psychology, engineering psychology, and program evaluation. It can introduce you to innovative job opportunities that lie outside the sphere of academia.

- *Potential earnings.* What are entry-level salaries, and how much can you hope to earn if you're exceptionally successful? What does the average person earn? What are the fringe benefits?
- *Potential status.* What is the social status associated with this occupation? Is it personally satisfactory for you?
- *Opportunities for advancement.* How do you "move up" in this field? Are there adequate opportunities for promotion and advancement?
- *Intrinsic job satisfactions.* Outside of money and formal fringe benefits, what can you derive in the way of personal satisfaction from this job? Will it allow you to have fun, help people, be creative, or shoulder responsibility?
- *Future outlook.* How is supply and demand projected to shape up in the future for this occupational area?

Understanding Job Satisfaction

In making a vocational choice, people, in a sense, make a prediction about the future. They project that the occupation they are entering will provide them with satisfaction. Since a vocational choice involves this sort of projection, it is useful to analyze the determinants of job satisfaction.

IMPORTANCE OF JOB SATISFACTION

Let me begin by emphasizing the tremendous importance of vocational satisfaction. Work plays a very significant role in our lives. The satisfactions and dissatisfactions associated with work can spill over with great impact into virtually any area of our lives.

Various lines of evidence demonstrate the importance of work to our general adjustment. For example, you may recall that in Chapter 1 we looked at Freedman's (1978) research on the correlates of happiness and learned that **job satisfaction** is a major determinant of general happiness. In Chapter 4 we learned that work-related problems are an extremely significant source of stress that show an alarmingly high relationship to coronary risk (House, 1974; Theorell, 1974).

Still other lines of evidence clearly show that work can have an enormous impact on our general well-being. One very dramatic piece of evidence suggests that if you're happy with your work, you're likely to live longer! Palmore (1969) found a positive correlation between job satisfaction and longevity. The importance of one's job is further highlighted by the fact that unemployment rates are a very significant predictor of suicide rates (Vigderhous & Fishman, 1978). Losing one's job also appears to be related to the likelihood of psychological disorders, sexual difficulties, alcoholism, and divorce (Dumont, 1977). Thus, you can see that vocational satisfaction is a crucial issue for many people. This reality underscores why it is so important to make a wise vocational choice. In thinking about vocations, it might be helpful to you to know what kinds of things make jobs satisfying for other people.

JOB SATISFACTION. *One's happiness and contentment with a particular occupational position.*

MEASURING JOB SATISFACTION

Before describing the factors associated with job satisfaction, I need to emphasize the great complexity of this issue. First, I should clarify that I am talking here about job satisfaction, not job *success*. Although there is some relation between job satisfaction and job performance, they are not the same thing. I will be focusing on what makes people subjectively *happy* with their work. Second, job satisfaction is a multidimensional concept that is not easily measured. A job has many aspects, and a person might be satisfied with one, such as promotion opportunities, and dissatisfied with another, such as job security. Third, and most important, *one's job satisfaction depends on more than just the nature of the job.* Two persons working at exactly the same job might display very different levels of satisfaction. This is because your satisfaction with your work may be influenced by (1) how well you "fit" in a particular job, (2) how much you have succeeded in your vocation in comparison with how much you aspired to, and (3) what reference group you compare yourself with (Crites, 1969). As you can see, then, job satisfaction is a very complex matter. Nonetheless, researchers have isolated some key factors that are related to job satisfaction for most people.

INGREDIENTS OF JOB SATISFACTION

Surprisingly, job satisfaction is not very strongly related to job *level.* Many people seem to assume that higher-status jobs lead to greater satisfaction. There may be a trend in that direction, but Seashore and Barnowe (1972) found that the "blue-collar blues" show up among plenty of higher-status white-collar workers as well.

If job level isn't the crucial factor, what *are* the main ingredients of job satisfaction? Quite a number of elements combine to produce job satisfaction. I will highlight some of the more important factors in this section. Although I will cite some individual studies, the discussion will be based primarily on an excellent review of research in this area by Michael Gruneberg (1979).

Challenge.   In their analysis of "blue-collar blues," Seashore and Barnowe (1972) found that people need challenge in their jobs. This makes sense in view of our earlier observation that people want to use their full potentials in their work. This point was reinforced further by results obtained in a large-scale survey about attitudes toward work (Renwick & Lawler, 1978). When asked to rate the importance of various aspects of their jobs, respondents ranked the "chance to learn new things" and the "opportunity to develop skills and abilities" third and fourth, respectively. The great importance of challenge in one's job illustrates why increasing underemployment may create serious problems in the work world. There is evidence that underemployed people tend to have low job satisfaction (Gooding, 1970). Much of their dissatisfaction may stem from a lack of personal challenge in their jobs.

Good pay.   When workers are asked to rate the importance of various job features, they generally rank pay much lower than you would probably expect. For instance, in the Renwick and Lawler survey, pay was ranked only 12th in importance out of 18 items. However, these low rankings may be somewhat misleading. Although workers often rank pay low in importance, it tends to be a major source of complaints, suggesting that people may be more concerned about pay than they themselves would like to believe.

Pay, by the way, is one of those things that tend to be evaluated on a relative basis. People are very sensitive to what *others* earn. The crucial issue for pay is not simply how many dollars you take home but, rather, how your paycheck stacks up in comparison with others' paychecks. Obviously, your choice of a reference group greatly influences your feelings about whether your income is adequate.

Security.   We saw earlier that being unemployed can have a devastating impact on one's psychological health. Given this reality, it is not surprising that people value security in their jobs. In surveys, this factor is sometimes ranked low in importance because we tend to take it for granted when there is no threat to our job. But job security becomes very important as soon as it is undermined.

Meaningfulness. Meaningfulness as it relates to work is rather difficult to define. Generally, when people talk about their work being meaningful, they seem concerned about whether it makes a real contribution to their society. This appears to be an important issue for many people. In the Renwick and Lawler (1978) survey, the "chance to accomplish something worthwhile" was ranked second in importance by the respondents.

Variety. Variety in a job is also an important consideration. People tend to find repetitive work very boring and dissatisfying. Life on an assembly line tends to be rather dull. Given a choice, most workers prefer task variety in their jobs.

Autonomy. A closely related consideration is job autonomy. Autonomy and variety tend to go hand in hand in work, and both are highly desired. In the Renwick and Lawler (1978) survey, "freedom on the job" was ranked fifth in importance.

Friendship. In Chapter 9 I discussed the prominent roles that affiliation and friendship play in our lives. For many people, friendship circles emerge largely out of interactions at work. Consequently, it is logical that the social aspects of a job are a prime determinant of job satisfaction. When interpersonal relationships at work are pleasant and rewarding, people are relatively likely to be content with their jobs.

Recognition. Whether it is provided through pay raises, promotions, or simply praise, people crave recognition for their work. Most of us need to have the value of our work externally validated by others, especially supervisors and co-workers. This element showed up as a very major source of job satisfaction in a classic study by Herzberg, Mausner, and Snyderman (1959).

Role clarity. A relatively obscure factor that turns out to be important to job satisfaction is role clarity. Workers like their job responsibilities to be clearly defined. When workers aren't sure what is expected of them, they tend to feel uncomfortable. Clear explanations of work requirements and performance criteria tend to promote job satisfaction.

RECOMMENDED READING

10.4 *What Color Is Your Parachute? A Practical Manual for Job-Hunters and Career-Changers*
by Richard Nelson Bolles (Ten Speed Press, revised yearly)

Richard Bolles is a clever, creative writer who has put together a landmark book on the process of hunting for a job. The book has been so successful that it's being updated yearly!

Although Bolles devotes some attention to the matter of career choice, this book focuses mainly on the task of hunting for a job. Unlike many similar books, it does not assume that you're a recent college graduate seeking your first job. Instead, it devotes equal time to people shifting careers later in life.

Bolles's writing is humorous and very opinionated. However, his opinions have merit because he has done his homework; the book is very thoroughly researched and documented. He destroys many myths about what does and does not work in seeking jobs. Bolles discusses a variety of practical topics, including where the jobs are, what will get you hired, how to get in to see the boss, whom to go see, and whom to avoid.

In a separate study, of those who sent out résumés, it was found that employers made one job-offer to a job-hunter for every 1470 résumés they received, on an average. That means that 1469 out of every 1470 résumés do not result in a job [1980, p. 181].

Job-hunters such as yourself, dear Reader, begin by thinking there are too few job markets (and therefore, too few jobs) "out there." Thus far, in this chapter, we have argued just the opposite. There are too many. If you try to hit them all (shotgun style) you will only diffuse your energies and your effectiveness. Better, far better, to try concentrating your energies and effectiveness. Rifle style [1980, p. 121].

Other factors.   The above list is certainly not exhaustive. There are additional factors that influence job satisfaction. Although these other factors appear to be less important than those just discussed, they may be of critical importance for some people. Other relevant considerations include quality of the physical working conditions, opportunities for advancement and promotion, opportunities to participate in broad policy-making decisions, technical competence of one's supervisors, and interpersonal competence of one's supervisors.

Summary

Development refers to age-related changes in behavior. In recent years, social scientists have begun to study development during the adult years. Most models of adult development are stage theories. Although such theories probably overestimate the uniformity of developmental patterns, they can be very useful descriptive models.

Physical development during adulthood leads to many obvious changes in physical appearance and sensory acuity. After age 30 there is a steady loss of active brain cells, but this loss has not been clearly related to reductions in cognitive functioning. Similarly, endocrine changes that occur appear to be only modestly related to midlife distress or to declining sexual activity during the later years. Unfortunately, health does tend to decline with increasing age for a variety of reasons.

Intelligence seems to remain fairly steady during most of adulthood. Memory retrieval, attentional capacity, speed of learning, and success in problem solving all tend to decline a little during old age, although most people remain capable of sound intellectual functioning. Insofar as personality is concerned, stability seems to outweigh change during adulthood.

Erikson's psychoanalytic theory of development focuses on the psychosocial crises that must be dealt with during each of eight successive stages. These crises center on transitions in social relations. Successful navigation through the adult stages in Erikson's model leads one to have a clear sense of identity, be capable of intimacy, be concerned about future generations, and face death with integrity. Building on Erikson's model, Havighurst proposes that there are developmental tasks that must be mastered during each stage.

Research by Gould and Levinson led to the emergence of two new and influential theories of adult development during the 1970s. Gould's theory emphasizes false assumptions that must be wrestled with, while Levinson's focuses on age-related changes in one's life structure. Although the models are far from identical, they have many congruent themes. Both propose that there are major life transitions around age 20, again around age 40, and probably around age 60.

Super has described in detail the unfolding of vocational development, asserting that vocational decisions are expressions of one's self-concept. According to Super, there are five major stages in the occupational life cycle: growth, exploration, establishment, maintenance, and decline.

One's vocational choice is not unlimited and may even be determined by chance factors. One has the potential for success in more than one occupation, and the perfect job does not exist. The process of vocational choice extends throughout life, but some decisions are not easily reversed. Vocational choice is influenced by a vast array of factors, especially one's personality. In making vocational decisions, one should consider one's personality, abilities, and interests. One's interests can be assessed through interest inventories, although the results should be regarded only as food for thought. In seeking information on jobs, one will usually be interested in the nature of the work, working conditions, entry requirements, potential earnings, potential status, opportunities for advancement, intrinsic satisfactions, and the future outlook for the occupational area. Job satisfaction appears to be very important: it has been related to happiness, stress reactions, and longevity. Job satisfaction is influenced by many variables, but certain factors are related to satisfaction with some consistency. These include challenge, good pay, meaningfulness, variety, autonomy, friendship, recognition, and role clarity.

In our upcoming application section, I will discuss the final phase of adult development—death. As we progress through adulthood, we tend to encounter the death of loved ones more and more frequently. To help you to better understand this sensitive topic, I will analyze attitudes about death, describe the process of dying, and discuss how to cope with the specter of death.

Confronting Death and Dying

True or false? Choose one.

_____ 1. The elderly fear death less than middle-aged people.
_____ 2. Grief over the death of one's spouse may hasten death in the bereaved.
_____ 3. All cultures are characterized by a purely negative view of death.
_____ 4. Experts maintain that it is best to delay telling someone that he or she is dying as long as possible.
_____ 5. When people know they are dying, it is best to avoid discussing it with them.

What are the correct responses to the questions above? Well, the first two statements appear to be true, while the last three appear to be largely false. However, there is some room for argument with respect to any of these five assertions. You will not find solid agreement among the so-called experts in this area on any of these five issues. The arguable nature of these assertions illustrates two realities about the topics of death and dying. First, this is a relatively new area of research, and we still have a great deal to learn. Extensive study of death and dying by social scientists began only in the 1970s. Our fund of knowledge in this area is surprisingly limited. Second, many of the issues in this area are value-laden ones that are not simple questions of fact. Beliefs about the "best" way to deal with death are greatly influenced by one's cultural background, religious orientation, and resulting values. Hence, some of these issues may remain arguable no matter how much research we do. Nonetheless, research on death and dying has increased substantially during the last decade or so, and social scientists have unearthed some interesting insights that are worthy of our consideration.

CULTURAL AND INDIVIDUAL ATTITUDES ABOUT DEATH

Research on death was relatively scarce until recently because modern Western society is characterized by a decidedly negative attitude about death. It is a taboo topic that most people are very reluctant to discuss. In dealing with death, the most common strategy in our culture is *avoidance*. Evidence of our collective inability to confront death comfortably is plentiful. It is apparent in how we talk about death—using euphemisms such as "he passed away" in order to avoid even the word itself. Our discomfort often leads us to unnecessarily quarantine the dying in hospitals and nursing homes in order to minimize our exposure to the specter of death. Even after death, our embalming procedures make the deceased look "lifelike" in order to further facilitate the denial of death. These are all manifestations of what Kastenbaum (1977) calls a **death system**—the collection of rituals and procedures used by a culture to handle death. Death systems vary from one culture to another. Ours happens to be rather negative and evasive in nature. It is dominated by a pervasive attitude of *fear*.

DEATH SYSTEM. *A culture's institutionalized way of dealing with death; includes attitudes, norms, rituals, and traditions.*

Negativism, avoidance, and fear are *not* universal features of all death systems. The Amish, for example, view death in a more calm and accepting fashion. They see death as a natural transition rather than as a dreaded adversary (Bryer, 1979). Thus, some cultures display relatively favorable attitudes about death. Viewing death in a positive light may strike you as somewhat strange, but it is possible. Consider this eloquent passage:

> Death produces another important paradox. Although it only occurs once, at the end of life, it seems to affect the whole course of individual development. It is a primary source of motivation for the living. Can you imagine life without death? Immortality transforms the meaning of life completely. Time, love, work—all our significant roles and values would be radically altered in a deathless universe. It might well be that a deathless universe is a lifeless one. Life draws its vitality, its intensity, its value, in some measure from its very perishability [Stevens-Long, 1984, p. 514].

Within our culture, *individuals* differ greatly in their attitudes about death. For example, anxiety about death is related to age and religion. There are conflicting findings about whether *preoccupation* with thoughts about death peaks in middle age or old age. However, the evidence is fairly clear that *fear* of death tends to decline after middle age (Bengtson, Cuellar, & Ragan, 1977). The reasons may be that older people gradually begin to feel they have lived a "full" life and that they gradually work through the meaning of death as they confront others' deaths more and more frequently. Religious affiliation isn't particularly influential, but a strong, deeply felt religious commitment (regardless of denomination) is associated with a lower level of death anxiety. Ultimately, fear of death is a highly individualized matter, greatly influenced by one's personality and family background (Templer, Ruff, & Franks, 1971).

CONTROVERSY OVER THE "RIGHT TO DIE"

Some aspects of our attitudes about death appear to be going through a rather controversial transition. Traditionally, we have valued life over death, no matter what the circumstances might be. However, recent medical advances have led many people to reconsider whether their commitment to life over death should be absolute. Medical progress has made it possible to prolong life extensively for many people suffering from some terminal illness. The use of medical technology to delay the inevitable is a natural outgrowth of our very negative view of death. However, many people argue that this prolongation effort adds to the dying person's physical and psychological suffering. These people also assert that life maintained by machines is often a demeaning and hollow imitation of the real thing and that extraordinary efforts to sustain the terminally ill may only serve to increase and draw out the anguish of loved ones. In light of these considerations, many individuals argue, people should be permitted to exercise their "right to die" in such circumstances.

EUTHANASIA. *The act of ending life (for those who are presumed terminally ill) in order to alleviate suffering. Commonly used to refer to "mercy killing," although the original meaning was simply "good death."*

Those who believe in the right to die advocate the practice of **euthanasia.** Most seem to favor the *passive* form of euthanasia, which involves permitting people to die by choosing not to use heroic measures to sustain life. Although the percentage of people who endorse the concept of passive euthanasia has increased substantially over the last several decades (Rogers, 1982), the practice is still highly controversial. This is not surprising, as the concepts of euthanasia and the right to die clash head on with our traditional abhorrence of death. Additionally, there is some justifiable concern that in our youth-worshipping culture, wherein old people are often viewed as burdensome, the use of euthanasia might gradually expand into a socially sanctioned system for prematurely dispatching the elderly.

DYING A "GOOD" DEATH: PLANNING AHEAD

LIVING WILL. *A document expressing an individual's desires about whether he or she should be kept alive by extraordinary efforts or life-sustaining machines if the situation arises. It is completed in case a person is prevented from making this decision because of his or her condition at the time.*

The debate over the right to die is a thorny ethical issue that we certainly will not resolve here. However, it does bring up another important matter that you should consider. *If* you have strong feelings about how you want to be treated if you hover on the brink of death, you should make these known to the appropriate people. Otherwise, if such a situation occurs, your deteriorated condition (you may be unconscious, for instance) may prevent you from having any input about the matter. Besides depriving yourself of your own right to decide, you may thrust an incredibly difficult conflict on your loved ones. The most effective way to make sure your wishes are known and heeded is to fill out a document known as a **living will,** which formally spells out your preferences (see Figure 10.2 on p. 364).

Most people have some ideas about how they would prefer to die. In describing a "good death," people tend to say that they would like it to be dignified, relatively painless, and reasonably quick, with loved ones present (Berger, 1983). Obviously, we cannot exert complete control over how we die. However, we *can* influence many aspects of the death process—if we have the courage to look ahead. Unfortunately, our collective avoidance of the topic of death means that relatively few of us make even the most basic plans for this inevitable event. Unless you just don't care, it would seem wise to *plan* for death by writing out your wishes on various relevant issues. Besides considering a living will, you may want to indicate what sort of funeral you would like, whether you prefer burial or cremation, and whether you would like to be an organ donor. Forms and checklists for organizing these plans can often be obtained from a local funeral home. All this may strike you as morbid (since you have been socialized in a death-avoidant culture), but it is an essential part of confronting the irrefutable fact that we all are mortal.

THE PROCESS OF DYING

Pioneering research on the experience of dying was conducted by Elisabeth Kübler-Ross (1969, 1970) during the 1960s. At first, her project met with immense resistance. Fellow physicians at the hospital where she worked were not inclined to cooperate with her requests to interview dying patients. Gradually, however, it became apparent that many such patients were quite enthusiastic about the discussions. They were sick of the "conspiracy of silence" that surrounds death and were pleased to get things out in the open, as Kübler-Ross explains:

> Suddenly, this big teaching hospital did not have a single dying patient!
> During the first year of this undertaking it required an average of ten hours per week to search for a patient—and to get permission from a physician. . . .
> In general, the very young physicians or the very old ones were more amenable to our requests, the nurses and nurses' aides the most interested, and the patients themselves the most enthusiastic. With few ex-

ceptions, the patients were surprised, amazed, and grateful. Some were plain curious and others expressed their disbelief that "a young, healthy doctor would sit with a dying old woman and really care to know what it is like." In the majority of cases the initial outcome was similar to opening floodgates. It was hard to stop them once the conversation was initiated and the patients responded with great relief to sharing some of their last concerns, expressing their feelings without fear of repercussions [Kübler-Ross, 1970, pp. 157–158].

Eventually, Kübler-Ross interviewed over 200 terminally ill patients and developed a model of the process of dying. According to her model, people evolve through a series of five stages as they confront their own death. These "stages" often overlap and coexist, however, so it is probably more accurate to simply characterize them as typical *reactions*, which may or may not unfold

TO MY FAMILY, MY PHYSICIAN, MY LAWYER, MY CLERGYMAN; TO ANY MEDICAL FACILITY IN WHOSE CARE I HAPPEN TO BE; TO ANY INDIVIDUAL WHO MAY BECOME RESPONSIBLE FOR MY HEALTH, WELFARE, OR AFFAIRS

Death is as much a reality as birth, growth, maturity, and old age—it is the one certainty of life. If the time comes when I, _____ , can no longer take part in decisions for my own future, let this statement stand as an expression of my wishes, while I am still of sound mind.

If the situation should arise in which there is no reasonable expectation of my recovery from physical or mental disability, I request that I be allowed to die and not be kept alive by artificial means or "heroic measures." I do not fear death itself as much as the indignities of deterioration, dependence, and hopeless pain. I therefore ask that medication be mercifully administered to me to alleviate suffering even though this may hasten the moment of death.

This request is made after careful consideration. I hope you who care for me will feel morally bound to follow its mandate. I recognize that this appears to place a heavy responsibility upon you, but it is with the intention of relieving you of such responsibility and of placing it upon myself in accordance with my strong convictions that this statement is made.

Signed _____

Date _____

Witness _____

Witness _____

Copies of this request have been given to

_____

_____

_____

_____

FIGURE 10.2   A living will.

sequentially. Huyck and Hoyer (1982, pp. 506–507) provide a succinct description of her model.

- *Stage 1: Denial.* Denial, shock, and disbelief are the first reactions to being informed of a serious, life-terminating illness. According to Kübler-Ross, few patients maintain this stance to the end.
- *Stage 2: Anger.* After denial, the patient often becomes nasty, demanding, difficult, and hostile. Asking and resolving the question "Why me?" can help the patient reduce resentment.
- *Stage 3: Bargaining.* In this stage the patient wants more time and asks for favors to postpone death. The bargaining may be carried out with the physician or, more frequently, with God. Kübler-Ross gives the example of a dying woman who asked to be relieved of her severe pain just for one day so that she could attend her son's wedding. The woman promised that if she could just see her son married, she would then be able to die in peace. She was taught self-hypnosis to control the pain and was permitted to leave the hospital for one day. She did not want to return. "Dr. Ross," she said, "don't forget, I have another son."
- *Stage 4: Depression.* Depression is a signal that the acceptance process has really begun. Kübler-Ross has referred to this stage as *preparatory grief—* the sadness is related to impending loss.
- *Stage 5: Acceptance.* Now the person has taken care of unfinished business. The patient has relinquished the unattainable and is now ready to die. He or she will want to be with close family members, usually a wife or husband and children; children want to be with their parents. The presence of someone warm, caring, and accepting is desired at this time, but verbal communication may be totally unnecessary.

Although doubts about the generality of Kübler-Ross's findings have been expressed (Shneidman, 1973), there is no question that she greatly improved our understanding of the process of dying and stimulated additional research by others that continues to add to our knowledge. In particular, her work has generated useful insights about how to deal with the dying person, an issue I turn to next.

DEALING WITH THE DYING PERSON

Having been raised in a death-avoidant culture, most of us tend to feel exceedingly awkward and uncomfortable when we interact with a person who is dying. This discomfort leads many of us to spend as little time as possible with the dying individual. Such an outcome is most unfortunate, as the dying person often *needs* support and affection more than ever. To alleviate some of this discomfort, Kübler-Ross (1969, 1974) and other researchers (Kastenbaum, 1977; Saunders, 1969) have offered some insights about how to better deal with the dying person. Some of these insights are summarized below.

1. The first issue that usually surfaces is whether the dying person should be told that he or she is dying. Most experts in this area today assert that honesty is the best policy. Many dying patients have a hunch about the reality of the situation anyway and like to get it out in the open. This gives patients time to tie up loose ends and to get ready for death.

2. Although they may know the reality of the situation at one level of consciousness, many patients initially respond to a terminal prognosis with denial. Kübler-Ross suggests that this is the first stage in an evolutionary process, but she cautions that you should not take her model too literally and feel compelled to usher the dying person on to subsequent stages. It is not your job to break down the defense of denial and destroy the person's hope. Let the dying person set his or her own pace in facing death.

3. If you are close to the dying person, it is very important that you try to spend a good deal of time with the individual, in spite of any discomfort you

might feel. When dying people are ignored, they understandably feel spurned and isolated. Their already precarious self-esteem will sink even lower. This is quite the opposite of what they need, which is to feel valued, loved, and significant. You can help by expressing your affection when you are with them.

4. People often wonder what they should talk about. Frequently you needn't worry about it much, because what many dying people need is a good *listener* to talk to. They need an opportunity to think things through out loud, to ventilate their feelings, to discuss their fears, and to express their regrets. Many will embark on a "life review" as they reminisce about the past. This is a natural step in working through the meaning of one's life and generally should be encouraged.

5. In these sessions, be prepared to encounter some anger and depression. These are common and natural reactions, according to Kübler-Ross. Realistically, your discussions may often be somewhat unpleasant. The dying person may direct some anger at you and may not offer to you the expressions of affection that *you need* at this time. You should not take this anger or apparent rejection personally. Dying people are obviously absorbed by their own concerns, and some will not show their normal sensitivity to others' feelings.

HOSPICE. *A program for dying patients that offers basic medical services aimed at alleviating pain and supporting home care, while working to fulfill the emotional needs of the patient and family. Hospices are sometimes associated with a traditional hospital but employ a nontraditional philosophy of care.*

6. The impersonal, institutional setting of the hospital is less than ideal as an environment in which to confront one's death. Many people say they would prefer to face death in the comfortable security of their own home. When possible, such wishes should generally be respected. To facilitate this end, many hospitals are developing **hospice** programs, which emphasize making the patient comfortable, rather than delaying death. These programs focus on the family as well as the patient through the provision of counseling. They work to facilitate home-based care for the terminally ill while minimizing pain and discomfort. The goal is to make the patient's final months as pleasant, comfortable, and meaningful as possible.

BEREAVEMENT, GRIEF, AND MOURNING

BEREAVEMENT. *The loss of a loved one through death; usually used with reference to close friends and relatives of the deceased.*

Bereavement refers to the loss of a loved one through death. Typically, the bereaved person experiences a mixture of strong emotions, including depression, anxiety, guilt, anger, despair, and apathy, which collectively constitute *grief*. Bereaved people often experience agitation, restlessness, difficulty in concentrating, and disturbed sleep. They yearn for the presence of the deceased and frequently think obsessively about the person. The emotional response to this extremely stressful event is often very, very strong. Accordingly, the bereaved quite frequently report many symptoms of physical distress that are associated with emotional arousal. Furthermore, in light of the stress/illness link that I have discussed repeatedly, it is not surprising that such persons are at high risk for serious illness. In fact, the grieving exhibit an elevated risk for death themselves during the first year after their bereavement (Clayton, 1971; Parkes, 1972).

Of course, the *intensity* of grief varies greatly from one person to another. The intensity of grieving is affected by a host of factors, including how close one was to the deceased, the age of the deceased, and the suddenness of the death (Stevens-Long, 1984). On the one hand, grief may be quite mild when an older person dies after a protracted illness. On the other hand, the unexpected loss of a young parent, child, or spouse can elicit massive and overwhelming grief that may leave the bereaved temporarily incapacitated.

MOURNING. *The actions and expressions of grief by one who has been bereaved.*

Mourning is a process involving the expression of one's grief in response to bereavement. This process often begins well before the actual death (assuming a preceding illness) and inevitably goes on long beyond the funeral. According to Kübler-Ross, the process of mourning unfolds sequentially, much like the process of dying. Parkes (1972) describes four phases in this evolutionary process. The first phase is dominated by *numbness*. Overt expressions of emotion are minimal because the person is paralyzed by shock. The second phase is a period of *yearning,* during which the individual is preoccupied with thoughts of the deceased. People think about "old times" and often think they see the face or hear the footsteps of the deceased. In the third stage, *dejection and despair* deepen as the reality of one's loss gradually sinks in. Life may seem meaningless as the depressed person often struggles with feelings of guilt and anger. Finally, in the fourth stage, *recovery* begins. People begin to reconstruct a new lifestyle for themselves. They fully accept the loss of their loved one and learn to live without either the real or fantasy presence of the deceased.

There are great individual differences among people in how rapidly they progress through the mourning process. This depends on a variety of factors, including all those that affect the intensity of the initial grief reaction, such as age of the deceased and suddenness of the death. As one might expect, the intensity of the initial grief (in the first few weeks) is a good predictor of how long the mourning process will last. Nonetheless, it is virtually impossible to offer any "norms" about how quickly one should progress through mourning. In one study of widows (Lopata, 1973), about half were in the recovery period after one year, while 20% indicated that they *never* expected to get over the loss of their husband.

DEALING WITH BEREAVEMENT

Dealing with bereavement is one of the toughest coping challenges that a person is likely to face. Unfortunately, there is nothing miraculous that you can do or say to lift the gloom that descends on the bereaved. However, experts (Clayton, 1971; Kübler-Ross, 1969, 1974; Parkes, 1972) do offer a few pieces of advice, which I will summarize briefly. They are outlined from the perspective of helping a bereaved friend (or relative) through the mourning process but are relevant to dealing with one's own bereavement as well.

- It is important to participate in the rituals surrounding death. Wakes, funerals, eulogies, sympathy letters, and the like serve important functions. Among other things, they underscore the reality of the death, permit socially sanctioned expressions of grief, affirm social bonds, and impose

---

RECOMMENDED READING

10.5 Widow

by Lyn Caine (William Morrow, 1974)

In this highly personal book, Lyn Caine writes about the death of her husband (from cancer, in his early fifties) and its aftermath. She writes in a compelling fashion about the deterioration of his health, her struggle with grief, resentment, and guilt, and her gradual metamorphosis. The author is not a psychologist, and the book is practical rather than technical. Caine does not provide any dazzling insights that can make one's confrontation with death easy. However, her very emotional story may have cathartic value for readers who have struggled with bereavement and can help anyone to achieve a better understanding of the experience of bereavement.

According to the little Webster's on my desk, condolence means "expression of sympathy with another in sorrow." But most of the condolence letters I received were anything but. Instead, they were expressions of personal awkwardness and discomfort, addressing themselves to the writer's distress, not to my sorrow or to our shared loss.

"I don't know what to say . . ."

"I'm bound to be lousy at offering polite condolences . . ."

"Several times I started to write expressing sympathy, but I can't find the words . . ."

"What I should say just won't come . . ."

"I feel even worse now . . ."

The brand-new widow, raw from loss, is in no mood to be told how awkward her loss makes others feel. Such a response from those around her is society's first step in convincing the widow that she is now a second-class citizen, because she makes other people uncomfortable.

None of my friends who sat down to write these duty letters wanted to make me feel bad. But I don't think they wanted to comfort me either. I am convinced that their main impetus was to discharge this distasteful duty, get it over with. No one is comfortable in the face of death [pp. 80–81].

some "closure" on the event. Hence, you should not shirk obligations of this sort, even though they may very well be unpleasant.

- The main thing that one can do for the bereaved is to provide social support. We have already discussed how social support can help people deal with stress in a variety of ways (see Chapter 3). Bereavement is an exceptionally stressful event, and social support can be especially helpful in dealing with it. In particular, it seems important to provide empathy for the bereaved.

- The bereaved should be encouraged to openly express their emotions. Open expression seems to move the mourning process along, while suppression seems to retard it. Unfortunately, in order to avoid awkward emotional moments, we often send signals to the bereaved that they should "bear up" and muffle their feelings.

- The bereaved should not be encouraged to bury their feelings of pain with drugs or alcohol. Kübler-Ross is ardently opposed to the common practice of sedating the bereaved. She feels that it is better for the bereaved to fully experience and express their grief.

- The bereaved should be discouraged from making quick decisions that commit them to dramatic new directions in life. They sometimes develop the illusory belief that sharp breaks with the past will bring their depression or confusion to an end. Thus, it may be prudent to suggest that they delay making *major* decisions about the future for a while.

IDEAS: REVIEW OF LEARNING OBJECTIVES

When you have mastered the material in this chapter, you should be able to do the following.

1. Describe the focus of stage theories and the assumptions underlying such theories.
2. Identify the basic problems with stage theories.
3. Explain how age roles and social clocks might affect behavior.
4. Discuss the significance of adult developmental trends in appearance, neurological functioning, and sensory acuity.
5. Discuss the significance of menopause in both sexes.
6. Describe adult developmental trends in health status.
7. Summarize evidence on adult developmental trends in intelligence and memory.
8. Summarize evidence on adult developmental trends in learning and problem solving.
9. Summarize evidence on adult developmental trends in personality.
10. Describe the innovations apparent in Erikson's theory of psychosocial development.
11. Briefly summarize the basic themes in stages 5 through 8 of Erikson's model of development.
12. Explain Havighurst's contributions to the understanding of adult development.
13. Describe Gould's sample and methodology and the basic idea that resulted from his study.
14. Describe Levinson's sample and methodology and the basic idea that resulted from his study.
15. Identify the key challenge during the early twenties, according to Levinson, and the nature of the Dream.
16. Identify the key conflict that occurs in the mid to late twenties, according to Levinson, and describe mentoring.
17. Describe Vaillant's research on the establishment of intimate relationships during the twenties and Levinson's research on the nature of the age-30 transition.
18. Summarize Levinson's view on the thirties decade.
19. Summarize key features of the midlife transition.
20. Summarize Levinson's and Gould's findings regarding the mid to late forties phase and the fifties decade.
21. Discuss the trends toward disengagement or activity during late adulthood.
22. Summarize Super's five-stage model of vocational development.
23. Discuss variations and qualifications relative to Super's model of vocational development.
24. List eight general principles regarding the vocational choice process.
25. List the personal characteristics that one should consider in making vocational decisions.
26. Discuss the value of occupational interest inventories as they relate to vocational choice.
27. List eight job or occupational characteristics that one should be concerned about in vocational decisions.
28. Explain how and why job satisfaction can be so important to one's adjustment.
29. List nine ingredients that tend to contribute to job satisfaction.
30. Describe our culture's attitude about death and how age and religion are related to individuals' attitudes about death.
31. Discuss the controversy over the "right to die."
32. Describe the five stages in the process of dying that were identified by Kübler-Ross.
33. Summarize advice offered on dealing with the dying person.
34. Describe the typical impact of bereavement.
35. Describe the four phases of the mourning process.
36. Summarize advice offered about dealing with bereavement.

TERMS: REVIEW OF NEW VOCABULARY

When you have mastered the material in this chapter, you should be able to define the following terms.

Age cohort	Death system	Hospice	Neuron
Ageism	Development	Intelligence	Senile dementia
Age role	Developmental psychology	Job satisfaction	Social clock
Aging	Developmental tasks	Living will	Stage
Androgyny	Euthanasia	Menopause	Underemployment
Bereavement	Gerontology	Mourning	Vocation

PEOPLE: REVIEW OF MAJOR THEORISTS AND RESEARCHERS

When you have mastered the material in this chapter, you should be able to summarize the principal contributions and/or ideas of the following people.

Erik Erikson	Robert Havighurst	Daniel Levinson	Donald Super
Roger Gould	Elisabeth Kübler-Ross		

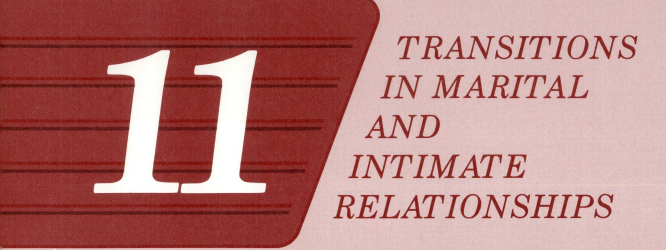

11

TRANSITIONS IN MARITAL AND INTIMATE RELATIONSHIPS

A proposal of marriage in our society tends to be a way in which a man sums up his social attributes and suggests to a woman that hers are not so much better as to preclude a merger or partnership in these matters.

ERVING GOFFMAN

In Box 11.1 I have reprinted another Bob Greene column. Because of the nature of his column, Mr. Greene is contacted by numerous people who have

---

11.1   HIS "MENOPAUSE" WAS A REAL CHANGE OF LIFE

SOME STORIES, you don't think there is another side.

BOB GREENE

Such a story was the one about Cindy, the 16-year-old girl whose father, a 50-year-old doctor, had abandoned his family to marry a much younger woman. Cindy wrote an open letter to the woman who had taken her father, and I printed it.

A lot of people responded by writing letters consoling Cindy, and asking me to forward the letters to her. That I expected.

What I didn't expect was the man who contacted me, being very hesitant about what he had to say.

Finally he said, "See, I'm in the same position as that girl's father. And for the first time, reading what she said, I began to feel guilty. And that made me mad. Because I've got nothing to feel guilty about."

I asked him to explain. He said that he was a man in his late 40s, from an affluent suburb, who had within the last year left his wife and three children to live with a woman in her 20s.

"I met her through my work," he said.

I stopped him to tell him that virtually every person who had responded to the column had voiced sympathy to Cindy and her family.

"I know, I know," he said. "I already told you, I felt sympathetic too. And that's wrong. Because the men have a side to be heard, too, and your article was unfair."

I told him to go ahead.

"Look, you get to be 46, 47 years old," he said. "You look at your life. You came out of school with a lot of dreams, and some of the dreams you got, some of them you didn't. Maybe most of them you didn't. You've got a wife you've known for so long it's hard to remember when you didn't know her. My own wife, I met in high school. You've got kids who are almost grown up themselves. The challenge is gone out of your work. If you're lucky, you've reached a position that's good. If you're not lucky, you haven't reached that position and you're never going to make it because the young kids are going to crawl right over you.

"You look at your life and it's all going to be downhill. There is nothing for you to look forward to, nothing really new. All you're expected to do is get up in the morning, go to your job, and spend the evening with the wife and kids. One night a week you bring home food from McDonald's. I've got a son who's 22, I've been taking him to McDonald's since he was a little one, and we're still eating food from McDonald's once a week.

"It's such a trap. And you feel everything slipping away from you. You know you're going to do everything you're expected to do until the morning you die. And then you meet a girl.

"The girl I now live with knew I was married when we first started going out. She let me know she knew it. Do you know how great that made me feel, that she was accepting me for myself? There were never any demands. She said she liked being with me. This was not a case of a woman stealing me away. She never said she would stop seeing me if I didn't leave home.

"Everyone talks about male menopause, and how it's the reason a guy does something like this. All right, let's accept it. Let's say I was in male menopause. I don't agree, but for the sake of argument let's say I was. Well . . . all I know is that she made me feel young again. That's not saying it strong enough. Listen, being with her was the difference between life and death. When I was at her place I was living, when I was at home I was dying.

"And it became a question of did I want to spend the rest of my life alive or dead? Did I do the right thing and wake up every morning of the rest of my life miserable, or did I do the thing that's supposed to be wrong and start my life over again?

"I agonized over it. I looked at my wife at night, and I looked at my children, and I wondered what kind of monster I was. But that was in my head. In my heart, I was aching to make myself happy. I had spent my entire adult life making a life for my wife and my children. Now I wanted to make a life for myself.

"The day that decided it, I was playing tennis with my new girl. I looked at her in her tennis dress, and she was so young and full of life. And without even wanting to, I thought what my wife would look like on the tennis court, and it repulsed me. Isn't that a terrible thing to admit? But that's how it happened, and from that day on I knew I was leaving.

"It cost me a lot of money. I expected that. And it cost me a lot of friends. Almost all of our old friends sided with my wife, which I can understand. Two of the kids won't speak to me, the other one will. That hurts a lot. Children you brought into the world.

"A lot of people pin guilt on me, but I've found out that guilt isn't such a terrible thing to live with. It's not like cancer. If I have some guilt, I have some guilt. I also have a whole new life. And if my reasons are selfish, so be it. If I can't be selfish in this life, then I can never be selfish.

"I'm happy. I'm the happiest I've been since I was a kid. I'm happier than I ever thought I had hope of being again."

I asked him if he thought that anyone who read his story would feel any sympathy toward him.

"I don't know," he said. "Probably not. But I can live without sympathy. I've got love."

moving, powerful stories to relate. In this case, it's a story about a marriage gone stale and the resulting departure by the husband. It is reprinted neither to endorse nor to condemn the man who has left his wife for a younger woman. Rather, it is here simply to drive home the enormous importance of intimate relationships in our lives. In referring to his decision to leave his wife, the man says "It became a question of did I want to spend the rest of my life alive or dead?" That rhetorical question illustrates just how much our emotional vitality depends on our intimate relationships.

In this chapter I will take a long look at marriage and other intimate relationships. I will review challenges to the traditional model of marriage and discuss why we marry and how we progress toward the selection of a mate. To shed light on marital adjustment, I will describe the life cycle of the family and then try to make you aware of key vulnerable spots in marital relations. I will also address issues related to divorce, cohabitation, remaining single, and being gay. Finally, in the application section, I will examine the "games" that intimate couples play in the context of their relationships.

Challenges to the Traditional Model of Marriage

The institution of marriage remains popular in spite of the fact that it seems to be under a savage assault from shifting social trends. This assault has prompted experts such as Morton Hunt (1977) to ask whether marriage might be in severe trouble as an institution. Although it appears that marriage will weather the storm, it seems worthwhile to review some of the changing patterns in intimate relationships that are currently presenting challenges to the traditional model of marriage.

1. *Increasing acceptability of singlehood.* The exceedingly negative stereotype of people who remain single, picturing them as lonely, frustrated, and unchosen, is gradually evaporating. An increasing proportion of the adult population under age 35 is remaining single (Stein, 1983). Although this trend may reflect longer postponement of marriage more than complete rejection of marriage, it appears that singlehood is becoming a more viable lifestyle.

2. *Increasing popularity of cohabitation.* Negative attitudes toward couples "living together" also appear to be declining in popularity. Although it is difficult to get accurate information on rates of cohabitation, census data suggest that the rate is skyrocketing (Glick & Spanier, 1980). One study of young men registered for the Selective Service (Clayton & Voss, 1977) found that 18% had participated in cohabitation for some period of time.

3. *Reduced premium on permanence.* The social stigma associated with divorce is also becoming less influential. This trend is probably both a cause and

KUDZU CARTOON REPRINTED BY PERMISSION: TRIBUNE MEDIA SERVICES, INC.

an effect of the dramatic increase in divorce rates. Furthermore, many social critics (for example, Bernard, 1973) are suggesting that expectations of permanence in marriage are simply unrealistic in our turbulent modern society.

4. *Changing sex roles.* The women's movement and economic pressures have led to substantial change in the role expectations of many men and women entering marriage today. The traditional breadwinner and homemaker roles for the husband and wife are being discarded by many couples. There is much greater diversity regarding current role models as well as much greater confusion about appropriate role expectations.

5. *Increasing extramarital sexual activity.* Media discussion of extramarital sex may have exaggerated its prevalence, but the frequency of extramarital coitus does appear to be on the upswing (Reiss, 1976). Thus, the once-sacred doctrine of sexual fidelity in marriage is being challenged by changing attitudes.

In summary, the institution of marriage is in a period of transition. While support for the traditional concept of monogamy remains strong, many social trends are modifying the way we think about marriage.

Moving toward Marriage

MARRIAGE. *A socially sanctioned union of sexually intimate adults. Traditionally, the arrangement includes economic interdependence, common residence, sexual exclusivity, and shared responsibility for children.*

Marriage involves the socially sanctioned union of sexually cohabiting adults. It is a pervasive social institution that, in one way or another, affects all of us. Although the institution of marriage is currently facing a number of challenges from the increasing rates of divorce, singlehood, and cohabitation, it remains extremely popular. In spite of all the new "alternatives" to marriage, experts project that over 90% of us will marry at least once in our lifetime (Skolnick, 1983).

THE MOTIVATION TO MARRY

There are a vast array of motivational factors that propel people into marriage. Foremost among these are the tremendous social pressure exerted on people to marry and the desire to participate in a socially sanctioned, mutually rewarding, intimate relationship. The multiplicity of motivational factors involved in the decision to marry is illustrated in Table 11.1, which summarizes research by Stein (1975, 1976). In his research, Stein interviewed single men and women aged 22 to 45 who were judged to be neither unattractive nor socially inept. As you can see in Table 11.1, there are many forces pushing and pulling us toward marriage or singlehood.

Although there are many good reasons for pursuing a marriage commitment, it should be noted that *people often marry for reasons that are less than ideal.* For example, a marriage motivated purely by physical attraction or the desire for a regular sexual outlet seems likely to be quite fragile. Similarly, marriages motivated by shame over being single, the belief that one "should" be married by a particular age, or the desire to escape an unsatisfactory home situation do not have a very solid base on which to build.

It is also worth noting that people vary greatly in the *strength* of their motivation to marry. Some people are desperately eager to marry, while others are reluctant to assume the responsibility or take the risk. Reiss (1976) has pointed out that marriage is a risky proposition. In deciding to get married, we must make a long-range projection about the future of the relationship. Obviously, it is difficult to predict 50 years of commitment on the basis of one or two years of premarital interaction. There is no way of making this projection with absolute assurance of accuracy. Instead, marriage requires a leap of faith. Variability in the threshold for this leap of faith is probably a major determinant of when and why people marry; yet we know very little about how this threshold is shaped or how it is related to personality.

TABLE 11.1 **The multiplicity of motivational forces involved in the decision to marry**

Peter Stein (1975) interviewed single people between 22 and 45 to ascertain the motivational factors that influence the decision to marry. *Pushes* toward marriage involve deficits felt by single persons; pushes toward singlehood involve deficits supposedly felt by married persons. *Pulls* are positive factors associated with marriage or singlehood. Reading across, the top boxes summarize motivational forces that typically propel people toward marriage. The bottom boxes summarize the factors that mediate in favor of remaining single. Although a particular person is not likely to weigh all the factors mentioned below, the list nicely illustrates the potential complexity of the decision to marry.

Pushes toward marriage	*Pulls toward marriage*
Economic security	Influence of parents
Influence from mass media	Desire for family
Pressure from parents	Example of peers
Need to leave home	Romanticization of marriage
Interpersonal and personal reasons	Love
Fear of independence	Physical attraction
Loneliness	Emotional attachment
Alternatives did not seem feasible	Security, social status, prestige
Cultural expectations, socialization	
Regular sex	
Guilt over singlehood	

Pushes toward singlehood	*Pulls toward singlehood*
Restrictions	Career opportunities
Suffocating one-to-one relationships, feeling trapped	Variety of experiences
Obstacles to self-development	Self-sufficiency
Boredom and unhappiness and anger	Sexual availability
Role playing and conformity to expectations	Exciting lifestyle
Poor communication with mate	Freedom to change and experiment
Sexual frustration	Mobility
Lack of friends, isolation, loneliness	Sustaining friendships
Limitations on mobility and available experience	Supportive groups
Influence of and participation in women's movement	Men's and women's groups
	Group living arrangements
	Specialized groups

SELECTING A MATE

Modern Western cultures are somewhat unusual in permitting free choice of one's marital partner. Most societies rely on parental arrangements and severely restrict the range of acceptable partners along religious and class lines (Stephens, 1963). Mate selection in American culture is a gradual process that begins with dating and moves on to sometimes lengthy periods of courtship. In this section, I will look at the impact of endogamy, homogamy, and personal ideals on marital choice, and I will review Murstein's S-V-R theory, which provides a good overview of the *process* of mate selection.

ENDOGAMY

ENDOGAMY. *Marriage within one's own social group, promoted by law, custom, or proximity.*

The term **endogamy** refers to the rather strong tendency of people to marry within their "social unit." Kephart (1977) reviews extensive evidence indicating that people tend to marry people of the same race, religion, ethnic background, and social class. This endogamy is promoted by cultural norms and by the way the proximity and similarity factors influence interpersonal attraction. Although endogamy appears to be declining in prevalence, it is clearly not a thing of the past, and it will remain influential for the foreseeable future.

HOMOGAMY

The term **homogamy** refers to the somewhat weaker tendency for people to marry others who have similar personal characteristics. Among other things, marital partners tend to be similar in age and education (Kando, 1978). In the 1970s, the median age difference shrank to 2.2 years. These age differences are not symmetric, as there is still a strong tendency for women *not* to get involved with younger men. As more and more people delay marriage until their thirties, this norm against dating younger men may begin to pose problems for women. Without the freedom to date younger men, they will find their pool of potential partners dwindling much more rapidly than males of similar age. In addition to age and education, there is evidence that married couples tend to be similar in level of physical attractiveness (Murstein, 1972) and in attitudes and values (Kerckhoff & Davis, 1962).

IDEALIZED IMAGES

If you are not married, you can probably describe in abundant detail the kind of person you would eventually like to marry. Most of us develop a pretty clear picture of the idealized man or woman we would like to have sweep us off our feet (Barnes & Buss, 1984). This idealized picture must necessarily influence our evaluation of potential mates. If a person does not compare very favorably with our ideal, this seems likely to undermine our attraction to that person. Some people may create problems for themselves by holding highly unrealistic ideals of perfection that will exclude virtually all potential partners.

STIMULUS-VALUE-ROLE THEORY

Bernard Murstein (1976) has developed a stimulus-value-role theory that provides an insightful overview of the ongoing process of marital selection. Murstein theorizes that we generally proceed through three stages, consecutively named the stimulus, value, and role stages, as we progress toward marriage.

During the first stage, our attraction to members of the other sex depends mainly on their *stimulus value*. At this point, *we focus on relatively superficial and easily identifiable characteristics of the other person.* Foremost among these are physical attractiveness, social status and prestige, and our initial perceptions of the individual's personality and competence. Murstein borrows from social exchange theory and argues that progress to the next stage depends on the pair's having relatively similar stimulus value so as to produce an "even" exchange. The two persons may derive their stimulus value from different characteristics—say, wealth and beauty. However, progress to stage 2 is thought to depend on their subjective perceptions of overall similarity in stimulus value.

If a pair of persons make it to the second stage, involving *value comparison*, the significance of stimulus variables may be reduced. *Further progress now depends on compatibility in values.* Typically, the pair will begin to explore each other's attitudes about religion, politics, sex, sex roles, leisure activities, and so forth. If fundamental incompatibilities are uncovered, the relationship will probably be stalled at stage 2 or may be terminated altogether. However, if the two persons discover similarity in values as they open up to each other, this will lead to additional self-disclosure and progress toward stage 3.

In the final *role stage*, people begin to think about marriage, and they therefore start evaluating whether the other person does a satisfactory job in the role of intimate companion. *Most people have definite expectations for this role, and they will begin to compare the potential partner's performance with these expectations.* At this point, people may focus on the distribution of power in their relationship, the reliability of emotional support, and the quality of their sexual liaison (if they have formed one). Although some people may marry after progressing through only the first *two* stages, Murstein maintains that marriage is generally delayed until couples are comfortable with role enactments in stage 3.

Making It Work: Issues in Marital Adjustment
MARITAL ADJUSTMENT ACROSS THE FAMILY LIFE CYCLE

FAMILY LIFE CYCLE. *An orderly sequence of stages that families progress through.*

The institutions of marriage and family are inevitably intertwined. With the advent of marriage, two persons add a new member to their already existing families and create an entirely new family. Typically, this new family forms the central core of one's existence as an adult. There are predictable patterns of development for families, just as there are for individuals. These patterns make up the **family life cycle,** a series of developmental stages that families tend to evolve through. In this section, I will describe the typical family life cycle in order to further enhance your understanding of the challenges and transitions that we encounter in adult life. This discussion will also allow me to address certain matters that relate to the issue of marital adjustment, a topic I will pursue in earnest in the following section.

SOCIOLOGY. *The scientific study of human society and its institutions.*

The family life cycle has been studied primarily by **sociologists** who have proposed a number of models (see Duvall, 1977) to describe family development. These models are basically pretty similar. For our purposes it will be sufficient to describe family development with the six-stage model outlined by Carter and McGoldrick (1980). Table 11.2 provides an overview of this model, spelling out the developmental tasks for the family during each stage of the life cycle. The table describes the patterns of progress for only one kind of family—a family with children that remains intact. Carter and McGoldrick have described variations on this basic pattern that are associated with remaining childless or going through a divorce. However, I will concentrate mainly on the basic modal pattern in this section and consider variations later. I should also mention that shifting social trends in marriage, divorce, and childbearing are producing some changes in the modal family life cycle (Norton, 1983). I will highlight some of these changes as we proceed through our description of the family life cycle.

A recent study (Anderson, Russell, & Schumm, 1983) suggests that the family life cycle is an important determinant of "marital quality." The researchers in this study defined marital quality as the spouses' overall *satisfaction* with their relationship. Examining this satisfaction across stages 2 through 6 in our model, they found a "U-shaped" relationship. In other words, satisfaction was greatest at the beginning and at the end of the family life cycle, with a noticeable decline in satisfaction occurring in the middle. Obviously, marital adjustment can be greatly affected by the nature of the challenges that couples have to confront at various points in the family life cycle.

BETWEEN FAMILIES: THE UNATTACHED YOUNG ADULT

I have already discussed the developmental tasks of young adulthood for *individuals* (in Chapter 10). In terms of the family life cycle, what is interesting about this stage is that it is being prolonged by more and more people. While the percentage of people who expect to forgo marriage altogether has increased only slightly, the percentage of young adults who are *postponing* marriage until their late twenties or midthirties has risen dramatically (Meyer, 1980). The frequent extension of this stage is probably due to a number of factors. Among the more prominent are the availability of new work and career options for women, disenchantment with the institution of marriage as people see divorces mushroom in number, and increased emphasis on the value of personal autonomy.

JOINING TOGETHER: THE NEWLY MARRIED COUPLE

In this phase, the newly married couple gradually settle into their new roles as husband and wife. This phase *can* be quite troublesome if the spouses come into the marriage with very different expectations about marital roles. This is probably happening more frequently than it used to, because of the current transitions that are taking place in regard to sex roles. *In general, however, this stage tends to be characterized by great happiness—the proverbial "marital bliss."* The study I mentioned earlier (Anderson et al., 1983), and various other studies (Campbell, 1975; Glenn & McLanahan, 1982) indicate that spouses' satisfaction with their relationship tends to be relatively high early in the marriage, before the arrival of the first child.

Traditionally, couples just *assumed* that they would proceed to have children—remaining childless by choice was virtually unthinkable. Indeed, this prechildren phase tended to be rather short, as most newly married couples

TABLE 11.2 **The stages of the family life cycle**

Family life cycle stage	*Emotional process of transition: Key principles*	*Second-order changes in family status required to proceed developmentally*
1. Between families: The unattached young adult	Accepting parent/offspring separation	a. Differentiation of self in relation to family of origin b. Development of intimate peer relationships c. Establishment of self in work
2. The joining of families through marriage: The newly married couple	Commitment to new system	a. Formation of marital system b. Realignment of relationships with extended families and friends to include spouse
3. The family with young children	Accepting new members into the system	a. Adjusting marital system to make space for child(ren) b. Taking on parenting roles c. Realignment of relationships with extended family to include parenting and grandparenting roles
4. The family with adolescents	Increasing flexibility of family boundaries to include children's independence	a. Shifting of parent/child relationships to permit adolescent to move in and out of system b. Refocus on midlife marital and career issues c. Beginning shift toward concerns for older generation
5. Launching children and moving on	Accepting a multitude of exits from and entries into the family system	a. Renegotiation of marital system as a dyad b. Development of adult to adult relationships between grown children and their parents c. Realignment of relationships to include in-laws and grandchildren d. Dealing with disabilities and death of parents (grandparents)
6. The family in later life	Accepting the shifting of generational roles	a. Maintaining own and/or couple functioning and interests in face of physiological decline; exploration of new familial and social role options b. Support for a more central role for middle generation c. Making room in the system for the wisdom and experience of the elderly; supporting the older generation without overfunctioning for them d. Dealing with loss of spouse, siblings, and other peers and preparation for own death. Life review and integration.

quickly went about the business of having their first child. However, in recent years more and more couples have found themselves struggling with a *conscious decision* on whether to have children. Voluntary childlessness has become a socially acceptable option, which is especially likely to receive serious consideration from couples when the wife has a successful and rewarding career (Lasswell & Lasswell, 1982).

Couples who choose to remain childless cite the great *costs* incurred in raising children. In addition to the substantial financial burden, they mention costs such as giving up educational or career opportunities, loss of time for leisure activities, reduced time for each other, loss of privacy and autonomy, and the increased stress associated with child rearing (Lamanna & Riedmann, 1981). In light of these considerable costs, it is not surprising that childless couples tend to report higher levels of marital satisfaction than couples with children (Polonko, Scanzoni, & Teachman, 1982).

Nonetheless, the vast majority of newly married individuals continue to plan on having children, although many expect to delay having their first child until their late twenties. In explaining their decision to have children, they cite many reasons, including the responsibility to procreate, the joy of watching youngsters mature, the sense of purpose that children create, and the satisfactions associated with emotional nurturance and the challenge of child rearing (Lamanna & Riedmann, 1981). In spite of the "costs" involved in raising children, most parents report no regret about their choice.

FAMILY WITH YOUNG CHILDREN

Although most parents are happy with their decision to have children, the fact remains that the arrival of the first child represents a *major* life transition for most couples. The transition is an abrupt one, and the disruption of old routines can sometimes create a full-fledged crisis (LeMasters, 1957). The inescapable fact is that raising children is a tough task. Doubts about how to handle the task are common. Disagreements about how to rear the children may create strain between parents. Additionally, child-related responsibilities often prevent one from pursuing old leisure activities, and new parents typically have far less time than before to devote to each other.

The key to making this transition less stressful may be to have *realistic expectations* about parental responsibilities. Kach and McGhee (1982) found that mothers with naive and inaccurate expectations about parenthood were the most likely to have difficulty in making the necessary adjustments. In other words, prospective parents need to realize that although children can be unparalleled sources of joy and satisfaction, they can also be a gigantic headache. It is also important to understand that children vary in how "easy" they are to raise, even when they are babies (Thomas & Chess, 1977).

Parenting is a very complex topic to which many entire books have been devoted. Suffice it to say that there are diverse "styles" of parenting that are differentially effective in yielding certain results (LeMasters, 1977). I don't have the space to even begin to delve into this topic in any detail beyond offering some *very* general advice: (1) parents should function as a "team," working out disagreements so that they do not end up working at cross-purposes, and (2) it is very important to maintain good communication with one's children.

FAMILY WITH ADOLESCENT CHILDREN

As children move into adolescence, parents are often making a major transition themselves—into middle age. This can mean turbulent times for both generations, and parent/child conflict during this stage is fairly typical (Davis, 1974). Emotionally charged clashes over values are not uncommon, and power struggles frequently ensue. Parental influence over the adolescent tends to decline. Many parents have great difficulty in adjusting to this reality. The adjustment would probably be easier if more parents would recognize that this is a normal (and often healthy) trend that should be expected.

LAUNCHING CHILDREN INTO THE ADULT WORLD

When a couple's children begin to reach their twenties, the family has to adapt to a multitude of exits and entries, as children leave and return, sometimes with spouses. It is a period during which the children have to progress from dependence to independence. That progression is sometimes complicated when parents have difficulty in "letting go." Young adults do need assistance and support during this stage, but some parents insist on continuing to take care of everything for their children. They have difficulty making the transition to relating on an adult-to-adult basis with their children. Frequently, this works out to be very counterproductive for the young adult who is discouraged from achieving necessary independence.

When parents get their children successfully launched into the adult world, they find themselves faced with an "empty nest." This was formerly thought to represent a difficult transition for many parents, especially mothers who were familiar only with the maternal role. Today, however, more women have experience with other roles outside the home, and most look forward to their "liberation" from child-rearing responsibilities (Rubin, 1979). In fact, as offspring gradually strike out on their own, couples' marital satisfaction tends to start climbing to higher levels once again (Campbell, 1975).

THE FAMILY IN LATER LIFE

The postparental period often provides couples with new freedom to devote attention to each other. Many couples take advantage of this opportunity and travel or develop new leisure interests. It can be a period of increased intimacy and great satisfaction for many people. Spouses do have to adapt to spending much more time with each other, but most seem to make the adjustment

The postparental years can be much more enjoyable than many people realize.

without major problems (Treas, 1983). Of course, age-related considerations that exist independent of the relationship, such as the increased likelihood of physical illness or financial problems, can make the later years stressful and troublesome. In general, however, the trend is for couples to report fairly high satisfaction until one of the spouses (usually the husband) dies.

AVOIDING THE QUICKSAND: POTENTIAL PROBLEM AREAS IN MARITAL ADJUSTMENT

An unavoidable reality of marriage is that the couple must confront a legion of problems together. During the courtship, the couple can usually focus mostly on pleasurable activities, but as a marital unit they must face many problems, such as arriving at acceptable role compromises, raising a family, and paying bills. *There is simply no such thing as a problem-free marriage.* Rather, successful marriages are built on the *conquest* of numerous problems that are virtually inevitable. In this section I will probe the major kinds of problems that are likely to emerge. Unfortunately, there are no simple solutions for these problems. However, in navigating your way through married life, it helps to know where the most perilous reefs are, and I can offer some general advice for confronting many potential difficulties.

UNREALISTIC EXPECTATIONS

Farson (1977) notes that many of us enter marriage with unrealistic expectations about how wonderful it's going to be. *With such high expectations, some disappointment is virtually a certainty.* Part of the problem is that the media romanticize love and marriage so much. Films and TV tend to focus on the excitement of falling in love, rather than the sacrifice of caring for a sick spouse. People who marry quickly are often "flying high" on the giddy euphoria of new-found love and have developed an idealized picture of their prospective mate. This idealized picture often turns out to be inaccurate when we see

---

11.2   PREDICTORS OF MARITAL SUCCESS

In view of the high premium placed on marital success, it is not surprising to find that a great deal of effort has been devoted to predicting marital success. This research has been plagued by one obvious problem: how do you measure such a complex phenomenon? Some studies have simply compared divorced and intact couples in regard to premarital characteristics. Other researchers have used elaborate scaling procedures to measure marital satisfaction. Even these instruments, however, appear to measure lack of conflict and complacency more than the quality of the marital coalition. Even though our measures of marital success are rather crude, some relations between predictor variables and success have been found. These relations are all statistically weak but nonetheless intriguing.

1. *Family backgound.* Marital adjustment of parents has been found to be correlated with marital satisfaction of their children. For a number of reasons, marital instability appears to run in families (Pope & Mueller, 1979).
2. *Age.* The age of the bride and groom is also related to the likelihood of success. Couples who

marry young have higher divorce rates (Bumpass & Sweet, 1972; Glick, 1957).
3. *Length of courtship.* Longer periods of courtship are associated with a greater probability of marital success (Locke, 1951). It is probably not the duration of courtship in itself that is critical here but, rather, the personal characteristics of the people who are cautious about making a marital commitment.
4. *Socioeconomic class.* The frequency of marital dissolution is higher in the working and lower classes than in the upper and middle classes (Hollingshead, 1968). There are probably many reasons, but the main one appears to be the greater economic stress in lower socioeconomic strata.
5. *Personality.* Generally, partners' personality characteristics are *not* predictive of success, with the exception of one very general characteristic, overall emotional health. The presence of serious psychological and emotional problems in one or both partners is associated with marital problems (Renne, 1973).

our new mate in a wider variety of less pleasant situations. Many a spouse has been toppled from a pedestal of perfection during the first year of marriage. This kind of frustrating letdown can best be avoided by trying to be realistic about a lover's qualities and by remembering that marriage has its downs as well as its ups. Such disappointment can also be reduced if lovers are open with each other during the courtship period and disclose their frailties instead of hiding them.

GAPS IN ROLE EXPECTATIONS

When a couple marry, they assume the roles of husband and wife. With each role go certain expectations that the partners hold about how the role occupant should behave. These expectations may vary greatly from one person to another. Gaps between the partners in their role expectations may cause serious problems. Tharp (1970) notes that agreement about marital roles is a major determinant of marital satisfaction. However, substantial differences in role expectations seem particularly likely in this era of transition in sex roles.

Who benefits from traditional roles?   Chapter 8 discussed the fact that many women maintain that the subservience inherent in the wife role is unfair to them. Empirical evidence on who benefits from marriage suggests that this assertion is accurate. It appears that men derive more benefit from marriage than women do. Married men report themselves to be happier than unmarried men and enjoy greater physical and mental health (Bradburn, 1969). In contrast, married women show *higher* rates of psychological disturbance than single women (Knupfer, Clark, & Room, 1966). Moreover, in comparing wives and husbands, Bernard (1973) notes that the wives report more marital frustration, more regret about their marriage, and more thought about divorce, and they rate themselves as less happy. Thus, it appears that the traditional model of marriage has provided more psychological gains for men than for women over the years.

The impact of transition in marital roles.   Marital role expectations are shaped significantly by our parents. Typically, our parents' relationship is the marital arrangement that we are most intimately acquainted with. The role expectations passed on by parents used to be fairly clear. Husbands were supposed to be the principal breadwinners, make the important decisions, and take care of certain household chores, such as car or yard maintenance. The wife was supposed to raise the children, cook, clean, and follow the leadership of her husband. In recent years, however, the advance of the women's movement and various other forces of social change have led to much revision of thinking about these roles. Traditional gender stereotypes have eroded, but only partly. The problem is that some people have changed their role conceptions and others have not. Osmond and Martin (1975) surveyed 480 undergraduates and found that, even in this relatively homogeneous and supposedly liberated sample, men were substantially more traditional than women about gender-role expectations.

Moreover, such expectations are dynamic and may often change over the course of a marriage. For instance, a woman might initially be quite happy with a traditional role but gradually come to find it unsatisfactory. Thus, even if spouses *enter* a marriage with similar role expectations, the potential exists for divergence in their beliefs. Any divergence between a couple regarding role expectations will set the stage for very significant conflict. Obviously, if a man expects his wife to have dinner ready every evening while she expects the two of them to divide cooking duties evenly, they are on a collision course.

In this era of transition regarding sex roles, it is imperative that couples discuss role expectations in depth before marriage. If substantial divergence exists, the potential for problems should be taken quite seriously. Many women tend to casually dismiss sex-role disagreements early in a relationship, thinking that the man will be reasonable and eventually change his overly traditional viewpoint. However, many women may be underestimating the strength of tradition in these time-honored views. These traditional models are often deeply ingrained and not easily changed.

Another related problem is that some men are "pseudo liberals" who are willing to accept some deviations from tradition—but only those that they like. For instance, many men are quite receptive about "letting" their wives work— as long as the wife can continue to raise the kids and do all the cooking and cleaning. Thus, many women get maneuvered into a double burden: they maintain a full-time career with all its work and stress, *and* they continue to be saddled with a grossly disproportionate share of the housework (Nickols & Metzen, 1982).

Although continued change in attitudes about marital roles appears inevitable, it would be foolish to argue that *everyone* should abandon the older customs. Many couples are quite happy with traditional arrangements. However, it does seem imperative that prospective partners be open about their expectations and that present partners be reasonably flexible in this era of change.

WORK AND CAREER ISSUES

In the traditional family, the principal focus for the male often lies outside the home, as he devotes his energy to being an effective breadwinner. One could speculate that job satisfaction and marital adjustment might be either positively *or* negatively related to each other. On the one hand, if a husband is highly involved in his career, he might have less time and energy to devote to his marriage and family. On the other hand, frustration associated with one's job might spill over to contaminate one's marriage.

The actual research evidence on this question suggests that the issue is indeed complex and that both scenarios described above are realistic possibilities. Evidence of a *positive* relationship between husbands' occupational success and marital adjustment was reported by Scanzoni (1970), who found higher marital satisfaction when a husband was moving upward in his career endeavors. Similarly, Ridley (1973) found a positive correlation between husbands' job satisfaction and marital adjustment. However, Ridley also found data suggestive of a *negative* relationship, reporting that husbands' high job *involvement* (amount of time devoted to the job beyond the routine workday) was related to *poor* marital adjustment.

Ridley's (1973) study, which focused on female teachers and their husbands, uncovered a similarly complex situation for women. For wives who considered their job a significant element in their lives, there was a positive correlation between job satisfaction and marital adjustment. However, for women who considered their job to be of secondary importance, job satisfaction and marital adjustment were unrelated.

There has been some speculation that wives' increasing entry into the work force might have some negative effects on marital adjustment. Thus far, however, the evidence suggests that this concern is largely unwarranted. Locksley (1980) found that both husbands' and wives' marital satisfaction was *not* related to wives' employment or their degree of interest in their job (see Box 11.3). Other studies find little evidence of any direct link between wives' employment and husbands' well-being (Fendrich, 1984).

MONEY

We learned in Chapter 1 that although money can't buy happiness, a significant *lack* of financial resources may undermine happiness. The situation is the same in regard to marital adjustment. Although having ample financial resources does not promote marital satisfaction, poverty can produce serious problems. Komarovsky (1977) writes movingly about the impact that poverty can have on a marriage. She notes how life can become "a constant struggle to meet the bills for rent, groceries, a pair of shoes, a winter coat and the TV set and the washing machine" (p. 336). Without money, families live in constant dread of financial drains such as illness, layoffs, or broken appliances. Husbands, viewing themselves as poor providers, see their self-esteem crumble. This problem is sometimes aggravated by disappointed wives who criticize their husbands. Spontaneity in communication may be impaired by an understandable reluctance to talk about the excessive stack of bills and the uncertain future. *Thus, it is clear that poverty produces significant stress for a*

11.3 WHEN WIVES WORK: DUAL OR DUELING CAREERS?

The proportion of married women employed outside the home has been mounting steadily since the 1950s. The percentage of working wives among those living with their husbands increased from 23.8% in 1950 to 43% in 1974 (Locksley, 1980) and is probably even higher today. As of 1980, a substantial majority (64%) of younger women (aged 25 to 34) were either working or seeking work (Hicks, Hansen, & Christie, 1983). In this era of inflation, it is becoming a virtual necessity that both marital partners work. This change in family functioning has stimulated concern on the part of both the participants themselves and social critics. Many people have wondered whether wives' employment might have a negative impact on their children or on the marital relationship itself.

Effects on the Children

Two thorough reviews of relevant research by Claire Etaugh suggest that maternal employment generally is *not* harmful to the children. The evidence indicates that the impact of maternal employment depends on the age and sex of the child, the mother's attitude, and various aspects of the employment (Etaugh, 1974). Nonetheless, it is clear that children *can* form a strong attachment to a working mother. Moreover, maternal employment was not found to be related to the adjustment of the children. Whether employed or not, mothers who are satisfied with their roles have the psychologically healthiest offspring. On the positive side, the daughters of working women tend to have higher-than-average career aspirations.

In another review, Etaugh (1980) scrutinized the impact on nonmaternal care (various kinds of day care) on preschool children. While acknowledging that the research evidence was characterized by certain shortcomings, she concluded that "high quality nonmaternal care does not appear to have adverse effects on the young child's maternal attachment, intellectual development, or socio-emotional behavior" (p. 309). In summary, then, it seems that it is the quality, not the quantity, of mother/child interaction that is crucial to successful child-rearing efforts.

Effects on the Marriage

Current evidence also suggests that wives' working is *not* related to the quality of the marital relationship itself. Locksley (1980) measured both husbands' and wives' estimates of their marital adjustment and their feelings of companionship. These variables were found to be unrelated to wives' employment or their degree of interest in their job. On the positive side of the ledger, Burke and Weir (1976) found that working wives reported *better* marital communication than nonworking wives, and Booth (1977) found that the additional income brought in by employed wives often helped to alleviate stress attributable to financial difficulties.

Although these results are reassuring, some theorists have argued that marital adjustment might be affected most negatively in those cases in which the wife has attained higher occupational prestige than her husband. However, even this seemingly plausible hypothesis has received only occasional support in research (Rubenstein, 1982). A recent review of research (Hiller & Philliber, 1982) suggests that higher occupational attainment by wives may damage marital adjustment primarily when spouses subscribe to traditional attitudes about sex roles. Relatively androgynous spouses seem to have less difficulty in adapting to this situation. Thus, it does not appear that wives' employment presents challenges for a married couple that cannot be overcome in most cases.

Effects on the Careers

The situation *can* get a bit complicated when both spouses have full-fledged *careers* that are centerpieces of their self-concepts. Careers (as opposed to jobs) generally require greater personal commitments as people try to seek long-range advancement. There is ample evidence that women may have to struggle with a residual sexist bias as they try to juggle career and family concerns. Lasswell and Lasswell (1982) summarize evidence that suggests that (1) both spouses tend to ascribe more importance to the husband's career, (2) high job involvement of wives causes more marital discord than high job involvement of husbands, and (3) wives compromise their career ambitions more than their husbands do. While all these trends are probably genuine, one study (Ferber & Huber, 1979) indicates that dual careers can have a negative impact on *both* partners' advancement. This study found that when both spouses held a doctorate, the academic productivity of both the husband and the wife suffered. Thus, there is reason to believe that the compromises required by dual careers may frequently undermine wives' career advancement and may sometimes retard husbands' career progress as well.

marital unit. Given this reality, it is important that prospective partners be realistic about their ability to finance a viable future.

Even when financial resources are plentiful, money can be a source of marital strain. Quarrels about how to spend money are common. They may become even more frequent as more working wives decide that they deserve more input into decisions about family finances. The best way to avoid troublesome battles over money is to engage in extensive planning of expenditures together.

INADEQUATE COMMUNICATION

Effective communication is crucial to the success of a marital coalition. The damaging role that poor communication can play was clearly demonstrated in a study by Beck and Jones (1973). They tabulated the frequency of various problems reported by couples who solicited help from 266 family counseling agencies in the United States. The results of the study are summarized in Figure 11.1. It should be readily apparent that *poor communication is the most common problem among these distressed couples,* with over 86% reporting communication difficulties.

Approaching the matter from a different angle, studies that compare communication patterns in happily as opposed to unhappily married couples (Navran, 1967; Yelsma, 1984) find that the happily married spouses (1) talk to each other more, (2) discuss a wider range of topics, (3) understand each other better, (4) discuss important decisions, personal problems, and disagreements more often, (5) less frequently express emotions by sulking or pouting, (6) know when to avoid certain subjects, and (7) display greater sensitivity to each other's nonverbal signals. Additionally, as mentioned in Chapter 7, high self-disclosure is associated with greater marital satisfaction (Hansen & Schuldt, 1984; Hendrick, 1981). Thus, it is apparent that good communication helps to promote successful marriages.

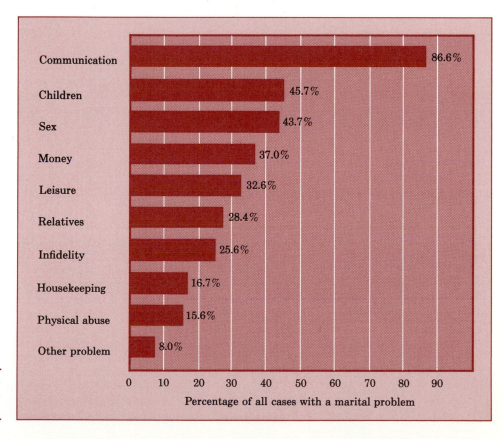

FIGURE 11.1 Problems reported by couples seeking family counseling.

As I have already discussed in Chapter 7, communication can be improved in many ways. Most of the advice offered in that chapter can be applied to marital communication. In particular, it is important to avoid defensiveness and to do the kinds of things that promote a positive climate for communication (see "Verbal Communication" in Chapter 7). Developing constructive approaches to conflict resolution is also critical.

PROBLEMS WITH IN-LAWS

According to Nass (1978), research on in-law conflict has diminished in recent years. This may indicate that in-law trouble is less of a problem in our more mobile society. The key points in Nass's summary of this research area include these: (1) the mother-in-law is more likely to generate conflict than the father-in-law, (2) men whose wives are better educated than themselves are especially prone to in-law strife, (3) overdependence on parents for advice or emotional support may stimulate discord in the marital union, and (4) in-law problems are aggravated if the parents are providing financial support for the younger couple.

SEXUAL PROBLEMS

There is a strong link between couples' marital satisfaction and their perception of the quality of their sexual relationship (Hunt, 1974). Although this link between marital and sexual satisfaction is quite strong, it is difficult to discern which is the cause and which is the effect. The assertion that sexual problems cause marital distress, though true, would be a gross oversimplification, since marital distress also causes sexual problems.

SEXUAL DYSFUNCTION.
An impairment in sexual functioning that causes distress for the person or couple.

Generally, marital sexual problems fall into one of two categories: (1) sexual dysfunction and (2) disagreement about the frequency or nature of sexual activity. **Sexual dysfunction** refers to inadequacies in the actual sexual functioning of the couple. Masters and Johnson (1970) believe that such problems are quite common. Negotiation of a mutually satisfactory compromise regarding the nature and frequency of sexual encounters is also a very common adjustment problem for married couples. I will discuss both these problems in Chapter 12.

The sexual problems described above are often intertwined with other marital problems. For instance, disagreement about the appropriate frequency of sex probably emerges primarily from differing role expectations. Poor communication between partners is often cited as playing a major role in sexual dissatisfaction.

JEALOUSY

JEALOUSY. *Applied to romantic relationships, a largely emotional reaction that occurs when one believes that there is a threat to one's intimate relationship. There is also social comparison jealousy, which involves envy of others' accomplishments.*

Romantic **jealousy** has been defined as a complex of thoughts, emotions, and behaviors that result from the perception of a threat to one's intimate relationship (Brehm, 1985). To put it in simpler terms, the "green-eyed monster" is aroused when you fear a loss of affection from a romantic partner. Although jealousy is a natural and sometimes legitimate reaction, there is evidence that the amount of jealousy in a marriage is *negatively* related to marital satisfaction (Bringle & Evenbeck, 1979).

Some people are more prone to get jealous than others. It appears that this jealousy-prone disposition is primarily a function of poor self-esteem. Highly jealous persons tend to have a negative self-concept, be relatively unhappy, and feel insecure, inadequate, and dependent in their intimate relationship (Bringle, 1981; White, 1981). Contrary to popular belief, it does not appear that women experience more jealousy than men (Adams, 1980). However, there is evidence (White, 1980a) that women intentionally induce and manipulate jealousy in their partner more often than men do.

Jealousy is usually triggered by some specific event. This usually involves either being left out of some activity involving your partner or anything that suggests, even remotely, that your partner's affection could be lost (Clanton &

Smith, 1977). In a recent study of over 50 jealousy-provoking circumstances (Salovey & Rodin, 1984), the situations that elicited the greatest romantic jealousy were these: (1) you find out your lover is having an affair, (2) someone goes out with the person you like, (3) someone seems to be getting closer to a person to whom you are attracted, (4) your boy- or girlfriend wants to see other people, and (5) your boy- or girlfriend visits the person he or she used to go out with.

Jealousy-prone persons often may be *imagining* a threat to their relationship where there is none. Such tendencies are likely to create unnecessary problems in the marital unit. Clanton and Smith (1977) point out that attempts to gain pervasive control over one's partner through jealousy tend to be resented. Correcting this problem is not easy, since it is usually rooted in a deep-seated negative self-concept. Efforts to correct the problem must focus on improving self-esteem and learning to think more rationally about one's relationship. People who are secure in a relationship are less likely to overreact when a spouse shows some interest in, or affection for, someone else. They are more likely to regard the event as normal and see the third person's interest in their spouse as an affirmation of their own good taste.

GROWING IN DIFFERENT DIRECTIONS

At several points in the book, I have mentioned the tendency for people to be drawn together by their similarity. However, unless the partners choose total stagnation, it is always possible that they will diverge in terms of their values and activity preferences. For instance, in the early years of a marriage, both members of a couple might enjoy a moderate amount of social entertaining with their friends. As the years wear on, one partner might find that activity tedious, while the other becomes even more highly motivated to pursue social encounters with other couples. Neither partner is wrong! This is a matter of personal taste, and they are simply evolving in different directions. However, this divergence can lead to bitter debate about how the couple should spend their time.

Although sometimes difficult, it is important that spouses allow each other room for personal growth. They should recognize that it is unrealistic to expect their partner to remain exactly the same forever. In this era, with recreational

---

11.4

RECOMMENDED READING
Finding Intimacy: The Art of Happiness in Living Together
by Herbert G. Zerof (Random House, 1978)

There are innumerable books that attempt to tell couples how to make it all work. Herbert Zerof's entry in this market appears to be superior to most of the others. Building on years of experience as a marriage counselor, Zerof offers practical and realistic suggestions for improving intimate relationships. A characteristic of the book that impressed me was Zerof's willingness to confront the *complexity* of achieving intimacy while keeping the book at a common-sense level. Sets of penetrating questions at the end of each chapter, which force the reader to probe into his or her own relationship, are also a nice feature.

In Chapter Three, Zerof outlines *ten reasons why romantic love confuses intimacy.* You'll have to read the book to get more details, but the ten reasons listed below should prove thought-provoking.

1. "Love" is unrealistic.
2. Love expects too much in return.
3. Love wants ownership.
4. Love wants unconditional acceptance.
5. Love expects you to be a mind reader.
6. Love fosters subservience.
7. Love expects you to take care of me.
8. Love refuses to change.
9. Love means I'm always right.
10. Love means you must pass all my tests [pp. 36–53].

As noted above, there are many books on how to promote marital success. In another outstanding one, *Becoming Partners: Marriage and Its Alternatives* (1972), Carl Rogers applies his unique humanistic perspective to the problem of achieving intimacy. You also might want to consult *Married, Etc.* (Suid et al., 1976), a sourcebook that reviews over 80 other books (some good, some bad) that are relevant in some way to making marriages work.

activities playing an increasingly large role in our lives, it seems essential that spouses tolerate individual activities, maybe even separate vacations. At the same time, it is important to strive to maintain some joint activities as well. Orthner (1975) found a strong link between a high level of joint leisure activity and positive marital satisfaction for both partners. Joint leisure activities appear to have great potential for encouraging open communication and role interchange.

WHEN THINGS GO SOUR: MARRIAGE COUNSELING

The previous section should make clear that *any* marriage may run into trouble. The way couples react to serious trouble has been changing in recent years. A decade or two ago, people were more likely than today to try to "tough it out." For the sake of the kids or social appearances, unhappy spouses would swallow their disappointments, repress their resentments, and continue to co-exist in a sometimes emotionally "empty" relationship. Currently, there is a new emphasis on achieving fulfillment in marriage. Hence, couples are much more likely to take active steps to pursue greater personal satisfaction.

When things go sour, one obvious option is divorce, discussed later in this chapter. Before choosing that option, however, more and more people are seeking professional **marriage counseling.** Therefore, a few comments on such counseling are in order.

MARRIAGE COUNSELING. *Professional help for people experiencing marital difficulties.*

1. It should be stressed that marriage counselors are not miracle workers; they have no simple solutions for complex and deep-seated problems. People sometimes report disappointment with their counseling experience because of unrealistic expectations.

2. The effectiveness of marriage counseling is very difficult to judge because it is hard to say what constitutes a success. The goal of such counseling is *not* simply to preserve the marriage; it may very well be that divorce is the most sensible course of action. That brings up one of the major contributions that marriage counseling can make to a couple. Decisions about divorce are exceedingly difficult to make. An objective third party (the counselor) can be very useful in aiding the couple to *rationally* evaluate the viability of their marriage.

3. Insofar as we know anything about the effectiveness of marital counseling, we do know that *joint participation* by the spouses is crucial to success (Cookerly, 1973). Little can be done if only one partner is involved in the counseling process. Another of the worthwhile things that a counselor can do is to help open up communication channels that have been dammed up by hostility. However, this obviously requires that both partners be involved.

4. The *quality* of marriage counseling varies tremendously. Relatively few states have adequate guidelines for licensing this kind of counseling, and McCary (1975) speculates that incompetent counselors may very well out-

number competent ones. Hence, in spite of possible embarrassment, it is important to "ask around" about marriage counselors instead of taking a random stab in the phone book.

Divorce

Any of the problems discussed in the previous section might lead a couple to consider divorce. People appear to vary greatly in their threshold for divorce, just as they do in their threshold for marriage. Some couples will tolerate a great deal of disappointment, distress, and bickering without seriously considering dissolution of their marriage. Other couples are ready to call their attorney as soon as it becomes apparent that their great expectations for marital bliss were somewhat unrealistic. Typically, however, divorce is the culmination of a gradual disintegration of the relationship brought about by an accumulation of many interrelated problems.

THE INCREASING RATE OF DIVORCE

Although relatively accurate statistics are available on divorce rates, it is still a rather complex problem to estimate the percentage of marriages ending in divorce. Scanzoni (1972) points out that the usually cited ratio of marriages in a year to divorces in the same year is highly misleading. It would be more instructive to follow people married in a particular year over a period of time, but little research of this nature has been done. In any case, it is clear that divorce rates have increased substantially in recent years. The incidence of divorce (per 100 population) *doubled* between 1965 and 1976 (Glick & Norton, 1978)! Although divorce rates appear to be leveling off, it is now estimated that *38% of first marriages and 45% of second marriages end in divorce* (Belkin & Goodman, 1980).

A wide variety of social trends have probably played a role in this phenomenon of increasing divorce. The stigma attached to divorce has gradually eroded. Religious organizations are becoming more tolerant of divorce, and marriage has thus lost some of its sacred quality. The declining fertility rate and the consequent smaller families probably make divorce a more viable possibility. Economic trends, such as increased mobility and the entry of more women into the work force, may put more stress on marriages while making wives more financially independent. New attitudes emphasizing individual self-fulfillment seem to have counteracted older attitudes that encouraged dissatisfied spouses to suffer in silence. Reflecting all these trends, *legal* barriers to divorce have also diminished.

DECIDING ON A DIVORCE

Divorce is usually a bone-jarring event for both spouses, which is often postponed repeatedly and is rarely executed without much forethought. It is difficult to generalize about the relative merit of divorce as opposed to remaining in an unsatisfactory marital situation. There is evidence that divorced women tend to be more depressed than married, single, or widowed women (Levinger, 1976). However, these divorced women may have been very depressed *before* the marital dissolution. McIntire and Nass (1974) compared couples whose marriages were stable and happy against couples whose marriages were stable but unhappy; they found people in the latter situation to be significantly lower on various measures of self-actualization. *These data suggest that sticking it out in an unhappy marriage is counterproductive to one's adjustment.* Renne (1971) made a more direct study of the relative consequences of divorce and concluded that marriage-related depression was somewhat likely to be lightened after a divorce and quite likely to be lightened by a successful second marriage. Thus, it appears that divorce is a realistic, though often painful, option, which has the potential for improving one's state of affairs.

Decisions about divorce must necessarily take into consideration the impact on any children involved. There has been much debate about whether it is to the children's benefit if the parents persevere and keep an unhappy marriage intact. There are some obvious reasons for arguing that marital strife may be psychologically damaging to the children. The research evidence indicates that this is a situation in which "you're damned if you do and damned if you don't." Comparing children from unbroken homes characterized by marital discord with children whose parents were divorced, Burchinal (1964) found little difference in the frequency of psychological problems. Unfortunately, children from *both* situations were prone to have difficulties in adjustment. In any case, the evidence does not support the notion that children are better off in a dissension-riddled but formally intact home (Slater & Haber, 1984). If anything, the preponderance of evidence suggests that when there is a great deal of conflict in the home, going ahead with the divorce is better for the children (Longfellow, 1979).

Although divorce may be better for the children in the long run, one should not underestimate the immense trauma that most children go through when their parents divorce. Evidence suggests that divorce may frequently be tougher on children than on the adults who are parting ways (Wallerstein & Kelly, 1980). The first year may be especially difficult. Common reactions among the children include anger, resentment, grief, anxiety, guilt over maybe having contributed to the breakup, and attention-seeking behavior such as whining, rebelling, and misbehaving (Hetherington, Cox, & Cox, 1978). The children's recovery and subsequent adjustment seem to depend primarily on the quality of their relationship with the custodial parent and on how well the custodial parent is adjusting to the divorce (Pett, 1982).

ADJUSTING TO DIVORCE

It is clear that divorce is an exceedingly stressful life event (Bloom, White, & Asher, 1979), often combining all four major sources of stress: frustration, conflict, pressure, and above all else, enormous change. The impact of a divorce is greatly affected by whether one is "leaving" or "being left." Generally, divorce tends to be more stressful and disruptive for women than for men (Campbell, 1975), although it can be devastating for either sex. Women are more likely to assume the responsibility of raising the children, while they are less likely to have a marketable skill with which to gain a reasonable income. According to Campbell, divorced women, as opposed to divorced men, report that they are under greater stress and feel more financially strapped. Obviously, newly divorced persons have numerous problems to confront. I will review some of these problems.

The crisis of change. One is hard-pressed to name events that produce more far-reaching change than divorce. Not only is one's lifestyle altered radically, but one's very sense of identity must be revised substantially. People tend to define themselves in terms of being somebody's spouse. Considerable psychological dislocation may occur when one has to suddenly revamp one's self-concept. The emotional crisis may peak long before the actual divorce, but the difficulties inherent in the postdivorce transitions in socializing, child rearing, and so forth may seem overwhelming.

Emotional problems. Weiss (1975) points out that a divorce may be preceded by much quarreling and reciprocal derogation by the partners. The disparaging remarks, although they may have been flung thoughtlessly in anger, are often difficult to dismiss. One or both of the former spouses may experience feelings of failure and shame, and self-confidence may sink to a dismal level. Divorced people may also be plagued by perplexing feelings of ambivalence toward their former partner. Feelings of continued attachment may be jumbled up with feelings of bitterness and anger. Separation distress often occurs, wherein one partner feels very lonely and longs for the presence of the former spouse. The difficulty that one experiences in accepting the termination of marriage tends to be relatively great when (1) the divorce was initiated by one's spouse, (2) the marriage was thought to be reasonably harmonious, and (3) parents and/or friends disapprove of the divorce (Thompson & Spanier, 1983).

Practical problems. The emotional difficulties are usually accompanied by a challenging variety of practical problems. If children are involved, arrangements for custody and support must be made. Both parents must adjust to a drastically different child-rearing situation. Patterns of socializing must be revamped. Old friendships with other couples are likely to decay. New friendships must be forged, and this is often made more challenging by the prejudice that still exists (though reduced) against divorced people in our society. In particular, divorced women have a problem in that they often are stereotyped as desperate for love and readily available for sex with a minimum of commitment.

Rebuilding. Although the difficulties inherent in divorce are substantial, they are *not* insurmountable. People do successfully retrench and rebuild. One should not feel reluctant to seek out professional therapeutic help or to solicit advice and support from relatives and friends. A need for some professional assistance should not be seen as an indication of personal inadequacy. In view of the enormous stress associated with most divorces, it seems eminently reasonable to pursue supportive therapy. During the rebuilding period there are four common syndromes that one should try to avoid (Cox, 1979):

RECOMMENDED READING

11.5 *Marital Separation*
by Robert S. Weiss (Basic Books, 1975)

As its title suggests, this book is intended for people struggling through the dissolution of their marriage or its aftermath. A sociologist who has pioneered seminars for the separated, Weiss writes in a warm and thoughtful manner about this event, which can be so incredibly traumatic. Weiss draws on both his clinical experience and his very thorough knowledge of relevant empirical data to put together a highly practical book. He illustrates his points in a particularly poignant manner by inserting quotes from separated people who have participated in his seminars. The book progresses in a very logical fashion, examining problems in the order in which they are likely to emerge as one's marriage dissolves.

Obsessive review is a constant, absorbing, sometimes maddening preoccupation that refuses to accept any conclusion. Often the preoccupation seems to have control of the individual's mind. His or her determination to think about other things is again and again frustrated as the preoccupation reenters with its own images and feelings. . . . Yet obsessive review can also fix on just those events that were most excruciatingly painful and refuse to relinquish them. One man replayed in his mind, as on an endless loop of film, the scene in which he had come home late one night to discover parked in front of his house a car belonging to his wife's boyfriend, and in the back seat of the car his wife and the boyfriend in an embrace. He could not accept the scene, nor could he forget it. It fit with nothing else; it made no sense; and yet it was more real for him than anything happening around him [pp. 79–80].

Another, more recent book on this topic is *The Divorce Book* by Matthew McKay, Peter D. Rogers, Joan Blades, and Richard Gosse (1984). Written by a pair of psychotherapists, an attorney, and an expert on single life, it is an extremely practical book. It deals not only with the emotional wounds of divorce but also with pragmatic considerations, such as legal issues, how to help children cope, how to share parental responsibilities, and how to return to dating. Like Weiss's book, this is highly recommended reading for those who are struggling with the dissolution of a marriage.

1. *Retreat.* Some people retreat into a shell of self-pity. It is important to gradually edge back into the interpersonal marketplace.
2. *Rebound.* Some people jump back into the interpersonal marketplace too quickly and too eagerly. Obsessive pursuit of a new love may blind one's judgment and lead to another poor relationship.
3. *Return.* Some people get paralyzed by foolish and unrealistic yearning for the return of the former spouse. It is better to face up to reality and get on with life.
4. *Resentment.* Some people get bogged down by excessive resentment of their former spouse. This anger and hostility can have a very negative effect on any children involved and may spill over and contaminate one's social relationships in general.

REMARRIAGE

Evidence that courtship opportunities for the divorced are adequate is provided by the statistics on remarriage. *Roughly three-quarters of divorced women and five-sixths of divorced men eventually remarry* (Glick, 1977). About half of these remarriages occur within three years of the divorce. Youth, financial stability, and a desire for the original divorce are all associated with relatively rapid remarriage (Hunt, 1966). How one assesses the success of remarriage depends on the standard of comparison. Divorce rates *are* higher for second than for first marriages. However, this may merely reflect the obvious fact that this group of people sees divorce as a reasonable alternative to an unsatisfactory marriage. In other words, it may be that their threshold for divorce is relatively low. *Nonetheless, studies of marital adjustment as well as research on divorce rates suggest that second marriages are somewhat less successful than first marriages* (Cherlin, 1981). Of course, if you consider that in this pool of people *all* the first marriages ran into serious trouble, then the second marriages look rather good by comparison. In fact, in one study (Albrecht, 1979) 88% of remarried individuals rated their second marriage as "much better" than their first.

It is more appropriate to evaluate remarriage by comparing divorced people who remarry against divorced people who do not. When Spanier and Furstenberg (1982) did this, they found that those who remarried were *not* any healthier or happier, on the average, than those who did not. However, they did find that the quality of one's second marriage *is* related to well-being, and many victims of divorce do eventually find happiness in a subsequent marriage.

Marriage-Related Innovations and Alternatives

I noted at the beginning of this chapter that the traditional model of marriage has been undermined by a variety of social trends. More and more people are choosing alternatives to marriage or innovative marital arrangements. I will discuss some of these in the present section.

COHABITATION

COHABITATION. *The sharing of a household by two unmarried, opposite-sex adults. Children may be present but usually are not.*

Although earlier rates of unmarried heterosexual **cohabitation** may have been underestimated, *it seems clear that recent years have witnessed a tremendous increase in the phenomenon of couples "living together."* In a sizable national sample of males, Clayton and Voss (1977) found that 18% of them had cohabited for six months or more at some point in their life, although only 5% of the men were involved in cohabitation at the time of the survey. Glick and Spanier (1980) estimated that slightly over 1 million couples were living together in the United States as of 1978. The phenomenon seems especially prevalent among college students. These students often report that their parents are not aware of their cohabitation and would not approve of it if they were (Bower & Christopherson, 1977).

The principal motivations for cohabitation among students in a study at Cornell University were security, companionship, and emotional satisfaction (Clatworthy, 1975). Even though the arrangement is not generally endorsed by our society, relatively few participants appear to experience substantial guilt (Macklin, 1974). Those who choose cohabitation tend to be relatively young, liberal (in values), nonreligious, high in self-esteem, and pragmatic (rather than romantic) about intimate relationships (Macklin, 1983; Newcomb, 1983).

Although many people see cohabitation as a threat to the institution of marriage, some theorists see it as a new stage in the courtship process—a sort of trial marriage. Consistent with the latter analysis, Bower and Christopherson (1977) found that 96% of their sample of cohabitants indicated that they would eventually like to marry. Thus, it appears that cohabitation does not represent a repudiation of marriage.

In discussing the advantages and disadvantages of cohabitation, Schulz and Rodgers (1980) point out that it may constitute an important opportunity for personal growth for many young people who can experiment with marital-like responsibilities. As a prelude to marriage, it eliminates the problem of entering marriage with unrealistic expectations and may permit some couples to "bail out" of relationships that might otherwise have led to unsuccessful marriages. While these are intriguing possibilities, the ten or so studies that have attempted to ascertain whether premarital cohabitation might improve the likelihood of subsequent marital success have consistently *failed* to find any such effect (Macklin, 1983). In fact, one recent study found premarital cohabitation linked to lower marital satisfaction (DeMaris & Leslie, 1984). Thus, although the vast majority of cohabitants speak very favorably of personal growth associated with the experience, there is presently no reason to believe that cohabitation improves couples' probability of marital success.

OPEN MARRIAGE

The term *open marriage* was coined by O'Neill and O'Neill (1972), who proposed it as an alternative to traditional marital arrangements, which they regarded as "closed." According to the O'Neills, traditional marriages emphasize the "possession" of one partner by the other, and a dominant sense of "we-ness" necessarily supplants individual identities. This approach is thought to lead to self-denial, submergence of one's individual needs, rigid role playing, and exclusive reliance on the spouse for sexual gratification and companionship. The O'Neills argue that this restrictive element in marriage is counterproductive because it limits spouses' personal growth and prevents them from gaining much-needed emotional support from outside the marital unit.

OPEN MARRIAGE. *A marital arrangement in which the partners are encouraged to develop individual social relationships and pursue relatively independent lifestyles.*

In contrast, **open marriage** emphasizes the following: *(1) flexibility in role expectations, especially traditional gender-based roles, (2) endorsement of intimate relationships with persons other than one's spouse, and (3) affirmation of the legitimacy of individual needs and desires in the marital union.* The O'Neills' analysis is provocative and has had some impact on attitudes toward marriage in our society. It is unfortunate that the term *open marriage* has been mistakenly stereotyped as synonymous with sexual promiscuity and an absence of legal matrimonial bonds. Although the O'Neills did suggest that sexual fidelity and legal obligations should be *optional* elements in a marriage, these highly publicized features of open marriage were not really at the core of the concept.

REMAINING SINGLE

The pressure to marry in our society is tremendous. We are socialized to believe that we are not "complete" until we have found our "other half" and

The "swinging single" experience may be, after all, a media-manufactured illusion.

entered into a partnership for life. We refer to people's *failure* to marry. In spite of this pressure, an increasing proportion of adults are remaining single (Stein, 1983).

Singlehood has been plagued by two very disparate stereotypes of the single life (Cargan & Melko, 1982). On the one hand, singles are portrayed as unattractive, socially inept, unlucky, frustrated, lonely, and bitter. They are seen as losers who did not succeed in snaring a mate. On the other hand, they are sometimes portrayed as suave, carefree swingers who are too busy enjoying the fruits of sexual promiscuity to be concerned about shouldering marital responsibilities. These stereotypes may describe a minority of single people, but they do a great injustice to the diversity that exists among those who are single.

Let us first dispose of the stereotypes and then discuss the dynamics of single life. Although it is usually true that unattractiveness and poor social skill limit one's appeal in the heterosexual marketplace, there are probably very few people for whom the situation is irrevocably hopeless. At the risk of sounding patronizing and cynical, I must argue that, regardless of how unattractive or socially inept a person might be, there is probably someone of the other sex who would be a reasonable match. Even though many singles have been indoctrinated by society to define themselves as failures and losers, it appears that most single people—in a broad sense, at least—have *chosen* to remain single. As attitudes shift in our society, more and more people are actively choosing to remain single to enhance their careers to avoid the stultifying marriages that they observe among their friends, or simply to maximize personal freedom and independence.

The "swinging single" stereotype also turns out to be highly misleading. The media-created image of the single person jauntily meandering through urban bars and nightclubs, meeting new friends, enjoying good times, and indulging in casual sex does not match the reality experienced by most people. Instead, Starr and Carns (1973) found that most women burned out on the singles-bar routine within six months, men persisting only somewhat longer. In interviewing single people, Gordon (1976) found that the singles-bar circuit was described as an experience in alienation and disappointment. Thus, the "swinging single" experience appears to be largely a media-manufactured illusion designed to lure singles' spending power into adult playgrounds that generally turn out to be barren of productive social encounters.

It does not appear that single people are plagued with a unique set of problems; they must cope with the same difficulties that confront most adults (Starr & Carns, 1973). However, there obviously are some special challenges. Since adult social interaction tends to revolve around couples, there may be some extra difficulty in developing a satisfactory friendship network. The absence of a spouse to lean on makes an independent personality a virtual necessity. Single men trying to climb the corporate ladder have some bias working against them, as they are seen as less stable than married men.

Generally, single people do rate themselves as less happy than married people (Campbell, 1975). Although society tends to be more tolerant of the single role for men than for women, it appears that women get along without men better than men get along without women. Single women report being more satisfied with their lives than single men do (Campbell, 1975). Additionally, you may recall previously discussed data indicating that single men are *less* psychologically healthy than married men while single women are *more* psychologically healthy than married women. However, physical illness, mental illness, and suicide are all more frequent among singles of either sex than among married people (Gove & Tudor, 1973; Verbrugge, 1979). Of course, it is difficult to separate cause and effect in this relationship. It seems more plausible that illness causes singlehood (by reducing one's appeal) rather than vice versa.

A NOTE ON GAY RELATIONSHIPS

HETEROSEXUAL.
Pertaining to sexual desire for, and erotic activity with, members of the opposite sex.

GAY. *A nonderogatory term that refers to homosexual men or women.*

HOMOSEXUAL. *Pertaining to sexual desire for, and erotic activity with, members of one's own sex.*

Up until this point, I have, for purposes of simplicity, focused my attention on **heterosexual** relationships. It is time now to acknowledge that I have been ignoring a significant minority group: **gay** men and women. It is difficult to estimate just how large this minority group is, because negative attitudes in our society about **homosexuality** continue to prevent many gays from "coming out of the closet." The best empirical data on the issue (which aren't very good) suggest that roughly 2% of women and 4–5% of men are *exclusively* homosexual (Gebhard, 1972; Hunt, 1974). More speculative estimates by some gay-rights activists range as high as 10% for both sexes. Although these estimates are highly speculative, they may not be unreasonable if one's definition of homosexuality does not require an exclusive and total commitment to same-sex relationships (Paul & Weinrich, 1982). Thus, there may be as many as 25 million gay people in the United States.

The fact that I have parceled off a separate section on gay relationships implies that their dynamics are somehow different from those seen in heterosexual relationships. Actually, this is probably less true than most heterosexuals might assume. In discussing gay couplings, Karla Jay (1977) argues that "we suffer from many of the same problems that beset heterosexual couples" (p. 253). Nonetheless, it is clear that intimate relationships among gays must necessarily be somewhat different, if only because marriage is not socially sanctioned for gays. In spite of the disparities that exist, little special advice based on empirical study is available for gays. Jay (1977) notes that "we have very little written directly for us. Often we are forced to read about how some heterosexuals have dealt with their problems, and then have to transfer their solutions onto our own relationship" (p. 254). Although this approach is less than ideal, I prefer to stress the similarities between gay and straight relationships and would therefore suggest that much of the material already presented in this chapter may be relevant to gay couples.

In the absence of special advice for gays, I will endeavor instead to review some of the research about the nature of gay relationships. At this point, I will focus on myths and realities regarding intimate relationships between gays.

There are a number of common beliefs about gay relationships that are not altogether accurate. First, many people assume that most gay couples adopt traditional masculine and feminine roles in their relationships, one partner behaving in a cross-sexed manner. This appears to be true in only a small minority of cases, and in fact, gay couples appear to be more flexible about role expectations than heterosexuals, as a whole (Harry, 1983).

Second, it is popularly believed that gays are exceptionally promiscuous, engaging in casual sex with a spectacular number of partners. To some extent, this is true for males but not for females. Lesbian women generally do not report having had an unusually high number of sexual partners and are far less likely than men to go "cruising" in public, seeking a sexual encounter (Bell & Weinberg, 1978). In a study of gay couples, Peplau (1981) found that 87% of the lesbian women reported that they had had sexual relations only with their intimate companion during the past six months. However, in the same study, fewer than half of the gay males reported a similar sexual exclusivity with their partner during the preceding six months. Moreover, in Bell and Weinberg's (1978) study, many males *did* report high rates of sexual activity. Among Caucasians, almost half claimed having had over *500* sexual partners, while another third of the men estimated that they had had between 100 and 500. Bell and Weinberg caution that these estimates may be exaggerated, and they emphasize that encounters with numerous partners are not universal among gay males. More significantly, Harry (1983) points out that sampling problems in such studies may lead to a substantial overestimate of sexual activity among gay men. In most studies of gay males, the samples are disproportionately young, as they are usually procured through gay organizations that tend to have youthful memberships. Since it is known that age is strongly related to sexual activity rates among gay men, this difficult-to-avoid sampling bias may exaggerate the level of promiscuity among male homosexuals.

Third, popular stereotypes suggest that gays only rarely get involved in long-term intimate relationships. In reality, Bell and Weinberg (1978) found that virtually all members of both sexes had been involved in at least one stable and lengthy affair. At the time of the survey, about one-half of the men and three-quarters of the women were committed to a stable relationship. While intimate relationships among gays are clearly less stable than marriages among straights, they may compare favorably with heterosexual cohabitation, which would be a more appropriate baseline for comparison. Bell and Weinberg attribute the relative instability of homosexual couplings primarily to the lack of legal sanctions.

Finally, an inevitable fate for any stereotyped group is that its members are all lumped together and simplistically assumed to be identical. In reality, there is much diversity among gays in regard to intimate relationships. Bell and Weinberg (1978) were able to differentiate five gay lifestyles, which were summarized by Victor (1980, p. 344) as follows:

1. *Close-coupled homosexuals* resemble happily married heterosexuals. They maintain a close relationship with another person and seek their sexual and emotional satisfaction primarily in that relationship. They have the fewest sexual problems and are the least likely to seek outside sexual partners. Although they do not have the highest level of sexual activity, they are the most likely to report being satisfied with their sex lives. They are also very unlikely to regret being homosexual.

2. *Open-coupled homosexuals* also live with a special sexual partner. However, they are less monogamous and more likely to seek sexual partners outside their relationship. Many of them seek sexual encounters without the knowledge of their special partner. They do more "cruising" (partner seeking in public places) and are more sexually active than the average respondent. In the study, this lifestyle was the one most common among men, while it was relatively rare among women. The women were more likely to be "close-coupled."

3. *Functional homosexuals* resemble swinging singles in their lifestyle. They are not particularly interested in finding a special partner with whom to establish an exclusive relationship. They are more interested in sexual pleasure and have more frequent sexual activity and more numerous partners than any other group of homosexuals. Functional homosexuals spend a great deal of time with many friends, cruise bars frequently for sexual partners, and are active participants in the gay subculture. They are the most likely homosexuals to ever have been arrested for an offense related to their homosexual behavior. Yet, functional homosexuals are less likely to regret being homosexual than any other group.

4. *Dysfunctional homosexuals* suffer from more regret about their homosexuality than any other group. They also report having more problems in sexual functioning (difficulties such as attaining erection or orgasm) than any other group. They tend to consider themselves sexually unattractive, report more difficulties in finding agreeable sexual partners, and worry more about being able to maintain affection for a partner. Nevertheless, the males report frequently cruising for sexual encounters. Many aspects of their lives, in addition to the sexual aspect, are beset with frustration.

5. *Asexual homosexuals* are withdrawn and socially isolated individuals. They score lowest on sexual interest and activity and rate their sexual attractiveness as very low. They tend to spend their leisure time alone and have infrequent contact with friends. They do less cruising than any other group except close-coupled homosexuals. Asexual homosexuals are not very interested in establishing a relationship with a special partner. Finally, asexual homosexuals rate themselves as being less exclusively homosexual and more bisexual than the other groups.

Summary

The traditional model of marriage is being challenged by the increasing acceptability of singlehood, the increasing popularity of cohabitation, the reduced premium on permanence, changing sex roles, and increasing extramarital sexual activity. Nonetheless, marriage remains quite popular.

People vary in the strength of their motivation to marry, and many are motivated by less-than-ideal reasons. Mate selection is influenced by endogamy, homogamy, and one's ideals. According to Murstein, the process of mate selection goes through three stages, which emphasize the stimulus value of the potential partner, value compatibility, and adequacy of role enactments.

Marital satisfaction and adjustment appear to be influenced by the family life cycle. Newly married couples tend to be very happy before the arrival of children. Today an increasing number of couples are choosing to remain childless, and more and more spouses are struggling with the decision whether to have children. The arrival of children is a major transition that is handled best by parents who have realistic expectations about the difficulties inherent in the task of raising children. Parenting is a complex art, which is facilitated when spouses work together. As children reach adolescence, parents should expect more conflict as their influence declines. They must learn to relate to their children as adults and help to launch them into the adult world. Once the children have struck out on their own, marital satisfaction tends to rise once again.

Traditional marriage roles appear to be advantageous to husbands. Gaps in expectations about roles, or unrealistic expectations in general, may create marital stress. Occupational dissatisfaction and a lack of money may also produce marital problems. Inadequate communication is the most commonly reported marital problem, while in-law problems appear to be declining. Sexual dysfunction, jealousy, and growing in different directions are other problems that are common in marital relationships.

Marriage counseling can open up communication channels and aid couples in evaluating the viability of their marriages. However, it varies in quality, cannot work miracles, and depends on the joint participation of the spouses. Divorce is becoming increasingly common for a variety of reasons. Unpleasant as divorce may be, the evidence suggests that toughing it out in an unhappy marriage is often worse. Divorce can create problems for children, but so does a strife-ridden intact home. Divorce is quite stressful and may lead to a variety of emotional and practical problems associated with the crisis of change. In rebuilding, people should try to avoid four syndromes: retreat, rebound, return, and resentment. A substantial majority of divorced people remarry. These second marriages have a somewhat lower probability of success than first marriages.

The prevalence of cohabitation has increased dramatically; nonetheless, it appears to be more of a prelude than an alternative to marriage. The O'Neills' concept of open marriage, emphasizing individual needs and relationships, has influenced current attitudes about marriage. Single people are often stereotyped as losers or carefree swingers. Both pictures are largely inaccurate. Although singles generally have the same adjustment problems as married couples, evidence suggests that singles tend to be slightly less happy and healthy. Gay relationships are characterized by great diversity. It is not true that gays usually assume traditional masculine and feminine roles or that they rarely get involved in long-term intimate relationships. Popular beliefs about gay promiscuity appear to be inaccurate for women, though less so for men. Bell and Weinberg have described five types of gay lifestyles.

The upcoming application section will focus on the manipulative games that couples tend to play. It is hoped that your awareness of these game-playing tendencies might reduce your propensity to get locked into such counterproductive patterns.

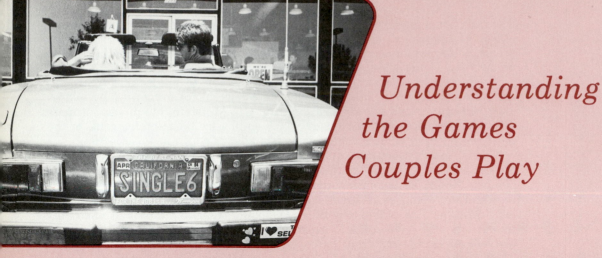

Understanding the Games Couples Play

Answer the following yes or no.

_____ 1. In intimate relationships, I sometimes catch myself being manipulative.

_____ 2. In interacting with my partner, I sometimes notice that we get into subtle little battles to demonstrate our superiority.

_____ 3. It often seems that people are operating with a "hidden agenda."

_____ 4. Many people seem to derive some sort of perverse satisfaction from laying "guilt trips" on others.

_____ 5. I sometimes think that life would be simpler if couples would tell each other what they were *really* thinking.

If you answered yes to several of the items above, you have noticed that people often tend to play "games" with each other. If you answered no to all the items, either you haven't *noticed* the games that we play, or you're hanging around with people from another planet. We all play games at least occasionally. This reality has been most insightfully analyzed by Eric Berne (1961, 1964, 1972), who developed an approach to understanding personality and interpersonal relations called **transactional analysis.**

Basically, games are manipulative interactions in which participants conceal their true motivations (I will provide a more formal definition after introducing you to the essentials of transactional analysis). Games are not limited to intimate relationships; we may play games with coworkers, neighbors, and even strangers. However, games become particularly problematic in intimate relationships, where authentic communication is especially important. Intimate couplings are also exceptionally vulnerable to games because there is much more opportunity, in terms of sheer time spent interacting, for *repetition* of destructive patterns of duplicity. Games are far from ideal in an intimate coupling. Over the long run, they are antagonistic to the growth of the relationship. Therefore, this application section will introduce you to the basics of transactional analysis, so that you can try to spot some of this game playing in your own intimate interactions.

EGO STATES IN TRANSACTIONAL ANALYSIS

EGO STATE. *In transactional analysis, an internal personality structure consisting of a coherent system of feelings. There are three such ego states, known as the Child, the Parent, and the Adult.*

Berne postulated the existence of three **ego states:** the Child, the Parent, and the Adult (when these terms are capitalized, they refer to the ego state; otherwise they refer to the actual status of child, parent, or adult). According to Berne, an ego state is a coherent system of internal feelings that manifests itself in a related set of coherent behavioral patterns. The theory states that we directly experience these ego states and that we shift in and out of them depending on the situation and our personal history. It is important to understand that there is no one-to-one correspondence between these ego states and a person's actual status. In other words, one does not have to be a child to experience the Child ego state or a parent to experience the Parent ego state.

THE CHILD

The Child ego state consists of a set of "recordings" of childhood experiences that we retain throughout adulthood. In certain situations we fall back into our old childlike patterns of spontaneity and irresponsibility. For instance, when faced with frustration, a person who used to throw temper tantrums in childhood might revert to this strategy as an adult. In so doing, the person is operating from the Child ego state. Although this particular example is somewhat negative, operating from the Child ego state is not inherently bad, and it should not be equated with behaving immaturely. On the positive side, it is entry into the Child ego state that facilitates fresh and spontaneous enjoyment of recreational activities.

THE PARENT

The Parent ego state also consists of residual recordings from childhood. However, these recordings largely involve assertions about right and wrong. They represent the values and mores adopted from one's parents and other authority figures. For example, suppose that you suddenly realized that you were reading this text too lackadaisically, without really digesting the information. If you proceeded to scold yourself for this lethargic attitude, you would be operating from the Parent ego state. The Parent in us jumps in with criticism when we transgress against the morals instilled by our parents. The Parent is like a solemn judge, handing down decisions about the acceptability of our behavior as well as the behavior of others.

THE ADULT

The Adult is rational and less emotional than the Child and Parent. We shift into the Adult ego state when we work diligently, when we dispassionately weigh alternative courses of action, when we systematically endeavor to solve a problem, and so forth. The Adult attempts to tune in to reality and to maximize efficiency. Like the ego as described by Freud, the Adult has "executive" responsibilities for making many important decisions, which often involve mediating between the Child and the Parent.

TYPES OF TRANSACTIONS

TRANSACTION. *The fundamental unit of social interaction in transactional analysis.*

COMPLEMENTARY TRANSACTION. *In transactional analysis, a situation wherein two persons communicate from compatible ego states. Specifically, the receiver responds from the ego state addressed by the source.*

A **transaction** is simply a unit of social interaction, consisting of an initial statement by a communicating source and a response by the receiver. There are several classes of transactions, depending on which ego states are communicating with each other.

In a **complementary transaction** the receiver responds from the same ego state that was addressed by the source. Two kinds of complementary transactions are possible. In Type I, the two persons are sending and receiving from the same ego state (see Figure 11.2). In other words, they communicate Adult-to-Adult, Child-to-Child, or Parent-to-Parent. In Type II, the two persons do *not* address each other as equals (see Figure 11.3). For example, the transaction might go Parent-to Child and Child-to-Parent or Child-to-Adult and Adult-to-Child. In either kind of complementary transaction people are cooperating in the communication effort.

In a **crossed transaction** the receiver does *not* cooperate and refuses to respond from the ego state addressed by the source. For example, an Adult-to-Adult transmission might be answered with a Parent-to-Child response. There are a variety of possible combinations for crossed transactions, as you can see from the four examples in Figure 11.4. Crossed transactions tend to undermine effective communication and may create tension between the persons involved.

Of greatest interest to us are **ulterior transactions,** which include hidden messages and provide the basis for most games. These transactions are characterized by duplicity and pretense. In ulterior transactions *two* messages are sent and received. At a superficial, social level there is the readily apparent,

CROSSED TRANSACTION. *In transactional analysis, a situation wherein two persons communicate from incompatible ego states. Specifically, the receiver does not respond from the ego state addressed by the source.*

ULTERIOR TRANSACTION. *In transactional analysis, a special kind of complementary transaction that includes hidden, or latent, messages intended to serve ulterior motives.*

Conversations

Students do not seem to work hard. They are quite lazy in many respects.

It's simply the way things are today. No one does more than he has to.

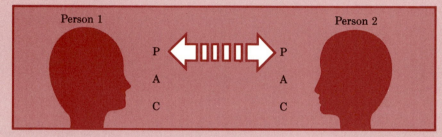

You should never go to that store again after what they did.

You are so right. They will probably always treat me that way.

Parent-Parent

What floor is the furniture on?

It's on the fifth floor.

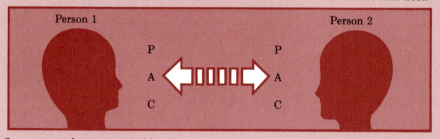

Sue seems to be preoccupied lately.

Let's go and talk to her.

Adult-Adult

My house is bigger than yours.

But mine has more windows.

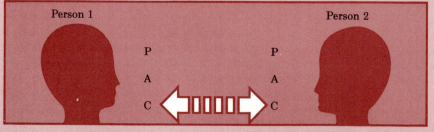

I wish I were the Lone Ranger.

Me too.

Child-Child

FIGURE 11.2 Complementary transactions, in which the two parties are addressing each other as equals.

manifest message. Beneath the surface, at the psychological level, there occurs a latent but more meaningful exchange. Often, the manifest transmission is Adult-to-Adult for the sake of appearances. Beneath the surface, however, an altogether different sort of communication may be taking place.

GAMES IN INTIMATE RELATIONSHIPS

GAME. *In transactional analysis, a series of manipulative interactions progressing toward a predictable outcome. Actors usually conceal their true motivations, and the game tends to promote feelings of antagonism.*

Now that I have reviewed the basics of transactional analysis, I can introduce you to a more formal definition of games. According to Berne, a **game** is "an ongoing series of complementary ulterior transactions progressing toward a well-defined, predictable outcome" (1964, p. 48). The crucial problem with

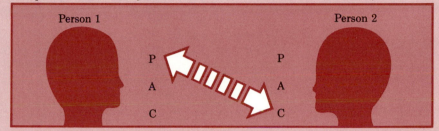

Conversations

You spent too much money for the dress.   But I really wanted it.

Person 1   Person 2

P   P
A   A
C   C

You must do things as I say.   You are always telling me what to do.

Parent-Child

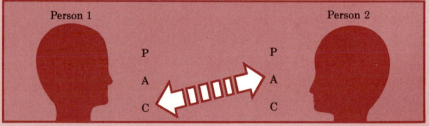

I'm feeling anxious. I don't think I can perform.   In my opinion, you have performed well in rehearsal. Why not try?

Person 1   Person 2

P   P
A   A
C   C

I'm really feeling happy about our new car. In fact, I'm absolutely delighted.   I understand how you feel. What did your brother say?

Child-Adult

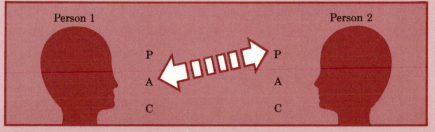

I'd like to quit smoking. Would you help me?   The first step is for you to start chewing gum.

Person 1   Person 2

P   P
A   A
C   C

FIGURE 11.3 Complementary relationships, in which one person plays the role that the other wants.

I wonder if I'll ever be any good at painting. Can you give me some tips?   Sure. Just follow the suggestions in the book and do what I tell you to.

Adult-Parent

games is that the outcome usually includes antagonism and disharmony between the persons involved.

There are many kinds of games, including what Berne calls life games, party games, marital games, and sexual games. Our parents start shaping our preferences for certain games during our childhood. In adulthood, we may carry these game-playing tendencies into our intimate relationships. A common problem for couples is that they tend to get into a rut. They play the same destructive games over and over, often without recognizing the repetitive patterns in their behavior. This section will describe some of the games that couples are especially likely to get locked into.

IF IT WEREN'T FOR YOU

This game is commonly played by marital partners or other couples who have been together for a while. In it, one spouse charges the other with restricting the first spouse's behavior. For example, one spouse might casually but cleverly bring up the fact that a friend will be receiving a graduate degree soon. The other partner might innocently respond "That's great." This sets the stage for the first spouse to assert "If it weren't for you, I could have gone to graduate school." Thus, an old source of disharmony may be resurrected. There are a number of potential payoffs for the initiator of this game. It may be that the first spouse didn't go to graduate school because he or she was terrified of the challenge. However, the self-deception in this game permits the

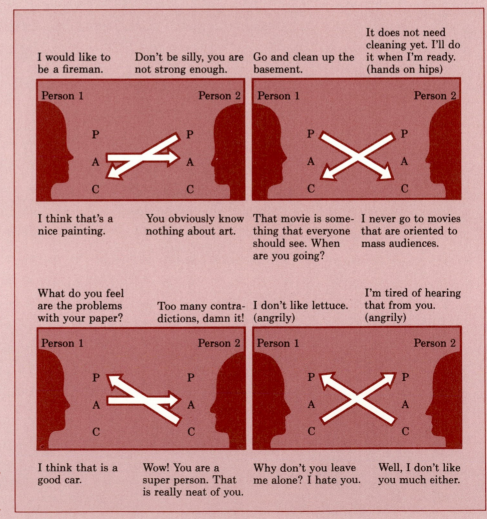

FIGURE 11.4 Examples of crossed transactions.

first spouse to deny hidden insecurities and thereby maintain greater self-esteem. The guilt laid on the second spouse also provides a bargaining advantage in subsequent transactions.

COURTROOM

This game requires the availability of a third party who gets thrust (often with much discomfort) into the center of the game. In the presence of one's partner, a person says to the third party "Let me tell you what this clown [turkey, ogre, or whatever] did yesterday." The "plaintiff" then launches into a distorted account of some allegedly terrible behavior of the other partner's. The aim here is obviously to make the "defendant" partner feel guilty so as to gain an advantage in future transactions. Part of the appeal of this game is that it's hard for the defendant not to play. Given the situation, the defendant has little choice but to mount a rebuttal.

CORNER

In this game, one partner corners the other in a "no-win" situation. For example, the initiator, who normally handles a particular household chore (example: buying the groceries), asks the other partner to assume the responsibility today. If the second partner says no, he or she is condemned for failing to take on an adequate share of household duties. However, when the second partner agrees and does the grocery shopping, the initiator finds fault with the job, asserting that "the asparagus looks terrible, you got the wrong kind of paper towels," and so forth. Thus, the second partner can't win either way. Regardless of which way the second partner goes, the initiator garners more appreciation for the chore that he or she normally handles.

THREADBARE

This game is used by one spouse to gain more control over family finances. The spouse makes some kind of apparently significant sacrifice, going without something that would require some expenditure, so as to make it difficult for the other spouse to spend money guilt-free. Let's say a husband continues to drive a shabby, old, beat-up car that he really could afford to replace. Driving the car appears to be a sacrifice and allows him to constantly harp about any money his wife spends on clothes. Often, the sacrifice only *appears* to be significant. The husband may not really care what kind of car he drives, but he will pretend that he does. If the car were important to him, he would probably find some other way to make his "sacrifice." This gimmick allows him to increase his proportional control over family expenditures.

WHY DON'T YOU—YES BUT

This is a game of "one-upmanship." One partner mentions a problem to the other, who innocently offers possible solutions—only to have them all rejected.

11.6

RECOMMENDED READING
Games People Play
by Eric Berne (Grove Press, 1964)

It's hard to believe that this classic best-seller is over 20 years old. Reviewers have called it "disturbing" and "chilling" because of the way it cuts through our social façades to lay bare the guile, sham, and fraud that characterize so much of our interpersonal behavior. There is one shortcoming, in that some of Berne's analyses assume the existence of traditional sex roles, which, of course, are fading today. With the exception of this minor problem, Berne's descriptions of 120 games remain shrewd and discerning.

Fortunately, the rewards of game-free intimacy, which is or should be the most perfect form of human living, are so great that even precariously balanced personalities can safely and joyfully relinquish their games if an appropriate partner can be found for the better relationship [p. 62].

Let's say a wife mentions some difficulty in correcting some problem behavior on the part of one of the children. The husband responds sincerely with a series of ideas, "Why don't you . . . ?" However, the issue was brought up not to *solicit* suggestions but to *reject* them. The wife has already thought of all the obvious possibilities and rattles off a putdown for each one with "Yes, but . . . ." This game allows the initiator to demonstrate his or her superiority while making the other party feel inadequate.

SWEETHEART

This is a simple little gambit wherein one partner tells a subtly derogatory story about the other partner, ending with "Isn't that right, sweetheart?" The pseudoaffectionate ending makes it a bit more difficult for the second spouse to issue a denial.

BEYOND GAMES

I have discussed only a small, illustrative sampling of the games described by Berne. However, this sampling should clarify for you the problems with games: they generally are hollow, deceitful, manipulative patterns of interaction that sabotage genuine intimacy and instead promote animosity and alienation.

Can we get away from game playing? According to Berne, the answer is yes. The key is to become *aware* of your counterproductive patterns of interaction. Berne felt that once couples gained insight into their games, they could choose not to play. Thus, by promoting this kind of insight, transactional analysis may aid people in achieving greater intimacy.

CHAPTER 11 REVIEW

IDEAS: REVIEW OF LEARNING OBJECTIVES

When you have mastered the material in this chapter, you should be able to do the following.

1. List five social trends that are undermining the traditional model of marriage.
2. Discuss several poor motivations for marriage.
3. Explain how endogamy, homogamy, and ideals affect mate selection.
4. Describe Murstein's stimulus-value-role theory.
5. Discuss how the family life cycle is related to marital satisfaction.
6. Discuss changing attitudes about the choice by couples to remain childless.
7. Discuss how the arrival of the first child in a family tends to affect marital interactions and satisfaction.
8. Discuss some common problems that surface as a family's children begin to reach adolescence.
9. Discuss some common problems that surface when it is time to launch children into the adult world.
10. Discuss marital satisfaction in the postparental years.
11. Discuss how unrealistic expectations might affect marital adjustment.
12. Explain who benefits from traditional marital roles.
13. Discuss how gaps in role expectations may lead to marital problems.
14. Summarize the evidence on the relation between occupational and marital satisfaction.
15. Describe the potential impact of poverty on a marriage.
16. Discuss the frequency of communication problems in troubled marriages and how happily married couples tend to differ from troubled couples in patterns of communication.
17. Discuss recent trends regarding in-law conflicts.
18. Discuss how sexual dysfunction is related to marital adjustment.
19. Discuss who tends to get jealous and how such jealousy may affect a relationship.
20. Describe how marital adjustment is affected by shared leisure activities.
21. Discuss factors that influence the "success" of marriage counseling.
22. Summarize current estimates of the divorce rate.
23. Summarize evidence on the predivorce and postdivorce adjustment of former spouses and their children.
24. List four sets of problems associated with divorce.
25. List four postdivorce syndromes to be avoided.
26. Summarize the data on remarriage.
27. Describe evidence on the prevalence of cohabitation and the characteristics of those who cohabit.
28. Discuss whether cohabitation is a serious threat to the institution of marriage and whether it improves the probability of subsequent marital success.
29. Describe the fundamental principles of open marriage.
30. Describe two inaccurate stereotypes of single life.
31. Discuss the adjustment, health, and happiness of single as opposed to married people.
32. Describe three myths about homosexual relationships.
33. List and describe the five types of homosexual relationships delineated by Bell and Weinberg.
34. Discuss how games may lead to problems in intimate relationships.
35. Describe the three ego states outlined by Berne.
36. Describe three types of transactions outlined by Berne.
37. Briefly describe the themes in If it weren't for you, Courtroom, and Corner.
38. Briefly describe the themes in Threadbare, Why don't you—Yes but, and Sweetheart.

TERMS: REVIEW OF NEW VOCABULARY

When you have mastered the material in this chapter, you should be able to define the following terms.

Cohabitation	Family life cycle	Jealousy	Transaction
Complementary transaction	Game	Marriage	Transactional analysis
	Gay	Marriage counseling	Ulterior transaction
Crossed transaction	Heterosexual	Open marriage	
Ego state	Homogamy	Sexual dysfunction	
Endogamy	Homosexual	Sociology	

PEOPLE: REVIEW OF MAJOR THEORISTS AND RESEARCHERS

When you have mastered the material in this chapter, you should be able to summarize the principal contributions and/or ideas of the following people.

Bell and Weinberg	Eric Berne	Bernard Murstein	O'Neill and O'Neill

12

THE DEVELOPMENT AND EXPRESSION OF SEXUALITY

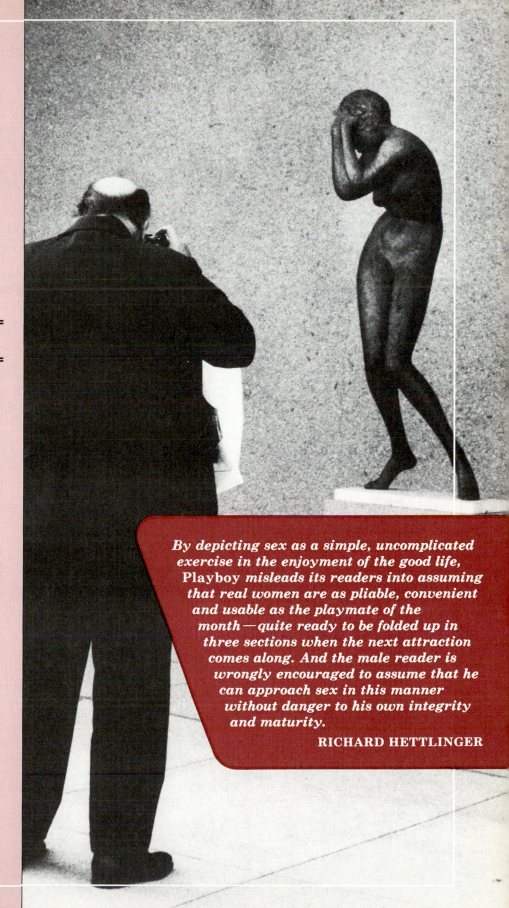

Summary

Applying Psychology to Your Life: Improving Sexual Satisfaction

GENERAL SUGGESTIONS

1. PURSUE ADEQUATE SEX EDUCATION
2. REVIEW YOUR SEXUAL VALUE SYSTEM
3. COMMUNICATE ABOUT SEX
4. AVOID GOAL SETTING AND SPECTATORING
5. ENJOY YOUR FANTASIES
6. BE SELECTIVE ABOUT SEX

SUGGESTIONS FOR SPECIFIC PROBLEMS

ERECTILE DIFFICULTIES
PREMATURE EJACULATION
ORGASMIC DIFFICULTIES IN WOMEN

By depicting sex as a simple, uncomplicated exercise in the enjoyment of the good life, Playboy misleads its readers into assuming that real women are as pliable, convenient and usable as the playmate of the month—quite ready to be folded up in three sections when the next attraction comes along. And the male reader is wrongly encouraged to assume that he can approach sex in this manner without danger to his own integrity and maturity.

RICHARD HETTLINGER

Sex. To some people it's a sport, to others an oppressive duty. For some it's recreation, for others it's business. Some find it a source of great intimacy and pleasure; others, a source of extraordinary anxiety and frustration. Whatever the case, sexuality plays a central role in the lives of most of us. In our culture, it sometimes seems that we are obsessed with sex. We joke and gossip about it constantly. Our magazines and novels are saturated with sex. The advertising business uses sex to sell us everything from toothpaste to automobiles. We have become gluttonous in our consumption of both pornography and books purporting to tell us how to improve our sex lives. In spite of all this, many lovers find it excruciatingly difficult to talk to each other about sex, and misconceptions about sexual behavior abound.

In this chapter I will consider how we express our sexuality and how this affects our adjustment. Specifically, I will look at the development of sexual identity, the interpersonal nature of sexual relationships, the psychology and physiology of sexual arousal, patterns of sexual behavior, and causes of problems in sexual functioning. In the application section at the end of the chapter, I will discuss some things that people can do to increase their sexual satisfaction.

Problems in Doing Research on Sexual Behavior

A recent sex survey published in *Cosmopolitan* magazine (Wolfe, 1980), with over 106,000 respondents, reports that "*Cosmo* girls" are "sexy and wild." Over 20% of the *Cosmo* girls indicated that they had engaged in sex with two or more partners at the same time; 25% reported that they had occasional lesbian encounters; 44% reported that they had had over ten sex partners in their lives; and 50% indicated that they had been involved in extramarital sex.

What is one supposed to make of such startling figures? Well, they are interesting, but they illustrate a current problem in the field of sex research. Every time you look up, someone is publishing a new sex survey indicating that people are wilder than ever before. However, these findings should be consumed with a grain of salt. Research data in *any* area of inquiry should not be viewed naively as representing the truth. Moreover, conducting research on sexual behavior is particularly problematic, and findings in this area must be interpreted with great caution. Several problems, though not unique to sex research, are especially troublesome in this area of inquiry. These include the following.

SAMPLING DIFFICULTIES

It is exceptionally difficult to get a sound, representative sample of respondents in sex research. You cannot *force* people to participate in such research; you have to depend on volunteers. However, many people are reluctant to discuss their sex lives. For example, two major sex surveys, those by Morton Hunt (1974) and Shere Hite (1976), had return rates of only 20% and 3%, respectively. The crucial problem here is that people who are willing to volunteer information about their sexual behavior differ systematically from those who are unwilling to do so. We have reason to believe that those who respond to sex surveys are more "liberal" and more sexually experienced than those who do not (Kaats & Davis, 1971). This sampling bias may have contributed to the surprising findings in the *Cosmopolitan* survey.

UNRELIABILITY OF SELF-REPORT

Sex research has consisted predominantly of surveys that have depended on subjects' self-reports about their sexual behavior. There are several problems with these self-reports. Some people may intentionally lie about their sexual behavior. Others may have difficulty in recalling how they behaved 10 or 20 years ago. People may also have difficulty in estimating how often they do this or how long they do that. In person-to-person interviews, shame and embarrassment may prevent people from responding accurately. Thus, there are many reasons to be cautious about accepting self-report data.

DIFFICULTY IN DOING DIRECT OBSERVATION

Given the problems inherent in self-reports, it would be nice if we could conduct more experiments and do more direct observation. However, this is difficult because people understandably desire privacy in their sexual encounters. Although some direct observation has been done (primarily by Masters & Johnson, 1966), sampling bias is probably *very* strong in such studies (Farkas, Sine, & Evans, 1978).

In summary, sex researchers have their work cut out for them. It is difficult to collect accurate data on sexual behavior. Because of these problems, you should evaluate sex research with more than the usual cautionary skepticism.

Development of Sexual Identity

There is immense variety in how people express their sexuality. Some people barely express it at all; rather, they work diligently to suppress sexual feelings and desires. At the other extreme, some people express their sexual urges with an ease that borders on abandon, as they casually meander through a lifetime "smorgasbord" of sexual encounters. Some need to turn the lights out before they can have sex, while others would like to be on camera with spotlights shining. Some cannot even bring themselves to use sexual words without massive embarrassment, while others guiltlessly engage in brutal sexual assault. The enormous diversity in human sexual behavior is best explained by examining how one's *sexual identity* develops.

KEY ASPECTS OF SEXUAL IDENTITY

SEXUAL IDENTITY. *The complex of personal qualities that determine one's sexual behavior; includes body image, sexual orientation, sexual values and ethics, and erotic preferences.*

I will use the term **sexual identity** to refer to the complex of personal qualities, self-perceptions, attitudes, and role commitments that determine one's sexual behavior. In other words, your sexual identity consists of those personal characteristics that guide and govern how you express your sexuality. This conception of sexual identity includes four key features or aspects.

1. *Body image.* Your body image simply involves how you see yourself physically. It is a part of your self-concept, and as you learned in Chapter 6, it may or may not be a very accurate reflection of physical reality. However, it definitely affects how you feel about yourself in the sexual domain. The widespread use of plastic surgery for breast enhancements, facelifts, "nose jobs," and so forth is a testimonial to the importance of body image. People who have their physical features altered often feel very differently about themselves sexually after the surgery.

BISEXUAL. *A sexual orientation wherein one desires erotic activity with members of either sex (in contrast to heterosexual or homosexual, defined in Chapter 11).*

2. *Sexual orientation.* Your sexual orientation is the direction in which you experience and channel sexual desires. The four basic sexual orientations are heterosexual, homosexual, **bisexual,** and **transsexual.** Although the vast majority of us are heterosexual, the alternative orientations are probably more common than most people realize.

TRANSSEXUAL. *A sexual orientation wherein there is a mismatch between gender identity and actual biological sex. Such people feel they are trapped in the body of the wrong sex. They frequently seek sex-change surgery.*

3. *Sexual values and ethics.* Because sexual interactions are very important, most cultures attempt to impose some morality-based constraints on how people behave sexually. Our society is no exception, and we are all trained to believe that certain expressions of sexuality are "right" while others are "wrong." The resulting attitudes about what is moral and immoral constitute

our sexual values and ethics. These standards of "appropriate" conduct exert tremendous influence over our sexual behavior.

4. *Erotic preferences.* Within the limits imposed by sexual orientation and values, there still are great differences among people in regard to exactly what they find arousing or enjoyable. Erotic preferences involve one's personal tastes in sexual activities. Your erotic preferences encompass your attitudes about self-stimulation, styles of foreplay and intercourse, oral sex, and a host of other approaches to sexual arousal and satisfaction.

One's sexual identity is shaped and reshaped gradually over an entire life-time (Kilmann, 1984). The years up through young adulthood are probably especially influential, although substantial changes in sexual identity can occur at later points in the life span. This shaping process involves a complex inter-play between physiological and psychosocial determinants.

PHYSIOLOGICAL SOURCES OF SEXUAL IDENTITY

SECONDARY SEX CHARACTERISTICS. *The physical characteristics, other than the genitals, that appear with maturation and distinguish the male from the female, such as a beard and deepened voice in males or breasts and menstruation in females.*

Obviously, your sexual identity is intimately tied to your gender, or biological sex. As the maturation process unfolds, **secondary sex characteristics** gradually appear and help most of us to further define ourselves sexually. Those who mature early often get a "jump" on age-mates and progress relatively rapidly toward a sexual identity (Masters, Johnson, & Kolodny, 1982). Additionally, one's overt physical characteristics, which are largely a product of genetic transmission, influence one's body image, which is a key feature of sexual identity. Those whose physical features correspond to the cultural ideals for their gender may struggle less than others with certain aspects of their sexual identity (Allgeier & Allgeier, 1984).

There is a great deal of speculation, but relatively little solid evidence, about the more subtle impact of hormone levels on sexual identity. We know that (1) there are clear differences between males and females in hormonal patterns, (2) hormonal fluctuations affect the development of secondary sex characteristics, (3) hormonal malfunctions during the prenatal period of development can interfere with the normal evolution of gender characteristics, and (4) hormone injections can moderate sexual desire in some people. All these findings clearly indicate that hormonal patterns can have important effects on sexual identity. However, the exact nature of these effects remains somewhat mysterious and controversial. For instance, we do not know whether normal differences between people in hormone levels significantly affect either sexual orientation or sexual appetite (Masters et al., 1982).

PSYCHOSOCIAL SOURCES OF SEXUAL IDENTITY

While physiological factors undoubtedly exert some influence, most experts believe that the contours of sexual identity are shaped mainly by psychosocial determinants (Money, 1980). It appears that sexual identity is molded in much the same way as the general sex differences in behavior discussed in Chapter 8. As you may recall, I concluded that socialization *processes* are critical in shaping sex differences and sex roles. In particular, I described how *imitation* of certain role models, *reinforcement* of "appropriate" behaviors, and *self-socialization,* or active information seeking, gradually produce the behavioral disparities that exist between males and females. Precisely the same learning processes are at work in the acquisition of sexual identity. I will illustrate these processes at work as I discuss the three main sources of socialization that influence sexual identity. These principal sources of sexual identity are essentially the same as the main sources of sex-role socialization listed in Chapter 8: the home, the school, and the media.

HOME/PARENTS

Parents and the home environment can affect the development of sexual identity throughout life but are especially influential in the early years, when they

Parental reactions to children's sex play may influence sexual identity in adulthood.

have little competition from other sources of socialization. Children usually engage in some sex play and exploration before they reach school age (Martinson, 1980). Many will experiment with self-stimulation of the genitals and will display their curiosity about sexual matters, asking questions such as "Where do babies come from?" Very young children are quite impressionable, and parental reactions to sexual exploration and curiosity at this stage can have a telling impact on sexual identity. When parents don't feel comfortable with their own sexuality, they often respond to youngsters' exploration with horror, dismay, and discouragement. They may severely punish innocent, exploratory sex play and squirm miserably when kids ask sexual questions. These sorts of reactions tend to convey to children that sex is a "dirty" activity and topic, and they may begin to feel guilty about their sexual urges and curiosity. Thus, parents who are not comfortable with their sexuality can begin to pass on that discomfort to their children at very early ages (Kilmann, 1984).

Ultimately, parents who make sex a "taboo" topic end up reducing their influence on their kids' evolving sexual identity. Their children inevitably turn elsewhere to seek information about sexuality. Thus, the "conspiracy of silence" about sex in the home often backfires by increasing the influence of peers, schools, and the media.

SCHOOLS/PEERS

Parents' inability to confront their kids' sexual curiosity leaves a huge void that is typically filled by a youngster's peer group. As you can see in Table 12.1, friends are the principal source of sex information for both males and females (Hunt, 1974). Of course, friends may be ill informed themselves, so that one's peer group can be a source of highly misleading misinformation. Furthermore, peers are unlikely to instill the same kinds of sexual ethics that parents tend to champion. Spanier (1977) found that girls who learned the facts of life from their mothers were less sexually active than girls who got their information from peers and other sources.

TABLE 12.1 Main source of sexual information, in percentages

	Males	Females
Friends	59	46
Reading	20	22
Mother	3	16
Father	6	1
School program	3	5
Adults outside home	6	4
Brothers, sisters	4	6
Other, and no answer	7	7

Schools may influence sexual identity through sex education programs. Evidence suggests (Spanier, 1977) that these programs sway students in the direction of the more conservative sexual values that most parents would espouse. However, many parents try to extend the conspiracy of silence regarding sex into the classroom and campaign against such programs.

MEDIA

As you may have noticed in Table 12.1, the second leading source of information on sex comes from the media domain—through reading (Hunt, 1974). Unfortunately, however, there are a great many popular books and magazines that perpetuate myths and miseducate their young readers. Moreover, magazines such as *Hustler* or pornographic novels are not likely to promote the kinds of sexual values that most parents would prefer.

Although youngsters may pick up the facts of life from reading, the video medium (TV and movies) may have more impact on norms for body image and sexual ethics. As discussed in Chapter 9, feelings about physical attractiveness can be distorted by the endless parade of physical beauty that we are exposed to in the video medium. Sexual relationships are portrayed extensively in movies and TV shows in ways that must necessarily influence the emerging sexual ethics of young people. Additionally, erotic preferences may be shaped by exposure to pornographic or even semipornographic books and films.

Interaction in Sexual Relationships

Sexual relationships are extremely important to most of us. Given this importance and their very emotional nature, sexual relationships tend to be highly charged sources of potential conflict. The fuse on this powder keg is often lit by the sparks that fly when incompatible sexual ethics clash. In this section, I will briefly discuss the dynamics of sexual relationships.

DIFFERING MOTIVES UNDERLYING SEXUAL INTERACTIONS

The first thing you should be aware of in contemplating sexual relationships is that people may unite sexually for entirely different reasons. Many different motives may lead people to enter sexual encounters and relationships. Two partners may *not* be motivated by the same desires or intentions. We have not yet studied whether mismatched motives increase the likelihood of trouble in a relationship, but that certainly would seem to be a logical possibility. Building on work by Neubeck (1972), Nass, Libby, and Fisher (1981, pp. 102–103) list 12 different motives that may underlie sexual interactions:

> *Affection*—longing for love, closeness, and the physical and emotional union that can be satisfied through sex;
>
> *Hostility*—for those of us who are taught that sex is dirty and degrading, using it as a way to degrade people we feel hostile toward, or sometimes using it as a weapon of retaliation against the same gender as a person who has hurt us;
>
> *Anxiety*—using sex as temporary relief from nonsexual frustrations or worries;
>
> *Boredom*—using sex to enhance a dull environment, routine activities, or even less "intimate" forms of sexmaking;
>
> *Duty*—feeling that it's our responsibility to have sex on schedule or to keep a partner from being uncomfortably frustrated (typically a female feels that she can't leave a male unsatisfied, and the notion that he could masturbate or that she might feel equally uncomfortable if highly aroused but not satisfied is missing from traditional scripts);
>
> *Mending wounds*—using sex as a way to make up after an argument or even to avoid dealing with it;
>
> *Accomplishment*—wanting to have sex as often as we think everyone else does, in every conceivable position, and perhaps break records with our "scores";
>
> *Adventure*—creatively desiring to explore beyond the bounds of our previous experiences;
>
> *Recreation*—having sex for fun and games or for creating pleasant sensations for each other;
>
> *Lust*—having passion for increasing and then gratifying sexual desires with a focus on sensual arousal, fantasies, and delight in touching and being touched;
>
> *Self-affirmation*—acting out our perceived sexual identity so that the other will notice and approve of it;
>
> *Altruism*—feeling that we give others sexual pleasure and enjoy doing so.

DIFFERING SEXUAL SCRIPTS

SCRIPT. *A culturally programmed set of expectations about how role-regulated relationships should be enacted and how they should evolve.*

In addition to differing in their motives for sex, people may be guided in their sexual relationships by very different *scripts*. "Script" is a relatively new concept, emerging out of work in transactional analysis, that refers to expectations that people hold for a series of interactions. Basically, a **script** is a person's mental map that outlines how a particular kind of relationship is supposed to unfold. It is a culturally programmed set of expectations about a role-regulated sequence of social transactions. Scripts in life are similar to theatrical scripts for movies or plays, which spell out exactly how actors will interact and what they will say. However, real-life scripts tend to be sketchier, allowing for more spontaneity, or "ad-libbing." Scripts are a product of lifelong learning and socialization. Scripts for sexual relationships are strongly influenced by sexual values and ethics.

Sexual scripts guide our conduct in sexual relationships.

Although scripts can be highly individualized, there are a handful of scripts that guide the behavior of most of us in the sexual arena. Nass et al. (1981, pp. 23–24) describe five common sexual scripts that modulate our conduct of sexual interactions in modern Western culture:

1. *Traditional religious script,* in which sex is acceptable only within marriage. In this script, all other sexual activities are taboo, especially for women. Sex means reproduction, though it may also have something to do with affection.

2. *Romantic script,* now the predominant one in our society, in which sex means love. According to this script, if we grow in love with someone, it's okay to "make love," either in or out of marriage. Without love, sex is a meaningless animal function. The eligible actors are two people who are in love, the ideal emotional state is uncontrollable loving passion, the words exchanged are assurances of affection, and all activities should appear to be spontaneous expressions of love. . . .

3. *Sexual friendship script,* in which people who are friends can also have an intimate sexual relationship. Although the association of the actors in this script is usually ongoing, typically it's not sexually exclusive.

4. *Casual/mutual horniness script,* increasingly publicized by the mass media, in which sex is defined as recreational fun. In this script, the actors are casual acquaintances who are mutually sexually aroused. Qualities that are looked for in sexmaking may include joy, playfulness, abandon, variety, and, increasingly, good technique....

5. *Utilitarian-predatory script,* in which people have sex for some reason other than sexual pleasure, reproduction, or love. In this script, the reasons for sex might include economic gain (as in prostitution), career advancement, or power achievement. For example, to achieve power, some male groups see sex as "scoring" and believe they enhance their status within the group by boasting of their sexual exploits. Militant feminists, too, may define heterosexual activity as a power play rather than as a quest for love or pleasure.

THE NEGOTIATION PROCESS

In light of the differing motives and scripts that we may bring into sexual interactions, it is not surprising that there is an inevitable process of negotiation in sexual relationships. You may not feel very comfortable with the word *negotiation* because its materialistic, bartering connotations conflict with the religious and romantic scripts that a great many of us embrace. Moreover, operating according to these scripts, we often keep the negotiation process veiled in a shroud of social ambiguity and subtlety. Nonetheless, sexual relationships inevitably require some negotiation between the partners. Couples have to negotiate whether, how often, and when they will have sex, who will take various initiatives, what kinds of erotic activities will take place, and what it all means to the social relationship. The negotiation process may not be explicit—but it's there.

MAKING SEXUAL CHOICES

In the context of this negotiation process, you have the responsibility to make choices about your sexual behavior. I cannot offer any simple advice for making these sexual choices. If I were to do so, I would be writing yet another sexual script for you to follow, when in fact I want to encourage you to write your own scripts. However, I will make a couple of very brief comments.

First, I want to encourage you to make conscious choices. Many of us take our sexual values, ethics, and scripts for granted. They are imposed on us by others, and we accept them passively. It is wiser for you to think things out on your own and make your own choices. Second, effective communication is of the utmost value in making the sexual negotiation process a healthy one. Thinking in terms of negotiation should help you to realize just how important open communication is in sexual interactions. Most of the advice in Chapter 7 on how to improve verbal and nonverbal communication can be applied in sexual relationships. In particular, you may want to think about how constructive conflict-resolution strategies can be employed in the sexual negotiation process.

The Human Sexual Response

We turn our attention now to the human sexual response itself. I will begin by reviewing Masters and Johnson's (1966) description of the four-stage sexual response cycle. I will then discuss some significant differences between women and men in their patterns of responding. Finally, I will review the main techniques for achieving sexual arousal. Throughout this section the principal aim will be to enhance your understanding of the psychology and physiology of sexual arousal.

THE SEXUAL RESPONSE CYCLE

WILLIAM MASTERS
AND VIRGINIA JOHNSON

The research team of William Masters and Virginia Johnson deserves enormous credit for expanding our understanding of the physiology of sexual arousal. Masters and Johnson used a variety of direct-observation techniques in a laboratory setting to probe the exact nature of the sexual response. Subjects were filmed and observed engaging in both masturbation and intercourse. Physiological recording devices were used to measure a variety of bodily changes during sex. Masters and Johnson even developed an artificial penile device equipped with a camera to explore physiological changes inside the vagina. These direct observations were supplemented by thorough interviews. The results of this research were summarized in a book entitled *Human Sexual Response* (1966).

Masters and Johnson divide the sexual response into four stages: excitement, plateau, orgasm, and resolution. It should be emphasized that these stages constitute a *descriptive model* involving somewhat arbitrary divisions. With the exception of orgasm, the transitions from one stage to another are not clearly marked, and other theorists (Kaplan, 1979) have suggested breaking the sequence into fewer (three) stages. More important, the description is a generalized one, outlining typical rather than inevitable patterns of response. You should keep in mind that there is considerable variability among people in their sexual response cycles.

It has proved useful to diagram sexual response cycles in a graphic format. You can see typical response patterns for females and males in Figures 12.1 and 12.2. These diagrams essentially graph the intensity of arousal at various points in time and provide a clear picture of how the sexual response typically progresses. A glance at these figures will give you an overview of what I am about to discuss in more detail.

EXCITEMENT PHASE

Sexual arousal may be elicited by an enormous variety of events, ranging from fantasy to genital stimulation. Whatever the source of the stimulation, the initial arousal is referred to as the excitement phase. During this phase, physiological changes tend to build relatively rapidly. In both sexes, muscle tension, respiration rate, heart rate, and blood pressure increase quickly.

VASOCONGESTION. *The engorgement of blood vessels. Vasocongestion in the genital area is an important feature of sexual arousal.*

In males, these changes are accompanied by erection of the penis, which is due to **vasocongestion.** Additionally, the scrotum thickens and rises, and the testes increase in size. Erection of the nipples takes place in some men.

In females, the vasocongestion response in the genital area produces a swelling and hardening of the clitoris, a swelling and opening up of the inner and outer lips of the vagina, and vaginal expansion and lubrication. Most women experience nipple erection and a swelling of the breasts. Some women also experience a skin flush, usually in the chest area.

PLATEAU PHASE

Generally, the plateau phase involves an intensification of the physiological changes that were triggered in the excitement phase. The name for this stage is somewhat misleading (as are Figures 12.1 and 12.2) in that it suggests that physiological arousal levels off. Actually, bodily reactions usually continue to build, but at a slower pace. For instance, muscle tension, respiration rate, heart rate, and blood pressure tend to continue their ascent.

Some important genital changes occur in women during the plateau phase. The outer third of the vagina swells to form what is called an "orgasmic plat-

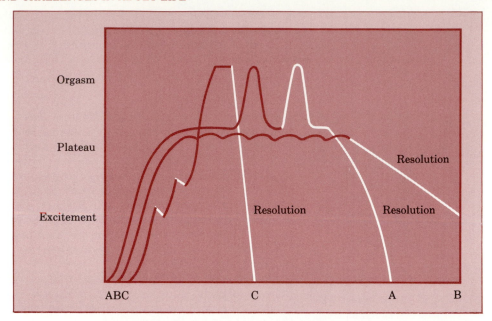

FIGURE 12.1   Female sexual response cycle.

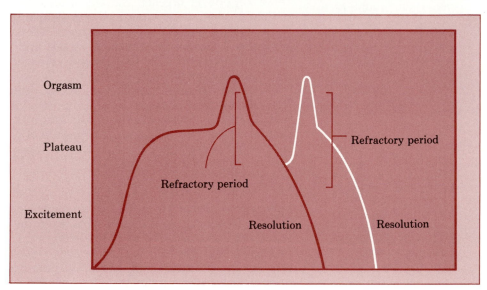

FIGURE 12.2   Male sexual response cycle.

form." This also produces a tightening of the vaginal entrance. Additionally, the clitoris shortens and withdraws under the clitoral hood. In males, the genital changes basically involve a continuation of reactions begun in the excitement phase. However, some men will secrete a bit of fluid at the tip of the penis during this phase. Although this fluid is not the ejaculate, it may contain sperm.

Sexual tension tends to build during the plateau phase, but it is altogether normal for arousal to fluctuate, especially when foreplay is lengthy. This is particularly apparent in males; their erection may diminish and increase in size several times. In females, this fluctuation may be reflected most obviously in changes in vaginal lubrication.

ORGASM PHASE

It is unlikely that any verbal description can do justice to the experience of an orgasm. Nonetheless, I'll try. Basically, in an **orgasm** sexual tension reaches

ORGASM. *The physiological peak of the sexual response cycle, which produces a release of sexual tension and involves a spastic response centered in the pelvic area; also called a climax.*

its peak intensity and is discharged in a very pleasant spasmodic response centered in the pelvic region.

In both sexes, heart rate, respiration rate, and blood pressure increase sharply. Muscle spasms usually occur throughout the body. A series of muscular contractions pulsate through the pelvic area. These contractions are separated by about .8 second. The first few are especially intense; they are followed by a series of lesser contractions. Orgasms tend to last a shade longer in women than in men.

EJACULATION. *The expulsion of semen from the penis. It is usually accompanied by orgasm.*

In males, the orgasm is accompanied by **ejaculation** of the seminal fluid. Masters and Johnson report that there is nothing comparable to ejaculation in women. However, a provocative, recent study (Sevely & Bennett, 1978) suggests that there *is* an analogous discharge of fluid in some women. Additional research (Belzer, Whipple, & Moger, 1984; Goldberg et al., 1983) has not yet settled this controversial new issue.

It appears that the subjective experience of an orgasm is very similar for men and women. In some clever studies (Vance & Wagner, 1976; Wiest, 1977), written descriptions of orgasmic experiences were given to readers without telling the readers which were provided by males and which by females. The descriptions were so much alike that even physicians and psychologists were unable to reliably identify the sex of the writers.

The sexes *do* differ in regard to the likelihood that they will reach orgasm. Masters and Johnson found that women are somewhat more likely than men to engage in intercourse without experiencing an orgasm (see pattern B in Figure 12.1). However, women may be *multiorgasmic* (see pattern A in Figure 12.1). I will discuss these sex differences in greater detail in a moment.

RESOLUTION PHASE

REFRACTORY PERIOD. *A period of time following an orgasm in males during which they are largely unresponsive to further sexual stimulation.*

This fourth and final phase involves a return to a nonaroused state. The physiological changes produced by sexual arousal subside, some very quickly, others more gradually. If an orgasm has not been experienced, the reduction in tension may be relatively slow and sometimes unpleasant. In males, after an orgasm, there is a **refractory period,** during which another orgasm is impossible. This refractory period varies tremendously in length and depends on the man's age and a host of other factors.

SEX DIFFERENCES IN SEXUAL RESPONSE

Overall, the sexual responses of women and men parallel each other fairly closely. The similarities clearly outweigh the differences. However, there are a few important differences that merit some attention. I referred to them briefly in the preceding discussion; I will now consider them in earnest.

FREQUENCY OF ORGASM IN INTERCOURSE

COITUS. *Sexual intercourse involving penile insertion into the vagina and (typically) pelvic thrusting.*

In the context of *intercourse,* or **coitus,** women are less likely than men to reach orgasm (Kinsey et al., 1953; Masters & Johnson, 1966). The gap between the sexes appears to have shrunk somewhat since Kinsey's data were collected. Nonetheless, Hunt (1974) still found that women achieve orgasm less consistently in intercourse than men.

There appear to be several reasons that women are less likely than men to achieve coital orgasms, and an understanding of these reasons may enhance the interaction of sexual partners. First, although most women report that intercourse is a very pleasant experience, evidence from *The Hite Report* (Hite, 1976) suggests that *coitus may not be the optimal mode of stimulation for many women.* Hite found that a sizable number of women who only rarely or never reached orgasm in intercourse were able to climax quite regularly through masturbation. This finding is presumably attributable to the fact that coitus provides rather indirect stimulation to the clitoris, while masturbation usually provides much more direct stimulation. Thus, arousal techniques other than coitus, such as manual or oral stimulation, may be more beneficial for many women. However, many couples are locked into a coital-centered sexual script wherein they assume that orgasms must or should be achieved through intercourse. This narrow point of view seems unfortunate, since it appears that women may not be as well suited to coital sex as men.

A second factor underlying this sex difference in frequency of orgasm involves the rapidity with which men and women reach a climax. Gebhard (1966) found that most men reach an orgasm after a mere 2 to 7 minutes of coitus, while most women require over 15 minutes of coital stimulation. This slower response in women is probably due to the indirect nature of clitoral stimulation in intercourse. This interpretation is supported by data (Kinsey et al., 1953) indicating that women require only about 4 minutes, on the average, to *masturbate* to orgasm. Since women tend to require lengthier intercourse than men to achieve orgasm, *it is likely that one reason for the lesser frequency of coital orgasm among females is often that the intercourse is too brief.*

A third consideration was discussed in Chapter 8. There I pointed out that more women than men are brought up to feel guilty about expressing their sexuality. Orgasm is more likely when a person approaches a sexual encounter with enthusiasm and vigor. Because of their greater guilt and ambivalence about sex, *women may be more prone than men to approach sex with a negative attitude,* which may undermine and sabotage sexual arousal.

In summary, there are several reasons that women display less coital orgasmic consistency than men. These reasons center primarily on differences in the value of coital stimulation and differences in sexual attitudes, rather than differences in genital sensitivity or response capability.

A related issue that should be raised here is *faking orgasms.* Hite (1976) found that many women have felt compelled to fake orgasm, presumably to make their male partners feel better about the encounter. Generally, this deceptive practice will be counterproductive in that it will simply perpetuate problems for the couple. Open and candid communication is much more likely to promote a satisfactory sexual relationship.

THE MALE REFRACTORY PERIOD

The most obvious disparity between men and women in sexual response involves the postorgasmic refractory period, seen exclusively in males. *During this refractory period, men are largely nonresponsive to additional stimulation.* The refractory period may vary from a few minutes to quite a number of hours and depends primarily on the man's age, becoming longer with advancing age. The physiological basis for the male refractory period is not understood. There is some evidence from animal studies (Barfield, Wilson, & McDonald, 1975) that suggests that it may be regulated by mechanisms in the brain.

MULTIPLE ORGASMS

Women, lacking the refractory period characteristic of males, are much more capable than men of achieving *multiple orgasms.* A person is said to be multiorgasmic if he or she experiences more than one climax in a very brief time. Just how brief the time limitation should be is the source of some debate.

It should be noted that *multiple orgasms are not extremely common in women.* In surveys (Athanasiou, Shaver, & Tavris, 1970; Kinsey et al., 1953), about 15% of female respondents report reaching multiple orgasms with some regularity. Thus, women should certainly not feel inadequate if they are not among what is actually a small minority of females who experience multiple orgasms. In males, multiorgasmic capacity appears to be quite rare. However, multiple orgasms in men have been observed in the laboratory (Robbins & Jensen, 1978).

ACHIEVING SEXUAL AROUSAL

THE MIND AS AN EROGENOUS ZONE

EROGENOUS ZONE. *An area of the body that is especially responsive to sexual stimulation.*

The term **erogenous zone** refers to an area of the body that is sexually sensitive or responsive. Areas such as the genitals and breasts usually come to mind when people think of erogenous zones. Although it is clear that these are, indeed, particularly sensitive areas for most people, it is worth noting that many individuals fail to appreciate the potential that lies in other areas of the body. Virtually *any* area of the body can function as an erogenous zone.

The ultimate erogenous zone is the mind. By this I mean to convey that one's mental set is extremely important in governing sexual arousal. Vigorous and skillful genital stimulation by a partner may have absolutely no impact if a person is not in the mood for sex. Conversely, fantasy in the absence of any other stimulation may produce great arousal. In fact, some people can elicit orgasms through fantasy alone (Kinsey et al., 1953).

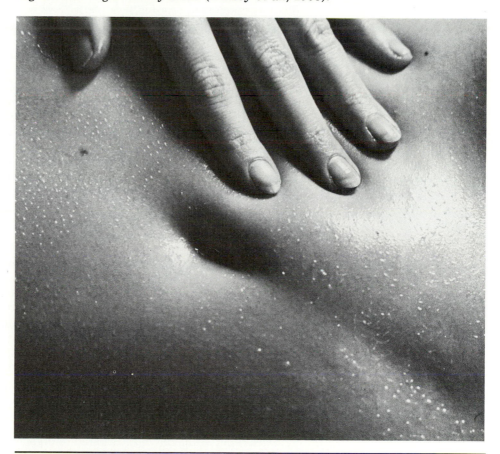

The ultimate erogenous zone is the mind.

Fantasy often occurs in conjunction with other modes of sexual stimulation. For example, most people fantasize while engaging in masturbation (Hunt, 1974). It should be emphasized that if someone fantasizes about a particular kind of encounter, such as being forced to have sex, it does not usually mean that the person would actually like to be involved in such an encounter. Recent research (Sue, 1979) indicates that it is also quite common for members of both sexes to fantasize *during* intercourse. Moreover, both sexes acknowledge that the principal goal of their coital fantasizing is the enhancement of sexual arousal. Some of the more common themes in these fantasies are listed in Table 12.2.

TABLE 12.2 **Fantasies during intercourse, in percentages**

Theme	Males	Females
A former lover	42.9	41.0
An imaginary lover	44.3	24.3
Oral-genital sex	61.2	51.4
Group sex	19.3	14.1
Being forced or overpowered into a sexual relationship	21.0	36.4
Others observing you engage in sexual intercourse	15.4	20.0
Others finding you sexually irresistible	55.2	52.8
Being rejected or sexually abused	10.5	13.2
Forcing others to have sexual relations with you	23.5	15.8
Others giving in to you after resisting at first	36.8	24.3
Observing others engaging in sex	17.9	13.2
A member of the same sex	2.8	9.4
Animals	0.9	3.7

Note: For comparison, the responses of "frequently" and "sometimes" were combined for both males and females to obtain the percentages above. The number of respondents answering for a specific fantasy ranged from 103 to 106 for males and from 105 to 107 for females.

SELF-STIMULATION

AUTOEROTICISM. *A term for sexual self-stimulation, or masturbation.*

Stimulation of one's own genitals is commonly called masturbation. Because the term carries a decidedly bad connotation, many writers on sexuality prefer to use terms such as *self-stimulation* or **autoeroticism.** Although self-stimulation is quite common in both sexes, it continues to be a controversial topic.

Attitudes.   The origin of negative attitudes about masturbation appears to lie primarily in Judeo-Christian religious dogma, which asserts that the only suitable basis for sexual acts is procreation. Thus, because of its nonreproductive nature, autoeroticism has traditionally been condemned as immoral. In the 19th and early 20th centuries, the medical establishment was influenced by this view of masturbation as an immoral act, and it was commonly assumed that self-stimulation was also harmful to one's physical and mental health. During this period, disapproval and suppression of masturbation were truly intense. Many antimasturbation devices were marketed to concerned parents. Children were forced to sleep in manacles, and some were fitted with genital cages (Diamond & Karlen, 1980).

Given this heritage, it is not surprising that much of the adult population in the United States continues to condemn self-stimulation. Although Kinsey, Pomeroy, and Martin (1948) discovered over three decades ago that a great many people masturbate with no apparent ill effects, guilt about self-stimulation remains quite common (Greenberg & Archambault, 1973).

Prevalence.   In spite of these negative attitudes, self-stimulation is very prevalent in our society. In Hunt's (1974) survey, 94% of males and 63% of females reported having masturbated to orgasm at least once. These figures are similar to those observed by Kinsey et al. (1948, 1953), who also found that males tend to begin masturbating at an earlier age than females.

Hunt's (1974) data indicate that self-stimulation remains common among adults even after marriage. Among younger married couples 72% of the husbands and 68% of the wives reported engaging in self-stimulation. It is believed that these marital partners generally do *not* talk to each other about their masturbation (Diamond & Karlen, 1980). Most of them probably assume that their partner would view it as a sign of sexual discontent. However, the great prevalence of self-stimulation among married couples indicates that, for most, it is not a response to dissatisfaction.

Value.   Experts on sexuality are gradually recognizing that self-stimulation is a normal, healthy, and sometimes important component of one's sexual behavior (Gadpaille, 1975). This route to sexual pleasure has obvious value when a sexual partner is unavailable. Moreover, many people are beginning to view self-stimulation as more than a poor substitute for "the real thing." It is becoming apparent that some people may derive more pleasure from masturbation than from coital sex (Hite, 1976). Additionally, sex therapists are discovering that self-stimulation can be very valuable in helping sexually troubled clients explore their sexual response (LoPiccolo & Lobitz, 1972). In summary, self-stimulation is a reasonable and potentially valuable mode of sexual expression. That is not to say that it should replace coitus and other joint sexual activities. However, it need not trigger the excessive guilt that it has in the past.

FOREPLAY

FOREPLAY. *Kissing, caressing, and other kinds of sexual stimulation that precede sexual intercourse.*

Foreplay may include a wide range of sexual activities (Hunt, 1974). Typically, it is initiated by kissing. This kissing is not limited to the mouth; it may be extended to virtually any area of a partner's body. Mutual caressing is also an integral element of foreplay for most couples. Like kissing, this tactile stimulation may be applied to any area of the body. As in any phase of sex, specific techniques are not as important as good communication. Satisfying foreplay hinges on partners' communicating about what feels good.

The importance of foreplay is often underestimated, especially by men. Part of the problem is that the term itself suggests that the initial stimulation is a mere preliminary to the main event. Some people get so wrapped up in their anticipation of the main event that they fail to appreciate the pleasure inherent in foreplay. It appears that this tendency may contribute to some sexual problems (Masters & Johnson, 1970). This evidence suggests that people would be wise to adopt the attitude that "half the fun is getting there." Foreplay can be enjoyed for its own sake.

Sexual partners often have differing expectations about the significance and appropriate length of foreplay (Hite, 1976). Ideally, these disparities should be brought out in the open and discussed. Partners who work to accommodate each other in this area are more likely to have a satisfactory sexual liaison than those who ignore such disparities.

COITUS

INTROMISSION. *Insertion of the penis into the vagina for the purpose of intercourse.*

Heterosexual intercourse involving insertion of the penis into the vagina is the most widely endorsed and widely practiced sexual act in our society. Kinsey and his associates (1948, 1953) found that it accounted for about 80–85% of the total sexual outlet for married couples. **Intromission** generally requires adequate vaginal lubrication, or it may be difficult and painful. In the absence of such lubrication, partners may choose to use artificial lubricants. The actual insertion should be a cooperative act.

Partners may use an infinite variety of positions in their intercourse. Many couples use more than one position in a single encounter. There are four positions that are employed most often. Of these, the man-above, or "missionary," position is the most common. When Kinsey's studies were done 30 years ago, many couples limited themselves to this position exclusively. Hunt's (1974) more recent data indicate that there is more variation today. In asking married couples about the other three common positions, Hunt found that 75% reported using the female-above position, 50% reported using the side-by-side position, and 40% reported using the rear-entry position.

Each position has its advantages and disadvantages (Masters & Johnson, 1966, 1970). Although people tend to be fascinated by the relative merits of coital positions, specific positions may not be as important as the tempo, depth, and angle of coital movements. Generally, variations in tempo, depth, and angle are appreciated by most people. *However, the most crucial consideration is that partners talk to each other about their preferences.*

OTHER TECHNIQUES

CUNNILINGUS. *Oral stimulation of the female genitals.*

FELLATIO. *Oral stimulation of the male genitals.*

Cunnilingus refers to oral stimulation of the female genitals; **fellatio** refers to oral stimulation of the penis. Partners may stimulate each other simultaneously, or one partner may stimulate the other without immediate reciprocation. Oral-genital sex may serve as a key element in foreplay, or it may constitute the main event in a sexual encounter. Oral sex is a major source of orgasms for many heterosexual couples. In homosexual relationships it plays a particularly central role. As with masturbation, there is a residue of negative attitudes toward oral sex. However, the prevalence of oral sex appears to have increased dramatically since the era of the Kinsey studies. Hunt (1974) found that 80% of married couples under age 35 and 90% under age 25 reported oral-genital contact. Similar figures were observed in the sizable and reasonably recent survey by Tavris and Sadd (1977). *Thus, it appears that oral sex is now a conventional component in most couples' sexual relationship.*

12.1 SEX AND DRUGS

Interest in aphrodisiacs—substances believed to increase sexual desire and performance—probably dates back to prehistoric times. Today, most people are aware that foods alleged to have aphrodisiac value, such as oysters, potatoes, and tomatoes, have no real impact on sexual functioning. However, new myths have grown up surrounding the effects of various drugs on sex drive.

Before reviewing the list of drugs for which claims have been made, several general points are in order. First, the consensus of the medical establishment is that there are no substances that can reliably increase sex drive through any direct physical mechanism. *In the traditional sense, then, there are no aphrodisiacs.* However, it *does* appear that certain drugs may increase sex drive or enhance subjective sexual pleasure in some people, some of the time, through *indirect psychological* mechanisms (Gawin, 1978). Second, while some drugs may have positive effects on sexual interactions, many may have negative effects. For example, *The Essential Guide to Prescription Drugs* (Long, 1977) lists some 19 classes of prescribed drugs believed to be associated with *reductions* in sex drive and potency. Drugs that have a negative impact on sexual functioning appear to outnumber those that may occasionally have positive effects. Third, many of the positive effects attributed to drugs may be due to the operation of a *self-fulfilling prophecy.* If you believe that some substance will improve a sexual encounter, it may very well do so by changing your mental set. The power of suggestion was demonstrated in a study (Wilson & Lawson, 1976) in which men were exposed to erotic materials after being given alcohol or a placebo drink that they *thought* contained alcohol. Both groups of men reported greater sexual arousal than did control groups, even though the men in one group only *believed* that they had drunk alcohol. With these thoughts in mind, let's review the actual effects of various drugs on sexual functioning.

1. *Alcohol.* Drinking alcohol can weaken sexual inhibitions in some people and thereby increase the likelihood of sexual activity. With their inhibitions reduced, some people may also enjoy sex more. However, alcohol is a depressant that commonly produces erectile difficulties in men and orgasmic difficulties in women.

2. *Barbiturates.* "Downers" operate in a manner very similar to alcohol. They may decrease sexual inhibitions, but they also undermine sexual arousal.

3. *Cocaine and amphetamines.* The effects of these drugs vary greatly from person to person. They are stimulants that create an energetic sense of well-being, accompanied by heightened sex drive in some individuals. Others report a lessened desire for sex. Some men report that these drugs delay their orgasm, thereby increasing their potency. Other men and women report erectile problems, orgasmic difficulties, and reductions in vaginal lubrication.

4. *Marijuana.* The effects of marijuana are very complex and individualized, and additional research is needed to fully understand them. The drug appears to affect the enjoyment of sex more than sexual desire. Many people report that the perceptual distortions produced by the drug increase their subjective enjoyment of sexual activities.

5. *Amyl nitrate.* This is a drug that changes blood flow and thereby affects genital vasocongestion. It also produces a brief period of time distortion, which may contribute to its reported effect of intensifying orgasms. However, it reduces orgasmic responsiveness for some people and may have dangerous effects on blood pressure.

6. *Spanish fly.* This powder derived from pulverized beetles produces an irritation in the urinary tract that leads to a reflex erection in males. It has no effect on actual sexual desire, and the erection may be quite painful. Moreover, the drug is very dangerous and may even be lethal.

7. *Vitamin E.* Contrary to some spectacular claims, there is no sound evidence that this vitamin affects sexual functioning.

The fact that oral sex was widely considered perverse until recently means that many people still have misgivings about it. In particular, among working-class couples it may be a source of conflict and hard feelings (Rubin, 1976). One partner (usually female) may often be coerced by the other into oral sex. Obviously, a reluctant participant is unlikely to derive much enjoyment from the act.

ANAL SEX. *A sexual act involving penile insertion into the anus and rectum; a fairly common practice among male homosexuals.*

Anal sex involves insertion of the penis into a partner's anus and rectum. Whereas oral and manual stimulation of the anal area are moderately common elements in foreplay, anal intercourse remains relatively uncommon. In the Hunt (1974) survey, only 6% of married couples under age 35 indicated that they engaged in anal sex with any regularity. Anal intercourse is substantially more popular among homosexual male couples than among heterosexual couples (Bell & Weinberg, 1978). However, even among gay men it ranks behind oral sex and mutual masturbation in prevalence.

Patterns of Sexual Behavior

In the previous section I focused on the sexual response itself. The principal interest was physiology and technique. In this section I will focus on how variables such as age, sex, and marital status are related to patterns of sexual behavior. In other words, I will be talking about the frequency with which particular groups of people engage in various sexual practices. Of course, the topics of sexual response and patterns of practice are difficult to separate, and I have already discussed many patterns of sexual behavior in my coverage of arousal techniques. Now, however, I will shift the emphasis away from the dynamics of sexual arousal and examine the "sexual revolution," along with patterns of premarital, marital, and extramarital sexual behavior.

HAS THERE BEEN A SEXUAL REVOLUTION?

It is commonly suggested in the popular media that we have undergone a "sexual revolution." If this is indeed true, it would make data on sexual behavior collected in the 1940s, the 1950s, and even the 1960s obsolete. Hence, before reviewing research on sexual behavior, it would seem prudent to put the sexual revolution in proper perspective.

It is altogether unclear what would constitute a *revolution* in sexual behavior. Presumably, a revolution would involve sudden, radical, and widespread changes in the expression of our sexuality. But what would qualify as sudden, radical, or widespread is a matter of opinion.

From your author's perspective, it would seem more accurate to characterize the changes in our sexual behavior as *evolutionary* rather than *revolutionary*. It appears that the sexual revolution has occurred more in our popular media than in our bedrooms. There *has* been some radical change in the openness with which sex is discussed and portrayed in magazines, movies, and TV shows. However, a comparison of survey data across recent decades suggests that our actual behavior has changed gradually rather than suddenly. The amount of change has probably been exaggerated by our tendency to talk more openly about sex. The extent of change may also be exaggerated by a curious tendency for people to underestimate the sexual activity of their parents (Pocs & Godow, 1977). This is probably why a sexual revolution has been heralded in *every* decade of the 20th century! Undoubtedly, there *has* been substantial change in our sexual behavior, but it appears to have been less abrupt and less spectacular than widely believed.

PREMARITAL SEX

PREVALENCE

Although there are some difficulties in comparing the relevant surveys, it is clear that *the prevalence of premarital sex has increased in the last couple of*

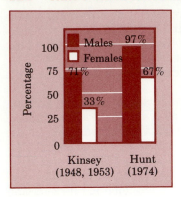

FIGURE 12.3 Percentages of people who had engaged in premarital sex, according to the Kinsey reports and the Hunt report.

decades (Robinson & Jedlicka, 1982). Evidence suggests (Hunt, 1974) that by age 25, 97% of the men in our society and 67% of the women have engaged in premarital coitus. As you can see in Figure 12.3, the comparable percentages reported in the Kinsey studies were substantially lower. Thus, premarital sex is rather commonplace today, and people entering marriage as virgins have become a rather small minority group (Tavris & Sadd, 1977). Although the gap is shrinking, males are still more likely than females to engage in premarital sex (Delamater & MacCorquodale, 1979).

The term *premarital sex* tends to conjure up images of furtive sex among teenagers. Of course, with more and more people delaying marriage until later ages, premarital sex may increasingly involve relationships between mature persons in their twenties and thirties. Obviously, the patterns and emotional implications of sex between a pair of 15-year-olds living with their parents and a pair of independent 30-year-old adults are likely to be quite different.

Although some of the increase in premarital sex may be attributable to later marriages, it nonetheless appears that premarital sex among teenagers *has* become more frequent. In fact, Zelnick and Kantner (1977) found a substantial upswing in the frequency of adolescent premarital sex in the brief period from 1971 to 1976.

In general, premarital sexual activity tends to be less frequent and less diverse than sexual activity in marriage (Victor, 1980). However, when participants are older and have more independence and privacy, their sexual relationships increasingly resemble those of married couples.

ATTITUDES

People hold a number of viewpoints regarding premarital sex. Ira Reiss (1960) has identified four common viewpoints.

1. *Abstinence.* This point of view assumes that premarital sex is wrong under any circumstances and that one should abstain from such activities.
2. *Permissiveness with affection.* This attitude is that premarital sex is acceptable *if* it takes place in the context of a stable, loving relationship.
3. *Permissiveness without affection.* This viewpoint endorses "casual" premarital sex between people who happen to be attracted to each other.
4. *Double standard.* This is the notion that premarital intercourse is OK for men but not for women.

Most parents and most institutions (churches, schools, and so forth) in our society at least formally endorse the abstinence viewpoint. At the same time, considerable dismay has been voiced by people who believe that the viewpoint of permissiveness without affection has become the norm. What does the actual evidence indicate? A careful examination of data from several surveys (Hunt, 1974; Tavris & Sadd, 1977; Zelnick & Kantner, 1977) suggests that *permissiveness with affection is probably the dominant standard in our society.* Even among relatively young women (20–24), Tavris and Sadd (1977) found that more than half had had just *one* premarital partner. The casual "one-night stands" that get so much attention in the media appear to be much less frequent than commonly believed. Across all ages, only 15% of the respondents in the Tavris and Sadd survey indicated that they had had more than five sex partners. Thus, concern about premarital "promiscuity" running rampant in our society appears to be overstated. Attitudes about premarital sex have undergone some change (Reiss, 1976), but casual sex is *not* the norm.

MARITAL SEX

IMPORTANCE IN MARRIAGE

Sex is a very important element in a marital union. There is ample evidence (Hunt, 1974; Tavris & Sadd, 1977) that couples' overall marital satisfaction is highly related to their satisfaction with their sexual relationship. For example,

Hunt found that 79% of married males who rated their marital relationship "very close" rated their sex life "very pleasurable." In contrast, only 12% of men who rated their marriage "not too close or very distant" rated their sex life "very pleasurable." Hunt's findings for females were generally similar (see Figure 12.4), and so it is fair to conclude that good sex and a good marriage tend to go hand in hand. Of course, it is difficult to ascertain whether this is a matter of good sex promoting good marriages or good marriages promoting good sex. In all probability, it's a two-way street. It seems likely that marital closeness is conducive to sexual pleasure *and* that sexual satisfaction increases marital satisfaction.

FREQUENCY AND PRACTICES

Married couples vary greatly in how often they have sex. *On the average,* couples in their twenties and thirties engage in sex about two or three times a week (Hunt, 1974; Westoff, 1974). It appears that marital sex has increased in frequency since the Kinsey studies, but only a very little bit. During the first five years of a marital relationship, the frequency of sex tends to decline to about half of its initial level. Couples report that this decline is due to increasing fatigue from work and child rearing and to growing familiarity with their sexual routine (Greenblatt, 1983).

Disagreement between marital partners about the appropriate frequency of sex is quite common. Levinger (1966) found that *54%* of his respondents reported some disagreement about the ideal frequency of sex. In this study, husbands were about twice as likely as wives to prefer more frequent sexual activity. As discussed in Chapter 8, this trend toward greater sexual desire in males is probably due to differences in upbringing rather than physiological differences between the sexes. In any case, it is clear that this is an issue that couples should try to negotiate in a reasonable manner. A key point is that this kind of disagreement is really quite normal and should not be a source of resentment.

It appears that the sexual practices of married couples have become more diversified than they were in Kinsey's era. A comparison of recent surveys with the Kinsey data suggests that couples today engage in lengthier foreplay and lengthier coitus, use oral-genital techniques of arousal more often, and use a greater variety of coital positions. Recent studies also suggest that husbands have become more concerned about their wives' sexual pleasure and that wives are reaching orgasm with greater frequency than they did a couple of generations ago (Hyde, 1982; Victor, 1980).

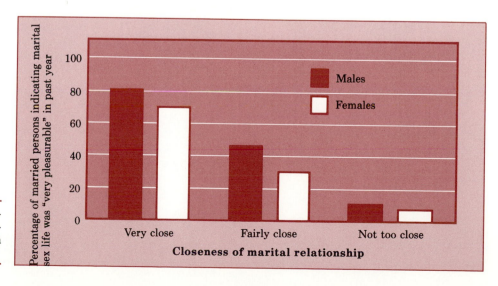

FIGURE 12.4   Relation between closeness of marital relationship and satisfaction with sex life.

EFFECTS OF AGING

Married couples' level of sexual activity tends to decline rather steadily during middle and late adulthood (Westoff, 1974; Wilson, 1975). *This decline appears to be due to couples' changing attitudes more than physiological factors.* Our youth-oriented culture tends to discourage sexual expression among older people. We are led to believe that sexual activity among the elderly is inappropriate, unimportant, and even repugnant. Many older couples seem to accept

---

12.2   THE CONTRACEPTION DILEMMA

For a variety of reasons, a great number of couples who do *not* want to conceive a child fail to use any contraceptive procedures (Byrne, 1979). The reasons for inadequate contraceptive efforts range from simple (laziness) to complex (guilt, inability to communicate about such touchy matters). Part of the problem is that many people lack accurate information about the great variety of alternatives. The following table, taken from Janet Shibley Hyde's (1982) *Understanding Human Sexuality,* provides a concise summary of the pros and cons of different methods of birth control.

Summary of information on methods of birth control

Method	Effectiveness rating	Theoretical failure rate, %	Actual failure rate, %	Death rate (per 100,000 women)	Yearly costs[a]	Advantages	Disadvantages
Birth control pills	Excellent	0.34	4–10	0.3–3.0	$72	Highly effective, not used at time of coitus, improved menstrual cycles	Cost, possible side effects, must be taken daily
IUD	Excellent	1–3	5	0.3–2.0	$25–$50	Requires no memory or motivation	Side effects, may be expelled
Condom	Very good	3	10	1.7[b]	$18–$60	Easy to use, protection from VD	Interference with coitus, continual expense
Diaphragm with cream or jelly	Very good	3	17	3.0[b]	$15–$30	No side effects, inexpensive	Aesthetic objections
Vaginal foam	Good	3	22	3.4[b]	$10–$30	Easy to use, availability	Messy, continual expense
Withdrawal	Fair	9	20–25		None	No cost	Requires high motivation
Rhythm (calendar method)	Poor to fair	13	21		None	No cost, accepted by Roman Catholic Church	Requires high motivation, prolonged abstinence, not all women can use
Unprotected intercourse	Poor	90	90	14[b]	None[c]		
Legal abortion	Excellent	0	0	3.2	$200–$400	Available when other methods fail	Expense, moral or psychological unacceptability
Sterilization, male	Excellent	<0.15	0.15		$150[d]	Is permanent and highly effective	Is permanent, psychological complications
Sterilization, female	Excellent	0.04	0.05		$200[d]	Is permanent and highly effective	Is permanent, expense, psychological complications

[a]Based on 150 acts of intercourse.
[b]Based on the death rate for pregnancies resulting from the method.
[c]But having a baby is expensive.
[d]These are one-time-only costs.

these attitudes at face value and assume that they ought not to be interested in sex.

It *is* true that a person's sexual response changes with age (Masters & Johnson, 1966). Arousal tends to build more slowly in both sexes, and orgasms tend to diminish in intensity. Males' refractory periods lengthen, and females' vaginal lubrication and elasticity decrease.

In spite of these changes, however, people in their sixties, seventies, and eighties remain capable of rewarding sexual encounters. For example, one study (Pfeiffer, Verwoerdt, & Wang, 1968) found continued sexual activity in more than 10% of couples over age 78. The married couples who remain sexually active in old age generally are those who had a particularly good sexual relationship when they were younger (Pfeiffer & Davis, 1972).

AVOIDING MONOTONY

Many married couples eventually have to struggle with the problem of monotony in their sexual relationship. There are no pat solutions for this problem. However, Janda and Klenke-Hamel (1980) offer three suggestions to help couples ward off monotony. First, they stress that couples should strive for open communication about their sexual desires and preferences. Second, they recommend that couples should throw their hearts into foreplay instead of making it a listless and lethargic preliminary to coitus. Third, they emphasize that couples should try to keep open minds about experimenting with new modes of sexual expression. Ultimately, all these suggestions are intended to promote *variety* in sexual practices, so that couples will be less likely to become bored with a standard routine.

EXTRAMARITAL SEX

TYPES

Extramarital sex, known more negatively as "adultery" or "cheating," involves a married person engaging in erotic activity with someone other than his or her spouse. Clanton (1973) has differentiated among three types of extramarital liaisons. In *clandestine extramarital sex* the nonmarital sexual activity is successfully kept secret from one's spouse. In *consensual extramarital sex* the spouse is aware of the nonmarital activity; he or she accepts it and may even approve of it. In "mate swapping" or "swinging" *both* spouses are actively involved in the extramarital sex. However, in some cases only *one* of the partners is active in extramarital relations. For example, a wife might approve of her husband's patronization of prostitutes. Finally, in *ambiguous extramarital sex* a spouse becomes aware of secretive nonmarital sexual activity but chooses not to confront the participating spouse with this reality. Typically, the activity is tolerated *without* approval, in order to avoid marital strife or a clash that might lead to divorce.

In our society, consensual extramarital sex remains relatively infrequent (Hyde, 1982) in spite of the media focus on "swinging" and related activities. Thus, most extramarital sex is of the clandestine or ambiguous variety. I will limit further discussion to these two types of extramarital activity.

PREVALENCE

The vast majority of people in our society continue to have largely negative attitudes about extramarital sex (Glenn & Weaver, 1979). Nonetheless, a substantial number get involved in extramarital activity. Roughly speaking, the data from various studies suggest that about 40–50% of American husbands and about 25–35% of American wives engage in extramarital activity at least once (Thompson, 1983). These figures may *not* mean that men are more likely than women to have an "affair." Much of the higher incidence of extramarital sex for males probably involves visits to prostitutes and very casual one-time-only encounters. These kinds of activities appear to be less frequent among women (Bell, Turner, & Rosen, 1975). Thus, if we define an "affair" as a repetitive encounter with someone other than a prostitute, it *may* be that the incidence of affairs is fairly similar for the two sexes.

MOTIVATIONS

Why do people pursue extramarital sexual encounters? There are many reasons, and I will review some of the more common ones.

First, it is clear that dissatisfaction with one's marriage is related to the likelihood of engaging in extramarital sex (Bell et al., 1975). People who are unhappy with their marriage may simply be seeking affection and emotional support (or something else) that their marriage is not providing. Marital dissatisfaction might also lead to extramarital activity that is an expression of anger. Sometimes spouses use affairs to retaliate against each other.

Second, there is evidence (Bell et al., 1975) that dissatisfaction with just the *sexual* aspect of one's marriage may instigate interest in extramarital sex. This applies to both sexes, although it is probably a more common motivational factor for husbands than for wives. In this situation, people are simply seeking sexual satisfaction that they are not deriving from their marital relationship.

Third, even when the sexual component of a marriage is satisfactory, some people desire new and different sexual experiences (Buunk, 1980). Interestingly, the evidence suggests that this pursuit of additional variety, excitement, and gratification may frequently lead to disappointment. Data from the Hunt (1974) survey suggest that extramarital sex may not be as "good" as marital sex. Hunt found that extramarital sex involves *less* variety in arousal techniques and is *less* frequently viewed as "very pleasurable" than marital sex! Hence, people seeking a new "sexual high" may often be in for a big letdown.

Fourth, I would be remiss if I did not mention that sometimes extramarital sexual activity occurs simply because two persons are attracted to each other. Erotic reactions to people other than one's spouse do not cease when one marries. Most people suppress these sexual desires because they value their marital relationship or because they consider extramarital sex immoral. Occasionally, however, a spontaneous attraction may be sufficiently powerful to override these considerations.

IMPACT

The impact of extramarital sexual activity on a marriage is highly varied, depending on the nature of the activity and the nature of the marriage. Generally speaking, extramarital sex probably has a destructive effect on most marriages. The deception and hypocrisy inherent in clandestine or ambiguous extramarital sex seem likely to undermine the trust and affection that are so important to a marriage. Of course, if one is motivated by marital dissatisfaction, these destructive tendencies may be of little concern.

However, extramarital affairs may sometimes have a positive effect on a marriage. Many participants inadvertently develop a new appreciation for the quality and importance of their marital union (Tavris & Sadd, 1977). Basically, many people who believe that "the grass is greener on the other side of the fence" learn that they actually have a "lush lawn."

Sexual Problems

If you think about it, sexual intercourse is really a pretty simple activity. Even lower organisms can execute the act with a minimum of difficulty. However, humans have managed to make sexual activity rather complicated, and many people suffer from sexual problems. In fact, Masters and Johnson (1970) *estimate* that as many as *half* of American couples may experience chronic sexual difficulties. Although this is a very rough estimate and may be way off, it is clear that sexual problems are not uncommon.

SEXUAL DYSFUNCTION.
An impairment in sexual functioning that causes distress for the person or couple.

Sexual dysfunction is a technical term that refers to any impairment in sexual functioning. This portion of the chapter will describe the various kinds of impairments that are common and discuss their causes. This discussion will be based primarily on work done by Masters and Johnson (1966, 1970, 1976) and Helen Singer Kaplan (1974, 1979).

Masters and Johnson argue that we should view a sexual problem as existing in the sexual unit rather than in one person or the other. Traditionally, people have taken a different view, assuming that the problem lies in *one* of the partners. Thus, people talk about a male's impotence or a female's frigidity. However, research by Masters and Johnson suggests that it is more accurate and appropriate to view sexual problems in the context of relationships. In other words, *sexual problems belong to couples rather than to individuals.* Although I concur fully with this perspective, I will discuss typical problems in men and women separately. This is merely a matter of organizational convenience, and you should keep in mind that sexual problems generally emerge out of partners' unique ways of relating to each other.

TYPICAL MALE PROBLEMS AND THEIR CAUSES

ERECTILE DIFFICULTIES

Definition.   Some men consistently have difficulty achieving and maintaining an erection sufficient for intercourse. This problem has traditionally been called *impotence.* Because this term has a decidedly negative—even demeaning—connotation, I prefer the term **erectile difficulties.**

ERECTILE DIFFICULTIES.
Persistent problems in achieving and/or maintaining an erection adequate for intercourse; also known as impotence.

Masters and Johnson (1970) distinguish between primary and secondary erectile difficulties. A man who has *never* had an erection sufficient for vaginal penetration is said to have *primary erectile difficulties.* A man who has experienced some coitus in the past but is currently having problems in achieving an erection is said to have *secondary erectile difficulties.* The secondary variety of this condition is far more common than the primary variety.

Causes.   It is now thought that Masters and Johnson (1970) greatly underestimated how often physiological factors contribute to erectile difficulties. Their original sampling suggested that organic factors were responsible for fewer than 10% of erectile problems. It is now clear that a host of diseases, including some common ones such as diabetes, can produce erectile problems as a side effect (Melman & Leiter, 1983). As new data come in, experts are revising their estimates, and many now project that physiological factors may contribute to as many as one-quarter of the cases of erectile dysfunction. Thus, most sex therapists recommend a thorough medical examination for males with erectile problems, in order to rule out (or discover) possible organic causes.

Although physiological conditions may cause erectile problems more frequently than originally believed, it is clear that psychological factors are of paramount importance in the majority of cases of secondary erectile dysfunction. Indeed, it appears that *the most common cause of erectile difficulties is anxiety about sexual performance.* There are many ways to acquire this anxiety. For some men, it comes from doubts about their masculinity that are deeply rooted in their upbringing. For other men, the anxiety is derived from doubts about the morality of their sexual desires. These men tend to come from highly religious homes where they were conditioned (either intentionally or inadvertently) to view sex as dirty and sinful.

Although this debilitating anxiety may be deeply rooted in a man's personality, it often is acquired through a gross overreaction to an occasional incident of sexual "failure." A male may fail to get aroused in a sexual encounter for any of a number of reasons that have nothing to do with his sexual potency. In a particular situation, arousal may be inhibited by fatigue, worry, tension, conflict with one's partner, a negative mood, too much alcohol, or the use of certain drugs. The reaction of *both* partners to these incidents is crucial. If either party turns the incident into a major catastrophe, the male may begin to get concerned about his sexual response. Seeds of doubt can be planted, which then undermine arousal in subsequent sexual encounters. *Thus, it is important for members of both sexes to realize that erectile difficulties are normal and understandable reactions to many situations* and that these difficulties do not necessarily indicate declining potency or lack of affection for one's partner. Unfortunately, with our current emphasis on sexual performance, people often create problems by overreacting and becoming unduly upset about occasional erectile problems.

PREMATURE EJACULATION

PREMATURE EJACULATION. *Persistent problems with the ejaculatory response occurring too rapidly in the context of intercourse.*

Definition. When a man consistently reaches his climax too quickly, he is said to be troubled by **premature ejaculation.** However, it is very difficult to say what is "too quick." Setting a time requirement is hopelessly arbitrary. Masters and Johnson (1970) suggest that a problem exists when a male is unable to "satisfy" his partner at least 50% of the time. Although this criterion is more defensible, I must argue that percentages are not nearly as important as the subjective feelings of the partners. It seems more reasonable to say that a problem with premature ejaculation exists if either partner feels that his or her sexual gratification is being significantly reduced by overly rapid ejaculation. Research suggests that this is a fairly common sexual problem.

Causes. A variety of factors may lead to premature ejaculation. For some men, it is simply a matter of not exerting any effort to prolong coitus. Typically, these men are not very concerned about the satisfaction of their female partner. Most of these men do not view their ejaculations as premature; however, their partners probably feel quite differently, although they may or may not voice their feelings.

If we assume that the man *is* concerned about his partner's satisfaction, problems may still emerge because *early sexual experiences often put an emphasis on the desirability of a rapid climax.* Furtive sex in the back seat of a car, quick efforts at masturbation, and experiences with prostitutes are examples of situations wherein a man typically attempts to achieve orgasm very quickly. With these kinds of initial experiences, many men become conditioned to climax quickly, and then later in life they have difficulty learning how to delay their orgasms.

Tension and excessive concern about self-control may also aggravate problems with premature ejaculation. In well-intentioned efforts to delay orgasm, some men concentrate on their sexual arousal in ways that only serve to speed up their climax. Thus, like erectile difficulties, premature ejaculation can become a self-fulfilling prophecy.

TYPICAL FEMALE PROBLEMS AND THEIR CAUSES

ORGASMIC DIFFICULTIES

ORGASMIC DIFFICULTIES. *Persistent problems among women in achieving orgasm in spite of the availability of some reasonable stimulation and the appearance of some arousal; also referred to as frigidity (which carries a negative connotation). Essentially the same problem occurs in men but is called retarded ejaculation.*

Definition. Women who are unhappy with their ability to achieve orgasm are said to be troubled by **orgasmic difficulties** (this is traditionally called frigidity). As with erectile difficulties, it is useful to distinguish between primary and secondary orgasmic difficulties. A woman with *primary orgasmic difficulties* has *never* experienced an orgasm through *any* kind of stimulation. Evidence (Kaplan, 1974) suggests that roughly 10% of American women are troubled by this condition. Women who formerly experienced orgasms but are presently unable to do so and women who experience orgasm only through noncoital techniques (oral, manual, and self-stimulation) are said to have *secondary orgasmic difficulties.* This category includes a substantial number of women, who have a diverse array of problems that produce highly varied amounts of subjective distress.

Causes. A host of psychological and situational factors may lead to orgasmic difficulties for women. Foremost among these, according to Masters and Johnson (1970), are *negative attitudes about sex*. In our society, many women have been taught that sex is a dirty, sinful, depraved activity that only men enjoy. Women trained in this manner are likely to approach sex with negative feelings of shame, guilt, and ambivalence. Such negative attitudes prevent many of these women from expressing their sexuality fully and freely. These feelings diminish their enjoyment of sex and inhibit their orgasmic response.

For many females, *inadequate stimulation* is the problem underlying their orgasmic difficulties. As discussed earlier, coitus appears to provide less than optimal stimulation for many women. However, many sexual partners are locked into a traditional coital model of sex and do not experiment with other modes of stimulation. Many couples' preoccupation with coital sex, especially when brief, may prevent women from receiving stimulation that would prove sufficient to trigger an orgasm.

Women appear more likely than men to have their sexual arousal and satisfaction undermined by a *lack of authentic affection* for their partner. Presumably, because of their values, affection tends to be more important in a sexual relationship for women than for men. Thus, when true affection is absent or gradually deteriorates, a woman is relatively likely to find her orgasmic response inhibited.

SPECTATORING. *A common cause of sexual problems wherein the person takes a detached view that detracts from enjoyment of the incoming sexual stimulation.*

Spectatoring also appears to be a fairly common problem for women. Orgasms are achieved most readily when there is a relaxed focus on the erotic stimulation. When one approaches sex with a grim determination to climax and analytically monitors what is going on, this detracts from incoming stimulation. Thus, an overconcern about climaxing produces orgasmic difficulties for some women.

INHIBITED SEXUAL DESIRE

INHIBITED SEXUAL DESIRE. *A general lack of interest in sex. Traditionally, the term* frigidity *was used to describe women who showed sexual apathy. However, this term is not preferred, because* frigidity *was also used to refer to orgasmic difficulties in women and because this syndrome may occur in males as well as females.*

Definition. People who display little or no interest in sex are said to be troubled by **inhibited sexual desire** (Kaplan, 1979). This syndrome may be manifested in either males or females but appears to be more common in women. It has been investigated extensively by Helen S. Kaplan, a prominent sex therapist.

Causes. Apathy about sex is probably caused by many of the same factors that lead to orgasmic difficulties in women. Negative attitudes about sex, whether the product of one's upbringing or of unsatisfactory sexual encounters, probably underlie most cases of inhibited sexual desire. Sexual apathy sometimes grows gradually as a by-product of sexual boredom or conflict with one's partner.

Summary

Research on sexual behavior is particularly difficult to do because of problems in getting a representative sample, the relative unreliability of self-report data, and barriers to direct-observation studies.

The great variety in sexual expression among people is due to differences in sexual identity. One's sexual identity is made up of body image, sexual orientation, sexual values and ethics, and erotic preferences. Although physiological factors such as hormonal fluctuations shape sexual identity, psychosocial determinants may be even more influential. Sources of socialization that shape sexual identity include home and parents, schools and peers, and the media.

People frequently enter into sexual interactions with differing motivations and sexual scripts. These differences understandably lead to conflicts that necessitate negotiation between sexual partners. Effective communication is the key to making this negotiation process a healthy one.

The physiology of the human sexual response was elucidated by the research team of Masters and Johnson. They analyzed the sexual response cycle into four phases: excitement, plateau, orgasm, and resolution. Men reach orgasm more consistently than women in intercourse. Several factors appear to underlie this sex difference. Men and women also differ in that men have a post-orgasmic refractory period and women have a much greater capacity for multiple orgasms.

Fantasy plays an important part in sexual arousal, and the mind is the ultimate erogenous zone. Negative attitudes about self-stimulation are rooted in religious dogma. In spite of these attitudes, self-stimulation is quite common, even among married people. Rather than viewing it as harmful, some experts believe that self-stimulation can be a valuable mode of sexual expression.

Foreplay may involve a wide range of erotic activities. Its importance is often underestimated, particularly by males. The key to satisfactory foreplay is good communication between the partners. Coitus is the most widely endorsed sexual act in our society. Four coital positions are commonly used. Although each has its advantages and disadvantages, positions by themselves are not a crucial determinant of sexual arousal. Oral-genital sex has become a common element in most young couples' sexual repertoire. However, it is sometimes a source of conflict in relationships. Anal sex continues to be a relatively infrequent practice among heterosexuals.

The widely heralded sexual revolution appears to be more media hype than reality. However, the prevalence and acceptability of premarital sex *have* increased. The quality of one's sexual relationship is intimately tied to the quality of one's marriage. Disagreements about the appropriate frequency of sex are common. Younger married couples tend to have sex about two or three times a week, but this frequency tends to decline with advancing age. This age-related decline in sexual activity appears to be due to attitudes more than changes in capacity.

Consensual extramarital sex remains uncommon in our society. Clandestine and ambiguous extramarital sex are much more prevalent. More men than women participate in extramarital sex; however, this gap may be shrinking. Marital dissatisfaction, sexual discontent, curiosity, and chance attractions motivate people to get involved in extramarital sex.

Masters and Johnson believe that sexual dysfunctions are quite common. Erectile difficulties are usually caused by excessive anxiety. Premature ejaculation may be attributable to lack of effort, early conditioning, or excessive tension. Female orgasmic difficulties are caused by negative attitudes about sex, inadequate stimulation, lack of feeling for the man involved, and spectatoring. Inhibited sexual desire appears to result from negative attitudes or sexual boredom.

In the upcoming application section I will talk about what you can do to avoid or overcome these kinds of sexual problems.

Improving Sexual Satisfaction

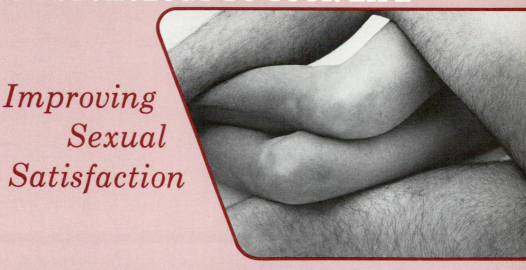

Answer the following questions yes or no.

_____ 1. I sometimes have difficulty expressing my sexuality freely and spontaneously.

_____ 2. I am not altogether satisfied with the sexual aspects of my life.

_____ 3. I am sometimes anxious about sexual encounters.

_____ 4. I would like to make some changes in my sex life.

_____ 5. I often have difficulty discussing sex.

If you answered yes to several of the above questions, you may be one of a great number of people who would like to improve their sexual functioning. Sexual problems are common. Fortunately, much can be done to remedy sexual difficulties. They do not have to be chronic sources of shame and frustration. In this application section I will discuss how couples can enhance their sexual satisfaction.

SEX THERAPY. *The professional treatment of sexual problems, disorders, or dysfunction.*

Most of the following advice is drawn from books on professional **sex therapy.** Sex therapists such as Masters and Johnson have reported tremendous success in treating most types of sexual problems. Although some critics (Zilbergeld & Evans, 1980) have suggested that the cure rates reported by Masters and Johnson are overly optimistic, it is nonetheless clear that sexual problems can be conquered with reasonable regularity.

Although professional sex therapy has a pretty impressive "track record," it is not for everyone. It is expensive, time-consuming, and, in some locations, difficult to find. Most couples can probably benefit from simply learning some of the key principles involved in sex therapy. In this section, I will offer some advice derived from selected principles of sex therapy. Space constraints preclude being as detailed as you might like. Therefore, I will make numerous suggestions for further readings that are more elaborate and detailed. It is hoped that this advice and the suggested readings may prove beneficial to some of you.

In the interests of simplicity and brevity, I will direct my advice to *couples.* In other words, I will assume that you have (or will have) a regular sexual partner with whom to work. This is not intended to suggest that people must have a regular partner in order to work toward improved sexual functioning. However, it *is* more complicated without a regular partner, and I don't have the space to deal with those complications.

I will also assume that there is a sincere bond of affection that provides the basis for your sexual partnership. It is virtually impossible to overestimate the importance of affection to a sexual relationship. In many cases, sexual difficulties are simply attributable to a lack of authentic affection between the partners. When that is the case, it is more a matter of "relationship problems" than "sexual problems."

GENERAL SUGGESTIONS

Let us begin with some general ideas about how to promote satisfactory sexual relationships. These suggestions are relevant even if you are altogether satisfied with your sexual partnership. Think of these ideas as "preventive medicine"; they can help you avoid sexual difficulties. They are derived from a number of books on sexuality, although one by Janet Shibley Hyde (1982) deserves special credit.

1. PURSUE ADEQUATE SEX EDUCATION

Although our society sometimes seems obsessed with sex, the fact is that a great number of people are terribly ignorant about sexuality. In a book entitled *Sexual Myths and Fallacies*, James McCary (1971) discussed over 80 inaccurate beliefs about sexuality that are relatively common. Misconceptions about sexuality abound, and many of these can impair sexual functioning. Hence, the first step toward promoting sexual satisfaction is to acquire accurate information about sex. As you are surely aware, the shelves of most bookstores are bulging with books on the topic. Unfortunately, many of these are riddled with inaccuracies and have helped to foster sexual ignorance. Your best bet is to pick up a college textbook on human sexuality. Three of the best are spotlighted in Box 12.3. Enrolling in an entire course on sexuality is an even better idea (more and more colleges are offering such courses today).

2. REVIEW YOUR SEXUAL VALUE SYSTEM

It is clear that many people's sexual problems are derived from a negative sexual value system. Many people are brought up to associate sex with immorality, depravity, and sin. This conditioning often leads to great guilt about sexual expression. Given this fact, you may want to rethink your sexual value system. Try to understand how your sexual values were acquired. Do they date back to your childhood? Were they *imposed* by your parents and society? Do they make good sense, given your values today? The idea here is simply to work out your *own* sexual ethics. If you want, it is your prerogative to go ahead and equate sex with immorality. I am merely suggesting that you think things through on your own, as an adult, with an understanding of the possible implications. A couple of books that can help you in reconsidering your sexual value system are mentioned in Box 12.4.

3. COMMUNICATE ABOUT SEX

In many homes a "conspiracy of silence" surrounds sex. Hence, many people learn that they shouldn't talk about sex, and they have great difficulty doing so, even with their partner. Good communication is extremely important in a sexual partnership. Your partner is not a mind reader. You have to share your thoughts and feelings with your partner in order to promote mutual satisfaction. It is important that you (1) ask questions if you have doubts about something, (2) provide *reasonably* candid feedback when you are asked about something (be diplomatic; total candor may be too much), and (3) learn to make *specific* requests for the kinds of experiences that you desire. For many couples, talking about sex isn't easy. You may want to break the ice by buying a book to discuss. There is also a superb chapter on sexual communication in the book by Crooks and Baur recommended in Box 12.3.

4. AVOID GOAL SETTING AND SPECTATORING

Sexual encounters generally work out better if you simply relax and enjoy yourself. If you set up goals, you set yourself up for failure. In particular, it is easy to get overly concerned about orgasms. This may lead to problems with spectatoring. Don't be detached and analytic. Remember, half of the fun lies in getting there.

5. ENJOY YOUR FANTASIES

Keep in mind the earlier point that the *mind* is the ultimate erogenous zone. Fantasy during sexual encounters is perfectly normal. Don't be afraid to use fantasy to enhance your sexual arousal.

6. BE SELECTIVE ABOUT SEX

Sexual encounters generally work out better when you have privacy and a relaxed atmosphere, when you are well rested, and when you are eager. If your heart isn't in it, it may be a good idea to take a "rain check." If you consistently have sex in bad situations, negative outcomes and negative feelings about your sexual partnership may result. Obviously, you cannot depend on having ideal situations all the time. There are many good reasons for going ahead with sexual encounters in less-than-ideal situations. However, it is good to be aware of the value of being selective.

12.3

RECOMMENDED READING
Textbooks on Human Sexuality

In assembling this chapter, your author consulted quite a number of textbooks on human sexuality, as well as the usual technical books and journal articles. Until recently there were only a handful of textbooks on human sexuality, since college courses devoted exclusively to the study of sex were rare. However, collegiate courses on sexuality are gradually popping up all over the country, and a host of new books to serve these courses are now available. In my opinion, three of these stand out above the others: *Understanding Human Sexuality* by Janet Shibley Hyde (McGraw-Hill, 1982), *Our Sexuality* by Robert Crooks and Karla Baur (Benjamin/ Cummings, 1983), and *Sexual Choice* by Gilbert Nass, Roger Libby, and Mary Pat Fisher (Wadsworth, 1981). All three of these books are accurate, thorough, and up to date, as are numerous other texts on human sexuality. What sets them apart is their clarity and their sensitivity to readers' personal needs. They are exceptionally well organized and written in an engaging, highly readable manner. Most important, they ad-

dress the personal and interpersonal aspects of sex without getting bogged down in physiology and the mechanics of reproduction. All three can provide you with an excellent introduction to the realities of human sexual expression.

Throughout most of recorded history, at least until about 100 years ago, religion (and rumor) provided most of the information that people had about sexuality.... It was against this background of religious understandings of sexuality that the scientific study of sex began in the late nineteenth century, although, of course, religious notions continue to influence our ideas about sexuality to the present day.... The scientific study of sex has still not emerged as a separate, unified academic discipline like biology or psychology or sociology. Rather, it tends to be interdisciplinary—a joint effort by biologists, psychologists, sociologists and anthropologists, and physicians [Hyde, 1982, pp. 3–6].

It is our belief that rigid gender role conditioning acts to limit each person's full range of human poten-

tial, producing a negative impact on our sexuality. For example, "appropriate" personality characteristics delegated to men and women may contribute to the notion that the man must always be the initiator and the woman must be the receiver. When this arrangement is the status quo, we believe it places tremendous responsibility on the male and severely limits the women's likelihood of discovering and meeting her own needs. It discourages the man from expressing his receptivity and the woman from experiencing her assertiveness [Crooks & Baur, 1983, p. 5].

Almost all human groups pay more explicit attention to women's looks than to men's. But definitions of female beauty vary. In many cultures, fat women are considered far more arousing than thin ones. Some societies think that a beautiful woman should be not only plump but also tall and strong. Breasts are important to female beauty in relatively few cultures, and their definitions of the beautiful breast vary. The shape thought to be ideal ranges from small and firm to long and droopy [Nass, Libby, & Fisher, 1981, p. 39].

SUGGESTIONS FOR SPECIFIC PROBLEMS

The following suggestions are drawn directly from a number of books on sex therapy (Barbach, 1975; Hartman & Fithian, 1974; Kaplan, 1974, 1975; Masters & Johnson, 1970). In the interests of brevity, I will discuss only the three most common sexual problems: erectile difficulties, premature ejaculation, and orgasmic difficulties in women.

The discussion will center on specific arousal techniques that have proved worthwhile for many couples. First, it should be emphasized that mechanically following certain arousal procedures will not guarantee success. Do not forget that the mind is the ultimate erogenous zone. In the final analysis, communication, cooperation, and a positive mental set are more important than positions and procedures.

ERECTILE DIFFICULTIES

The key to overcoming psychologically based erectile difficulties is to decrease the male partner's anxiety about performance and then restore his confidence in his sexual response. It is usually a good idea for the man to bring the problem out in the open and make clear to his female partner that it is not lack of affection for her that is causing the difficulties. It is crucial that the woman be supportive and sympathetic rather than hostile and demanding.

12.4

RECOMMENDED READING
Books That May Help You Improve Your Sex Life

With the new-found emphasis on achieving sexual satisfaction, more and more people are interested in reading books designed to help them cope with problems or spice up their sex life. Many of the available books are of inferior quality, but a number of them are potentially worthwhile. Below you will find a brief list of some of the better books.

General Interest
The Joy of Sex: A Gourmet Guide to Lovemaking by Alex Comfort (Simon & Schuster, 1972). This popular best-seller is essentially a "how to" manual that explains an exceptionally wide range of arousal techniques. Its strengths include clever but noncondescending writing, ample illustrations, and a creative variety of topics. It is not as strong on how to deal with specific problems as some other books.

Sexual Awareness: A Practical Approach by Barry McCarthy, Mary Ryan, and Fred Johnson (Boyd & Fraser, 1975). This is a nicely done guide for increasing sexual satisfaction. It places a great deal of emphasis on improving self-awareness.

Making Love: How to Be Your Own Sex Therapist by Patricia Raley (Dial Press, 1976). This is a very personal book that begins by having you take a look at your sexual history and attitudes. It is loaded with probing personal questions for the reader. It devotes a good deal of attention to confronting sexual problems. It is nicely illustrated with many very explicit and erotic photos, and it does not assume that you are heterosexual.

For Women with Orgasmic Difficulties
For Yourself: The Fulfillment of Female Sexuality by Lonnie G. Barbach (Doubleday, 1975). Barbach has written a sensitive, flexible book for women troubled by orgasmic difficulties. The book is laced with warm anecdotes that should help the reader feel more comfortable with this touchy topic. The book examines the reasons for the repression of female sexuality and offers a therapeutic program centering on self-stimulation.

Becoming Orgasmic: A Sexual Growth Program for Women by Julia Heiman, Leslie LoPiccolo, and Joseph LoPiccolo (Prentice-Hall,

1976). Joseph LoPiccolo was a pioneer in the therapeutic use of self-stimulation for women. This book is very thorough and covers a wide range of topics. The writing style is low-key but maybe a little less personal than that of Barbach's book.

For Those Who Want to Reassess Their Sexual Values
Sex without Guilt by Albert Ellis (Lyle Stuart, 1958). If you believe you are troubled by an excessively negative sexual value system, it may help to read a book that persuasively advocates more liberal attitudes about sex. Ellis, the architect of rational-emotive therapy, does a nice job of challenging traditional repressive views of sex. Although quite old, the book remains somewhat controversial.

Sex after the Sexual Revolution by Helen Colton (Association Press, 1972). This book also focuses primarily on sexual ethics. It provides a penetrating analysis of how our attitudes are acquired and why sexual values are changing. It's a good book for helping you to think out your own sexual value system.

SENSATE FOCUS. *A sex-therapy procedure wherein partners take turns pleasuring each other with guided verbal feedback. It is often done with certain kinds of stimulation temporarily prohibited.*

Masters and Johnson suggest something called **sensate focus** as an early part of the treatment of erectile difficulties. In sensate-focus exercises, one partner caresses the other, who simply lies back and enjoys it, while giving the first partner instructions and feedback about what feels good. The partners take turns, alternately giving and receiving stimulation. In the early phases, they are usually forbidden to touch the genitals. Attempts at intercourse are also forbidden. Sensate focus encourages communication between the partners, increases their appreciation for nongenital foreplay, and helps each to learn what the partner likes.

It is hoped that the prescription against genital stimulation and intercourse will free the male partner from feelings of pressure to perform. He doesn't have a *need* or *duty* to achieve an erection. With this pressure removed, many men find that they get aroused quite spontaneously.

Eventually, over a number of sexual encounters, the couple start including genital stimulation in their sensate focus, but coitus remains banned. Verbal feedback about what feels good should continue. With appropriate genital stimulation and a continued lack of pressure, *most* men will begin to experience erections. Attempts to put these to use immediately in intercourse remain prohibited. Instead, stimulation should be halted briefly, so that the erection subsides. Then stimulation should be renewed so that arousal occurs once again. Repeated arousals in a single session can convince a man that his erection is not "lost for the evening" when it first withers.

When the man has begun to regain confidence in his sexual response, the couple may proceed to intromission. The relaxed nature of the side-by-side position is often optimal for these initial attempts, and it is usually best if the woman handles the penile insertion. In many cases it is a good idea to lie still and simply appreciate the continued erection. If the arousal remains stable, the couple can progress to actual intercourse. At this point, the man should be allowed to be "selfish" and focus exclusively on his own arousal. For many men, all it takes is a couple of successful encounters, and their confidence is restored.

PREMATURE EJACULATION

Men troubled by "premature" ejaculation may range from those who climax almost instantly to those who are unable to last the 10 to 15 minutes that their partner requires. In the latter case there are a number of simple things that can be done.

1. It helps to reduce muscular tension in the male. The popular "missionary position" tends to do the opposite: it maximizes tension. Hence, it's a good idea to use other positions in order to try to delay the male's climax.

2. Often it helps if you simply slow down the coital movements. This may be particularly valuable if the man can learn to recognize when ejaculation is near. If he can learn the physical sensations that signal an impending climax, he can pause altogether for a few moments, and the impulse may pass.

3. This problem can sometimes be solved indirectly by discarding the traditional coital model, which prescribes that orgasms must come through intercourse only. If the female partner is responsive to oral or manual stimulation, these can be used to provide her with a climax either before or after the coitus. Sometimes, if couples change their attitudes about intercourse being the main event, this reduces the pressure on the male, and they may find that coitus starts lasting longer. There is also something to be said for having two or more encounters in a single "session" of sex. After the initial orgasm, most men will climax more slowly in subsequent efforts at intercourse.

The squeeze technique is a procedure that has proved useful to many men troubled by virtually instant ejaculation, as well as many others who have simply been interested in learning to delay their climax. In this procedure, the female partner stimulates the male until he feels near ejaculation. When he is on the verge of orgasm, he signals his partner, and she halts stimulation and firmly squeezes the tip of the penis for a few seconds. With proper timing and application, this squeeze should prevent the forthcoming ejaculation, usually with some resulting loss in the erection. After waiting a brief period, the couple can then repeat the entire procedure. In severe cases, this procedure may be repeated frequently over a period of several weeks. This deceptively simple procedure can be useful in several ways. It helps the male learn to recognize preorgasmic sensations accurately and it gets the couple communicating and cooperating on a mutual problem. Most important, it helps the male to gradually learn ejaculatory self-control.

ORGASMIC DIFFICULTIES IN WOMEN

Females' orgasmic difficulties are often rooted in an exceedingly negative sexual value system. When this is the case, a restructuring of one's values may be crucial to conquering this problem. There are also some specific procedures that may help women either to make the initial orgasmic breakthrough or to increase their orgasmic consistency.

It is usually recommended that women who have never had an orgasm try to make their initial breakthrough with noncoital techniques. Self-stimulation is usually the key to this effort. Many previously nonorgasmic women who have never experimented with masturbation are surprised to find that they can achieve orgasms through self-stimulation. Some excellent books (see Box 12.4) offer elaborate suggestions about how to make self-stimulation a rewarding, guilt-free experience. In many cases, after the initial breakthrough is made, the orgasmic responsiveness can be transferred to interactions with one's partner.

Some women are troubled by orgasmic difficulties only in the context of coitus. If the partners are not locked into a coital model of sex, this need not be seen as a problem. However, since most couples are eager to experience orgasms through traditional intercourse, this pattern is usually viewed as a problem.

The sensate-focus exercises that are useful for men with erectile difficulties may also be valuable for women troubled by secondary orgasmic difficulties. The communication in the sensate-focus exercise can greatly improve the male's understanding of what his female partner desires in the way of erotic stimulation. Practicing the sensate focus can also reduce spectatoring tendencies in the woman, which may be undermining her orgasmic responsiveness. As the sensate focus proceeds gradually to genital stimulation, it is often a good idea for the female to take the male's hand in hers and show him exactly what kind of caressing she likes. Additional strategies that may increase the probability of coital orgasms include the following.

- It is often best if the woman decides when she is ready for intromission. She knows when her arousal is peaking better than the male.
- It is a good idea to use the female-above position. In addition to providing good clitoral stimulation, it allows the woman to control the thrusting in whatever way she finds most pleasurable.
- If desired, there is no reason that manual stimulation of the clitoral area cannot be included in a coital encounter.

CHAPTER 12 REVIEW

IDEAS: REVIEW OF LEARNING OBJECTIVES

When you have mastered the material in this chapter, you should be able to do the following.

1. Describe three problems in doing research on sexual behavior.
2. List and describe four key aspects of sexual identity.
3. Explain how physiological factors may influence the development of sexual identity.
4. List and discuss three psychosocial sources of influence on sexual identity.
5. Provide some examples of differing motives that may propel people into sexual relationships.
6. Describe five common sexual scripts in our culture.
7. Discuss the role of negotiation in sexual interactions.
8. Briefly describe the four phases in the human sexual response cycle.
9. Discuss three reasons that women tend to reach orgasm less frequently than men in coitus.
10. Describe sex differences in regard to the postorgasmic refractory period and multiple orgasms.
11. Discuss the role of fantasy in sexual arousal.
12. Discuss attitudes about self-stimulation.
13. Summarize data on the prevalence of self-stimulation.
14. Explain why foreplay is a source of discord for some couples.
15. Discuss the importance of sexual positions in coitus.
16. Summarize data on the prevalence of oral and anal sex.
17. Evaluate the concept of "the sexual revolution."
18. Summarize data on the prevalence of premarital sex.
19. Describe four attitudes toward premarital sex.
20. Discuss the link between marital and sexual satisfaction.
21. List some changes in marital sexual practices since the Kinsey studies.
22. Explain the impact of age on marital sexual activity.
23. Describe three types of extramarital sexual relationships.
24. Summarize data on the prevalence of extramarital sex.
25. List four common motivations for extramarital sex.
26. Describe primary and secondary erectile difficulties.
27. Discuss the causes of erectile difficulties in men.
28. Explain why it is difficult to define premature ejaculation.
29. Discuss the causes of premature ejaculation.
30. Describe primary and secondary orgasmic difficulties.
31. Discuss the causes of orgasmic difficulties in women.
32. Discuss the nature and causes of inhibited sexual desire.
33. List six general suggestions for improving sexual functioning.
34. Describe sensate-focus exercises.
35. Describe strategies for coping with erectile difficulties.
36. Describe strategies for overcoming problems with premature ejaculation.
37. Describe strategies for overcoming female orgasmic difficulties.

TERMS: REVIEW OF NEW VOCABULARY

When you have mastered the material in this chapter, you should be able to define the following terms.

Anal sex
Autoeroticism
Bisexual
Coitus
Cunnilingus
Ejaculation
Erectile difficulties

Erogenous zone
Fellatio
Foreplay
Inhibited sexual desire
Intromission
Orgasm
Orgasmic difficulties

Premature ejaculation
Refractory period
Script
Secondary sex
  characteristics
Sensate focus
Sex therapy

Sexual dysfunction
Sexual identity
Spectatoring
Transsexual
Vasocongestion

PEOPLE: REVIEW OF MAJOR THEORISTS AND RESEARCHERS

When you have mastered the material in this chapter, you should be able to summarize the principal contributions and/or ideas of the following people.

Morton Hunt
Helen S. Kaplan

Kinsey and associates

Masters and Johnson

Ira Reiss

Crisis and Growth

PART

PSYCHOLOGICAL DISORDERS

Summary

Applying Psychology to Your Life: Understanding and Preventing Suicide

INCIDENCE OF SUICIDE

MYTHS ABOUT SUICIDE

EVALUATING SUICIDAL POTENTIAL

PREVENTING SUICIDE

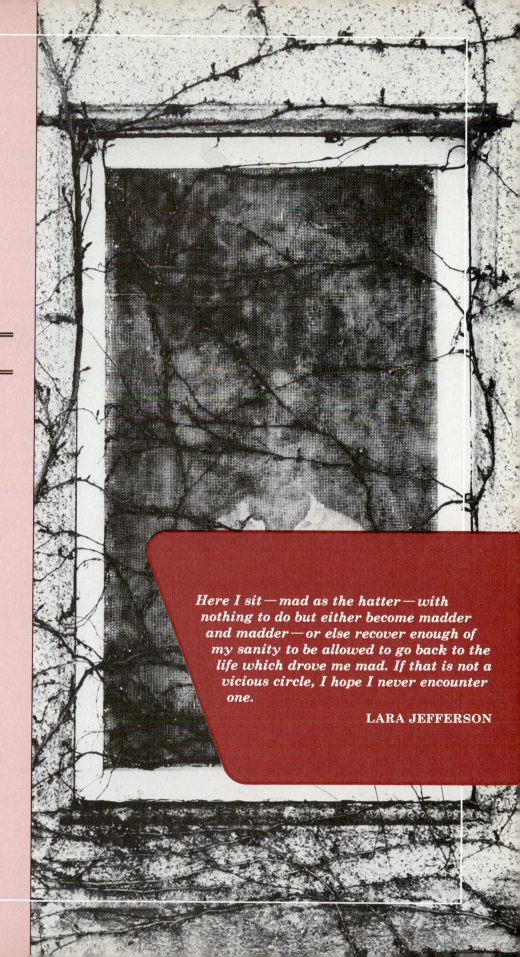

Here I sit — mad as the hatter — with nothing to do but either become madder and madder — or else recover enough of my sanity to be allowed to go back to the life which drove me mad. If that is not a vicious circle, I hope I never encounter one.

LARA JEFFERSON

A main premise of this book is that at one time or another every one of us has to struggle with psychological problems. Thus far I have directed your attention to common problems that most of us are likely to encounter in everyday life. For instance, I've talked about frustration, conflict, pressure, self-control, and loneliness; I've analyzed difficulties in communication, intimate relationships, sexuality, and vocational progress. I am now going to consider a less common class of problems, often called "psychological disorders." These disorders are relatively tough, sometimes overwhelming challenges to one's adjustment. Though less common than the "everyday" problems I've discussed up until now, they are far more widespread than most people realize. In their milder forms they are *not* rare. No one is immune to psychological disorders. Consequently, a thorough understanding of the full range of the adjustment process cannot be achieved without looking at how psychological disorders develop and progress.

I will begin my coverage of psychological disorders by discussing some preliminary issues. I will clarify the nature of psychological disorders, take a look at the "medical model" of such disorders, and try to sort out other, related issues. The bulk of the chapter will be devoted to describing particular disorders and analyzing their causes. At the end of the chapter, in the application section, I will examine the tragic phenomenon of suicide.

Preliminary Issues

Misconceptions about psychological disorders abound. Therefore, before describing the various types of psychological disorders and their development, I need to clear up some preliminary issues. This section will address three important questions: What are psychological disorders, how common are they, and what is the role of psychodiagnosis?

WHAT ARE PSYCHOLOGICAL DISORDERS?

What exactly are psychological disorders? This is a deceptively simple question. We have a great number of terms that we use almost interchangeably when we discuss psychological disorders. We talk about psychopathology, mental illness, deviance, abnormality, and maladaptive behavior. In less formal terms, we refer to people as "crazy," "deranged," "nuts," and "insane." The great variety of terms used is probably attributable to the fact that psychological disorders encompass a great variety of very different kinds of problems. There are a number of distinct reasons that people may be said to have a psychological disorder. In a moment, I will discuss some of the more common criteria used in labeling people as disordered. Please note that I am *not* going to provide you with a *definition* of psychological disorders. The matter is too complex for a simple definition. In lieu of a definition, I will describe the criteria of mental illness.

CRITERIA OF PSYCHOLOGICAL DISORDERS

No single criterion for diagnosing mental illness is applicable to all cases and situations. I will list the four most common criteria of psychological disorders. Sometimes these criteria are overlapping in that all four might apply to a particular case. However, people are often labeled disordered when only one criterion is met.

Social deviance. Often people are labeled psychologically disordered because their behavior deviates in significant ways from what their society considers normal or acceptable (Ullmann & Krasner, 1975). Although norms regarding appropriate behavior vary somewhat from one culture to another, all societies have such norms. When people ignore these standards and expecta-

TRANSVESTITISM. *A psychological disorder wherein a person achieves sexual arousal by dressing in the clothing of the opposite sex.*

tions, they may be labeled mentally ill. For example, **transvestitism** is considered a psychological disorder because a man who wears a dress, brassiere, and nylons is deviating from our culture's norms.

Personal distress. Often people get themselves labeled mentally ill because they report that they are subjectively experiencing great personal distress (Goldstein, Baker, & Jamison, 1980). This is often the criterion met by people who are troubled by anxiety or depression. These people go to mental-health professionals and indicate that they are suffering from psychological pain of some kind.

Maladaptive behavior. Often people are judged to have a psychological disorder because their behavior prevents optimal or even reasonable functioning (Coleman, Butcher, & Carson, 1984). For example, a person who stays home most of the time because of his or her **agoraphobia** obviously cannot lead a very full life. This person's behavior is not so much deviant as it is maladaptive. It interferes with what is considered normal functioning. Similarly, people who are dependent on drugs are said to be disordered because their addiction is maladaptive.

AGORAPHOBIA. *A fear of being in open or public places.*

Irrationality. Often it is the irrational nature of a person's behavior that leads to the diagnosis of a psychological disorder (Reiss et al., 1977). If you were to insist that you have been fighting space wars with vampires for centuries, people would doubt your contact with reality. You would undoubtedly be labeled abnormal. We regard people as mentally ill when their thoughts or behavior don't make sense to us.

As you can see, there are several criteria that may be applied in diagnosing psychological disorders. *You should be aware that all these criteria involve value judgments that depend on one's culture or personal background.* Behavior that appears irrational or maladaptive to one person may seem quite reasonable to another. Behavior that is considered deviant in one society may be quite acceptable in another. A problem that creates great personal distress for one person might not merit a raised eyebrow from another. Thus, there are

Agoraphobia, a fear of public places, is more widespread than most people realize.

no "value-free" criteria of psychological disorders, just as there are no value-free criteria of psychological health.

THE MEDICAL MODEL OF PSYCHOLOGICAL DISORDERS

Does it make sense to view a psychological disorder as a disease? This is a very controversial question. *The medical model proposes that it is useful to view psychological disorders as if they were diseases or sicknesses.* This view is the basis for the term *mental illness.* The medical model has been the dominant conception of psychological disorders for quite a long time, having gained acceptance in the 18th and 19th centuries.

The advent of the medical model clearly represented progress over earlier models of disordered behavior. Previous models were largely moralistic. People who behaved strangely were thought to be witches, possessed by demons, or victims of God's punishment. Their disorders were "treated" by chants, rituals, exorcisms, and so forth. When their behavior was exceptionally bizarre, they were candidates for chains, dungeons, torture, and death (see Figure 13.1). With the rise of the medical model, treatment of people with psychological disorders changed drastically. As victims of illness or disease, they were offered sympathy and relatively humane treatment instead of barbaric cruelty. Ineffectual efforts at treatment, such as exorcism, gradually gave way to scientific investigation of the causes and cures of mental illness. Thus, the medical model clearly constituted an advance over previously primitive conceptual models.

In recent years, however, the medical model has been attacked for a variety of reasons. Critics suggest that it may have outlived its usefulness. A particularly vocal critic has been Thomas Szasz, author of *The Myth of Mental Illness* (1961). Szasz argues that abnormal behavior involves a deviation from social norms rather than an illness. He contends that such deviations involve moral and social problems rather than medical problems. According to Szasz, the medical model converts ethical questions about what is acceptable behavior into medical questions. Under the guise of "healing the sick," this conversion allows societies to incarcerate deviants and enforce their norms of conformity. Thus, Szasz maintains that psychological disorders are really "problems in living" rather than illnesses.

The medical model has been criticized on other grounds as well (Korchin, 1976). Among other problems, the following are consistently noted.

1. The medical model implies that psychological disorders are caused mainly by biological malfunctions. Although biological factors often play a role in psychological disorders, psychological and social factors are extremely important in a majority of cases. Strict adherence to the medical model may lead some clinicians to overlook the potentially crucial role of social and psychological factors.

2. The medical model encourages victims of psychological disorders to adopt the passive role of patient. In this passive role they wait for someone else to do the work to effect a cure. This passivity can be problematic even when an illness is purely physical. In psychological disorders, such passivity can be fatal to any hopes of therapeutic gains. Generally, people with psychological problems have to be actively involved in therapeutic efforts, or there is little hope for improvement.

3. The medical model suggests erroneously that judgments about psychological disorders are value-free. I have already discussed the fact that this is not true. The popularity of this misconception is attributable to the widespread notion that psychological disorders are diseases.

So, what position will this chapter take in regard to the medical model? An intermediate position, neither accepting nor discarding the model entirely. Undoubtedly, there are significant problems with the medical model. In spite of these problems, however, the disease model is not easy to replace. Other pro-

FIGURE 13.1 One common "cure" for demon possession was burning.

posed models also have significant flaws. For example, Szasz's concept of "problems of living" is hopelessly vague. This conceptual category could include anything from severe schizophrenia to difficulties in beating rush-hour traffic.

My position is that the disease analogy is useful, as long as one understands that it is only an analogy. I fully concur with Szasz that most psychological disorders are not really diseases. However, I believe that systematic analysis of psychological disorders *can* be facilitated by using medical concepts such as etiology, prognosis, and therapy. Even clinicians who decry the medical model turn around and use this terminology.

The crucial consideration here is that you remember that the medical/disease model is only an analogy. Bear in mind that psychological disorders are not actually illnesses. They usually are not caused by physiological factors exclusively. The passive role of medical patient is not well suited to psychotherapy. Evaluations of psychological disorders are not value-free. And finally, treatment of psychological disorders is not the exclusive province of physicians.

MYTHS ABOUT PSYCHOLOGICAL DISORDERS

The above discussion of the medical model should have cleared up some misconceptions that you may have held about psychological disorders. However, there are still other myths about mental illness that need to be exposed as such. I will review four myths about abnormal behavior discussed by Kazdin (1980) and/or Kleinmuntz (1980).

Myth 1: People with psychological disorders are very bizarre and very different. This is true only in a small minority of cases, usually involving relatively severe disorders. Most people with psychological disorders are indistinguishable from the rest of us. There is a fine line between normal and abnormal behavior. This line is not easily drawn. It is difficult to specify just how depressed one has to be to have a mood disorder or just how paranoid one has to be to have a paranoid disorder or just how dependent on drugs one has to be to have a substance-abuse disorder. Even mental-health professionals may have difficulty distinguishing normal from abnormal behavior (Rosenhan, 1973).

Myth 2: People with psychological disorders are often violent and dangerous. This is true only very rarely. In fact, mentally ill people may not be any more violence-prone than the rest of the population. This myth exists because the occasional incidents of violence involving the mentally ill tend to get a great deal of media attention.

Myth 3: Psychological disorders should be a source of shame. People tend to see a psychological disorder as a manifestation of personal weakness. This leads many people to feel very ashamed and guilty when they develop such an affliction. In reality, psychological disorders are a function of many considerations—genetic predisposition, family background, social background, and so forth—over which we have little or no control. The mentally ill should not be blamed for their disorders any more than people are blamed for developing leukemia or cancer. One should not feel ashamed of a psychological disorder; mental illness can strike anyone.

Myth 4: Psychological disorders are incurable. Admittedly, there are significant numbers of mentally ill people for whom treatment is largely a failure. However, they are greatly outnumbered by people who *do* get better, either spontaneously or through treatment. Even the most debilitating psychological disorders *can* be treated successfully. The next chapter will discuss the various modes of treatment and their relative merits.

HOW COMMON ARE PSYCHOLOGICAL DISORDERS?

Solid information on the frequency of psychological disorders is not available. All the relevant studies have some sampling problems, and they vary greatly in their criteria of mental illness. Therefore, one can make only very rough estimates of the prevalence of psychological disorders in American culture.

These estimates tend to startle many people, and it is fair to say that *psychological disorders are more common than most people believe.* The best studies available suggest that about one-fifth of the population exhibits clear signs of psychological disorders while, at the other end of the continuum, about one-fifth appears to merit a clean bill of health (Altrocchi, 1980). Think about those figures for a moment. They suggest that four-fifths of the population is troubled by at least a moderate disturbance! Raw numbers are just as surprising. As of 1978 it was estimated that the United States contained 1 million people with schizophrenic disorders, 2 million severely depressed people, 6 million emotionally disturbed children, 10 million alcoholics, 20 million neurotics, and over 53 million people with mild to moderate depression (Coleman et al., 1980).

Although these figures are only crude estimates, it is clear that psychological disorders—in their milder forms, at least—are quite common. As you can see, when I said that mental illness can strike anyone, I meant it seriously and literally.

WHAT IS THE ROLE OF CLASSIFICATION AND DIAGNOSIS?

During the past hundred years, a great deal of research effort has been invested in devising elaborate systems for classifying psychological disorders. This work began in the 19th century with pioneering efforts by Emil Kraepelin, Eugen Bleuler, and Sigmund Freud. A modern landmark was reached in 1952 when the American Psychiatric Association unveiled its *Diagnostic and Statistical Manual of Mental Disorders,* known more briefly as DSM-I. This was a fairly thorough classification system describing some 60 disorders. A revised version (DSM-II), expanded to cover 145 disorders, was issued in 1968.

After much field testing, the current version (DSM-III) was officially put to work in 1980. Expanded still further, it describes over 200 kinds of disorders.

NEUROSIS. *A class of disorders in DSM-II involving mild to moderately severe disturbances in functioning; marked by ineffective, defensive efforts to cope with anxiety.*

Some changes in this most recent version have triggered considerable controversy. For instance, the time-honored and widely used term **neurosis** has been discarded. The architects of the new system decided that the ten different neuroses described in DSM-II didn't have enough in common to merit a single label. Accordingly, they broke up the old grouping into several new categories and dumped the term *neurosis*. Another source of controversy is the inclusion of many new problems not conventionally thought of as forms of mental illness. For example, DSM-III includes conditions such as a shyness disorder, an academic underachievement disorder, a tobacco-use disorder (distress derived from excessive smoking), and caffeinism (dependence on coffee). Critics argue that problems such as these should not be defined as illnesses. However, critics of the *old* system (DSM-II) complained because it omitted many problems such as these which were in fact being treated by clinicians.

These debates vividly illustrate an important point that I have made repeatedly. Assessments of psychological disorders are *not* value-free. In spite of this controversy, I will largely follow the DSM-III system in describing the various kinds of psychological disorders. As long as one remembers that the disease analogy is only an analogy, there is much to be said for the more comprehensive approach of DSM-III. The new system is also an improvement in certain technical ways, which I shall discuss as this chapter progresses. Before I begin these descriptions, however, I need to address certain problems inherent in any effort at classification and diagnosis.

PROBLEMS WITH PSYCHODIAGNOSIS

PSYCHODIAGNOSIS. *The task or process of identifying and classifying psychological disorders.*

The entire enterprise of **psychodiagnosis,** whether it be based on DSM-I, II, or III, has long been under assault from a number of vantage points. I will discuss three lines of criticism.

Labeling. First, some critics (Goffman, 1961; Laing, 1967) are troubled by the fact that diagnosis necessarily involves pinning potentially derogatory labels on people. Unfortunately, these labels can become self-fulfilling prophecies. Some people labeled paranoid or alcoholic seem to accept the designation and proceed to live out the role created for them. Many of these labels also carry a social stigma that is difficult to shake. Someone labeled as an addict or schizophrenic may, even after a full recovery, have difficulty in finding work or even friends. Others may relate to such a person with caution and distrust. This prejudice against people labeled mentally ill can further complicate the problems they already have.

Pseudo explanations. Other critics (Ullmann & Krasner, 1975) argue that the technical-sounding medical labels used in psychodiagnosis create an illusion that we understand more than we really do. For instance, let's say a fellow arrives in a psychologist's office exhibiting schizophrenic symptoms such as withdrawal, inappropriate emotion, delusions, and hallucinations. He is diagnosed as schizophrenic. Later, his bewildered family asks "Doctor, why does he behave in these strange ways?" The doctor may often reply "Because he is schizophrenic." That explanation may *sound* reasonable, but it is really a pseudo explanation produced by circular reasoning. It is *not* accurate to say that he is withdrawn, delusional, and hallucinatory *because* he is schizophrenic. Quite the opposite is true. He is schizophrenic because he is withdrawn, delusional, and hallucinatory. Schizophrenia is only a descriptive category; it is not an explanation.

Lack of reliability. Numerous studies (Beck, 1962; Spitzer & Wilson, 1980) indicate that psychodiagnosis is not nearly as reliable as we would like ideally. Recall from Chapter 2 that reliability refers to consistency in measurement or, in this case, diagnosis. Research shows that clinicians *often* disagree on the appropriate diagnosis for a particular person. Whereas the more severe disorders can be diagnosed with reasonable reliability, the milder disorders tend to generate much disagreement. This technical problem may be partly remedied by the new diagnostic system. A major goal of DSM-III was to provide more specific, elaborate, detailed, and objective diagnostic criteria so as to improve diagnostic reliability.

VALUE OF PSYCHODIAGNOSIS

Because of the problems discussed in the previous section, many theorists advocate abandoning the diagnostic enterprise altogether. Admittedly, the questions they raise are serious ones; in particular, the problems associated with labeling are especially worrisome. However, I believe that it would be an overreaction to renounce all efforts at classification and diagnosis.

In spite of its flaws, psychodiagnosis has great value. Maher (1970) points out that *a classification system is a prerequisite for scientific research on any topic, including psychological disorders.* We saw in Chapter 1 that the first goal of science is measurement and description. A classification system provides this measurement and description, which are *essential* to moving forward toward an understanding of the phenomena under study. One cannot lump all psychological disorders together without giving up all hope of understanding them better.

Additionally, *a sound classification system can serve three very important purposes* (Goldstein et al., 1980). Armed with a diagnosis, a clinician can make learned, empirically based guesses about (1) the probable causes, or etiology, of the disorder, (2) the likely future course of the disorder (prognosis), and (3) the optimal therapeutic treatment for the disorder. Although these analyses are admittedly conjectural, they are certainly better than nothing, which is what a clinician would have without a diagnostic system.

In conclusion, there is little to be gained by abandoning psychodiagnosis. People who behaved strangely were stigmatized long before DSM-I, II, and III were developed. Pseudo explanations of psychological disorders were even more prevalent, and more primitive, before the advent of modern psychodiagnosis. Rather than giving up on psychodiagnosis, we must confront the challenge of improving it.

THE SCOPE OF OUR COVERAGE

I am now ready to start describing the various forms of psychological disorders. My primary goal in the rest of the chapter will be to acquaint you with how these disorders may *develop.* This is the issue that is most relevant to our topic, the dynamics of adjustment. Therefore, the descriptions of the disorders themselves will be as brief as possible. This will allow us to focus more on the etiology of the disorders. **Etiology** is a technical term for how a disorder

---

13.1 THE "MEDICAL STUDENTS' DISEASE"

As you read about the various psychological disorders described in this chapter, you may begin to see some of yourself in the descriptions. You may come to the startling and disconcerting conclusion that you have a phobic disorder or a problem with paranoia or schizophrenic characteristics. If this happens, *don't* be alarmed. This is a common tendency when reading about patterns of mental illness. Most people probably go through it to some extent. In fact, it is a common tendency with physical disorders as well. Medical students often feel that they are coming down with many of the diseases that they learn about. Thus, this affliction is often called the "medical students' disease."

Actually, there is a lesson to be learned from this tendency. It illustrates a point made repeatedly throughout this chapter—that the line between "normality" and "abnormality" is a very slender one, which is quite difficult to draw.

ETIOLOGY. *The apparent causation or developmental history of a disorder.*

appears to have developed. Although there are many paths that may lead to a particular psychological disorder, some are more common than others. I will try to identify some of these common paths for you, so that you can better understand the stress and strain of the adjustment process.

Coverage of the different kinds of psychological disorders will not be exhaustive. Because of space limitations, I will omit some kinds of disorders that are only of borderline relevance to the thematic orientation of this book. For example, I will not discuss mental disorders that have a purely organic (physical) basis. Nor will I cover childhood disorders or psychosexual disorders. The role of psychological factors in physical disease was already covered in Chapter 4, and so I will not tackle that issue here. In spite of these omissions, I will describe a wide range of problems, including the following eight classes of disorders: (1) anxiety disorders, (2) somatoform disorders, (3) dissociative disorders, (4) mood disorders, (5) schizophrenic disorders, (6) paranoid disorders, (7) personality disorders, and (8) substance-use disorders.

Anxiety Disorders

We all experience anxiety from time to time. As discussed in Chapter 3, anxiety is a natural and common emotional reaction to many kinds of stress. For some people, however, anxiety becomes a chronic problem. These people experience excessive levels of anxiety with disturbing regularity. More important, their intense anxiety states generally tend to have an irrational quality to them: the anxiety does not seem appropriate to the circumstances.

SPECIFIC SYNDROMES

ANXIETY DISORDERS. *Disturbances wherein behavior is dominated by feelings of tension and apprehension; includes phobic, obsessive-compulsive, and generalized anxiety disorders. All these were classified as neuroses in DSM-II.*

The **anxiety disorders** include three syndromes that were previously known as neuroses (in DSM-I and II). Although the behavioral manifestations of the specific syndromes can be quite different, they share continuity in that one's behavior comes to be dominated by anxiety.

GENERALIZED ANXIETY DISORDER

GENERALIZED ANXIETY DISORDER. *An anxiety disorder marked by a chronic, high level of tension and apprehension.*

The **generalized anxiety disorder** involves a chronic, high level of anxiety that is not tied to any specific threat. Because of its nonspecific nature, this anxiety is often called "free-floating anxiety." People with this disorder worry constantly about yesterday's mistakes and tomorrow's problems. They hate having to confront decisions, and they brood perpetually about the decisions that they do make. Their incessant worry is often accompanied by physiological symptoms, including sustained muscular tension, diarrhea, and high blood pressure. Insomnia and nightmares are common. Some of these people are prone to anxiety attacks, wherein they are suddenly overwhelmed by an extremely intense state of panic that typically is brief.

13.2 *PERSONAL EXPERIENCE: GENERALIZED ANXIETY DISORDER*

At times I felt that it would never stop. It hurt, like a burning in my guts . . . like a knife ripping away at my flesh . . . like a scream inside me that couldn't get out. I couldn't sit still, I walked around the house, looked at the walls, tore up magazines. I would start to cry, then choke back the tears 'cause they frightened me more. I thought that I was falling apart. I can remember hearing Mary [his wife] say something to me. I yelled at her to go away. God . . . I can't even talk about it without feeling scared. It's like being afraid of something so terrible that no power in the world can help you. It's like being sure that you are going to die a horrible death and knowing that it is going to happen today. It's worse than dying, I'm sure. I wanted to die to make it stop. The medicine helped a little, but just remembering . . . [excerpted from Duke & Nowicki, 1979, pp. 239–240].

PHOBIC DISORDER

PHOBIC DISORDER. *An anxiety disorder marked by a persistent and irrational fear of an object or situation that presents no realistic danger.*

In a **phobic disorder** the excessive anxiety has a specific focus. A *phobia* is a recurring, irrational fear of some object or situation that doesn't represent a real threat. A phobia can develop about virtually anything (see Table 13.1), but certain phobias are especially common. Particularly frequent is *agoraphobia*, fear of going out into public places. This fear often escalates to the point that people become "prisoners" confined to their homes. Other common phobias include claustrophobia (fear of small, enclosed places), pyrophobia (fear of places catching on fire), ocholophobia (fear of large crowds), and social phobias (fears of particular interpersonal situations). Many people with phobias realize that their fears are irrational, but they feel powerless to prevent them. When confronted by a phobic object, they are likely to react with a severe attack of anxiety.

TABLE 13.1   Some types of phobias

Acrophobia	Fear of high places	Nyctophobia	Fear of darkness
Agoraphobia	Fear of open spaces	Ombrophobia	Fear of rain
Androphobia	Fear of men	Pathophobia	Fear of disease
Aviophobia	Fear of flying	Phobophobia	Fear of fear
Claustrophobia	Fear of closed or narrow spaces	Sitophobia	Fear of food
Hydrophobia	Fear of water	Thanatophobia	Fear of death
Iatrophobia	Fear of doctors	Toxophobia	Fear of being poisoned
Lalophobia	Fear of speaking (in public)	Xenophobia	Fear of strangers
Mysophobia	Fear of dirt or contamination		

OBSESSIVE-COMPULSIVE DISORDER

OBSESSIVE-COMPULSIVE DISORDER. *An anxiety disorder marked by persistent intrusions of unwanted thoughts (obsessions) and uncontrollable urges to engage in certain actions (compulsions).*

The defining feature of an **obsessive-compulsive disorder** is the presence of obsessions and/or compulsions. Obsessions are thoughts that repeatedly intrude on one's consciousness in a distressing fashion. Compulsions are actions that one feels compelled to carry out repeatedly. Obsessions and compulsions usually appear as a dual package, but not always. Obsessions often center on inflicting harm on others, suicide, or sexual acts considered immoral. People bothered by obsessions quite understandably feel that they have lost control of their thought processes or their mind. As you can readily imagine, this is a disturbing feeling, which arouses great anxiety. Compulsions typically involve senseless rituals that temporarily relieve anxiety. Common examples include frequent handwashing, tying a tie a certain number of times, or repetitively cleaning things that are already clean.

13.3 *PERSONAL EXPERIENCE: OBSESSIVE-COMPULSIVE DISORDER*

I can tell you how it is when I'm being obsessive. It is a tiring experience. I've always been an organizer ... so that from the time I get up in the morning until I go to sleep at night I'm thinking about what's going to happen. I worry, but I can take it and it's not too bad ... but it's when those terrible thoughts come into my head that I become afraid. The thoughts are all different, and they're sickening and terrible. Like when I was outside with my child, I thought of what would happen if my metal rake slipped and flew over and hit my child in the head. I don't know why I would think of this. It made me feel like a crazy person, and then I'm worried sick the rest of the day that I'm going to think that thought again. Here's another example of what I mean. While eating dinner the thought suddenly came to me ... how would it look if I drove my fork through the eye of my husband ... I mean my husband's eye. I can see the fork puncture the eye and the liquid squirts out ... and then I break out in a cold sweat and have to leave the table. Why in God's name would I think such things? I love my child and my husband. I'm a kind person ... I go to church ... It makes me feel crazy and different. Even telling you makes me feel weird about myself [excerpted from Duke & Nowicki, 1979, p. 255].

ETIOLOGY

PHYSIOLOGICAL FACTORS

At present, there is no clear evidence that genetic or biological factors contribute to the development of the anxiety disorders (Rosenthal, 1970). However, many theorists *suspect* that genetically inherited differences in autonomic nervous system (ANS) sensitivity may affect susceptibility to these disorders (Martin, 1971). According to this notion, people with a highly reactive ANS would be particularly vulnerable to anxiety-related problems. There is also an interesting theory (Seligman, 1971) that humans are programmed by their evolutionary history so as to be predisposed to develop phobias to particular classes of stimuli (for example, snakes, heights). Although these conjectural analyses appear quite plausible, it seems likely that physiological factors play only a small role in the origin of anxiety disorders.

PSYCHOLOGICAL FACTORS

Child-rearing considerations. Many people are predisposed to anxiety disorders by events in their childhood (Kleinmuntz, 1980). There are many ways in which parents can inadvertently foster anxiety in their offspring. One way is by a simple *modeling* effect. For example, if a father hides in a closet every time it storms, his children are quite likely to acquire an intense fear of storms (astraphobia). Some parents, often trying to live out their ambitions vicariously through their children, place excessive demands on their daughters and sons. Because these overly demanding parents are rarely satisfied with their kids' performance, the children develop feelings of inadequacy and inferiority, often accompanied by anxiety. Parents who are overprotective may prevent their children from acquiring needed social skills. This lack of social finesse may be a source of great anxiety later in life.

Conditioning. Many of our fears and anxieties are probably *acquired* through respondent conditioning and then *maintained* through operant conditioning (Mowrer, 1947). According to this analysis, an originally neutral stimulus (let's say an elevator) is paired with a frightening event (let's say it suddenly drops half a floor) and thus becomes a conditioned stimulus eliciting anxiety. The person then starts avoiding the anxiety-producing stimulus of elevators, and this avoidance response is reinforced by anxiety reduction. Thus, an elevator phobia might be acquired and maintained through conditioning processes. This analysis is undermined by research (Marks, 1977) showing that most people with phobias *cannot* recall or identify a traumatic conditioning experience that led to the phobia. However, this failure may be attributable to repressive efforts or to poor memory of childhood trauma buried deep in the past.

Conflict. Freud's (1959) theory that inner conflicts may generate excessive anxiety still appears to have merit. Freud saw many patients whose conflicting feelings about sexual behavior led to intense anxiety. Of course, the conflict does not have to center on sexuality. Another potentially anxiety-arousing source of conflict is the desire to trust someone in an intimate relationship, which may be pitted against a fear of getting "burned." Conflict may be particularly important in the development of obsessive-compulsive disorders. Worrisome conflicts may often generate profound feelings of guilt. This guilt, in turn, seems to generate obsessive-compulsive behavior.

Somatoform Disorders

Somatoform disorders involve psychological problems that become manifested in physical symptoms for which no authentic organic basis can be found.

SOMATOFORM DISORDERS. *A group of disturbances wherein some kind of physical symptom is manifested for which no organic cause can be identified, leading to a strong suspicion that the symptom is psychogenic in origin.*

People with somatoform disorders show up initially in the offices of physicians practicing internal medicine or neurology rather than in the offices of psychologists or psychiatrists. These people are *not* faking illness. Patients who are practicing conscious deception are said to be **malingering.** Unlike malingerers, victims of somatoform disorders subjectively experience their symptoms of physical malady. There are a number of closely related syndromes in this category.

SPECIFIC SYNDROMES

SOMATIZATION DISORDER

MALINGERING. *Deliberate faking or exaggeration of an illness for some personal gain.*

SOMATIZATION DISORDER. *A somatoform disorder wherein the person is characterized by a recurrent history of very diverse medical complaints.*

The **somatization disorder** is seen mostly in women who report experiencing a truly spectacular succession of minor physical ailments. They complain regularly but vaguely about a mixed collection of physical problems and usually have a long and complicated history of medical treatment from many physicians. These people are said to "cling to ill health." The distinguishing features are (1) the recurrent history of chronic medical complaints and (2) the *diversity* of the complaints, which eventually implicate nearly every organ system in the body. In somatization, people experience a mixed bag of gastrointestinal, cardiovascular, pulmonary, neurological, respiratory, and genitourinary symptoms. The improbable nature of such a smorgasbord of symptoms is a key diagnostic clue that can alert a physician to the psychological basis for the patient's problems.

CONVERSION DISORDER

CONVERSION DISORDER. *A somatoform disorder in which the person typically experiences a significant loss of physiological function (with no apparent organic basis) in a single organ system.*

People with **conversion disorders** typically produce more extensive simulations of more severe ailments than people suffering from somatization. Their ailments often involve a loss of some normal physiological function, which is usually limited to only one affected organ system. This disorder used to be known as hysterical conversion. That name was based on Freud's belief that the afflicted person was *converting* a sexual conflict into a physical disorder. Although analyses of etiology are more complex today, a variation on the original name has been retained.

In conversion reactions people unconsciously duplicate physical diseases, thus disrupting their lifestyles in significant ways. Common disorders include partial or complete loss of vision, partial or complete loss of hearing, paralysis, tremors, tics, severe laryngitis, mutism, epilepticlike convulsions, respiratory difficulties, and headaches. These disorders appear to be physical, but medical probing fails to uncover any physiological basis for the symptoms. Sometimes these individuals do a "sloppy" job of simulating their disorders. For instance, people who go into epileptic seizures rarely lose bladder control in the manner that authentic epileptics do. (See Figure 13.2 for another example.) These poor simulations can easily be detected and diagnosed as conversion disorders. However, in recent years, the public's increasing medical sophistication has led to better mimicry.

PSYCHOGENIC PAIN DISORDER

PSYCHOGENIC PAIN DISORDER. *A somatoform disorder in which the physical symptoms are limited to chronic pain of unknown origin.*

A syndrome that is very similar to conversion is the **psychogenic pain disorder.** Here, too, patients display physical symptoms that appear to have a psychological, rather than organic, basis. However, in this case there is no loss of function, just inexplicable pain.

HYPOCHONDRIA

Hypochondriacs are excessively preoccupied with their health, which they believe to be quite precarious. They worry constantly about contracting virtually every illness that they've ever heard about. Usually they've heard about

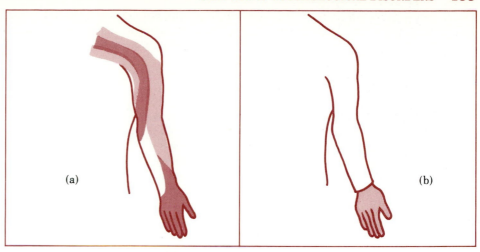

FIGURE 13.2 An example of a conversion disorder: glove anesthesia. A patient who complained of numbness in the hand might be diagnosed as suffering from conversion disorder if the area of the hand affected showed that a disorder of the nervous system was not responsible. The skin areas served by nerves in the arm are shown in (a). The "glove anesthesia" shown in (b) could not result from damage to these nerves.

HYPOCHONDRIA. *A somatoform disorder marked by excessive worry about the possibility of contracting a physical illness and a general preoccupation with health concerns.*

quite a variety of diseases, because they read a great deal of popular medical literature. Hypochondriacs compulsively monitor their physical condition, looking for signs of serious illness. Any tiny alteration from their physical norm leads them to conclude that they have contracted some catastrophic disease. When assured by medical specialists that they do not have a severe illness, they tend to be skeptical and disbelieving. They frequently assume that the physician is incompetent and go shopping for another doctor.

ETIOLOGY

PHYSIOLOGICAL FACTORS

These disorders are influenced by physiological factors in that they often grow out of real illnesses. Hypochondriacal obsessions with health often develop after a serious bout with an authentic illness. Conversion reactions may appear in conjunction with actual physical problems that are greatly exaggerated (Coleman, 1976).

PSYCHOLOGICAL FACTORS

Personality. Certain types of personalities seem to be particularly likely to develop these disorders. People with histrionic personalities (see Table 13.3 on p. 466), characterized by suggestibility, excitability, egocentricity, and excessive dramatization tendencies, are prime candidates for somatoform disorders (Ziegler, 1970).

Avoidance. Manufacturing an illness is a superb way to avoid having to face up to life's stresses. More than anything else, somatoform disorders probably involve efforts to avoid confronting significant problems, such as marital discord, social inadequacies, or career frustrations. When you're sick, others cannot place exacting demands on you.

SECONDARY GAINS. *Benefits derived from adopting the role of ill person, including increased attention and sympathy and a decrease in demands placed on the person.*

Maintenance factors. Attention is a very potent reinforcer for most people, especially those who don't get enough of it. When people become ill, they command the attention of prestigious doctors, as well as their family and friends. This attention usually aggravates the problem by reinforcing the illness-simulating behavior. The disordered behavior is further supported by the sympathy that one tends to get from others. These maintenance factors are often called **secondary gains.**

Dissociative Disorders

DISSOCIATIVE DISORDERS. *Disturbances in which behavior is disrupted by a loss of contact with portions of one's memory; includes amnesia, fugue, and multiple personality.*

Dissociative disorders are very dramatic syndromes in which people lose contact with portions of their consciousness or memory. These disorders generally appear to have a sudden onset, although careful probing often reveals that they have been fermenting for years. All the dissociative disorders are extremely rare. Their prevalence is greatly exaggerated because they often involve bizarre cases that generate an enormous volume of publicity. Entire movies, such as *The Three Faces of Eve,* and popular books, such as *Sybil* (Schreiber, 1973), have been devoted to these fascinating cases. These disorders used to be included among the neuroses but now have their own category.

SPECIFIC SYNDROMES

AMNESIA AND FUGUE

AMNESIA. *A pathological loss of memory; may be caused by psychological or organic factors or both.*

FUGUE. *A dissociative disorder marked by amnesia and flight from the scene of stress; often leads to the beginning of a "new life" elsewhere.*

Amnesia is a sudden memory loss that is too extensive to be attributed to normal forgetfulness. For example, a person might have a blank memory for several days following a traumatic incident, such as a serious fire or an auto accident. The memory loss may cover anything from a few hours to an entire lifetime, although the latter is rare. When people forget substantial portions of their lives, their memory losses tend to be quite selective. They forget unpleasant events and elements of their identity, such as their name or their residence, but they remember how to read, drive a car, or type. In **fugue** states people forget who they are, wander away from home, and often acquire a new identity. Essentially, fugue consists of amnesia plus flight from the scene of stress.

MULTIPLE PERSONALITY

MULTIPLE PERSONALITY. *A dissociative disorder in which a person manifests two or more distinct personalities.*

Multiple personality involves the coexistence in one person of two or more largely complete, and usually very different, personalities. In multiple personality, the divergences in behavior go far beyond those that we all display in playing different roles for different people or situations. Generally, the original personality is not aware of the existence of the secondary personalities, but the secondary personalities are usually familiar with the original personality and have varying amounts of awareness of each other. The secondary personalities tend to have traits that are quite foreign to the original personality. For instance, an inhibited, shy, introverted person might develop a flamboyant, extroverted secondary personality. Transitions between personalities tend to be sudden and are often brought on by stress.

ETIOLOGY

We know relatively little about the etiology of dissociative disorders (Bellack, 1980). This is probably due mainly to their rarity. Another problem involves the ambiguity of these disorders. Some skeptics believe that many people with these disorders are consciously pretending to forget or pretending to develop new personalities (Berman, 1975). Indeed, there is evidence (Kiersch, 1962) that these syndromes are faked with some regularity. However, various lines of evidence (Condon, Ogston, & Pacoe, 1969; Osgood & Luria, 1957) suggest that at least some cases are authentic. In any event, psychological rather than biological factors appear to be crucial in the development of these disorders.

SEVERE STRESS

Dissociative disorders tend to emerge in the presence of severe stress that functions as a precipitating cause. They seem to represent an extreme reaction to stress that is perceived as overwhelming. The stress may involve some unexpected event that is very traumatizing, or it may involve a gradual accumulation of many chronic problems.

AVOIDANCE VIA REPRESSION

Like the somatoform disorders, the dissociative disorders often constitute elaborate efforts to avoid confronting one's problems. However, the mechanism of avoidance is different. Instead of adopting the sick role, the person avoids facing up to difficulties by *repressing* the existence of those difficulties (Nemiah, 1978). Thus, dissociative phenomena entail wholesale use of the defense mechanism of repression. There is some reason to believe that people who are subjected to excruciating emotional trauma in childhood are particularly likely to use this radical defensive strategy.

Mood Disorders

AFFECTIVE DISORDERS.
Affect *refers to mood or emotion. See Mood disorders.*

We all have our ups and downs in terms of mood. Life would be dull indeed if one's emotional tenor were a constant. All of us experience depression occasionally, and all of us have days that we sail through on an emotional high. Although such fluctuations are natural, some people are prone to severe distortions of mood known as **affective disorders.**

SPECIFIC SYNDROMES

MOOD DISORDERS. *A group of disorders in which there is a prominent and persistent disturbance in mood, or emotional tenor; also known as affective disorders.*

MANIC-DEPRESSIVE PSYCHOSIS. *Term used in DSM-II to refer to severe disturbance marked by excessive mania, excessive depression, or alternation between both of these. In DSM-III, this is called bipolar mood disorder.*

The classification of **mood disorders** underwent a significant reorganization with the development of DSM-III. A previously used distinction between neurotic depression and psychotic depression has largely been discarded. The old distinction was based on the belief that there were basic differences in the nature and etiology of severe (psychotic) and moderate (neurotic) depression. It is now believed, however, that these differences are merely a matter of degree, and the two syndromes are currently lumped together under affective disorders. In addition to depression, this category includes the **manic-depressive psychosis,** which has been renamed the bipolar mood disorder.

DEPRESSIVE DISORDER

DEPRESSIVE DISORDER. *A mood disorder in which feelings of sadness, dejection, and despair dominate one's behavior. The severity of this disorder varies tremendously, ranging from mild depression to a depressive stupor.*

DELUSION. *A belief that appears to be out of contact with reality; a distortion of fact.*

HALLUCINATION. *A sensory perception in the absence of a real external stimulus; a sensory distortion. It may occur in any of the senses, but auditory and visual hallucinations are most commonly reported.*

The line between normal and abnormal depression is very difficult to draw, and ultimately it entails a subjective judgment. Crucial considerations in this judgment include the persistence of the depression and its disruptive effects. If the depression significantly alters customary functioning for a period of a couple of weeks, there is reason for concern. Even after the threshold for a **depressive disorder** has clearly been crossed, there is a great deal of variation among people in the intensity of their depression.

Complaints about feeling sad, dejected, and discouraged are the heart of the depressive syndrome, but many other symptoms may also appear. Depressed people tend to lose interest in activities from which they used to derive pleasure. They quit going bowling or give up needlepoint. Appetite and sleep disturbances are common. Usually, they experience reduced appetite and suffer from insomnia, although a minority shift the other way, toward excessive eating and sleeping. People with depression often seem to lack energy; they frequently move slowly and talk slowly. Indecisiveness, anxiety, irritability, and brooding are commonly observed. Self-esteem typically sinks like a rock; an unrealistic sense of worthlessness comes to dominate one's self-concept. In severe cases of depression, **delusions** are common, and **hallucinations** are occasionally observed. The delusions often concern deteriorating physical health or far-fetched assumptions of guilt for events long past. In exceptionally severe cases, people display total indifference and extreme disorientation, often remaining bedridden indefinitely. Depressive disorders are often *episodic.*

That means that the periods of depression come and go. A person might be quite depressed for several months, return to an even emotional keel for a while, and then become severely depressed again.

BIPOLAR (MANIC-DEPRESSIVE) DISORDER

BIPOLAR MOOD DISORDER. *A mood disorder characterized by the experience of both manic and depressive states; formerly known as manic-depressive disorder, circular type, in DSM-II. In DSM-III, anyone with at least one manic episode is classified as having a bipolar mood disorder. Those who display only episodes of depression are said to have a major depressive disorder.*

People with **bipolar mood disorders** experience both depression and its opposite, a manic state. This disorder also tends to be episodic, and anyone who has had at least one identified manic episode is put into this category. In a manic episode, the person's mood becomes elevated to the point of euphoria although, paradoxically, the person is often very easy to irritate. Self-esteem skyrockets in unrealistic ways, and exorbitant plans are made. The person bubbles over with enthusiasm, optimism, and energy. Sleep disruption is common, and a person may go for days without sleep. In a manic state people talk rapidly, shift topics wildly, and rarely let others get a word in edgewise. Judgment is typically impaired, and the person may spend money frantically, gamble impetuously, or become much more reckless than usual in regard to sexual behavior. In severe cases, people become delusional, hallucinatory, and incoherent.

The hallmark of the bipolar affective disorder is excessive fluctuation in mood. These mood swings may be patterned in many different ways. Some people experience only one or two manic or depressive episodes in their lifetime. Others may shift back and forth between both extremes in the same day. However, this kind of circularity is unusual.

ETIOLOGY

The etiology of mood disorders is complex. There are probably a number of routes into these disorders. Moreover, each route may involve intricate interactions among a variety of biological and psychological factors.

CONCORDANCE. *When a pair of related persons both display the same disorder, they are said to be concordant. They are said to be discordant if one displays the disorder and the other does not. A concordance rate is an index of what percentage of the relatives both manifest the disorder under study.*

PHYSIOLOGICAL FACTORS

Genetic vulnerability. There is ample evidence that genetic considerations influence the likelihood of developing mood disorders. A standard strategy for assessing the contribution of genetic factors to a disorder is to compare identical and fraternal twins in regard to the likelihood that *both* members of a pair have the disorder. When both twins develop a particular disorder, they are said to be **concordant** for that disorder. *If identical twins show higher concordance rates for a disorder than fraternal twins, this difference strongly suggests that genetic factors are operative in the disorder. This inference is*

13.4 *PERSONAL EXPERIENCE: BIPOLAR MOOD DISORDER*

When it's beginning to happen, I can feel it. It's like a wave of feeling suddenly overwhelming me. When I was depressed last year, all I can remember is the sense of worthlessness I felt. I couldn't believe that anyone could care about me or try to help me. I just wanted to die. My doctor gave me this note that I wrote then: "Dear Doctor_____, Please don't waste your time on me. Please help the ones who deserve to live. I wish you and your wife well in your new home in San Jose. When they take me to my grave I'll feel relieved. Death will be my punishment for the evil I've done to you and to my fellow man."

It scares me to even read such a note and even more to realize that I wrote it. But my most recent episode was an uncontrollable high—I mean, happiness with no bound. It started at a party I was at over New Year's Eve—always a tough time for me to get through, anyway. I felt that wave, that uncontrollable surge of feeling, and I was there before I knew it. I couldn't stop myself from moving around, talking, singing, and carrying on. I felt like I could lick the world, I felt that the whole world thought I was something special. I really liked that feeling, but again, I've been told by Dr._____ that I was acting crazy and out of control. He said that I went around making believe that I was a dog looking for a fire hydrant and that I wet my pants. It sounds funny to think of it now. Thank goodness for the lithium therapy—it brought me down. I wish I knew what prompted the attacks.... At least they've all gone away—so far [excerpted from Duke & Nowicki, 1979, p. 198].

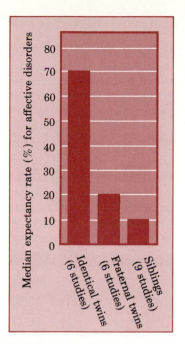

FIGURE 13.3 Expectancy rates for affective disorders among relatives of index cases diagnosed as manic-depressive or affective psychotic.

derived from the fact that pairs of identical (one-egg) twins are more genetically similar to each other than are pairs of fraternal twins. Essentially, the higher concordance rates for identical twins are attributed to their greater genetic correspondence. When this strategy is used to investigate mood disorders, the studies consistently find higher concordance rates for identical twins than for fraternal twins (Page, 1975; Price, 1972; see Figure 13.3). Other approaches to researching this issue also indicate that genetic factors play a role in the etiology of mood disorders (Rosenthal, 1970).

These findings do *not* mean that people directly inherit the mood disorder itself. *What people may inherit is a heightened vulnerability to these disorders.* In other words, your hereditary endowment may make you especially susceptible to mood disorders. The biological basis for this vulnerability has not been determined. However, experts suspect that it may involve a predisposition to experience certain biochemical changes in the brain.

Biochemical changes. There is strong evidence that there is a biochemical basis for many mood disorders. This is why the mechanism of genetic transmission is thought to involve biochemistry.

What is the nature of this evidence? The brain functions electrochemically, and chemical substances known as neurotransmitters play key roles in normal brain functioning. Research (Schildkraut, 1965) suggests that a shortage of one of these neurotransmitters, *norepinephrine,* may produce depression, while an excess of this substance may lead to manic states. More recent research (Baldessarini, 1975; Kety, 1975) suggests that this analysis may be oversimplified. Abnormal levels of at least two other neurotransmitters appear to contribute to the biochemical foundation for mood disorders. Thus, the exact complexities are yet to be worked out, but it is clear that biochemical changes tend to accompany depression.

Currently, we are not sure whether these biochemical changes occur spontaneously, occur as a physiological response to life stress, or both. A study with monkeys (Kraemer & McKinney, 1979) suggests that these biochemical alterations may be caused by stressful events.

PSYCHOLOGICAL FACTORS

Personality. A number of theories suggest that certain kinds of personalities are particularly susceptible to mood disorders. Psychoanalytic theorists (Abraham, 1948; Freud, 1959) argue that *people who bottle up their hostility may end up turning that hostility inward on themselves* and thus become depressed. Freudian theory also suggests that children who experience the loss of a significant love object (such as death of a parent) may be sensitized to such losses, so that a similar loss of love in adulthood might trigger depression. There is some support for these hypotheses, although the evidence is highly tentative (Reiss et al., 1977).

Other theorists (Lewinsohn, 1974) maintain that *inadequate social skills* put people on the road to depression. According to this notion, depression-prone people lack the social skill necessary to acquire many important kinds of reinforcement (good friends, desirable spouses, top jobs, and so forth). This paucity of reinforcers would be understandably depressing.

Still other theorists (Cohen et al., 1954) assert that *excessive emphasis on achievement and success* may make people vulnerable to mood disorders. According to this hypothesis, overly demanding parents may have unrealistically high expectations for a child, which the child has difficulty in meeting. This failure to live up to parental expectations may then undermine the child's self-esteem. The resulting sense of failure and negative self-concept then makes the person a prime candidate for a mood disorder. This analysis has some merit, and there is reason to believe that its relevance is not limited to mood disorders (Becker, Spielberger, & Parker, 1963). Thus, well-intentioned parents who are overly demanding may predispose their offspring to a host of psychological disorders.

Another line of thought suggests that the roots of depression may often lie in excessive *dependency* (McCranie & Bass, 1984) on others for approval, support, and a sense of worth. Extreme dependency puts one in a very precarious position; negative feedback or rejection from important others can be devastating and ultimately depressing. This pathological level of dependency is thought to be fostered in childhood by parents who express affection inconsistently while exercising strict control over the child and demanding complete conformity to parental authority.

Cognition. Aaron Beck (1972) has theorized that depression is brought on by thought disturbances. *He believes that people create depression by thinking negatively* in ways that Albert Ellis would characterize as "irrational" (see Chapter 5). Specifically, he asserts that depression-prone people (1) attribute their failures to personal inadequacies without considering circumstantial explanations, (2) focus on negative feedback from others while ignoring positive feedback, and (3) make pessimistic assumptions about the future. According to Beck, this negative thinking leads to depression. Many studies (for example, Cofer & Wittenborn, 1980; Vestre, 1984) provide support for this cognitive explanation of depression.

LEARNED HELPLESSNESS. *A syndrome described by Seligman involving passive behavior produced by prolonged exposure to unavoidable aversive events; used as a model to explain depression in humans.*

Learned helplessness. Seligman's (1974) model of **learned helplessness** (see Chapter 5) has also been used to explain depression. *According to this model, people who are exposed to aversive events that they are powerless to prevent will develop a sense of helplessness because they view the world around them as uncontrollable.* This learned helplessness then leads to apathy, withdrawal, and depression. This model has been the subject of a great deal of theoretical debate, much of it highly critical (Buchwald, Coyne, & Cole, 1978; Costello, 1978).

ATTRIBUTION. *An inference drawn about the causes of behavior.*

In light of some of this criticism, the learned-helplessness model of depression has been revised and made more cognitive (Seligman, 1983). You may recall from Chapter 6 that we routinely make **attributions** in order to explain our own behavior and the behavior of others. The new theory of learned helplessness proposes that uncontrollable, aversive events may exert their impact by altering patterns of attribution. They may promote (in some people) an attributional style in which people consistently attribute their setbacks to internal rather than external causes. If failures are routinely attributed to personal shortcomings (rather than situational factors), self-esteem is bound to suffer, and depression may also be likely (Garber & Hollon, 1980).

Precipitating stress. It was once believed that mood disorders often appeared mysteriously "out of nowhere." In other words, it was thought that mood disorders were not tied closely to environmental stresses. However, more recent attention to more precise measurement of personal stress suggests that the mood disorders are like other disorders—they usually are triggered by significant stress (Barrett, 1979; Paykel, 1973).

Schizophrenic Disorders

SCHIZOPHRENIC DISORDERS. *A group of severe disturbances dominated by irrational thought processes and poor reality contact; also marked by a deterioration in behavior, disturbed affect, hallucinations, delusions, and withdrawal.*

Schizophrenic disorders involve rather severe disruptions of normal functioning. In fact, schizophrenic persons are said to be **psychotic** because they often seem to be out of touch with reality. Interpreted literally, the term *schizophrenic* means "split mind." It was coined by Bleuler (1911), who thought that the disorder was characterized by a split between the mind and reality, as well as an overall fragmenting of mental functioning. The term is widely misused in the popular media, where the split-mind notion is assumed to refer to the split-personality syndrome, which I covered under dissociative

PSYCHOSIS. *A class of disorders in DSM-II. In DSM-III it is more of a generic term referring to any disturbance so severe as to produce impaired contact with reality.*

disorders. As we have already seen, this rare syndrome, in which two or more personalities are manifested, is actually called multiple personality. Schizophrenia is an altogether different kind of disorder.

People with schizophrenic disorders display some of the same symptoms seen in people with relatively severe affective disorders. The two sets of disorders share some psychotic features but are differentiated as follows. Schizophrenic disorders are dominated by a *thought disturbance,* which spills over to disrupt perceptual, social, and emotional processes. In contrast, mood disorders are dominated by an *emotional disturbance,* which spills over to disrupt perceptual, social, and thought processes.

SPECIFIC SYNDROMES

There are a number of forms of schizophrenia, which differ in significant ways. In fact, there has been some debate about whether these different syndromes should be lumped together under the single term *schizophrenia.* Before I describe these specific syndromes, I will outline some of the general characteristics of schizophrenic disorders.

GENERAL CHARACTERISTICS

Although no single characteristic is inevitably present in schizophrenia, there are some general characteristics that are *usually* present (see Table 13.2).

TABLE 13.2 Signs and symptoms recorded in schizophrenia patients worldwide

Signs and symptoms	Percentage of patients
Lack of insight that patient is mentally ill	97
Presence of auditory hallucinations	74
Ideas of reference (everything has personal meaning)	67
Suspiciousness	66
Flatness of affect (mood)	65
Voices speaking to patient	64
Delusions of persecution	64
Thoughts controlled by others	52

Deterioration of behavior. Schizophrenia usually involves a noticeable deterioration in the quality of one's routine functioning in areas such as work, interpersonal relations, and personal care. This prominent deterioration of behavior highlights the severity of the schizophrenic disorders.

Irrational thought processes. Deterioration of one's thought processes is a central feature of the schizophrenic syndromes. Highly irrational beliefs called *delusions* are common. For example, affected persons frequently believe that their private thoughts are being broadcast to other people or that thoughts are being injected into their mind against their will. Delusions of persecution, wherein people feel that others are spying on them, plotting against them, and mistreating them, are common. So, too, are delusions of grandeur, wherein people often come to view themselves as great political or religious leaders. In addition to delusions, there is often a degeneration in one's train of thought. People with schizophrenic disorders often shift wildly from one topic to another in a manner that is irrationally disjointed and sometimes incoherent.

Hallucinations. A variety of perceptual distortions may occur in schizophrenia. The most common by far are auditory hallucinations. Schizophrenics often hear nonexistent people talking to them. These voices may provide a running commentary on the person's behavior, and they are often quite insulting.

Disturbed affect.   The emotional responsiveness of the schizophrenic may be fouled up in a couple of ways. Some display a blunting or flattening of affect so that they seem emotionless. Others show inappropriate emotional responses that don't jibe with the situation or with what they're saying.

Other features.   Schizophrenics may also exhibit a wide variety of other, less central characteristics. These include a disruption of one's sense of self or individuality; peculiarities in communication, such as inventing words or rambling on without saying anything; withdrawal from social relationships; difficulties in following through on goal-directed activities; and abnormal motor behavior, such as rocking back and forth constantly or becoming immobilized.

SCHIZOPHRENIC SUBTYPES

Paranoid type.   This is a fairly common form of schizophrenia. As its name implies, this disorder is dominated by **paranoia,** or delusions of perse-

Delusions and hallucinations are common features of schizophrenia.

PARANOIA. *Feelings of being persecuted; the dominant symptom in several psychological disorders.*

cution. Paranoid schizophrenics come to believe, usually gradually, that they have innumerable enemies who want to harass and oppress them. The paranoid schizophrenic may become suspicious of friends and relatives or may attribute the persecution to unknown persons. These people are convinced that they are being watched and manipulated in malicious ways. To make sense of this persecution, they often develop delusions of grandeur. They believe that they must have enormous importance of some kind to merit this attention from others. Paranoid schizophrenics tend to be argumentative, erratic, and prone to jealousy.

Catatonic type. Striking motor disturbances usually dominate the picture in catatonic schizophrenia. Some catatonics go into an extreme form of withdrawal called a catatonic stupor, in which they may become virtually motionless and seemingly oblivious to their environment. Others go into a state of catatonic excitement in which they may be wildly impulsive, hyperactive, incoherent, and dangerous. Some show rapid alternation between these two dramatic extremes. The catatonic type is not particularly common in Western cultures, and the incidence of the disorder seems to be declining.

Disorganized type. Also relatively uncommon is the disorganized type of schizophrenia, which involves a particularly severe deterioration of behavior. Prominent features in this syndrome include emotional indifference, frequent incoherence, extreme social withdrawal, and bizarre delusions and hallucinations.

Undifferentiated type. People who are clearly schizophrenic but who cannot be placed into one of the three previous categories are said to have an undifferentiated schizophrenic disorder. They may display a smorgasbord of symptoms from all three of the other subtypes of schizophrenia.

Schizoaffective disorder. In addition to the four subtypes listed above, there is a hybrid category for people who show schizophrenic symptoms as well as clear signs of a severe mood disorder. This blended disorder may mean that people can suffer from two kinds of psychoses simultaneously.

RECOMMENDED READING

13.5 **The Eden Express**
by Mark Vonnegut (Praeger Publishers, 1975)

This is a very personalized account of the author's descent into schizophrenia. It is highly readable, vivid, sometimes humorous, and occasionally frightening. Most people have a difficult time imagining what it would be like to slowly lose touch with reality. Vonnegut describes his gradual disintegration in a graphic and altogether nontechnical manner. This autobiographical tale is illuminating in that it can greatly increase your insight into one of the most severe of all psychological disorders.

Small tasks became incredibly intricate and complex. It started with pruning the fruit trees. One saw cut would take forever. I was completely absorbed in the sawdust floating gently to the ground, the feel of the saw in my hand, the incredible patterns in the bark, the muscles in my arm pulling back and then pushing forward. Everything stretched infinitely in all directions. Suddenly it seems as if everything was slowing down and I would never finish sawing the limb. Then by some miracle that branch would be done and I'd have to rest, completely blown out. The same thing kept happening over and over. Then I found myself being unable to stick with any one tree. I'd take a branch here, a couple there. It seemed that I had been working for hours and hours but the sun hadn't moved at all [pp. 76–77].

At other times suicidal longings came from desperate unhappiness, but everything was so confused I couldn't do a decent job of it. I'd become convinced that something like sitting in a certain chair, looking crosseyed at a psychedelic poster while I chanted Om and clicked my heels together, would do the trick. It became very hard for me to tell when I was committing suicide and when I wasn't [p. 117].

ETIOLOGY

Like the mood disorders, schizophrenic disorders appear to develop through a complex interaction of numerous biological and psychological factors.

PHYSIOLOGICAL FACTORS

Genetic vulnerability.   Evidence is plentiful that hereditary factors play a role in the development of schizophrenic disorders. Twin studies such as those discussed earlier under "Mood Disorders" consistently show much higher concordance rates for identical than fraternal twins (Gottesman & Shields, 1972; Kringlen, 1967). Adoption studies also indicate that a genetic predisposition for schizophrenia is likely (Heston, 1966; Wender et al., 1974). In these adoption studies, researchers track the development of children of schizophrenic parents who are adopted into "normal" homes. Although reared in reasonably healthy homes, these offspring of schizophrenic parents become schizophrenic themselves more often than matched controls. Collectively, these lines of research suggest that people may inherit a genetically transmitted vulnerability to schizophrenic disorders (Gottesman, 1978).

Biochemical changes.   Like the mood disorders, schizophrenic disorders may be partly attributable to biochemical changes in the brain. The evidence linking these disorders to biochemical changes is not as clear as it is for the mood disorders. Nonetheless, there is reason to believe that abnormal levels of certain neurotransmitters may contribute to the onset of schizophrenia (Davis, 1978; Meltzer & Stahl, 1976).

Neurological deficits.   Various studies (Pogue-Geile & Oltmanns, 1980; Shakow, 1962) suggest that schizophrenics have difficulty in focusing their attention. Basically, it appears that they are too easily distracted by irrelevant stimuli. Some theorists believe that their bizarre behavior is due mainly to an inability to filter out unimportant stimuli. These kinds of problems with attentional and perceptual processes have led some experts to theorize that neurological impairments may underlie schizophrenic disorders. Consistent with this hypothesis, researchers *have* found a higher-than-average incidence of neurological deficits in schizophrenic populations (Mosher, Pollin, & Stabenau, 1971). Thus, it is possible that neurological anomalies *may* contribute to the development of schizophrenia. As yet, however, no one has shown exactly how these neurological deficits might be linked to schizophrenic disorders.

PSYCHOLOGICAL FACTORS

Pathogenic family dynamics.   Hundreds of studies have attempted to relate family dynamics to the development of schizophrenia. Although many of these studies have been methodologically flawed (Fontana, 1966), a general picture has emerged of the kind of family life that appears to nurture the development of schizophrenia.

Schizophrenics tend to come most frequently from homes characterized by a negative emotional climate. Persons with these disorders often emerge from homes where authentic love is a rare commodity (Lidz, 1973; Wynne et al., 1958). In some cases, the hostility is out in the open; the parents battle frequently and bitterly. These parents viciously undermine each other's worth as human beings, and the threat of marital dissolution hangs in the air constantly. In other cases the parents work at pretending to have a happy, harmonious home, but the children are quite aware of the latent hostility that seethes beneath the surface. Thus, the homes of schizophrenics might be characterized as emotional wastelands, if not savage battlegrounds.

This negative emotional climate tends to be accompanied by unhealthy *distortions in role relationships*. Often the family roles are defined in exceedingly rigid ways that outlaw any spontaneity. Domination of one parent by the other is common. The children are often used as pawns in the parents' psychological warfare. Not having their emotional needs met adequately by their spouses, many parents encourage maladaptive emotional dependency in their children.

Exactly how these unhealthy family dynamics promote schizophrenia is not clear. It is suspected that they may foster emotional withdrawal, significant inner conflicts, insecurity, inadequate social skills, and a view of the world as a hostile, perilous place.

Training in irrationality.   Lidz (1973) emphasizes how the pathogenic family patterns discussed above lead to training in irrationality. According to this notion, there is a great deal of ambiguous communication in these homes. Bateson et al. (1956) note that *parents often send double-edged, contradictory messages to their children.* For example, a parent might be both loving and rejecting at two different levels of communication. The confusion engendered by these incompatible "double bind" messages may lead children to doubt their perceptual skills or to doubt the rationality of the world around them.

Social ineptitude.   Some investigators (Cameron & Magaret, 1951) have noted that schizophrenics tend to be rather unskilled socially. Because of this social ineptitude, schizophrenics may receive little in the way of positive reinforcement from their interpersonal behaviors. Some theorists believe that this lack of a payoff for interpersonal interactions may lead schizophrenics to turn inward into their own fantasy world.

Precipitating stress.   The importance of precipitating stress in the onset of schizophrenic disorders is not very clear. One very influential theory of schizophrenia (Zubin & Spring, 1977) assumes that stress plays a key role in triggering schizophrenic episodes. There *is* some evidence (Brown, 1972) to support this intuitively plausible hypothesis. Overall, however, evidence that stress is crucial seems notably lacking. Thus, the exact role of precipitating stress in the etiology of schizophrenic disorders remains to be worked out.

Paranoid Disorders
SPECIFIC SYNDROMES

PARANOID DISORDERS. *Disturbances marked by intricate systems of delusion of persecution and/or grandeur, but without the severe personality disintegration seen in paranoid schizophrenia.*

Sometimes people develop serious problems with intense paranoia that are *not* accompanied by a schizophrenic deterioration of personality. Like paranoid schizophrenics, people with **paranoid disorders** develop irrational beliefs that others are conspiring against them, spying on them, stealing from them, poisoning them, spreading malicious rumors about them, and just generally mistreating them. These people tend to be jealous, resentful, angry, and suspicious. However, they do not display the overall deterioration in behavior seen in paranoid schizophrenia. They generally do not become incoherent, withdraw emotionally, or report hallucinations. Although their social interactions may be disrupted by the paranoia, their occupational and intellectual functioning may be unimpaired.

ETIOLOGY

At present there is no evidence linking the paranoid disorders to biological factors. Instead, they appear to grow out of interpersonal incompetence and extreme feelings of inferiority (Coleman et al., 1984). People who develop these disorders tend to come from authoritarian, rigid, emotionally cold, and heavily disciplined homes. They develop seclusive, suspicious, humorless personalities marked by concern about being inferior. Their unappealing personalities may make them the target of some *real* mistreatment. When this is combined with a history of failure in crucial endeavors, they begin, usually gradually, to develop feelings of being persecuted. Essentially, they try to preserve their precarious self-esteem by attributing their failures to an elaborate conspiracy working against them.

Personality Disorders

I have emphasized throughout this chapter that the line between normal and disordered behavior is very difficult to draw. This is especially true of personality disorders. **Personality disorders** involve patterns of personality that are judged to be maladaptive in a relatively moderate way. *People with these disorders exhibit extreme or exaggerated personality traits that are regarded as substantially less than optimal in terms of psychological health.* Their behavior generally is not severely disturbed, and most will never seek professional help, but their adjustment is usually of borderline quality.

This category includes tremendous diversity, in that DSM-III describes 11 personality disorders (see Table 13.3). Many of these are moderate versions of more severe or full-blown disorders that I have already discussed. For example, the label *compulsive personality disorder* is applied to people who are excessively rigid, conventional, formal, and preoccupied with trivia. These people show obsessive-compulsive traits but do not display a full-fledged obsessive-compulsive disorder. In a similar fashion, many of the other personality disorders involve low-grade versions of more serious disturbances.

There is, however, one personality disorder that shares little continuity with

TABLE 13.3 **Personality disorders**

Paranoid personality disorder	Pervasive and unwarranted suspiciousness and mistrust of people; overly sensitive; prone to jealousy
Schizoid personality disorder	Defective capacity for forming social relationships; absence of warm, tender feelings for others
Schizotypal personality disorder	Oddities of thinking, perception, and communication that resemble schizophrenia but are not severe enough to be schizophrenia
Histrionic personality disorder	Overly dramatic behavior; exaggerated expressions of emotion; egocentric attention seeking
Narcissistic personality disorder	Grandiose sense of self-importance; preoccupation with success fantasies; expectation of special treatment; lack of interpersonal empathy
Antisocial personality disorder	Chronic violation of the rights of others; failure to accept social norms, form attachments to others, or sustain consistent work behavior; exploitive and reckless
Borderline personality disorder	Instability in self-image, mood, and interpersonal relationships; impulsive and unpredictable
Avoidant personality disorder	Excessive sensitivity to potential rejection, humiliation, or shame; socially withdrawn in spite of desire for acceptance from others
Dependent personality disorder	Excessive lack of self-reliance and self-esteem; passively allows others to make all decisions; constantly subordinates own needs to others' needs
Compulsive personality disorder	Preoccupation with organization, rules, schedules, lists, trivial details; extremely conventional, serious, and formal; unable to express warm emotions
Passive-aggressive personality disorder	Indirect resistance to demands for adequate social and occupational performance; tendency to procrastinate, dawdle, and "forget"

previously discussed syndromes and therefore merits our attention. This is the psychopathic, or antisocial, personality disorder. I will focus exclusively on it in this section because it is so different from the other personality disorders and because we know much more about it.

PSYCHOPATHIC PERSONALITY SYNDROME

PSYCHOPATHIC PERSONALITY DISORDER. *A personality disorder marked by impulsive, callous, manipulative, hostile, irresponsible, and amoral behavior. Also called the* antisocial personality disorder.

ANTISOCIAL PERSONALITY DISORDER. *Same as* psychopathic personality disorder. *Antisocial personality is the formal* diagnostic label.

The **psychopathic,** or **antisocial, personality** is characterized by a notable lack of moral development, coupled with great hostility and aggressiveness (Millon, 1981). (*Antisocial personality* and *psychopathic personality* are synonyms. I will use the latter term because *antisocial* implies erroneously that people with this disorder are asocial.) People with this disorder use, manipulate, and exploit others without experiencing much guilt or anxiety. They are deceitful, cynical, and shameless. Often they are very skilled or "smooth" in social relations and become quite adept at manipulating others. They tend to be articulate, funny, and superficially charming. This charm allows them to cultivate others' liking. They put up a great façade and then take advantage of people in any way they can. As you can readily imagine, they make excellent "con artists." Although many of them get involved in illegal activities, relatively few end up in prisons or jails. Psychopaths rarely experience authentic affection for others. Instead, they fake affection in order to exploit people. They also tend to be impulsive and irresponsible. They can tolerate very little frustration, and they tend to pursue immediate gratification of their desires. Generally speaking, they make lousy workers, disloyal friends, and terrible spouses. Males develop psychopathic personalities far more often than females. The picture just sketched is a general one. Not all psychopaths will display each and every characteristic discussed.

ETIOLOGY OF THE PSYCHOPATHIC PERSONALITY

PHYSIOLOGICAL FACTORS

Psychopathic personalities lack the inhibitions that most of us have about violating the rights of others. Their generally uninhibited nature has led some experts (Eysenck, 1960) to theorize that they might acquire conditioned inhibitions more slowly or less easily than others and that there might be a physiological basis for this tendency. Indeed, there *is* evidence that many psychopaths have a relatively unresponsive autonomic nervous system (Hare, 1976). As with other syndromes, this unresponsiveness would simply create a *predisposition* toward developing psychopathic disorders.

PSYCHOLOGICAL FACTORS

Emotional deprivation. A number of studies have linked the psychopathic personality to emotional deprivation in childhood (Oltman & Friedman, 1967; Robins, 1966). Psychopaths seem particularly likely to emerge from homes where they have experienced a parental loss (through death or divorce) or parental rejection. It is thought that this emotional deprivation in childhood might undermine affected persons' capacity to feel real affection for others, leading to a calloused approach to interpersonal relationships.

Inadequate socialization. Even when both parents are present and truly affectionate, they may do a poor job of socializing their children to be respectful, truthful, responsible, and unselfish. This is a difficult challenge for even the most concerned parents, and there is evidence that psychopaths tend to come from homes where discipline is inconsistent, ineffective, or nonexistent (Meyer, 1980). Psychopaths also tend to come from homes where one or both parents exhibit psychopathic tendencies (Robins, 1966). In these situations, the psychopathic parents probably provide poor discipline and model antisocial, exploitive behavior.

Cultural factors. Many theorists believe that psychopathic personality disorders develop more frequently in lower-socioeconomic-class neighborhoods characterized by alienation, frustration, and disorganization (Coleman et al., 1984). Although the evidence on this hypothesis is not as strong as one might expect (Kleinmuntz, 1980), it has considerable plausibility. It seems logical to expect that such neighborhoods would nurture hostility and resentment. Furthermore, they may provide more psychopathic role models than more affluent neighborhoods. However, additional evidence is needed on these hypotheses.

Substance-Use Disorders

Problems associated with drug use are called substance-use disorders in DSM-III. I have already discussed the effects of various psychoactive drugs in Chapter 4, where I pointed out that the mere use of even an illicit drug does not, in and of itself, constitute a disorder. In this section I will try to spell out what qualifies as a drug-related behavioral disorder.

According to DSM-III, a **substance-use disorder** is distinguished by one

RECOMMENDED READING

13.6   You Are Not Alone: Understanding and Dealing with Mental Illness — A Guide for Patients, Families, Doctors and Other Professionals by Clara C. Park and Leon N. Shapiro (Little, Brown, 1976)

Although psychological disorders are much more commonplace than is widely believed, the topic of "mental illness" is shrouded in mystery for most people. It is not a subject that we discuss openly, casually, or routinely. Available readings tend to be dry, clinical descriptions of pathological syndromes and their causes. Worthwhile *practical* advice for people suffering from psychological problems and their friends and families is not easily found. However, this book by Park and Shapiro does a superb job of discussing practical considerations in dealing with mental illness.

To the best of my knowledge, it has not been a big-selling self-help book. That is probably easily explained in light of its appearance. It does look like a ponderous, academic book that one would expect (at a glance) to be theoretical and dull, rather than practical and interesting. However, once you get past the footnotes and spartan appearance, there is a wealth of useful insights inside. Moreover, the writing is surprisingly lively and marked by excellent clarity.

The book is very thorough, exploring all the relevant issues. Some of the basic stuff, on the nature of disorders, causes, diagnosis, and therapy, can be found in other books that are well written. However, some of the topics are rarely discussed elsewhere in such a practical and cogent fashion. Among other things, the authors discuss:

- The kinds of mental-health services that are available in most communities.
- What the different service agencies can deliver.
- How to sift through the services available in your community.
- How to deal with the mentally ill friend or relative.
- How to cope with your own distress about having a mentally ill relative.
- How to avoid having the family contribute to the problem rather than the solution.
- How to explain mental illness to children.
- Confidentiality in therapy.
- What mental hospitals are like.
- Legal issues such as involuntary commitment, insanity, and patients' rights.
- Insurance and financial considerations.

If you need information along these lines, you should seriously think about reading this book. I give it "four stars" for thoroughness, practicality, realism, willingness to tackle awkward issues, and high-quality advice.

PERHAPS IT HAPPENS SUDDENLY. The telephone call is from an unknown doctor; your son, who when you last heard from him had just got engaged to a lovely girl, is in the university hospital, hallucinating and incoherent. Or it happens slowly. Your wife's eccentricities have increased so gradually that you are scarcely aware of how far you must go out of your way, these days, to get along with her, or of the exhaustion that is leading you to the agonized recognition that something you've been trying not even to think about has got to be done.... However it comes, it throws up walls around you, as all your neighbors, it seems, go about their business of living with an ordinariness which seems suddenly enviable. There may be a hundred people with a similar experience of trouble living within a mile of you—indeed, if you live in a city, there certainly are—but the families of the mentally ill have a low visibility. Exhaustion and misery, if not shame and a conviction of guilt, may keep the knowledge of their plight even from their close friends [p. 4].

SUBSTANCE-USE DISORDERS. *Pathological patterns of drug use marked by frequent intoxication, noticeable impairment of functioning, and psychological and/or physiological dependence.*

or more of the following three characteristics: (1) a pattern of pathological use involving frequent intoxication, a felt need for daily use, and inability to control use (in other words, psychological dependence), (2) a significant impairment of social or occupational functioning that is attributable to the drug use, and (3) physiological dependence marked by serious problems associated with withdrawal of the drug. In summary, then, substance-use disorders exist when a person's psychological and/or physiological dependence on a drug leads to a disruption of normal functioning.

SPECIFIC SYNDROMES

There are quite a number of drugs that *may* eventually lead to substance-use disorders. The prime candidates are the following classes of drugs (see Chapter 4 for a fuller discussion of risks associated with each drug). Alcohol, barbiturate/sedative drugs, and opium derivatives all have the potential to create either physiological or psychological dependence. Cocaine and amphetamines have a high potential for psychological dependence and may show some ambiguous signs reminiscent of physiological dependence when the drug is withdrawn. Although physiological addiction is not a problem, cannabis derivatives, such as marijuana, have a moderate potential for creating adjustment problems. Dependency is only rarely a problem with hallucinogenic substances, but psychological dependence *is* possible. Caffeine and tobacco clearly have a great potential for psychological dependence, and there is some evidence that they may sometimes produce physiological dependence as well. These last two drugs only rarely produce a disruption in social or occupational functioning, but the dependency may create considerable personal distress.

Substance-use disorders do not necessarily center on only one drug, although they often do. Many people use a multiplicity of drugs (Douglass, Khavari, & Farber, 1980). Thus, substance-use disorders often involve overlapping problems attributable to the use of several drugs.

ETIOLOGY

There are a number of theories and some interesting studies on the etiology of substance-use disorders. This section will discuss some of the causal factors that appear to be related to development of these disorders. *Please note that I will be trying to shed some light on why drug-related disorders develop, not simply why people use drugs. These are two different issues.* For example, boredom, curiosity, and peer-group pressure may lead to the use of certain drugs, but factors such as these are highly unlikely to lead, by themselves, to the excessive level of use characteristic of substance-use disorders.

PHYSIOLOGICAL FACTORS

There is evidence that some people may carry a biologically based predisposition to at least some substance-use disorders. Most of this evidence concerns alcoholism. It has long been known that alcoholism tends to run in families. Until recently, however, most theorists did not ascribe this to genetic considerations (Rose & Burks, 1968). Instead, it was believed that alcoholic parents increased the likelihood of their children's becoming alcoholic through poor parenting and modeling effects. It now appears, however, that there may be a genetic basis for alcoholism. Recent studies (Goodwin, 1976; Holden, 1985) provide impressive evidence that some people may inherit a genetically transmitted *vulnerability* to problems with alcohol.

There are no comparable findings on any other classes of drugs. However, animal studies provide some interesting evidence on opium derivatives. Nichols (1965) discovered that susceptibility to morphine addiction can be bred into rats across generations. Claghorn, Ordy, and Nagy (1965) found that rhesus monkeys vary in their eagerness to consume morphine. Though highly tentative, this evidence suggests that there could be a biologically based vulnerability to opiate addiction in humans.

PSYCHOLOGICAL FACTORS

Association with other disorders. Substance-use problems in some people appear to be a derivative effect of other, more basic disorders. For instance, alcoholism may often be an outgrowth of depression (Weissman et al., 1977), opiate addiction is often associated with psychopathic personality disorders (Ling et al., 1973), and chronic use of hallucinogens seems to be related to significant identity problems (Welpton, 1968). Thus, drug dependence may *sometimes* be a dramatic symptom of more deeply rooted psychological disorders.

Stress. Excessive drug use may often be precipitated by significant stress in one's life. Laboratory studies show that subjects exposed to social stress consume more alcohol than control subjects do (Marlatt & Rose, 1980). Other studies have related actual alcoholism (Curlee, 1969) and opiate addiction (Cloward & Ohlin, 1966) to stressful life events. Several classes of drugs (alcohol, barbiturates, opiates) are capable of relieving feelings of anxiety. Many people probably turn to these drugs in times of stress in order to reduce tension and temporarily escape from unpleasant realities.

Reinforcement. The simplest explanation of drug abuse is often overlooked. People get wrapped up in analyzing the role of alienation, rebellion, peer pressure, and so forth and ignore the simple fact that most abused drugs produce very pleasant states of consciousness. Wikler (1965) points out that each drug ingestion is reinforced in a powerful way by the pleasant state it induces. The euphoric effects associated with abused drugs are highly gratifying. Given the immediate, potent, and consistent reinforcement provided by many drugs, it is not surprising that many people get "hooked" on them. This explanation is supported by the fact that monkeys, who presumably are not psychopathic, alienated, or under peer pressure, will become addicted to heroin if given the opportunity (Schuster, 1975).

Culture. We live in a very drug-oriented culture. Although we pay lip service to the dangers of drugs, we are taught from early childhood that our problems can be solved by popping pills. Enormous amounts of money are spent on advertising to convince people that they can improve their lives by consuming a vast array of legal drugs. There is evidence that the drug-consumption patterns displayed by parents exert considerable influence over their children's subsequent habits. For instance, Smart and Fejer (1972) found that adolescents whose mothers used tranquilizers were three to seven times more likely to use similar drugs than children whose mothers did not use tranquilizers.

Given these demonstrated modeling effects, it is not surprising that drug-abuse patterns vary along cultural lines. For instance, alcoholism is relatively common among the French and the Irish but quite rare among Mormons and Muslims (Coleman et al., 1984). Within American culture, there are interesting subcultural variations in substance abuse. For example, heroin addiction is most common in deteriorating neighborhoods in large cities, whereas barbiturate-related problems are seen more in the suburbs.

Summary

There is no simple way to define psychological disorders. Four criteria commonly used when people are labeled disordered are social deviance, personal distress, maladaptive behavior, and irrationality. The medical model assumes that it is useful to view mental disorders as if they were diseases. This model has been criticized on the grounds that (1) it turns ethical questions about deviance into medical questions, (2) it overlooks the importance of psychosocial factors in mental disorders, (3) it encourages adoption of the passive patient role, and (4) it suggests that judgments about mental disorders are value-free. Although there are serious problems with the medical model, the analogy is useful if one remembers that it is only an analogy.

Misconceptions about psychological disorders are quite common. Contrary to popular myths, people with psychological disorders usually are not particularly bizarre or dangerous. These disorders should not be a source of shame, and they are often curable. Although it is difficult to get solid data on the prevalence of psychological disorders, it is clear that they are far more common than is widely believed.

The current controversies about the official psychodiagnostic system, DSM-III, illustrate that judgments about psychological disorders are not value-free. There are some problems inherent in psychodiagnosis. The most serious is the stigma produced by labeling people mentally ill. Other problems include poor reliability and the tendency to create pseudo explanations of psychological disorders. Nonetheless, a diagnostic classification system is essential to a scientific approach to psychological disorders. The challenge is to improve our diagnostic system so that we can make better statements about etiology, prognosis, and treatment.

The anxiety disorders include the generalized anxiety disorder, phobic disorders, and obsessive-compulsive disorders. These disorders may be more probable in people who have a highly reactive autonomic nervous system. Parents who are overly demanding, who are overprotective, or who model anxiety may promote these disorders. Problems with anxiety may also be attributable to conditioning and the presence of inner conflict.

Somatoform disorders include somatization, conversion, the psychogenic pain disorder, and hypochondria. These disorders often emerge after an authentic physical illness, especially in highly suggestible, histrionic personalities. Somatoform disorders often constitute an avoidance strategy that may be supported by secondary gains, such as attention and sympathy.

Dissociative disorders include amnesia, fugue, and multiple personality. We know relatively little about the etiology of these very rare disorders. The presence of severe stress and efforts to promote avoidance through repression may play a role in the development of these disorders.

The principal mood disorders are depression and the bipolar affective disorder. Twin studies suggest that there may be a genetic vulnerability to these disorders; it appears to involve biochemical changes in the brain. People who repress their hostility, who have inadequate social skills, or who place excessive emphasis on success may be particularly prone to affective disorders. Although stress usually plays a role in the mood disorders, depression may be primarily a matter of negative thinking or learned helplessness.

Schizophrenic disorders are characterized by a deterioration in behavior, irrational thought processes, hallucinations, and disturbed affect. In addition to the blended schizoaffective disorder, there are paranoid, catatonic, disorganized, and undifferentiated subtypes of schizophrenia. Evidence suggests that there is a genetic vulnerability to schizophrenia, perhaps involving biochemical or neurological abnormalities. Pathogenic family dynamics involving a negative emotional climate, distorted role relationships, and training in irrationality may contribute to the development of schizophrenic disorders. Social inadequacies and precipitating stress may also play a role in the etiology of these disorders.

Paranoid disorders involve excessive paranoia without a schizophrenic deterioration in behavior. These disorders may be promoted by social ineptitude and feelings of inferiority. Personality disorders constitute moderate disturbances in personality. The psychopathic personality disorder involves manipulative, deceitful, exploitive, and amoral patterns of behavior. Although physiological factors may play an etiological role, it seems that this disorder is due mainly to emotional deprivation, poor socialization, and subcultural alienation. Substance-use disorders are sometimes associated with psychopathy or depression. Stress, reinforcement, and cultural endorsements of drug use appear to promote these disorders.

In the upcoming application section we will take a look at a deadly problem: suicide. I will try to improve your understanding of this unfortunate phenomenon and discuss suicide prevention.

Understanding and Preventing Suicide

Answer the following true or false.

_____ 1. Suicide is committed only by people with severe psychological disorders.

_____ 2. People who talk about suicide don't actually commit suicide.

_____ 3. Suicides usually take place with little or no warning.

_____ 4. People who attempt suicide are fully intent on dying.

_____ 5. People who are suicidal remain so forever.

The five statements above are all basically false. They are myths about suicide that I will dispose of momentarily. First, however, let me try to convey to you the great magnitude of this tragic problem.

INCIDENCE OF SUICIDE

Suicide is one of the top ten causes of death in the United States. Suicides actually outnumber murders, although the latter usually get far more attention and publicity. Moreover, the official statistics on suicide are thought to grossly underestimate the scope of the problem. Many people committing suicide disguise it as an accident so that their survivors can avoid embarrassment or collect on life insurance. In other instances it is the survivors who try to cover up the true nature of the death. In any case, experts estimate that there may be five to eight times as many suicides as are actually recorded. Thus, although it is impossible to know the true incidence of suicide, it is substantially more common than is widely believed.

Suicide efforts are not evenly distributed across all segments of society (Frederick, 1978). Suicide may strike anywhere, but some groups are at higher risk than others. *Sex*, for instance, is a paradoxical variable. On the one hand, about three times more women than men *attempt* suicide. On the other hand, males attempting suicide are much more likely to actually kill themselves than females are. *Age* is also related to suicide rates. Generally, the risk of suicide rises as people get older. In recent years, however, there has been a dramatic increase in the prevalence of suicide in the under-25 age group. The incidence of suicide also varies according to one's *marital status*. Married people commit suicide less frequently than divorced, bereaved, or single people. Finally, some *occupations* appear to be at higher risk than others. Suicide rates are particularly high among lawyers, dentists, pharmacists, and physicians (especially psychiatrists).

It should be emphasized that suicide is a double-edged tragedy. First, and most obvious, there is the unnecessary loss of a human life. That loss is made particularly lamentable by the fact that someone has willingly taken his or her own life. It is hard to imagine the sense of despair that must precipitate such a desperate action. Second, and less obvious, there is the impact on the victim's loved ones. Suicide rarely occurs in a social vacuum. Often it is precipitated by conflict with other people, such as parents, children, or a spouse, who are left with a mixture of grief and guilt. The impact of suicide on the deceased person's survivors can be devastating. Typically, the survivors feel ashamed, resentful, confused, remorseful, guilty, and depressed.

MYTHS ABOUT SUICIDE

EDWIN SHNEIDMAN

I opened this application section with five assertions about suicide that are largely false. I will now examine these myths about suicide, outlined by Edwin Shneidman and his colleagues (1970).

Myth 1: Suicide is committed only by people with severe psychological disorders. Only a small minority of those who commit suicide have a diagnosed psychological disorder. Suicide rates *are* relatively high among people with psychological disorders (especially the mood disorders), but most victims of suicide appear to be "normal."

Myth 2: People who talk about suicide don't actually commit suicide. Undoubtedly, there are many people who talk about suicide without ever going through with it. Nonetheless, there is no group at higher risk for suicide than those who openly discuss the possibility.

Myth 3: Suicides usually take place with little or no warning. It is estimated that eight out of ten suicide attempts are preceded by some kind of warning. These warnings may range from clear threats of suicide to more vague statements, such as "You won't have me around to worry about anymore."

Myth 4: People who attempt suicide are fully intent on dying. It appears that only about 3–5% of those who attempt suicide definitely want to die. About one-third of the people seem to be ambivalent—they intend to leave it up to fate. About two-thirds appear to have no interest in dying! They merely want to send out a very dramatic distress signal, and they try to arrange their suicide effort so that rescue is quite likely. These variations in intent probably explain why only about one out of eight suicide attempts actually ends in death.

Myth 5: People who are suicidal remain so forever. Most people who become suicidal do so for a relatively brief period. If they manage to ride through the crisis, thoughts of suicide *may* disappear completely.

EVALUATING SUICIDAL POTENTIAL

LETHALITY. *A term referring to the seriousness of a person's potential to attempt suicide.*

The first step toward preventing a suicide is to recognize that a suicidal potential exists. If the person makes clear, verbal threats, this is relatively easy. Many people, however, drop only subtle hints or make veiled threats that are hard to interpret. Moreover, even when clear threats are made, one needs to know how to judge whether there is any immediate danger. For these reasons, researchers have tried to pinpoint correlates of suicidal **lethality** so that people can better assess a person's suicide potential.

There is no sure way to predict whether a person will attempt suicide (Murphy, 1984). However, the following criteria may be helpful in assessing suicidal lethality (Shneidman et al., 1970; Wekstein, 1979).

1. *The nature of any verbal threat.* As already discussed, people who openly threaten suicide are a very high-risk group. Even if they have threatened suicide before without following through, their threat should not be ignored. Many people who *do* kill themselves have a history of such "empty threats." The immediate danger is greatest when a threat includes a clear, detailed plan involving a particularly deadly method.

2. *Emotional tenor.* Although a minority of suicidal persons have a diagnosed psychological disorder, a majority show signs of significant depression before their suicide attempt. People who express feelings of futility, hopelessness, and helplessness may be particularly suicide-prone. Irrationally negative statements about the future are a bad diagnostic sign.

3. *Presence of severe stress.* Suicide attempts are often precipitated by extremely stressful life events, such as loss of a loved one, marital discord, physical illness, career problems, or financial setbacks. Thus, a person's suicide potential tends to be greater when the person is being assaulted by overwhelming stress.

4. *Self-destructiveness.* Some people have a history of self-destructiveness, involving such things as excessive drug abuse, ignoring medical advice, or engaging in dangerous activities. When such people show signs of suicidal intent, their suicidal potential should be taken very seriously.

5. *Changes in behavior.* Sometimes people who have decided to kill themselves start behaving differently. They may become serene after going through a period of emotional turmoil. Occasionally, they start giving away some of their most precious possessions. Their eating and sleeping habits may change noticeably.

6. *Social support.* In evaluating someone's suicide potential, it is important to consider the person's overall social situation. The presence of supportive family and friends tends to counteract suicidal tendencies. Conversely, people who feel socially isolated and alienated have a greater suicide potential.

PREVENTING SUICIDE

There is no simple and reliable way to prevent someone from committing suicide. Wekstein (1979) makes the point that "perhaps nobody really knows *exactly* what to do when dealing with an imminent suicide" (p. 129). However, I can offer some general guidelines that may be useful if you ever have to help someone through a suicidal crisis (Farberow, 1974; Lester & Lester, 1971; Shneidman et al., 1970).

1. *Provide empathy and social support.* First and foremost, you must show the suicidal person that you care. People are often driven to contemplate suicide because they see the world around them as indifferent and unsupportive. Hence, you must demonstrate to the person that you are authentically concerned. Even if you barely know the person, you must provide empathy. Suicide threats are often a last-ditch cry for help. It is therefore imperative that you offer to help.

2. *Identify and clarify the crucial problem.* The suicidal person is often very confused and feels lost in a sea of frustration and problems. It is a good idea to try to help the person sort through this confusion and identify the crucial problem. Once it is isolated, the crucial problem may not seem quite so overwhelming. It also is useful to point out that the person's confusion is clouding his or her ability to rationally judge the seriousness of the problem.

3. *Suggest alternative courses of action.* People considering suicide often see it as the "only solution" to their problem. This is obviously an irrational view. Try to chip away at this premise by offering other solutions to the problem that has been identified as crucial. Suicidal people are often too distraught and disoriented to do this on their own. Therefore, you have to do it for them. Don't be overbearing about it, but try to display an air of confidence.

4. *Capitalize on any doubts.* For most people, life is not easy to give up; they are racked by doubts about the wisdom of their decision. Many people will voice their unique reasons for doubting whether they should take the suicidal path. Zero in on these doubts; they may be your best arguments for life over suicide. For instance, if a person expresses concern about how his or her suicide will affect family members, capitalize on this concern.

5. *Encourage professional consultation.* Most mental-health professionals have at least some experience with suicidal crises and can usually be quite helpful. Encourage the suicidal person to seek this professional help. Many large metropolitan areas have suicide prevention centers with 24-hour hotlines. These centers are staffed with people who have been specially trained to deal with suicidal problems. It is important to try to get the person to accept some kind of professional help. The contemplation of suicide indicates that the person is suffering from some deeply rooted psychological distress. Given this reality, professional consultation is essential.

14

PSYCHOTHERAPY

CHAPTER 13 REVIEW

IDEAS: REVIEW OF LEARNING OBJECTIVES

When you have mastered the material in this chapter, you should be able to do the following.

1. List four criteria of psychological disorders.
2. Explain the meaning of the "medical model" of psychological disorders.
3. Summarize critics' views on the medical model.
4. List four myths about psychological disorders.
5. Discuss the prevalence of psychological disorders.
6. Explain three problems that are associated with psychodiagnosis and classification of mental disorders.
7. Explain the potential value of psychodiagnosis.
8. Describe generalized anxiety disorders, phobic disorders, and obsessive-compulsive disorders.
9. Explain how physiological factors may be related to the etiology of anxiety disorders.
10. Explain how psychological factors may be related to the development of anxiety disorders.
11. Describe the somatization, conversion, and psychogenic pain disorders and hypochondria.
12. List the physiological and psychological factors that appear to be related to the etiology of somatoform disorders.
13. Describe the syndromes of amnesia, fugue, and multiple personality.
14. Describe two factors thought to be involved in the etiology of dissociative disorders.
15. Describe the two major mood disorders: depression and the bipolar affective disorder.
16. Explain how physiological factors may be related to the development of mood disorders.
17. Summarize how psychological factors may be related to the etiology of mood disorders.
18. List the general characteristics of schizophrenic disorders.
19. Describe the paranoid and catatonic subtypes of schizophrenia.
20. Describe the disorganized and undifferentiated subtypes of schizophrenia and schizoaffective disorders.
21. Describe three physiological factors that have been related to the etiology of schizophrenic disorders.
22. Explain how family dynamics may be related to the development of schizophrenic disorders.
23. Describe three other psychological considerations that may be involved in the etiology of schizophrenic disorders.
24. Describe paranoid disorders.
25. Discuss the etiology of paranoid disorders.
26. Describe the general nature of personality disorders.
27. Describe the psychopathic personality disorder.
28. Discuss the etiology of psychopathic personality disorders.
29. List three criteria of substance-use disorders.
30. Describe evidence relating physiological factors to some substance-use disorders.
31. Summarize how psychological factors may be related to the etiology of substance-use disorders.
32. Summarize how age, sex, and marital status are related to the incidence of suicide.
33. List five myths about suicide.
34. List six factors that can aid you in evaluating a person's suicide potential.
35. List five steps that may help to prevent someone from attempting suicide.

TERMS: REVIEW OF NEW VOCABULARY

When you have mastered the material in this chapter, you should be able to define the following terms.

Affective disorders
Agoraphobia
Amnesia
Antisocial personality disorder
Attribution
Anxiety disorders
Bipolar mood disorder
Concordance
Conversion disorder
Delusion

Depressive disorder
Dissociative disorders
Etiology
Fugue
Generalized anxiety disorder
Hallucination
Hypochondria
Learned helplessness
Lethality
Malingering

Manic-depressive psychosis
Mood disorders
Multiple personality
Neurosis
Obsessive-compulsive disorder
Paranoia
Paranoid disorders
Personality disorders
Phobic disorder

Psychodiagnosis
Psychogenic pain disorder
Psychopathic personality disorder
Psychosis
Schizophrenic disorders
Secondary gains
Somatization disorder
Somatoform disorders
Substance-use disorders
Transvestitism

PEOPLE: REVIEW OF MAJOR THEORISTS AND RESEARCHERS

When you have mastered the material in this chapter, you should be able to summarize the principal contributions and/or ideas of the following people.

Aaron Beck

Edwin Shneidman

Thomas Szasz

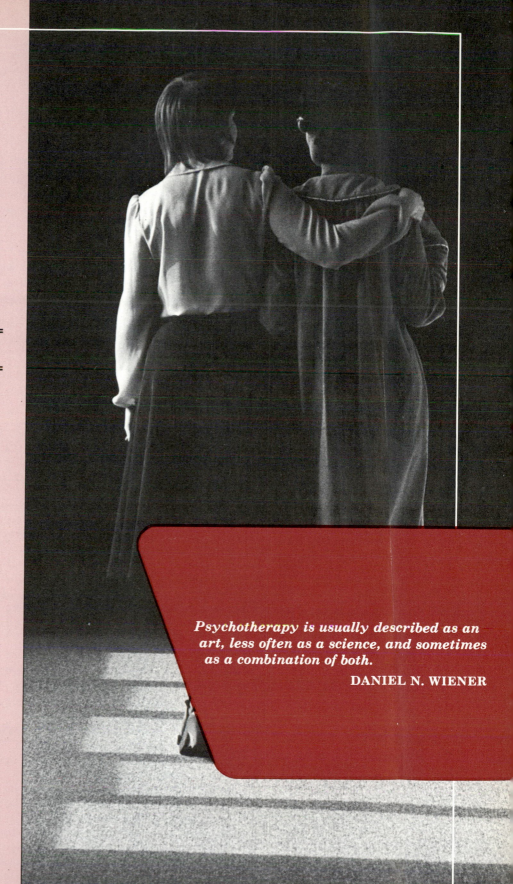

Summary

Psychotherapy is usually described as an art, less often as a science, and sometimes as a combination of both.

DANIEL N. WIENER

"I thought that therapists were magicians—knew the right answers—and if I just did what I was 'supposed' to, my life would be better. I now know that the process of therapy is difficult work demanding honesty with yourself as well as with the therapist."

"My preconceptions came mostly from the media, i.e. couches, male therapists with beards, drugs, shock therapy, white straitjackets, and very expensive private doctors" [Robson & Edwards, 1980, p. 19].

What do you know about psychotherapy? If you're like most people, including the two quoted above, you probably have many misconceptions about the nature of psychotherapy. People are led to believe that psychotherapy is only for "crazy" people, that therapists have magical powers that allow them to "see through" people, that therapists tell people how to live their lives, and that therapy can solve all one's problems. All these beliefs are incorrect. In this chapter I will endeavor to give you an accurate, down-to-earth picture of the complex process of psychotherapy. I begin by discussing the nature of psychotherapy, who seeks it, and who provides it. I then describe the many, very different approaches to doing psychotherapy. In the application section, I address practical questions about seeking psychotherapy.

Preliminary Questions

WHAT IS PSYCHOTHERAPY?

PSYCHOTHERAPY. *A general term that refers to any treatment procedure to help people with psychological disorders or distress.*

Psychotherapy can be defined as the process by which mental-health professionals try to help people suffering from psychological problems. Briefly, psychotherapy is the treatment of psychological disorders and/or psychological distress. A person receiving psychotherapy does *not* necessarily have a clearly identified psychological disorder. People who are only vaguely dissatisfied with their lives often seek therapy. What people in therapy have in common is this: they feel troubled, and they have sought professional help.

The mental-health professionals who provide this help are a diversified lot. Collectively, I will refer to them simply as therapists. In a moment, I will discuss the different kinds of professional training that one might have in order to serve as a therapist.

The therapeutic process itself is also highly diversified. There are numerous approaches to therapy. What unites them is their ultimate goal. They all strive to produce constructive behavioral changes in order to alleviate psychological problems. This chapter will review five general approaches to providing psychotherapy:

1. *Psychoanalytic approaches.* These approaches are based on the theories of Sigmund Freud and his followers. They emphasize probing into the client's unconscious in order to achieve insight into the nature of the client's problems.
2. *Humanistic approaches.* These approaches are based on the humanistic philosophy described in Chapter 2. They work to promote personal growth by pursuing insights about the structure and meaning of one's self-concept.
3. *Behavioristic approaches.* These approaches, based on the principles of learning, place little emphasis on attainment of personal insights. There are a variety of specific procedures intended for use with specific kinds of problems, which attempt to directly modify behavior.
4. *Group-oriented approaches.* Although therapy is usually conducted on an individualized basis, it is sometimes worthwhile to work with a group of people. These approaches usually emphasize pursuing insights about interpersonal processes.

5. *Physiological approaches.* These approaches involve intervention into a client's physiological functioning for therapeutic purposes. The most widely used procedures are the prescription of drugs and electroconvulsive shock therapy.

WHO SEEKS THERAPY?

As already noted, therapy is sought by people who feel "troubled." The nature of that trouble varies greatly from one person to another. People pursue professional help in order to cope better with a vast array of problems. The two most common presenting symptoms are excessive anxiety and depression (Lichtenstein, 1980).

The typical sequence of events that leads a client into a therapist's office has been broken into four stages (Kadushin, 1969). The first stage consists in recognizing that one has a significant personal problem. In the second stage, the person discusses his or her problem with friends, relatives, and other persons without professional training. Their attitudes about seeking professional therapy are of critical importance. If they discourage the idea, the person often will try to ride through the turmoil without pursuing professional help. If they support the idea of seeking therapy, the person is likely to move on to the third stage and select the kind of "helping profession" that appears most appropriate. The fourth stage then involves choosing a particular therapist or clinic. Of course, it should be noted that a sizable number of people are *coerced* into therapy. In most cases this coercion involves gentle pressure from a spouse, friend, co-worker, or supervisor. In some cases, however, people are ordered to enter therapy by the courts or by their employer.

People vary tremendously in their willingness to seek psychotherapy. *Unfortunately, it appears that far too few receive the therapy they need.* Studies estimating the prevalence of psychological problems in our society (Srole et al., 1962) suggest that only a small fraction of psychologically troubled people receive professional therapy. Many people who could benefit greatly from therapy do not seek it because (1) they are unaware of its availability, (2) they erroneously believe that its cost is prohibitive, and (3) they see use of therapy as an admission of personal weakness. Generally, men are less likely than women to enter therapy, and people from the lower socioeconomic classes seek therapy less frequently than those from the upper classes (Lichtenstein, 1980).

WHO PROVIDES THERAPY?

The general public is often confused by the diverse array of professionals who offer psychotherapy services. The provision of psychotherapy is not limited to a single profession. Rather, therapy may be provided by psychologists, psychiatrists, psychoanalysts, and psychiatric social workers. In this section I will try to clear up some of this confusion by describing the various mental-health professions.

Psychologists. Clinical or counseling psychologists are trained to provide psychotherapy. In most states a person must have a doctoral degree (Ph.D., Psy.D., or Ed.D.) in order to independently offer professional services as a psychologist. Doctoral programs generally require four or five years of study beyond a bachelor's degree. Admission to these programs is usually very competitive, and the schools can afford to be very selective.

Psychologists are trained to conduct research and do psychological testing as well as psychotherapy. Most of their training takes place on a university campus, where they take courses, engage in research, and acquire some practical experience. Additionally, they are usually required to serve a year-long internship, which provides a great deal of supervised clinical experience.

Psychologists are quite diverse in their approaches to therapy. Generally,

Psychologists receive extensive training in the conduct of psychotherapy.

they tend to emphasize humanistic, behavioristic, and group-oriented approaches.

In addition to doctoral-level psychologists, there are also master's-level psychologists who provide psychological testing and therapeutic services. A master's program generally requires only two years of study and is less rigorous and research-oriented than a doctoral program. In most states master's-level psychologists work in institutional settings, supervised by a doctoral-level psychologist or a psychiatrist. Generally, master's-level psychologists are no longer permitted to go into private practice, although those who had practices established before the standards were changed (in the 1960s) are allowed to continue to work independently.

Psychiatrists. Psychiatrists are physicians who have an M.D. degree and have specialized in the treatment of psychological disorders. Their training requires four years of course work in a medical school and four years of residency at an approved hospital. Thus, they have eight years of training beyond their bachelor's degree. Admission to medical school is intensely competitive.

During the four years of medical school, psychiatrists receive general training in medicine that is essentially the same as for physicians going into other specialties, such as internal medicine, surgery, or pediatrics. Some critics (Schofield, 1964) have argued that this general medical training is rather poor preparation for learning to do psychotherapy. Since most medical students majored in chemistry or biology as undergraduates, many psychiatrists-to-be graduate from medical school with only very scanty instruction in the behavioral sciences. Their crucial training takes place during their four years of residency. This intense, on-the-job training gives them an enormous amount of supervised clinical experience.

Psychiatrists may choose to employ virtually any approach to psychotherapy. The physiological approaches are exclusively their province. Only a physician may prescribe therapeutic drugs or electroconvulsive shock therapy. Psychiatrists are much more likely than psychologists to use psychoanalytic approaches in the tradition of Freud. They are less likely than psychologists to use humanistic, behavioristic, or group-oriented approaches to therapy, but some psychiatrists do use these approaches.

Psychoanalysts.   As their name suggests, psychoanalysts do psychoanalytic therapy. Usually they are psychiatrists who have pursued additional training in psychoanalysis. However, they may be clinical psychologists or other kinds of professionals who have sought psychoanalytic training. In any case, they base their approach to therapy on the theories of Sigmund Freud and his followers.

Psychiatric social workers.   Psychiatric social workers usually have a master's degree in social work, although some have a doctorate. They often work as part of a team with a psychologist or psychiatrist. On these teams, their main function is to work with the family of a disturbed person to improve the client's integration into the community. However, they increasingly work independently in providing a wide range of therapeutic services.

Psychoanalytic Approaches to Therapy

Let us turn now to the first of the five approaches to therapy that we will be examining. Sigmund Freud was a great pioneer whose work has had an enormous influence on the evolution of systems of psychotherapy. Trained as a neurologist, Freud became interested in the treatment of nervous disorders in the 1880s. The treatments available at that time were decidedly primitive, and so he began to develop his own unique techniques. Through a painstaking process of trial and error, he experimented with numerous procedures while working as a therapist for some 50 years in Vienna. His system of therapy, known as psychoanalysis, came to dominate psychiatry and remains extremely influential today (Greenley, Kepecs, & Henry, 1981). In discussing psychoanalytic approaches, I will begin by describing classical psychoanalysis, as practiced by Freud. I will then outline modern trends seen in various neo-Freudian revisions of psychoanalytic therapy.

CLASSICAL PSYCHOANALYSIS

PSYCHOANALYSIS. *The psychoanalytic, or Freudian, approach to therapy, which emphasizes the recovery of unconscious conflicts through techniques such as free association and transference.*

Though still available, classical **psychoanalysis** is not widely practiced anymore, primarily because, in its classical format, psychoanalysis is exceedingly expensive and time-consuming for the client. In the classical version of psychoanalysis, the client is expected to show up for four one-hour sessions per week (Freud saw his patients six days a week) over a period of three to five years. Few clients are willing or able to make that kind of commitment today. Nonetheless, classical psychoanalysis is worth describing because it provided the foundation for the great variety of psychoanalytic therapies that survive it. The following description will be based on discussions by Lichtenstein (1980) and Blanck (1976).

ORIGINS OF NEUROSIS

Classical psychoanalysis was based on certain assumptions about the origins of neurotic behavior. *Freud believed that neurosis was caused by unresolved conflicts that were being fought out at deep levels of one's unconscious.* These conflicts were believed to be derived from fixations on poorly resolved conflicts during early childhood. It was thought that these inner conflicts often centered on sexual and aggressive impulses emanating from the id. According to Freudian theory, the client avoids confronting these conflicts through the use of defense mechanisms. Nonetheless, because defense mechanisms are only a partial solution, anxiety may surface at a conscious level. It is this chronic anxiety that usually propels someone into therapy.

PROBING THE UNCONSCIOUS

Given the assumptions about neurotic behavior described above, the logic of psychoanalysis is quite straightforward. *The analyst attempts to probe the hazy depths of the unconscious in order to help the client "discover" the unresolved conflicts causing his or her neurosis.* The analyst functions initially as a "psychological detective" trying to piece together a complex personality puzzle. In this effort to explore the unconscious, the therapist relies on two techniques: free association and dream analysis. In **free association** clients lie on a couch and let their mind wander freely, expounding on anything that comes to mind, regardless of how trivial, silly, or embarrassing it might be. It is critical that the clients let everything pour out without any conscious censorship. When all censorship is inhibited, these free associations can provide important clues about the contents of the unconscious. In **dream analysis,** clients are trained to remember their dreams, which they then report to the therapist. These dreams are thought to be rather direct expressions of the unconscious. The therapist then analyzes the content of the dreams in order to gain insight into the workings of the unconscious.

RESISTANCE

In psychoanalysis, it is expected that clients will often display **resistance** to the therapeutic efforts. *Resistance involves largely unconscious defensive maneuvers intended to hinder the progress of therapy.* It may seem perplexing that a client would try to thwart the helping process, but there is a very good reason for this unfortunate tendency. The unconscious conflicts that the therapist is searching for were buried in the unconscious because they were scary and painful. Because of their frightening nature, many clients would rather leave them buried. Resistance may be manifested in a variety of ways. Patients

FREE ASSOCIATION. *A psychoanalytic technique in which clients express their thoughts and feelings freely and spontaneously with as little censorship as possible; used to gain access to the unconscious.*

DREAM ANALYSIS. *A procedure wherein a therapist interprets the meaning of the symbolic content in clients' dreams.*

RESISTANCE. *A psychoanalytic concept referring to defensive maneuvers by a client in therapy, used to avoid confronting painful material.*

14.1 *AN EXAMPLE OF PSYCHOANALYTIC THERAPY*

In psychoanalysis, the patient (analysand) usually attends up to five sessions of 45 to 60 minutes each week. Initially, the analyst and the analysand may speak face to face, but after a period of time the patient is usually directed to lie on a couch facing away from the therapist, who typically sits off to the side, out of the patient's vision. At this point, the fundamental rule of free association is applied: the patient is asked to report, without censoring or inhibiting, all feelings, ideas, associations, and thoughts that come to mind. The therapist listens intently and makes infrequent comments and interpretations, as seen in this excerpt from a psychoanalytic session:

Therapist: We can begin.
Client: Last night I thought about not coming back today. I felt you were really bored with what I was saying. You never say anything to me, and I feel sometimes like I'm wasting my time and money. (Pause.) You see I wait for an answer and I don't get one! I really get mad when you do that.

Therapist: Like when you were a child and you wanted your father to listen to you and to take care of your troubles?
Client: (Pause.) Yes—sort of—that made me think of my father. I remember a time when we were at a lake for the summer. I was on the boat dock feeding bread to the fish and he came out and sat down beside me. He looked at me with such great love in his eyes. I feel like crying just thinking about it. He would do that when I didn't ask for it. But when I cried for help from him, he would say, "Try to do it yourself." Why? Why?
Therapist: And I ask you to do it yourself, too. And I don't even look at you with love in my eyes.
Client: I feel alone—like a child. . . . You're right. I do wonder if you really care about me. Do you? (Pause.) You won't answer me. So, DAMMIT, I get so angry at you, but I did at him too. I miss him [Duke & Nowicki, 1979, p. 561].

may show up late for their sessions, argue with their therapist, and merely pretend to free-associate. Often, they will talk eagerly and extensively about issues that are irrelevant to their problem in order to avoid discussing the truly sensitive issues. An important element of psychoanalysis is the therapist's efforts to gradually break down this resistance.

TRANSFERENCE

Transference develops when clients start relating to their therapist in ways that mimic important relationships in their lives. For example, a client might start behaving toward the therapist as if the therapist were a parent or lover. As transference emerges, the client's free associations will drift more and more toward an interest in the therapist's personal life. The therapist's handling of these transference feelings is complicated, difficult, and important. The idea is to use the transference relationship as a model of how the client relates to certain crucial people. This endeavor can help the client gain critical insights and can give the client an opportunity to develop new modes of relating to people.

INTERPRETATION

Another critical process in psychoanalysis is the interpretation of the material presented. The therapist does not provide an interpretation for everything. Occasionally, however, the analyst does make suggestions about the possible meaning of certain kinds of information. For example, a therapist might suggest that a client's unwillingness to discuss feelings toward his mother might be significant, or a therapist might point out that a client is using a particular defense mechanism.

Interpretations involve confronting clients with new ideas. Contrary to popular belief, these interpretations usually do not constitute devastating revelations for the client. Rather, interpretation is an ongoing process throughout psychoanalysis that moves forward slowly, bit by bit. If an analyst tries to move too quickly and too deeply with an interpretation, the client may be overwhelmed and will probably reject the new idea. Instead, it is important for the therapist to move forward slowly, offering interpretations that may be just out of the client's own reach. The ultimate goal of these interpretations is to help the client gradually gain insight into the nature of his or her unconscious conflicts and defenses. It is believed that this insight will promote the resolution of key conflicts and the discarding of counterproductive defenses.

MODIFIED PSYCHOANALYTIC APPROACHES

Classical psychoanalysis was geared for a particular kind of clientele that Freud was seeing in Vienna some 80 years ago. As psychoanalytic practitioners fanned out across Europe and America, many found that it was necessary to adapt psychoanalysis to different cultures, changing times, and new kinds of patients. Thus, there developed a great many variations on Freud's original approach to psychoanalysis. Some of these adaptations, such as those by Carl Jung (1917), Alfred Adler (1927), and Otto Rank (1945), were sweeping revisions based on fundamental differences in theory. Others, such as those by Karen Horney (1937), Harry Stack Sullivan (1953), and Erik Erikson (1963), involved more subtle changes of emphasis. Still others (Stekel, 1950) simply involved efforts to streamline the process of psychoanalysis. Hence, today we have a rich diversity of psychoanalytic approaches to therapy that vary in many ways from classical psychoanalysis. Although I cannot review all these new variations on psychoanalysis, I can outline some of the major trends seen in modern approaches to psychoanalytic therapy (Kutash, 1976).

First, most new approaches have tried to reduce the cost and the time commitment required by psychoanalysis. Many therapists see their clients only once a week instead of the traditional four or five times a week. Furthermore, it is no longer assumed that it will take three to five years to accomplish significant therapeutic gains.

Second, psychoanalytic approaches have been modified so as to be relevant to a greater variety of clients. Classical psychoanalysis was considered appropriate only for certain kinds of neurosis—a rather narrow range of disorders. Modern approaches have been extended to encompass all forms of neurosis and some psychoses and may also be applied to people who simply wish to experience personal growth.

Third, the goals of psychoanalysis now go beyond the mere discovery of repressed conflicts and defenses. Considerably less attention is devoted to probing the mysterious workings of the unconscious. Instead, the focus is on the conscious processes of the ego. In addition to helping clients reappraise unhealthy modes of adjustment, the therapist actively works to facilitate the acquisition of new ways of relating to people and healthier life patterns.

Fourth, with the reduced emphasis on probing the unconscious, the client/therapist interaction has changed significantly. Analysts no longer depend on the process of free association, which was truly "free" only very rarely anyway. The couch has been supplanted by face-to-face interaction that simply emphasizes genuine communication and candor. In this face-to-face interaction the therapist tries to take advantage of subtle nonverbal clues that may be provided by the client.

Fifth, modern psychoanalysis no longer assumes that personal problems are rooted in conflict centering on sex and aggression. It now recognizes that there is a much greater diversity of reasons for neurotic behavior.

Sixth, modern psychoanalytic approaches put much less emphasis on delving into a client's past and trying to reconstruct early childhood experiences. Instead, the emphasis is on understanding the client's present problems and conflicts and his or her current social network.

Humanistic Approaches to Therapy

The humanistic approaches to psychotherapy are united by a general philosophy about the human condition. As you may recall from Chapter 2, this humanistic philosophy takes an optimistic view of human nature, emphasizes the importance of subjective reality, and assumes that humans have rational abilities to consciously choose their courses of action. Actually, quite a few approaches to therapy fall under the humanistic banner. Among the more prominent are client-centered therapy (Rogers, 1951), Gestalt therapy (Perls, 1969), rational-emotive therapy (Ellis, 1973), transactional analysis (Berne, 1961), reality therapy (Glasser, 1965), logotherapy (Frankl, 1967, 1969), and existential therapy (May, 1969). For purposes of illustration, I will describe two of the most widely used systems: Carl Rogers's client-centered therapy and Fritz Perls's Gestalt therapy.

INSIGHT THERAPY. *Any therapy involving a verbal relationship with a mental-health professional that has as its primary goal improved self-understanding.*

Like the psychoanalytic therapies, the humanistic therapies are **insight therapies.** In other words, their main goal is to help clients pursue a better understanding of their personality and behavior. However, humanistic approaches seek different kinds of insights, and they stalk them with altogether different methods.

CLIENT-CENTERED THERAPY

Carl Rogers's approach to psychotherapy is called **client-centered therapy** because the client sets the pace and determines the focus and direction of the therapy. It may seem surprising that the troubled layperson is put in charge of the therapy in this way. Rogers (1961) provides a compelling justification for this deviation from form.

CLIENT-CENTERED THERAPY. *An approach to therapy, developed by Carl Rogers, that emphasizes the client's role in directing the therapy and provision of a supportive therapeutic climate.*

It is the client who knows what hurts, what directions to go, what problems are crucial, what experiences have been deeply buried. It began to occur to me that unless I had a need to demonstrate my own cleverness and learning, I would do better to rely upon the client for the direction of movement in the process [pp. 11–12].

ORIGINS OF PSYCHOLOGICAL PROBLEMS

According to Rogers's theory, most personal distress is attributable to inconsistency between one's self-concept and one's subjective experience of reality. This inconsistency, which is called **incongruence,** makes the person feel threatened and leads to defensive maneuvers. This incongruence is believed to be rooted in clients' excessive dependency on others for approval and affection. In any case, this threatening incongruence restricts one's self-awareness and stifles one's potential for personal growth.

INCONGRUENCE. *In Rogers's theory of personality, any disparity between one's self-concept and actual experience.*

GOALS OF THERAPY

In order to solve the kinds of problems described above, a client-centered therapist tries to facilitate insights that are quite different from the repressed conflicts that the psychoanalyst tries to uncover. A principal goal is to help clients realize that they don't have to worry constantly about pleasing others. They are encouraged to respect their own feelings and values. Another goal is to help clients restructure their self-concept in ways that correspond to reality, while promoting self-acceptance. Ultimately, the goal is to foster self-determination and release the client's potential for self-actualization.

THERAPEUTIC CLIMATE

According to Rogers, the *process* of therapy is not as important as the *climate* in which the therapy takes place. *Rogers believes that it is critical for the therapist to create a warm, supportive atmosphere that will liberate the client's natural tendencies toward self-actualization.* The agent of change is the client; the therapist merely provides an environment conducive to this change. The therapist must provide three conditions in order to create a climate that will nurture personal growth:

1. *Genuineness.* It is critical that the therapist be genuine. In other words, he or she must communicate with the client in an honest and spontaneous fashion. The therapist must avoid phoniness and defensiveness. Clients must feel that they are being related to in an authentic manner.

14.2 *AN EXAMPLE OF CLIENT-CENTERED THERAPY*

As is shown in the following example of a client-centered-therapy interaction, this type of therapy sounds simple but is in fact difficult to perform effectively. Note that the therapist reflects feelings to the client, doing nothing more than stating for the client how the therapist perceives the client's feelings. The direction of the conversation rests with the client.

Client: I really feel bad today . . . just terrible.
Therapist: You're feeling pretty bad.
Client: Yeah, I'm angry and that's made me feel bad, especially when I can't do anything about it. I just have to live with it and shut up.
Therapist: You're very angry and feel like there's nothing you can safely do with your feelings.

Client: Uh-huh. I mean . . . if I yell at my wife she gets hurt. If I don't say anything to her I feel tense.
Therapist: You're between a rock and a hard place—no matter what you do, you'll wind up feeling bad.
Client: I mean she chews ice all day and all night. I feel stupid saying this. It's petty, I know. But when I sit there and try to concentrate I hear all these slurping and crunching noises. I can't stand it . . . and I yell. She feels hurt—I feel bad—like I shouldn't have said anything.
Therapist: So when you finally say something you feel bad afterward.
Client: Yeah, I can't say anything to her without getting mad and saying more than I should. And then I cause more trouble than it's worth [Duke & Nowicki, 1979, p. 565].

2. *Unconditional positive regard.* It also is imperative that the therapist show complete, nonjudgmental acceptance of the client as a person. The therapist should provide warmth and caring for the client with no strings attached. This does not mean that the therapist must approve of everything that the client does or says. A therapist can disapprove of a particular behavior while continuing to value the client as a human being.

3. *Accurate empathy.* Finally, the therapist must provide accurate empathy for the client. This means that the therapist must be able to understand the client's world from the client's point of view. Furthermore, the therapist must be sufficiently articulate to successfully communicate this understanding to the client.

THERAPEUTIC PROCESS

As already noted, the process of the therapeutic interaction is less important than the provision of a supportive climate. As the treatment proceeds, the therapist does not take a particularly active role. The client and therapist are viewed as equals, psychodiagnosis is avoided, and little guidance is provided. Interpretation and advice are taboo. There is no probing into the unconscious or delving into the past. Sessions are held only once or twice a week, and the therapy usually does not last longer than a year.

So just what does the therapist do? *Primarily, the therapist provides feedback in order to help clients sort out their feelings.* The therapist's key task is **clarification.** Client-centered therapists are supposed to function like human mirrors; they should reflect back a client's statements with increased clarity. Wexler (1974) suggests that a client-centered therapist serves as a substitute information processor for the client. This is necessary because the client's defensiveness and rigidity have led to confusion. The therapist helps the client sort out this confusing jumble of feelings by summarizing the obscure themes apparent from the client's ramblings. In addition to this clarification, the therapist helps clients become more aware of their feelings. This is accomplished by encouraging clients to express their feelings openly without the fear of being judged. Thus, through these relatively passive processes, client-centered therapists try to promote authenticity and self-determination.

CLARIFICATION. *A key process in Rogers's client-centered therapy, wherein the therapist helps clients see their problems more clearly.*

GESTALT THERAPY

GESTALT THERAPY. *An approach to therapy pioneered by Fritz Perls and characterized by a humanistic orientation. Historically, there was another Gestalt school of thought, centered in Europe in the early part of this century. The two schools are largely unrelated, the historical forerunner focusing mainly on the study of perceptual processes.*

Gestalt therapy was developed by Fritz Perls (1969), a charismatic figure who promoted his approach to therapy through compelling professional workshops rather than through research and writing. The therapy, which can be used with either individuals or groups, is a curious hybrid of psychoanalytic, humanistic, and existential ideas.

ORIGINS OF PSYCHOLOGICAL PROBLEMS

Although he used very different terminology, Perls's view of the roots of personal distress resembles Rogers's. Like Rogers, Perls believed that many people were troubled by the fact that they were not in touch with their "true" selves. According to Perls, problems emerge when people block out certain aspects of themselves rather than accepting the full Gestalt (the whole picture). This defensive behavior thwarts personal growth.

PRINCIPLES

The main goal of Gestalt therapy is to improve clients' awareness and their willingness to accept responsibility for their own lives. This requires, first of all, that the therapist refuse to take responsibility for the client's life. Many clients eagerly hope to put themselves into the hands of their therapist. Gestalt therapists are trained to reject these overtures toward dependency. Although Gestalt therapists will work to be supportive, they will not let clients lean on them too much, because the clients need to learn to take responsibility for their own lives.

Whereas a client-centered therapist plays a relatively passive role, a Gestalt therapist plays an active, assertive role. Gestalt therapists *confront* clients about their defensive maneuvers. They don't engage in a great deal of interpretation; rather, they simply try to draw attention to the sources of a client's problems.

A tremendous emphasis is placed on keeping the client in the "here and now." Clients are not permitted to dwell on the past or the future. Instead, they are constantly reminded to focus on the immediate present. Many communication gimmicks are used to keep the client/therapist interaction very present-oriented.

TECHNIQUES

In trying to penetrate a client's defenses, a Gestalt therapist focuses extensively on nonverbal clues. It is assumed that verbal statements are often misleading and self-serving. Therefore, nonverbal communication may provide important information about a client's *true* feelings.

Gestalt therapists depend a great deal on exercises and games that they put their clients through. These games usually involve role playing, wherein the client may act out a conversation with someone else, reverse roles and take the point of view of another person, or even pretend to be a particular part of his or her personality.

Gestalt therapists also make use of clients' dreams, especially recurring dreams. They believe that certain dream elements represent fragments of the client's personality that are being blocked out. Often, they will have the client reenact the dream several times from the perspective of different actors in the dream.

The Gestalt approach to therapy is often applied to groups. However, Gestalt therapists use group situations somewhat differently than other group therapists do. Most group therapists promote group interaction and encourage members to function in a therapeutic role, offering advice and insight to one another. In contrast, Gestalt therapists more or less conduct individual therapy in front of a group. Group members take turns being in the "hot seat" that makes them the temporary focus of this therapeutic endeavor. Clients have considerable freedom in signing up for these group workshops. Thus, entry into and exit from therapy are relatively flexible with the Gestalt approach.

Behavioristic Approaches to Therapy

A third approach to therapy emerged from the behavioristic tradition. You may recall from Chapter 2 that behaviorism has been an important school of thought in psychology since the 1920s. However, not until the 1950s did the behaviorists divert some of their energy to the development of therapeutic interventions. Until then, behaviorists were content to focus their attention on theoretical rather than practical issues, conducting laboratory research to identify general principles of behavior. Although a few behaviorists made occasional excursions into the clinical realm before the 1950s, modern behavioral therapy was born in 1958 with the publication of Joseph Wolpe's *Psychotherapy by Reciprocal Inhibition*. Since then, there has been an explosion of interest in behavioral approaches to psychotherapy. Today, more and more psychotherapists are using behavioral approaches, especially those who work with children (O'Leary, 1984). Behavioral interventions have been developed for virtually all kinds of psychological problems and disorders (Turner, Calhoun, & Adams, 1981).

BEHAVIOR THERAPY. *An approach to therapy emphasizing application of the principles of learning; often distinguished from insight therapy because the focus is on directly changing behavior rather than achieving insight.*

Behavior therapy shares a great deal of kinship with behavior modification or self-modification procedures (see Chapter 5). Behavior therapy and self-modification are based on the same philosophy and share many of the same principles and procedures. In fact, any division between behavior therapy and self-modification is arbitrary. Essentially, under self-modification I described some of the simpler procedures that relatively untrained people can apply to themselves in order to deal with everyday problems. Under behavior therapy I will discuss more complex procedures that are often used by professionals to help people solve more severe behavioral problems. You shouldn't be surprised when you see some overlap between self-modification and behavior therapy; they are really the same thing in different guises. Most of the procedures I discussed under self-modification are frequently used by professional behavior therapists, and many of the procedures I will describe under behavior therapy could conceivably be used in self-modification efforts.

GENERAL PRINCIPLES

Behavior therapy consists in applying the principles of learning in systematic efforts to help people with psychological problems. Like self-modification, it involves using the principles of respondent conditioning, operant conditioning, and observational learning in order to change behavior in therapeutic ways. Behavior therapy is based on a number of assumptions, the first three of which also provide the basis for self-modification (see Chapter 5).

1. *Adjustment is situationally specific.* As we saw in Chapter 5, behaviorists believe that most people are well adjusted in some areas of their lives and more poorly adjusted in other areas. For example, a person might be quite competent in most respects but have a severe problem with alcohol consumption. Because adjustment is situationally specific, the behaviorist argues that it is unnecessary (not to mention unrealistic) for a therapist to try to change the client's entire personality.

2. *Behavior is learned.* It is assumed that a person's behavior is governed by her or his experience, or learning history. No matter how pathological or disordered one's behavior might be, the behaviorist believes that this undesirable behavior is the result of one's past conditioning. Furthermore, even very pathological behavior is assumed to be controlled by environmental contingencies.

3. *What has been learned can be unlearned.* The same learning processes that account for the acquisition of unhealthy patterns of behavior can be used in therapeutic efforts to improve behavior. Thus, behavior therapists attempt to change clients' behavior by applying the principles of conditioning.

4. *Therapeutic efforts should focus on specific behavioral problems.* Like self-modification, behavior therapy focuses directly on specific target behaviors that are observable. Psychoanalytic and humanistic approaches to therapy generally assume that problem behaviors are symptoms of underlying disorders. Accordingly, psychoanalytic and humanistic therapists help the client pursue insight, which is supposed to reshape personality, which, in turn, is supposed to promote healthy behavioral change. In contrast, the behaviorists assume that insight is largely irrelevant. Behavior therapists work with their clients to identify specific problem behaviors that the clients would like to see changed.

5. *Specific therapeutic procedures should be linked to specific problems.* Once the specific troublesome behaviors have been targeted, the behavior therapist designs a program to directly modify these behaviors. The nature of the therapeutic program depends very much on the kind of problem that has been identified. In contrast to psychoanalytic and humanistic approaches, there is no single process of behavior therapy that is applied with most clients. Instead, there are a great variety of specific therapeutic procedures that are thought to be useful for particular problems.

6. *Therapeutic progress should be monitored carefully.* Behavioral therapists strongly affirm the value of carefully monitoring therapeutic progress. Of course, therapists of *any* theoretical persuasion pay attention to how the therapy is working. However, behaviorists tend to differ from other therapists in two ways. First, they put a greater emphasis on the importance of measuring therapeutic outcomes. Second, because they have relatively concrete and specific therapeutic goals, they can usually be much more precise than other therapists in this effort to measure therapeutic progress.

SPECIFIC BEHAVIORAL TREATMENTS

Behavior therapy uses quite a number of specific behavioral techniques, since clients show quite a diversity of behavioral problems. Consequently, the discussion that follows will be illustrative rather than exhaustive.

SYSTEMATIC DESENSITIZATION

SYSTEMATIC DESENSITIZATION. *A behavior-therapy procedure used to reduce clients' anxiety responses.*

Systematic desensitization is the treatment technique that really launched the entire behavior-therapy movement. Developed by Joseph Wolpe (1958, 1973), the technique is intended for use with clients who are troubled by excessive anxiety. *The treatment assumes that debilitating anxiety in response to certain stimuli or situations is acquired through classical conditioning.* The treatment attempts to weaken the conditioned association between the crucial stimuli and the response of anxiety.

This weakening process involves three steps. First, the therapist helps the client build an anxiety hierarchy. This is a list of specific fear-arousing stimuli that center on a particular source of anxiety, such as flying, academic tests, the other sex, or some animal. The client ranks the individual stimuli according to how much anxiety they elicit, from least to most anxiety-arousing. An example of such an anxiety hierarchy can be seen in Box 14.3.

14.3   *AN ANXIETY HIERARCHY FOR SYSTEMATIC DESENSITIZATION*

Here is an example of a hierarchy of a woman with a fear of heights and a penchant for hiking (from Rudestam, 1980, pp. 42–43).

Degree of fear	
5	I am standing on the balcony on the top floor of an apartment tower.
10	I am standing on a stepladder in the kitchen to change a light bulb.
15	I am walking on a ridge. The edge is hidden by shrubs and treetops.
20	I am sitting on the slope of a mountain, looking out over the horizon.
25	I am crossing a bridge 6 feet above a creek. The bridge consists of an 18-inch-wide board with a handrail on one side.
30	I am riding a ski lift 8 feet above the ground.
35	I am crossing a shallow, wide creek on an 18-inch-wide board, 3 feet above water level.
40	I am climbing a ladder outside the house to reach a second-story window.
45	I am pulling myself up a 30° wet, slippery slope on a steel cable.
50	I am scrambling up a rock, 8 feet high.
55	I am walking 10 feet on a resilient, 18-inch-wide board, which spans an 8-foot-deep gulch.
60	I am walking on a wide plateau, 2 feet from the edge of a cliff.
65	I am skiing an intermediate hill. The snow is packed.
70	I am walking over a railway trestle.
75	I am walking on the side of an embankment. The path slopes to the outside.
80	I am riding a chair lift 15 feet above the ground.
85	I am walking up a long, steep slope.
90	I am walking up (or down) a 15° slope on a 3-foot-wide trail. On one side of the trail the terrain drops down sharply; on the other side is a steep upward slope.
95	I am walking on a 3-foot-wide ridge. The slopes on both sides are long and more than 25° steep.
100	I am walking on a 3-foot-wide ridge. The trail slopes on one side. The drop on either side of the trail is more than 25°.

JOSEPH WOLPE

During the sessions devoted to constructing the anxiety hierarchy, the therapist will usually begin the second phase of the therapy, which involves relaxation training. Different therapists will use different relaxation procedures. Whatever procedures are employed, it is critical that the client learn to engage in deep and thorough relaxation, especially on command from the therapist.

In the third phase of the treatment, the client tries to work up through the hierarchy, starting with the least anxiety-arousing stimulus and imagining each stimulus while learning to remain relaxed. The therapy proceeds step by step through the anxiety hierarchy over a number of sessions. For each step, the client is told to relax and then asked to imagine the anxiety-producing situation as vividly as possible. If the client experiences substantial anxiety, he or she drops the imaginary scene and concentrates on relaxation. The client keeps repeating this process until he or she can imagine the scene with little or no anxiety. Once the anxiety associated with a particular scene is conquered, the client tackles the next stimulus in the anxiety hierarchy. Gradually, the client moves through the hierarchy, learning to cope with stimuli that arouse more and more anxiety. After stimuli are conquered in the client's imagination, the client is encouraged to confront these stimuli in real life. It is hoped that the imaginal desensitization will reduce anxiety enough so that clients will be able to confront situations that they used to avoid. Usually, these real-life confrontations will prove harmless, and the person's anxiety response will be further reduced.

The principle at work here is simple. Anxiety and relaxation are incompatible responses. If a person can be reconditioned so that a stimulus elicits relaxation, this counters the fear response. The treatment may strike you as too simple to work, but there is plenty of evidence that it is an effective procedure for alleviating problems with anxiety (Leitenberg, 1976). For example, Table 14.1 summarizes the results of one study (Paul, 1966) on the efficacy of desensitization. There is some debate about whether imaginal desensitization can be effective by itself or whether it is necessary to have benign exposures to the real stimuli (Lazarus & Wilson, 1976). In any case, it is clear that systematic desensitization is a powerful technique for dealing with excessive anxiety.

TABLE 14.1 **Proportion of cases in various improvement categories following treatment for stage fright**

Treatment	Number of cases	Unimproved	Slightly improved	Improved	Much improved
Desensitization	15	0%	0%	14%	86%
Insight	15	7	47	27	0
Attention (placebo)	15	20	33	47	0
No treatment (control)	29	55	28	17	0

AVERSION THERAPY

AVERSION THERAPY. *A behavior-therapy procedure used to reduce the frequency of an undesirable response. It involves pairing the stimulus that elicits the response with an aversive stimulus.*

Aversion therapy is by far the most controversial behavioral treatment. Aversion therapy is used to reduce the frequency of maladaptive or undesirable responses. In this treatment, the unwanted response is paired with an aversive stimulus, such as an electrical shock, a nausea-inducing drug, or a verbal insult. For example, alcoholic clients have been given electrical shocks each time they sip a drink during specially arranged therapy sessions (Vogler et al., 1970).

Aversion therapy has been used successfully to reduce the frequency of a great variety of maladaptive behaviors, including alcohol and drug use, cigarette smoking, overeating, sexual deviance, self-mutilation, stuttering, writer's cramp, gambling, and shoplifting (Lazarus & Wilson, 1976; Sandler, 1975). Although aversion therapy is a potentially powerful technique, it should be used only with willing clients and only when nonaversive alternatives appear unlikely to be effective (Sandler, 1975).

TOKEN ECONOMIES

TOKEN ECONOMY. *In behavior therapy or behavior modification, a system employing symbolic reinforcers, which can later be converted into authentic reinforcement.*

You may recall from Chapter 5 that a **token economy** is a system for doling out symbolic reinforcers, which may subsequently be traded for real positive reinforcers. While a token economy can be very effective in self-modification efforts, it has also proved very worthwhile in the management of institutionalized people (Paul & Lentz, 1977), and such programs are widely used (Atthowe, 1973).

A common and significant problem with chronic psychiatric patients is that they tend to be apathetic and listless. This makes a chronic psychiatric ward rather difficult to run efficiently and is antagonistic to the patients' ultimate recovery. This apathy has been successfully counteracted with well-designed token economy systems. In these token economies, institutional residents are rewarded for such things as taking care of personal hygiene, cleaning their rooms, helping with ward maintenance, treating one another respectfully, and cooperating with hospital personnel. Even very severely disturbed persons often respond well to these token economy interventions.

COGNITIVE RESTRUCTURING

COGNITIVE RESTRUCTURING. *A behavior-therapy procedure that tries to change clients' ways of thinking about their lives in order to alter their behavior.*

In recent years, behavior therapists have focused more on their clients' thought processes, or cognitions. Borrowing from Albert Ellis's rational-emotive therapy, which emerged out of the humanistic orientation, they have recognized that clients' belief systems are often crucial determinants of their maladaptive behavior. In **cognitive restructuring** (Beck, 1976; Meichenbaum, 1977) therapists try to change the way clients think about important things. More specifically, they work to change clients' self-talk. Essentially, the therapist helps clients identify self-defeating statements that they are prone to make when confronting certain challenges, such as exams, social interactions, or job interviews. *The therapist then helps clients modify their self-talk so as to promote more adaptive behavior.* The therapist may use a variety of strategies in this endeavor. What is unique about cognitive restructuring is the target behavior to be modified. In cognitive restructuring, the behavioral target is covert verbalizations. Behaviorists *used* to view such verbalizations as too private and unobservable to be of interest to them. But the new cognitive emphasis among behaviorists has led to a reevaluation of this position. This movement offers the possibility of more integration between traditional insight therapies and behavioral approaches to therapy.

Group-Oriented Approaches to Therapy

GROUP THERAPY. *Therapeutic endeavors intended to ameliorate psychological disorders, conducted simultaneously with a group of people.*

Psychotherapy does not have to be conducted on an individualized, one-to-one basis. In many instances therapy is conducted simultaneously with a group of clients. Although group-oriented approaches to therapy date back to the turn of the century, **group therapy** came of age in the 1950s and 1960s. During this period, the expanding demand for therapeutic services forced clinicians to use group-oriented techniques. At the same time, these clinicians began to realize that group therapy was more than a cheap substitute for individual therapy. Gradually, it was recognized that group therapy has its own unique strengths and advantages.

There is, of course, no single approach to group therapy. All three major schools of thought in psychology have adapted their ideas to the group-treatment situation. A psychoanalytic theoretical orientation provided the basis for one of the earliest and most popular approaches to group therapy. This was the **psychodrama** technique, developed by Jacob Moreno in Vienna in the 1920s. Moreno (1946) had clients act out problems and conflicts with a group of people in order to arrive at new insights and gain access to blocked feelings.

PSYCHODRAMA. *A relatively old approach to group therapy wherein clients use role playing in order to practice and foster healthier behavior.*

More recently, the behaviorists have adapted some of their specific procedures for use with a group. For example, clients plagued by similar fears and anxieties have been treated collectively with systematic desensitization (Fishman & Newes, 1971). Assertiveness training groups provide another example of a group treatment grounded in the behavioristic tradition. In these groups, the techniques of modeling and behavioral rehearsal are used to help clients increase their assertiveness (Fensterheim, 1972).

The humanistic school of thought has been the biggest champion of group-oriented approaches to psychotherapy. Numerous approaches to group therapy have been spawned by the humanistic movement. For example, we have already seen that Gestalt therapy is frequently done in a group setting. Eric Berne's transactional analysis approach is also widely used for group therapy. Furthermore, the much-publicized encounter group movement was based largely on the ideas of Carl Rogers.

ENCOUNTER GROUP. *A group experience designed to promote personal growth and not intended to ameliorate a specific and clearly recognized psychological disorder. Such groups generally strive to enhance participants' interpersonal awareness.*

Some theorists distinguish between group therapy, on the one hand, and encounter groups, sensitivity groups, and human-relations groups, on the other. According to this distinction, *group therapy* involves the professional treatment of people who exhibit manifest psychological problems. In contrast, **encounter groups** are designed for people who believe themselves to be psychologically healthy but who are seeking an expansion of awareness and personal growth. This distinction is somewhat artificial in that these two approaches share a great deal in terms of clientele, goals, and procedures. Nonetheless, there are enough differences in emphasis to merit making a very loose distinction. In this chapter, I will limit myself to a discussion of group therapy. I will discuss the encounter movement in Chapter 15.

THE PROCESS OF GROUP THERAPY

As already noted, group therapy may be conducted in a variety of ways. In spite of this diversity, a number of generalizations can be made about the process of group therapy (Korchin, 1976).

GROUP COMPOSITION

A therapy group typically consists of about eight participants. The clients are usually seated in a circle so that they can see one another as well as the therapist. The participants are usually screened by the therapist, but therapists vary greatly in terms of whom they see as a good candidate for group therapy.

Group therapy is much more than a cheap substitute for individual therapy.

Most therapists exclude severely psychotic persons who are likely to be disruptive. There is considerable debate about whether it is better to have a homogeneous group (people who are similar in age, sex, and presenting problem) or a heterogeneous group. Practical difficulties usually dictate that groups be at least moderately heterogeneous. Once assembled, a therapy group may be closed off to new members, or it may be open to adding new participants when they appear appropriate.

ROLE OF THE THERAPIST

In a group situation, the therapist's role tends to be subtle. Generally, the therapist is *not* viewed as the exclusive source of wisdom in the group. Although the therapist may make inquiries and interpretations, the participants may also function in this "therapeutic" role. *Many therapists try to stay in the background and focus primarily on promoting group cohesiveness.* They model therapeutic behaviors for other participants and try to ensure that the group climate stays healthy and supportive. The therapist always retains a special status in the group, but the therapist and clients are on much more equal footing in group therapy than in individual therapy. The leader in group therapy must be prepared to express emotions, share feelings, and cope with challenges from group members.

ROLE OF THE PARTICIPANTS

In group therapy, the participants are not passive recipients of therapeutic endeavors. *Rather, they are actively involved in the therapeutic process, functioning as therapists for one another.* Group members describe their problems, trade viewpoints, share experiences, and discuss coping strategies. Most critically, they provide acceptance and emotional support for one another.

In this supportive atmosphere, group members work at peeling away the social masks that cover their insecurities. Once these problems or flaws are uncovered, members work at correcting them. As members come to value one another's opinions, they work hard to display healthy changes so as to win the group's approval.

ADVANTAGES OF GROUP THERAPY

I mentioned earlier that group therapy is not merely a cheap substitute for individual therapy. Group therapy has many unique strengths, and it is expected that the use of group-oriented approaches will continue to increase in the 1980s (Scheidlinger, 1984). Obviously, one of the big advantages of group therapy is that this approach extends the therapist's reach to a greater number of people. Group-oriented approaches do save time and money. More people receive therapy, and they often pay less for it. However, there are other advantages as well when therapy is conducted on a group basis. Irvin Yalom (1975), who has studied group therapy extensively, has described many of these advantages. I will focus on those that are largely unique to group, as opposed to individual, therapy.

1. One nice feature of group therapy is that participants quickly realize that their misery is not unique. Clients often start individual or group therapy feeling very sorry for themselves and thinking that they alone have a terribly burdensome cross to bear. In the group situation, they quickly see that they are not unique and that many others have similar problems. This tends to be a reassuring discovery.

2. Many psychological problems essentially turn out to be difficulties in relating effectively to other people. Group therapy provides an opportunity for participants to work on their social skills in a relatively "safe" environment. Participants can practice their interpersonal skills in a nonthreatening, sup-

portive climate. Individual therapy does not provide the same kind of opportunity to develop social skills. Moreover, in the group situation, the therapist can see clients relating to one another and can detect interpersonal inadequacies to be worked on that might not show up in individual therapy.

3. In group therapy, participants have an opportunity to both give and receive emotional support. In giving support to other group members, participants come to feel that they have value as human beings. The support that members receive from one another can also be of tremendous value.

4. Finally, it should be pointed out that many kinds of problems are particularly suitable for treatment in a group context. For example, group-therapy techniques have been applied very profitably to marital and family problems. In fact, many psychotherapists specialize exclusively in marital or family therapy. Peer self-help groups are another very profitable application of group-therapy techniques. In peer self-help groups, people who have a problem in common get together regularly to help one another out. The original peer self-help group was Alcoholics Anonymous. Today, similar groups, made up of drug addicts, former psychiatric patients, single parents, and so forth, work with or without professional guidance in order to help members deal with particular problems.

Physiological Approaches to Therapy

Numerous psychological disorders are treated through physiological interventions, such as the prescription of drugs. Such physiological interventions assume that psychological disorders are caused, at least in part, by biological malfunctions. For some disorders this assumption clearly has merit. You may recall from Chapter 13 that physiological factors are implicated in the etiology of various psychological disorders. I will discuss two general kinds of physiological treatment: the drug therapies and electroconvulsive shock therapy. These therapies are *medical* treatments that are used exclusively by physicians.

THERAPEUTIC INTERVENTIONS WITH DRUGS

Like group therapy, psychopharmacology came of age in the 1950s. During these years, rapid gains were made in the treatment of psychological disorders with drugs. Today, chemical treatments are firmly entrenched as a principal therapeutic tool used by psychiatrists.

A great number of drugs are used for therapeutic purposes. This diverse array of drugs could be organized in a number of different ways. I will place the various drugs into three categories: antianxiety drugs, antipsychotic drugs, and antidepressant drugs.

ANTIANXIETY DRUGS

Popping pills to relieve anxiety is a rather common activity these days. The drugs involved in this widely used coping strategy are the antianxiety agents. The most popular of these are Valium (generic name: diazepam) and Librium (chlordiazepoxide). The barbiturate sedatives are also used for this purpose, especially when sleeping problems are present. Collectively, these drugs are often called "tranquilizers." Generally, they are prescribed for people with neurotic anxiety, moderate tension, or psychosomatic problems. These drugs exert their effects almost immediately and can be fairly effective in alleviating feelings of anxiety (Greenblatt & Shader, 1974).

ANTIPSYCHOTIC DRUGS

The antipsychotic drugs are used primarily with schizophrenics and people

with severe mood disorders. They calm psychotic hyperactivity, reduce mental confusion, and eliminate hallucinations and delusions. These drugs work gradually, with patients usually responding within two days to two weeks; further improvement may occur for several months. Among the more commonly used drugs in this category are Thorazine (chlorpromazine), Serpasil (reserpine), Haldol (haloperidol), and Lithane (lithium carbonate). These drugs have proved tremendously valuable, in that they have permitted many people with severe disorders to return to the community instead of being housed indefinitely in psychiatric facilities (Freedman et al., 1976). However, the relapse rates tend to be fairly high when these drugs are discontinued.

ANTIDEPRESSANT DRUGS

Antidepressant drugs are used to elevate mood in order to bring people out of depression. Among the more prominent antidepressant agents are Elavil (amitriptyline) and Nardil (phenelzine). Like the antipsychotic drugs, they exert their effects gradually rather than immediately. Like any treatment, they are not 100% effective, but they do have a pretty good track record for relieving depression (Davis, 1973).

PROBLEMS WITH DRUG THERAPIES

Drug therapies have proved quite useful in the treatment of psychological disorders. Drugs can produce very impressive therapeutic gains in a relatively brief time. However, the efficacy and value of drug therapies are often overestimated by both clients and clinicians. The drug therapies are not without their problems.

Side effects from the drugs present one very significant problem. The drugs used for therapeutic purposes are usually powerful drugs that exert many effects in addition to the intended curative effects. These side effects range from

---

14.4 BLENDING APPROACHES TO THERAPY: ECLECTICISM AND MULTIMODAL THERAPY

As you have probably gathered by now, there are a great many very different approaches to conducting psychotherapy. Although most of the more influential approaches are mentioned in this chapter, our coverage really does not extend below the "tip of the iceberg." Raymond Corsini's (1981) *Handbook of Innovative Psychotherapies* lists *241* different systems of therapy, including such approaches as aqua-energetics therapy, dance therapy, nude therapy, reparenting therapy, and transcendence therapy.

While new approaches to therapy seem to come and go like clothing fads, attracting a lot of attention along the way, a very significant trend seems to have crept into the field of psychotherapy largely unnoticed. There seems to be a trend away from strong loyalty to individual schools of thought (Gallatin, 1982). The era of exclusive use of one system, complete rejection of all other systems, and ferocious factional fighting about which systems work best may gradually be drawing to a close. In a 1976 survey of psychologists' therapeutic orientations (Garfield & Kurtz, 1976), researchers were surprised to find that a majority of respondents described themselves as *eclectic* in approach. Eclecticism involves selecting what appears to be the best from a variety of systems or approaches. Thus, eclectic therapists use ideas, insights, and techniques from a variety of sources—and adjust their approach to the unique needs of each individual client. Eclecticism requires a creative blending of a number of different theoretical perspectives.

Many eclectic therapists simply borrow ideas somewhat haphazardly from a variety of orientations as they see fit, but some theorists are working to develop systematic approaches to being eclectic. The most notable thus far is the system originated by Arnold Lazarus (1981) called multimodal therapy.

In Lazarus's scheme, therapy is viewed as an educational process, rather than a disease-correcting medical treatment. The therapist plays the role of a knowledgeable mentor for the client. Personal problems are assumed to be multidimensional and are analyzed in terms of seven dimensions: overt behaviors, emotions, sensations, imagery, cognitions, interpersonal aspects, and biological considerations. The therapy is organized around four processes: assessment of the problems, development of an individually tailored intervention plan, implementation of the plan, and ongoing evaluation and refinement of the plan. An enormous range of intervention techniques are used, depending on the nature of the client's problems.

annoying to deadly. Potential side effects of antipsychotic drugs include blurred vision, constipation, diarrhea, allergic reactions, lethargy, changes in blood pressure, respiratory problems, seizures, and insomnia (Long, 1977). A moderately common side effect of certain antipsychotic drugs (the neuroleptics) is a syndrome known as **tardive dyskinesia** (Baldessarini, 1980). This is a serious neurological disorder marked by a chronic impairment of motor coordination, involuntary spastic movements, and tremors. Given these possible side effects, it is clear that some patients can take therapeutic drugs more easily than other patients.

Another problem is possible psychological or physiological dependence. Some of the drugs present little problem in this regard, but others are exceedingly dangerous. In particular, people are prone to become dependent on many of the antianxiety agents (Lickey & Gordon, 1983).

Still another shortcoming is that drug therapies often produce rather "superficial" curative effects. For example, gobbling up Valium does not really solve one's problems with anxiety. It merely gets rid of some unpleasant symptoms temporarily. Indeed, this temporary relief may lull patients into an attitude of complacency that prevents them from working toward a more permanent solution. In a similar vein, patients on antipsychotic or antidepressant drugs often suffer a relapse when the drug is discontinued (Lickey & Gordon, 1983). Thus, drug-based solutions to psychological problems are often short-lived. For this reason, it is usually a good idea to use drug therapy in conjunction with other kinds of psychotherapy.

ELECTROCONVULSIVE THERAPY

In the 1930s, Von Meduna concluded that epilepsy and schizophrenia could not coexist in the same body. On the basis of this *inaccurate* assumption, Von Meduna theorized that it might be therapeutic to artificially induce epileptic-like seizures in people with psychological disorders. Initially, a drug (Metrazol) was used to trigger these seizures, but it was soon replaced by electricity, yielding modern **electroconvulsive therapy (ECT)**.

In ECT, electrodes are attached to the skull over the temporal lobes of the brain. A 70- to 130-volt current is then applied for less than a half-second. This triggers a brief (5–20 seconds) convulsive seizure, during which the patient loses consciousness. Patients usually return to normal in an hour or two, depending on the collection of drugs that they were given before the treatment. Various drugs are regularly administered before ECT treatments to alleviate patients' fears and to reduce the likelihood of spinal fractures caused by the convulsion. Patients typically receive between 6 and 20 treatments as inpatients at a hospital. In recent years, there has been a trend toward using unilateral shock (to just one side of the brain) because it appears safer than bilateral shock (Salzman, 1978).

THERAPEUTIC EFFECTS

There is much controversy about the therapeutic effectiveness of ECT. Reported improvement rates range from 15 to 90% (Friedberg, 1976). This spectacular variability in results is probably due to the fact that ECT studies tend to be methodologically unsound. Barton (1977) could find only *six* studies among hundreds on ECT that used appropriate control groups to assess therapeutic gains. The poor methodology and highly contradictory results of ECT research make it very difficult to draw a conclusion about the therapeutic efficacy of ECT. There are ardent proponents who maintain that it is a remarkably effective treatment procedure (Fink, 1979), and there are equally ardent opponents who argue that it is no better than a **placebo** treatment (Friedberg, 1976). Although ECT was once considered appropriate for manic disorders, schizophrenia, depression, and a range of other problems, even most

TARDIVE DYSKINESIA. *A neurological disorder associated with the use of neuroleptic antipsychotic drugs. It involves a chronic deterioration of motor coordination.*

ELECTROCONVULSIVE THERAPY (ECT). *A physiological treatment involving administration of electrical shock to a client in order to trigger a convulsion, which is believed to be therapeutic.*

PLACEBO. *In pharmacology, a placebo is a substance with no real effect that is given to some subjects in order to control for the effects of expectations in testing the efficacy of some drug. In general usage, placebo effects refers to a situation wherein subjects experience some change or improvement from an empty, fake, or ineffectual treatment.*

proponents now recommend it only for severe depression. Thus, its principal use today is in the treatment of depression, although some psychiatrists still use it for other syndromes (Gill & Lambourn, 1981; Kendell, 1981).

Curiously, insofar as ECT may be effective, no one knows *why*. Evidence suggests that the occurrence of a cortical seizure is critical to the treatment, but we don't really understand how a seizure might be therapeutic (Salzman, 1978). *In summary, about the only conclusion that one can draw is that the effectiveness of ECT is highly debatable.* There seems to be enough favorable evidence (Scovern & Kilmann, 1980) to justify the continued use of ECT in treating depression. However, we really do not know just how effective it is for this purpose. This does *not* make ECT unique among psychotherapies. However, it is especially problematic in the case of ECT because ECT carries an unusual number of risks.

RISKS

There is disagreement not only about the effectiveness of ECT but also about the risks associated with the procedure. ECT does not appear to be harmless. It is well documented that ECT may produce memory losses. These losses include amnesia for recent events and difficulties in remembering new information (Salzman, 1978). Everyone acknowledges that memory losses are a common side effect of shock therapy. However, ECT proponents (Weeks, Freeman, & Kendell, 1981) assert that these losses usually last only a month or two;

14.5   *PERSONAL EXPERIENCE WITH SHOCK THERAPY: A VISIT TO THE COLONEL*

What can I tell you about the shock treatments that I went through? I can't tell you about all the terrors involved, they seem to be too personal, locked too far away inside of me. Even if I could bring them back, I could never make you feel their intensity. This same thing seems to hold true for the emotions involved. All that leaves me to tell you is what happened. I am not saying this is what all shock is about, or that it happens this way everywhere. I am saying that this is what happened to me in this particular institution.

Slang for shock in that institution was known as "gettin' Kentucky fried" and being taken to shock was known as "a visit to the Colonel." I was going for a visit.

Along the way, I always started making deals with God, "if you get me out of this one, . . ." They never worked out. When the deals fell through, I started making every promise I knew I could keep, and just to be safe, a few I knew I couldn't. Looking back, it all seems kind of funny. At the time, I was sure they were trying to kill me.

The room where it was done was in the very center of the ward. This was not surprising. Almost all of our shock was done as a disciplinary measure, our very lives revolved around staff's ability to enforce discipline and order upon us. So, to me, it was not too surprising that the Colonel set up shop where he did.

When the door opened, the intense whiteness of the fluorescent lights blinded me. Staff took advantage of this by leading me to the gurney where I was to lie down. By the time my eyes adjusted, I was on my back with several pair of hands holding me down.

I don't remember ever seeing the Colonel's face; if I did, its image is lost to me now. He always stood out of sight at the head end of the gurney. Anyway, by now I had other things on my mind.

A mouthpiece was crammed rather indelicately into place, and the conductant was smeared on my temples. There was some technical talk and someone said "now" (I wanted desperately to say wait a moment). And then there it was—one of the most excruciating pains I have ever felt. My back arched in an attempt to jump off the gurney, all the air squeezed out of my lungs, my legs flexed until they felt as if they would break, my head felt as if it would pop off. I was out of control, it was not me anymore.

I don't know how long it took, but I finally passed out. When I opened my eyes again, I had the headache of headaches. I was confused, I couldn't connect two thoughts.

The next two or three days were a nightmare of confusion and awkward movements, always feeling like a thought was there, on the tip of your tongue, but not able to grab it. The more you grabbed at it, the more elusive it became, and the more frustrated you became.

Eventually, I returned to normal, but before that happened, I would go through a deep dark depression. I could fight the system, I could fight Staff, I could fight the drugs, the aides, and the other patients.

I could not fight this. I was beaten. My thoughts were exactly that, mine. Before shock they were untouched, now they had been reached and, worse still, disorganized externally. The depression then seemed to come from a sense of defeat, of being violated, and of being mentally raped.

How can I make you feel that?

Quoted by permission from a former student.

critics of ECT maintain that the losses are often permanent. Breggin (1979), for instance, presents impressive evidence that long-term cognitive disruption occurs in at least some ECT patients. The issue is complex, since it appears that the severity of memory disruption is probably related to the number of shock treatments received. In any case, it is clear that at least some risk of mental deterioration is associated with the use of ECT. There is also evidence (Templer, Ruff, & Armstrong, 1973) that ECT may produce permanent brain damage.

Although ECT is probably not as damaging as its more outspoken critics maintain (Weiner, 1984), the evidence certainly provides reason for concern. Additionally, it should be pointed out that ECT can be dangerous for patients with undiagnosed heart problems (Malamud & Zheutlin, 1953). Controversy about the use of ECT is also fueled by the fact that most patients subjectively find it to be exceedingly unpleasant (even terrifying) and the inexcusable reality that it is sometimes used as a disciplinary maneuver in mental hospitals to "keep patients in line" (Breggin, 1979; see Box 14.5).

RECOMMENDED USE

In view of the risks associated with electroconvulsive shock therapy, a majority of experts currently recommend that physicians use the treatment reluctantly and sparingly. Specifically, they suggest that ECT should be confined to severe cases of depression that have not responded to other types of treatment. In line with these suggestions, there has been a trend toward more conservative use of ECT (Weiner, 1984). Unfortunately, a minority of psychiatrists appear to be rather injudicious in their use of ECT, prescribing a great number of treatments for a wide variety of patients without trying other alternatives first (Friedberg, 1976). Some states are now developing legislation to curtail this overuse of ECT. This anti-ECT movement is becoming as controversial as ECT itself. Although I concur that the overuse of ECT is a significant problem that merits attention, I am not sure that legislation is the answer. Realistically, most lawmakers do *not* have any training that prepares them for making judgments about medical or psychological care. I find the vision of politicians and bureaucrats dictating the parameters of medical/psychological treatment very unappealing.

Summary

Psychotherapy is the treatment of psychological disorders and/or psychological distress. Many people seek professional help for a great variety of problems; there are probably many more who could benefit from therapy but never receive any.

Therapists come from a variety of professional backgrounds. Psychologists, psychiatrists, psychoanalysts, and psychiatric social workers are the principal providers of psychotherapy. Each of these groups tends to approach therapy somewhat differently.

Psychoanalytic approaches to therapy assume that neurosis originates from unresolved conflicts lurking in the unconscious. Therefore, in psychoanalysis, free association and dream analysis are used to probe the unconscious. When this probing hits sensitive areas, resistance can be expected. The transference relationship may be used to overcome this resistance so that the client can accept interpretations that lead to insight. The classical version of psychoanalysis is not widely practiced anymore, but there are many modified versions of psychoanalysis operating today.

Like psychoanalytic therapies, humanistic therapies pursue insight. Rogers's client-centered therapy assumes that problems are derived from incongruence between one's self-concept and reality. Accordingly, a client-centered therapist tries to help clients restructure their self-concept and improve self-acceptance. This is done by providing a therapeutic climate including genuineness, empathy, and unconditional positive regard. The process of therapy emphasizes clarification of the client's feelings. Perls's Gestalt therapy also works toward helping clients get in touch with their true feelings. Gestalt therapists confront clients about their defensive maneuvers and encourage them to take full responsibility for their own lives. In this endeavor, they often use group and role-playing techniques.

Behavioristic approaches to therapy assume that (1) adjustment is situationally specific, (2) behavior is learned, (3) what has been learned can be unlearned, (4) therapeutic efforts should focus on specific problems, (5) specific procedures should be linked to specific problems, and (6) therapeutic progress should be evaluated carefully. Systematic desensitization, a treatment for excessive anxiety, has proved very effective. It involves the construction of an anxiety hierarchy, relaxation training, and step-by-step movement through the hierarchy, pairing relaxation with each stimulus. In aversion therapy, an unwanted response is reduced by pairing it with an unpleasant stimulus. The token economy, which is a system for doling out symbolic reinforcers, has proved very useful with a variety of institutionalized populations. In cognitive restructuring, therapists try to modify clients' self-talk.

All three major schools of thought in psychology, but especially the humanists, have adapted their ideas to the treatment of people in groups. Therapy groups can be composed in a variety of ways, but there is usually some screening by the therapist. Most group therapists play a relatively subtle role, staying in the background and trying to promote group cohesiveness and a therapeutic climate. The participants provide mutual support and share problems, experiences, and coping strategies. Essentially, they act as therapists for one another. Group therapy is not simply a poor substitute for individual therapy. Group therapy offers people an opportunity to see that their problems are not unique and allows them to work on their social skills in a nonthreatening environment where they provide emotional support for one another. Many kinds of problems are particularly suited to treatment in a group context.

Psychological disorders may also be treated with physiological interventions. A great variety of drugs are prescribed for therapeutic purposes. These include antianxiety drugs, antipsychotic drugs, and antidepressant drugs. Although drug therapies can be very effective, there are potential problems, such as side effects and drug dependency. Also, drugs sometimes provide a rather superficial solution for personal problems. Electroconvulsive shock therapy (ECT) is used to trigger a cortical seizure that is alleged to have therapeutic value for some disorders, especially depression. There is a great deal of debate about the therapeutic effectiveness of ECT. There is also heated argument about possible risks associated with its use.

The application section of this chapter will discuss practical considerations that are relevant to seeking professional therapy. This discussion may be helpful if you ever have to seek psychotherapy for yourself, a friend, or a family member.

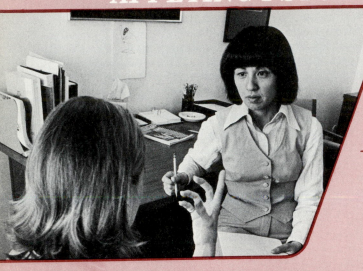

Seeking Psychotherapy

Answer the following true or false.

_____ 1. Psychotherapy is an art as well as a science.
_____ 2. A therapist's school of thought or approach to therapy is relatively unimportant.
_____ 3. Psychotherapy can be harmful or damaging to a client.
_____ 4. Psychotherapy can be inexpensive.
_____ 5. It is a good idea to "shop around" for a therapist.

All of the above statements are essentially true. If you missed a few of them, don't feel bad. Most people are rather naive about the practicalities of seeking professional psychotherapy. The task of finding an appropriate therapist can be very complex. Should you see a psychologist or a psychiatrist? Should you opt for individual therapy or group therapy? Should you see a Gestalt therapist or a behavior therapist? Do you want a male or a female therapist? The unfortunate part of all this is that people seeking psychotherapy often feel overwhelmed by personal problems. The last thing they may need or want is to be confronted by yet another complex problem.

Nonetheless, the importance of finding a good therapist who is appropriate for you cannot be overestimated. There is evidence (Strupp, Hadley, Gomes-Schwartz, 1977) that psychotherapy can sometimes be damaging to clients. This is probably due most of the time to a therapist's incompetence or to a mismatch between the therapy and the client. Although a great many very talented therapists are available, psychotherapy, like any other profession, has incompetent practitioners as well. Therefore, you should "shop around" for a skilled therapist, just as you would for a good attorney or a good mechanic. In this application section I will try to give you some information that will be helpful if you ever have to seek psychotherapy for yourself or someone else.

WHEN SHOULD A PERSON SEEK PROFESSIONAL THERAPY?

There is no simple answer to this question. Obviously, people *consider* the possibility of professional therapy when they are psychologically distressed. However, there *are* other alternatives for dealing with psychological distress.

First, there is much to be said for trying to solve problems yourself. In fact, most therapists do not try to solve your problems for you; instead, they try to help you solve them yourself. Hence, you should usually seek professional help only after you have made an active effort to conquer personal problems on your own. There is also something to be said for seeking advice from your friends, family, members of the clergy, and so forth. Insights about personal problems do not belong exclusively to people with professional degrees. Many nonprofessionals can be very perceptive about the intricacies of life. So when should you seek professional help? You should probably think seriously about professional therapy (1) when you have no one to lean on, (2) when the people you lean on (or associate with) suggest it, (3) when you feel helpless and overwhelmed, or (4) when your life is seriously disrupted by your personal problems. Of course, you do not have to be "falling apart" in order to benefit from psychotherapy. You may want to pursue therapy simply because you want to get more out of your life.

WHERE DOES ONE GO FOR PROFESSIONAL THERAPY?

Professional therapy can be found in a wide variety of settings. Contrary to general belief, most therapists are not in private practice. Many work in institutional settings. Therapeutic services can be obtained from any of the following:

1. *Private practitioners.* Self-employed therapists are listed in the Yellow Pages under their professional category, such as psychologist or psychiatrist. Private practitioners tend to be relatively expensive, but they also tend to be more experienced than therapists in other settings.

2. *Community mental-health centers.* Community mental-health centers have salaried psychologists, psychiatrists, and social workers on staff. They provide a variety of services to people on an outpatient basis. They often have staff available on weekends and at night to deal with emergencies.

3. *Hospitals.* Several kinds of hospitals may provide therapeutic services. There are both public and private mental hospitals that specialize in the care of people with psychological problems. Additionally, many general hospitals have a psychiatric ward for the treatment of psychological disorders. Although these hospitals may concentrate primarily on inpatient treatment, many provide outpatient treatment as well.

4. *Human-services agencies.* Various social service agencies employ psychotherapists. Depending on your community, you may find agencies that deal with family problems, juvenile problems, drug problems, and so forth.

5. *Schools and workplaces.* Most high schools and colleges have counseling centers where their students can get help with personal problems. Similarly, some large businesses offer in-house counseling to their employees.

Therapy can be obtained in many settings, and the exact configuration of services available will vary from one community to another. To find out what your community has to offer, it is a good idea to consult friends and the local phone book. Community mental-health centers and human-services agencies are usually very helpful in explaining the range of services available in a particular area.

IS THE THERAPIST'S PROFESSIONAL TRAINING IMPORTANT?

Generally, the individual's professional training is not a crucial consideration in selecting a therapist. Many talented therapists come from all three of the principal therapeutic professions (psychology, psychiatry, and social work). It is true that only a psychiatrist can prescribe drugs for disorders that merit drug therapy. However, some critics (Wiener, 1968) argue that many psychiatrists are too quick to try drugs to solve everything. In any case, a psychologist or social worker will refer you to a psychiatrist if he or she believes drug therapy would be helpful. It's not a bad idea to inquire about a therapist's degrees in order to verify that he or she *does* have professional training. But the nature of that training isn't all that important.

IS THE THERAPIST'S SCHOOL OF THOUGHT OR APPROACH IMPORTANT?

This is a complex question. Logically, one would expect that different approaches to therapy might be differentially effective for certain kinds of problems. However, there is little evidence to support this belief (Korchin, 1976). A therapist's school of thought is probably not nearly as important as his or her personal characteristics. Some therapists are better than others, but this appears to be due more to differences in their personal skills than to differences in their theoretical orientation. Although the therapist's school of thought does not appear to be very important, there is one thing that a client should be concerned about. Some therapists are locked into their theoretical orientation to such a degree that they have pat answers for everything and fail to see a client's unique qualities. These inflexible therapists tend to twist everything so that it fits their preconceived notions. This sort of inflexibility can interfere with the progress of therapy.

IS THE THERAPIST'S SEX IMPORTANT?

This depends on your attitudes. If *you* feel that the therapist's sex is important, then for you it is. The therapeutic relationship must be characterized by trust and rapport. If you won't feel comfortable with a therapist because of her or his sex, that could inhibit the therapeutic process. Hence, you should feel free to look for a therapist of a particular sex.

IS THERAPY ALWAYS EXPENSIVE?

No. Psychotherapy does not have to be prohibitively expensive. Private practitioners tend to be the most expensive, charging between $25 and $100 per (50-minute) hour. These fees may seem high, but they are very much in line with those of similar professionals, such as attorneys or physicians. As already discussed, however, private practitioners are not the only sources of therapeutic services. Community mental-health centers and social service agencies are usually supported by tax dollars and can therefore charge lower fees. Many of these organizations employ a "sliding scale," wherein clients are charged according to how much they can afford to pay. Thus, most communities have relatively inexpensive opportunities for psychotherapy. Moreover, many health insurance plans provide partial reimbursement for the cost of psychotherapy.

WHAT SHOULD YOU LOOK FOR IN A PROSPECTIVE THERAPIST?

In searching for a therapist, you should not be bashful about asking prospective therapists some questions about their training, approach, fees, and so forth. Many clients are timid about this because they expect a negative reaction from the therapist. However, these are reasonable questions, and the vast majority of therapists will be most accommodating. Those who are not accommodating may be too rigid or pompous to be very good therapists anyway. You may ask your preliminary questions over the phone. Therapists are usually willing to talk to prospective clients for five or ten minutes on the phone in order to provide some general information about their services. If things appear promising, you may decide to make an appointment for an interview (you often have to pay for this). In this interview the therapist will gather more

INSIDE WOODY ALLEN CARTOON COPYRIGHT © 1977 KING FEATURES SYNDICATE, INC. ALL RIGHTS RESERVED.

information on your problem in order to decide whether she or he can be helpful to you. At the same time, you should be making a similar judgment about whether *you* believe this person could help you with your problems.

So what do you look for in a therapist? First, you should look for personal warmth and sincere concern. You want somebody whom you can be open and candid with. Try to judge whether you will be able to talk to this person in a relatively nondefensive manner. Second, look for empathy and understanding. Does the person listen thoughtfully and display an understanding of what is troubling you? Third, look for self-confidence on the part of the therapist. A self-assured therapist will not try to intimidate you with jargon or boast need-lessly about what he or she can do for you. Without doing these things, a confident therapist will communicate to you a sense of competence. When all is said and done, you pretty much have to *like* your therapist. If you don't like the person, you will not be able to establish the rapport needed for an effective therapeutic relationship.

WHAT CAN YOU EXPECT FROM PSYCHOTHERAPY?

It is important to have realistic expectations about psychotherapy, or you will probably be disappointed. Some people expect miracles. They expect to feel better quickly with little effort. Many clients expect their therapist to take over running their lives for them. They tend to be irritated when the therapist refuses to encourage this kind of dependency.

14.6 *RECOMMENDED READING*
The Psychotherapy Maze
by Otto Ehrenberg and Miriam Ehrenberg (Holt, Rinehart & Winston, 1977)

This book is billed as a "consumer's guide to the ins and outs of therapy." The Ehrenbergs provide a frank and down-to-earth discussion of the practicalities of psychotherapy. Most books on therapy are devoted almost exclusively to explaining different theoretical approaches to therapy. The Ehrenbergs go far beyond this in their book. They tackle practical issues such as how to select a therapist, how to make therapy work, and how to judge whether therapy is

doing you any good. They also discuss mundane but important details such as fees, insurance, missed sessions, and emergency phone calls. The Ehrenbergs' goal is to make therapy less intimidating and mysterious. They succeed handsomely in this endeavor.

While everybody who is committed to therapy wants to change, when therapy brings you to the point where the possibility of change becomes real, strong pulls emerge from within

to keep you the way you are. Long-standing life-styles cannot be given up, even if they have caused much suffering, without the anxiety of losing the familiar and the fear of confronting the unknown. Abandoning old patterns of existence when you are not sure that you can make it any other way is a frightening prospect. When therapy brings you to this point, you may want to run from it [p. 151].

As Ehrenberg and Ehrenberg (1977) point out, "Psychotherapy takes time, effort and courage" (p. 5). It is a slow process; your problems will not melt away instantly. It is hard work: your therapist is only a facilitator; *you* have to confront the challenge of changing your own behavior. And it may not be pleasant; you may have to face up to some painful truths about yourself.

ONCE YOU'RE IN THERAPY—WHAT IF YOU'RE DISSATISFIED?

If you feel that your therapy isn't going anywhere, you should probably discuss these feelings with your therapist. Don't be surprised, however, if the therapist suggests that it may be your fault. It seems that the psychoanalytic concept of resistance has some validity. Clients often do have a difficult time facing up to their problems. This tendency can lead to a lack of cooperation on the part of the client. Thus, if your therapy isn't progressing very well, you may have to decide whether this is due to your resistance or to other problems. This is not an easy decision, since you are not an unbiased observer. Ehrenberg and Ehrenberg (1977) suggest that negative feelings about therapy are likely to be a manifestation of resistance when (1) you have nothing specific or concrete to complain about, (2) your attitude about therapy changes suddenly, (3) you have had the same problem with other therapists in the past, (4) your conflicts with the therapist are similar to those that you have with other people in your life, or (5) you start hiding things from your therapist.

Given the likelihood that the cause of your dissatisfaction may be your own resistance, you should not be too quick to terminate therapy if you're dissatisfied. However, there is always the possibility that your therapist is not very skilled or that the two of you are incompatible. If you just can't develop a reasonable rapport with your therapist, you should feel free to terminate your therapy.

IDEAS: REVIEW OF LEARNING OBJECTIVES

When you have mastered the material in this chapter, you should be able to do the following.

1. List the five general approaches to psychotherapy covered in the chapter.
2. Describe the sequence of events that leads a client into therapy.
3. Briefly describe the four professions that provide psychotherapy.
4. Describe the view of classical psychoanalysis on the origins of neurosis and discuss the probing of the unconscious.
5. Explain the psychoanalytic concepts of resistance, transference, and interpretation.
6. List six trends in modified approaches to psychoanalysis.
7. Discuss the origins of psychological problems and the goals of therapy as viewed by the client-centered therapist.
8. Describe the three aspects of therapeutic climate believed to be important by Rogers.
9. Describe therapeutic process in client-centered therapy.
10. Summarize the principles and techniques employed by Gestalt therapy.
11. List the six general principles that form the basis for behavior therapy.
12. Describe the three phases of systematic desensitization and discuss its effectiveness.
13. Describe the purpose and nature of aversion therapy.
14. Describe the nature and uses of token economies.
15. Describe cognitive restructuring.
16. Distinguish between group therapy and encounter groups.
17. Describe the process of group therapy.
18. List four advantages of group therapy.
19. List the three general kinds of drugs used for psychotherapeutic purposes.
20. Discuss the problems associated with drug therapies.
21. Describe ECT and discuss its therapeutic effects.
22. Discuss the risks associated with ECT.
23. Summarize information on when a person should seek psychotherapy.
24. List the five settings in which professional therapy can be found.
25. Discuss how important a therapist's professional training, school of thought, or sex might be.
26. Summarize information on what one should look for in a prospective therapist.
27. Discuss what one should think about when dissatisfied with professional therapy.

TERMS: REVIEW OF NEW VOCABULARY

When you have mastered the material in this chapter, you should be able to define the following terms.

Aversion therapy
Behavior therapy
Clarification
Client-centered therapy
Cognitive restructuring
Dream analysis

Electroconvulsive therapy
Encounter group
Free association
Gestalt therapy
Group therapy
Incongruence

Insight therapy
Placebo
Psychoanalysis
Psychodrama
Psychotherapy
Resistance

Systematic desensitization
Tardive dyskinesia
Token economy
Transference

PEOPLE: REVIEW OF MAJOR THEORISTS AND RESEARCHERS

When you have mastered the material in this chapter, you should be able to summarize the principal contributions and/or ideas of the following people.

Sigmund Freud
Jacob Moreno

Fritz Perls
Carl Rogers

Joseph Wolpe

Irvin Yalom

15 ESOTERIC APPROACHES TO PERSONAL GROWTH

These ads from the *Village Voice* illustrate the bewildering array of personal-growth opportunities available in most large cities.

What do hypnosis, skydiving, Buddhist meditation, calligraphy, square dancing, Kundalini yoga, encounter groups for Catholic gays, a psychochirology workshop, and a transvestite boutique have in common? Advertisements for all these "services" and many others as well can often be found together in "alternative" newspapers, which are popular in many large American cities. Amongst such a hodgepodge, one might find some very legitimate and worthwhile opportunities for guidance toward personal growth. At the same time, given the overwhelming nature of this huge hodgepodge of services, it is no wonder that many people are very confused about the merits of such things as yoga, meditation, and biofeedback.

This chapter will examine a number of unusual or esoteric routes to growth. These are approaches that are not well understood by the general public. In fact, many people assume that these approaches are worthless fads or clever frauds because they are so often lumped with approaches that *do* appear to have little or no merit. I will focus mainly on methodologies that have real value. However, I will also comment repeatedly on the problematic issue of charlatanism, which crops up frequently when many of these esoteric approaches are discussed. The principal approaches that I will review are (1) encounter groups, (2) biofeedback, (3) hypnosis, and (4) spiritual pathways from the East. Some of these methods could have been discussed in the previous chapter, on psychotherapy, since they are tools that are frequently used by professional therapists. However, treating these intriguing topics in a separate chapter allows much more thorough coverage.

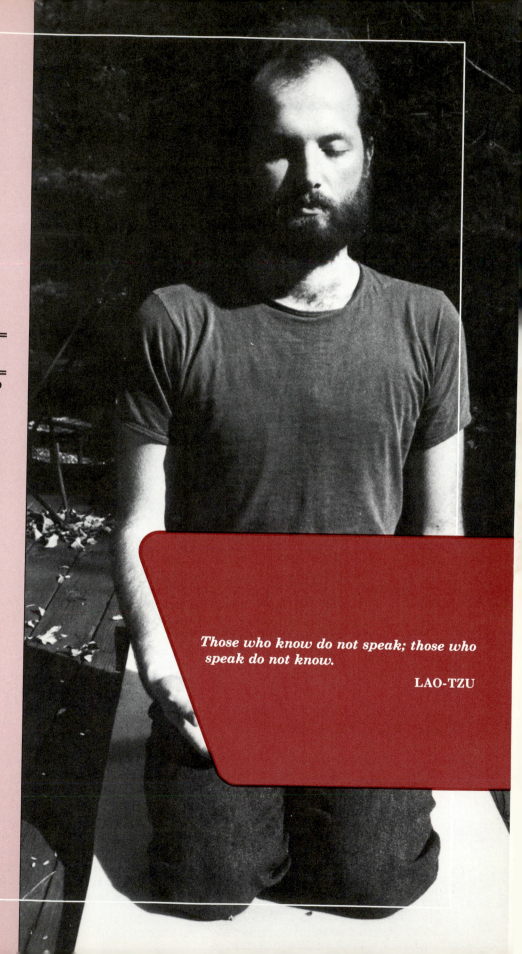

Summary

Applying Psychology to Your Life: An Epilogue on the Pursuit of Self-Improvement

Those who know do not speak; those who speak do not know.

LAO-TZU

Encounter Groups

In the previous chapter I made a distinction between group therapy and encounter groups. According to this distinction, *group therapy* involves a group leader who is a mental-health professional and participants who have sought professional help because they are troubled by some significant personal distress. In contrast, an **encounter group** may be led by someone with little or no professional training and may be made up largely of apparently "normal" participants who are motivated only by curiosity or a desire to undergo a group "experience."

DESCRIPTION

ENCOUNTER GROUP. *A group experience designed to promote personal growth and not intended to ameliorate a specific and clearly recognized psychological disorder. Such groups generally strive to enhance participants' interpersonal awareness.*

A great variety of group experiences have been offered under the banner of the human-potential movement. Massarik (1972) provides an illustrative list of some 39 types of group experiences that might be included under the generic term *encounter groups*. On this list, one will find such things as T-groups, sensitivity training groups, nude encounter groups, sensory awareness groups, marathons, conflict management labs, confrontation groups, and self-management groups. Obviously, the encounter group category encompasses a diverse array of experiences that vary in goals, techniques, approaches, styles, and results. This enormous diversity makes it difficult to describe a typical encounter group. Nonetheless, I can sketch a general picture.

An encounter group is supposed to provide an intense, intimate interpersonal experience. The leader or group facilitator usually runs the group in a relatively democratic manner. In larger groups there may be a coleader. Group size usually ranges between 8 and 20. Typically, the participants have had little prior contact. Some groups meet only once, usually for a relatively long period, such as an entire day or weekend. Other groups may meet repeatedly, usually weekly, for a more brief period, such as an hour or two.

Generally, encounter groups work toward making participants more aware of their own feelings and needs, as well as the feelings and needs of others. To produce this improvement in interpersonal awareness, the group tries to foster an atmosphere that values honesty, openness, and candor. In particular, members are encouraged to express emotions and feelings that social restrictions often force them to bottle up. Participants provide affection for one another, but they are also expected to be critical when members try to hide behind social masks. The basic idea is to get people to shed their dependence on such masks. Thus, participants are quick to zero in on one another's self-deceptions. To facilitate this goal, exercises are often used to improve members' sensitivity to nonverbal communication.

OUTCOMES

Given the enormous variety of group techniques, it is difficult to draw general conclusions about the impact of encounter groups. However, a superb large-scale study by Lieberman, Yalom, and Miles (1973) has provided some interesting insights about the effects of encounter groups. In this study, college-student volunteers were randomly assigned to one of 17 encounter groups. Participants' personality and attitudes were measured before the group experience, soon after the experience, and six to eight months later. Ratings of participants' changes in personality were also obtained from the group leaders, from friends, and from fellow participants.

The results of the study were complex. Overall, they suggested that *encounter groups can be either beneficial or harmful*. Subjectively, a majority (65%) of the participants felt that their encounter experiences were beneficial. Typically, these subjects reported improvements in spontaneity, honesty, and self-awareness. Interestingly, however, these estimates of personal benefits tended to dwindle with time. Many participants who thought very highly of their experiences soon afterward were much less enthusiastic six to eight months later.

Although participants' personal feelings about an encounter experience are very important, they also are very biased. Therefore, Lieberman et al. (1973) combined self-ratings with ratings from friends, fellow participants, and leaders to arrive at a more objective "composite change index." *On this more objective measure, roughly one-third of the participants showed positive changes in personality, values, and attitudes.* Another third failed to show any significant personal change. The remaining subjects either dropped out of their group or showed changes that were evaluated as *negative*.

Among the 18% of the participants who displayed negative changes, about half were regarded as full-fledged encounter group *casualties* who were damaged by the experience. Thus, the encounter experiences were harmful and destructive for about 9% of the subjects. Generally, these casualties suffered losses in self-esteem and felt less trustful toward others. As one might expect, these casualties were generally caused by verbal attacks on, or rejection of, the group member. A rather disturbing finding was that most group leaders were rather insensitive to the existence of casualties in their group. The untrained coparticipants were more likely to spot when somebody was seriously hurt.

FACTORS INFLUENCING OUTCOMES

The 17 groups studied by Lieberman et al. (1973) were not equally effective. Some had little impact on their members; others produced powerful experiences. Lieberman and his colleagues tried to sort out which factors were related to positive and negative outcomes.

LEADER CHARACTERISTICS

The theoretical or ideological allegiance of the leader was *not* consistently related to outcomes. It was not unusual for a particular theoretical approach, such as a Gestalt or psychoanalytic orientation, to yield *both* very positive and very negative outcomes. *However, leadership style was found to be influential.* Good leaders were moderately directive and provided a moderate amount of emotional stimulation by challenging, confronting, and exhorting group members. These good leaders provided considerable emotional support in the form of praise, affection, encouragement, and protection. They also showed skill in helping group members interpret their experiences.

15.1 RECOMMENDED READING
Inside Groups: A Practical Guide to Encounter Groups and Group Therapy
by Thomas R. Verny (McGraw-Hill, 1974)

As its title implies, this is a nontechnical book, aimed at the layperson, that attempts to provide some insight about encounter groups. Verny begins by providing some historical background on the group movement. He then examines the nature of encounter groups and discusses what they can and cannot do. He describes various approaches to encounter and talks about what to look for in a group leader. Although the topic necessarily brings forth some psychobabble, the book is a thorough and readable treatment of the encounter group phenomenon and will greatly enhance the reader's sophistication in these matters.

It is crucial for a new participant to understand clearly what he wants to gain from his group experience. Unless a serious attempt is made by him to work out—first in his own head and then with his group leader—what his goals are, his chances of gaining significantly from the group are poor indeed [p. 67].

Growth groups have a unique way of thinking and relating, as well as a language and an ethic of their own. It is sometimes difficult, therefore, for a neophyte to become a full-fledged member in good standing. The initiation rites, like all rites of passage, can be quite an ordeal—but they don't need to be [p. 71].

GROUP CHARACTERISTICS

Surprisingly, relatively few links are found between group characteristics and outcomes. The allegedly important variable of emotional intensity was *not* found to be related to either good or bad outcomes. Similarly, a confrontational atmosphere proved to be unrelated to group yield. The most important variable was the endorsement of "open boundaries," meaning that the group permitted the discussion of a wide range of topics. Open boundaries were associated with positive outcomes. Interestingly, there was a slight tendency for groups that met for a few lengthy sessions to be more productive than groups that met often but more briefly.

PARTICIPANT CHARACTERISTICS

The relation of participant characteristics to outcomes was exceedingly complex. This complexity is illustrated by the fact that people who clearly gained from the group experience and psychiatric casualties were *similar* in certain key characteristics, such as entering with poor self-esteem. Thus, members' personal qualities were not very consistent predictors of outcomes.

CRITIQUE

There is no doubt that encounter groups can provide worthwhile learning experiences. The objective evidence of this found by Lieberman et al. (1973) only adds to thousands upon thousands of personal testimonials. It is clear that some people become more sensitive to others, improve their self-awareness, learn how to express themselves more honestly, increase their capacity for deeper relationships, and so forth. The encounter group is an important social invention with a wide range of potential applications. Encounter groups are not a frivolous fad, and they will not disappear in the foreseeable future.

However, the evidence strongly indicates that caution should be exercised before leaping headlong into the human-potential movement. In encounter groups, people are encouraged to shed their defenses, open up, and become more vulnerable. In other words, they are asked to take a risk. In some cases this risk may backfire. Some people are not equipped to handle the candid, sometimes brutal feedback that they get from other members. The Lieberman et al. (1973) results indicate that some people are seriously harmed by their encounter group experience.

Given this reality, it is very important to have a skilled leader and a supportive group. Unfortunately, the human-potential movement seems to have drawn more than its share of charlatans and bumblers for leaders. This is probably because there is a minimal regulation of the encounter industry. Virtually anyone can advertise himself or herself as a group facilitator. It would seem wise to try to check the background of a group and its leader before joining. One should certainly inquire about the leader's professional training. A formal degree is no guarantee of skilled leadership, but it does provide some reassurance. If possible, it is probably a good idea to ask to observe the leader with a group before joining. In any case, one should move slowly and cautiously into the encounter group scene.

Biofeedback

Like encounter groups, biofeedback has received much publicity in recent years. Glowing newspaper reports on biofeedback suggest that it is a panacea for a great variety of medical and psychological problems. Prominent psychologists, such as Neal Miller (1985), who pioneered biofeedback research, predict that biofeedback techniques will be used more and more to "enhance the remarkable capacity we have to control our bodies" (p. 59).

DEFINITION

BIOFEEDBACK SYSTEM.
A procedure wherein a person's physiological processes are monitored and information about those processes is "fed back" to the person. A biofeedback system is used to achieve some control over involuntary bodily functions.

Just what is biofeedback? It is really not very mysterious. A **biofeedback system** is set up when a physiological recording device is used to monitor some bodily function, and information about that bodily process is fed back to the person. The intriguing part is this: armed with precise information about bodily functions, people are able to learn to exert far more control over them than previously thought possible. For example, many people have trouble with high blood pressure. This can be a serious medical problem for which drugs are often prescribed. Obviously, it would be nice if such people could learn to control their blood pressure. Evidence (Shapiro, Schwartz, & Tursky, 1972) indicates that biofeedback *can* be used to train people to control their blood pressure. Thus, you can see why people are enthusiastic about the potential of biofeedback. The reason for this excitement is that biofeedback systems are usually applied to bodily processes that were thought to be beyond voluntary control. Many of these bodily processes are intimately involved in our physiological response to stress. In Chapters 3–5 we learned the value of short-circuiting this bodily response to stress. It appears that biofeedback may be an excellent tool for achieving this goal.

APPLICATIONS

NEAL MILLER

CONTROL OF BRAIN ACTIVITY

As you know, an instrument called an electroencephalograph (EEG) can be used to monitor the electrical activity of the brain. Different brain-wave patterns are associated with different states of consciousness (see Figure 15.1). People are generally not able to produce a particular brain wave on command. With biofeedback training, however, people can learn to display remarkable control over their brain-wave activity.

In a typical experiment (Kamiya, 1969) the recording electrodes of the EEG are attached to the subject's skull, and the EEG signals are transformed into an auditory signal, such as a tone that increases or decreases in volume. This tone provides the biofeedback. It is explained to the subject that the tone is tuned into his or her brain-wave activity. The subject is then instructed to raise or lower the tone. Usually, the biofeedback system is set up so that the subject is asked to produce alpha waves, which range between 8 and 12 cycles per second. Most subjects quickly become fairly proficient at producing alpha activity. When asked afterward how they accomplish this, most have difficulty in explaining their technique.

The alpha-feedback studies generated considerable publicity because subjects reported that the alpha state was associated with a very pleasant psychological "high." Subjects described the state as one of tranquility, serenity, increased awareness, and relaxation. Furthermore, studies suggested that learning to produce alpha could improve task performance (Nowlis & Kamiya, 1970), memory (Green, Green, & Walters, 1970), and ability to tolerate pain (Gannon & Sternbach, 1971). These claims now appear greatly overstated (Lawrence & Johnson, 1977). Although alpha feedback may not be the panacea it once was believed to be, research is proceeding on other possible applications of biofeedback to the control of brain activity. For example, there is suggestive evidence (Sterman, 1977) that epilepsy and insomnia may be treatable with EEG biofeedback.

CONTROL OF CARDIOVASCULAR ACTIVITY

Our cardiovascular system appears to be particularly susceptible to the ravages of stress; Chapter 3 discussed the rather disturbing link between stress and heart disease. Hence, it comes as no surprise that researchers are very interested in the ability to acquire cardiovascular control through biofeedback training. Most of the attention has focused on the treatment of hypertension,

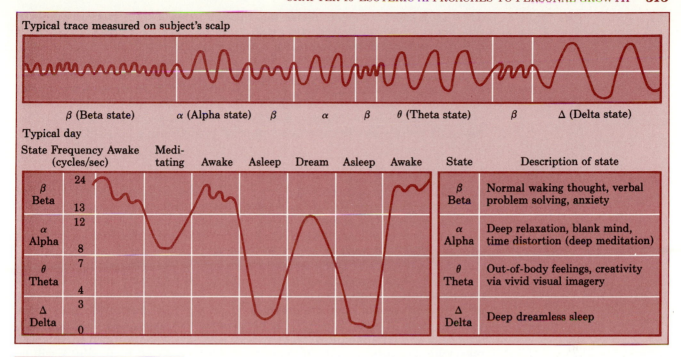

Typical trace measured on subject's scalp

β (Beta state)	α (Alpha state)	β	α	β	θ (Theta state)	β	Δ (Delta state)

Typical day

State	Frequency Awake (cycles/sec)	Medi-tating	Awake	Asleep	Dream	Asleep	Awake	State	Description of state
β Beta	24 — 13							β Beta	Normal waking thought, verbal problem solving, anxiety
α Alpha	12 — 8							α Alpha	Deep relaxation, blank mind, time distortion (deep meditation)
θ Theta	7 — 4							θ Theta	Out-of-body feelings, creativity via vivid visual imagery
Δ Delta	3 — 0							Δ Delta	Deep dreamless sleep

FIGURE 15.1 Brain-wave patterns seen under a variety of mental states: wakefulness, meditation, sleep, and dreaming. The state associated with each wave pattern is described on the right.

or high blood pressure. This very common affliction substantially increases coronary risk.

There is considerable evidence that subjects with hypertension can exert some control over their blood pressure. However, it is easier to increase blood pressure than to send it downward (Shapiro, Mainardi, & Surwit, 1977). Moreover, it remains to be shown that such decreases will be durable enough to correct the hypertensive problem (Blanchard, 1979). Nonetheless, the research in this area is promising, and many experts are optimistic that biofeedback can make a contribution to the treatment of hypertension.

Another line of research indicates that biofeedback can be used to train subjects to modify their heart rate. In one study, the average subject could increase heart rate by 13 beats per minute (see Lawrence & Johnson, 1977). These changes are not spectacular, but they do show that direct control over one's heart rate is possible. Although we can only speculate at this point, such control may have some value in reducing the likelihood of stress-related coronary problems.

CONTROL OF SKIN TEMPERATURE

Various studies have shown that people can be trained to exert some control over skin temperature at designated points on their body. The most frequent demonstration has been of control over hand temperature (Taub, 1977). This may seem a rather trifling finding, but it appears that voluntary control of finger temperature may be helpful in alleviating migraine headaches (Wickramasekera, 1973). Apparently, the changes in blood flow necessary to increase finger temperature somehow reduce the incidence and severity of the headaches. Additional research is needed to understand the mechanisms underlying these demonstrations.

CONTROL OF MUSCLE RELAXATION

The level of skeletal-muscular tension at various points on one's body can be measured by an instrument called an **electromyograph (EMG).** When this device is used to provide subjects with feedback about their level of muscular tension, the subjects can acquire considerable control over this physiological function (Budzynski & Stoyva, 1969). Essentially, biofeedback training with an

ELECTROMYOGRAPH (EMG). *A physiological recording device that monitors muscle tonus, or level of muscular tension.*

EMG is an exceptionally effective way to learn to relax. At numerous points in this book I have discussed the great value of learning to relax effectively. Effective relaxation may be helpful in the treatment of a host of stress-related problems. Promising results have been obtained with EMG feedback in the treatment of anxiety (Raskin, Bali, & Peeke, 1981), tension headaches (Blanchard & Andrasik, 1982), and hypertension (Lustman & Sowa, 1983). Moreover, the broad potential of EMG biofeedback was demonstrated in a recent study (McGowan, Haynes, & Wilson, 1981) that showed that EMG training could reduce certain aspects of subjects' response to a stressful stimulus.

CRITIQUE

It is easy to get excited about the subject of biofeedback—so easy, in fact, that many researchers who should have known better made overly extravagant projections in the 1960s and early 1970s. Swept up by this enthusiasm, biofeedback proponents did not inspect studies very closely for methodological flaws and engaged in grandiose speculation about possible implications. For instance, the benefits of alpha feedback were greatly exaggerated.

A more sober brand of optimism seems to be dominant today. It is now recognized that placebo effects and other experimental artifacts led to some unreplicable results. Furthermore, it is becoming clear that although we can learn to exert more control over our physiology than previously realized, there are limits to our capabilities. Nonetheless, research is continuing at a dizzying pace with promising results in many areas. It is clear that biofeedback will be an important technique for battling stress in the future. One of the nice features of biofeedback is its apparent harmlessness. It can be used to deal with many problems that are often treated with drugs, many of which produce a wide variety of undesirable side effects. Although more evidence is needed, it seems that side effects will not be a problem with biofeedback treatments.

While I have been emphasizing the potential utility of biofeedback in the treatment of adjustment problems, I should add that its potential goes far beyond the scope of our concern in this text. Biofeedback techniques are also proving useful in the rehabilitative treatment of purely physical problems, such as cerebral palsy, polio, nerve injury, and other neuromuscular disorders (Cataldo, Bird, & Cunningham, 1978; Keefe & Surwit, 1978). It also appears that biofeedback may be a useful tool for basic research on how physiological systems within the body interact. Thus, I can project with some confidence that in future years biofeedback will play an increasingly important role in both psychological and biomedical fields.

15.2

RECOMMENDED READING
New Mind, New Body
by Barbara Brown (Harper & Row, 1974)

If you're interested in biofeedback, this is probably the most readable introduction to this area of research. Brown, who has done some pioneering work in the area, has put together an exciting summary of biofeedback research. She also engages in some provocative speculation about future applications of biofeedback in medicine, psychotherapy, and education. As an enthusiastic advocate of biofeedback, Brown may be overly optimistic about the future, and some of her interpretations are more controversial than she indicates. Nonetheless, the book makes for very enjoyable reading.

Scientists have a double standard about publicity. In their hearts they crave it, but in their public stance they eschew its leveling effect, offering the intellect of the elite to the uneducated common society. They argue that, in biomedical science, the public will appropriate the secrets of science, misuse them, and come to harm and be disappointed. Their emotional-intellectual double standard has been delightfully exposed during the unusually long period of publicity that biofeedback has enjoyed. Several prominent bioscientists guardedly asked me how I was able to get in touch with so many media people. While the scientists were scheming to entice the media in their direction, they were publicly abhorring the rampant publicity about biofeedback [pp. 42–43].

Hypnosis

HYPNOSIS. *A technique that produces heightened suggestibility and a narrowing of attention.*

Hypnosis has a long and checkered history. It all began with an 18th-century Austrian physician by the name of Anton Mesmer. Practicing in Paris, he claimed to effect cures of various maladies by harnessing animal magnetism. He attained considerable popularity, but the local authorities ran him out of town on the grounds that it was all a hoax. Although officially discredited, practitioners of "mesmerism" persisted in plying their trade. Eventually, a Scottish physician, James Braid, became interested in the trancelike state that could be induced by the mesmerists. He didn't buy the magnetism theory of mesmerism, but he thought that the trance might be useful to accomplish anesthesia for surgery. It was Braid who renamed the phenomenon "hypnotism," borrowing from the Greek word for sleep. With a new name and a modest bit of scientific credibility, hypnotism gained some acceptance from the medical profession. Just as it was catching on as a technique for inducing general anesthesia, more reliable chemical anesthetics were discovered, and interest dwindled again.

Since then, hypnotism has led a curious dual existence. On the one hand, it has been the subject of numerous scientific studies, many of them by intellectual giants in the fields of psychology and medicine, including Sigmund Freud, Clark Hull, and Ernest Hilgard. Furthermore, it has enjoyed considerable use as a clinical tool by physicians, dentists, and psychologists for over 100 years. Among psychologists, for instance, a recent survey indicated that over 40% had used hypnotic techniques at some point in their career (Kraft & Rodolfa, 1982). However, an assortment of entertainers and quacks have continued in the tradition of Mesmer, using hypnotism for parlor tricks and charlatanism. Hence, the general public is understandably confused. I will try to clear up some of that confusion in this section.

HYPNOTIC INDUCTION

INDUCTION TECHNIQUES

Virtually everyone has seen a hypnotic induction enacted with the infamous swinging pendulum. Actually, there are a great many techniques for inducing the hypnotic trance. One excellent text (Kroger, 1977) lists over 20 techniques. Generally, it is the hypnotist's verbal behavior that plays a crucial role in the induction. The hypnotist confidently suggests to the subject that he or she is relaxing. Repetitively, softly, subjects are told that they are getting tired, drowsy, sleepy, and so forth. Usually, the hypnotist graphically describes bodily sensations that should be occurring: subjects are told that their arms are going limp, their feet are getting warm, their eyelids are getting very, very heavy. Gradually, the power of suggestion takes over, and the subject is hypnotized.

ERNEST HILGARD

SUSCEPTIBILITY

People differ in how well they respond to hypnotic induction. Ernest and Josephine Hilgard have done extensive research on this variation in hypnotic susceptibility. Not everyone can be hypnotized. About 10% of the population doesn't respond well at all. At the other extreme, only about 10% of subjects can achieve very deep trances. Responsiveness can be estimated by the *Stanford Hypnotic Susceptibility Scale* (SHSS). The distribution of scores on the SHSS can be seen in Figure 15.2.

What kind of person is highly susceptible to hypnosis? There is no single personality type that responds well. However, Hilgard (1970) has found some interesting correlations between certain characteristics and SHSS scores. People who can become deeply engrossed in intense experiences tend to be more susceptible. People who have a vivid imagination and strong fantasy

JOSEPHINE HILGARD

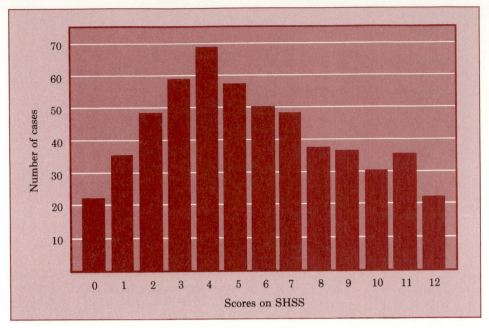

FIGURE 15.2 Distribution of first-session scores among 533 Stanford University students on the Stanford Hypnotic Susceptibility Scale.

involvement also tend to score high on the SHSS. Interestingly, people who experienced a lot of severe punishment in childhood tend to show good hypnotic susceptibility. It has been speculated that this punishment may have led such people to rely heavily on fantasy and may have made them relatively submissive.

HYPNOTIC PHENOMENA

Stage hypnotists usually concentrate on making their subjects behave foolishly. Obviously, instigating foolish behavior is hardly a noteworthy accomplishment. Underlying some of this silliness, however, are some interesting phenomena that can be induced through hypnosis.

1. *Anesthesia.* Under the influence of hypnosis, subjects can withstand rather remarkable amounts of pain. This analgesic effect has been put to use by some physicians and dentists, who use hypnosis as a substitute for anesthetic drugs. There is some debate about whether subjects fail to experience the pain or merely inhibit the normal response to the pain.

2. *Sensory distortions and hallucinations.* Hypnotized subjects may be led to experience auditory or visual hallucinations, hearing sounds or seeing things that are not there. They may also have their sensations distorted so that something sweet tastes sour or something with an unpleasant odor smells fine.

3. *Age regression.* A common hypnotic demonstration is to regress subjects to their childhood. These subjects often appear to display remarkable memories of trivial details relating to childhood experiences and will behave as if they were in fact much younger.

4. *Antisocial behavior.* Generally, it is believed to be difficult to get hypnotized subjects to do something inconsistent with their morality. Nonetheless, lab subjects have been induced to throw what they believed to be nitric acid into the face of the research assistant. Similarly, stage hypnotists are sometimes successful in getting people to disrobe in public. Thus, it is not out of the realm of possibility that a hypnotized person might be prompted into engaging in some antisocial behavior.

5. *Posthypnotic suggestions and amnesia.* Suggestions made during a hypnotic trance may influence a subject's behavior after the trance is lifted. The most common posthypnotic suggestion is to tell subjects that they will remem-

ber nothing that happened during their trance. Such subjects usually claim to remember nothing, as ordered.

THEORIES OF HYPNOSIS

THEODORE BARBER

Although there are many theories that purport to explain hypnosis, the reality is that we don't understand the phenomenon very well. The most crucial theoretical issue is whether hypnosis involves a true altered state of consciousness or some spectacular role playing.

ROLE-PLAYING EXPLANATIONS

Martin Orne (1970) and other theorists (Barber, 1969; Sarbin & Lim, 1963) believe that being hypnotized simply leads people to act out the role of hypnotic subject. According to this notion, people get caught up in their role and try to behave as they believe they are expected to, in order to please the hypnotist.

Two lines of evidence support this analysis. *First, it has been shown that some of the seemingly dramatic hypnotic phenomena can be duplicated by nonhypnotized subjects.* For example, nonhypnotized subjects can be suspended rigidly by only their heads and feet between two chairs (see Figure 15.3), duplicating hypnotic catalepsy (Meeker & Barber, 1971). Similarly, Orne and Evans (1965) showed that nonhypnotized subjects could easily be induced to throw so-called nitric acid into a stranger's face, just like hypnotized subjects. Furthermore, there is evidence (Barber & Hahn, 1962) that nonhypnotized subjects can display pain tolerance similar to that of hypnotized subjects. Such findings make hypnotic phenomena both less impressive and less mysterious. With these results in mind, Theodore Barber argues that we do not need to hypnotize an altered state of consciousness to explain feats that waking subjects can duplicate.

The second line of evidence involves demonstrations that hypnotized subjects often engage in faking. For example, Orne (1951) regressed hypnotized subjects to their sixth birthday and asked them to describe it. As usual, they responded with very detailed descriptions that appeared to represent great feats of memory. However, instead of accepting this information at face value, Orne compared it with information that he obtained from the subjects' parents. It turned out that many of the subjects' memories were inaccurate and invented! Orne also managed to get some psychological tests taken by some of his subjects when they were much younger. He regressed them to the appropri-

FIGURE 15.3 When instructed to lie between two chairs, suspended only by the head and feet, a hypnotized subject will do so. But so can you! Try it. Audiences think the effect is amazing simply because they do not question it.

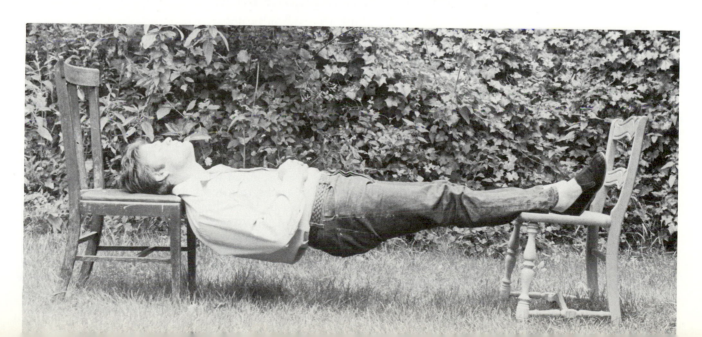

ate age and readministered the tests. The hypnotized subjects were *not* able to replicate the response patterns of their youth.

In summary, the role-playing explanation of hypnosis suggests that the power of suggestion leads subjects to go overboard being cooperative. This in itself is no small accomplishment, and it does not indicate that hypnosis is meaningless or useless. However, it certainly does take some of the romance and mystery away from hypnosis.

HYPNOSIS AS AN ALTERED STATE OF CONSCIOUSNESS

This theory proposes that hypnotic phenomena are attributable to the trance state that subjects enter. Proponents of the trance theory argue that it is doubtful that role playing can explain all hypnotic phenomena. They argue that even the most cooperative subjects are unlikely to endure surgery without a chemical anesthetic just to please their physician and live up to their role. They also point to evidence on physiological reactions that would seem to be difficult to produce at will. For example, there are studies (Pattie, 1941) wherein blisters have formed after a hypnotist suggested that a red-hot iron (usually a mere finger) was being applied to a subject's arm! Finally, the altered-state proponents like to cite studies (McGlashlin, Evans, & Orne, 1969) in which hypnotized subjects showed greater pain endurance than waking subjects who were simply led to believe that they would not experience pain.

PRACTICAL APPLICATIONS

Hypnosis may or may not involve a true altered state of consciousness. Either way, hypnosis involves harnessing the power of suggestion in ways that can be quite useful. For example, hypnosis can be very helpful with people who suffer from chronic pain. Physicians are reluctant to put such people on painkilling drugs because of side effects associated with long-term use. Hypnosis may be a worthwhile substitute for drugs in some such cases (Hilgard & Hilgard, 1975).

Hypnosis may also be useful in the treatment of self-control problems such as smoking and overeating (Crasilneck & Hall, 1975). As we have already seen, such problems can be very stubborn. However, posthypnotic suggestions can be used to increase subjects' self-control. For example, subjects can be given a posthypnotic suggestion that they will no longer crave cigarettes. Using four sessions for such a purpose, Crasilneck and Hall (1968) reported an 82% success rate after a posttreatment period of at least one year. Although most other hypnotherapy studies on smoking have not been *that* successful, it appears that hypnosis can contribute to the correction of some self-control problems.

CRITIQUE

In the skilled hands of a trained professional, hypnosis can be a very effective tool. That qualification, however, brings up one of the potential problems with hypnosis. There are a lot of incompetent eccentrics out there who fancy themselves hypnotists and offer their services as such. When wielded clumsily by a poorly trained person, hypnosis can be a bit dangerous. The situation is somewhat similar to the one that we have with encounter groups. There is little governance or licensing of either hypnotists or group facilitators. This anarchy seems more perilous in the case of hypnosis. Many encounter group leaders who lack formal training and degrees nonetheless seem to be fairly skilled and sensitive. Hypnotism, however, seems to attract more than its share of half-baked imbeciles and bizarre fanatics. Accordingly, if you feel that hypnotherapy might be beneficial to you, you should seek out a fully credentialed professional—either a psychologist or a physician.

The other limitation on the utility of hypnosis is that not everyone is a good hypnotic subject. Although most people can be hypnotized, significant personal problems can be overcome through hypnosis only with very responsive subjects. Thus, hypnosis does not work for a lot of people.

Let us end this section, however, on a note of optimism. Hypnosis *can* be very effective with some people and some problems. In particular, it appears to have potential for tackling many of the everyday self-control problems that plague so many of us.

Spiritual Pathways from the East

Recent years have seen an explosion of interest in spiritually based pathways to growth rooted in ancient Eastern religions, such as Buddhism, Hinduism, Taoism, and Sufism. Westerners have become positively infatuated with Oriental mysticism. Gurus peddling enlightenment have long enjoyed popularity in major cities, such as New York or San Francisco. But today, they're everywhere: Peoria, Kalamazoo, Bakersfield. There is no shortage of converts, and they come from all walks of life.

Why do we have this sudden rush to achieve transcendence? Well, in some respects, it may represent an idea whose time has come. As discussed in Chapter 1, we live in an era of unparalleled social mutation. Social change proceeds at a whirlwind pace. In the 1950s, the eminent anthropologist Margaret Mead predicted that increasingly rapid cultural change might lead to a "turn inward" to seek peace and serenity. Further, we live in an action-oriented society in which we tend to race about pell-mell working arduously to fulfill our material needs and desires. It is beginning to dawn on many people that this racehorse mentality only leaves them gutted by stress. Recognizing this reality, people are turning to Eastern disciplines because they offer a different world view. They value contemplation, intuition, and spirituality over action, rationality, and materialism. The great psychoanalytic theorist Carl Jung argued decades ago that there was much to be said for this alternative world view.

Turning to a more cynical line of thought, it may be that Eastern disciplines are gaining popularity because they have been repackaged into watered-down Westernized versions and marketed with sophisticated Western advertising techniques. Eastern mystics have come to the West seeking converts for decades. However, they used to simply lecture where invited, and they tended to emphasize the great sacrifice and self-discipline required to achieve spiritual growth. Nowadays, proponents of movements such as transcendental meditation shrewdly create good publicity, cleverly seek endorsements from celebrities, relentlessly plaster posters all over universities, and deceptively suggest that learning how to meditate is as easy as brushing your teeth. Thus, the accelerating popularity of Eastern religions may be due to this curious marriage of East and West. Of course, some critics (Ornstein, 1976) have suggested that these blended versions of Eastern disciplines may offer far less in the way of self-realization than the ancient originals.

In this section, we will examine several very popular pathways to growth derived from Eastern traditions. Specifically, we'll take a look at transcendental meditation, Zen Buddhism, and yoga. I have chosen these three because they are the most widely practiced of such disciplines in the Western world. In focusing on these three, I am omitting many others, such as Sufism or Tibetan Buddhism. This omission in not intended to suggest that the other approaches are less worthwhile. In fact, one might argue that their lesser contamination by Western success *may* make them *more* worthwhile.

TRANSCENDENTAL MEDITATION

DESCRIPTION

Transcendental meditation (TM) is a form of meditation derived from the Hindu religion. It was popularized in this country by Maharishi Mahesh

TRANSCENDENTAL MEDITATION (TM). *A form of meditation that involves repetitive chanting of, and focusing of attention on, a specially assigned mantra.*

MANTRA. *In transcendental meditation, a Sanskrit word that one uses as a focus of attention for one's meditative thoughts.*

Yogi, who divorced the meditative technique from its original religious trappings. The meditation procedure is deceptively simple. The meditator is supposed to sit in a comfortable position with eyes closed and silently focus attention exclusively on a **mantra,** a specially assigned Sanskrit word. This exercise in mental discipline is to be practiced twice daily for 20 minutes. The technique has been described as "diving from the active surface of the mind to its quiet depths" (Bloomfield & Kory, 1976, p. 49). The procedure is supposed to help one achieve a "heightened awareness" or "pure consciousness."

A regular practitioner of TM is said to experience some spectacular benefits. It has been alleged that TM will improve one's learning, creativity, perceptiveness, energy level, health, interpersonal relationships, and general happiness while reducing tension and anxiety caused by stress (Bloomfield & Kory, 1976; Henderson, 1975; Schwartz, 1974). These are not exactly humble claims. Moreover, TM proponents assert that they have scientific evidence to support their claims.

REPRESENTATIVE RESEARCH

In fact, there *are* scientific studies that reflect rather favorably on TM. However, the research does *not* document all the extraordinary claims mentioned above. The most impressive research relates to physiological changes during meditation. Wallace and Benson (1972) found that during meditation there were decreases in subjects' oxygen consumption, carbon dioxide elimination, respiration rate, and blood lactate, while skin resistance increased and alpha waves became more prominent in brain activity (see Figure 15.4). Collectively, these changes suggest that the meditator enters a potentially beneficial physiological state characterized by alertness, relaxation, and suppression of emotional arousal. Although Gary Schwartz (1974) notes that some of these changes have not been replicated in other studies, the data suggest that an effective meditator (an important qualification) enters an intriguing physiological state.

The long-range effects of repeated entry into this physiological state are difficult to document. The crucial problem is that if you want to evaluate a

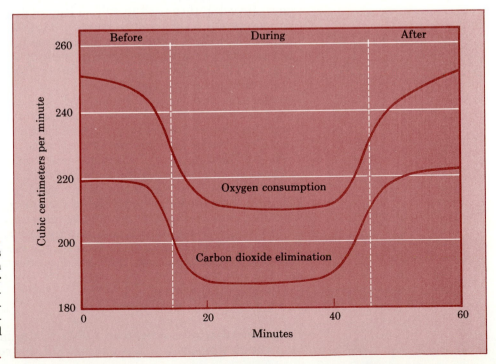

FIGURE 15.4 The effects of transcendental meditation on oxygen consumption (upper line) and carbon dioxide elimination (lower curve). The observed decline in these functions provides physiological evidence of relaxation.

person's happiness or energy level, you have to ask that person for a self-rating. These self-ratings are likely to be quite biased in that TM practitioners *want* and *expect* to see their happiness and energy level improve. Thus, improvement in such self-ratings has dubious value in supporting the claims about the benefits of TM. The unfortunate reality is that the bulk of the empirical research on meditation is methodologically weak (Shapiro, 1981).

Nonetheless, the research on TM *is* favorable. After three months of TM, subjects were found to rate themselves as happier, more energetic, less fatigued, and more creative (Otis, 1974). There are also reports (see Schwartz, 1974) that meditators improve on measures of self-actualization. Furthermore, there is evidence that meditators can handle more life stress without getting ill than comparable nonmeditators and that meditators recover from bodily arousal relatively quickly (see Goleman, 1976).

In summary, the empirical evidence on TM does stack up on the favorable side of the ledger. However, it should be pointed out that the advertising brochures on TM greatly exaggerate the scientific support for TM. These brochures suggest that there is a great deal of crystal-clear evidence verifying *all* the alleged benefits of TM. Actually, there is a smattering of ambiguous evidence that supports *some* of the TM claims.

ZEN

DESCRIPTION

Zen is a philosophy of life derived from the precepts of Buddhism and Taoism. Though rooted in ancient religions of India and China, Zen gained its greatest acceptance in Japan, where it is still an important religious force. In North America, the Zen philosophy gained some popularity in the 1960s through the writings of Alan Watts (1957). In contrast to TM, there is no single, central organization for Zen in America. Instead, there are numerous local organizations sprinkled all over the continent.

ZEN. *A philosophy of life and collection of meditative practices derived from the ancient religions of Buddhism and Taoism.*

The **Zen** philosophy of life is complex and not easily summarized. Among other things, it emphasizes an attitude of detachment toward life. One should experience events without getting too caught up in them. One should not become too dependent on satisfactions derived from the pleasant events in life, and one should not become overly upset about the unpleasant events. One should just "experience" them.

Zen also puts considerable emphasis on self-exploration, or the effort to come to know oneself better. Paradoxically, however, Zen discourages the rational, linear Western mode of thinking. A key principle of Zen is that one should trust intuition and act spontaneously without engaging in excessive analysis and contemplation.

SATORI. *The principal goal of Zen, involving a state of profound insight and heightened awareness.*

A disciple of Zen works toward achieving **satori,** a nonintellectual form of insight involving "total awareness." Satori is thought to be achieved suddenly, but only with great difficulty, normally after many years of Zen training. The Zen disciple pursues satori primarily through meditative techniques. Zen meditation is performed sitting with eyes open. Typically, the disciple directs meditative thoughts either to self-exploration or to the consideration of a **koan.** A koan is a paradoxical question or riddle that forces one to give up rational thought processes—an answerless question, such as "What is the sound of one hand clapping?" or "Where does your fist go when you open your hand?" Once satori has been achieved, one is thought to go through life with heightened awareness, greater spontaneity, and greater detachment.

KOAN. *In Zen, a paradoxical question for contemplation.*

REPRESENTATIVE RESEARCH

Research on Zen is minimal for two reasons. First, the Zen way does not value the rational, intellectual mode of thinking that provides the basis for Western science. Unlike TM proponents, Zen practitioners would never dream of seeking scientific support for the utility of their discipline. Such a move would

Eastern pathways to spiritual growth have become increasingly popular.

be antagonistic to the essence of the Zen philosophy. Second, Western scientists are put off by the highly subjective nature of Zen's principal goal, satori. Understandably, scientists tend not to be interested in things they cannot measure.

So, from the rational-scientific perspective of this book, what can I offer in the way of an evaluation of Zen? Well, I can comment on the goals of Zen and summarize the little bit of research that is available. Let us begin with the comment. Many of the objectives of Zen would certainly be applauded by proponents of humanistic psychology, such as Abraham Maslow or Carl Rogers. You may recall from Chapter 2 that Rogers's and Maslow's views of psychological health endorse intuition, spontaneity, and increased awareness. These characteristics are highly valued by Zen. In fact, the Zen description of the person who has achieved satori sounds very much like humanistic descriptions of the healthy personality. Indeed, it is easy to see how stressful events might be less harmful if one could achieve the sense of detachment advocated by the Zen way. Thus, the goals of Zen seem to have considerable merit from the point of view of Western psychology.

Although the research on Zen is limited, it *is* favorable. Studies (Kasamatsu & Hirai, 1969; Yamaoka, 1968) indicate that experienced Zen disciples show quick and dramatic changes in EEG when they meditate. During meditation, Zen masters show persistent alpha waves of increased amplitude. Moreover, it was found that the effectiveness of Zen masters in controlling their brain activity was closely related to their length of training. Disciples who had the most experience and training showed the largest EEG changes. Thus, there is evidence to suggest that Zen meditation might produce beneficial alterations in one's consciousness.

YOGA

DESCRIPTION

HATHA YOGA. *A form of yoga that attempts to promote physical health, primarily through the practice of breathing exercises and bodily postures.*

Yoga, derived from Hindu traditions, is a system of beliefs and practices intended to achieve a union between the individual self and the Universal Self. Actually, there are many systems of yoga. Some emphasize meditation, others self-contemplation or prayer. The kind of yoga most popular in the West is **Hatha Yoga.** This is actually one of the "lower" forms of yoga in that it emphasizes attainment of physical health in order to advance to "higher," more

---

15.3
RECOMMENDED READING
The Nature of Human Consciousness
edited by Robert Ornstein (W. H. Freeman, 1973)

If the spiritual pathways from the East intrigue you, you might find this volume quite interesting. Ornstein is a Western-trained psychologist who is interested in consciousness. He has assembled a diverse collection of articles that offer a variety of perspectives on spiritual pathways, as well as other topics. Ornstein is particularly enamored of Sufism, with five readings expounding on this subject. Empirical studies of meditation are mixed in with nontechnical articles on how to meditate. There are also some classic articles on hemi-

spheric specialization in the brain, perception, biofeedback, and paranormal phenomena.

To the completely orthodox mind, nothing could be further from "Psychology" than strange men repeating "magic" words over and over, or Yoga masters in unusual postures, or a dervish spinning, or a Zen monk puzzling over a seemingly unanswerable question such as "What is the size of the real you?"

Yet there are two major modes of knowing, and in the cultures of Japan, the Middle East, India, people

who were concerned with the central questions of psychology—consciousness—studied their local system of psychology, Buddhism, Sufism, Yoga, among others. These are inwardly directed systems, focused on personal rather than an intellectual knowledge, concerned with intuition, if you will, rather than verbal intellectuality. Only within the past few years have scientists begun to recognize that this inward personal knowledge is an essential complement to normal intellection [pp. 213–214].

spiritual forms of yoga. The underlying notion is that a healthy body is necessary to have a healthy mind capable of pursuing spiritual growth.

Practitioners of Hatha Yoga strive to improve their physical health through postures called **asanas** and through breathing exercises called **pranayama**. Most American instruction in yoga is devoted exclusively to these exercises. Generally, Westerners pay little homage to the spiritual aspects of yoga.

ASANAS. *In yoga, the various bodily postures that can be assumed in order to meditate and promote physical health.*

PRANAYAMA. *In yoga, the various breathing exercises that can be used in order to promote physical health.*

REPRESENTATIVE RESEARCH

Scientific research on yoga has focused mainly on examining the authenticity of claims about remarkable physical feats performed by yogis, such as fire-walking or stopping one's heart. Barber (1970) points out that these physical feats are not really a common element in yogic practice and that many of the people who attempt such feats are "self-styled yogis" who are more interested in theatrics than in spiritual growth. In any case, most of these physical feats have turned out to be less impressive than originally believed. For example, it was found that yogis who could allegedly stop their heart actually only slowed it down in such a way that their heartbeats could not be detected by a stethoscope (Wenger & Bagchi, 1961).

There is no research on everyday benefits that might be derived from the regular practice of yoga. We do know that practitioners of yogic meditation show EEG changes similar to those resulting from other forms of meditation (Anand, Chhina, & Singh, 1969). There is also reason to believe that yogic breathing exercises may enhance autonomic control in ways that could be beneficial to physical and mental health (Wenger & Bagchi, 1961). Finally, although it is impossible to say whether yogic postures are better or worse than more conventional exercises, there is much to be said for regular exercise of virtually any kind (see Chapter 5).

CRITIQUE

The spiritual pathways to growth that have been transplanted from the East are difficult to evaluate. Their very nature makes them foreign to the methods of Western science. Evaluation is also rendered difficult by the fact that it is tough to distinguish the bona fide gurus from the con artists, quacks, and impostors.

Basically, it appears that these spiritual pathways can prove to be very rewarding for some people. However, one should be wary of the oversell that often characterizes these quasi-religious movements. Though not the only of-

---

RECOMMENDED READING

15.4 *Integral Yoga—Hatha*

by Yogiraj Sri Swami Satchidananda (Holt, Rinehart and Winston, 1970)

This is a simple, straightforward introduction to Hatha Yoga. It is not a diluted, Westernized version. The author, an authentic Swami, immigrated to the United States in 1966, only four years before assembling this book. In spite of its authenticity, the book is quite digestible for those of us with a typical Western mind set. The book focuses on bodily postures, methods for deep relaxation, control of breathing, cleansing processes, and systems of mental concentration. It is well illustrated, with the Swami himself performing the multitude of exercises.

As the Yoga asanas and Yogic breathing are practiced, increasing the vitality of the body, there will follow a considerable decrease in harmful acts such as smoking and drinking. Many, many yoga practitioners have told me that, surprisingly enough to them, they had un-consciously lost the desire to smoke and drink. For that reason, I have never asked any of my students to give up habits such as the above-mentioned, nor have I used a "don't do this," "don't do that" method of training. To expect a student to get rid of his harmful habits before even starting Yoga practice would be like a doctor asking his patients to cure themselves of their ailments before receiving his treatment [from the Introduction].

fender, the TM movement provides an excellent example of this oversell. TM proponents claim that one must have "hands-on" training (which they happen to provide only for a very substantial fee) in order to learn to meditate, that TM is the *only* beneficial way to meditate, and that their training makes it easy to learn how to meditate. Such assertions involve bending the truth more than a little bit. Unfortunately, half-truths and gross exaggerations are not uncommon among people peddling transcendence and enlightenment.

Summary

This chapter reviews a variety of esoteric approaches to personal growth. Encounter groups provide intense, intimate interpersonal experiences. Such groups strive to improve participants' interpersonal awareness. Although most participants have favorable reactions to their experiences, objective research suggests that only about one-third of the people really show positive gains. Unfortunately, a substantial portion also experience negative changes. Encounter group outcomes are influenced more by leaders' style than by their theoretical orientation. The most important group characteristic seems to be flexibility, or open boundaries on discussion. Participant characteristics are very inconsistently related to outcomes. Because of the possibility of encounter group "casualties," it is probably a good idea to be cautious when joining such groups.

Biofeedback involves providing information about bodily functions to a person so that the person can attempt to exert some control over those bodily functions. It has been shown that people can learn to control brain-wave activity, cardiovascular activity, skin temperature, and level of muscular tension. Although the initial optimism about the practical applications of biofeedback has sobered a bit, the technique appears to have great potential for reducing the ravages of stress.

Hypnotic induction can be accomplished by a variety of procedures. Some people are hypnotized much more readily than others. Those with high hypnotic susceptibility typically can engross themselves in intense experiences, have a vivid imagination, and often have been punished extensively as children. Hypnosis can produce anesthesia, sensory distortions, and age regression. Sometimes people will display what appears to be antisocial behavior. Many theorists believe that hypnotic phenomena are produced simply through intensive role playing by the subjects. Other theorists argue that hypnotic phenomena are attributable to an altered state of consciousness. Hypnosis does appear to have potential for dealing with self-control problems, although one should be concerned about incompetent practitioners, who may be dangerous.

Spiritual pathways borrowed from Eastern religions recently enjoyed a surge in popularity. This may be due to the fact that they meet an important need, or it may be due to advances in their marketing. TM is a very simple approach to meditation that is supposed to produce spectacular benefits. Research currently available does suggest that TM produces a potentially worthwhile physiological state. Evidence on the psychological benefits of TM is favorable but not nearly as strong as TM proponents imply. Zen is a philosophy of life emphasizing detachment, contemplation, and self-exploration. A Zen disciple pursues higher awareness, primarily through meditative paths. Scientific evidence on Zen is minimal, although research does show that Zen meditators can control their brain-wave activity. In the West, most practice of yoga involves Hatha Yoga. This form of yoga is intended to improve physical health through postures and breathing exercises. There is little research on the benefits of yogic practice, but there are findings that suggest that the meditation and breathing exercises may be worthwhile.

In the upcoming application section I will focus on the current obsession with the pursuit of self-improvement. Specifically, I will offer some advice to help you avoid common pitfalls on the way to self-realization.

An Epilogue on the Pursuit of Self-Improvement

I began this book, 15 chapters ago, with the assertion that the basic challenge of modern life has become the search for a sense of direction and a strategy for self-fulfillment. I discussed how the recent proliferation of self-help books indicates that we are a nation obsessed with self-improvement. In the ensuing 15 chapters I have tried to shed some light on the psychological demands of modern life, and I have exposed you to a vast array of self-improvement systems, ranging from relaxation exercises to assertiveness training to psychotherapy to meditation. I hope that the enormous variety of self-improvement systems is less bewildering to you now than when you began this book. In this final application section, I will make one last effort to better prepare you to judge the merits of various self-improvement systems. Specifically, I will offer some advice about what to look for when you become intrigued by some pathway to personal growth. Although most of this advice follows logically from points I have made repeatedly, some of it is borrowed from an excellent discussion by Henderson (1975).

1. *Don't jump into something too quickly.* In the great search for self-improvement, it is all too easy to get excited about something that promises some hope. Don't let early enthusiasm carry you into something that you haven't checked out thoroughly. Try to read up on the approach, talk to the people involved, and talk to previous participants. If the approach has anything worthwhile to offer, it will still be available tomorrow. There is no need to act rashly.

2. *Watch out for exploitive charlatans.* People searching for a sense of direction are often easy marks for con artists. Because of this reality, there are an awful lot of con artists out there peddling self-realization. This is one of the reasons that it is a good idea to deliberate and be cautious when thinking about joining some self-improvement organization. Also, bear in mind that cost may not be a good indication of quality. Often, higher costs are merely associated with bigger hoaxes.

3. *Beware of egotistical "superstars."* A number of teachers, leaders, and therapists desire "followers" as a source of gratification for their overinflated egos. They are more interested in feeling important than in helping others. Such persons, although they may be authentically brilliant, are unlikely to be of much help to you.

4. *Remember that personal growth requires real effort.* You should be wary of anyone or any organization offering instant improvement. It just doesn't work that way. Even relatively small changes in lifestyle take a lot of work. Self-improvement usually proceeds painstakingly slowly. Old patterns of behavior give way only very begrudgingly. Promises of instant improvement are almost inevitably empty promises.

5. *After choosing an approach to growth, give it a chance.* As just noted, personal growth does not come easily. Even when you are on a good pathway for you, you should be prepared for setbacks and derailments. Don't give up too easily or too quickly. Stay with an improvement plan long enough to see whether it works.

IDEAS: REVIEW OF LEARNING OBJECTIVES

When you have mastered the material in this chapter, you should be able to do the following.

1. Describe what encounter groups tend to be like.
2. Summarize evidence on how participants are affected by encounter groups.
3. Summarize evidence on factors that influence encounter group outcomes.
4. Discuss why caution is advisable in seeking encounter group experiences.
5. Describe the nature and purpose of biofeedback systems.
6. Summarize evidence on biofeedback-produced control of brain activity.
7. Briefly summarize the biofeedback work done on the control of cardiovascular activity, skin temperature, and muscle relaxation.
8. Describe hypnotic induction and discuss hypnotic susceptibility.
9. List five hypnotic phenomena mentioned in the text.
10. Explain the role-playing and altered-consciousness theories of hypnosis.
11. Discuss practical applications of hypnosis.
12. Discuss precautions and limitations relative to the use of hypnosis.
13. Describe transcendental meditation (TM) and its alleged benefits.
14. Summarize research on TM.
15. Describe the Zen philosophy.
16. Summarize research on Zen.
17. Describe the practice of yoga.
18. Summarize research on yoga.
19. List five guidelines recommended in pursuing self-improvement.

TERMS: REVIEW OF NEW VOCABULARY

When you have mastered the material in this chapter, you should be able to define the following terms.

Asanas	Encounter group	Mantra	Transcendental meditation
Biofeedback system	Hatha Yoga	Pranayama	Zen
Charlatanism	Hypnosis	Satori	
Electromyograph	Koan		

PEOPLE: REVIEW OF MAJOR THEORISTS AND RESEARCHERS

When you have mastered the material in this chapter, you should be able to summarize the principal contributions and/or ideas of the following people.

Ernest and Josephine Hilgard	Lieberman, Yalom, and Miles	Neal Miller Martin Orne	Gary Schwartz Alan Watts

REFERENCES

Abraham, K. (1948). *Selected papers of Karl Abraham* (3rd ed.). London: Hogarth Press.

Adams, G., & Huston, T. (1975). Social perception of middleaged persons varying in physical attractiveness. *Developmental Psychology, 11,* 657–658.

Adams, V. (1980). Getting at the heart of jealous love. *Psychology Today, 13*(12), 38–47, 102, 105–106.

Ader, R. (1980). Psychosomatic and psychoimmunologic research. *Psychosomatic Medicine, 42*(3), 307–321.

Adler, A. (1927). *Practice and theory of individual psychology.* New York: Harcourt, Brace & World.

Adler, A. (1939). *Social interest.* New York: Putnam.

Adler, R., & Towne, N. (1975). *Looking out/looking in: Interpersonal communication.* San Francisco: Rinehart Press.

Aiken, L. R. (1963). The relationships of dress to selected measures of personality in undergraduate women. *Journal of Social Psychology, 59,* 119–128.

Alberti, R. E., & Emmons, M. L. (1974). *Your perfect right: A guide to assertive behavior.* San Luis Obispo, Calif.: Impact.

Albrecht, S. L. (1979). Correlates of marital happiness among the remarried. *Journal of Marriage and the Family, 41,* 857–867.

Alexander, C. N., & Knight, G. W. (1971). Situated identities and social psychological experimentation. *Sociometry, 34,* 65–82.

Al-Issa, I. (1982). Sex-differences in psychopathology. In I. Al-Issa (Ed.), *Culture and psychopathology.* Baltimore: University Park Press.

Allgeier, E. R., & Allgeier, A. R. (1984). *Sexual interactions.* Lexington, Mass.: Heath.

Allport, G. W. (1937). *Personality: A psychological interpretation.* New York: Holt.

Altman, I., & Taylor, D. (1973). *Social penetration: The development of interpersonal relationships.* New York: Holt, Rinehart and Winston.

Altrocchi, J. (1980). *Abnormal behavior.* New York: Harcourt Brace Jovanovich.

American Psychiatric Association. (1952). *Diagnostic and statistical manual of mental disorders* (1st ed.). Washington, D.C.: American Psychiatric Association.

American Psychiatric Association. (1968). *Diagnostic and statistical manual of mental disorders* (2nd ed.). Washington, D.C.: American Psychiatric Association.

American Psychiatric Association. (1980). *Diagnostic and statistical manual of mental disorders* (3rd ed.). Washington, D.C.: American Psychiatric Association.

Anand, B. K., Chhina, G. S., & Singh, B. (1969). Some aspects of electroencephalographic studies in Yogis. In C. T. Tart (Ed.), *Altered states of consciousness.* New York: Wiley.

Anderson, C. A., Horowitz, L. M., & French, R. D. (1983). Attributional style of lonely and depressed people. *Journal of Personality and Social Psychology, 45*(1), 127–136.

Anderson, N. H. (1968). Likableness ratings of 555 personality trait words. *Journal of Personality and Social Psychology, 9* 272–279.

Anderson, S. A., Russell, C. S., & Schumm, W. R. (1983). Perceived marital quality and family life-cycle categories: A further analysis. *Journal of Marriage and the Family, 45*(1), 127–139.

Angrist, S., & Almquist, E. (1975). *Careers and contingencies: How college women juggle with gender.* New York: Dunellen.

Anisman, H. (1978). Neurochemical changes elicited by stress. In H. Anisman & G. Bignami (Eds.), *Psychopharmacology of adversely motivated behavior.* New York: Plenum.

Applbaum, R. L., & Anatol, K. W. E. (1974). *Strategies for persuasive communication.* Columbus, Ohio: Charles E. Merrill.

Archer, R. L. (1979). Role of personality and the social situation. In G. J. Chelune & associates, *Self-disclosure: Origins, patterns, and implications of openness in interpersonal relationships.* San Francisco: Jossey-Bass.

Argyle, M. (1975). *Bodily communication.* New York: International Universities Press.

Argyle, M., & Dean, J. (1965). Eye-contact, distance, and affiliation. *Sociometry, 28,* 289–304.

Arieti, S., & Arieti, J. (1977). *Love can be found: A guide to the most desired and most elusive emotion.* New York: Harcourt Brace Jovanovich.

Armstrong, B., & Doll, R. (1975). Environmental factors and cancer incidence and mortality in different countries, with special reference to dietary practices. *International Journal of Cancer, 15,* 617–631.

Aronson, E., & Linder, D. (1965). Gain and loss of esteem as determinants of interpersonal attractiveness. *Journal of Experimental Social Psychology, 1,* 156–171.

Aronson, E., Willerman, B., & Floyd, J. (1966). The effect of pratfall on increasing interpersonal attractiveness. *Psychonomic Science, 4,* 157–158.

Asch, S. E. (1946). Forming impressions of personality. *Journal of Abnormal and Social Psychology, 41,* 258–290.

Atchley, R. C. (1977). *The social forces in later life* (2nd ed.). Belmont, Calif.: Wadsworth.

Athanasiou, R., Shaver, P., & Tavris, C. (1970). Sex. *Psychology Today, 4*(2), 39–52.

Atthowe, J. M. (1973). Behavior innovation and persistence. *American Psychologist, 28,* 34–41.

Austin, R. B., Jr. (1976). *How to make it with another person.* New York: Macmillan.

Bach, G. R., & Wyden, P. (1969). *The intimate enemy: How to fight fair in love and marriage.* New York: William Morrow.

Baker, G. H. B. (1982). Life events before the onset of rheumatoid arthritis. *Psychotherapy and Psychosomatics, 38,* 173–177.

Baker, T. (1980). Sex differences in social behavior. In L. Berkowitz (Ed.), *A survey of social psychology.* New York: Holt, Rinehart and Winston.

Baldessarini, R. J. (1975). Biogenic amine hypotheses in affective disorders. In F. F. Flach & S. C. Praghi (Eds.), *The nature and treatment of depression.* New York: Wiley.

Baldessarini, R. J. (1980). Drugs and the treatment of psychiatric disorders. In A. G. Gilman, L. S. Goodman, & A. Gilman (Eds.), *The pharmacological basis of therapeutics* (6th ed.). New York: Macmillan.

Balswick, J., & Avertt, C. P. (1977). Differences in expressiveness: Gender, interpersonal orientation, and perceived expressiveness as contributing factors. *Journal of Marriage and the Family, 39,* 121–127.

Bandura, A. (1977). *Social learning theory.* Englewood Cliffs, N.J.: Prentice-Hall.

Bandura, A., Ross, D., & Ross, S. (1963). Imitation of film-mediated aggressive models. *Journal of Abnormal and Social Psychology, 66,* 3–11.

Bandura, A., & Walters, R. H. (1963). *Social learning and personality development.* New York: Holt, Rinehart and Winston.

Barbach, L. G. (1975). *For yourself: The fulfillment of female sexuality.* Garden City, N.Y.: Doubleday.

Barber, T. X. (1969). *Hypnosis: A scientific approach.* New York: Van Nostrand.

Barber, T. X. (1970). *LSD, marihuana, yoga, and hypnosis.* Chicago: Aldine.

Barber, T. X., & Hahn, K. W. (1962). Physiological and subjective responses to pain producing stimulation under hypnotically-suggested and waking-imagined "analgesia." *Journal of Abnormal Psychology, 65,* 411–418.

Bardwick, J. M. (1971). *The psychology of women: A study of biocultural conflicts.* New York: Harper & Row.

Bardwick, J. M. (1973). Women's liberation: Nice idea, but it won't be easy. *Psychology Today, 6*(12), 26–33, 110–111.

Barfield, R., Wilson, C., & McDonald, P. (1975). Sexual behavior: Extreme reduction of postejaculatory refractory period by midbrain lesions in male rats. *Science, 189,* 147–149.

Barnes, E. J. (1972). The black community as the source of positive self-concept for black children: A theoretical perspective. In R. L. Jones (Ed.), *Black psychology.* New York: Harper & Row.

Barnes, M. L., & Buss, D. M. (1984, August). *Preferences in mate selection.* Paper presented at the meeting of the American Psychological Association, Toronto, Ontario.

Barofsky, I. (1981). Issues and approaches to the assessment of the cancer patient. In C. K. Prokop & L. A. Bradley (Eds.), *Medical psychology: Contributions to behavioral medicine.* New York: Academic Press.

Baron, P. H. (1974). Self-esteem, ingratiation, and evaluation of unknown others. *Journal of Personality and Social Psychology, 30,* 104–109.

Baron, R. A., & Byrne, D. (1977). *Social psychology: Understanding human interaction.* Boston: Allyn & Bacon.

Barrett, J. E. (1979). The relationship of life events to the onset of neurotic disorders. In J. E. Barrett, R. M. Rose, & G. L. Klerman (Eds.), *Stress and mental disorder.* New York: Raven Press.

Barrett, J. E., Rose, R. M., & Klerman, G. L. (Eds.). (1979). *Stress and mental disorder.* New York: Raven Press.

Barton, J. L. (1977). ECT in depression: The evidence of controlled studies. *Biological Psychiatry, 12,* 687–695.

Bateson, G., Jackson, D. D., Haley, J., & Weakland, J. (1956). Toward a theory of schizophrenia. *Behavioral Science, 1,* 251–264.

Baum, C., Kennedy, D. L., Forbes, M. D., & Jones, J. K. (1985). Drug use and expenditures in 1982. *Journal of the American Medical Association, 353*(3), 382–386.

Beardslee, D. C., & O'Dowd, D. D. (1962). Students and the occupational world. In N. Sanford (Ed.), *The American college.* New York: Wiley.

Beck, A. T. (1962). Reliability of psychiatric diagnosis: A critique of systematic studies. *American Journal of Psychiatry, 119,* 210–216.

Beck, A. T. (1972). *Depression: Causes and treatment.* Philadelphia: University of Pennsylvania Press.

Beck, A. T. (1976). *Cognitive therapy and the emotional disorders.* New York: International Universities Press.

Beck, D. F., & Jones, M. A. (1973). *Progress on family problems: A nationwide study of clients' and counselors' views on family agency services.* New York: Family Service Association of America.

Beck, S. B. (1979). Women's somatic preferences. In M. Cook & G. Wilson (Eds.), *Love and attraction.* New York: Pergamon Press.

Becker, J., Spielberger, C. D., & Parker, J. B. (1963). Value achievement and authoritarian attitudes in psychiatric patients. *Journal of Clinical Psychology, 19,* 57–61.

Belkin, G. S., & Goodman, N. (1980). *Marriage, family, and intimate relationships.* Chicago: Rand McNally.

Bell, A. P., & Weinberg, M. S. (1978). *Homosexualities: A study of diversity among men and women.* New York: Simon & Schuster.

Bell, R. R. (1979). *Marriage and family interaction.* Homewood, Ill.: Dorsey Press.

Bell, R. R., Turner, S., & Rosen, L. (1975). A multivariate analysis of female extramarital coitus. *Journal of Marriage and the Family, 37,* 375–383.

Bellack, A. S. (1980). Anxiety and neurotic disorders. In A. E. Kazdin, A. S. Bellack, & M. Hersen (Eds.), *New perspectives in abnormal psychology.* New York: Oxford University Press.

Belsky, M. S., & Gross, L. (1975). *How to choose and use your doctor.* New York: Arbor House.

Belzer, E. G., Jr., Whipple, B., & Moger, W. (1984). On female ejaculation. *Journal of Sex Research, 20*(4), 403–406.

Bem, D. J. (1965). An experimental analysis of self-persuasion. *Journal of Experimental Social Psychology, 1,* 199–218.

Bem, D. J. (1972). Self-perception theory. In L. Berkowitz (Ed.), *Advances in experimental social psychology* (Vol. 6). New York: Academic Press.

Bem, S. L. (1975). Androgyny vs. the tight little lives of fluffy women and chesty men. *Psychology Today, 9*(4), 58–62.

Beneke, W. M., & Harris, M. B. (1972). Teaching self-control of study behavior. *Behavior Research and Therapy, 10,* 35–41.

Bengtson, V. L., Cuellar, J. B., & Ragan, P. K. (1977). Stratum contrasts and similarities in attitudes toward death. *Journal of Gerontology, 32*(1), 76–88.

Benson, H. (1975). *The relaxation response.* New York: William Morrow.

Berger, K. S. (1983). *The developing person through the life span.* New York: Worth.

Berkowitz, L. (1969). The frustration-aggression hypothesis revisited. In L. Berkowitz (Ed.), *Roots of aggression: A re-exami-*

nation of the frustration-aggression hypothesis. New York: Atherton Press.

Berkowitz, L. (1980). *A survey of social psychology.* New York: Holt, Rinehart and Winston.

Berkun, M., Bialek, H., Kern, R., & Yagi, K. (1962). Experimental studies of psychological stress in man. *Psychological Monographs, 76,* 1–39.

Berland, T. (1980). *Diets '80: Rating the diets.* Skokie, Ill.: Publications International.

Berlo, D. K. (1960). *The process of communication: An introduction to theory and practice.* New York: Holt, Rinehart and Winston.

Berman, E. (1975). Tested and documented split personality: Veronica and Nelly. *Psychology Today, 9*(3), 78–81.

Bernard, J. (1973). *The future of marriage.* New York: Bantam Books.

Berne, E. (1961). *Transactional analysis in psychotherapy.* New York: Ballantine Books.

Berne, E. (1964). *Games people play.* New York: Grove Press.

Berne, E. (1972). *What do you say after you say hello?* New York: Grove Press.

Berscheid, E., & Walster, E. (1974). Physical attractiveness. In L. Berkowitz (Ed.), *Advances in experimental social psychology* (Vol. 7). New York: Academic Press.

Berscheid, E., & Walster, E. (1978). *Interpersonal attraction.* Reading, Mass.: Addison-Wesley.

Bettelheim, B. (1943). Individual and mass behavior in extreme situations. *Journal of Abnormal and Social Psychology, 38,* 417–452.

Bickman, L. (1971). The effect of social status on the honesty of others. *Journal of Social Psychology, 85,* 87–92.

Birren, J. E., Woods, A. M., & Williams, M. V. (1980). Behavioral slowing with age: Causes, organization and consequences. In L. W. Poon (Ed.), *Aging in the 1980s: Psychological issues.* Washington, D.C.: American Psychological Association.

Blake, R. R., & Mouton, J. S. (1964). *The managerial grid.* Houston: Gulf Publishing.

Blanchard, E. B. (1979). Biofeedback and the modification of cardiovascular dysfunctions. In R. J. Gatchel & K. P. Price (Eds.), *Clinical applications of biofeedback: Appraisal and status.* New York: Pergamon Press.

Blanchard, E. B., & Andrasik, F. (1982). Psychological assessment and treatment of headache: Recent developments and emerging issues. *Journal of Consulting and Clinical Psychology, 50,* 859–879.

Blanck, G. (1976). Psychoanalytic technique. In B. B. Wolman (Ed.), *The therapist's handbook.* New York: Van Nostrand Reinhold.

Blank, A. S., Jr. (1982). Stresses of war: The example of Viet Nam. In L. Goldberger & S. Breznitz (Eds.), *Handbook of stress: Theoretical and clinical aspects.* New York: Free Press.

Blau, P. M., Gustad, J. W., Jessor, R., Parnes, H. S., & Wilcock, R. C. (1956). Occupational choice: A conceptual framework. *Industrial Labor Relations Review, 9,* 531–543.

Blau, Z. S. (1971). *Old age in a changing society.* New York: D. Van Nostrand.

Bleuler, E. (1911). *Dementia praecox or the Group F schizophrenias.* New York: International Universities Press.

Block, J. (1981). Some enduring and consequential structures of personality. In A. I. Rabins, J. Aronoff, A. Barclay, & R. Zucker (Eds.), *Further explorations in personality.* New York: Wiley.

Block, J. D. (1980). *Friendship: How to give it, how to get it.* New York: Macmillan.

Block, J. H. (1976). Issues, problems, and pitfalls in assessing sex differences: A critical review of *The Psychology of Sex Differences. Merrill-Palmer Quarterly, 22,* 283–308.

Bloom, B. L., White, S. W., & Asher, S. J. (1979). Marital disruption as a stressful life event. In G. Levinger & O. C. Moles (Eds.), *Divorce and separation.* New York: Basic Books.

Bloomfield, H. H., & Kory, R. B. (1976). *Happiness: The TM program, psychiatry, and enlightenment.* New York: Simon & Schuster.

Bolles, R. N. (1980). *What color is your parachute? A practical manual for job-hunters and career-changers.* Berkeley, Calif.: Ten Speed Press.

Booth, A. (1977). Wives' employment and husbands' stress: A replication and refutation. *Journal of Marriage and the Family, 39,* 645–650.

Boshell, B. R. (1974). Metabolic aspects of obesity. In F. J. Stare (Ed.), *Obesity: Data and directions for the 70s.* New York: Medcom.

Bossard, J. H. S. (1931). Residential propinquity as a factor in mate selection. *American Journal of Sociology, 38,* 219–224.

Boston Women's Health Book Collective. (1973). *Our bodies, ourselves: A book by and for women.* New York: Simon & Schuster.

Boston Women's Health Book Collective. (1984). *The new our bodies, ourselves: A book by and for women.* New York: Simon & Schuster.

Bower, D. W., & Christopherson, V. A. (1977). University student cohabitation: A regional comparison of selected attitudes and behavior. *Journal of Marriage and the Family, 39,* 447–453.

Bower, G. H. (1973). Educational applications of mnemonic devices. In K. O. Doyle, Jr. (Ed.), *Interaction: Readings in human psychology.* Boston: Heath.

Bower, G. H., & Clark, M. C. (1969). Narrative stories as mediators of serial learning. *Psychonomic Science, 14,* 181–182.

Bower, G. H., Clark, M. C., Lesgold, A. M., & Winzenz, D. (1969). Hierarchical retrieval schemes in recall of categorized word lists. *Journal of Verbal Learning and Verbal Behavior, 8,* 323–343.

Bower, S. A., & Bower, G. H. (1976). *Asserting yourself: A practical guide for positive change.* Reading, Mass.: Addison-Wesley.

Bowlby, J. (1958). The nature of the child's tie to his mother. *International Journal of Psychoanalysis, 39,* 350–373.

Bradburn, N. M. (1969). *The structure of psychological well-being.* Chicago: Aldine.

Bradley, C. (1979). Life events and the control of diabetes mellitus. *Journal of Psychosomatic Research, 23,* 159–162.

Bradley, G. W. (1978). Self-serving biases in the attribution process: A re-examination of the fact or fiction question. *Journal of Personality and Social Psychology, 35,* 56–71.

Brady, J. V. (1958). Ulcers in "executive" monkeys. *Scientific American, 199,* 95–99.

Bramwell, S. T., Masuda, M., Wagner, N. N., & Holmes, T. H. (1975). Psychosocial factors in athletic injuries: Development and application of the Social and Athletic Readjustment Rating Scale (SARRS). *Journal of Human Stress, 1*(2), 6–20.

Braude, M. C., & Szara, S. (Eds.). (1976). *Pharmacology of marihuana.* New York: Raven Press.

Brecher, E. M., & the editors of *Consumer Reports.* (1972). *Licit and illicit drugs.* Boston: Little, Brown.

Breggin, P. R. (1979). *Electroshock: Its brain-disabling effects.* New York: Springer.

Brehm, S. S. (1985). *Intimate relationships.* New York: Random House.

Brett, J. M. (1980). The effect of job transfer on employees and their families. In C. L. Cooper & R. Payne (Eds.), *Current concerns in occupational stress.* New York: Wiley.

Brewer, M. (1975). Erhard Seminars Training: "We're gonna tear you down and put you back together." *Psychology Today, 9*(3), 35–40, 82, 88–89.

Brill, N. W., & Christie, R. L. (1974). Marihuana use and psychosocial adaptation: Follow-up study of a collegiate population. *Archives of General Psychiatry, 31,* 713–719.

Bringle, R. G. (1981). Conceptualizing jealousy as a disposition. *Alternative Lifestyles, 4*(3), 274–290.

Bringle, R. G., & Evenbeck, S. (1979). The study of jealousy as a dispositional characteristic. In M. Cook & G. Wilson (Eds.), *Love and attraction*. New York: Pergamon Press.

Briscoe, M. E., Woodyard, M. D., & Shaw, N. E. (1967). Personality impression change as a function of the favorableness of first impressions. *Journal of Personality, 35*, 343–357.

Broadbent, W. W. (1976). *How to be loved*. Englewood Cliffs, N.J.: Prentice-Hall.

Brothers, J. (1978). *How to get whatever you want out of life*. New York: Ballantine.

Broverman, I. K., Vogel, S. R., Broverman, D. M., Clarkson, F. E., & Rosenkrantz, P. S. (1972). Sex roles stereotypes: A current appraisal. *Journal of Social Issues, 28*, 59–78.

Brown, B. B. (1974). *New mind, new body*. New York: Harper & Row.

Brown, D. G. (1972). Stress as a precipitant of eczema. *Journal of Psychosomatic Research, 16*, 321–327.

Brown, G. W. (1972). Life events and psychiatric illness: Some thoughts on methodology and causality. *Journal of Psychosomatic Research, 16*, 311–320.

Bruning, J. L., & Albott, W. (1974). Funny, you don't look Cecil. *Human Behavior, 3*(3), 56–57.

Bryer, K. B. (1979). The Amish way of death: A study of family support systems. *American Psychologist, 34*(3), 255–261.

Buchwald, A. M., Coyne, K. C., & Cole, C. S. (1978). A critical evaluation of the learned helplessness model of depression. *Journal of Abnormal Psychology, 87*, 180–193.

Budzynski, T., & Stoyva, J. (1969). An instrument for producing deep muscle relaxation by means of analog information feedback. *Journal of Applied Behavior Analysis, 2*, 231–237.

Buhler, C., & Allen, M. (1972). *Introduction to humanistic psychology*. Monterey, Calif.: Brooks/Cole.

Bumpass, L. L., & Sweet, J. A. (1972). Differentials in marital instability: 1970. *American Sociological Review, 37*, 754–767.

Burchinal, L. G. (1964). Characteristics of adolescents from unbroken, broken, and reconstituted families. *Journal of Marriage and the Family, 26*, 44–51.

Burke, R. J., & Weir, T. (1976). Relationship of wives' employment status to husband, wife, and pair satisfaction and performance. *Journal of Marriage and the Family, 38*, 279–287.

Buscaglia, L. (1982). *Living, loving & learning*. Thorofare, N.J.: Charles B. Slack.

Buunk, B. (1980). Extramarital sex in the Netherlands: Motivations in social and marital context. *Alternative Lifestyles, 3*(1), 11–39.

Buxton, M. N., Arkel, Y., Lagos, J., Deposito, F., Lowenthal, H., & Simring, S. (1981). Stress and platelet aggregation in hemophiliac children and their family members. *Research Communications in Psychology, Psychiatry and Behavior, 6*(1), 21–48.

Byrne, D. (1971). *The attraction paradigm*. New York: Academic Press.

Byrne, D. (1979). Determinants of contraceptive values and practices. In M. Cook & G. Wilson (Eds.), *Love and attraction*. New York: Pergamon Press.

Byrne, D., Ervin, C. R., & Lamberth, J. (1970). Continuity between the experimental study of attraction and real-life computer dating. *Journal of Personality and Social Psychology, 16*, 157–165.

Caine, L. (1974). *Widow*. New York: William Morrow.

Cameron, N., & Magaret, A. (1951). *Behavior pathology*. Boston: Houghton Mifflin.

Cameron, R., & Meichenbaum, D. (1982). The nature of effective coping and the treatment of stress related problems: A cognitive-behavioral perspective. In L. Goldberger & S. Breznitz (Eds.), *Handbook of stress: Theoretical and clinical aspects*. New York: Free Press.

Campbell, A. (1975). The American way of mating: Marriage si, children only maybe. *Psychology Today, 8*(12), 37–43.

Campbell, A. (1981). *The sense of well-being in America: Recent patterns and trends*. New York: McGraw-Hill.

Campbell, A. M. G., Evans, M., Thompson, M. L. G., & Williams, M. J. (1971). Cerebral atrophy in young cannabis smokers. *Lancet, 2*, 1219–1224.

Cargan, L., & Melko, M. (1982). *Singles: Myths and realities*. Beverly Hills, Calif.: Sage.

Carmichael, S., & Hamilton, C. V. (1967). *Black power: The politics of liberation in America*. New York: Random House.

Carnegie, D. (1936). *How to win friends and influence people*. New York: Simon & Schuster.

Carter, E. A., & McGoldrick, M. (1980). The family life cycle and family therapy: An overview. In E. A. Carter & M. McGoldrick (Eds.), *The family life cycle: A framework for family therapy*. New York: Gardner Press.

Cary, M. S. (1978). The role of gaze in the initiation of conversation. *Social Psychology, 41*, 269–271.

Cash, T. F., & Derlega, V. J. (1978). The matching hypothesis: Physical attractiveness among same-sexed friends. *Personality and Social Psychology Bulletin, 4*, 240–243.

Cataldo, M. F., Bird, B. L., & Cunningham, C. E. (1978). Experimental analysis of EMG feedback in treating cerebral palsy. *Journal of Behavioral Medicine, 1*(1), 311–322.

Cattell, R. B. (1965). *The scientific analysis of personality*. Baltimore: Penguin Books.

Cheek, J. M., & Busch, C. M. (1981). The influence of shyness on loneliness in a new situation. *Personality and Social Psychology Bulletin, 7*(4), 572–577.

Chelune, G. J. (1979). Measuring openness in interpersonal communication. In G. J. Chelune & associates, *Self-disclosure: Origins, patterns, and implications of openness in interpersonal relationships*. San Francisco: Jossey-Bass.

Cherlin, A. (1981). *Marriage, divorce, remarriage*. Cambridge, Mass.: Harvard University Press.

Chesler, P. (1972). *Women and madness*. Garden City, N.Y.: Doubleday.

Chittenden, G. E. (1973). An experimental study in measuring and modifying assertive behavior in young children. *Monographs of the Society for Research in Child Development, 7*(No. 31).

Christodoulou, G. N., Alevizos, B. H., & Konstantakakis, E. (1983). Peptic ulcers in adults: Psychopathological, environmental, characterological and hereditary factors. *Psychotherapy and Psychosomatics, 39*, 55–62.

Claghorn, J. L., Ordy, J. M., & Nagy, A. (1965). Spontaneous opiate addiction in rhesus monkeys. *Science, 149*, 440–441.

Clanton, G. (1973). The contemporary experience of adultery: Bob and Carol and Updike and Rimmer. In R. W. Libby & R. N. Whitehurst (Eds.), *Renovating marriage*. Danville, Calif.: Consensus Publishers.

Clanton, G., & Smith, L. G. (1977). The self-inflicted pain of jealousy. *Psychology Today, 10*(10), 44–47, 80–82.

Clatworthy, N. M. (1975). Living together. In N. Glazer-Malbin (Ed.), *Old family/new family*. New York: D. Van Nostrand.

Clayton, P. J. (1971). Bereavement: Concepts of management. *Psychiatry, 59*, 63.

Clayton, R. R., & Voss, H. L. (1977). Shacking up: Cohabitation in the 1970's. *Journal of Marriage and the Family, 39*, 273–284.

Cleary, P. J. (1980). A checklist for life event research. *Journal of Psychosomatic Research, 24*, 199–207.

Clifford, M. M., & Walster, E. (1973). The effects of physical attractiveness on teachers' expectations. *Sociology of Education, 46*, 248–258.

Cloward, R. A., & Ohlin, L. E. (1966). *Delinquency and opportunity: A theory of delinquent gangs*. Glencoe, Ill.: Free Press.

Cobb, S., & Rose, R. M. (1973). Hypertension, peptic ulcer, and diabetes in air traffic controllers. *Journal of the American Medical Association, 224*, 489–492.

Cofer, D., & Wittenborn, J. (1980). Personality characteristics of formerly depressed women. *Journal of Abnormal Psychology, 89*, 309–314.

Cohen, F. (1979). Personality, stress and the development of physical illness. In G. C. Stone, F. Cohen, N. E. Adler, & associates, *Health psychology—A handbook.* San Francisco: Jossey-Bass.

Cohen, M. B., Baker, G., Cohen, R. A., Fromm-Reichmann, F., & Weigert, E. V. (1954). An intensive study of twelve cases of manic-depressive psychosis. *Psychiatry, 17*, 103–137.

Cohen, S. (1977). Angel dust. *Journal of the American Medical Association, 238*, 515–516.

Cohen, S., Lessin, P. J., Hahn, P. M., & Tyrrell, E. D. (1976). A 94-day cannabis study. In M. C. Braude & S. Szara (Eds.), *Pharmacology of marihuana.* New York: Raven Press.

Cohen, S. I., & Hajioff, J. (1972). Life events and the onset of acute closed-angle glaucoma. *Journal of Psychosomatic Research, 16*, 335–341.

Coleman, J. C. (1969). *Psychology and effective behavior.* Glenview, Ill.: Scott, Foresman.

Coleman, J. C. (1979). *Contemporary psychology and effective behavior.* Glenview, Ill.: Scott, Foresman.

Coleman, J. C., Butcher, J. N., & Carson, R. C. (1980). *Abnormal psychology and modern life* (6th ed.). Glenview, Ill.: Scott, Foresman.

Coleman, J. C., Butcher, J. N., & Carson, R. C. (1984). *Abnormal psychology and modern life* (7th ed.). Glenview, Ill.: Scott, Foresman.

Colgrove, M., Bloomfield, H. H., & McWilliams, P. (1976). *How to survive the loss of a love: 58 things to do when there is nothing to be done.* New York: Lion Press.

Colton, H. (1972). *Sex after the sexual revolution.* New York: Association Press.

Combs, B. J., Hales, D. R., & Williams, B. K. (1980). *An invitation to health: Your personal responsibility.* Menlo Park, Calif.: Benjamin/Cummings.

Comfort, A. (Ed.). (1972). *The joy of sex: A gourmet guide to lovemaking.* New York: Simon & Schuster.

Condon, W. S., Ogston, W. D., & Pacoe, L. V. (1969). Three faces of Eve revisited: A study of transient microstrabismus. *Journal of Abnormal Psychology, 74*, 618–620.

Conrad, C. C. (1976, May). How different sports rate in promoting physical fitness. *Medical Times*, pp. 4–5.

Cookerly, J. R. (1973). The outcome of the six major forms of marriage counseling compared: A pilot study. *Journal of Marriage and the Family, 35*, 608–612.

Cooper, C. L. (1984). The social-psychological precursors to cancer. *Journal of Human Stress, 10*(1), 4–11.

Coopersmith, S. (1967). *The antecedents of self-esteem.* San Francisco: W. H. Freeman.

Corsini, R. J. (1981). *Handbook of innovative psychotherapies.* New York: Wiley.

Costa, P. T., & McCrae, R. R. (1980). Still stable after all these years: Personality as a key to some issues in aging. In P. B. Baltes & O. G. Brim (Eds.), *Life span development and behavior* (Vol. 3). New York: Academic Press.

Costello, C. G. (1978). A critical view of Seligman's laboratory experiments on learned helplessness and depression in humans. *Journal of Abnormal Psychology, 87*, 21–31.

Cox, F. D. (1979). *Human intimacy: Marriage, the family, and its meaning.* St. Paul, Minn.: West.

Cox, H. (1977). Eastern cults and Western culture: Why young Americans are buying Oriental religions. *Psychology Today, 11*(2), 36–42.

Cox, S. (1976). *Female psychology: The emerging self.* Chicago: Science Research Associates.

Cozby, P. C. (1973). Self-disclosure: A literature review. *Psychological Bulletin, 79*, 73–91.

Crasilneck, H. B., & Hall, J. A. (1968). The use of hypnosis in controlling cigarette smoking. *Journal of the Southern Medical Association, 61*, 99–102.

Crasilneck, H. B., & Hall, J. A. (1975). *Clinical hypnosis: Principles and applications.* New York: Grune & Stratton.

Crawford, F. A., Hammon, J. W., Jr., & Shingleton, W. W. (1971).

The stress ulcer syndrome: A clinical and pathological review. *American Journal of Surgery, 121*, 644–649.

Crites, J. O. (1969). *Vocational psychology.* New York: McGraw-Hill.

Crooks, R., & Baur, K. (1983). *Our sexuality.* Menlo Park, Calif.: Benjamin/Cummings.

Cumming, E. (1963). Further thoughts on the theory of disengagement. *International Social Science Journal, 15*, 377–393.

Cunningham, J. D. (1981). Self-disclosure intimacy: Sex, sex of target, cross-national, and "generational" differences. *Personality and Social Psychology Bulletin, 7*(2), 314–319.

Curlee, J. (1969). Alcoholism and the "empty nest." *Bulletin of the Menninger Clinic, 33*, 165–171.

Curran, J. P. (1975). Convergence toward a single sexual standard? *Social Behavior & Personality, 43*, 528–539.

Cutrona, C. E. (1982). Transition to college: Loneliness and the process of social adjustment. In L. A. Peplau & D. Perlman (Eds.), *Loneliness: A sourcebook of current theory, research and therapy.* New York: Wiley.

Dambrot, F. H., Papp, M. E., & Whitmore, C. (1984). The sex-role attitudes of three generations of women. *Personality and Social Psychology Bulletin, 10*(3), 469–473.

Dansby, P. G. (1972). Black pride in the seventies: Fact or fantasy. In R. L. Jones (Ed.), *Black psychology.* New York: Harper & Row.

Davis, J. M. (1973). Drug therapy. In E. A. Spiegel (Ed.), *Progress in neurology and psychiatry.* New York: Grune & Stratton.

Davis, J. M. (1978). Dopamine theory of schizophrenia: A two-factor theory. In L. C. Wynne, R. L. Cromwell, & S. Matthysse (Eds.), *The nature of schizophrenia: New approaches to research and treatment.* New York: Wiley.

Davis, K. (1974). The sociology of parent-youth conflict. In R. L. Coser (Ed.), *The family: Its structures and functions.* New York: St. Martin's Press.

Davis, K. E. (1985). Near and dear: Friendship and love compared. *Psychology Today, 19*(2), 22–30.

Davitz, J. R. (1969). *The language of emotion.* New York: Academic Press.

Dawkins, R. (1971). Selective neurone death as a possible memory mechanism. *Nature, 229*, 117–118.

Dawley, H. H., Jr., & Wenrich, W. W. (1976). *Achieving assertive behavior: A guide to assertive training.* Monterey, Calif.: Brooks/Cole.

Deaux, K. (1972). To err is humanizing: But sex makes a difference. *Representative Research in Social Psychology, 3*, 20–28.

Deese, J., & Hulse, S. H. (1967). *The psychology of learning.* New York: McGraw-Hill.

Delamater, J., & MacCorquodale, P. (1979). *Premarital sexuality: Attitudes, relationships, behavior.* Madison: University of Wisconsin Press.

DeMaris, A., & Leslie, G. R. (1984). Cohabitation with the future spouse: Its influence upon marital satisfaction and communication. *Journal of Marriage and the Family, 46*(1), 77–84.

Dement, W. C. (1960). The effect of dream deprivation. *Science, 131*, 1705–1707.

Dennis, W. (1966). Age and creative productivity. *Journal of Gerontology, 21*(1), 1–8.

DePaulo, B. M., Lanier, K., & Davis, T. (1983). Detecting the deceit of the motivated liar. *Journal of Personality and Social Psychology, 45*(5), 1096–1103.

Derlega, V. J., & Chaikin, A. L. (1975). *Sharing intimacy: What we reveal to others and why.* Englewood Cliffs, N.J.: Prentice-Hall.

Derlega, V. J., & Grezlak, J. (1979). Appropriateness of self-disclosure. In G. J. Chelune & associates, *Self-disclosure: Origins, patterns, and implications of openness in interpersonal relationships.* San Francisco: Jossey-Bass.

Dermer, M., & Thiel, D. (1975). When beauty may fail. *Journal of Personality and Social Psychology, 31*, 1168–1176.

Derogatis, L. R. (1982). Self-report measures of stress. In L. Goldberger & S. Breznitz (Eds.), *Handbook of stress: Theoretical and clinical aspects*. New York: Free Press.

Diamond, M. (1977). Human sexual development: Biological foundations for social development. In F. A. Beach (Ed.), *Human sexuality in four perspectives*. Baltimore: Johns Hopkins University Press.

Diamond, M., & Karlen, A. (1980). *Sexual decisions*. Boston: Little, Brown.

DiMatteo, M. R., & Friedman, H. S. (1982). *Social psychology and medicine*. Cambridge, Mass.: Oelgeschlager, Gunn & Hain.

Dion, K. L., Berscheid, E., & Walster, E. (1972). What is beautiful is good. *Journal of Personality and Social Psychology, 24*, 285–290.

Dishotsky, N. I., Loughman, W. D., Mogar, R. E., & Lipscomb, W. R. (1971). LSD and genetic damage: Is LSD chromosome damaging, carcinogenic, mutagenic, or teratogenic? *Science, 172*, 431–440.

Dixon, N. F. (1980). Humor: A cognitive alternative to stress? In I. G. Sarason & C. D. Spielberger (Eds.), *Stress and anxiety* (Vol. 7). Washington, D.C.: Hemisphere.

Dohrenwend, B. S. (1973). Life events as stressors: A methodological inquiry. *Journal of Health and Social Behavior, 14*, 167–175.

Dohrenwend, B. S., Krasnoff, L., Askenasy, A. R., & Dohrenwend, B. P. (1978). Exemplification of a method for scaling life events: The PERI life events scale. *Journal of Health and Social Behavior, 19*, 205–229.

Dollard, J., Doob, L. W., Miller, N. E., Mowrer, O. H., & Sears, R. R. (1939). *Frustration and aggression*. New Haven, Conn.: Yale University Press.

Dollard, J., & Miller, N. E. (1950). *Personality and psychotherapy*. New York: McGraw-Hill.

Donelson, E. (1973). *Personality: A scientific approach*. Pacific Palisades, Calif.: Goodyear.

Douglass, F. M., IV, Khavari, K. A., & Farber, P. D. (1980). Three types of extreme drug users identified by a replicated cluster analysis. *Journal of Abnormal Psychology, 89*, 240–249.

Douglass, J. H. (1967). Mental health aspects of the effects of discrimination upon children. *Young Children, 22*, 298–305.

Dudycha, G. J. (1936). An objective study of punctuality in relation to personality and achievement. *Archives of Psychology, 204*, 1–53.

Duke, M., & Nowicki, S., Jr. (1979). *Abnormal psychology: Perspectives on being different*. Monterey, Calif.: Brooks/Cole.

Dumont, M. P. (1977). Is mental health possible under our economic system? No. *Psychiatric Opinion, 14*, 9–11, 32–33, 44–45.

Dunn, J. P., & Cobb, S. (1962). Frequency of peptic ulcer among executives, craftsmen, and foremen. *Journal of Occupational Medicine, 4*, 343–348.

Dusek, D., & Girdano, D. A. (1980). *Drugs: A factual account*. Reading, Mass.: Addison-Wesley.

Dutton, D., & Aron, A. (1974). Some evidence for heightened sexual attraction under conditions of high anxiety. *Journal of Personality and Social Psychology, 30*, 510–517.

Duvall, E. (1977). *Marriage and family development*. Philadelphia: Lippincott.

Dyer, W. W. (1976). *Your erroneous zones*. New York: Thomas Y. Crowell.

Eagly, A. H. (1978). Sex differences in influenceability. *Psychological Bulletin, 85*, 86–116.

Eagly, A. H., & Whitehead, G. I. (1972). Effect of choice on receptivity to favorable and unfavorable evaluations of one's self. *Journal of Personality and Social Psychology, 22*, 223–230.

Ebbinghaus, H. (1913). *Memory: A contribution to experimental psychology* (H. A. Ruger & E. C. Bussenius, trans.). New York: Columbia University. (Original work published 1885)

Efran, J. S., & Broughton, A. (1966). Effect of expectancies for social approval on visual behavior. *Journal of Personality and Social Psychology, 4*, 103–107.

Efran, M. (1974). The effect of physical appearance on the judgment of guilt, interpersonal attraction, and severity of recommended punishment in a simulated jury task. *Journal of Research in Personality, 8*, 45–54.

Egan, G. (1986). *The skilled helper: Model, skills, and methods for effective helping*. Monterey, Calif.: Brooks/Cole.

Egan, K. J., Kogan, H. N., Garber, A., & Jarrett, M. (1983). The impact of psychological distress on the control of hypertension. *Journal of Human Stress, 9*(4), 4–10.

Ehrenberg, O., & Ehrenberg, M. (1977). *The psychotherapy maze*. New York: Holt, Rinehart and Winston.

Eibl-Eibesfeldt, I. (1975). *Ethology: The biology of behavior*. New York: Holt, Rinehart and Winston.

Eiswirth, N. A., Smith, D. E., & Wesson, D. R. (1973). Cocaine: Champagne of uppers. In D. E. Smith & D. R. Wesson (Eds.), *Uppers and downers*. Englewood Cliffs, N.J.: Prentice-Hall.

Ekman, P. (1975). The universal smile: Face muscles talk every language. *Psychology Today, 9*(4), 35–39.

Ekman, P., & Friesen, W. V. (1969). The repertoire of nonverbal behavior: Categories, origins, usage, and coding. *Semiotica, 1*, 49–98.

Ekman, P., & Friesen, W. V. (1974). Detecting deception from the body or face. *Journal of Personality and Social Psychology, 29*, 288–298.

Ekman, P., & Friesen, W. V. (1975). *Unmasking the face*. Englewood Cliffs, N.J.: Prentice-Hall.

Eliot, R. S., & Breo, D. L. (1984). *Is it worth dying for?* New York: Bantam.

Ellis, A. (1958). *Sex without guilt*. New York: Lyle Stuart.

Ellis, A. (1973). *Humanistic psychotherapy: The rational-emotive approach*. New York: Julian Press.

Ellis, A. (1977). *Reason and emotion in psychotherapy*. Secaucus, N.J.: Lyle Stuart.

Ellis, A., & Harper, R. A. (1975). *A new guide to rational living*. Englewood Cliffs, N.J.: Prentice-Hall.

Ensor, P. G., Henkel, B. O., & Means, R. K. (1977). *Personal health: Confronting your health behavior*. Boston: Allyn & Bacon.

Epstein, S. P. (1978). Avoidance-approach: The fifth basic conflict. *Journal of Consulting and Clinical Psychology, 46*, 1016–1022.

Epstein, S. P. (1979). The stability of behavior: On predicting most of the people much of the time. *Journal of Personality and Social Psychology, 37*, 1097–1126.

Epstein, S. P. (1982). Conflict and stress. In L. Goldberger & S. Breznitz (Eds.), *Handbook of stress: Theoretical and clinical aspects*. New York: Free Press.

Epstein, S. P. (1983). Natural healing processes of the mind: Graded stress inoculation as an inherent coping mechanism. In D. H. Meichenbaum & M. E. Jaremko (Eds.), *Stress reduction and prevention*. New York: Plenum.

Epstein, S. P., & Roupenian, A. (1970). Heart rate and skin conductance during experimentally induced anxiety: The effect of uncertainty about receiving a noxious stimulus. *Journal of Personality and Social Psychology, 16*, 20–28.

Erikson, E. H. (1963). *Childhood and society* (2nd ed.). New York: Norton.

Erikson, E. H. (1968). *Identity: Youth and crisis*. New York: Norton.

Etaugh, C. F. (1974). Effects of maternal employment on children: A review of recent research. *Merrill-Palmer Quarterly, 20*, 71–98.

Etaugh, C. F. (1980). Effects of nonmaternal care on children: Research evidence and popular views. *American Psychologist, 35*, 309–319.

Etaugh, C. F., Collins, G., & Gerson, A. (1975). Reinforcement of sex-typed behaviors of 2-year-old children in a nursery school setting. *Developmental Psychology, 11*, 255.

Exline, R. (1963). Explorations in the process of person perception: Visual interaction in relation to competition, sex, and need for affiliation. *Journal of Personality, 31,* 1–20.

Eysenck, H. J. (1960). Classification and the problems of diagnosis. In H. J. Eysenck (Ed.), *Handbook of abnormal psychology.* New York: Basic Books.

Eysenck, H. J. (1967). *The biological basis of personality.* Springfield, Ill.: Charles C Thomas.

Farberow, N. L. (1974). *Suicide.* Morristown, N.J.: General Learning Press.

Farkas, G. M., Sine, L. F., & Evans, I. M. (1978). Personality, sexuality, and demographic differences between volunteers and nonvolunteers for a laboratory study of male sexual behavior. *Archives of Sexual Behavior, 7,* 513–520.

Farson, R. (1977). Why good marriages fail. In J. E. DeBurger (Ed.), *Marriage today: Problems, issues, and alternatives.* Cambridge, Mass.: Schenkman.

Fast, J. (1970). *Body language.* New York: M. Evans.

Fast, J. (1977). *The body language of sex, power, and aggression.* New York: M. Evans.

Fast, J., & Bernstein, M. (1983). *Sexual chemistry: What it is, how to use it.* New York: M. Evans.

Fasteau, M. F. (1974). *The male machine.* New York: McGraw-Hill.

Featherstone, H. J., & Beitman, B. D. (1984). Marital migraine: A refractory daily headache. *Psychosomatics, 25*(1), 30–38.

Fendrich, M. (1984). Wives' employment and husbands' distress: A meta-analysis and a replication. *Journal of Marriage and the Family, 46*(4), 871–879.

Fensterheim, H. (1972). Behavior therapy: Assertive training in groups. In C. Sager & H. Kaplan (Eds.), *Progress in group and family therapy.* New York: Brunner/Mazel.

Ferber, M., & Huber, J. (1979). Husbands, wives and careers. *Journal of Marriage and the Family, 41,* 315–325.

Ferree, M. M. (1976). The confused American housewife. *Psychology Today, 10*(4), 76–80.

Festinger, L. (1954). A theory of social comparison processes. *Human Relations, 7,* 117–140.

Festinger, L. (1957). *A theory of cognitive dissonance.* Stanford, Calif.: Stanford University Press.

Festinger, L., Schachter, S., & Back, K. (1950). *Social pressures in informal groups: A study of human factors in housing.* New York: Harper.

Fidell, L. S. (1970). Empirical verification of sex discrimination in hiring practices in psychology. *American Psychologist, 25,* 1094–1098.

Fink, M. (1979). *Convulsive therapy: Theory and practice.* New York: Raven Press.

Fisher, W. A., & Byrne, D. (1978). Sex differences in response to erotica? Love versus lust. *Journal of Personality and Social Psychology, 36,* 117–125.

Fishman, S., & Newes, N. (1971). Standard desensitization method in group treatment. *Journal of Counseling Psychology, 18,* 520–527.

Fitts, W. (1972). *The self concept and psychopathology.* Nashville, Tenn.: Counselor Recording and Tests.

Flanders, J. P. (1976). *Practical psychology.* New York: Harper & Row.

Folkins, C. H., & Sime, W. (1981). Physical fitness training and mental health. *American Psychologist, 36,* 373–389.

Folkman, S. (1984). Personal control and stress and coping processes: A theoretical analysis. *Journal of Personality and Social Psychology, 46*(4), 839–852.

Folkman, S., & Lazarus, R. S. (1980). An analysis of coping in a middle-aged community sample. *Journal of Health and Social Behavior, 21,* 219–239.

Folkman, S., Schaefer, C., & Lazarus, R. S. (1979). Cognitive processes as mediators of stress and coping. In V. Hamilton & D. M. Warburton (Eds.), *Human stress and cognition: An information processing approach.* New York: Wiley.

Fontana, A. (1966). Familial etiology of schizophrenia: Is a scientific methodology possible? *Psychological Bulletin, 66,* 214–228.

Forbes, R. (1979). *Life stress.* Garden City, N.Y.: Doubleday.

Foy, D. W., Sipprelle, R. C., Rueger, D. B., & Carroll, E. M. (1984). Etiology of posttraumatic stress disorder in Vietnam veterans: Analysis of premilitary, military, and combat exposure influences. *Journal of Consulting and Clinical Psychology, 52*(1), 79–87.

France, K. (1984, August). *Competitive versus noncompetitive thinking during exercise: Effects on norepinephrine levels.* Paper presented at the meeting of the American Psychological Association, Toronto, Ontario.

Frankl, V. E. (1962). *Man's search for meaning.* Boston: Beacon Press.

Frankl, V. E. (1967). *Psychotherapy and existentialism.* New York: Washington Square Press.

Frankl, V. E. (1969). *The will to meaning.* New York: New American Library.

Frederick, C. J. (1978). Current trends in suicidal behavior in the United States. *American Journal of Psychotherapy, 32,* 172–200.

Freedman, A. M., Kaplan, H. I., & Sadock, B. J. (1976). *Modern synopsis of comprehensive textbook of psychiatry/II.* Baltimore: Williams & Wilkins.

Freedman, J. L. (1978). *Happy people.* New York: Harcourt Brace Jovanovich.

Freeman, R. B. (1976). *The over-educated American.* New York: Academic Press.

Fretz, B. R., & Stang, D. J. (1980). *Preparing for graduate study in psychology: Not for seniors only.* Washington, D.C.: American Psychological Association.

Freud, S. (1924). *A general introduction to psychoanalysis.* New York: Boni and Liveright. (Original work published 1920)

Freud, S. (1953). *The interpretation of dreams. Standard Edition,* Vols. 4 and 5. London: Hogarth Press. (Original work published 1900)

Freud, S. (1959). *Collected papers* (Vols. 1–5). New York: Basic Books.

Freud, S. (1960). *The psychopathology of everyday life. Standard Edition,* Vol. 6. London: Hogarth Press. (Original work published 1901)

Friedan, B. (1964). *The feminine mystique.* New York: Dell.

Friedberg, J. (1976). *Shock treatment is not good for your brain.* San Francisco: Glide Publications.

Friedewald, W. T. (1982). Current nutrition issues in hypertension. *Journal of the American Dietetic Association, 80,* 17.

Friedman, H. S. (1983). Social perception and face-to-face interaction. In D. Perlman & P. C. Cozby (Eds.), *Social psychology.* New York: Holt, Rinehart and Winston.

Friedman, H. S., Prince, L. M., Riggio, R. E., & DiMatteo, M. R. (1980). Understanding and assessing nonverbal expressiveness: The affective communication test. *Journal of Personality and Social Psychology, 39*(2), 333–351.

Friedman, M., & Rosenman, R. F. (1974). *Type A behavior and your heart.* New York: Knopf.

Friedman, M., Rosenman, R. H., Straus, R., Wurm, M., & Kositchek, R. (1968). The relationship of behavior pattern A to the state of coronary vasculature: A study of fifty-one autopsy subjects. *American Journal of Medicine, 44,* 525–537.

Friedman, S. B., Ader, R., & Glasgow, L. A. (1965). Effects of psychological stress in adult mice inoculated with coxsackie B viruses. *Psychosomatic Medicine, 27,* 361–368.

Fries, H., Nillius, J., & Petersson, F. (1974). Epidemiology of secondary amenorrhea. *American Journal of Obstetrics and Gynecology, 118,* 473–479.

Frieze, I. H., Parsons, J. E., Johnson, P. B., Ruble, D. N., & Zellman, G. L. (1978). *Women and sex roles: A social psychological perspective.* New York: Norton.

Frodi, A., Macaulay, J., & Thome, P. R. (1977). Are women always less aggressive than men? A review of the experimental literature. *Psychological Bulletin, 84,* 634–660.

Froelicher, V., Jensen, D., Genter, F., Sullivan, M., McKirnan, D., Witztum, K., Scharf, J., Strong, M. L., & Ashburn, W. (1984). A randomized trial of exercise training in patients with coronary heart disease. *Journal of the American Medical Association, 252*(10), 1291–1297.

Fromm, E. (1941). *Escape from freedom.* New York: Rinehart.

Fromm, E. (1947). *Man for himself.* New York: Rinehart.

Fromm, E. (1955). *The sane society.* New York: Rinehart.

Fromm, E. (1956). *The art of loving.* New York: Harper & Row.

Gadpaille, W. J. (1975). *The cycles of sex.* New York: Scribner's.

Gallatin, J. (1982). *Abnormal psychology: Concepts, issues, trends.* New York: Macmillan.

Gannon, L., & Sternbach, R. A. (1971). Alpha enhancement as a treatment for pain: A case study. *Journal of Behavior Therapy and Experimental Psychiatry, 2,* 209–213.

Garber, J., & Hollon, S. D. (1980). Universal versus personal helplessness in depression: Belief in uncontrollability or incompetence. *Journal of Abnormal Psychology, 89,* 56–66.

Garfield, S. L., & Kurtz, R. (1976). Clinical psychologists in the 1970s. *American Psychologist, 31,* 1–9.

Garrity, T. F., Marx, M. B., & Somes, G. W. (1978). The relationship of recent life change to seriousness of later illness. *Journal of Psychosomatic Research, 22,* 7–12.

Gatchel, R. J., & Baum, A. (1983). *An introduction to health psychology.* Reading, Mass.: Addison-Wesley.

Gaudry, E., & Spielberger, C. D. (1971). *Anxiety and educational achievement.* New York: Wiley.

Gawin, F. H. (1978). Pharmacological enhancement of the erotic: Implications of an expanded definition of aphrodisiacs. *Journal of Sex Research, 14,* 107–117.

Gay, G. R., & Way, E. L. (1972). Pharmacology of the opiate narcotics. In D. E. Smith & G. R. Gay (Eds.), *"It's so good, don't even try it once": Heroin in perspective.* Englewood Cliffs, N.J.: Prentice-Hall.

Gebhard, P. H. (1966). Factors in marital orgasm. *Journal of Social Issues, 22,* 88–95.

Gebhard, P. H. (1972). Incidence of overt homosexuality in the United States and Western Europe. In J. Livengood (Ed.), *National Institute of Mental Health Task Force on Homosexuality: Final report and background papers.* Washington, D.C.: U.S. Government Printing Office.

Georgas, J., Giakoumaki, E., Georgoulias, N., Koumandakis, E., & Kaskarelis, D. (1984). Psychosocial stress and its relation to obstetrical complications. *Psychotherapy and Psychosomatics, 41,* 200–206.

Giambra, L. M., & Arenberg, D. (1980). Problem solving, concept learning, and aging. In L. W. Poon (Ed.), *Aging in the 1980s: Psychological issues.* Washington, D.C.: American Psychological Association.

Gibb, J. R. (1961). Defensive communication. *Journal of Communication, 11,* 141–148.

Gibbins, K. (1969). Communication aspects of women's clothes and their relation to fashionability. *British Journal of Social and Clinical Psychology, 8,* 301–312.

Giffin, K., & Patton, B. R. (1971). *Fundamentals of interpersonal communication.* New York: Harper & Row.

Gilder, G. F. (1973). *Sexual suicide.* New York: Quadrangle Books.

Gill, D., & Lambourn, J. (1981). The indications for ECT: A profile of its use. In R. L. Palmer (Ed.), *Electroconvulsive therapy: An appraisal.* Oxford: Oxford University Press.

Gillies, J. (1976). *Friends: The power and potential of the company you keep.* New York: Coward, McCann & Geoghegan.

Gilmer, B. V. H. (1975). *Applied psychology: Adjustments in living and work.* New York: McGraw-Hill.

Ginzberg, E. (1952). Toward a theory of occupational choice. *Occupations, 30,* 491–494.

Ginzberg, E. (1972). Toward a theory of occupational choice: A restatement. *Vocational Guidance Quarterly, 20,* 169–176.

Glaser, M. (1984). Rx activity solid despite new products trickle: 45th annual prescription survey. *Drug Topics, 128*(6), 28–42.

Glass, D. C. (1978). Pattern A behavior and uncontrollable stress. In T. M. Dembroski, S. M. Weiss, J. L. Shields, S. G. Haynes, & M. Feinleib (Eds.), *Coronary-prone behavior.* New York: Springer-Verlag.

Glasser, W. (1965). *Reality therapy.* New York: Harper & Row.

Glasser, W. (1969). *Schools without failure.* New York: Harper & Row.

Glenn, N. D., & McLanahan, S. (1982). Children and marital happiness: A further specification of the relationship. *Journal of Marriage and the Family, 44*(1), 63–72.

Glenn, N. D., & Weaver, C. N. (1979). Attitudes toward premarital, extramarital, and homosexual relations in the U.S. in the 1970s. *Journal of Sex Research, 15,* 108–118.

Glenn, R. N., & Janda, L. H. (1977). Self-ideal discrepancy and acceptance of false personality interpretations. *Journal of Personality Assessment, 41,* 311–316.

Glick, P. C. (1957). *American families.* New York: Wiley.

Glick, P. C. (1977). Updating the life cycle of the family. *Journal of Marriage and the Family, 39,* 5–13.

Glick, P. C., & Norton, A. J. (1978). Marrying, divorcing, and living together in the U.S. today. In H. Z. Lopata (Ed.), *Family factbook.* Chicago: Marquis.

Glick, P. C., & Spanier, G. B. (1980). Married and unmarried cohabitation in the United States. *Journal of Marriage and the Family, 42,* 19–30.

Goethals, G. R., & Darley, J. M. (1977). Social comparison theory: An attributional approach. In J. M. Suls & R. L. Miller (Eds.), *Social comparison processes: Theoretical and empirical perspectives.* Washington, D.C.: Hemisphere/Halsted.

Goffman, E. (1956). The nature of deference and demeanor. *American Anthropologist, 58,* 473–502.

Goffman, E. (1959). *The presentation of self in everyday life.* Garden City, N.Y.: Doubleday Anchor.

Goffman, E. (1961). *Asylums: Essays on the social situation of mental patients and other inmates.* Garden City, N.Y.: Doubleday.

Goffman, E. (1971). *Relations in public.* New York: Basic Books.

Goldberg, D. C., Whipple, B., Fishkin, R. E., Waxman, H., Fink, P. J., & Weisberg, M. (1983). The Grafenberg spot and female ejaculation: A review of initial hypotheses. *Journal of Sex & Marital Therapy, 9*(1), 27–37.

Goldberg, H. (1976). *The hazards of being male: Surviving the myth of masculine privilege.* New York: Nash.

Goldman, W., & Lewis, P. (1977). Beautiful is good: Evidence that the physically attractive are more socially skillful. *Journal of Experimental Social Psychology, 13,* 125–130.

Goldstein, M. J. (1959). The relationship between coping and avoiding behavior and response to fear-arousing propaganda. *Journal of Abnormal and Social Psychology, 58,* 247–252.

Goldstein, M. J., Baker, B. L., & Jamison, K. R. (1980). *Abnormal psychology: Experiences, origins, and interventions.* Boston: Little, Brown.

Goleman, D. (1976). Meditation helps break the stress spiral. *Psychology Today, 9*(9), 82–86, 93.

Goleman, D. (1978). Special abilities of the sexes: Do they begin in the brain? *Psychology Today, 12*(6), 48–59, 120.

Gooding, J. (1970, July). The fraying white collar. *Fortune,* pp. 78–81, 108.

Goodman, M. J., Stewart, C. J., & Gilbert, F. (1977). Patterns of menopause. *Journal of Gerontology, 32,* 291–298.

Goodman, N., & Feldman, K. A. (1975). Expectations, ideals and reality: Youth enters college. In S. E. Dragastin & G. H. Elder (Eds.), *Adolescence in the life cycle.* Washington, D.C.: Hemisphere.

Goodwin, D. W. (1976). *Is alcoholism hereditary?* New York: Oxford University Press.

Gordon, S. (1976). *Lonely in America.* New York: Touchstone.

Gorzynski, J. G., Holland, J., Katz, J. L., Weiner, H., Zumoff, B.,

Fukushima, D., & Levin, J. (1980). Stability of ego defenses and endocrine responses in women prior to breast biopsy and ten years later. *Psychosomatic Medicine, 42*, 323–328.

Gottesman, I. I. (1978). Schizophrenia and genetics: Where are we? Are you sure? In L. C. Wynne, R. L. Cromwell, & S. Matthysse (Eds.), *The nature of schizophrenia: New approaches to research and treatment.* New York: Wiley.

Gottesman, I. I., & Shields, J. (1972). *Schizophrenia and genetics.* New York: Academic Press.

Gottschalk, L. A., Welch, W. D., & Weiss, J. (1983). Vulnerability and immune response: An overview. *Psychotherapy and Psychosomatics, 39*, 23–25.

Gould, R. (1976). Measuring masculinity by the size of a paycheck. In D. S. David & R. Brannon (Eds.), *The forty-nine percent majority: The male sex role.* Reading, Mass.: Addison-Wesley.

Gould, R. L. (1972). The phases of adult life: A study in developmental psychology. *American Journal of Psychiatry, 129*, 521–531.

Gould, R. L. (1978). *Transformations: Growth and change in adult life.* New York: Simon & Schuster.

Gove, W. R., & Tudor, J. F. (1973). Adult sex roles and mental illness. *American Journal of Sociology, 78*, 812–835.

Grayson, R. R. (1972). Air controllers syndrome: Peptic ulcer in air traffic controllers. *Illinois Medical Journal, 142*, 111–115.

Green, E. E., Green, A. M., & Walters, E. D. (1970). Self-regulation of internal states. In J. Rose (Ed.), *Progress of cybernetics: Proceedings of the International Congress of Cybernetics.* London: Gordon & Breach.

Greenberg, J., & Archambault, F. (1973). Masturbation, self-esteem, and other variables. *Journal of Sex Research, 9*, 41–51.

Greenberg, J. S. (1983). *Comprehensive stress management.* Dubuque, Iowa: William C. Brown.

Greenblat, C. S. (1983). The salience of sexuality in the early years of marriage. *Journal of Marriage and the Family, 45*(2), 289–299.

Greenblatt, D., & Shader, R. (1974). *Benzodiazepines in clinical practice.* New York: Raven Press.

Greene, W. A., & Swisher, S. N. (1969). Psychological and somatic variables associated with the development and course of monozygotic twins discordant for leukemia. *Annals of the New York Academy of Sciences, 164*, 394–408.

Greenley, J. R., Kepecs, J. G., & Henry, W. E. (1981). Trends in urban American psychiatry: Practice in Chicago in 1962 and 1973. *Social Psychiatry, 16*, 123–128.

Greeno, J. G. (1964). Paired-associate learning with massed and distributed repetitions of items. *Journal of Experimental Psychology, 67*, 286–295.

Greenwald, J. (1973). *Be the person you were meant to be.* New York: Simon & Schuster.

Grob, G. N. (1983). Disease and environment in American history. In D. Mechanic (Ed.), *Handbook of health, health care, and the health professions.* New York: Free Press.

Groninger, L. D. (1971). Mnemonic imagery and forgetting. *Psychonomic Science, 23*, 161–163.

Grotevant, H. D., Scarr, S., & Weinberg, R. A. (1978). Are career interests inheritable? *Psychology Today, 11*(10), 88–90.

Gruneberg, M. M. (1979). *Understanding job satisfaction.* New York: Wiley.

Gurin, P., Gurin, G., Lao, R. C., & Beattie, M. (1969). Internal-external control in the motivational dynamics of Negro youth. *Journal of Social Issues, 25*(3), 29–53.

Hall, C. S., & Lindzey, G. (1978). *Theories of personality.* New York: Wiley.

Hall, E. T. (1959). *The silent language.* Garden City, N.Y.: Doubleday.

Hall, E. T. (1966). *The hidden dimension.* Garden City, N.Y.: Doubleday.

Hall, J. A. (1978). Gender effects in decoding nonverbal cues. *Psychological Bulletin, 85*, 845–857.

Hallie, P. P. (1971). Justification and rebellion. In N. Sanford & C. Comstock (Eds.), *Sanctions for evil.* San Francisco: Jossey-Bass.

Halpern, H. M. (1982). *How to break your addiction to a person.* New York: McGraw-Hill.

Hamachek, D. E. (1978). *Encounters with the self.* New York: Holt, Rinehart and Winston.

Hammond, E. C., & Horn, D. (1984). Smoking and death rates—Report on 44 months of followup of 187,783 men. *Journal of the American Medical Association, 251*(21), 2840–2853.

Hansen, J. E., & Schuldt, W. J. (1984). Marital self-disclosure and marital satisfaction. *Journal of Marriage and the Family, 46*(1), 923–926.

Harari, H., & McDavid, J. W. (1973). Name stereotypes and teacher expectations. *Journal of Educational Psychology, 65*, 222–225.

Hare, R. D. (1976). Psychopathy. In P. H. Venables & M. J. Christie (Eds.), *Research in psychophysiology.* New York: Wiley.

Harlow, H. F. (1958). The nature of love. *American Psychologist, 13*, 673–685.

Harlow, H. F. (1959). Love in infant monkeys. *Scientific American, 200*, 68–74.

Harris, L. J. (1980). Lateralized sex differences: Substrates and significance. *Behavioral and Brain Sciences, 3*, 236–237.

Harris, T. (1967). *I'm OK—you're OK.* New York: Harper & Row.

Harry, J. (1983). Gay male and lesbian relationships. In E. D. Macklin & R. H. Rubin (Eds.), *Contemporary families and alternative lifestyles: Handbook on research and theory.* Beverly Hills, Calif.: Sage.

Hartley, J. T., Harker, J. O., & Walsh, D. A. (1980). Contemporary issues and new directions in adult development of learning and memory. In L. W. Poon (Ed.), *Aging in the 1980s: Psychological issues.* Washington, D.C.: American Psychological Association.

Hartman, W. E., & Fithian, M. A. (1974). *Treatment of sexual dysfunction: A bio-psycho-social approach.* New York: Jason Aronson.

Harvey, J. H., Town, J. P., & Yarkin, K. L. (1981). How fundamental is "the fundamental attribution error"? *Journal of Personality and Social Psychology, 40*(2), 346–349.

Havighurst, R. J. (1972). *Developmental tasks and education.* New York: McKay.

Havighurst, R. J., Neugarten, B., & Tobin, S. (1968). Disengagement and patterns of aging. In B. Neugarten (Ed.), *Middle age and aging.* Chicago: University of Chicago Press.

Hawes, G. R. (1979). *Careers tomorrow: Leading growth fields for college graduates.* New York: New American Library.

Healey, E. S., Kales, A., Monroe, L. J., Bixler, E. O., Chamberlin, K., & Soldatos, C. R. (1981). Onset of insomnia: Role of life-stress events. *Psychosomatic Medicine, 43*(5), 439–451.

Heider, F. (1958). *The psychology of interpersonal relations.* New York: Wiley.

Heiman, J. R. (1975). The physiology of erotica: Women's sexual arousal. *Psychology Today, 8*(11), 90–94.

Heiman, J. R., LoPiccolo, L., & LoPiccolo, J. (1976). *Becoming orgasmic: A sexual growth program for women.* Englewood Cliffs, N.J.: Prentice-Hall.

Hemsley, G. D., & Doob, A. N. (1978). The effect of looking behavior on perceptions of a communicator's credibility. *Journal of Applied Social Psychology, 8*, 136–144.

Henderson, C. W. (1975). *Awakening: Ways to psychospiritual growth.* Englewood Cliffs, N.J.: Prentice-Hall.

Hendrick, S. S. (1981). Self-disclosure and marital satisfaction. *Journal of Personality and Social Psychology, 40*, 1150–1159.

Hennig, M., & Jardim, A. (1978). *The managerial woman.* New York: Simon & Schuster.

Herzberg, F., Mausner, B., & Snyderman, B. B. (1959). *The motivation to work.* New York: Wiley.

Heston, L. (1966). Psychiatric disorders in foster home reared children of schizophrenic mothers. *British Journal of Psychiatry, 112,* 819–825.

Hetherington, M., Cox, M., & Cox, R. (1978). The aftermath of divorce. In J. Stevens & M. Matthews (Eds.), *Mother-child, father-child relations.* Washington, D.C.: National Association for the Education of Young Children.

Heun, L. R., & Heun, R. E. (1975). *Developing skills for human interaction.* Columbus, Ohio: Charles E. Merrill.

Hicks, M. W., Hansen, S. L., & Christie, L. A. (1983). Dual career/dual work families: A systems approach. In E. D. Macklin & R. H. Rubin (Eds.), *Contemporary families and alternative lifestyles: Handbook on research and theory.* Beverly Hills, Calif.: Sage.

Hilgard, E. R., & Hilgard, J. R. (1975). *Hypnosis in the relief of pain.* Los Altos, Calif.: Kaufmann.

Hilgard, J. R. (1970). *Personality and hypnosis: A study of imaginative involvement.* Chicago: University of Chicago Press.

Hill, C. T., Rubin, Z., & Peplau, L. A. (1976). Breakups before marriage: The end of 103 affairs. *Journal of Social Issues, 32,* 147–168.

Hiller, D. V., & Philliber, W. W. (1982). Predicting marital and career success among dual-worker couples. *Journal of Marriage and the Family, 44*(1), 53–62.

Hinsie, L. E., & Campbell, R. J. (1970). *Psychiatric dictionary.* New York: Oxford University Press.

Hiroto, D. S. (1974). Locus of control and learned helplessness. *Journal of Experimental Psychology, 102,* 187–193.

Hite, S. (1976). *The Hite report.* New York: Macmillan.

Hoffman, M. L. (1977). Sex differences in empathy and related behaviors. *Psychological Bulletin, 84,* 712–722.

Hokanson, J. E., & Burgess, M. (1962). The effects of three types of aggression on vascular processes. *Journal of Abnormal and Social Psychology, 65,* 446–449.

Holden, C. (1985). Genes, personality and alcoholism. *Psychology Today, 19*(1), 38–44.

Holland, J. L. (1973). *Making vocational choices.* Englewood Cliffs, N.J.: Prentice-Hall.

Hollingshead, A. B. (1968). Class differences in family stability. In M. B. Sussman (Ed.), *Sourcebook in marriage and the family.* Boston: Houghton Mifflin.

Hollister, L. E. (1978). Psychotomimetic drugs in man. In L. L. Iversen, S. D. Iversen, & S. H. Snyder (Eds.), *Handbook of psychopharmacology* (Vol. 11). New York: Plenum.

Holmes, T. H. (1979). Development and application of a quantitative measure of life change magnitude. In J. E. Barrett, R. M. Rose, & G. L. Klerman (Eds.), *Stress and mental disorder.* New York: Raven Press.

Holmes, T. H., & Masuda, M. (1974). Life change and illness susceptibility. In B. S. Dohrenwend & B. P. Dohrenwend (Eds.), *Stressful life events: Their nature and effects.* New York: Wiley.

Holmes, T. H., & Rahe, R. H. (1967). The Social Readjustment Rating Scale. *Journal of Psychosomatic Research, 11,* 213–218.

Holroyd, K. A., & Lazarus, R. S. (1982). Stress, coping and somatic adaptation. In L. Goldberger & S. Breznitz (Eds.), *Handbook of stress: Theoretical and clinical aspects.* New York: Free Press.

Holter, H. (1975). Sex roles and social change. In M. T. S. Mednick, S. S. Tangri, & L. W. Hoffman (Eds.), *Women and achievement: Social and motivational analyses.* Washington, D.C.: Hemisphere.

Horner, M. (1968). *Sex differences in achievement motivation and performance in competitive and non-competitive situations.* Unpublished doctoral dissertation, University of Michigan.

Horner, M. (1969). Fail: Bright women. *Psychology Today, 3*(6), 36–38, 62.

Horney, K. (1937). *The neurotic personality of our time.* New York: Norton.

Horney, K. (1973). On the genesis of the castration complex in women. In J. B. Miller (Ed.), *Psychoanalysis and women.* New York: Brunner/Mazel. (Original work published 1922)

Horowitz, M. J. (1979). Psychological response to serious life events. In V. Hamilton & D. M. Warburton (Eds.), *Human stress and cognition: An information processing approach.* New York: Wiley.

Horowitz, M. J., & Solomon, G. F. (1978). Delayed stress response syndromes in Viet Nam veterans. In C. R. Figley (Ed.), *Stress disorders among Viet Nam veterans: Theory, research and treatment.* New York: Brunner/Mazel.

House, J. S. (1974). Occupational stress and coronary heart disease: A review and theoretical integration. *Journal of Health and Social Behavior, 15,* 12–25.

House, J. S. (1981). *Work stress and social support.* Reading, Mass.: Addison-Wesley.

Howard, J. A. (1984). Social influences on attribution: Blaming some victims more than others. *Journal of Personality and Social Psychology, 47*(3), 494–505.

Howard, S. M., & Kubis, J. F. (1964). Ego identity and some aspects of personal adjustment. *Journal of Psychology, 58,* 459–466.

Hoyer, W. J., & Plude, D. J. (1980). Attentional and perceptual processes in the study of cognitive aging. In L. W. Poon (Ed.), *Aging in the 1980s: Psychological issues.* Washington, D.C.: American Psychological Association.

Hughes, M., & Gove, W. R. (1981). Playing dumb. *Psychology Today, 15*(10), 74–80.

Hunt, M. (1966). *The world of the formerly married.* New York: McGraw-Hill.

Hunt, M. (1974). *Sexual behavior in the 1970s.* Chicago: Playboy Press.

Hunt, M. (1977). Is marriage in trouble? In J. E. DeBurger (Ed.), *Marriage today: Problems, issues, and alternatives.* Cambridge, Mass.: Schenkman.

Hunt, W. A., & Matarazzo, J. D. (1982). Changing smoking behavior: A critique. In R. J. Gatchel, A. Baum, & J. E. Singer (Eds.), *Handbook of psychology and health.* Vol. 1: *Clinical psychology and behavioral medicine, overlapping disciplines.* Hillsdale, N.J.: Erlbaum.

Hurlock, E. B. (1974). *Personality development.* New York: McGraw-Hill.

Hurst, M. W., Jenkins, C. D., & Rose, R. M. (1978). The assessment of life change stress: A comparative and methodological inquiry. *Psychosomatic Medicine, 40,* 126–141.

Huseman, R. C., Lahiff, J. M., & Hatfield, J. D. (1976). *Interpersonal communication in organizations.* Boston: Holbrook Press.

Huyck, M. H., & Hoyer, W. J. (1982). *Adult development and aging.* Belmont, Calif.: Wadsworth.

Hyde, J. S. (1982). *Understanding human sexuality* (2nd ed.). New York: McGraw-Hill.

Hyde, J. S., & Rosenberg, B. G. (1980). *Half the human experience: The psychology of women.* Lexington, Mass.: Heath.

IMS. (1983). *National prescription audit.* Ambler, Pa.: IMS America Ltd.

Ineichen, B. (1979). The social geography of marriage. In M. Cook & G. Wilson (Eds.), *Love and attraction.* New York: Pergamon Press.

Insel, P. M., & Roth, W. T. (1976). *Health in a changing society.* Palo Alto, Calif.: Mayfield.

Isherwood, J., Adam, K. S., & Hornblow, A. R. (1982). Readjustment, desirability, expectedness, mastery and outcome dimensions of life stress suicide attempt and auto-accident. *Journal of Human Stress, 8*(1), 11–18.

Iverson, M. A. (1964). Personality impressions of punitive stimulus persons of differential status. *Journal of Abnormal and Social Psychology, 68,* 617–626.

Jacobs, L., Berscheid, E., & Walster, E. (1971). Self-esteem and attraction. *Journal of Personality and Social Psychology, 17,* 84–91.

Jacobs, T. J., & Charles, E. (1980). Life events and the occurrence of cancer in children. *Psychosomatic Medicine, 42*(1), 11–24.

Jakubowski-Spector, P. (1973). Facilitating the growth of women through assertive training. *Counseling Psychologist, 4,* 75–86.

Janda, L. H., & Klenke-Hamel, K. E. (1980). *Human sexuality.* New York: D. Van Nostrand.

Janis, I. L. (1958). *Psychological stress.* New York: Wiley.

Janis, I. L. (1983). Stress inoculation in health care. In D. H. Meichenbaum & M. E. Jaremko (Eds.), *Stress reduction and prevention.* New York: Plenum.

Jay, K. (1977). Surviving gay coupledom. In E. S. Morrison & V. Borosage (Eds.), *Human sexuality: Contemporary perspectives.* Palo Alto, Calif.: Mayfield.

Jeffrey, D. B., & Lemnitzer, N. (1981). Diet, exercise, obesity and related health problems: A macroenvironmental analysis. In J. M. Ferguson & C. B. Taylor (Eds.), *The comprehensive handbook of behavioral medicine. Vol. 2: Syndromes and special areas.* Jamaica, N.Y.: Spectrum.

Johnson, D. W. (1972). *Reaching out: Interpersonal effectiveness and self-actualization.* Englewood Cliffs, N.J.: Prentice-Hall.

Johnson, D. W., & Johnson, F. (1975). *Joining together.* Englewood Cliffs, N.J.: Prentice-Hall.

Johnson, M. L., Burke, B. S., & Mayer, J. (1956). Relative importance of inactivity and overeating in the energy balance of obese high school girls. *American Journal of Clinical Nutrition, 4,* 37–44.

Johnson, P. B., Updyke, W. F., Schaefer, M., & Stolberg, D. C. (1975). *Sport, exercise, and you.* New York: Holt, Rinehart and Winston.

Jones, E. E. (1964). *Ingratiation.* New York: Appleton-Century-Crofts.

Jones, E. E., & Davis, K. (1965). From acts to dispositions: The attribution process in person perception. In L. Berkowitz (Ed.), *Advances in experimental social psychology* (Vol. 2). New York: Academic Press.

Jones, E. E., Gergen, K. J., & Davis, K. (1962). Some reactions to being approved or disapproved as a person. *Psychological Monographs, 76*(Whole No. 521).

Jones, E. E., & Nisbett, R. E. (1971). *The actor and the observer: Divergent perceptions of the causes of behavior.* Morristown, N.J.: General Learning Press.

Jones, R. T. (1978). Marihuana: Human effects. In L. L. Iversen, S. D. Iversen, & S. H. Snyder, *Handbook of psychopharmacology* (Vol. 12). New York: Plenum.

Jones, W. H. (1984, August). *Situational factors in shyness.* Paper presented at the meeting of the American Psychological Association, Toronto, Ontario.

Jones, W. H., Hobbs, S. A., & Hockenbury, D. (1982). Loneliness and social skill deficits. *Journal of Personality and Social Psychology, 42*(4), 682–689.

Jones-Witters, P., & Witters, W. (1983). *Drugs and society: A biological perspective.* Monterey, Calif.: Wadsworth Health Sciences.

Jordaan, J. P. (1974). Life stages as organizing modes of career development. In E. L. Herr (Ed.), *Vocational guidance and human development.* Boston: Houghton Mifflin.

Jourard, S. M. (1961). Age trends in self-disclosure. *Merrill-Palmer Quarterly, 7,* 191–197.

Jourard, S. M. (1964). *The transparent self.* New York: Van Nostrand Reinhold. (2nd ed., 1971.)

Jourard, S. M. (1971). *Self-disclosure: An experimental analysis of the transparent self.* New York: Wiley.

Jourard, S. M. (1974). *Healthy personality: An approach from the viewpoint of humanistic psychology.* New York: Macmillan.

Jourard, S. M., & Landsman, M. J. (1960). Cognition, cathexis, and the "dyadic effect" in men's self-disclosing behavior. *Merrill-Palmer Quarterly, 6,* 178–186.

Julien, R. M. (1975). *A primer of drug action.* San Francisco: W. H. Freeman.

Jung, C. G. (1917). *Analytical psychology.* New York: Moffat, Yard.

Jung, C. G. (1933). *Modern man in search of a soul.* New York: Harcourt, Brace & World.

Jung, C. G. (1960). The transcendent function. In *Collected works* (Vol. 8). Princeton, N.J.: Princeton University Press. (Original work published 1916)

Jung, C. G. (Ed.). (1964). *Man and his symbols.* Garden City, N.Y.: Doubleday.

Kaats, G., & Davis, K. (1971). Effects of volunteer biases in studies of sexual behavior and attitudes. *Journal of Sex Research, 7,* 26–34.

Kach, J. A., & McGhee, P. E. (1982). Adjustment of early parenthood: The role of accuracy of preparenthood experiences. *Journal of Family Issues, 3*(3), 375–388.

Kadushin, C. (1969). *Why people go to psychiatrists.* New York: Atherton Press.

Kalant, H., & Kalant, O. J. (1979). Death in amphetamine users: Causes and rates. In D. E. Smith (Ed.), *Amphetamine use, misuse, and abuse.* Boston: G. K. Hall.

Kamiya, J. (1969). Operant control of the EEG rhythm and some of its reported effects on consciousness. In C. T. Tart (Ed.), *Altered states of consciousness.* New York: Wiley.

Kandel, D. B. (1978). Similarity in real-life adolescent friendship pairs. *Journal of Personality and Social Psychology, 36,* 306–312.

Kando, T. M. (1978). *Sexual behavior and family life in transition.* New York: Elsevier.

Kanin, E. J., Davidson, K. R., & Scheck, S. R. (1970). A research note on male-female differentials in the experience of heterosexual love. *Journal of Sex Research, 6,* 64–72.

Kanner, A. D., Coyne, J. C., Schaefer, C., & Lazarus, R. S. (1981). Comparison of two modes of stress management: Daily hassles and uplifts versus major life events. *Journal of Behavioral Medicine, 4,* 1–39.

Kaplan, H. S. (1974). *The new sex therapy: Active treatment of sexual dysfunction.* New York: Brunner/Mazel.

Kaplan, H. S. (1975). *The illustrated manual of sex therapy.* New York: A & W Visual Library.

Kaplan, H. S. (1979). *Disorders of sexual desire and other new concepts and techniques in sex therapy.* New York: Simon & Schuster.

Kaplan, W., & Kimball, C. (1982). The risks and course of coronary artery disease: A biopsychosocial perspective. In T. Millon, C. Green, & R. Meagher (Eds.), *Handbook of clinical health psychology.* New York: Plenum.

Karling, M., Coffman, T. L., & Walters, G. (1969). On the fading of social stereotypes: Studies in three generations of stereotypes. *Journal of Personality and Social Psychology, 13,* 1–16.

Kasamatsu, A., & Hirai, T. (1969). An electroencephalographic study of Zen meditation. In C. T. Tart (Ed.), *Altered states of consciousness.* New York: Wiley.

Kasl, S. V., & Cobb, S. (1970). Blood pressure changes in men undergoing job loss: A preliminary report. *Psychosomatic Medicine, 32,* 19–38.

Kastenbaum, R. J. (1977). *Death, society and human experience.* St. Louis: Mosby.

Kazdin, A. E. (1980). Basic concepts and models of abnormal behavior. In A. E. Kazdin, A. S. Bellack, & M. Hersen (Eds.), *New perspectives in abnormal psychology.* New York: Oxford University Press.

Keefe, F. J., & Surwit, R. S. (1978). Electromyographic biofeedback: Behavioral treatment of neuromuscular disorders. *Journal of Behavioral Medicine, 1*(1), 13–24.

Kelley, H. H. (1950). The warm-cold variable in first impressions of persons. *Journal of Personality, 18,* 431–439.

Kelley, H. H. (1967). Attribution theory in social psychology. In D. Levine (Ed.), *Nebraska Symposium on Motivation* (Vol. 15). Lincoln: University of Nebraska Press.

Kelley, H. H. (1971). *Attribution in social interaction.* Morristown, N.J.: General Learning Press.

Kelley, K., Byrne, D., Przybyla, D. P. J., Eberly, C., Eberly, B., Greendlinger, V., Wan, C. K., & Gorsky, J. (1984, August). *Chronic self-destructiveness: Conceptualization, measurement and construct validity.* Paper presented at the meeting of the American Psychological Association, Toronto, Ontario.

Kelly, G. A. (1955). *The psychology of personal constructs* (Vols. 1 & 2). New York: Norton.

Keltner, J. W. (1973). *Elements of interpersonal communication.* Belmont, Calif.: Wadsworth.

Kendell, R. E. (1981). The contribution of ECT to the treatment of affective disorders. In R. L. Palmer (Ed.), *Electroconvulsive therapy: An appraisal.* Oxford: Oxford University Press.

Kenrick, D. T., & Gutierres, S. E. (1980). Contrast effects and judgments of physical attractiveness: When beauty becomes a social problem. *Journal of Personality and Social Psychology, 38,* 131–140.

Kephart, W. M. (1977). *The family, society, and the individual.* Boston: Houghton Mifflin.

Kerckhoff, A. C., & Davis, K. E. (1962). Value consensus and need complementarity in mate selection. *American Sociological Review, 27,* 295–303.

Kety, S. (1975). Biochemistry of the major psychoses. In A. M. Freedman, H. I. Kaplan, & B. J. Sadock (Eds.), *Comprehensive textbook of psychiatry.* Baltimore: Williams & Wilkins.

Keyes, R. (1973). *We the lonely people: Searching for community.* New York: Harper & Row.

Kiecolt-Glaser, J. K., Garner, W., Speicher, C., Penn, G. M., Holliday, J., & Glaser, R. (1984). Psychosocial modifiers of immunocompetence in medical students. *Psychosomatic Medicine, 46*(1), 7–14.

Kieffer, J. A. (1982). So much for the great American dream of retiring early. *Generations, 6*(4), 7–9.

Kiersch, T. A. (1962). Amnesia: A clinical study of 98 cases. *American Journal of Psychiatry, 119,* 57–60.

Kiesler, C. A., & Pallack, M. (1976). Arousal properties of dissonance manipulations. *Psychological Bulletin, 83,* 1014–1025.

Kiesler, S. B., & Baral, R. L. (1970). The search for a romantic partner: The effects of self-esteem and physical attractiveness on romantic behavior. In K. J. Gergen & D. Marlowe (Eds.), *Personality and social behavior.* Reading, Mass.: Addison-Wesley.

Kilmann, P. R. (1984). *Human sexuality in contemporary life.* Boston: Allyn & Bacon.

Kimmel, D. C. (1980). *Adulthood and aging: An interdisciplinary, developmental view.* New York: Wiley.

Kinsbourne, M. (1980). If sex differences in brain lateralization exist, they have yet to be discovered. *Behavioral and Brain Sciences, 3,* 241–242.

Kinsey, A. C., Pomeroy, W. B., & Martin, C. E. (1948). *Sexual behavior in the human male.* Philadelphia: Saunders.

Kinsey, A. C., Pomeroy, W. B., Martin, C. E., & Gebhard, P. H. (1953). *Sexual behavior in the human female.* Philadelphia: Saunders.

Kinsman, R. A., Dirks, J. F., & Jones, N. F. (1982). Psychomaintenance of chronic physical illness: Clinical assessment of personal styles affecting medical management. In T. Millon, C. Green, & R. Meagher (Eds.), *Handbook of clinical health psychology.* New York: Plenum.

Kissen, D. M. (1963). Personality characteristics in males conducive to lung cancer. *British Journal of Medical Psychology, 36,* 27–36.

Kleinke, C. L. (1977). Compliance to requests made by gazing and touching experimenters in field settings. *Journal of Experimental Social Psychology, 13,* 218–223.

Kleinke, C. L., Meeker, R. B., & LaFong, C. (1974). Effects of gaze, touch, and use of name on evaluation of "engaged" couples. *Journal of Research in Personality, 7,* 368–373.

Kleinmuntz, B. (1980). *Essentials of abnormal psychology.* San Francisco: Harper & Row.

Kline, P. (1972). *Fact and fantasy in Freudian theory.* London: Methuen.

Klonoff, H. (1974). Marijuana and driving in real-life situations. *Science, 186,* 317–324.

Knupfer, G., Clark, W., & Room, R. (1966). The mental health of the unmarried. *American Journal of Psychiatry, 122,* 841–851.

Kobasa, S. C. (1979). Stressful life events, personality, and health: An inquiry into hardiness. *Journal of Personality and Social Psychology, 37,* 1–11.

Kobasa, S. C. (1982). The hardy personality: Toward a social psychology of stress and health. In G. S. Sanders & J. Suls (Eds.), *Social psychology of health and illness.* Hillsdale, N.J.: Erlbaum.

Kobasa, S. C., Maddi, S. R., & Kahn, S. (1982). Hardiness and health: A prospective study. *Journal of Personality and Social Psychology, 42*(1), 168–177.

Kobasa, S. C., & Pucetti, M. C. (1983). Personality and social resources in stress resistance. *Journal of Personality and Social Psychology, 45*(4), 839–850.

Kohen, A. I. (1975). Occupational mobility among middle-aged men. In U.S. Department of Labor, Manpower R&D Monograph 15, *The preretirement years.* Vol. 4: *A longitudinal study of the labor market experience of men.* Washington, D.C.: U.S. Government Printing Office.

Kohlberg, L. (1966). A cognitive-developmental analysis of children's sex-role concepts and attitudes. In E. E. Maccoby (Ed.), *The development of sex differences.* Stanford, Calif.: Stanford University Press.

Kolodny, R. C., Masters, W. H., Kolodner, R. M., & Toro, G. (1974). Depression of plasma testosterone levels after chronic intensive marihuana use. *New England Journal of Medicine, 291,* 872–874.

Komarovsky, M. (1976). *Dilemmas of masculinity: A study of college youth.* New York: Norton.

Komarovsky, M. (1977). The effects of poverty upon marriage. In J. E. DeBurger (Ed.), *Marriage today: Problems, issues, and alternatives.* Cambridge, Mass.: Schenkman.

Koocher, G. P. (1971). Swimming, social competence, and personality change. *Journal of Personality and Social Psychology, 18,* 275–278.

Koplan, J. P., Powell, K. E., Sikes, R. K., Shirley, R. W., & Campbell, C. C. (1982). An epidemiologic study of the benefits and risks of running. *Journal of the American Medical Association, 248*(23), 3118–3121.

Korchin, S. J. (1976). *Modern clinical psychology.* New York: Basic Books.

Kraemer, G. W., & McKinney, W. T. (1979). Interactions of pharmacological agents which alter biogenic amine metabolism and depression. *Journal of Affective Disorders, 1,* 33–54.

Kraft, W. A., & Rodolfa, E. R. (1982). The use of hypnosis among psychologists. *American Journal of Clinical Hypnosis, 24*(4), 249–257.

Kramer, M., Rosen, B. M., & Willis, E. M. (1973). Definitions and distributions of mental disorders in a racist society. In C. V. Willie, B. M. Kramer, & B. S. Brown (Eds.), *Racism and mental health.* Pittsburgh: University of Pittsburgh Press.

Krantz, D. L. (1977). The Santa Fe experience: In search of a new life—radical career change in a special place. In S. B. Sarason (Ed.), *Work, aging and social change: Professionals and the one life—one career imperative.* New York: Free Press.

Krantz, D. S., Glass, D. C., Contrada, R., & Miller, N. E. (1981). *Behavior and health: National Science Foundation's second five-year outlook on science and technology.* Washington, D.C.: U.S. Government Printing Office.

Kremers, J. (1960). *Scientific psychology and naive psychology.*

Nijmegen, Netherlands: Drukkerij Gebrakt Janssen.

Kringlen, E. (1967). *Heredity and environment in the functional psychosis: An epidemiological clinical twin study.* Oslo: Universits Forlaget.

Kroger, W. S. (1977). *Clinical and experimental hypnosis.* Philadelphia: Lippincott.

Krohne, H. W. (1978). Individual differences in coping with stress and anxiety. In C. D. Spielberger & I. G. Sarason (Eds.), *Stress and anxiety* (Vol. 5). Washington, D.C.: Hemisphere.

Krueger, D. W. (1981). Stressful life events and the return to heroin use. *Journal of Human Stress, 7*(2), 3–8.

Krueger, W. C. F. (1929). The effect of overlearning on retention. *Journal of Experimental Psychology, 12,* 71–78.

Kruglanski, A. W. (1975). The endogenous-exogenous partition in attribution theory. *Psychological Review, 82,* 387–406.

Kübler-Ross, E. (1969). *On death and dying.* New York: Macmillan.

Kübler-Ross, E. (1970). The dying patient's point of view. In O. G. Brim, Jr., H. E. Freeman, S. Levine, & N. A. Scotch (Eds.), *The dying patient.* New York: Russell Sage Foundation.

Kübler-Ross, E. (1974). *Questions and answers on death and dying.* New York: Macmillan.

Kuehnle, J., Mendelson, J. H., Davis, K. R., & New, P. F. J. (1977). Computerized tomographic examination of heavy marihuana smokers. *Journal of the American Medical Association, 237,* 1231–1232.

Kuntzleman, C. T., and the editors of *Consumer Guide.* (1980). *Rating the exercises.* New York: Penguin Books.

Kutash, S. B. (1976). Modified psychoanalytic therapies. In B. B. Wolman (Ed.), *The therapist's handbook.* New York: Van Nostrand Reinhold.

Lacy, W. B., & Hendricks, J. (1980). Developmental models of adult life: Myth or reality? *International Journal of Aging and Human Development, 11*(2), 89–110.

Laing, R. D. (1967). *The politics of experience.* New York: Ballantine Books.

Lakein, A. (1973). *How to get control of your time and your life.* New York: Peter H. Wyden.

Lal, N., Ahuja, R. C., & Madhukar (1982). Life events in hypertensive patients. *Journal of Psychosomatic Research, 26*(4), 441–445.

Lamanna, M. A., & Riedmann, A. (1981). *Marriage and families: Making choices throughout the life cycle.* Belmont, Calif: Wadsworth.

Landy, D., & Sigall, H. (1974). Beauty is talent. *Journal of Personality and Social Psychology, 29,* 299–304.

Lange, A. J., & Jakubowski, P. (1976). *Responsible assertive behavior.* Champaign, Ill.: Research Press.

LaRocco, J. M., House, J. S., & French, J. R. P., Jr. (1980). Social support, occupational stress, and health. *Journal of Health and Social Behavior, 21,* 202–218.

Larwood, L., & Gattiker, U. (1984, August). *A comparison of the career paths used by successful men and women.* Paper presented at the meeting of the American Psychological Association, Toronto, Ontario.

Lasswell, M., & Lasswell, T. E. (1982). *Marriage and the family.* Lexington, Mass.: Heath.

Lavrakas, P. J. (1975). Female preferences for male physiques. *Journal of Research in Personality, 9,* 324–334.

Law, D. K., Dudrick, S. J., & Abdou, N. I. (1973). Immunocompetence of patients with protein-calorie malnutrition: The effects of nutritional repletion. *Annals of Internal Medicine, 79,* 545–550.

Lawler, K. A. (1980). Cardiovascular and electrodermal response patterns in heart rate reactive individuals during psychological stress. *Psychophysiology, 17*(5), 464–470.

Lawrence, G. H., & Johnson, L. C. (1977). Biofeedback and performance. In G. E. Schwartz & J. Beatty (Eds.), *Biofeedback: Theory and research.* New York: Academic Press.

Lawson, E. D. (1971). Hair color, personality, and the observer.

Psychological Reports, 28, 311–322.

Lazarus, A. A. (1981). *The practice of multimodal therapy.* New York: McGraw-Hill.

Lazarus, A. A., & Wilson, G. T. (1976). Behavior modification: Clinical and experimental perspectives. In B. B. Wolman (Ed.), *The therapist's handbook.* New York: Van Nostrand Reinhold.

Lazarus, R. S. (1969). *Patterns of adjustment and human effectiveness.* New York: McGraw-Hill.

Lazarus, R. S. (1976). *Patterns of adjustment.* New York: McGraw-Hill.

Lazarus, R. S. (1981). Little hassles can be hazardous to health. *Psychology Today, 15*(7), 58–62.

Lazarus, R. S., & Folkman, S. (1984). *Stress, appraisal and coping.* New York: Springer.

Leavitt, F. (1982). *Drugs and behavior.* New York: Wiley.

Lee, J. A. (1974). The styles of loving. *Psychology Today, 8*(5), 43–51.

Lehne, G. K. (1976). Homophobia among men. In D. S. David & R. Brannon (Eds.), *The forty-nine percent majority: The male sex role.* Reading, Mass.: Addison-Wesley.

Leitenberg, H. (1976). Behavioral approaches to treatment of neuroses. In H. Leitenberg (Ed.), *Handbook of behavior modification and behavior therapy.* Englewood Cliffs, N.J.: Prentice-Hall.

LeMasters, E. E. (1957). Parenthood as crisis. *Marriage and Family Living, 19,* 352–355.

LeMasters, E. E. (1977). *Parents in modern America.* Homewood, Ill.: Dorsey Press.

Lerner, M. J. (1970). The desire for justice and reactions to victims. In J. Macaulay & L. Berkowitz (Eds.), *Altruism and helping behavior: Social psychological studies of some antecedents and consequences.* New York: Academic Press.

Lesgold, A. M., & Goldman, S. R. (1973). Encoding uniqueness and the imagery mnemonic in associative learning. *Journal of Verbal Learning and Verbal Behavior, 12,* 193–202.

LeShan, L. (1966). An emotional life-history pattern associated with neoplastic disease. *Annals of the New York Academy of Sciences, 125,* 780–793.

Lester, G., & Lester, D. (1971). *Suicide: The gamble with death.* Englewood Cliffs, N.J.: Prentice-Hall.

Levenson, H., Hirschfeld, M. L., Hirschfeld, A., & Dzubay, B. (1983). Recent life events and accidents: The role of sex differences. *Journal of Human Stress, 9*(1), 4–11.

Levinger, G. (1966). Systematic distortion in spouses' reports of preferred and actual sexual behavior. *Sociometry, 29,* 291–299.

Levinger, G. (1974). A three-level approach to attraction: Toward an understanding of pair relatedness. In T. L. Huston (Ed.), *Foundations of interpersonal attraction.* New York: Academic Press.

Levinger, G. (1976). A social psychological perspective on marital dissolution. *Journal of Social Issues, 32,* 21–43.

Levinson, D. J., Darrow, C. M., Klein, E. G., Levinson, M. H., & McKee, B. (1974). The psychosocial development of men in early adulthood and the midlife transition. In D. F. Ricks, A. Thomas, & M. Roff (Eds.), *Life history research in psychopathology* (Vol. 3). Minneapolis: University of Minnesota Press.

Levinson, D. J., Darrow, C. M., Klein, E. G., Levinson, M. H., & McKee, B. (1978). *The seasons of a man's life.* New York: Knopf.

Levitin, T., Quinn, R. P., & Staines, G. L. (1971). Sex discrimination against the American working woman. *American Behavioral Scientist, 15,* 237–254.

Lewinsohn, P. M. (1974). A behavioral approach to depression. In R. J. Friedman & M. M. Katz (Eds.), *The psychology of depression: Contemporary theory and research.* New York: Halsted Press.

Lewinsohn, P. M., Mischel, W., Chapline, W., & Barton, R. (1980). Social competence and depression: The role of illusory self-perceptions. *Journal of Abnormal Psychology, 89,* 203–212.

Lichtenstein, E. (1980). *Psychotherapy: Approaches and applications.* Monterey, Calif.: Brooks/Cole.

Lickey, M. E., & Gordon, B. (1983). *Drugs for mental illness: A revolution in psychiatry.* New York: W. H. Freeman.

Lidz, T. (1973). *The origin and treatment of schizophrenic disorders.* New York: Basic Books.

Lieberman, M. A., Yalom, I. D., & Miles, M. B. (1973). *Encounter groups: First facts.* New York: Basic Books.

Lindgren, H. C. (1969). *The psychology of college success: A dynamic approach.* New York: Wiley.

Ling, W., Holmes, E. D., Post, G. R., & Litaker, M. B. (1973). A systematic psychiatric study of the heroin addict. In *Proceedings of the Fifth National Conference on Methadone Treatment* (Vol. 1). New York: NAPAN.

Litewka, J. (1977). The socialized penis. In E. S. Morrison & V. Borosage (Eds.), *Human sexuality: Contemporary perspectives.* Palo Alto, Calif.: Mayfield.

Litwack, M., & Resnick, M. R. (1984). *The art of self-fulfillment.* New York: Simon & Schuster.

Livson, F. B. (1976). Patterns of personality development in middle-aged women: A longitudinal study. *International Journal of Aging and Human Development, 7*(2), 107–115.

Locke, H. J. (1951). *Predicting adjustment in marriage: A comparison of a divorced and a happily married group.* New York: Holt, Rinehart and Winston.

Locksley, A. (1980). On the effects of wives' employment on marital adjustment and companionship. *Journal of Marriage and the Family, 42,* 337–346.

Locksley, A., & Colten, M. E. (1979). Psychological androgyny: A case of mistaken identity? *Journal of Personality and Social Psychology, 37,* 1017–1031.

Long, J. W. (1977). *The essential guide to prescription drugs.* New York: Harper & Row.

Longfellow, C. (1979). Divorce in context: Its impact on children. In G. Levinger & O. C. Moles (Eds.), *Divorce and separation.* New York: Basic Books.

Lopata, H. Z. (1973). *Widowhood in an American city.* Cambridge, Mass.: Schenkman.

LoPiccolo, J., & Lobitz, C. (1972). The role of masturbation in the treatment of sexual dysfunction. *Archives of Sexual Behavior, 2,* 163–171.

Lorayne, H., & Lucas, J. (1974). *The memory book.* New York: Ballantine Books.

Lott, D. F., & Sommer, R. (1967). Seating arrangements and status. *Journal of Personality and Social Psychology, 7,* 90–95.

Lowenthal, M. F., & Chiriboga, D. (1972). Transition to the empty nest: Crises, challenge or relief? *Archives of General Psychiatry, 26,* 8–14.

Lowenthal, M. F., Thurnher, M., Chiriboga, D., & associates. (1975). *Four stages of life: A comparative study of women and men facing transitions.* San Francisco: Jossey-Bass.

Luke, B. (1984). *Principles of nutrition and diet therapy.* Boston: Little, Brown.

Lustman, P. J., & Sowa, C. J. (1983). Comparative efficacy of biofeedback and stress inoculation for stress reduction. *Journal of Clinical Psychology, 31,* 191–197.

Macklin, E. D. (1974). Cohabitation in college: Going very steady. *Psychology Today, 8*(6), 53–59.

Macklin, E. D. (1983). Nonmarital heterosexual cohabitation: An overview. In E. D. Macklin & R. H. Rubin (Eds.), *Contemporary families and alternative lifestyles: Handbook on research and theory.* Beverly Hills, Calif.: Sage.

Maccoby, E. E., & Jacklin, C. N. (1974). *The psychology of sex differences.* Stanford, Calif.: Stanford University Press.

Maher, B. A. (1970). *Introduction to research in psychopathology.* New York: McGraw-Hill.

Mahl, G. F. (1968). Gestures and body movements in interviews. In J. M. Shlien (Ed.), *Research in psychotherapy* (Vol. 3).

Washington, D.C.: American Psychological Association.

Mahoney, M. J. (1971). The self-management of covert behavior: A case study. *Behavior Therapy, 2,* 575–578.

Mahoney, M. J. (1979). *Self-change: Strategies for solving personal problems.* New York: Norton.

Major, B., Deaux, K., & Carnevale, P. J. D. (1981). A different perspective on androgyny: Evaluations of masculine and feminine personality characteristics. *Journal of Personality and Social Psychology, 41*(5), 988–1001.

Malamud, N., & Zheutlin, A. (1953). Fatal cardiac complications during electroshock treatment. *Journal of Nervous and Mental Disease, 117,* 458–464.

Malcolm X (with Alex Haley). (1965). *The autobiography of Malcolm X.* New York: Grove Press.

Mandler, G. (1979). Thought processes, consciousness and stress. In V. Hamilton & D. M. Warburton (Eds.), *Human stress and cognition: An information processing approach.* New York: Wiley.

Manuck, S. B., & Garland, F. N. (1980). Stability of individual differences in cardiovascular reactivity. *Physiology and Behavior, 24*(3), 621–624.

Manz, W., & Lueck, H. (1968). Influence of wearing glasses on personality ratings. *Perceptual and Motor Skills, 27*(3), 704.

Marecek, J. (1978). Psychological disorders in women: Indices of role strain. In I. H. Frieze, J. E. Parsons, P. B. Johnson, D. N. Ruble, & G. L. Zellman, *Women and sex roles: A social psychological perspective.* New York: Norton.

Marks, G. (1984). Thinking one's abilities are unique and one's opinions are common. *Personality and Social Psychology Bulletin, 10*(2), 203–208.

Marks, I. (1977). Phobias and obsessions: Clinical phenomena in search of laboratory models. In J. D. Maser & M. E. P. Seligman (Eds.), *Psychopathology: Experimental models.* San Francisco: W. H. Freeman.

Marlatt, G. A., & Rose, F. (1980). Addictive disorders. In A. E. Kazdin, A. S. Bellack, & M. Hersen (Eds.), *New perspectives in abnormal psychology.* New York: Oxford University Press.

Marlowe, D., & Gergen, K. (1969). Personality and social interaction. In G. Lindzey & E. Aronson (Eds.), *The handbook of social psychology* (Vol. 3). Reading, Mass.: Addison-Wesley.

Marsh, H. W., & Parker, J. W. (1984). Determinants of student self-concept: Is it better to be a relatively large fish in a small pond even if you don't learn to swim well? *Journal of Personality and Social Psychology, 47*(1), 213–231.

Martin, B. (1971). *Anxiety and neurotic disorders.* New York: Wiley.

Martin, R. A., & Lefcourt, H. M. (1983). Sense of humor as a moderator of the relation between stressors and moods. *Journal of Personality and Social Psychology, 45*(6), 1313–1324.

Martin, R. A., & Poland, E. Y. (1980). *Learning to change: A self management approach to adjustment.* New York: McGraw-Hill.

Martinson, F. M. (1980). Childhood sexuality. In B. B. Wolman & J. Money (Eds.), *Handbook of human sexuality.* Englewood Cliffs, N.J.: Prentice-Hall.

Maslach, C., & Jackson, S. E. (1981). The measurement of experienced burnout. *Journal of Occupational Behavior, 2,* 99–113.

Maslow, A. (1954). *Motivation and personality.* New York: Harper & Row.

Maslow, A. (1962). *Toward a psychology of being.* Princeton, N.J.: Van Nostrand.

Maslow, A. (1970). *Motivation and personality* (2nd ed.). New York: Harper & Row.

Mason, J. W. (1975). A historical view of the stress field, Part II. *Journal of Human Stress, 1,* 22–36.

Massarik, F. (1972). Standards for group leadership. In L. N. Solomon & B. Berzon (Eds.), *New perspectives on encounter groups.* San Francisco: Jossey-Bass.

Masters, W. H., & Johnson, V. E. (1966). *Human sexual response.* Boston: Little, Brown.

Masters, W. H., & Johnson, V. E. (1970). *Human sexual inadequacy*. Boston: Little, Brown.

Masters, W. H., & Johnson, V. E. (1976). *The pleasure bond*. New York: Bantam Books.

Masters, W. H., Johnson, V. E., & Kolodny, R. C. (1982). *Human sexuality*. Boston: Little, Brown.

Matarazzo, J. D. (1980). Behavioral health and behavioral medicine: Frontiers for a new health psychology. *American Psychologist, 35*, 807–817.

May, R. (1969). *Love and will*. New York: Dell.

Mayer, J. (1980). The bitter truth about sugar. In C. Borg (Ed.), *Annual editions: Readings in health*. Guilford, Conn.: Dushkin.

McCann, I. L., & Holmes, D. S. (1984). Influence of aerobic exercise on depression. *Journal of Personality and Social Psychology, 46*(5), 1142–1147.

McCarthy, B., Ryan, M., & Johnson, F. (1975). *Sexual awareness: A practical approach*. San Francisco: Boyd & Fraser.

McCary, J. L. (1971). *Sexual myths and fallacies*. New York: Schocken Books.

McCary, J. L. (1975). *Freedom and growth in marriage*. Santa Barbara, Calif.: Hamilton.

McCary, J. L., & McCary, S. P. (1982). *McCary's human sexuality* (4th ed.). Belmont, Calif.: Wadsworth.

McCoy, P. K., & Mewaldt, S. P. (1984, August). *A comparison of sleep in high- and low-frequency nappers*. Paper presented at the meeting of the American Psychological Association, Toronto, Ontario.

McCrae, R. R. (1984). Situational determinants of coping responses: Loss, threat and challenge. *Journal of Personality and Social Psychology, 46*(4), 919–928.

McCranie, E. W., & Bass, J. D. (1984). Childhood family antecedents of dependency and self-criticism: Implications for depression. *Journal of Abnormal Psychology, 93*(1), 3–8.

McDavid, J. W., & Harari, H. (1966). Stereotyping of names in popularity of grade school children. *Child Development, 37*, 453–459.

McGeoch, J. A. (1930). The influence of associative value upon the difficulty of nonsense-syllable lists. *Journal of Genetic Psychology, 37*, 421–426.

McGlashlin, T. H., Evans, F. J., & Orne, M. T. (1969). The nature of hypnotic analgesic and placebo response to experimental pain. *Psychosomatic Medicine, 31*, 227–246.

McGlone, J. (1980). Sex-differences in human brain asymmetry: A critical review. *Behavioral and Brain Sciences, 3*, 215–263.

McGowan, W. T., Haynes, S. N., & Wilson, C. W. (1981). Frontal electromyographic feedback: Stress attenuation and generalization. In D. Shapiro, J. Stoyva, J. Kamiya, T. X. Barber, N. E. Miller, & G. E. Schwartz (Eds.), *Biofeedback and behavioral medicine 1979/80: Therapeutic applications and experimental foundations*. Chicago: Aldine.

McGrath, J. E. (1977). Settings, measures, and themes: An integrative review of some research on social-psychological factors in stress. In A. Monat & R. S. Lazarus (Eds.), *Stress and coping: An anthology*. New York: Columbia University Press.

McGuire, W. (1969). The nature of attitudes and attitude change. In G. Lindzey & E. Aronson (Eds.), *The handbook of social psychology*. Cambridge, Mass.: Addison-Wesley.

McIntire, W. G., & Nass, G. D. (1974). Self-actualizing qualities of low and high happiness stable marriages. *Research in the Life Sciences* (University of Maine at Orono), *21*, 5.

McKay, M., Rogers, P. D., Blades, J., & Gosse, R. (1984). *The divorce book*. Oakland, Calif.: New Harbinger Publications.

McKinley, J. (1978, September). Pusher in the gray-flannel suit. *Playboy*, pp. 165–166, 178, 180, 228, 230.

Mead, M. (1950). *Sex and temperament in three primitive societies*. New York: Mentor Books.

Mechanic, D. (1972). Social psychologic factors affecting the presentation of bodily complaints. *New England Journal of Medicine, 286*, 1132–1139.

Meeker, W. R., & Barber, T. X. (1971). Toward an explanation of stage hypnosis. *Journal of Abnormal Psychology, 77*, 61–70.

Mehrabian, A. (1969). Significance of posture and position in the communication of attitude and status relationships. *Psychological Bulletin, 71*, 359–372.

Mehrabian, A. (1971). *Silent messages*. Belmont, Calif.: Wadsworth.

Mehrabian, A. (1972). *Nonverbal communication*. Chicago: Aldine/Atherton.

Mehrabian, A. (1976). *Public spaces and private places*. New York: Basic Books.

Mehrabian, A., & Ferris, J. (1967). Inference of attitudes from nonverbal communication in two channels. *Journal of Consulting and Clinical Psychology, 31*, 248–252.

Meichenbaum, D. H. (Ed.). (1977). *Cognitive behavior modification: An integrative approach*. New York: Plenum.

Meichenbaum, D. H., & Turk, D. (1982). Stress, coping and disease: A cognitive-behavioral perspective. In R. W. J. Neufeld (Ed.), *Psychological stress and psychopathology*. New York: McGraw-Hill.

Mello, N. K., & Mendelson, J. H. (1978). Alcohol and human behavior. In L. L. Iversen, S. D. Iversen, & S. H. Snyder (Eds.), *Handbook of psychopharmacology* (Vol. 12). New York: Plenum.

Melman, A., & Leiter, E. (1983). The urologic evaluation of impotence (male excitement phase disorder). In H. S. Kaplan (Ed.), *The evaluation of sexual disorders: Psychological and medical aspects*. New York: Brunner/Mazel.

Meltzer, H., & Stahl, S. (1976). The dopamine hypothesis of schizophrenia: A review. *Schizophrenia Bulletin, 1976, 21*, 19–26.

Mendelson, J. H., Rossi, A. M., & Meyer, R. E. (1974). *The use of marihuana: A psychological and physiological inquiry*. New York: Plenum.

Meyer, P. H. (1980). Between families: The unattached young adult. In E. A. Carter & M. McGoldrick (Eds.), *The family life cycle: A framework for family therapy*. New York: Gardner Press.

Meyer, R. E. (1975). Psychiatric consequences of marihuana use: The state of the evidence. In J. R. Tinklenberg (Ed.), *Marijuana and health hazards: Methodologic issues in current research*. New York: Academic Press.

Meyer, R. G. (1980). The antisocial personality. In R. H. Woody (Ed.), *Encyclopedia of clinical assessment* (Vol. 1). San Francisco: Jossey-Bass.

Michelozzi, B. N. (1980). *Coming alive from nine to five: The career search handbook*. Palo Alto, Calif.: Mayfield.

Miklich, D. R., Rewey, H. H., Weiss, J. H., & Kolton, S. (1973). A preliminary investigation of psychophysiological responses to stress among different subgroups of asthmatic children. *Journal of Psychosomatic Research, 17*, 1–8.

Milam, J. R., & Ketcham, K. (1981). *Under the influence: A guide to the myths and realities of alcoholism*. New York: Bantam.

Miller, D. C., & Form, W. H. (1951). *Industrial sociology*. New York: Harper & Row.

Miller, G. A., & Selfridge, J. A. (1950). Verbal context and the recall of meaningful material. *American Journal of Psychology, 63*, 176–185.

Miller, G. P. (1978). *Life choices: How to make the critical decisions—about your education, career, marriage, family, life style*. New York: Thomas Y. Crowell.

Miller, L. C., Berg, J. H., & Archer, R. L. (1983). Openers: Individuals who elicit intimate self-disclosure. *Journal of Personality and Social Psychology, 44*(6), 1234–1244.

Miller, N. E. (1959). Liberalization of basic S-R concepts: Extension to conflict behavior, motivation, and social learning. In S. Koch (Ed.), *Psychology: A study of a science* (Vol. 2). New York: McGraw-Hill.

Miller, N. E. (1985). Rx: Biofeedback. *Psychology Today, 19*(2), 54–59.

Millett, K. (1970). *Sexual politics.* Garden City, N.Y.: Doubleday.

Millman, J., & Pauk, W. (1969). *How to take tests.* New York: McGraw-Hill.

Millon, T. (1981). *Disorders of personality DSM-III: Axis II.* New York: Wiley.

Mirkin, G., & Hoffman, M. (1978). *The sports medicine book.* Boston: Little, Brown.

Mischel, W. (1969). Continuity and change in personality. *American Psychologist, 24,* 1012–1018.

Mischel, W. (1970). Sex-typing and socialization. In P. H. Mussen (Ed.), *Carmichael's manual of child psychology* (Vol. 2). New York: Wiley.

Mischel, W. (1973). Toward a cognitive social learning conceptualization of personality. *Psychological Review, 80,* 252–283.

Mittleman, R. E., & Wetli, C. V. (1984). Death caused by recreational cocaine use. *Journal of the American Medical Association, 252*(14), 1889–1893.

Modan, B. (1977). Role of diet in cancer etiology. *Cancer, 40,* 1887–1891.

Money, J. (1980). *Love and love-sickness.* Baltimore: Johns Hopkins Press.

Money, J., & Ehrhardt, A. A. (1972). *Man and woman, boy and girl: Differentiation and dimorphism of gender identity.* Baltimore: Johns Hopkins University Press.

Monge, R. H. (1973). Developmental trends in factors of adolescent self-concept. *Developmental Psychology, 8,* 382–393.

Monge, R. (1975). Structure of the self-concept from adolescence through old age. *Experimental Aging Research, 1*(2), 281–291.

Moos, R. H. (1968). Psychological aspects of oral contraceptives. *Archives of General Psychiatry, 30,* 853–867.

Moos, R. H., & Billings, A. G. (1982). Conceptualizing and measuring coping resources and processes. In L. Goldberger & S. Breznitz (Eds.), *Handbook of stress: Theoretical and clinical aspects.* New York: Free Press.

Moreno, J. L. (1946). *Psychodrama.* New York: Beacon.

Morgan, M. (1982). Television and adolescents' sex role stereotypes: A longitudinal study. *Journal of Personality and Social Psychology, 43,* 947–955.

Morse, S., & Gergen, K. J. (1970). Social comparison, self-consistency, and the concept of self. *Journal of Personality and Social Psychology, 16,* 148–156.

Mosher, C. R., Pollin, W., & Stabenau, J. R. (1971). Identical twins discordant for schizophrenia: Neurological findings. *Archives of General Psychiatry, 24,* 422–430.

Moss, H. A. (1967). Sex, age, and state as determinants of mother-infant interaction. *Merrill-Palmer Quarterly, 13,* 19–36.

Mowrer, O. H. (1947). On the dual nature of learning—reinterpretation of "conditioning" and "problem-solving." *Harvard Educational Review, 17,* 102–148.

Munroe, R. L., & Munroe, R. H. (1975). *Cross-cultural human development.* Monterey, Calif.: Brooks/Cole.

Murphy, G. E. (1984). The prediction of suicide: Why is it so difficult? *American Journal of Psychotherapy, 38*(3), 341–349.

Murray, H. A. (1938). *Explorations in personality.* Englewood Cliffs, N.J.: Prentice-Hall.

Murstein, B. I. (1971). Critique of models of dyadic attraction. In B. I. Murstein (Ed.), *Theories of attraction and love.* New York: Springer.

Murstein, B. I. (1972). Physical attractiveness and marital choice. *Journal of Personality and Social Psychology, 22,* 8–12.

Murstein, B. I. (1976). *Who will marry whom? Theories and research in marital choice.* New York: Springer.

Myers, D. G. (1980). *Inflated self: Human illusions and the Biblical call to hope.* New York: Seabury Press.

Nahas, G. G., Suciu-Foca, N., Armand, J. P., & Morishima, A. (1974). Inhibition of cellular mediated immunity in marihuana smokers. *Science, 183,* 419–420.

Nass, G. D. (1978). *Marriage and the family.* Reading, Mass.: Addison-Wesley.

Nass, G. D., Libby, R. W., & Fisher, M. P. (1981). *Sexual choices: An introduction to human sexuality.* Monterey, Calif.: Wadsworth Health Sciences.

Nathan, P. E., & Harris, S. L. (1975). *Psychopathology and society.* New York: McGraw-Hill.

National Institute on Alcohol Abuse and Alcoholism (1980). *Facts about alcohol and alcoholism.* Washington, D.C.: U.S. Government Printing Office.

Navran, L. (1967). Communication and adjustment in marriage. *Family Process, 6,* 173–184.

Nemiah, J. C. (1978). Psychoneurotic disorders. In A. M. Nicholi, Jr. (Ed.), *Harvard guide to modern psychiatry.* Cambridge, Mass.: Belknap Press.

Nepenthe. (1978). Opiate addicts average ten years of drug use before treatment. C.A.D.R.E. survey. Seattle: University of Washington Alcoholism Institute.

Neubeck, G. (1972). The myriad motives for sex. *Sexual Behavior, 2*(7), 51–56.

Neugarten, B. L. (1968). *Middle age and aging.* Chicago: University of Chicago Press.

Neugarten, B. L., & associates. (1964). *Personality in middle and late life: Empirical studies.* New York: Atherton Press.

Neugarten, B. L., & Hagestad, G. (1976). Age and the life course. In R. Binstock & E. Shanas (Eds.), *Handbook of aging and the social sciences.* New York: Van Nostrand Reinhold.

Newcomb, M. D. (1983). Relationship qualities of those who live together. *Alternative Lifestyles, 6*(2), 78–102.

Newman, M., & Berkowitz, B. (1976). *How to be awake and alive.* Westminster, Md.: Ballantine Books.

Nias, D. K. B. (1979). Marital choice: Matching or complementation. In M. Cook & G. Wilson (Eds.), *Love and attraction.* New York: Pergamon Press.

Nichols, J. R. (1965). How opiates change behavior. *Scientific American, 212,* 80–86.

Nickols, S. Y., & Metzen, E. J. (1982). Impact of wife's employment upon husband's housework. *Journal of Family Issues, 3*(2), 199–216.

Nielsen, J. M. (1978). *Sex in society: Perspectives on stratification.* Belmont, Calif.: Wadsworth.

Nierenberg, G. I., & Calero, H. H. (1971). *How to read a person like a book—and what to do about it.* New York: Hawthorn Books.

Nikelly, A. G. (1977). *Achieving competence and fulfillment.* Monterey, Calif.: Brooks/Cole.

Noguchi, T. T., & Nakamura, G. R. (1978). Phencyclidine-related deaths in Los Angeles County, 1976. *Journal of Forensic Science, 25*(3), 503–507.

Noller, P. (1980). Misunderstandings in marital communication: A study of couples' nonverbal communication. *Journal of Personality and Social Psychology, 39*(6), 1135–1148.

Nora, J. J., & Fraser, F. C. (1974). *Medical genetics: Principles and practice.* Philadelphia: Lea & Febiger.

Norton, A. J. (1983). Family life cycle: 1980. *Journal of Marriage and the Family, 45*(2), 267–275.

Novaco, R. W., Stokols, D., Campbell, J., & Stokols, J. (1979). Transportation, stress and community psychology. *American Journal of Community Psychology, 7*(4), 361–380.

Nowlis, D. P., & Kamiya, J. (1970). The control of electroencephalographic alpha rhythms through auditory feedback and the associated mental activity. *Psychophysiology, 6,* 476–484.

Nurnberger, J. I., & Zimmerman, J. (1970). Applied analysis of human behavior: An alternative to conventional motivational inferences and unconscious determination in therapeutic programming. *Behavior Therapy, 1,* 59–69.

O'Connell, V., & O'Connell, A. (1974). *Choice and change: An introduction to the psychology of growth.* Englewood Cliffs, N.J.: Prentice-Hall.

O'Leary, K. D. (1984). The image of behavior therapy: It is time to take a stand. *Behavior Therapy, 15,* 219–233.

O'Leary, V. E. (1977). *Toward understanding women.* Monterey, Calif.: Brooks/Cole.

Oltman, J., & Friedman, S. (1967). Parental deprivation in psychiatric conditions, III. *Diseases of the Nervous System, 28,* 289–303.

O'Malley, P. M., & Bachman, J. G. (1979). Self-esteem and education: Sex and cohort comparisons among high school seniors. *Journal of Personality and Social Psychology, 37,* 1153–1159.

O'Neill, N., & O'Neill, G. (1972). *Open marriage.* New York: Avon Books.

Orne, M. T. (1951). The mechanisms of hypnotic age regression: An experimental study. *Journal of Abnormal and Social Psychology, 46,* 213–225.

Orne, M. T. (1970). Hypnosis, motivation, and the ecological validity of the psychological experiment. In W. J. Arnold & M. M. Page (Eds.), *Nebraska Symposium on Motivation* (Vol. 18). Lincoln: University of Nebraska Press.

Orne, M. T., & Evans, F. J. (1965). Social control in psychological experiments: Antisocial behavior and hypnosis. *Journal of Personality and Social Psychology, 1,* 189–200.

Ornstein, R. E. (1972). *The psychology of consciousness.* San Francisco: W. H. Freeman.

Ornstein, R. E. (Ed.). (1973). *The nature of human consciousness.* San Francisco: W. H. Freeman.

Ornstein, R. E. (1976). Eastern psychologies: The container vs. the contents. *Psychology Today, 10*(4), 36–43.

Orth-Gomer, K., & Ahlbom, A. (1980). Impact of psychological stress on ischemic heart disease when controlling for conventional risk factors. *Journal of Human Stress, 6*(1), 7–15.

Orthner, D. K. (1975). Leisure activity patterns and marital satisfaction over the marital career. *Journal of Marriage and the Family, 37,* 91–102.

Osgood, C. E., & Luria, Z. (1957). Case report: A blind analysis of a case of multiple personality using the semantic differential. In C. H. Thigpen & H. M. Cleckley, *The three faces of Eve.* New York: McGraw-Hill.

Osmond, M. W., & Martin, P. Y. (1975). Sex and sexism: A comparison of male and female sex-role attitudes. *Journal of Marriage and the Family, 37,* 744–758.

Osti, R. M. A., Trombini, G., & Magnani, B. (1980). Stress and distress in essential hypertension. *Psychotherapy and Psychosomatics, 33,* 193–197.

Otis, L. S. (1974). The facts on transcendental meditation, Part III: If well-integrated but anxious, try TM. *Psychology Today, 7*(11), 45–46.

Packard, V. (1972). *A nation of strangers.* New York: McKay.

Page, J. D. (1975). *Psychopathology.* Chicago: Aldine.

Paige, K. E. (1973). Women learn to sing the menstrual blues. *Psychology Today, 7*(4), 41–46.

Palmblad, J. (1981). Stress and immunologic competence: Studies in man. In R. Ader (Ed.), *Psychoneuroimmunology.* New York: Academic Press.

Palmore, E. (1969). Predicting longevity: A follow-up controlling for age. *Gerontologist, 9,* 247–250.

Palmore, E. (1975). *The honorable elders.* Durham, N.C.: Duke University Press.

Park, C. C., & Shapiro, L. N. (1976). *You are not alone: Understanding and dealing with mental illness—a guide for patients, families, doctors and other professionals.* Boston: Little, Brown.

Parkes, C. M. (1972). *Bereavement: Studies of grief in adult life.* New York: International Universities Press.

Parlee, M. B. (1973). The premenstrual syndrome. *Psychological Bulletin, 80,* 454–465.

Parlee, M. B., & the editors of *Psychology Today.* (1979). The friendship bond: PT's survey report on friendship in America. *Psychology Today, 13*(4), 43–54, 113.

Parsons, T. (1979). Definitions of health and illness in light of the American values and social structure. In E. G. Jaco (Ed.),

Patients, physicians and illness: A sourcebook in behavioral science and health. New York: Free Press.

Passer, M. W., & Seese, M. (1983). Life stress and athletic injury: Examination of positive versus negative events and three moderator variables. *Journal of Human Stress, 9,* 11–16.

Pattie, F. A. (1941). The production of blisters by hypnotic suggestions: A review. *Journal of Abnormal and Social Psychology, 36,* 62–72.

Pauk, W. (1962). *How to study in college.* Boston: Houghton Mifflin.

Paul, G. L. (1966). *Insight versus desensitization in psychotherapy.* Stanford, Calif.: Stanford University Press.

Paul, G. L., & Lentz, R. J. (1977). *Psychosocial treatment of chronic mental patients: Milieu versus social-learning programs.* Cambridge, Mass.: Harvard University Press.

Paul, W., & Weinrich, J. D. (1982). Whom and what we study: Definition and scope of sexual orientation. In W. Paul, J. D. Weinrich, J. C. Gonsiorek & M. E. Hotvedt (Eds.), *Homosexuality: Social, psychological and biological issues.* Beverly Hills, Calif.: Sage.

Pauling, L. C. (1970). *Vitamin C and the common cold.* San Francisco: W. H. Freeman.

Pauling, L. C. (1980). Vitamin C therapy of advanced cancer. *New England Journal of Medicine* [Letters], *302,* 694.

Pavlov, I. P. (1906). The scientific investigation of the psychical faculties or processes in the higher animals. *Science, 24,* 613–619.

Paykel, E. S. (1973). Life events and acute depression. In J. P. Scott & E. C. Senay (Eds.), *Separation and depression.* Washington, D. C.: American Association for the Advancement of Science.

Paykel, E. S. (1974). Life stress and psychiatric disorder. In B. S. Dohrenwend & B. P. Dohrenwend (Eds.), *Stressful life events: Their nature and effects.* New York: Wiley.

Pedhazur, E. J., & Tetenbaum, T. J. (1979). Bem sex-role inventory: A theoretical and methodological critique. *Journal of Personality and Social Psychology, 37,* 996–1016.

Peplau, L. A. (1981). What homosexuals want in relationships. *Psychology Today, 15*(3), 28–38.

Peplau, L. A., & Perlman, D. (1979). Blueprint for a social psychological theory of loneliness. In M. Cook & G. Wilson (Eds.), *Love and attraction.* New York: Pergamon Press.

Perkins, D. V. (1982). The assessment of stress using life events scales. In L. Goldberger & S. Breznitz (Eds.), *Handbook of stress: Theoretical and clinical aspects.* New York: Free Press.

Perls, F. S. (1969). *Gestalt therapy verbatim.* Lafayette, Calif.: Real People Press.

Perry, D. G., & Bussey, K. (1979). The social learning theory of sex differences: Imitation is alive and well. *Journal of Personality and Social Psychology, 37,* 1699–1712.

Peters, R. K., Cady, L. D., Jr., Bischoff, D. P., Bernstein, L., & Pike, M. C. (1983). Physical fitness and subsequent myocardial infarction in healthy workers. *Journal of the American Medical Association, 249*(22), 3052–3056.

Pett, M. G. (1982). Correlates of children's social adjustment following divorce. *Journal of Divorce, 5*(4), 25–39.

Pettigrew, T. F. (1973). Racism and the mental health of white Americans: A social psychological view. In C. V. Willie, B. M. Kramer, & B. S. Brown (Eds.), *Racism and mental health.* Pittsburgh: University of Pittsburgh Press.

Pettigrew, T. F. (1979). The ultimate attribution error: Extending Allport's cognitive analysis of prejudice. *Personality and Social Psychology Bulletin, 5,* 461–476.

Pfeiffer, E., & Davis, G. L. (1972). Determinants of sexual behavior in middle and old age. *Journal of American Geriatric Society, 20,* 82–87.

Pfeiffer, E., Verwoerdt, A., & Wang, H. S. (1968). Sexual behavior in aged men and women. *Archives of General Psychiatry, 19,* 757–758.

Phelps, S., & Austin, N. (1975). *The assertive woman.* San Luis

Obispo, Calif.: Impact.

Pickens, R., Meisch, R. A., & Thompson, T. (1978). Drug self-administration: An analysis of the reinforcing effects of drugs. In L. L. Iversen, S. D. Iversen, & S. H. Snyder (Eds.), *Handbook of psychopharmacology* (Vol. 12). New York: Plenum.

Pines, A. M., Aronson, E., & Kafry, D. (1981). *Burnout: From tedium to personal growth.* New York: Free Press.

Pivar, W. H. (1978). *The whole earth textbook: A survival manual for students.* Philadelphia: Saunders.

Pleck, J. H., & Sawyer, J. (1974). *Men and masculinity.* Englewood Cliffs, N.J.: Prentice-Hall.

Plutchik, R., Williams, M. H., Jerrett, I., Karasu, T. B., & Kane, C. (1978). Emotions, personality and life stresses in asthma. *Journal of Psychosomatic Research, 22,* 425–431.

Pocs, O., & Godow, A. G. (1977). Can students view parents as sexual beings? *Family Coordinator, 26,* 31–36.

Pogue-Geile, M. F., & Oltmanns, T. F. (1980). Sentence perception and distractibility in schizophrenic, manic, and depressed patients. *Journal of Abnormal Psychology, 89,* 115–124.

Polonko, K. A., Scanzoni, J., & Teachman, J. D. (1982). Childlessness and marital satisfaction: A further assessment. *Journal of Family Issues, 3*(4), 545–573.

Pope, H. G., Jr., Ionescu-Pioggia, M., & Cole, J. O. (1981). Drug use and life-style among college undergraduates. *Archives of General Psychiatry, 38,* 588–591.

Pope, H., & Mueller, C. W. (1979). The inter-generational transmission of marital instability: Comparisons by race and sex. In G. Levinger & O. C. Moles (Eds.), *Divorce and separation.* New York: Basic Books.

Powell, J. (1969). *Why am I afraid to tell you who I am?* Niles, Ill.: Argus Communications.

Powell, L. H., Friedman, M., Thoresen, C. E., Gill, J. J., & Ulmer, D. K. (1984). Can the Type A behavior pattern be altered after myocardial infarction? A second year report from the recurrent coronary prevention project. *Psychosomatic Medicine, 46*(4), 293–313.

Prasad, J. S. (1980). Effect of vitamin E supplementation on leukocyte function. *American Journal of Clinical Nutrition, 33,* 606–608.

Price, R. H. (1972). *Abnormal behavior: Perspectives in conflict.* New York: Holt, Rinehart and Winston.

Purkey, W. W. (1970). *Self-concept and school achievement.* Englewood Cliffs, N.J.: Prentice-Hall.

Rabbitt, P. (1977). Changes in problem solving ability in old age. In J. E. Birren & K. W. Schaie (Eds.), *Handbook of the psychology of aging.* New York: Van Nostrand Reinhold.

Rabkin, J. G., & Streuning, E. L. (1976). Life events, stress and illness. *Science, 194,* 1013–1020.

Rahe, R. H. (1972). Subjects' recent life changes and their near-future illness reports: A review. *Annals of Clinical Research, 4,* 393–397.

Rahe, R. H. (1979). Life change events and mental illness: An overview. *Journal of Human Stress, 5,* 2–10.

Rahe, R. H., & Arthur, R. H. (1978). Life change and illness studies. *Journal of Human Stress, 4*(1), 3–15.

Rahe, R. H., & Holmes, T. H. (1965). Social, psychologic and psychophysiologic aspects of inguinal hernia. *Journal of Psychosomatic Research, 8,* 487–491.

Rahe, R. H., & Lind, E. (1971). Psychosocial factors and sudden cardiac death: A pilot study. *Journal of Psychosomatic Research, 15,* 19–24.

Raley, P. E. (1976). *Making love: How to be your own sex therapist.* New York: Dial Press.

Rank, O. (1945). *Will therapy; and truth and reality.* New York: Knopf.

Rapaport, D. (1967). On the psychoanalytic theory of thinking. In M. M. Gill (Ed.), *The collected papers of David Rapaport.* New York: Basic Books.

Raskin, R., Bali, L. R., & Peeke, H. V. (1981). Muscle biofeedback and transcendental meditation: A controlled evaluation of efficacy in the treatment of chronic anxiety. In D. Shapiro, J. Stoyva, J. Kamiya, T. X. Barber, N. E. Miller, & G. E. Schwartz (Eds.), *Biofeedback and behavioral medicine 1979/80: Therapeutic applications and experimental foundations.* Chicago: Aldine.

Raugh, M. R., & Atkinson, R. C. (1975). A mnemonic method for learning a second-language vocabulary. *Journal of Educational Psychology, 67,* 1–16.

Reedy, M. N. (1983). Personality and aging. In D. S. Woodruff & J. E. Birren (Eds.), *Aging: Scientific perspectives and social issues.* Monterey, Calif.: Brooks/Cole.

Reis, H. T., Wheeler, L., Spiegel, N., Kernis, M. H., Nezlek, J., & Perri, M. (1982). Physical attractiveness in social interaction: II. Why does appearance affect social experience? *Journal of Personality and Social Psychology, 43*(5), 979–996.

Reiss, I. L. (1960). *Premarital sexual standards in America.* New York: Free Press.

Reiss, I. L. (1976). *Family systems in America.* Hinsdale, Ill.: Dryden Press.

Reiss, S., Peterson, R. A., Eron, L. D., & Reiss, M. M. (1977). *Abnormality: Experimental and clinical approaches.* New York: Macmillan.

Renne, K. S. (1971). Health and marital experience in an urban population. *Journal of Marriage and the Family, 33,* 338–350.

Renne, K. S. (1973). Correlates of dissatisfaction in marriage. In M. E. Lasswell & T. E. Lasswell (Eds.), *Love, marriage, family.* Glenview, Ill.: Scott, Foresman.

Renwick, P. A., & Lawler, E. E. (1978). What you really want from your job. *Psychology Today, 11*(12), 53–65, 118.

Repetti, R. L. (1984). Determinants of children's sex-stereotyping: Parental sex-role traits and television viewing. *Personality and Social Psychology Bulletin, 10*(3), 457–468.

Richmond, J. B., & Lustman, S. L. (1955). Autonomic function in the neonate: I. Implications for psychosomatic theory. *Psychosomatic Medicine, 17,* 269–275.

Ridley, C. A. (1973). Exploring the impact of work satisfaction and involvement on marital interaction when both partners are employed. *Journal of Marriage and the Family, 1973, 35,* 229–237.

Riedel, S., & McKillip, J. (1979, May). *Friends, lovers, and physical attractiveness.* Paper presented at the meeting of the Midwestern Psychological Association, Chicago.

Riesman, D. (1950). *The lonely crowd.* New Haven, Conn.: Yale University Press.

Ringer, R. J. (1978). *Winning through intimidation.* New York: Fawcett.

Robbins, M. B., & Jensen, G. D. (1978). Multiple orgasm in males. *Journal of Sex Research, 14,* 21–26.

Robbins, S. L., & Cotran, R. S. (1979). *Pathologic basis of disease.* Philadelphia: Saunders.

Roberts, S. O. (1971). Some mental and emotional health needs of Negro children and youth. In R. Wilcox (Ed.), *The psychological consequences of being a black American.* New York: Wiley.

Robins, L. N. (1966). *Deviant children grown up.* Baltimore: Williams & Wilkins.

Robinson, F. P. (1970). *Effective study* (4th ed.). New York: Harper & Row.

Robinson, I. E., & Jedlicka, D. (1982). Change in sexual attitudes and behavior of college students from 1965 to 1980: A research note. *Journal of Marriage and the Family, 44*(1), 237–240.

Robson, E., & Edwards, G. (1980). *Getting help: A woman's guide to therapy.* New York: E. P. Dutton.

Rodin, J. (1981). Obesity: Why the losing battle? In B. B. Wolman (Ed.), *Psychological aspects of obesity: A handbook.* New York: Van Nostrand Reinhold.

Roe, A. (1956). *The psychology of occupations.* New York: Wiley.

Rogers, C. R. (1951). *Client-centered therapy: Its current practice, implications, and theory.* Boston: Houghton Mifflin.

Rogers, C. R. (1959). A theory of therapy, personality, and interpersonal relationships, as developed in the client-centered framework. In S. Koch (Ed.), *Psychology: A study of a science* (Vol. 3). New York: McGraw-Hill.

Rogers, C. R. (1961). *On becoming a person: A therapist's view of psychotherapy.* Boston: Houghton Mifflin.

Rogers, C. R. (1972). *Becoming partners: Marriage and its alternatives.* New York: Delacorte Press.

Rogers, C. R. (1977). *Carl Rogers on personal power.* New York: Delacorte Press.

Rogers, D. (1982). *The adult years: An introduction to aging.* Englewood Cliffs, N.J.: Prentice-Hall.

Rose, A., & Burks, B. (1968). Roundup of current research: Is the child really the father of the man? *Trans-action, 5,* 6.

Rosen, B. C. (1959). Race, ethnicity, and the achievement syndrome. *American Sociological Review, 24,* 47–60.

Rosen, R. D. (1977). *Psychobabble.* New York: Atheneum.

Rosenberg, M. (1965). *Society and the adolescent self-image.* Princeton, N.J.: Princeton University Press.

Rosenberg, M. (1979). *Conceiving the self.* New York: Basic Books.

Rosenfeld, L. B., Civikly, J. M., & Herron, J. R. (1979). Anatomical and psychological sex differences. In G. J. Chelune & associates, *Self-disclosure: Origins, patterns, and implications of openness in interpersonal relationships.* San Francisco: Jossey-Bass.

Rosenhan, D. (1973). On being sane in insane places. *Science, 179,* 250–258.

Rosenman, R. H., & Chesney, M. A. (1982). Stress, Type A behavior, and coronary disease. In L. Goldberger & S. Breznitz (Eds.), *Handbook of stress: Theoretical and clinical aspects.* New York: Free Press.

Rosenstock, I. M., & Kirscht, J. P. (1979). Why people seek health care. In G. C. Stone, F. Cohen, N. E. Adler, & associates, *Health psychology—a handbook.* San Francisco: Jossey-Bass.

Rosenthal, D. (1970). *Genetic theory and abnormal behavior.* New York: McGraw-Hill.

Ross, J. J. (1965). Neurological findings after prolonged sleep deprivation. *Archives of Neurology, 12,* 399–403.

Ross, L. (1977). The intuitive psychologist and his shortcomings: Distortions in the attribution process. In L. Berkowitz (Ed.), *Advances in experimental social psychology* (Vol. 10). New York: Academic Press.

Ross, L., Greene, D., & House, P. (1977). The "false consensus effect": An egocentric bias in social perception and attribution processes. *Journal of Experimental Social Psychology, 13,* 279–301.

Rotter, J. B. (1966). Generalized expectancies for internal vs. external reinforcement. *Psychological Monographs, 80*(1, Whole No. 609).

Rotter, J. B. (1972). Beliefs, social attitudes, and behavior: A social learning analysis. In J. B. Rotter, J. E. Chance, & E. J. Phares (Eds.), *Applications of a social learning theory of personality.* New York: Holt, Rinehart and Winston.

Rowley, G. L. (1974). Which examinees are most favoured by the use of multiple choice tests? *Journal of Educational Measurement, 11,* 15–23.

Rubenstein, C. M. (1982). Real men don't earn less than their wives. *Psychology Today, 16*(11), 36–41.

Rubenstein, C. M., & Shaver, P. (1979, September). *The experience of loneliness: A factor analytic exploration.* Paper presented at the meeting of the American Psychological Association, New York City.

Rubin, L. B. (1976). *Worlds of pain: Life in the working class family.* New York: Basic Books.

Rubin, L. B. (1979). *Women of a certain age: The midlife search for self.* New York: Harper & Row.

Rubin, Z. (1970). Measurement of romantic love. *Journal of Personality and Social Psychology, 16,* 265–273.

Rubin, Z. (1973). *Liking and loving: An invitation to social psychology.* New York: Holt, Rinehart and Winston.

Rubin, Z., Peplau, L. A., & Hill, C. T. (1981). Loving and leaving: Sex differences in romantic attachments. *Sex Roles, 7*(8), 821–835.

Rudestam, K. E. (1980). *Methods of self-change: An ABC primer.* Monterey, Calif.: Brooks/Cole.

Rule, B. G., & Percival, E. (1971). The effects of frustration and attack on physical aggression. *Journal of Experimental Research in Personality, 5,* 111–118.

Rytina, N. F. (1981). Occupational segregation and earnings differences by sex. *Monthly Labor Review, 104,* 49–53.

Sackett, D. L., & Snow, J. C. (1979). The magnitude of compliance and noncompliance. In R. B. Haynes, D. W. Taylor, & D. L. Sackett (Eds.), *Compliance and health care.* Baltimore: Johns Hopkins University Press.

Safilios-Rothschild, C. (1977). *Love, sex, and sex roles.* Englewood Cliffs, N.J.: Spectrum Books.

Salovey, P., & Rodin, J. (1984, August). *The structure of jealousy-provoking situations.* Paper presented at the meeting of the American Psychological Association, Toronto, Ontario.

Salzman, C. (1978). Electroconvulsive therapy. In A. M. Nicholi, Jr. (Ed.), *The Harvard guide to modern psychiatry.* Cambridge, Mass.: Harvard University Press.

Sandler, J. (1975). Aversion methods. In F. H. Kanfer & A. P. Goldstein (Eds.), *Helping people change: A textbook of methods.* New York: Pergamon Press.

Sarason, I. G. (1960). Empirical findings and theoretical problems in the use of anxiety scales. *Psychological Bulletin, 57,* 403–415.

Sarason, I. G. (1984). Stress, anxiety and cognitive interference: Reactions to tests. *Journal of Personality and Social Psychology, 46*(4), 929–938.

Sarason, I. G., Johnson, J. H., & Siegel, J. M. (1978). Assessing the impact of life changes: Development of the Life Experiences Survey. *Journal of Consulting and Clinical Psychology, 46,* 932–946.

Sarason, I. G., Levine, H. M., & Sarason, B. R. (1982). Assessing the impact of life changes. In T. Millon, C. Green, & R. Meagher (Eds.), *Handbook of clinical health psychology.* New York: Plenum.

Sarbin, T. R., & Lim, D. T. (1963). Some evidence in support of the role-taking hypothesis in hypnosis. *International Journal of Clinical Hypnosis, 11,* 98–103.

Sarnacki, R. E. (1979). An examination of test-wiseness in the cognitive test domain. *Review of Educational Research, 49,* 252–279.

Satchidananda, Y. S. S. (1970). *Integral Yoga—Hatha.* New York: Holt, Rinehart and Winston.

Saunders, C. (1969). The moment of truth: Care of the dying person. In E. Pearson (Ed.), *Death and dying: Current issues in the treatment of the dying person.* Cleveland, Ohio: Case Western Reserve University Press.

Scannell, D. P. (1960). Prediction of college success from elementary and secondary school performance. *Journal of Educational Psychology, 51,* 130–134.

Scanzoni, J. H. (1970). *Opportunity and the family.* New York: Free Press.

Scanzoni, J. H. (1972). *Sexual bargaining.* Englewood Cliffs, N.J.: Prentice-Hall.

Scarf, M. (1979). The more sorrowful sex. *Psychology Today, 12*(11), 45–52, 89–90.

Schachter, S. (1959). *The psychology of affiliation.* Stanford, Calif.: Stanford University Press.

Schachter, S. (1964). The interaction of cognitive and physiological determinants of emotional state. In L. Berkowitz (Ed.), *Advances in experimental social psychology* (Vol. 1). New York: Academic Press.

Schachter, S. (1971). *Emotion, obesity, and crime.* New York: Academic Press.

Schaie, K. W. (1983). Age changes in adult intelligence. In D. S. Woodruff & J. E. Birren (Eds.), *Aging: Scientific perspectives and social issues.* Monterey, Calif.: Brooks/Cole.

Schaie, K. W., & Geiwitz, J. (1982). *Adult development and aging*. Boston: Little, Brown.

Scheflen, A. E. (1965). *Stream and structure of communicational behavior*. Philadelphia: Eastern Pennsylvania Psychiatric Institute.

Scheflen, A. E., & Scheflen, A. (1972). *Body language and social order: Communication as behavioral control*. Englewood Cliffs, N.J.: Prentice-Hall.

Scheidlinger, S. (1984). Group psychotherapy in the 1980s: Problems and prospects. *American Journal of Psychotherapy, 38*(4), 494–504.

Schein, E. H. (1978). *Career dynamics: Matching individual and organizational needs*. Reading, Mass.: Addison-Wesley.

Schildkraut, J. J. (1965). The catecholamine hypothesis of affective disorders: A review of supporting evidence. *American Journal of Psychiatry, 122*, 509–522.

Schmidt, N., & Sermat, V. (1983). Measuring loneliness in different relationships. *Journal of Personality and Social Psychology, 44*(5), 1038–1047.

Schneider, D. (1973). Implicit personality theory: A review. *Psychological Bulletin, 79*, 294–309.

Schofield, W. (1964). *Psychotherapy: The purchase of friendship*. Englewood Cliffs, N.J.: Prentice-Hall.

Schreiber, F. R. (1973). *Sybil*. Chicago: Henry Regnery.

Schroeder, D. H., & Costa, P. T., Jr. (1984). Influence of life event stress on physical illness: Substantive effects or methodological flaws? *Journal of Personality and Social Psychology, 46*(4), 853–863.

Schultz, N. R., Jr., & Moore, D. (1984). Loneliness: Correlates, attributions, and coping among older adults. *Personality and Social Psychology Bulletin, 10*(1), 67–77.

Schulz, D. A., & Rodgers, S. F. (1980). *Marriage, the family and personal fulfillment*. Englewood Cliffs, N.J.: Prentice-Hall.

Schuster, C. R. (1975). Drugs as reinforcers in monkey and man. *Pharmacology Review, 27*, 511.

Schwartz, G. E. (1974). The facts on transcendental meditation, Part II: TM relaxes some people and makes them feel better. *Psychology Today, 7*(11), 39–44.

Scovern, A., & Kilmann, P. (1980). Status of electroconvulsive therapy: Review of the outcome literature. *Psychological Bulletin, 87*, 260–303.

Sears, R. R., Hovland, C. I., & Miller, N. E. (1940). Minor studies of aggression: I. Measurement of aggressive behavior. *Journal of Psychology, 9*, 275–294.

Seashore, S. E., & Barnowe, J. T. (1972). Collar color doesn't count. *Psychology Today, 6*(3), 53–54, 80–82.

Seeman, M. (1971). The urban alienations: Some dubious theses from Marx to Marcuse. *Journal of Personality and Social Psychology, 19*, 135–143.

Seligman, M. E. P. (1971). Phobias and preparedness. *Behavior Therapy, 2*, 307–321.

Seligman, M. E. P. (1974). Depression and learned helplessness. In R. J. Friedman & M. M. Katz (Eds.), *The psychology of depression. Contemporary theory and research*. New York: Wiley.

Seligman, M. E. P. (1983). Learned helplessness. In E. Levitt, B. Lubin, & J. Brooks (Eds.), *Depression: Concepts, controversies, and some new facts*. Hillsdale, N.J.: Erlbaum.

Selye, H. (1936). A syndrome produced by diverse nocuous agents. *Nature, 138*, 32.

Selye, H. (1956). *The stress of life*. New York: McGraw-Hill.

Selye, H. (1974). *Stress without distress*. New York: Lippincott.

Selye, H. (1975). Confusion and controversy in the stress field. *Journal of Human Stress, 1*, 37–44.

Selye, H. (1976). *The stress of life* (2nd ed.). New York: McGraw-Hill.

Sevely, J. L., & Bennett, J. W. (1978). Concerning female ejaculation and the female prostate. *Journal of Sex Research, 14*, 1–20.

Shakow, D. (1962). Segmental set. *Archives of General Psychiatry, 6*, 1–17.

Shank, J. C. (1983). Disease incidence and prevalence. In R. B. Taylor (Ed.), *Family medicine: Principles and practice*. New York: Springer-Verlag.

Shapiro, D. H., Jr. (1981). Meditation and psychotherapeutic effects: Self-regulation strategy and altered state of consciousness. In D. Shapiro, J. Stoyva, J. Kamiya, T. X. Barber, N. E. Miller, & G. E. Schwartz (Eds.), *Biofeedback and behavioral medicine 1979/80: Therapeutic applications and experimental foundations*. Chicago: Aldine.

Shapiro, D. H., Jr., Mainardi, J. A., & Surwit, R. S. (1977). Biofeedback and self-regulation in essential hypertension. In G. E. Schwartz & J. Beatty (Eds.), *Biofeedback: Theory and research*. New York: Academic Press.

Shapiro, D. H., Jr., Schwartz, G. E., & Tursky, B. (1972). Control of diastolic blood pressure in man by feedback and reinforcement. *Psychophysiology, 9*, 296–304.

Sharma, B. P. (1975). Cannabis and its users in Nepal. *British Journal of Psychiatry, 127*, 550–552.

Shatan, C. F. (1978). Stress disorders among Viet Nam veterans: The emotional content of combat continues. In C. R. Figley (Ed.), *Stress disorders among Viet Nam veterans: Theory, research and treatment*. New York: Brunner/Mazel.

Shaver, P., & Freedman, J. (1976). Your pursuit of happiness. *Psychology Today, 10*(3), 26–29, 31–32, 75.

Shaver, P., & Rubenstein, C. M. (1979, September). *Living alone, loneliness, and health*. Paper presented at the meeting of the American Psychological Association, New York City.

Shaw, M. E., & Costanzo, P. R. (1970). *Theories in social psychology*. New York: McGraw-Hill.

Sheldon, W. J. (with the collaboration of S. S. Stevens). (1942). *The varieties of temperament: A psychology of constitutional differences*. New York: Harper.

Sherman, J. A. (1967). Problem of sex differences in space perception and aspects of intellectual functioning. *Psychological Review, 74*, 290–299.

Sherman, J. A. (1971). *On the psychology of women: A survey of empirical studies*. Springfield, Ill.: Charles C Thomas.

Sherman, J. A. (1978). *Sex-related cognitive differences*. Springfield, Ill.: Charles C Thomas.

Sherrod, D. R. (1971). Selective perception of political candidates. *Public Opinion Quarterly, 35*, 554–562.

Shertzer, B. (1977). *Career planning: Freedom to choose*. Boston: Houghton Mifflin.

Shick, J. F. E., & Smith, D. E. (1970). Analysis of the LSD flashback. *Journal of Psychedelic Drugs, 3*, 82–90.

Shields, S. A. (1975). Functionalism, Darwinism, and the psychology of women: A study in social myth. *American Psychologist, 30*, 739–754.

Shneidman, E. S. (1973). *Deaths of man*. New York: Quadrangle.

Shneidman, E. S., Farberow, N. L., & Litman, R. E. (Eds.). (1970). *The psychology of suicide*. New York: Science House.

Shoemaker, M. E., & Satterfield, D. O. (1977). Assertion training: An identity crisis that's coming on strong. In R. E. Alberti (Ed.), *Assertiveness: Innovations, applications, issues*. San Luis Obispo, Calif.: Impact.

Shuter, R. (1979). *Understanding misunderstandings: Exploring interpersonal communication*. New York: Harper & Row.

Siegel, J. M., Johnson, J. H., & Sarason, I. G. (1979). Life changes and menstrual discomfort. *Journal of Human Stress, 5*, 41–46.

Siegler, I. C., Nowlin, J. B., & Blumenthal, J. A. (1980). Health and behavior: Methodological considerations for adult development and aging. In L. W. Poon (Ed.), *Aging in the 1980s: Psychological issues*. Washington, D.C.: American Psychological Association.

Sigall, H., & Landy, D. (1973). Radiating beauty: The effects of having a physically attractive partner on person perception. *Journal of Personality and Social Psychology, 28*, 218–224.

Singer, J. L., & Singer, D. G. (1981). *Television, imagination and aggression: A study of preschoolers*. Hillsdale, N.J.: Erlbaum.

Siscovick, D. S., Weiss, N. S., Fletcher, R. H., & Lasky, T. (1984). The incidence of primary cardiac arrest during vigorous exercise. *New England Journal of Medicine, 311*(14), 874–877.

Skinner, B. F. (1938). *The behavior of organisms.* New York: Appleton-Century-Crofts.

Skinner, B. F. (1971). *Beyond freedom and dignity.* New York: Knopf.

Sklar, L. S., & Anisman, H. (1981). Contributions of stress and coping to cancer development and growth. In K. Bammer & B. H. Newberry (Eds.), *Stress and cancer.* Toronto: C. J. Hogrefe.

Skolnick, A. S. (1983). *The intimate environment: Exploring marriage and the family.* Boston: Little, Brown.

Slater, E. J., & Haber, J. D. (1984). Adolescent adjustment following divorce as a function of familial conflict. *Journal of Consulting and Clinical Psychology, 52*(5), 920–921.

Sloan, W. W., Jr., & Solano, C. H. (1984). The conversational style of lonely males with strangers and roommates. *Personality and Social Psychology Bulletin, 10*(2), 293–301.

Slobin, D. I., Miller, S. H., & Porter, L. W. (1968). Forms of address and social relations in a business organization. *Journal of Personality and Social Psychology, 8,* 289–293.

Slochower, J. (1976). Emotional labelling of overeating in obese and normal weight individuals. *Psychosomatic Medicine, 38,* 131–139.

Smart, R. G., & Fejer, D. (1972). Relationships between parental and adolescent drug use. In W. Keup (Ed.), *Drug abuse: Current concepts and research.* Springfield, Ill.: Charles C Thomas.

Smith, K. C., & Kleinman, A. (1983). Beyond the biomedical model: Integration of psychosocial and cultural orientations. In R. B. Taylor (Ed.), *Family medicine: Principles and practice.* New York: Springer-Verlag.

Snyder, M. (1979). Self-monitoring processes. In L. Berkowitz (Ed.), *Advances in experimental social psychology* (Vol. 12). New York: Academic Press.

Snyder, M. (1981). Impression management: The self in social interaction. In L. S. Wrightsman & K. Deaux (Eds.), *Social psychology in the 80s.* Monterey, Calif.: Brooks/Cole.

Snyder, M., & Gangestad, S. (1982). Choosing social situations: Two investigations of self-monitoring processes. *Journal of Personality and Social Psychology, 43*(1), 123–135.

Snyder, S. H. (1979). Amphetamine psychosis: A "model schizophrenia" mediated by catecholamines. In D. E. Smith (Ed.), *Amphetamine use, misuse, and abuse.* Boston: G. K. Hall.

Solano, C. H., Batten, P. G., & Parish, E. A. (1982). Loneliness and patterns of self-disclosure. *Journal of Personality and Social Psychology, 43*(3), 524–531.

Solnick, R., & Corby, N. (1983). Human sexuality and aging. In D. S. Woodruff & J. E. Birren (Eds.), *Aging: Scientific perspectives and social issues.* Monterey, Calif.: Brooks/Cole.

Solomon, G. E., & Amkraut, A. A. (1981). Psychoneuroendocrinological effects of the immune response. *Annual Review of Microbiology, 35,* 155–184.

Solomon, G. E., Amkraut, A. A., & Kasper, P. (1974). Immunity, emotions and stress. *Psychotherapy and Psychosomatics, 23,* 209–217.

Sommer, R. (1967). Small group ecology. *Psychological Bulletin, 67,* 145–152.

Sommer, R. (1969). *Personal space.* Englewood Cliffs, N.J.: Prentice-Hall.

Spanier, G. B. (1977). Sources of sex information and premarital sexual behavior. *Journal of Sex Research, 13*(2), 73–88.

Spanier, G. B., & Furstenberg, F. F., Jr. (1982). Remarriage after divorce: A longitudinal analysis of well-being. *Journal of Marriage and the Family, 44*(3), 709–720.

Spence, J., & Helmreich, R. (1978). *Masculinity and femininity.* Austin: University of Texas Press.

Spitzer, R., & Wilson, P. (1980). Nosology and the official psychiatric nomenclature. In A. Freedman, H. Kaplan, & B. Sadock (Eds.), *Comprehensive textbook of psychiatry II* (3rd ed.). Baltimore: Williams & Wilkins.

Srole, L., Langner, T. S., Michael, S. T., Opler, M. K., & Rennie,
T. A. C. (1962). *Mental health in the metropolis: The Midtown Manhattan Study* (Vol. 1). New York: McGraw-Hill.

Stare, F. J. (Ed.). (1974). *Obesity: Data and directions for the 70s.* New York: Medcom.

Starr, J. R., & Carns, D. E. (1973). Singles in the city. In H. Z. Lopata (Ed.), *Marriage and families.* New York: D. Van Nostrand.

Steger, J., & Fordyce, W. (1982). Behavioral health care in the management of chronic pain. In T. Millon, C. Green, & R. Meagher (Eds.), *Handbook of clinical health psychology.* New York: Plenum.

Stein, P. J. (1975). Singlehood: An alternative to marriage. *Family Coordinator, 24,* 489–503.

Stein, P. J. (1976). *Single.* Englewood Cliffs, N.J.: Prentice-Hall.

Stein, P. J. (1983). Singlehood. In E. D. Macklin & R. H. Rubin (Eds.), *Contemporary families and alternative lifestyles.* Beverly Hills, Calif.: Sage.

Stekel, W. (1950). *Techniques of analytical psychotherapy.* New York: Liveright.

Stephens, W. N. (1963). *The family in cross-cultural perspective.* New York: Holt, Rinehart and Winston.

Sterman, M. B. (1977). Clinical implications of EEG biofeedback training: A critical appraisal. In G. E. Schwartz & J. Beatty (Eds.), *Biofeedback: Theory and research.* New York: Academic Press.

Stern, G. S., McCants, T. R., & Pettine, P. W. (1982). Stress and illness: Controllable and uncontrollable life events' relative contributions. *Personality and Social Psychology Bulletin, 8*(1), 140–145.

Sternberg, R. J., & Grajek, S. (1984). The nature of love. *Journal of Personality and Social Psychology, 47*(2), 312–329.

Sternberg, R. J., & Soriano, L. J. (1984). Styles of conflict resolution. *Journal of Personality and Social Psychology, 47*(1), 115–126.

Stevens, J. H., Turner, C. W., Rhodewalt, F., & Talbot, S. (1984). The Type A behavior pattern and carotid artery atherosclerosis. *Psychosomatic Medicine, 46*(2), 105–113.

Stevens-Long, J. (1984). *Adult life: Developmental processes.* Palo Alto, Calif.: Mayfield.

Stone, A. A., & Neale, J. M. (1984). New measures of daily coping: Development and preliminary results. *Journal of Personality and Social Psychology, 46*(4), 892–906.

Stoner, C., & Parke, J. (1977). *All Gods children: The cult experience—salvation or slavery?* Radnor, Pa.: Chilton.

Streib, G. F., & Schneider, C. J. (1971). *Retirement in American society: Impact and process.* Ithaca, N.Y.: Cornell University Press.

Strickberger, M. W. (1976). *Genetics.* New York: Macmillan.

Strupp, H. H., Hadley, S. W., & Gomes-Schwartz, B. (1977). *Psychotherapy for better or worse: The problem of negative effects.* New York: Jason Aronson.

Stuart, J. C., & Brown, B. M. (1981). The relationship of stress and coping ability to incidence of diseases and accidents. *Journal of Psychosomatic Research, 25*(4), 255–260.

Stuart, R. B., & Davis, B. (1972). *Slim chance in a fat world: Behavioral control of obesity.* Champaign, Ill.: Research Press.

Sue, D. (1979). Erotic fantasies of college students during coitus. *Journal of Sex Research, 15,* 299–305.

Suedfeld, P. (1979). Stressful levels of environmental stimulation. In I. G. Sarason & C. D. Spielberger (Eds.), *Stress and anxiety* (Vol. 6). Washington, D.C.: Hemisphere.

Suid, R., Bradley, B., Suid, M., & Eastman, J. (1976). *Married, etc.* Reading, Mass.: Addison-Wesley.

Sullivan, H. S. (1953). *The interpersonal theory of psychiatry.* New York: Norton.

Super, D. E. (1953). A theory of vocational development. *American Psychologist, 8,* 185–190.

Super, D. E. (1957). *The psychology of careers.* New York: Harper & Row.

Super, D. E. (1972). Vocational development theory: Persons, positions and process. In J. M. Whitely & A. Resnikoff (Eds.),

Perspectives on vocational development. Washington, D.C.: American Personnel and Guidance Association.

Svensson, J., & Theorell, T. (1983). Life events and elevated blood pressure in young men. *Journal of Psychosomatic Research, 27*(6), 445–456.

Swensen, C. H., Jr. (1973). *Introduction to interpersonal relations.* Glenview, Ill.: Scott, Foresman.

Szasz, T. S. (1960). The myth of mental illness. *American Psychologist, 15,* 113–118.

Szasz, T. S. (1961). *The myth of mental illness.* New York: Harper & Row.

Taub, E. (1977). Self-regulation of human tissue temperature. In G. E. Schwartz & J. Beatty (Eds.), *Biofeedback: Theory and research.* New York: Academic Press.

Taub, J. M., & Burger, R. J. (1969). Extended sleep and performance: The Rip Van Winkle effect. *Psychonomic Science, 16,* 204–205.

Tavris, C., & Offir, C. (1977). *The longest war: Sex differences in perspective.* New York: Harcourt Brace Jovanovich.

Tavris, C., & Sadd, S. (1977). *The Redbook report on female sexuality.* New York: Delacorte Press.

Taylor, D. A., Altman, I., & Sorrentino, B. (1969). Interpersonal exchange as a function of rewards and costs and situational factors: Expectancy confirmation-disconfirmation. *Journal of Experimental Social Psychology, 5,* 324–339.

Templer, D. I., Ruff, C. F., & Armstrong, G. (1973). Cognitive functioning and degree of psychosis in schizophrenics given many electroconvulsive treatments. *British Journal of Psychiatry, 123,* 441–443.

Templer, D. I., Ruff, C., & Franks, C. (1971). Death anxiety: Age, sex, and parental resemblance in diverse populations. *Developmental Psychology, 4*(1), 108.

Terborg, J. R., & Ilgen, D. R. (1975). A theoretical approach to sex discrimination in traditionally male occupations. *Organizational Behavior and Human Performance, 13,* 352–376.

Tharp, R. G. (1970). Psychological patterning in marriage. In A. L. Grey (Ed.), *Man, woman, and marriage.* New York: Atherton Press.

Theorell, T. (1974). Life events before and after the onset of a premature myocardial infarction. In B. S. Dohrenwend & B. P. Dohrenwend (Eds.), *Stressful life events: Their nature and effects.* New York: Wiley.

Thomas, A., & Chess, S. (1977). *Temperament and development.* New York: Brunner/Mazel.

Thomas, K. (1976). Conflict and conflict management. In M. D. Dunnette (Ed.), *Handbook of industrial and organizational psychology.* Chicago: Rand McNally.

Thompson, A. P. (1983). Extramarital sex: A review of the research literature. *Journal of Sex Research, 19*(1), 1–22.

Thompson, L., & Spanier, G. B. (1983). The end of marriage and acceptance of marital termination. *Journal of Marriage and the Family, 45*(1), 103–113.

Thornton, B. (1984). Defensive attribution of responsibility: Evidence for an arousal-based motivational bias. *Journal of Personality and Social Psychology, 46*(4), 721–734.

Toffler, A. (1970). *Future shock.* New York: Random House.

Tomkins, S. S. (1966). Psychological model for smoking behavior. *American Journal of Public Health, 56,* 17–20.

Torrance, E. P. (1965). *Constructive behavior: Stress, personality, and mental health.* Belmont, Calif.: Wadsworth.

Totman, R., Kiff, J., Reed, S. E., & Craig, J. W. (1980). Predicting experimental colds in volunteers from different measures of recent life stress. *Journal of Psychosomatic Research, 24,* 155–163.

Treas, J. (1983). Aging and the family. In D. S. Woodruff & J. E. Birren (Eds.), *Aging: Scientific perspectives and social issues.* Monterey, Calif.: Brooks/Cole.

Triandis, M. C., & Vassiliou, V. (1967). Frequency of contact and stereotyping. *Journal of Personality and Social Psychology, 7,* 316–328.

Trimble, J. E. (1974, September). *Say goodbye to the Hollywood Indian: Results of a nationwide survey of the self-image of the American Indian.* Paper presented at the meeting of the American Psychological Association, New Orleans.

Troll, L. E. (1982). *Continuations: Adult development and aging.* Monterey, Calif.: Brooks/Cole.

Tucker, I. F. (1970). *Adjustment: Models and mechanisms.* New York: Academic Press.

Turner, B. (1981). Sex-related differences in aging. In B. B. Wolman & G. Stricker (Eds.), *Handbook of developmental psychology.* Englewood Cliffs, N.J.: Prentice-Hall.

Turner, S. M., Calhoun, K. S., & Adams, H. E. (Eds.). (1981). *Handbook of clinical behavior therapy.* New York: Wiley.

Twerski, A. J. (1978). *Like yourself—and others will too.* Englewood Cliffs, N.J.: Prentice-Hall.

Ullmann, L. P., & Krasner, L. (1975). *A psychological approach to abnormal behavior.* Englewood Cliffs, N.J.: Prentice-Hall.

Underwood, B. J. (1961). Ten years of massed practice on distributed practice. *Psychological Review, 68,* 229–247.

Vaillant, G. E. (1977). *Adaptation to life.* Boston: Little, Brown.

Valins, S. (1966). Cognitive effects of false heart-rate feedback. *Journal of Personality and Social Psychology, 4,* 400–408.

Vance, E. B., & Wagner, N. N. (1976). Written descriptions of orgasm: A study of sex differences. *Archives of Sexual Behavior, 5,* 87–98.

Vanek, J. (1974). Time spent in housework. *Scientific American, 231,* 116–120.

VanGorp, G., Stempfle, J., & Olson, D. (1969). Dating, attitudes, expectations, and physical attractiveness. Unpublished paper, University of Michigan. Cited in H. Harari & R. M. Kaplan, *Psychology: Personal and social adjustment.* New York: Harper & Row, 1977.

Vaughan, E. (1977). Misconceptions about psychology among introductory psychology students. *Teaching of Psychology, 4,* 138–141.

Verbrugge, L. M. (1979). Marital status and health. *Journal of Marriage and the Family, 41,* 267–285.

Verderber, K. S., & Verderber, R. F. (1977). *Inter-act: Using interpersonal communication skills.* Belmont, Calif.: Wadsworth.

Verinis, J., & Roll, S. (1970). Primary and secondary male characteristics. *Psychological Reports, 26,* 123–126.

Verny, T. R. (1974). *Inside groups: A practical guide to encounter groups and group therapy.* New York: McGraw-Hill.

Vestre, N. D. (1984). Irrational beliefs and self-reported depressed mood. *Journal of Abnormal Psychology, 93*(2), 239–241.

Veterans Administration. (1981). *Legacies of Viet Nam: Comparative adjustment of veterans and their peers.* Washington, D.C.: U.S. Government Printing Office.

Victor, J. S. (1980). *Human sexuality: A social psychological approach.* Englewood Cliffs, N.J.: Prentice-Hall.

Vigderhous, G., & Fishman, G. (1978). The impact of unemployment and familial integration on changing suicide rates in the U.S.A., 1920–1969. *Social Psychiatry, 13,* 239–248.

Vogler, R. E., Lande, S. E., Johnson, G. R., & Martin, P. L. (1970). Electrical aversion conditioning with chronic alcoholics. *Journal of Consulting and Clinical Psychology, 34,* 302–307.

Von Baeyer, C. L., Sherk, D. L., & Zanna, M. P. (1981). Impression management in the job interview: When the female applicant meets the male (chauvinist) interviewer. *Personality and Social Psychology Bulletin, 7*(1), 45–51.

Vonnegut, M. (1975). *The Eden express.* New York: Praeger.

Vourakis, C., & Bennett, G. (1979). Angel dust: Not heaven sent. *American Journal of Nursing, 79,* 649–653.

Wadden, T. A., Stunkard, A. J., Brownell, K. D., & VanItallie, T. B. (1983). The Cambridge diet. *Journal of the American Medical Association, 250*(20), 2833–2834.

Walk, R. D. (1956). Self ratings of fear in a fear-invoking situation. *Journal of Abnormal and Social Psychology, 52,* 171–178.

Wallace, R. K., & Benson, H. (1972). The physiology of meditation. *Scientific American, 226,* 84–90.

Wallerstein, J., & Kelly, J. (1980). *Surviving the breakup: How children actually cope with divorce*. New York: Basic Books.

Wallis, C. (1984, August 6). Why joggers are running scared. *Time*, p. 58.

Walsh, D. A. (1983). Age differences in learning and memory. In D. S. Woodruff & J. E. Birren (Eds.), *Aging: Scientific perspectives and social issues*. Monterey, Calif.: Brooks/Cole.

Walster, E. (1965). The effect of self-esteem on romantic liking. *Journal of Experimental Social Psychology, 1*, 189–197.

Walster, E., Aronson, V., Abrahams, D., & Rottmann, L. (1966). Importance of physical attractiveness in dating behavior. *Journal of Personality and Social Psychology, 4*, 508–516.

Walster, E., & Walster, G. W. (1976). Interpersonal attraction. In B. Seidenberg & A. Sandowsky (Eds.), *Social psychology: An introduction*. New York: Free Press.

Walster, E., & Walster, G. W. (1978). *A new look at love*. Reading, Mass.: Addison-Wesley.

Walster, E., Walster, G. W., Piliavin, J., & Schmidt, L. (1973). Playing hard-to-get: Understanding an elusive phenomenon. *Journal of Personality and Social Psychology, 26*, 113–121.

Wassmer, A. C. (1978). *Making contact*. New York: Dial.

Watson, D. L., & Friend, R. (1969). Measurement of social-evaluative anxiety. *Journal of Consulting and Clinical Psychology, 33*(4), 448–457.

Watson, D. L., & Tharp, R. G. (1972). *Self-directed behavior: Self-modification for personal adjustment*. Monterey, Calif.: Brooks/Cole.

Watson, D. L., & Tharp, R. G. (1985). *Self-directed behavior: Self-modification for personal adjustment* (4th ed.). Monterey, Calif.: Brooks/Cole.

Watson, J. B. (1913). Psychology as the behaviorist views it. *Psychological Review, 20*, 158–177.

Wattenberg, W. W., & Clifford, C. (1964). Relation of self-concept to beginning achievement in reading. *Child Development, 35*, 461–467.

Watts, A. (1957). *The way of Zen*. New York: Random House.

Webb, W. B. (1973). Sleep and dreams. In B. B. Wolman (Ed.), *Handbook of general psychology*. Englewood Cliffs, N.J.: Prentice-Hall.

Webb, W. B., & Agnew, H. W., Jr. (1968). Measurement and characteristics of nocturnal sleep. In L. A. Abt & B. F. Riess (Eds.), *Progress in clinical psychology* (Vol. 7). New York: Grune & Stratton.

Wechsler, D. (1958). *The measurement of adult intelligence*. Baltimore: Williams & Wilkins.

Weeks, D., Freeman, C. P. L., & Kendell, R. E. (1981). Does ECT produce enduring cognitive deficits? In R. L. Palmer (Ed.), *Electroconvulsive therapy: An appraisal*. Oxford: Oxford University Press.

Weg, R. B. (1978). The physiology of sexuality in aging. In R. Solnick (Ed.), *Sexuality and aging*. Los Angeles: University of Southern California Press.

Weinberg, C. (1979). *Self creation*. New York: Avon.

Weinberg, J., & Levine, S. (1980). Psychobiology of coping in animals: The effects of predictability. In S. Levine & H. Ursin (Eds.), *Coping and health*. New York: Plenum.

Weiner, H. (1978). Emotional factors. In S. C. Werner & S. H. Ingbar (Eds.), *The thyroid*. New York: Harper & Row.

Weiner, R. D. (1984). Does electroconvulsive therapy cause brain damage? *Behavioral and Brain Sciences, 7*, 1–53.

Weinrach, S. G. (1979). *Career counseling: Theoretical and practical perspectives*. New York: McGraw-Hill.

Weinstein, N. D. (1984). Why it won't happen to me: Perceptions of risk factors and susceptibility. *Health Psychology, 3*(5), 431–458.

Weiss, J. M. (1970). Somatic effects of predictable and unpredictable shock. *Psychosomatic Medicine, 32*, 397–408.

Weiss, R. S. (1973). *Loneliness: The experience of emotional and social isolation*. Cambridge, Mass.: M.I.T. Press.

Weiss, R. S. (1975). *Marital separation*. New York: Basic Books.

Weissman, M. M., Pottenger, M., Kleber, H., Ruben, H. L., Wil-liams, D., & Thompson, D. (1977). Symptom pattern in primary and secondary depression. *Archives of General Psychiatry, 34*, 854–862.

Weiten, W., Armstrong, F., & Dixon, J. (1984, May). *Pressure as a form of stress and its relationship to psychological symptomatology*. Paper presented at the meeting of the Midwestern Psychological Association, Chicago.

Weiten, W., Clery, J., & Bowbin, G. (1980, September). *Test-wiseness: Its composition and significance in educational measurement*. Paper presented at the meeting of the American Psychological Association, Montreal.

Weiten, W., & Dixon, J. (1984, August). *Measurement of pressure as a form of stress*. Paper presented at the meeting of the American Psychological Association, Toronto, Ontario.

Weiten, W., & Etaugh, C. F. (1974). Lateral eye-movement as a function of cognitive mode, question sequence, and sex of subject. *Perceptual and Motor Skills, 38*, 1203–1206.

Wekstein, L. (1979). *Handbook of suicidology*. New York: Brunner/Mazel.

Wells, L. E., & Marwell, G. (1976). *Self-esteem: Its conceptualization and measurement*. Beverly Hills, Calif.: Sage.

Welpton, D. R. (1968). Psychodynamics of chronic lysergic acid diethylamide use. *Journal of Nervous and Mental Disease, 147*, 377–385.

Wender, P. H., Rosenthal, D., Kety, S. S., Schulsinger, F., & Welner, J. (1974). Cross-fostering: A research strategy for clarifying the role of genetic and experimental factors in the etiology of schizophrenia. *Archives of General Psychiatry, 30*, 121–128.

Wenger, M. A., & Bagchi, B. K. (1961). Studies of autonomic functions in practitioners of yoga in India. *Behavioral Science, 6*, 312–323.

Westoff, C. (1974). Coital frequency and contraception. *Family Planning Perspectives, 6*, 136–141.

Wexler, D. (1974). A cognitive theory of experiencing, self-actualization, and therapeutic process. In D. Wexler & L. Rice (Eds.), *Innovations in client-centered therapy*. New York: Wiley.

White, G. L. (1980a). Inducing jealousy: A power perspective. *Personality and Social Psychology Bulletin, 6*(2), 222–227.

White, G. L. (1980b). Physical attractiveness and courtship progress. *Journal of Personality and Social Psychology, 39*(4), 660–668.

White, G. L. (1981). Some correlates of romantic jealousy. *Journal of Personality and Social Psychology, 49*(2), 129–147.

White, G. L., Fishbein, S., & Rutstein, J. (1981). Passionate love and the misattribution of arousal. *Journal of Personality and Social Psychology, 41*, 56–62.

White, R. W. (1959). Motivation reconsidered: The concept of competence. *Psychological Review, 66*, 297–333.

Whitley, B. E., Jr. (1983). Sex role orientation and self-esteem: A critical meta-analytic review. *Journal of Personality and Social Psychology, 44*(4), 765–778.

Whitney, E. N., & Cataldo, C. B. (1983). *Understanding normal and clinical nutrition*. St. Paul, Minn.: West.

Whitney, E. N., & Hamilton, E. M. N. (1977). *Understanding nutrition*. St. Paul, Minn.: West.

Wickramasekera, I. E. (1973). Temperature feedback for the control of migraine. *Journal of Behavior Therapy and Experimental Psychiatry, 4*, 343–345.

Wiener, D. N. (1968). *A practical guide to psychotherapy*. New York: Harper & Row.

Wiest, W. (1977). Semantic differential profiles of orgasm and other experiences among men and women. *Sex Roles, 3*, 399–403.

Wiggins, J. S., Wiggins, N., & Conger, J. C. (1968). Correlates of heterosexual somatic preference. *Journal of Personality and Social Psychology, 10*, 82–89.

Wikler, A. (1965). Conditioning factors in opiate addiction and relapse. In D. M. Wilmer & G. G. Kassebaum (Eds.), *Narcotics*. New York: McGraw-Hill.

Wilcox, B. L. (1981). Social support, life stress, and psychological adjustment. *American Journal of Community Psychology, 9*(4), 371–386.

Wilder, C. S. (1971). Chronic conditions and limitations of activity and mobility: United States, July 1965 to June 1967. *U.S. Vital and Health Statistics, 10*(6).

Williams, D. A., Lewis-Faning, E., Rees, L., Jacobs, J., & Thomas, A. (1958). Assessment of the relative importance of the allergic, infective and psychological factors in asthma. *Acta Allergologista, 12,* 376–385.

Williams, J. E., Bennett, S. M., & Best, D. L. (1975). Awareness and expression of sex stereotypes in young children. *Developmental Psychology, 11,* 635–642.

Williams, N. A., & Deffenbacher, J. L. (1983). Life stress and chronic yeast infections. *Journal of Human Stress, 9*(1), 26–31.

Wilson, G. T., & Lawson, D. M. (1976). Expectancies, alcohol, and sexual arousal in male social drinkers. *Journal of Abnormal Psychology, 85,* 587–594.

Wilson, W. C. (1975). The distribution of selected sexual attitudes and behaviors among the adult population of the United States. *Journal of Sex Research, 11,* 46–64.

Winch, R. F. (1958). *Mate selection: A study of complementary needs.* New York: Harper & Row.

Wing, S., & Manton, K. G. (1983). The contribution of hypertension to mortality in the U.S.: 1968, 1977. *American Journal of Public Health, 73*(2), 140–144.

Witkin, H. A. (1964). Origins of cognitive style. In C. Sheerer (Ed.), *Cognition: Theory, research, and promise.* New York: Harper & Row.

Wolf, S., & Goodell, H. (1968). *Stress and disease.* Springfield, Ill.: Charles C Thomas.

Wolfe, L. (1980). The sexual profile of that *Cosmopolitan* girl. *Cosmopolitan, 189*(3), 254–257, 263–265.

Wolpe, J. (1958). *Psychotherapy by reciprocal inhibition.* Stanford, Calif.: Stanford University Press.

Wolpe, J. (1973). *The practice of behavior therapy.* New York: Pergamon Press.

Wolpe, J. (1981). Behavior therapy versus psychoanalysis: Therapeutic and social implications. *American Psychologist, 36,* 159–164.

Women on Words and Images. (1972). *Dick and Jane as victims: Sex stereotyping in children's readers.* Princeton, N.J.: Women on Words and Images.

Woods, P. J. (Ed.). (1976). *Career opportunities for psychologists: Expanding and emerging areas.* Washington, D.C.: American Psychological Association.

Woods, P. J. (Ed.). (1979). *The psychology major: Training and employment strategies.* Washington, D.C.: American Psychological Association.

Woolfolk, R. L., & Richardson, F. C. (1978). *Stress, sanity, and survival.* New York: Sovereign/Monarch.

Worchel, P. (1957). Catharsis and relief of hostility. *Journal of Abnormal and Social Psychology, 55,* 238–243.

Wyler, A. R., Masuda, M., & Holmes, T. H. (1971). Magnitude of life events and seriousness of illness. *Psychosomatic Medicine, 33,* 115–122.

Wylie, R. C. (1961). *The self concept: A critical survey of pertinent research literature.* Lincoln: University of Nebraska Press.

Wylie, R. C. (1968). The present status of self-theory. In E. F. Borgatta & W. W. Lambert (Eds.), *Handbook of personality theory and research.* Chicago: Rand McNally.

Wynne, L. C., Ryckoff, I. M., Day, J., & Hirsch, S. I. (1958). Pseudomutuality in the family relations of schizophrenics. *Psychiatry, 21,* 205–220.

Yalom, I. D. (1975). *The theory and practice of group psychotherapy.* New York: Basic Books.

Yamaoka, T. (1968). Psychological study of mental self-control. In Y. Akishige (Ed.), *Psychological studies in Zen.* Fukoka, Japan: Kyushu University.

Yelsma, P. (1984). Marital communication, adjustment and perceptual differences between "happy" and "counseling" couples. *American Journal of Family Therapy, 12*(1), 26–36.

Yerkes, R. M., & Dodson, J. D. (1908). The relation of strength of stimulus to rapidity of habit formation. *Journal of Comparative and Neurological Psychology, 18,* 459–482.

Young, J. (1979, September). *Cognitive therapy and loneliness.* Paper presented at the meeting of the American Psychological Association, New York City.

Zaccaria, J. (1970). *Theories of occupational choice and vocational development.* New Hampshire: Time Share Corporation.

Zajonc, R. B. (1968). Attitudinal effects of mere exposure. *Journal of Personality and Social Psychology,* Monograph Supplement, *9*(2, Pt. 2), 2–27.

Zanna, M., Goethals, G. R., & Hill, J. (1975). Evaluating a sex-rated ability: Social comparison with similar others and standard setters. *Journal of Experimental Social Psychology, 11,* 86–93.

Zegans, L. S. (1982). Stress and the development of somatic disorders. In L. Goldberger & S. Breznitz (Eds.), *Handbook of stress: Theoretical and clinical aspects.* New York: Free Press.

Zeiss, A. M. (1980). Aversiveness versus change in the assessment of life stress. *Journal of Psychosomatic Stress, 24,* 15–19.

Zelnick, M., & Kantner, J. F. (1977). Sexual and contraceptive experience of young unmarried women in the United States, 1976 and 1971. *Family Planning Perspectives, 9,* 55–71.

Zerof, H. G. (1978). *Finding intimacy: The art of happiness in living together.* New York: Random House.

Ziegler, F. J. (1970). Hysterical conversion reactions. *Postgraduate Medicine, 47,* 174–179.

Zilbergeld, B., & Evans, M. (1980). The inadequacy of Masters and Johnson. *Psychology Today, 14*(3), 28–34, 37–43.

Zimbardo, P. G. (1977). *Shyness: What it is, what to do about it.* Reading, Mass.: Addison-Wesley.

Zimkin, N. V. (1961). Stress during muscular exercise and the state of nonspecifically increased resistance. *Physiology Journal of the U.S.S.R., 47,* 814.

Zubin, J., & Spring, B. J. (1977). Vulnerability: A new view of schizophrenia. *Journal of Abnormal Psychology, 86,* 103–126.

Zuckerman, M. (1974). The sensation-seeking motive. In B. Maher (Ed.), *Progress in experimental personality research.* New York: Academic Press.

Zuckerman, M. (1978). The search for high sensation. *Psychology Today, 11*(9), 38–46, 96–99.

Zunin, L., & Zunin, N. (1972). *Contact: The first four minutes.* New York: Ballantine Books.

NAME INDEX

SUBJECT INDEX

This page constitutes an extension of the copyright page.

CHAPTER 1: **10,** Box 1.1 from *All God's Children: The Cult Experience—Salvation or Slavery?,* by C. Stoner and J. Parke. Copyright 1977 by the authors. Reprinted by permission of the Chilton Book Company, Radnor, Pennsylvania. **12,** Box 1.2 courtesy of Daniel Henninger and the *Wall Street Journal.* **22,** Box 1.4 adapted from *Psychology: An Introduction to a Behavioral Science,* by H. Lindgren and D. Byren. Copyright 1975 by John Wiley & Sons. Reprinted by permission. *Photographs:* **xi, 1,** and **3,** T. D. Lovering, Stock Boston, Inc. **4,** Robert Houser, Photo Researchers, Inc. **6,** courtesy of Erich Fromm. **25,** Jeff Albertson, Stock Boston, Inc. **28,** Frank Siteman, Taurus Photos, Inc. **29,** Frank Siteman, Stock Boston, Inc.

CHAPTER 2: **43,** Figure 2.1 from *Psychology: A Scientific Study of Human Behavior, Fifth Edition,* by L. S. Wrightsman, C. K. Sigelman, and F. H. Sanford. Copyright © 1961, 1965, 1970, 1975, 1979, by Wadsworth Publishing Company, Inc. Reprinted by permission of Brooks/Cole Publishing Company, Monterey, California. **52,** Figure 2.3 from *Psychology: Its Principles and Meanings, Third Edition,* by Lyle E. Bourne, Jr., and Bruce R. Ekstrand. Copyright © 1976, 1979 by Holt, Rinehart and Winston. Reprinted by permission of Holt, Rinehart and Winston, CBS College Publishing. **73,** Box 2.1 from "Measurement of Social-Evaluative Anxiety," by D. Watson and R. Friend. In *Journal of Consulting and Clinical Psychology, 33*(4), pp. 448–457. Copyright 1969 by the American Psychological Association. Reprinted by permission. *Photographs:* **xi, 1,** and **37,** Arthur Tress, Magnum Photos, Inc. **43,** National Library of Medicine. **53,** Culver Pictures, Inc. **55,** Harvard University News Office. **57,** courtesy of Albert Bandura. **60,** Douglas A. Land. **61,** Marcia Roltner. **64,** Ellis Herwig, Stock Boston, Inc. **69,** Laimute E. Druskis, Taurus Photos, Inc.

CHAPTER 3: **85,** Table 3.1 from the "Social Readjustment Rating Scale," by T. H. Holmes and R. H. Rahe. Reprinted with permission from *Journal of Psychosomatic Research,* Vol. 11, pp. 213–218. Copyright 1967 by Pergamon Press, Ltd. **92,** Figure 3.3 from *Invitation to Psychology,* by J. P. Houston and V. Benassi. Copyright 1979 by Academic Press. Reprinted by permission. **94,** Figure 3.5 from *Psychology: A Scientific Study of Human Behavior, Fifth Edition,* by L. S. Wrightsman, C. K. Sigelman, and F. H. Sanford. Copyright © 1962, 1965, 1970, 1975, 1979 by Wadsworth Publishing Company, Inc. Reprinted by permission of Brooks/Cole Publishing Company, Monterey, California. **108–111,** Table 3.2 from "Assessing the Impact of Life Changes," by I. G. Sarason, H. M. Levine, and B. R. Sarason. In T. Millon, C. Green, and R. Meagher (Eds.), *Handbook of Clinical Health Psychology,* pp. 377–400. Copyright 1982 by Plenum Publishing Corporation. Reprinted by permission. *Photographs:* **xii, 1,** and **77,** Ray Ellis, Photo Researchers, Inc. **79,** courtesy of Richard Lazarus. **80,** Arthur Grace, Stock Boston, Inc. **95,** Karsh Ottawa, Woodfin Camp & Associates. **98,** Leonard Freed, Magnum Photos, Inc. **102,** Jose A. Fernandez, Woodfin Camp & Associates. **106,** Mark Jones, Jeroboam, Inc.

CHAPTER 4: **142,** Figure 4.5 from "Drug Use and Life-Style among College Undergraduates," by H. G. Pope, Jr., M. Ionescu-Pioggia, and J. O. Cole. In *Archives of General Psychiatry,* 1981, *38,* 588–591. Copyright 1981, American Medical Association. Reprinted by permission. **147,** Figure 4.6 from *Barbiturates: Their Use, Misuses and Abuse,* by D. R. Wesson and D. E. Smith. Copyright 1977 by Human Sciences Press. Reprinted by permission. **153,** Figure 4.7 from "Subjective Benefits and Drawbacks of Marijuana and Alcohol," by W. T. Roth, J. Tinklenberg, and B. Kopell. In *The Therapeutic Potential of Marijuana,* by S. Cohen and R. C. Stillman (Eds.). Copyright 1976 by Plenum Publishing Corporation. Reprinted by permission. *Photographs:* **xii, 1,** and **115,** Arthur Tress, Photo Researchers, Inc. **124,** Alan Carey, The Image Works, Inc. **127,** Arthur Tress, Photo Researchers, Inc. **137,** Paul Conklin, Monkmeyer Press Photo Service. **139,** Magnum Photos, Inc. **141,** Arthur Tress, Photo Researchers, Inc. **152,** Ed Buryn, Jeroboam, Inc.

CHAPTER 5: **174,** Box 5.3 Copyright © 1962 by the Institute for Rational Living, published by arrangement with Lyle Stuart. **181,** Procedures for eliciting the relaxation response from *The Relaxation Response* (pp. 114–115), by Herbert Benson, M.D., with Miriam Z. Klipper. Copyright © 1975 by William Morrow and Company, Inc., and Bill Adler

Inc. By permission of the publishers. **187,** Box 5.5 adapted from "How Different Sports Rate in Promoting Physical Fitness," by C. C. Conrad. In *Medical Times,* May 1976, 4–5, copyright 1976 by Romaine Pierson Publishers. Reprinted by permission. **196,** Figure 5.2 reproduced from *Self-Change: Strategies for Solving Personal Problems,* by Michael J. Mahoney, with the permission of W. W. Norton & Company, Inc. Copyright © 1979 by W. W. Norton & Company, Inc. **197,** List from *Self-Directed Behavior: Self-Modification for Personal Adjustment, Fourth Edition,* by D. L. Watson and R. L. Tharp. Copyright © 1972, 1977, 1981, 1985 by Wadsworth, Inc. Reprinted by permission of Brooks/Cole Publishing Company, Monterey, California. *Photographs:* **xiii, 1,** and **159,** Michael Murphy, Photo Researchers, Inc. **163,** courtesy of Martin Seligman. **172,** courtesy of Albert Ellis. **178,** Paul Fusco, Magnum Photos, Inc. **180,** Ron Cooper, EKM-Nepenthe. **186,** Rick Mansfield, The Image Works, Inc. **190** (top), courtesy of David Watson. **190** (bottom), courtesy of Roland Tharp. **190,** Frank Keillor.

CHAPTER 6: **214,** Box 6.1 from *Encounters with the Self, Second Edition,* by Don E. Hamachek. Copyright © 1971, 1978 by Holt, Rinehart and Winston, Inc. Reprinted by permission of Holt, Rinehart and Winston, CBS College Publishing. **228,** Table 6.1 adapted from "On the Fading of Social Stereotypes: Studies in Three Generations of Stereotypes," by M. Karling, T. L. Coffman, and G. Walters. In *Journal of Personality and Social Psychology,* 1969, *13,* 1–16. Copyright 1969 by the American Psychological Association. **230,** Box 6.5 from *The Autobiography of Malcolm X,* by Malcolm X, with the assistance of Alex Haley. Copyright © 1964 by Alex Haley and Malcolm X. Copyright © 1965 by Alex Haley and Betty Shabazz. Reprinted by permission of Random House, Inc. *Photographs:* **xiii, 207,** and **209,** Mimi Forsyth, Monkmeyer Press Photo Service. **216,** Jane Scherr, Jeroboam, Inc. **220,** Emilio Mercado, Jeroboam, Inc. **221,** courtesy of Mark Snyder. **232,** Menschenfreund, Taurus Photos, Inc.

CHAPTER 7: **244,** Box 7.1 adapted from *Unmasking the Faces,* by P. Ekman and W. V. Friesen. Copyright 1975 by Prentice-Hall, Inc. Reprinted by permission of the authors. **252,** Box 7.3 from *Contact: The First Four Minutes,* by L. Zunin and N. Zunin. Copyright 1972 by Nash Publishing Corp. Reprinted by permission. **253,** Box 7.4 excerpted from *Time Lurches On,* by Ralph Schoenstein. Copyright © 1961, 1962, 1963, 1964, 1965 by Ralph Schoenstein. Reprinted by permission of Doubleday & Company, Inc. **266,** Quotations from *Dilemmas of Masculinity: A Study of College Youth,* by M. Komarovsky. Copyright 1976 by W. W. Norton. Reprinted by permission. *Photographs:* **xiv, 207,** and **237,** Peter Vandermark, Stock Boston, Inc. **238,** Elizabeth Hamlin, Stock Boston, Inc. **241,** Gatewood, The Image Works, Inc. **244,** courtesy of Paul Eckman. **245,** Erika Stone. **247** (left), Robert Burroughs, Jeroboam, Inc. **247** (right), Peter Menzel, Stock Boston, Inc. **248,** Allan L. Price, Rapho/Photo Researchers, Inc. **260,** David Hurn, Magnum Photos, Inc.

CHAPTER 8: **267,** Table 8.1 from "Sex Role Stereotypes: A Current Appraisal," by I. K. Broverman, S. R. Vogel, D. M. Broverman, F. E. Clarkson, and P. S. Rosenkrantz. In *Journal of Social Issues,* 1972, *28,* 59–78. Copyright 1972 by Plenum Publishing Corp. Reprinted by permission. **269,** Figure 8.2 from Form AA, 1962, *Identical Blocks,* by R. E. Stafford and H. Gullikson. Reprinted by permission of the authors. **270,** Figure 8.3 reproduced by special permission from *The Group Embedded Figures Test,* by Phillip Oltman, Evelyn Raskin, and Herman Witkin. Copyright 1971 by Consulting Psychologists Press, Inc., Palo Alto, California 94306. **290,** Box 8.7 reprinted from *Asserting Yourself: A Practical Guide for Positive Change,* by Sharon Anthony Bower and Gordon H. Bower. Copyright © 1976 by Addison-Wesley Publishing Co., Reading, Massachusetts. *Photographs:* **xiv, 207,** and **265,** Erika Stone. **277,** Leonard Freed, Magnum Photos, Inc. **280** (top), courtesy of Sandra Bem. **280** (bottom), Martha Stewart. **287,** Ian Berry, Magnum Photos, Inc. **289,** Laimute E. Druskis, Taurus Photos, Inc.

CHAPTER 9: **296,** Box 9.1 (and photo) copyright © 1978 by Bob Greene. Reprinted by permission of Tribune Company Syndicate, Inc. **298,** Figure 9.1 adapted from *The Psychology of Affiliation,* by S. Schachter. Copyright 1959 by Stanford University Press. Reprinted by permission. **302,** Table 9.2 from "Men and Women Report Their Views on Masculinity," by Carol Tavris. Reprinted from *Psychology Today* Magazine. Copyright © 1977 Ziff-Davis Publishing Company. **304,** Table 9.3

from "What's Sexiest about Men?" by H. Smith. In *Cosmopolitan*, January 1975, pp. 112–113. **305,** Table 9.4 from "Likableness Ratings of 555 Personality Trait Words," by N. H. Anderson. In *Journal of Personality and Social Psychology*, 1968, *9,* 272–279. Copyright 1968 by the American Psychological Association. **307,** Figure 9.2 from "Gain and Loss of Esteem as Determinants of Interpersonal Attractiveness," by E. Aronson and D. Linder. In *Journal of Experimental Social Psychology*, 1965, *1,* 156–171. Copyright 1965 by the American Psychological Association. **309,** Figure 9.3 from "Attraction as a Linear Function of Proportion of Positive Reinforcements," by D. Byrne and D. Nelson. In *Journal of Personality and Social Psychology*, 1965, *1,* 659–663. Copyright 1965 by the American Psychological Association. **311,** Figure 9.4 from "The Friendship Bond," by Mary Brown Parlee and the Editors of *Psychology Today*. Reprinted from *Psychology Today* Magazine. Copyright © 1979 by Ziff-Davis Publishing Company. **320,** Table 9.5 from Paper presented at the annual convention of the American Psychological Association, September 2, 1979. An expanded version of this paper appears in *New Directions in Cognitive Therapy*, edited by Emery, Hollon, and Bedrosian, Guilford Press, 1981, and in *Loneliness: A Sourcebook of Current Theory, Research, and Therapy*, by L. A. Peplau and D. Perlman (Eds.). Copyright 1982 by John Wiley & Sons, Inc. Reprinted by permission of John Wiley & Sons, Inc., and Jeffrey Young. **323,** Table 9.6 reprinted from *Shyness: What It Is, What to Do about It*, by Philip G. Zimbardo. Copyright © 1977 by permission of Addison-Wesley Publishing Co., Reading, Massachusetts. *Photographs:* **xv, 207,** and **295,** Alex Harris, Archive Pictures, Inc. **303,** Ellis Herwig, Stock Boston, Inc. **312,** Chester Higgins, Jr., Rapho/Photo Researchers. **316,** Charles Gatewood, The Image Works, Inc. **322,** Frank Siteman, Taurus Photos, Inc. **323,** courtesy of Philip Zimbardo.

CHAPTER 10: **334,** Table 10.1 from "Chronic Conditions and Limitations of Activity and Mobility: United States, July 1965 to June 1967," by C. S. Wilder. In *U.S. Vital and Health Statistics*, 1971, *10*(6). **336,** Table 10.2 from "Age and Creative Productivity," by W. Dennis. In *Journal of Gerontology*, 1966, *21*(1), 1–8. **338,** Table 10.3 adapted from *Identity and the Life Cycle*, by Erik H. Erikson, by permission of W. W. Norton & Company, Inc., and The Hogarth Press Ltd. Copyright © 1980 by W. W. Norton & Company, Inc. Copyright © 1959 by Universities Press, Inc. **347,** Table 10.5 cited in *Theories of Occupational Choice and Vocational Development*, by J. Zaccaria, pp. 51–52. Copyright 1970 by Time Share Corporation, New Hampshire. **354,** Figure 10.1 reprinted from *Manual for the Strong-Campbell Interest Inventory*, Form T325 of the *Strong Vocational Interest Blank, Third Edition*, by David P. Campbell and Jo-Ida C. Hansen, with the permission of the publishers, Stanford University Press. Copyright © 1974, 1977, 1981 by the Board of Trustees of the Leland Stanford Junior University. **364,** Figure 10.2 courtesy of the Euthanasia Educational Council, New York. *Photographs:* **xv, 327,** and **329,** Charles Gatewood, The Image Works, Inc. **333,** Alan Carey, The Image Works, Inc. **337,** Harvard University Archives. **346,** Abigail Heiman, Archive Pictures, Inc. **352** (left), Don McCullin, Magnum Photos, Inc. **352** (right), Ron Wolfson, LGI. **361,** Dan Hulburt.

CHAPTER 11: **372,** Box 11.1 (and photo) copyright © 1978 by Bob Greene. Reprinted by permission of Tribune Company Syndicate, Inc. **375,** Table 11.1 adapted from Peter J. Stein, "Singlehood: An Alternative to Marriage," *The Family Coordinator*, 24:4 Copyright 1975 by the National Council on Family Relations. This chart also appears in Peter J. Stein (Ed.), *Single Life: Unmarried Adults in Social Context*. N.Y.: St. Martin's Press, 1981 (p. 18). Reprinted by permission. **385,** Figure 11.1 reproduced from *Progress on Family Problems: A Nationwide Study of Clients' and Counselors' Views on Family Agency Services*, by Dorothy Fahs Beck and Mary Ann Jones, by permission of the publisher. Copyright 1973 by Family Service Association of America, New York. **396,** Summary of gay lifestyles from *Homosexualities*, by Alan P. Bell and Martin S.

Weinberg. Copyright © 1978 by Alan P. Bell and Martin S. Weinberg. Reprinted by permission of Simon & Schuster, Inc. **400, 401,** and **402,** Figures 11.2, 11.3, and 11.4 from Anthony F. Grasha, *Practical Applications of Psychology, Second Edition*. Copyright © 1983 by Little, Brown and Company, Inc. Reprinted by permission. *Photographs:* **xvi, 327,** and **371,** Kent Reno, Jeroboam, Inc. **380,** Alan Carey, The Image Works, Inc. **394,** Bill Bachman, Photo Researchers, Inc. **398,** Robert V. Eckert, Jr., EKM-Nepenthe.

CHAPTER 12: **420,** Table 12.2 from "The Erotic Fantasies of College Students during Coitus," by David Sue. Reprinted by permission from *The Journal of Sex Research*, 1979, *15,* p. 303. **425,** Figure 12.3 copyright © 1974 by Morton Hunt. Reprinted by permission of Playboy Enterprises International Books, Inc. **426,** Box 12.2 from *Understanding Human Sexuality*, by J. S. Hyde. Copyright 1979 by McGraw-Hill Book Company. Reprinted by permission. *Photographs:* **xvi, 327,** and **407,** Erika Stone. **411,** Hella Hammid, Photo Researchers, Inc. **413,** Eric Kroll, Taurus Photos, Inc. **415,** Erwitt, Magnum Photos, Inc. **419,** Bob Footnorap, Jeroboam, Inc. **433,** Frank Siteman.

CHAPTER 13: **447,** Figure 13.1 courtesy of the Bancroft Rare Books Library, University of California, Berkeley. **455,** Figure 13.2 from *Psychology Today: An Introduction, Third Edition*. Copyright © 1975 by Random House, Inc. Reprinted by permission of the publisher. **458,** Box 13.4 from *Abnormal Psychology: Perspectives on Being Different*, by M. Duke and S. Nowicki. Copyright © 1979 by Wadsworth, Inc. Reprinted by permission of Brooks/Cole Publishing Company, Monterey, California. **461,** Table 13.2 adapted from "The International Pilot Study of Schizophrenia," by N. Sartorius, R. Shapiro, and A. Jablensky. In *Schizophrenia Bulletin*, 1974, Vol. 11, p. 30. Reprinted by permission of the U.S. National Institute of Mental Health. **463,** Box 13.5 from *The Eden Express*, by Mark Vonnegut. Copyright © 1975 by Praeger Publishers, Inc. Reprinted by permission of Holt, Rinehart and Winston, Publishers. *Photographs:* **xviii, 441,** and **443,** Bernard Pierre, Wolff, Magnum Photos, Inc. **445,** Yan Lukas, Photo Researchers, Inc. **447,** Bancroft Rare Books Library, University of California, Berkeley. **462,** Richard Hutchings, Photo Researchers, Inc. **473,** Picatti, Jeroboam, Inc. **474,** Sid Avery & Associates.

CHAPTER 14: **484,** Box 14.1 and Box 14.2 from *Abnormal Psychology: Perspectives on Being Different*, by M. Duke and S. Nowicki. Copyright © 1979 by Wadsworth, Inc. Reprinted by permission of Brooks/Cole Publishing Company, Monterey, California. **491,** Box 14.3 from *Methods of Self Change: An ABC Primer*, by K. E. Rudestam. Copyright © 1980 by Wadsworth, Inc. Reprinted by permission of Brooks/Cole Publishing Company, Monterey, California. **492,** Table 14.1 adapted from *Insight versus Desensitization in Psychotherapy*, by G. L. Paul. Copyright 1966 by Stanford University Press. Reprinted by permission. *Photographs:* **xviii, 441,** and **479,** Robert Pacheco, EKM-Nepenthe. **482,** Alex Webb, Magnum Photos, Inc. **492,** courtesy of Joseph Wolpe. **494,** Mark Antman, The Image Works, Inc. **502,** Frank Siteman.

CHAPTER 15: **515,** Figure 15.1 from *The Study of Psychology*, by J. Rubinstein. Copyright 1975 by Dushkin Publishing Group, Inc. Reprinted by permission. **518,** Figure 15.2 from *Hypnotic Susceptibility*, by Ernest R. Hilgard, © 1965 by Harcourt Brace Jovanovich, Inc. Reprinted by permission of the publisher. **522,** Figure 15.4 adapted from "The Physiology of Meditation," by Robert Keith Wallace and Herbert Benson. Copyright © 1972 by Scientific American, Inc. All rights reserved. *Photographs:* **xviii, 441,** and **509,** Charles Gatewood, The Image Works, Inc. **514,** courtesy of Neil Miller. **517** (both), News and Publications Service, Stanford University. **519,** courtesy of Theodore Barber. **519,** Kira Godbe. **524,** Arthur Grace, Stock Boston, Inc. **527,** David R. Frazier.